CRIC

PREFACE

This annual, the 60th under the *Playfair* banner initiated by the late Peter West in 1948, goes to press on the eve of the opening match of the Ninth World Cup. Even if Peter had dreamt that this title would still be in existence well into the next century, he could never have foreseen the scale of the Caribbean carnival about to focus on the world's top limited-overs cricketers for nearly two months.

Those who specialise in the longer game have been allowed a well-earned rest as there will have been no Test cricket between 28 January and the start of England's four-match series against West Indies on 17 May. That and the subsequent three-match rubber against India offer possibly a final chance for us to admire the exhilarating strokeplay of Brian Lara and Sachin Tendulkar, two of the most prolific batsmen of all time. This hiatus, the longest since 1971-72, has also provided statisticians with a rare opportunity to compile the Test records while knowing that they will not be out of date until six weeks after publication.

On 30 May *Test Match Special* will celebrate its golden jubilee; continuous ball-by-ball commentary commenced at Edgbaston in a remarkable match against the 1957 West Indians. Birmingham's first Test for 28 years saw England concede a first-innings lead of 288 (Sonny Ramadhin 7 for 49 and 'Collie' Smith 161) before Peter May (285 not out) and Colin Cowdrey (154) added 411 together, still England's highest stand for any wicket, as Ramadhin toiled for 98 overs, the longest bowling stint in any first-class innings. The series will also mark the end of a remarkable 35-year reign as *TMS* producer by Peter Baxter.

Last season saw Sussex win their second Championship on the back of another outstanding campaign by their ace leg-spinner, Mushtaq Ahmed, after a telling display of accurate seam bowling by James Kirtley had clinched victory in the last Lord's final under the Cheltenham and Gloucester banner.

Special congratulations must go to Mark Ramprakash. His aggregate of 2278 runs speaks for itself. His first-class average of 103.54 has been surpassed only by Sir Donald Bradman (115.66 in 1938) among those scoring 1000 runs in a season and he set world records by scoring 2000 runs in only 20 innings, by posting scores of at least 150 in five successive matches and by reaching double figures in each of his 24 innings. His exceptional performances in a smaller indoor arena saw him succeed Darren Gough as the winner of television's *Strictly Come Dancing*. As I watched some fairly abject batting performances by England in Australia this winter, I could not help wondering how 'Rampers' would have dealt with their ageing attack. David Steele, that gritty battler who wore down far more formidable Australian and West Indian attacks in the mid-Seventies, lamented the lack of footwork and basic technique. An exception was Ian Bell, victim of my poisoned chalice *Playfair* cover award, who came of age with three successive hundreds against Pakistan last summer.

Debate about the recent Ashes tour is far from over. While England would undoubtedly have fared better had the series occurred a year later with half the opposition in retirement and possibly with Michael Vaughan and Simon Jones available, they were inadequately prepared and the victims of some bizarre choices of selection. That said, Australia were stronger than in 2005 with the inclusion of Mike Hussey and Stuart Clark, and defeat had motivated them to an extraordinary degree. Even for an Englishman, Australia provided a series full of entertainment and drama, not to mention many delights away from the cricket.

BILL FRINDALL
Urchfont, Wiltshire
12 March 2007

ACKNOWLEDGEMENTS AND THANKS

HEADLINE
Rhea Halford (Editorial Assistant)
David Mitchell (proofs)

LETTERPART
Lorraine Byfield
Chris Leggett
Caroline Leggett

CAREER RECORDS
Philip Bailey
Cricket Archive
Robin Abrahams
Debbie Frindall

ECB
Alan Fordham

COUNTY SCORER/STATISTICIANS
John Brown (Derbyshire)
Brian Hunt (Durham)
Tony Choat (Essex)
Andrew Hignell (Glamorgan)
Keith Gerrish Gloucestershire)
Tony Weld (Hampshire)
Jack Foley (Kent)
Alan West (Lancashire)
Graham York (Leicestershire)
Don Shelley (Middlesex)
Tony Kingston (Northamptonshire)
Gordon Stringfellow (Nottinghamshire)
Gerry Stickley (Somerset)
Mike Charman (Sussex)
Keith Booth (Surrey)
David Wainwright (Warwickshire)
Neil Smith (Worcestershire)
Roy Wilkinson (Yorkshire)

UNIVERSITIES
Ray Markham (Cambridge)
Graeme Fowler (Durham)
Margaret Folwell (Loughborough)
Neil Harris (Oxford)

TASTATS
Ric Finlay
David Fitzgerald

OVERSEAS
Rajesh Kumar (India)
Andrew Samson (South Africa)
Charlie Wat (Australia)

COUNTY ADMINISTRATIONS
David Houghton (Derbyshire)
Pat Walton (Durham)
Nancy Fuller (Essex)
Caryl Watkin (Glamorgan)
Mark Alleyne (Gloucestershire)
Tim Tremlett (Hampshire)
Carolyn Dunne (Kent)
Diana Lloyd (Lancashire)
Elaine Pickering (Leicestershire)
Emma Channon (Middlesex)
Lyndsey Hutchings (Northamptonshire)
Mick Newell (Nottinghamshire)
Sally Donoghue (Somerset)
Stephen Howes (Surrey)
Francesca Watson (Sussex)
Keith Cook (Warwickshire)
Steve Rhodes (Worcestershire)
Liz Sutcliffe (Yorkshire)

DUCKWORTH/LEWIS – A BRIEF EXPLANATION

The Duckworth/Lewis (D/L) method has been around now for 10 years and it is generally accepted as being a very fair method for resetting targets in interrupted one-day matches. However, ask a typical cricket fan as to how the calculations are done and the fallback excuse of not being good at maths at school is frequently trotted out. But if you can work out how much tax you have to pay on your net income then D/L calculations are well within your grasp.

You may well have heard that the D/L method is based on the idea of resources – these are the combination of wickets and overs that a team has for their innings. However, it's not just the numbers of these that matter; it is also their relative value – wickets and overs have different relative importance as an innings progresses. For example, having lots of wickets in hand without overs left in which to use them is of little value, just as if lots of overs remain they have little value if there are no wickets left with which to use them. In conducting their innings, teams need to manage these twin resources in order to maximise the total they set or maximise their chances of winning the match. Through some neat behind-the-scenes mathematics and statistical analysis of hundreds of matches, Duckworth and Lewis have produced a table that represents the average percentages remaining of their twin resources of a 50-over innings. In the extract of the table supplied you will see that teams start with all 50 overs and 10 wickets – and therefore 100% of their resources. As an innings progresses a team receives its overs, loses its wickets and thereby consumes its resources. The table works always in overs left – in that way it can be used for matches that are shorter than 50 overs – and tells us what percentage of their combined resources remains.

Wickets lost:	0	2	4	6	9
Overs remaining:-					
50	100.0	85.1	62.7	34.9	4.7
40	89.3	77.8	59.5	34.6	4.7
30	75.1	67.3	54.1	33.6	4.7
25	66.5	60.5	50.0	32.6	4.7
20	56.6	52.4	44.6	30.8	4.7
10	32.1	30.8	28.3	22.8	4.7
5	17.2	16.8	16.1	14.3	4.6

Suppose that a team have batted for 45 overs and have lost 6 wickets. With 5 overs left, for 6 wickets lost the table shows they have 14.3% of their resources remaining. If their innings is now terminated, these resources are lost and they have had available for their innings 100–14.3 = 85.7% resources compared with the 100% for a complete 50-over innings.

These figures came into play in a crucial Group match of the 2003 World Cup in South Africa. Against the host nation, Sri Lanka scored 268 in their 100% resources of 50 overs. Rain began to fall and abandonment looked likely at the end of the 45th over of South Africa's innings. Charts of the D/L method were consulted and the relevant figure was obtained through the comparative resources of the two teams. The calculation was 268×85.7/100=229.676. This meant that in order to win SA needed to reach 230 by the end of the 45th over if the match were abandoned. A score of 229 would be the score to tie.

How would South Africa know this? You will have seen the D/L par score displayed on scoreboards. These numbers come from the par-score sheet that is distributed during the interval to team camps, match officials and the media. The par-score is given for the end of every one of the combinations of overs left and wickets lost (and even on a ball-by-ball basis). This sheet is clearly labelled as the score needed to tie. In the World Cup match the SA camp told the batsmen, Boucher and Klusener, that they needed to get to 229 by the end of the over. Thanks to a six from Boucher off the penultimate ball of the over, they achieved this – and to avoid losing his wicket, which would have raised the par-score, Boucher blocked the last ball. Play was duly abandoned at the end of the over but the dismay in the SA camp was palpable when it was finally realised that the 229 the batsmen had been told to score was in fact the score to *tie* and not to *win* the match. So a tie it was and the misreading of the clear information available led to the elimination of the host nation from the tournament.

Whenever a stoppage occurs within an innings, the table provides the information by which to calculate the resources lost. Suppose that there are 20 overs left with only 4 wickets down and a stoppage reduces the innings by 10 overs so there are now only 10 overs left on the resumption. You will see from the table that the team went off with 44.6% resources left and came back with 28.3% left. The stoppage would have cost them 44.6–28.3 = 16.3% of their resources so that they would have available 100–16.3 = 83.7% resources for their innings if there are no more stoppages (but if there are, the resources available are further reduced in the same way) and, in most cases, the target comes from reducing the first innings score in proportion to the resources available as in the World Cup example.

Sometimes teams start with fewer than 50 overs either due to a shorter match competition, such as the Pro40, or due to a delayed start. For a 25-over innings, for instance, teams start with 66.5% resources compared with a 50-over innings. Although they have half the overs they still have all 10 wickets and therefore more than half their resources – the table says about two-thirds compared with a 50-over innings. Any loss of overs would reduce this further in the same way and using the same figures as in the table.

So you see that it really is simple to calculate targets following interruptions during the second innings. The method is simply to adjust the first innings score in proportion to the resources available to the two teams – rounding up to win and one fewer to tie.

A distinctive feature of the D/L method compared with previous methods of adjusting targets is that it compensates the team batting first for stoppages within their innings – their batting strategy has been based on the full 50 overs and so to have it curtailed is usually a disadvantage. The D/L method usually sets an enhanced target, that is, a target which is quite a few runs more than the team batting first scored. This has the effect of compensating them for the unexpected shortening of the first innings and the advantage that the team batting second have from knowing in advance of their shorter innings.

How this is achieved, together with further detailed descriptions of the Duckworth/Lewis method and some frequently asked questions, can be found at the Cricinfo website: www.cricinfo.com/db/ABOUT_CRICKET/RAIN_RULES/ and a booklet is available from Acumen Books at www.acumenbooks.co.uk/ducklew.htm.

Although rain is usually the cause of stoppages and D/L adjusted targets, interruptions have occurred for several other causes including sandstorms, snow, floodlight failures, crowd disturbances and on one occasion due to the sun!

Cases at the higher levels of the game usually run to 80-100 per year and total well over 700 since the method's first use on 1st January 1997 in which England lost to Zimbabwe when they would have won by the old, unfair average run-rate method.

There have been some advances in the methodology since January 1997. With higher totals being more prevalent, teams need to score a bigger percentage of their runs in the earlier stages of their innings than those suggested by the standard tables. Consequently, higher scores lead to the need for the table to be adjusted and this needs the computer to do the calculations. Whereas what is now known as the Standard Edition, using a single table of resources as described here, is used at lower levels of the game where computers aren't necessary or available, the higher levels of the game now use the more advanced computerised version called the Professional Edition. In this edition, the computer in effect produces a different table of resources for every match, but thereafter the calculations are the same as described here.

ENGLAND v WEST INDIES

SERIES RECORDS

1928 to 2004

HIGHEST INNINGS TOTALS

England	in England	619-6d	Nottingham	1957
	in West Indies	849	Kingston	1929-30
West Indies	in England	692-8d	The Oval	1995
	in West Indies	751-5d	St John's	2003-04

LOWEST INNINGS TOTALS

England	in England	71	Manchester	1976
	in West Indies	46	Port-of-Spain	1993-94
West Indies	in England	54	Lord's	2000
	in West Indies	47	Kingston	2003-04

HIGHEST MATCH AGGREGATE	1815 for 34 wickets	Kingston	1929-30
LOWEST MATCH AGGREGATE	309 for 29 wickets	Bridgetown	1934-35

HIGHEST INDIVIDUAL INNINGS

England	in England	285*	P.B.H.May	Birmingham	1957
	in West Indies	325	A.Sandham	Kingston	1929-30
West Indies	in England	291	I.V.A.Richards	The Oval	1976
	in West Indies	400*	B.C.Lara	St John's	2003-04

HIGHEST AGGREGATE OF RUNS IN A SERIES

England	in England	506	(av 42.16)	G.P.Thorpe (*6 Tests*)	1995
	in West Indies	693	(av 115.50)	E.H.Hendren	1929-30
West Indies	in England	829	(av 118.42)	I.V.A.Richards	1976
	in West Indies	798	(av 99.75)	B.C.Lara	1993-94

RECORD WICKET PARTNERSHIPS – ENGLAND

1st	212	C.Washbrook (102)/R.T.Simpson (94)	Nottingham	1950
2nd	291	A.J.Strauss (137)/R.W.T.Key (221)	Lord's	2004
3rd	303	M.A.Atherton (135)/R.A.Smith (175)	St John's	1993-94
4th	411	P.B.H.May (285*)/M.C.Cowdrey (154)	Birmingham	1957
5th	150	A.J.Stewart (143)/G.P.Thorpe (84)	Bridgetown	1993-94
6th	205	M.R.Ramprakash (154)/G.P.Thorpe (103)	Bridgetown	1997-98
7th	197	M.J.K.Smith (96)/J.M.Parks (101*)	Port-of-Spain	1959-60
8th	217	T.W.Graveney (165)/J.T.Murray (112)	The Oval	1966
9th	109	G.A.R.Lock (89)/P.I.Pocock (13)	Georgetown	1967-68
10th	128	K.Higgs (63)/J.A.Snow (59*)	The Oval	1966

RECORD WICKET PARTNERSHIPS – WEST INDIES

1st	298	C.G.Greenidge (149)/D.L.Haynes (167)	St John's	1989-90
2nd	287*	C.G.Greenidge (214*)/H.A.Gomes (92*)	Lord's	1984
3rd	338	E.de C.Weekes (206)/F.M.M.Worrell (167)	Port-of-Spain	1953-54
4th	399	G.St A.Sobers (226)/F.M.M.Worrell (197*)	Bridgetown	1959-60
5th	265	S.M.Nurse (137)/G.St A.Sobers (174)	Leeds	1966
6th	282*	B.C.Lara (400*)/R.D.Jacobs (107*)	St John's	2003-04
7th	155*	G.St A.Sobers (150*)/B.D.Julien (121)	Lord's	1973
8th	99	C.A.McWatt (54)/J.K.Holt (48*)	Georgetown	1953-54
9th	150	E.A.E.Baptiste (87*)/M.A.Holding (69)	Birmingham	1984
10th	70	I.R.Bishop (44*)/D.Ramnarine (19)	Georgetown	1997-98

BEST INNINGS BOWLING ANALYSIS

England	in England	8-103	I.T.Botham	Lord's	1984
	in West Indies	8- 53	A.R.C.Fraser	Port-of-Spain	1997-98
West Indies	in England	8- 92	M.A.Holding	The Oval	1976
	in West Indies	8- 45	C.E.L.Ambrose	Bridgetown	1989-90

BEST MATCH BOWLING ANALYSIS

England	in England	12-119	F.S.Trueman	Birmingham	1963
	in West Indies	13-156	A.W.Greig	Port-of-Spain	1973-74
West Indies	in England	14-149	M.A.Holding	The Oval	1976
	in West Indies	11- 84	C.E.L.Ambrose	Port-of-Spain	1993-94

HIGHEST AGGREGATE OF WICKETS IN A SERIES

England	in England	34	(av 17.47)	F.S.Trueman	1963
	in West Indies	27	(av 18.66)	J.A.Snow	1967-68
		27	(av 18.22)	A.R.C.Fraser	1997-98
West Indies	in England	35	(av 12.65)	M.D.Marshall	1988
	in West Indies	30	(av 14.26)	C.E.L.Ambrose	1997-98

RESULTS SUMMARY
ENGLAND v WEST INDIES – IN ENGLAND

		Series			Lord's			Manchester			The Oval			Nottingham			Birmingham			Leeds		
	Tests	*E*	*WI*	*D*	*E*	*WI*	*D*	*E*	*WI*	*D*	*E*	*WI*	*D*	*E*	*WI*	*D*	*E*	*WI*	*D*	*E*	*WI*	*D*
1928	3	3	–	–	1	–	–	1	–	–	1	–	–	–	–	–	–	–	–	–	–	–
1933	3	2	–	1	1	–	–	–	–	1	1	–	–	–	–	–	–	–	–	–	–	–
1939	3	1	–	2	1	–	–	–	–	1	–	–	1	–	–	–	–	–	–	–	–	–
1950	4	1	3	–	–	1	–	1	–	–	–	1	–	–	1	–	–	–	–	–	–	–
1957	5	3	–	2	1	–	–	–	–	–	1	–	–	–	–	1	–	–	1	1	–	–
1963	5	1	3	1	–	–	1	–	1	–	–	1	–	–	–	–	1	–	–	–	1	–
1966	5	1	3	1	–	–	1	–	1	–	1	–	–	–	1	–	–	–	–	–	1	–
1969	3	2	–	1	–	–	1	1	–	–	–	–	–	–	–	–	–	–	–	1	–	–
1973	3	–	2	1	–	1	–	–	–	–	–	1	–	–	–	–	–	–	1	–	–	–
1976	5	–	3	2	–	–	1	–	1	–	–	1	–	–	–	1	–	–	–	–	1	–
1980	5	–	1	4	–	–	1	–	–	1	–	–	1	–	1	–	–	–	–	–	–	1
1984	5	–	5	–	–	1	–	–	1	–	–	1	–	–	–	–	–	1	–	–	1	–
1988	5	–	4	1	–	1	–	–	1	–	–	1	–	–	–	1	–	–	–	–	1	–
1991	5	2	2	1	–	–	1	–	–	–	1	–	–	–	1	–	–	1	–	1	–	–
1995	6	2	2	2	1	–	–	1	–	–	–	–	1	–	–	1	–	1	–	–	1	–
2000	5	3	1	1	1	–	–	–	–	1	1	–	–	–	–	–	–	1	–	1	–	–
2004	4	4	–	–	1	–	–	1	–	–	1	–	–	–	–	–	1	–	–	–	–	–
	74	25	29	20	7	4	6	5	5	4	7	6	3	–	4	4	2	4	2	4	6	1

ENGLAND v WEST INDIES – IN WEST INDIES

		Series			Bridgetown			Port-of-Spain			Georgetown			Kingston			St John's		
	Tests	*E*	*WI*	*D*	*E*	*WI*	*D*	*E*	*WI*	*D*	*E*	*WI*	*D*	*E*	*WI*	*D*	*E*	*WI*	*D*
1929-30	4	1	1	2	–	–	1	1	–	–	–	1	–	–	–	1	–	–	–
1934-35	4	1	2	1	1	–	–	–	1	–	–	–	1	–	1	–	–	–	–
1947-48	4	–	2	2	–	–	1	–	–	1	–	1	–	–	1	–	–	–	–
1953-54	5	2	2	1	–	1	–	–	–	1	1	–	–	1	1	–	–	–	–
1959-60	5	1	–	4	–	–	1	1	–	1	–	–	1	–	–	1	–	–	–
1967-68	5	1	–	4	–	–	1	1	–	1	–	–	1	–	–	1	–	–	–
1973-74	5	1	1	3	–	–	1	1	1	–	–	–	1	–	–	1	–	–	–
1980-81	4	–	2	2	–	1	–	–	1	–	–	–	–	–	–	1	–	–	1
1985-86	5	–	5	–	–	1	–	–	2	–	–	–	–	–	1	–	–	1	–
1989-90	4	1	2	1	–	1	–	–	–	1	–	–	–	1	–	–	–	1	–
1993-94	5	1	3	1	1	–	–	–	1	–	–	1	–	–	1	–	–	–	1
1997-98	6	1	3	2	–	–	1	1	1	–	–	1	–	–	–	1	–	1	–
2003-04	4	3	–	1	1	–	–	1	–	–	–	–	–	1	–	–	–	–	1
	60	13	23	24	3	4	6	6	7	5	1	4	4	3	5	6	–	3	3
Totals	134	38	52	44															

ENGLAND v INDIA

SERIES RECORDS

1932 to 2002

HIGHEST INNINGS TOTALS

England	in England	653-4d	Lord's	1990
	in India	652-7d	Madras	1984-85
India	in England	628-8d	Leeds	2002
	in India	591	Bombay	1992-93

LOWEST INNINGS TOTALS

England	in England	101	The Oval	1971
	in India	102	Bombay	1981-82
India	in England	42	Lord's	1974
	in India	83	Madras	1976-77

HIGHEST MATCH AGGREGATE	1614 for 30 wickets	Manchester	1990
LOWEST MATCH AGGREGATE	482 for 31 wickets	Lord's	1936

HIGHEST INDIVIDUAL INNINGS

England	in England	333	G.A.Gooch	Lord's	1990
	in India	207	M.W.Gatting	Madras	1984-85
India	in England	221	S.M.Gavaskar	The Oval	1979
	in India	224	V.G.Kambli	Bombay	1992-93

HIGHEST AGGREGATE OF RUNS IN A SERIES

England	in England	752	(av 125.33)	G.A.Gooch	1990
	in India	594	(av 99.00)	K.F.Barrington	1961-62
India	in England	602	(av 100.33)	R.Dravid	2002
	in India	586	(av 83.71)	V.L.Manjrekar	1961-62

RECORD WICKET PARTNERSHIPS – ENGLAND

1st	225	G.A.Gooch (116)/M.A.Atherton (131)	Manchester	1990
2nd	241	G.Fowler (201)/M.W.Gatting (207)	Madras	1984-85
3rd	308	G.A.Gooch (333)/A.J.Lamb (139)	Lord's	1990
4th	266	W.R.Hammond (217)/T.S.Worthington (128)	The Oval	1936
5th	254	K.W.R.Fletcher (113)/A.W.Greig (148)	Bombay	1972-73
6th	171	I.T.Botham (114)/R.W.Taylor (43)	Bombay	1979-80
7th	125	D.W.Randall (126)/P.H.Edmonds (64)	Lord's	1982
8th	168	R.Illingworth (107)/P.Lever (88*)	Manchester	1971
9th	103	C.White (94*)/M.J.Hoggard (32)	Nottingham	2002
10th	70	P.J.W.Allott (41*)/R.G.D.Willis (28)	Lord's	1982

RECORD WICKET PARTNERSHIPS – INDIA

1st	213	S.M.Gavaskar (221)/C.P.S.Chauhan (80)	The Oval	1979
2nd	192	F.M.Engineer (121)/A.L.Wadekar (87)	Bombay	1972-73
3rd	316	G.R.Viswanath (222)/Yashpal Sharma (140)	Madras	1981-82
4th	249	S.R.Tendulkar (193)/S.C.Ganguly (128)	Leeds	2002
5th	214	M.Azharuddin (110)/R.J.Shastri (111)	Calcutta	1984-85
6th	130	S.M.H.Kirmani (43)/Kapil Dev (97)	The Oval	1982
7th	235	R.J.Shastri (142)/S.M.H.Kirmani (102)	Bombay	1984-85
8th	128	R.J.Shastri (93)/S.M.H.Kirmani (67)	Delhi	1981-82
9th	104	R.J.Shastri (93)/Madan Lal (44)	Delhi	1981-82
10th	63	A.B.Agarkar (109*)/A.Nehra (19)	Lord's	2002

BEST INNINGS BOWLING ANALYSIS

England	in England	8-31	F.S.Trueman	Manchester	1952
	in India	7-46	J.K.Lever	Delhi	1976-77
India	in England	6-35	L.Amar Singh	Lord's	1936
	in India	8-55	M.H.Mankad	Madras	1951-52

BEST MATCH BOWLING ANALYSIS

England	in England	11- 93	A.V.Bedser	Manchester	1946
	in India	13-106	I.T.Botham	Bombay	1979-80
India	in England	10-188	C.Sharma	Birmingham	1986
	in India	12-108	M.H.Mankad	Madras	1951-52

HIGHEST AGGREGATE OF WICKETS IN A SERIES

England	in England	29	(av 13.31)	F.S.Trueman	1952
	in India	29	(av 17.55)	D.L.Underwood	1976-77
India	in England	17	(av 34.64)	S.P.Gupte	1959
	in India	35	(av 18.91)	B.S.Chandrasekhar	1972-73

RESULTS SUMMARY

ENGLAND v INDIA – IN ENGLAND

		Series			Lord's			Manchester			The Oval			Leeds			Nottingham			Birmingham		
	Tests	*E*	*I*	*D*	*E*	*I*	*D*	*E*	*I*	*D*	*E*	*I*	*D*	*E*	*I*	*D*	*E*	*I*	*D*	*E*	*I*	*D*
1932	1	1	–	–	1	–	–	–	–	–	–	–	–	–	–	–	–	–	–	–	–	–
1936	3	2	–	1	1	–	–	–	–	1	1	–	–	–	–	–	–	–	–	–	–	–
1946	3	1	–	2	1	–	–	–	–	1	–	–	1	–	–	–	–	–	–	–	–	–
1952	4	3	–	1	1	–	–	1	–	–	–	–	1	1	–	–	–	–	–	–	–	–
1959	5	5	–	–	1	–	–	1	–	–	1	–	–	1	–	–	1	–	–	–	–	–
1967	3	3	–	–	1	–	–	–	–	–	–	–	–	1	–	–	–	–	–	1	–	–
1971	3	–	1	2	–	–	1	–	–	1	–	1	–	–	–	–	–	–	–	–	–	–
1974	3	3	–	–	1	–	–	1	–	–	–	–	–	–	–	–	–	–	–	1	–	–
1979	4	1	–	3	–	–	1	–	–	–	–	–	1	–	–	1	–	–	–	1	–	–
1982	3	1	–	2	1	–	–	–	–	1	–	–	1	–	–	–	–	–	–	–	–	–
1986	3	–	2	1	–	1	–	–	–	–	–	–	–	–	1	–	–	–	–	–	–	1
1990	3	1	–	2	1	–	–	–	–	1	–	–	1	–	–	–	–	–	–	–	–	–
1996	3	1	–	2	–	–	1	–	–	–	–	–	–	–	–	–	–	–	1	1	–	–
2002	4	1	1	2	1	–	–	–	–	–	–	–	1	–	1	–	–	–	1	–	–	–
	45	23	4	18	10	1	3	3	–	5	2	1	6	3	2	1	1	–	2	4	–	1

ENGLAND v INDIA – IN INDIA

		Series			Bombay			Calcutta			Madras			Delhi			Kanpur			Bangalore			Chandigarh			Ahmedabad		
	Tests	*E*	*I*	*D*	*E*	*I*	*D*	*E*	*I*	*D*	*E*	*I*	*D*	*E*	*I*	*D*	*E*	*I*	*D*	*E*	*I*	*D*	*E*	*I*	*D*	*E*	*I*	*D*
1933-34	3	2	–	1	1	–	–	–	–	1	1	–	–	–	–	–	–	–	–	–	–	–	–	–	–	–	–	–
1951-52	5	1	1	3	–	–	1	–	–	1	–	1	–	–	–	1	1	–	–	–	–	–	–	–	–	–	–	–
1961-62	5	–	2	3	–	–	1	–	1	–	–	1	–	–	–	1	–	–	1	–	–	–	–	–	–	–	–	–
1963-64	5	–	–	5	–	–	1	–	–	1	–	–	1	–	–	1	–	–	1	–	–	–	–	–	–	–	–	–
1972-73	5	1	2	2	–	–	1	–	1	–	–	1	–	1	–	–	–	–	1	–	–	–	–	–	–	–	–	–
1976-77	5	3	1	1	–	–	1	1	–	–	1	–	–	1	–	–	–	–	–	–	1	–	–	–	–	–	–	–
1979-80	1	1	–	–	1	–	–	–	–	–	–	–	–	–	–	–	–	–	–	–	–	–	–	–	–	–	–	–
1981-82	6	–	1	5	–	1	–	–	–	1	–	–	1	–	–	1	–	–	1	–	–	1	–	–	–	–	–	–
1984-85	5	2	1	2	–	1	–	–	–	1	1	–	–	1	–	–	–	–	1	–	–	–	–	–	–	–	–	–
1992-93	3	–	3	–	–	1	–	–	1	–	–	1	–	–	–	–	–	–	–	–	–	–	–	–	–	–	–	–
2001-02	3	–	1	2	–	–	–	–	–	–	–	–	–	–	–	–	–	–	–	–	–	1	–	1	–	–	–	1
	46	10	12	24	2	3	5	1	3	5	3	4	2	3	–	4	1	–	5	–	1	2	–	1	–	–	–	1
Totals	91	33	16	42																								

TOURING TEAMS REGISTER 2007

Neither West Indies nor India had selected their 2007 touring teams at the time of going to press. The following players had represented those teams in Test matches since 1 September 2006.

WEST INDIES

Full Names	*Birthdate*	*Birthplace*	*Team*	*Type*	*F-C Debut*
BRADSHAW, Ian David Russell	09.07.74	Christ Church	Barbados	LHB/LFM	1997-98
BRAVO, Dwayne John	07.10.83	Santa Cruz	Trinidad	RHB/RFM	2001-02
CHANDERPAUL, Shivnarine	16.08.74	Unity Village	Guyana	LHB/LB	1991-92
COLLINS, Pedro Tyrone	12.08.76	Boscobelle	Barbados	RHB/LFM	1996-97
COLLYMORE, Corey Dalanelo	21.12.77	Boscobelle	Barbados	RHB/RFM	1998-99
EDWARDS, Fidel Henderson	06.02.82	St Peter	Barbados	RHB/RF	2001-02
GANGA, Daren	14.01.79	Barrackpore	Trinidad	RHB/OB	1996-97
GAYLE, Christopher Henry	21.09.79	Kingston	Jamaica	LHB/OB	1998-99
HINDS, Wavell Wayne	07.09.76	Kingston	Jamaica	LHB/RM	1995-96
LARA, Brian Charles	02.05.69	Cantaro, Santa Cruz	Trinidad	LHB/LBG	1987-88
LAWSON, Jermaine Jay Charles	13.01.82	Spanish Town	Jamaica	RHB/RFM	2000-01
LEWIS, Rawl Nicholas	05.09.74	Union Village, Grenada	Windward Is	RHB/LBG	1991-92
MOHAMMED, Dave	08.10.79	Princes Town	Trinidad	LHB/SLC	2000-01
MORTON, Runako Shakur	22.07.78	Rawlins, Nevis	Leeward Is	RHB/OB	1996-97
POWELL, Daren Brentlyle	15.04.78	Malvenn	Jamaica	RHB/RFM	2000-01
RAMDIN, Denesh	13.03.85	Freeport, Couva	Trinidad	RHB/WK	2003-04
SAMUELS, Marlon Nathaniel	05.01.81	Kingston	Jamaica	RHB/OB	1996-97
SARWAN, Ramnaresh Ronnie	23.06.80	Wakenaam Island	Guyana	RHB/LB	1995-96
SMITH, Dwayne Romel	12.04.83	Storey Gap	Barbados	RHB/RM	2001-02
SMITH, Devon Sheldon	21.10.81	Sauters, Grenada	Windward Is	LHB/OB	1998-99
TAYLOR, Jerome Everton	22.06.84	St Elizabeth	Jamaica	RHB/RF	2002-03

INDIA

Full Names	*Birthdate*	*Birthplace*	*Team*	*Type*	*F-C Debut*
AGARKAR, Ajit Bhalchandra	04.12.77	Bombay	Bombay	RHB/RFM	1996-97
CHAWLA, Piyush	24.12.88	Aligarh	Uttar Pradesh	LHB/LBG	2005-06
DHONI, Mahendra Singh	07.07.81	Ranchi	Jharkhand	RHB/WK	1999-00
DRAVID, Rahul	11.01.73	Indore	Karnataka	RHB/OB/WK	1990-91
GAMBHIR, Gautam	14.10.81	Delhi	Delhi	LHB/LB	1999-00
GANGULY, Sourav Chandidas	08.07.72	Calcutta	Bengal	LHB/RM	1989-90
HARBHAJAN SINGH	03.07.80	Jullundur	Punjab	RHB/OB	1997-98
JAFFER, Wasim	16.02.78	Bombay	Bombay	RHB/OB	1996-97
KAIF, Mohammad	01.12.80	Allahabad	Uttar Pradesh	RHB/OB	1997-98
KARTHIK, Krishankumar Dinesh	01.06.85	Madras	Tamil Nadu	RHB/WK	2002-03
KHAN, Zaheer	07.10.78	Shrirampur	Baroda	RHB/LFM	1999-00
KUMBLE, Anil	17.10.70	Bangalore	Karnataka	RHB/LBG	1989-90
LAXMAN, Vangipurappu Venkata Sai	01.11.74	Hyderabad	Hyderabad	RHB/OB	1992-93
PATEL, Munaf Musa	12.07.83	Ikhar	Maharashtra	RHB/RFM	2003-04
PATHAN, Irfan Khan	27.10.84	Baroda	Baroda	LHB/LMF	2000-01
SEHWAG, Virender	20.10.78	Delhi	Delhi	RHB/OB	1997-98
SINGH, Rudra Pratap	06.12.85	Rae Bareli	Uttar Pradesh	RHB/LMF	2003-04
SINGH, Vikram Rajvir	17.09.84	Chandigarh	Punjab	RHB/RMF	2004-05
SREESANTH, Shanthakumaran	06.02.83	Kothamangalam	Kerala	RHB/RFM	2002-03
TENDULKAR, Sachin Ramesh	24.04.73	Bombay	Bombay	RHB/RM/LB/OB	1988-89
YUVRAJ SINGH	12.12.81	Chandigarh	Punjab	LHB/LM/SLA	1996-97

THE FIRST-CLASS COUNTIES REGISTER, RECORDS AND 2006 AVERAGES

Career statistics are to the end of the 2006 season.
Test Match and LOI career bests have been updated to 1 March 2007.

ABBREVIATIONS – General

*	not out/unbroken partnership
b	born
BB	Best innings bowling analysis
Cap	Awarded 1st XI County Cap
f-c	first-class
HS	Highest Score
l-o	limited-overs
LOI	Limited-Overs Internationals
Tests	Official Test Matches
F-c Tours	Overseas tours involving first-class appearances

Awards

PCA 2006	Professional Cricketer's Association Player of 2006
Wisden 2005	One of *Wisden Cricketers' Almanack's* Five Cricketers of 2005
YC 2006	Cricket Writers' Club Young Cricketer of 2006

ECB Competitions

ARU	Anglia Ruskin University
BHC	Benson & Hedges Cup (1972-2002)
CC	Liverpool Victoria County Championship
CGT	Cheltenham & Gloucester Trophy
NL	National League
NWT	NatWest Trophy (1981-2000)
P40	PRO 40 League
SL	Sunday League (1969-98)
T20	Twenty20 Competition

Education

BHS	Boys' High School
C	College
CFE	College of Further Education
CHE	College of Higher Education
CS	Comprehensive School
GS	Grammar School
HS	High School
I	Institute
IHE	Institute of Higher Education
RGS	Royal Grammar School
S	School
SFC	Sixth Form College
SM	Secondary Modern School
SS	Secondary School
TC	Technical College
T(H)S	Technical (High) School
U	University
UMIST	University of Manchester Institute of Science and Technology
UWIC	University of Wales Institute, Cardiff

Playing Categories

LBG	Bowls right-arm leg-breaks and googlies
LF	Bowls left-arm fast
LFM	Bowls left-arm fast-medium
LHB	Bats left-handed
LM	Bowls left-arm medium pace
LMF	Bowls left-arm medium fast
OB	Bowls right-arm off-breaks
RF	Bowls right-arm fast
RFM	Bowls right-arm fast-medium
RHB	Bats right-handed
RM	Bowls right-arm medium pace
RMF	Bowls right-arm medium-fast
RSM	Bowls right-arm slow-medium
SLA	Bowls left-arm leg-breaks
SLC	Bowls left-arm 'Chinamen'
WK	Wicket-keeper

Teams (see also p 130)

ACT	Australian Capital Territory
ADBP	Agricultural Development Bank of P
B	Bangladesh
CD	Central Districts
EP	Eastern Province
GW	Griqualand West
HK	Hong Kong
K	Kenya
KRL	Khan Research Laboratories
NBP	National Bank of Pakistan
ND	Northern Districts
NSW	New South Wales
NT	Northern Transvaal
(O)FS	(Orange) Free State
PIA	Pakistan International Airlines
PTC	Pakistan Telecommunication Co
Q	Queensland
REDCO	Really Efficient Development Co
SAU	South African Universities
Tas	Tasmania
Vic	Victoria
WA	Western Australia
WAPDA	Water & Power Development Auth.
WP	Western Province

DERBYSHIRE

Formation of Present Club: 4 November 1870
Inaugural First-Class Match: 1871
Colours: Chocolate, Amber and Pale Blue
Badge: Rose and Crown
County Champions: (1) 1936
Gillette/NatWest/C & G Trophy Winners: (1) 1981
Benson and Hedges Cup Winners: (1) 1993
Pro 40/National League (Div 1) Winners: (0); best – 4th (Div 2) 2002
Sunday League Winners: (1) 1990
Twenty20 Cup Winners: (0) best – Quarter-Finalist 2005.

Chief Executive: Tom Sears, County Cricket Ground, Nottingham Road, Derby DE21 6DA • Tel: 01332 383211/388101 • Fax: 01332 290251 • Email: post@derbyshire.com • Web: www. derbyshire.com

Director of Cricket: D.L.Houghton. **Captain**: S.M.Katich. **Vice-Captain**: tba. **Overseas Players**: T.R.Birt and S.M.Katich. **2007 Beneficiary**: G.Welch. **Head Groundsman**: Neil Godrich. **Scorer**: John M.Brown. ‡ New registration. NQ Not qualified for England.

ADNAN, Muhammad **Hassan** SYED (M.A.O. College, Lahore), b Lahore, Pakistan 15 May 1974. 5'10". RHB, OB. Islamabad 1994-95, 2000-01. WAPDA 1997-98 to 2004-05 (as an overseas player 2002-03 to 2004-05). Gujranwala 1997-98 to 1998-99. Lahore 2003-04. Played 49 f-c matches in Pakistan before his Derbyshire debut in 2003; cap 2004. 1000 runs (1): 1380 (2004). HS 191 v Somerset (Taunton) 2005. BB 1-4 (CC). LO HS 113* v NZ (Derby) 2004. LO BB 2-13 v Leics (Derby) 2004 (NL). T20 HS 54. T20 BB 1-18.

‡BALLANCE, Gary Simon (Peterhouse BS, Marondera, Zimbabwe; Harrow S), b Harare, Zimbabwe 22 Nov 1989. Nephew of D.L.Houghton (Rhodesia/Zimbabwe 1978-79 to 1997-98; Director of Cricket). 5'10". LHB, LB. LO HS 73 v Hants (Southampton) 2006 (P40).

NQBIRT, Travis Rodney (Sale Catholic C), b Sale, Victoria, Australia 9 Dec 1981. 5'11". LHB, RM. Tasmania 2004-05 to date. Australia A 2006. Derbyshire debut 2006. 1000 runs (1): 1059 (2006). HS 181 v Glos (Bristol) 2006. BB 1-24 v Surrey (Oval) 2006. LO HS 145 Tas v S Aus (Hobart) 2004-05. LO BB2-15 v Glos (Derby) 2006 (P40). T20 HS 34.

BORRINGTON, Paul Michael (Repton S; Chellarton S), b Nottingham 24 May 1988. Son of A.J.Borrington (Derbyshire 1971-80). 5'10". RHB, OB. Debut 2005. HS 38 v Surrey (Derby) 2006.

NQBOTHA, Anthony Greyvensteyn (Maritzburg C; Maritzburg Technikon), b Pretoria, South Africa 17 Nov 1976. 6'0". LHB, SLA. Natal/KwaZulu Natal 1995-96 to 1998-99. EP/Easterns 1999-00 to 2002-03. Derbyshire debut/cap 2004. HS 156* v Yorks (Derby) 2005. BB 8-53 Natal B v Northerns B (Pretoria) 1997-98. CC BB 6-104 v Lancs (Manchester) 2005. LO HS 60* Easterns v EP (Benoni) 2001-02. LO BB 5-60 v West Indies A (Derby) 2006. T20 HS 25*. T20 BB 2-16.

‡CUSDEN, Simon Mark James (Simon Langton GS, Canterbury), b Canterbury 21 Feb 1985. 6'5". RHB, RFM. Kent 2004-06. HS 12* K v Sussex (Canterbury) 2004. BB 4-68 K v Northants (Canterbury) 2004. LO HS 3 (NL). LO BB 1-29 (NL).

DEAN, Kevin James (Leek HS; Leek CFE), b Derby 16 Oct 1975. 6'5". LHB, LMF. Debut (Derbyshire) 1996; cap 1998; benefit 2006. MCC 2002. HS 54* v Worcs (Derby) 2002. 50 wkts (2): most – 83 (2002). BB 8-52 v Kent (Canterbury) 2000. 2 hat-tricks (1998, 2000). LO HS 16* v Glamorgan(Cardiff) 1998 (SL) and 16* v Middx (Derby) 2002 (NL). LO BB 5-32 v Glos (Derby) 1996 (SL). T20 HS 8*. T20 BB 2-14.

‡ NQ**HARVEY, Ian** Joseph (Wonthaggi TC), b Wonthaggi, Victoria, Australia 10 Apr 1972. 5'10". RHB, RMF. Victoria 1993-94 to 2004-05. Gloucestershire 1999-2003, 2006;cap 1999. Yorkshire 2004-05. Cape Cobras 2005-06. Joined Derbyshire 2007 as a Kolpak registration. *Wisden* 2003. **LOI** (A): 73 (1997-98 to 2004); HS 48* v WI (Kingston) 2003; BB 4-16 v B (Darwin) 2003. F-c Tour: NZ 1994-95 (Aus Academy). HS 209* Y v Somerset (Leeds) 2005. BB 8-101 Aus A v SA A (Adelaide) 2002-03. UK BB 6-19 (10-32 match) Gs v Sussex (Hove) 2000. Hat-trick (Victoria 2001-02). LO HS 112 Gs v Somerset (Taunton) 2006 (CGT). LO BB 5-19 Gs v Northants (Bristol) 2000 (NL). T20 HS 109. T20 BB 3-28.

HUNTER, Ian David (Fyndoune Community C, Sacriston; Durham New C), b Durham City 11 Sep 1979. 6'2". RHB, RMF. Durham 2000-03. Derbyshire debut 2004. HS 65 Du v Northants (Northampton) 2002. De HS 48 v Somerset (Taunton) 2006. BB 5-63 v Du (Chester-le-St) 2005. LO HS 39 Du v Leics (Leicester) 2002 (BHC). LO BB 4-29 Du v Essex (Ilford) 2000 (NL). T20 HS 25*. T20 BB 3-26.

‡**KATICH, Simon** Mathew (Trinity C, WA; U of WA), b Middle Swan, Midland, W Australia 21 Aug 1975. 6'0". LHB. SLC. W Australia 1996-97 to 2001-02. NSW 2002-03 to date. Durham 2000; cap 2000. Yorkshire 2002 (one match). Hampshire 2003-05; cap 2003. **Tests** (A): 23 (2001 to 2005-06); HS 125 v I (Sydney) 2003-04; BB 6-65 v Z (Sydney) 2003-04. **LOI** (A): 45 (2000-01 to 2006-07); 107* v SL (Brisbane) 2005-06. F-c Tours (A): E 2001, 2005; NZ 2004-05; I 2004-05; SL 1999-00, 2003-04. 1000 runs (2+3): most – 1301 (2003-04). HS 228* WA v S Aus (Perth) 2000-01. UK HS 168* A v MCC (Arundel) 2001. CC HS 143* v Yorks (Scarborough) 2003. BB 7-130 NSW v Vic (Melbourne) 2002-03. UK BB 4-21 H v Northants (Southampton) 2003. LO HS 136* NSW v Vic (Bowral) 2003-04. LO BB 3-21 Aus A v SA (Adelaide) 2001-02. T20 HS 59*.

LUNGLEY, Tom (St John Houghton SS; SE Derbyshire C), b Derby 25 Jul 1979. 6'1". LHB, RM. Debut (Derbyshire) 2000. HS 47 v Warwks (Derby) 2001. BB 4-101 v Glamorgan (Swansea) 2003. LO HS 45 v Essex (Chelmsford) 2001 (NL). LO BB 4-28 v Essex (Derby) 2001 (NL). T20 HS 25. T20 BB 4-13.

NEEDHAM, Jake (Nottingham Bluecoat S, Aspley), b Portsmouth, Hants 30 Sep 1986. 6'1". RHB, OB. Debut (Derbyshire) 2005. HS 29 v Essex (Chelmsford) 2006. BB 2-42 v Essex (Derby) 2005 – on debut. LO HS 14 v Glos (Derby) 2006 (P40). LO BB 1-29 (P40).

PAGET, Christopher David (Repton S), b Stafford 2 Nov 1987. 6'0". RHB, OB. Debut (Derbyshire) 2004. No f-c appearances 2005-06. HS 7 v Yorks (Leeds) 2004. BB 3-63 v WI (Derby) 2004. CC BB – . LO HS – and BB 1-61 v West Indies A (Derby) 2006.

PIPE, David **James** (Queensbury S, Bradford), b Bradford, Yorks 16 Dec 1977. 5'11". RHB, WK. Worcestershire 1998-2005. Derbyshire debut 2006. HS 104* Wo v Hants (Southampton) 2003. De HS 89 v Leics (Leicester) 2006. LO HS 56 Worcs CB v Kent CB (Kidderminster) 2000 (NWT). Held 8 catches Wo v Herts (Hertford) 2001 (CGT) to equal l-o record. T20 HS29*.

‡**RANKIN, William Boyd** (Strabane GAS; Harper Adams UC), b Londonderry, Co Derry, N Ireland 5 Jul 1984. 6'8". LHB, RMF. Brother of R.J.Rankin (Ireland U-19 – 2003-04). Debut (Ireland) 2006-07. Middlesex summer contract 2004-05. Derbyshire summer contract 2006. LOI (Ireland): 1 (2006-07); HS – and BB – v Bermuda (Nairobi). HS – and BB 4-56 Ireland v UAE (Abu Dhabi) 2006-07. LO HS 5* Ireland A v UAE (Abu Dhabi) 2006. LO BB 1-25 v Kent (Canterbury) 2006 (P40).

‡**REDFERN, Daniel** James (Adam's GS, Newport, Shropshire), b Shrewsbury, Shropshire 18 Apr 1990. 5"9". LHB, OB. Awaiting f-c debut. LO HS 6 (P40).

NQ**SMITH, Gregory** Marc (St Stithins C), b Johannesburg, S Africa 20 Apr 1983. 5'9". RHB, RM/OB. Debut (SA Academy) 2003-04. Griqualand West 2003-04. Derbyshire debut 2006. HS 86 v Glos (Derby) 2006. BB 2-60 GW v Border (E London) 2003-04. De BB 1-18. LO HS 57 v West Indies A (Derby) 2006. LO BB 2-44 v Worcs (Worcester) 2006 (P40).

STUBBINGS, Stephen David (Frankston HS, Aus; Swinburne U, Aus), b Huddersfield, Yorks 31 Mar 1978. 6'3". LHB, OB. Debut (Derbyshire) 1997; cap 2001. 1000 runs (3): most 1126 (2005). HS 151 v Somerset (Taunton) 2005. LO HS 110 v Northants (Northampton) 2006 (CGT). T20 HS 57.

TAYLOR, Christopher Robert (Benton Park HS, Rawdon), b Leeds 21 Feb 1981. 6'4". RHB, RMF. Yorkshire 2001-05. Derbyshire debut 2006. HS 121* v Glamorgan (Cardiff) 2006. LO HS 111* v Durham (Derby) 2006 (CGT). T20 HS 25.

WAGG, Graham Grant (Ashlawn S, Rugby), b Rugby, 28 Apr 1983. 6'0". RHB, LM. Warwickshire 2002-04; contract terminated after ECB imposed a 15-month ban, expiring 1 Jan 2006, for taking cocaine. Derbyshire debut 2006. F-c Tour (Eng A): I 2003-04. HS 94 v Surrey (Derby) 2006. BB 6-38 v Somerset (Taunton) 2006. LO HS 45 Eng A v Karnataka (Bangalore) 2003-04. LO BB 4-50 v Kent (Birmingham) 2002 (NL). T20 HS 27. T20 BB 3-24.

WELCH, Graeme (Hetton CS), b Durham City 21 Mar 1972. 5'11½". RHB, RM. Warwickshire 1994-2000; cap 1997. Derbyshire debut/cap 2001; captain 2006; benefit 2007. F-c Tour: SA 1994-95 (Wa). HS 115* v Leics (Oakham) 2004. 50 wkts (4); most 65 (1997). BB 6-30 v Durham (Chester-le-St) 2001. LO HS 82 v Sussex (Hove) 2004 (NL). LO BB 6-31 v Middx (Derby) 2002 (NL). T20 HS 53. T20 BB 2-87.

‡**WESTON,** William **Philip** Christopher (Durham S), b Durham City 16 Jun 1973. Brother of R.M.S.Weston (Durham, Derbyshire & Middlesex 1995-2003); Son of M.P.Weston (Durham; England RFU). 6'3". LHB, LM. Worcestershire 1991-2002; cap 1995. Gloucestershire 2003-06; cap 2004. F-c Tours (Wo): Z 1993-94, 1996-97. 1000 runs (4); most – 1389 (1996). HS 205 Wo v Northants (Northampton) 1997. BB 2-39 Wo v P (Worcester) 1992. CC BB (Gs) 1-8. LO HS 134 Wo v Derbys (Derby) 2001 (NL). LO BB (Wo) 1-2 (SL). T20 HS 73*.

WHITE, Wayne Andrew (John Poet S, Etwall; Nottingham Trent U), b Derby 22 Apr 1985. 6'2". RHB, RMF. Debut (Derbyshire) 2005. HS 19* and BB 4-35 v Surrey (Derby) 2006. LO HS – . LO BB 1-38 (P40).

RELEASED/RETIRED

(Having made a first-class County appearance in 2006)

Di VENUTO, M.J. – *see DURHAM.*

GODDARD, Lee James (Batley GS; Huddersfield TC; Loughborough U), b Dewsbury, Yorks 22 Oct 1982. 5'10". RHB, WK. Loughborough UCCE 2003. Derbyshire 2004, 2006. HS 91 v Surrey (Derby) 2006. LO HS 36 v Kent (Canterbury) P40.

GRAY, Andrew Kenneth Donovan, b Armadale, W Australia 19 May 1974. RHB, OB. British passport. Yorkshire 2001-04. Derbyshire 2005-06. HS 104 Y v Somerset (Taunton) 2003. De HS 77* v Somerset (Derby) 2005. BB 4-128 Y v Surrey (Oval) 2001. De BB 3-56 v Yorks (Leeds) 2005. LO HS 30* Y v Leics (Leicester) 2003 (NL). LO BB 4-34 Y v Kent (Leeds) 2002 (NL). T20 HS 13. T20 BB 3-18.

JONES, P.S. – *see SOMERSET.*

NORTH, M.J. – *see GLOUCESTERSHIRE.*

SHEIKH, Mohammad Avez (Broadway S), b Birmingham 2 Jul 1973. 6'0". LHB, RM. Warwickshire 1997-2003. Derbyshire debut 2004. HS 58* Wa v Northants (Northampton) 2000. De HS 55 v Essex (Derby) 2005. BB 5-65 v Surrey (Oval) 2006. LO HS 50* v Scot (Derby) 2004 (NL). LO BB 4-17 Wa v Yorks (Birmingham) 2001 (NL). T20 HS 20. T20 BB 2-20.

R.J.Browning (*see NORTHAMPTONSHIRE*) and B.J.France left the staff having not made a first-class appearance in 2006.

COUNTY CAPS AWARDED IN 2006

Derbyshire	None
Durham	None
Essex	M.L.Pettini, T.J.Phillips, R.N.ten Doeschate
Glamorgan	D.S.Harrison
Gloucestershire	V.Banerjee, D.O.Brown, D.A.Burton, H.J.H.Marshall
Hampshire	J.H.K.Adams, J.T.A.Bruce, M.A.Carberry, B.V.Taylor, D.J.Thornely
Kent	J.M.Kemp
Lancashire	B.J.Hodge
Leicestershire	None
Middlesex	N.R.D.Compton, C.E.W.Silverwood, S.B.Styris
Northamptonshire	L.Klusener, M.S.Panesar
Nottinghamshire	C.E.Shreck
Somerset	C.L.White
Surrey	N.D.Doshi, Mohammad Akram
Sussex	Yasir Arafat
Warwickshire	A.G.R.Loudon
Worcestershire	P.A.Jaques, Z.Khan, R.J.Sillence, L.Vincent
Yorkshire	T.T.Bresnan, G.J.Kruis

Durham no longer operate a capping system. Gloucestershire award caps on first-class debut. Worcestershire award club colours on Championship debut.

DERBYSHIRE 2006

RESULTS SUMMARY

	Place	Won	Lost	Tied	Drew	No Result
County Championship (2nd Division)	**5th**	4	4		8	
All First-Class Matches		4	5		9	
C & G Trophy (North Conference)	5th	5	4			
Pro40 League (2nd Division)	8th	1	6			1
Twenty20 Cup (North Division)	5th	2	5			1

COUNTY CHAMPIONSHIP AVERAGES

BATTING AND FIELDING

Cap		*M*	*I*	*NO*	*HS*	*Runs*	*Avge*	*100*	*50*	*Ct/St*
–	M.J.North	3	6	1	161	465	93.00	2	2	6
–	T.R.Birt	12	20	2	181	967	53.72	3	5	7
2000	M.J.Di Venuto	13	22	1	161*	1110	52.85	3	6	18
–	L.J.Goddard	4	6	2	91	209	52.25	-	1	8
2001	S.D.Stubbings	16	28	1	124	951	35.22	2	6	10
–	D.J.Pipe	12	19	4	89	500	33.33	-	3	39/6
–	C.R.Taylor	13	23	–	121	719	31.26	2	3	9
2004	M.H.S.Adnan	16	26	–	117	776	29.84	1	4	3
–	M.A.Sheikh	8	12	3	51*	264	29.33	–	1	1
–	G.M.Smith	5	9	1	86	227	28.37	–	1	4
–	G.G.Wagg	9	14	1	94	317	24.38	–	1	3
2004	A.G.Botha	10	17	–	100	374	22.00	1	3	12
2001	G.Welch	13	20	3	94	336	19.76	–	2	6
–	A.K.D.Gray	7	10	2	29	133	16.62	–	–	–
–	P.S.Jones	16	21	6	34*	227	15.13	–	–	2
–	I.D.Hunter	13	13	6	48	102	14.57	–	–	6
1998	K.J.Dean	3	4	2	18	19	9.50	–	–	–

Also batted: (1 match each): P.M.Borrington 18, 38; J.Needham 0, 29; W.A.White 18*, 19*.

BOWLING

	O	M	R	W	Avge	Best	5wI	10wM
P.S.Jones	494.4	99	1804	56	32.21	6- 25	1	–
G.Welch	347.3	86	1071	30	35.70	4- 33	–	–
G.G.Wagg	213.2	34	904	24	37.66	6- 38	1	–
I.D.Hunter	336	71	1242	32	38.81	4- 47	–	–
A.G.Botha	294.3	67	981	24	40.87	6-117	1	–
M.A.Sheikh	201.5	58	591	14	42.21	5- 65	1	–
A.K.D.Gray	168.4	35	552	12	46.00	3-106	–	–
Also bowled:								
W.A.White	21	4	83	6	13.83	4- 35	–	–

M.H.S.Adnan 9-0-37-1; T.R.Birt 25-2-118-2; K.J.Dean 53-11-231-2; J.Needham 15-1-88-0; M.J.North 42-8-91-1; G.M.Smith 46.5-6-182-2; S.D.Stubbings 1-0-2-0.

The First-Class Averages (pp 130–146) give the records of Derbyshire players in all first-class matches for the county (Derbyshire's other opponents being Oxford UCCE and the Sri Lankans).

DERBYSHIRE RECORDS

FIRST-CLASS CRICKET

Highest Total	For 707-7d		v	Somerset	Taunton	2005
	V 662		by	Yorkshire	Chesterfield	1898
Lowest Total	For 16		v	Notts	Nottingham	1879
	V 23		by	Hampshire	Burton upon T	1958
Highest Innings	For 274	G.A.Davidson	v	Lancashire	Manchester	1896
	V 343*	P.A.Perrin	for	Essex	Chesterfield	1904

Highest Partnership for each Wicket

1st	322	H.Storer/J.Bowden	v	Essex	Derby	1929
2nd	417	K.J.Barnett/T.A.Tweats	v	Yorkshire	Derby	1997
3rd	316*	A.S.Rollins/K.J.Barnett	v	Leics	Leicester	1997
4th	328	P.Vaulkhard/D.Smith	v	Notts	Nottingham	1946
5th	302*†	J.E.Morris/D.G.Cork	v	Glos	Cheltenham	1993
6th	212	G.M.Lee/T.S.Worthington	v	Essex	Chesterfield	1932
7th	258	M.P.Dowman/D.G.Cork	v	Durham	Derby	2000
8th	198	K.M.Krikken/D.G.Cork	v	Lancashire	Manchester	1996
9th	283	A.Warren/J.Chapman	v	Warwicks	Blackwell	1910
10th	132	A.Hill/M.Jean-Jacques	v	Yorkshire	Sheffield	1986

† *346 runs were added for this wicket in two separate partnerships*

Best Bowling	For	10- 40	W.Bestwick	v	Glamorgan	Cardiff	1921
(Innings)	V	10- 45	R.L.Johnson	for	Middlesex	Derby	1994
Best Bowling	For	17-103	W.Mycroft	v	Hampshire	Southampton	1876
(Match)	V	16-101	G.Giffen	for	Australians	Derby	1886

Most Runs – Season	2165	D.B.Carr	(av 48.11)	1959
Most Runs – Career	23854	K.J.Barnett	(av 41.12)	1979-98
Most 100s – Season	8	P.N.Kirsten		1982
Most 100s – Career	53	K.J.Barnett		1979-98
Most Wkts – Season	168	T.B.Mitchell	(av 19.55)	1935
Most Wkts – Career	1670	H.L.Jackson	(av 17.11)	1947-63
Most Career W-K Dismissals	1304	R.W.Taylor	(1157 ct; 147 st)	1961-84
Most Career Catches in the Field	563	D.C.Morgan		1950-69

LIMITED-OVERS CRICKET

Highest Total	**CGT**	365-3		v	Cornwall	Derby	1986
	P40	304-3		v	Kent	Maidstone	2005
	T20	195-8		v	Yorkshire	Leeds	2005
Lowest Total	**CGT**	79		v	Surrey	The Oval	1967
	P40	61		v	Hampshire	Portsmouth	1990
	T20	98		v	Lancs	Manchester	2005
Highest Innings	**CGT**	173*	M.J.Di Venuto	v	Derbys CB	Derby	2000
	P40	141*	C.J.Adams	v	Kent	Chesterfield	1992
	T20	83	J.Moss	v	Yorks	Leeds	2005
Best Bowling	**CGT**	8-21	M.A.Holding	v	Sussex	Hove	1988
	P40	6- 7	M.Hendrick	v	Notts	Nottingham	1972
	T20	4-13	T.Lungley	v	Notts	Derby	2003

DURHAM

Formation of Present Club: 23 May 1882
Inaugural First-Class Match: 1992
Colours: Navy Blue, Yellow and Maroon
Badge: Coat of Arms of the County of Durham
County Champions: (0); 7th (Div 1) 2006
Gillette/NatWest/C & G Trophy Winners: (0); best – 2nd in N Conference 2006
Benson and Hedges Cup Winners: (0); best – quarter-finalist 1998, 2000, 2001
Pro 40/National League (Div 1) Winners: (0); best – 8th (Div 1) 2002, 2006
Sunday League Winners: (0); best – 7th 1993
Twenty20 Cup Winners: (0); best – 4th in Group 2004

Chief Executive: David Harker, County Ground, Riverside, Chester-le-Street, Co Durham DH3 3QR • Tel: 0191 387 1717 • Fax: 0191 387 1616 • Email: marketing@durham-ccc.co.uk • Web: www.durhamccc.co.uk

Director of Cricket: *tba*. **First XI Coach**: Geoff Cook. **Captain**: D.M.Benkerstein. **Vice-Captain**: P.D.Collingwood. **Overseas Player**: M.J.Di Venuto. **2007 Beneficiary**: P.D.Collingwood. **Testimonial**: A.Walker. **Head Groundsman**: David Measor. **Scorer**: Brian Hunt. ‡ New registration. NQ Not qualified for England.

Durham initially awarded caps immediately after their players joined the staff but revised this policy in 1998, again capping players on merit, past 'awards' having been nullified. Durham abolished both their capping and 'awards' systems after the 2005 season.

NQ**BENKENSTEIN,** Dale Martin (Durban HS; Michaelhouse HS), b Salisbury, Rhodesia 9 Jun 1974. Son of M.M.Benkenstein (Rhodesia, Natal B 1970-71 to 1980-81); brother of twins B.R. (Natal B 1993-94) and B.N. Benkenstein (Natal B, GW 1994-95 to 1996-97). 5'9". RHB, RM/OB. Natal/KwaZulu-Natal 1993-94 to 2003-04. Dolphins 2004-05 to date. MCC 2004. British passport. Durham debut 2005; captain 2006 to date. **LOI** (SA): 23 (1998-99 to 2002-03); HS 69 v WI (Cape Town) 1998-99; BB 3-5 v K (Colombo) 2002-03. F-c Tours (SA A): WI 2000; NZ 1998-99 (SA); SL 1995 (SA U-24), 1998. 1000 (2); most – 1500 (2006). HS 259 KZ-Natal v Northerns (Durban) 2001-02. Du HS 162* v Derby (Chester-le-St) 2005. BB 4-16 Dolphins v Warriors (Durban) 2005-06. Du BB 4-29 v Northants (Northampton) 2005. LO HS 107* Natal v North West (Fochville) 1997-98. LO BB 4-16 v Surrey (Chester-le-St) 2005. T20 HS 56*. T20 BB 3-10.

NQ**BREESE, Gareth** Rohan (Wolmer's BHS, Kingston; Kingston U of Technology, Jamaica), b Montego Bay, Jamaica 9 Jan 1976. 5'7". RHB, OB. Jamaica 1995-96 to 2005-06 captain/overseas player 2003-04 to 2005-06. British passport (Welsh father). Durham debut 2004; cap 2005. **Tests** (WI): 1 (2002-03); HS 5 and BB 2-108 v I (Madras) 2002-03. F-c Tours (WI): E 2002 (WI A); I 2002-03. HS 165* v Somerset (Taunton) 2004. BB 7-60 Jamaica v Barbados (Bridgetown) 2000-01. Du BB 5-41 (10-151 match) v Yorks (Scarborough) 2004 – scored 35 and 68 to complete match double. LO HS 52* v Middx (Chester-le-St) 2004. LO BB 4-24 Jamaica v Barbados (Bridgetown) 2005-06. T20 HS 24*. T20 BB 4-14.

‡NQ**CLAYDON, Mitchell** Eric (Westfield Sports HS, Sydney), b Fairfield, NSW, Australia 25 Nov 1982. 6'4". LHB, RMF. Yorkshire 2005-06. HS 38 and CC BB 1-42 Y v Durham (Chester-le-St) 2006. BB 1-27 Y v Bangladesh A (Leeds) 2005. LO HS 9 Y v Worcs (Worcester) 2006 (CGT). LO BB 2-41 Y v Derbys (Leeds) 2006 (CGT). T20 HS 12*. T20 BB 2-6.

COETZER, Kyle James (Aberdeen GS), b Aberdeen, Scotland 14 Apr 1984. 5'11". RHB, RM. Debut (Durham) 2004, 2006. Scotland 2004. HS 133* Scot v Kenya (Abu Dhabi) 2004. Du HS 67 v Glamorgan (Cardiff) 2004. LO HS 30 Durham CB v Glamorgan (Darlington) 2003 (CGT).

COLLINGWOOD, Paul David (Blackfyne CS; Derwentside C), b Shotley Bridge 26 May 1976. 5'11". RHB, RMF. Debut (Durham) 1996 v Northants (Chester-le-St) taking wicket of D.J.Capel with his first ball before scoring 91 and 16; cap 1998; benefit 2007. MBE 2005. **ECB central contract 2007. Tests**: 20 (2003-04 to 2006-07); HS 206 v A (Adelaide) 2006-07; BB 1-33. **LOI**: 112 (2001 to 2006-07); HS 120* v A (Melbourne) 2006-07; BB 6-31 v B (Nottingham) 2005 – first to score a hundred (112*) and take six wickets in same **LOI**. F-c Tours: A 2006-07; WI 2003-04; I 2005-06; P 2005-06; SL 2003-04. 1000 runs (2); most – 1120 (2005), inc six hundreds (Du record). HS 206 (*see Tests*). Du HS 190 v SL (Chester-le-St) 2002 and 190 v Derbys (Derby) 2005. BB 5-52 v Somerset (Stockton) 2005. LO HS 120* (*see LOI*). LO BB 6-31 (*see LOI*). T20 HS 46. T20 BB 4-22.

DAVIES, Anthony **Mark** (Northfield CS, Billingham; Stockton SFC), b Stockton-on-Tees 4 Oct 1980. 6'3". RHB. RMF. Debut (Durham) 2002; cap 2005. HS 62 v Somerset (Stockton) 2005. 50 wkts (1): 50 (2004). BB 6-32 v Worcs (Chester-le-St) 2005. LO HS 31* v Warwks (Chester-le-St) 2002 (NL). LO BB 4-13 v Sussex (Chester-le-St) 2001 (NL). T20 HS 6. T20 BB 2-14.

‡ [NQ]**Di VENUTO, Michael** James (St Virgil's C; Hobart), b Hobart, Australia 12 Dec 1973. 6'0". LHB, RM/LBG. Tasmania 1991-92 to date. Sussex 1999; cap 1999. Derbyshire 2000-06; cap 2000; appointed captain for 2004 but missed entire season – back surgery. **LOI** (A): 9 (1996-97 to 1997-98); HS 89 v SA (Johannesburg) 1996-97. F-c Tours: Z 1995-96 (Tas); Sc/Ire 1998 (Aus A). 1000 runs (6): most – 1538 (2002). HS 230 De v Northants (Derby) 2002. BB (Tas) 1-0. CC BB (Sx) 1-3. LO HS 173* v Derbys CB (Derby) 2000 (NWT). LO BB (Tas) 1-10. T20 HS 95*. T20 BB 3-19.

GIBSON, Ottis Delroy (Ellerslie SS), b Sion Hill, Bridgetown, Barbados 16 Mar 1969. 6'2". RHB, RFM. Barbados 1990-91 to 1997-98. Border 1992-93 to 1994-95. Glamorgan 1994-96; cap 1994. Griqualand West 1998-99 to 1999-00. Gauteng 2000-01. Leicestershire 2004-05; cap 2004. Durham debut 2006. Staffordshire 2001. **Tests** (WI): 2 (1995 to 1998-99); HS 37 v SA (Cape Town)1998-99; BB 2-81 v E (Lord's) 1995. **LOI** (WI): 15 (1995 to 1996-97); HS 52 v A (Brisbane) 1995-96; BB 5-40 v SL (Perth) 1995-96. F-c Tours (WI): E 1995; A 1995-96; SA 1997-98 (WI A), 1998-99; SL 1996-97 (WI A). HS 155 v Yorks (Leeds) 2006. 50 wkts (2): most – 60 (1994, 2004). BB 7-55 Border v Natal (Durban) 1994-95. CC BB 6-43 (11-141 match) Le v Notts (Leicester) 2004. Du BB 6-110 v Kent (Stockton) 2006. LO HS 102* Staffs v Northumb (Jesmond) 2001 (CGT). LO BB 5-19 Border v GW (Kimberley) 1992-93. T20 HS 18. T20 BB 2-20.

‡**GIDMAN, William** Robert Simon (Wycliffe C), b High Wycombe, Bucks 14 Feb 1985. Younger brother of A.P.R.Gidman (*see GLOUCESTERSHIRE*). LHB, RM. MCC YC 2004-06. Awaiting f-c debut. HS LO 12 Gs CB v Surrey CB (Bristol) 2002.

HARMISON, Ben William (Ashington HS), b Ashington, Northumb 9 Jan 1986. Younger brother of S.J.Harmison. 6'5". LHB, RMF. Debut (Durham) 2006, scoring 110 v Oxford UCCE (Oxford). Scored 105 in his second match (v West Indies A). HS 110 (*see above*). LO HS 57 v Notts (Chester-le-St) 2006 (P40). LO BB 1-51 v Bangladesh A (Chester-le-St) 2005 – on 1st XI debut. T20 HS 5.

HARMISON, Stephen James (Ashington HS), b Ashington, Northumb 23 Oct 1978. Elder Brother of B.W.Harmison. 6'4". RHB, RF. Debut (Durham) 1996; cap 1999. *Wisden* 2004. MBE 2005. **ECB central contract 2007. Tests**: 49 (2002 to 2006-07); HS 42 v SA (Cape Town) 2004-05 – first No. 11 to top-score for England; BB 7-12 (9-73 match) v WI (Kingston) 2003-04. **LOI**: 46 (2002-03 to 2006-07); HS 13* v NZ (Chester-le-St) 2003; BB 5-33 v A (Bristol) 2005; hat-trick v I (Nottingham) 2004. F-c Tours: A 2002-03, 2005-06 (RW), 2006-07; SA 1998-99 (Eng A), 2004-05; WI 2003-04; I 2005-06; P 2005-06; Z 1998-99 (Eng A); B 2003-04. HS 42 (*see Tests*). Du HS 36 v Kent (Canterbury) 1998. 50 wkts (3); most – 64 (1999). BB 7-12 (*see Tests*). Du BB 6-52 (9-84 match) v Lancs (Manchester) 2005. Hat-trick v Worcs (Chester-le-St) 2005. LO HS 17 v Lancs (Manchester) 2006 (CGT). LO BB 5-33 (*see LOI*). T20 HS – . T20 BB 1-13.

IQBAL, Moneeb Mohammed (Hillhead HS; Anniesland C, Glasgow), b Glasgow, Scotland 28 Feb 1986. Brother-in-law of Mohammad Ramzan (Pakistan &etc 1986-87 to 2003-04). RHB, LB. Debut (Durham) 2006. HS 20 and CC BB 2-57 v Kent (Stockton) 2006. BB 4-36 v OU (Oxford) 2006. LO HS – .

KILLEEN, Neil (Greencroft CS; Derwentside C; Teesside U), b Shotley Bridge 17 Oct 1975. 6'2". RHB, RMF. Debut (Durham) 1995; cap 1999; benefit 2006. MCC 1999-2000. Tour (MCC) B 1999-00. HS 48 v Somerset (Chester-le-St) 1995. 50 wkts (1): 58 (1999). BB 7-70 v Hants (Chester-le-St) 2003. LO HS 32 v Middx (Lord's) 1996 (SL). LO BB 6-31 v Derbys (Derby) 2000 (NL). T20 HS 17*. T20 BB 4-7.

MUCHALL, Gordon James (Durham S), b Newcastle upon Tyne, Northumb 2 Nov 1982. 6'0". RHB, RM. Northumberland 1999. Debut (Durham) 2002; cap 2005. F-c Tours (ECB Acad): SL 2002-03. HS 219 v Kent (Canterbury) 2006. BB 3-26 v Yorks (Leeds) 2003. LO HS 101* v Yorks (Leeds) 2005 (NL). LO BB 1-15 (NL). T20 HS 64*. T20 BB 1-8.

MUSTARD, Philip (Usworth CS), b Sunderland 8 Oct 1982. 5'11". LHB, WK. Debut (Durham) 2002. HS 130 v Kent (Canterbury) 2006. LO HS 84 v Essex (Chester-le-St) 2006 (P40). T20 HS 67*.

ONIONS, Graham (St Thomas More RC S, Blaydon), b Gateshead 9 Sep 1982. 6'1". RHB, RMF. Debut (Durham) 2004. HS 40 v Warwks (Birmingham) 2006. BB 5-45 v Middx (Lord's) 2006. LO HS 11 v Notts (Chester-le-St) 2006 (P40). LO BB 3-39 v Derbys (Derby) 2005 (NL). T20 HS 31. T20 BB 3-25.

PARK, Garry Terence (Eshowe HS, Natal; Anglia Ruskin U), b Empangeni, Zululand, South Africa 19 Apr 1983. 5'7". RHB, WK, RM. Cambridge UCCE 2003-05. Debut (Durham) 2006. Cambridgeshire 2005. HS 100* v Yorks (Leeds) 2006. LO HS 32 v Bangladesh A (Chester-le-St) 2005.

PLUNKETT, Liam Edward (Nunthorpe SS; Teesside Tertiary C), b Middlesbrough, Yorks 6 Apr 1985. 6'3". RHB, RFM. Debut (Durham) 2003. **Tests**: 6 (2005-06 to 2006); HS 28 v P (Lord's) 2006; BB 3-17 v SL (Birmingham) 2006. **LOI**: 22 (2005-06 to 2006-07); HS 56 v P (Lahore) 2005-06; BB 3-24 v A (Sydney) 2006-07. F-c Tours: I 2005-06; P 2005-06. HS 74* v Somerset (Stockton) 2005. 50 wkts (1): 51 (2005). BB 6-74 v Hants (Chester-le-St) 2004. LO HS 56 (*see LOI*). LO BB 4-28 v Surrey (Chester-le-St) 2005 (NL). T20 HS 8. T20 BB 2-18.

SCOTT, Gary Michael (Hetton CS), b Sunderland 21 Jul 1984. 6'0". RHB, OB. Durham (Durham) 2001 – youngest Durham f-c debutant (17y 19d), 2005. HS 133 v Oxford UCCE (Oxford) 2006. CC HS 77 v Yorks (Leeds) 2006. BB 2-39 v Warwks (Chester-le-St) 2006. LO HS 100 Durham CB v Herefords (Darlington) 2002 (CGT). LO BB 2-24 v Warwks (Birmingham) 2006 (P40). T20 HS 31. T20 BB 3-27.

‡**SMITH, William** Rew (Bedford S; Collingwood C, Durham), b Luton, Beds 28 Sep 1982. 5'9". RHB, OB. Debut 2002. Durham UCCE 2003-05; captain 2004-05. British U 2004-05. Notts 2nd XI debut 1999 when aged 16y 309d. Bedfordshire 1999-2002. HS 156 DU v Somerset (Taunton) 2005, sharing opening partnership of 304 with A.J.Maiden. CC HS 141 v Middx (Lord's) 2006. BB 3-34 DU v Leics (Leicester) 2005. CC BB –. LO HS 95* Nt v Scot (Nottingham) 2006 (CGT). T20 HS 55.

STONEMAN, Mark Daniel (Whickham CS), b Newcastle-upon-Tyne, Northumb 26 Jun 1987. 5'11". LHB, RM. Staff 2006 – awaiting f-c debut.

NQ**THORP, Callum** David (Servite C, Tuart Hill, Perth), b Mount Lawley, Perth, Australia 11 Feb 1975. 6'3". British passport (English parents). RHB, RMF. W Australia 2002-03 to 2003-04. Durham debut 2005. HS 75 and BB 6-55 (11-97 match) v Hants (Southampton) 2006. LO HS 52 v B (Chester-le-Street) 2005. LO BB 6-17 v Scot (Edinburgh) 2006 (CGT). T20 HS 13. T20 BB 2-32.

NQ**WISEMAN, Paul** John (Auckland IT), b Takapuna, Auckland, New Zealand 4 May 1970. 6'1". RHB, OB. Auckland 1991-92 to 1992-93. Otago 1994-95 to 2000-01. Canterbury 2001-02 to 2005-06. Derbyshire debut 2006. Tests (NZ): 25 (1998 to 2004-05); HS 36 v SA (Hamilton) 2003-04; BB 5-82 v SL (Colombo) 1997-98 – on debut. **LOI** (NZ): 15 (1997-98 to 2003); HS 16 v SL (Colombo) 1998; BB 4-45 v Z (Nairobi) 2000-01. Tours (NZ): A 2004-05; SA 1997 (NZ Acad), 2004-05 (NZ A); I 1999-00, 2003-04; SL 1998, 2003, 2005-06 (NZ A); Z 1997-98, 2000-01; B 2004-05. HS 130 Canterbury v ND (Hamilton) 2005-06. UK/Du HS 6* and BB 1-127 v Y (Leeds) 2006. BB 9-13 Canterbury v CD (Christchurch) 2004-05. LO HS 65* Canterbury v Auckland (Christchurch) 2001-02. LO BB 4-45 (*see LOI*). T20 HS – . T20 BB 2-20.

RELEASED/RETIRED

(Having made a first-class County appearance in 2006)

BRIDGE, Graeme David (Southmoor S, Sunderland), b Sunderland 4 Sep 1980. 5'8". RHB, SLA. Durham 1999-2006. HS 52 v Leics (Chester-le-St) 2004. BB 6-84 v Hants (Chester-le-St) 2001. LO HS 50* v Leics (Leicester) 2002 (BHC). LO BB 4-20 v Hants (Chester-le-St) 2003 (NL). T20 HS 11*. T20 BB 2-16.

LEWIS, Jonathan James Benjamin (King Edward VI S, Chelmsford; Roehampton IHE), b Isleworth, Middx 21 May 1970. 5'9½". RHB, RSM. Essex 1990-96; cap 1994; scored 116* on debut v Surrey (Oval). Durham 1997-2006; cap 1998; captain 2000 (*part*) to 2004; benefit 2004. 1000 runs (4); most – 1252 (1997). HS 210* v OU (Oxford) 1997 – on Du debut. CC HS 160* v Derbys (Chester-le-St) 1997. BB 1-73 v Surrey (Chester-le-St) 1998. LO HS 102 v Glos (Cheltenham) 1997 (NL). T20 HS 49*. T20 BB – .

NQ**LEWIS, Mic**hael Llewellyn (Parade C, Bundoora, Vic), b Greensborough, Victoria, Australia 29 Jun 1974. 6'0". RHB, RFM. Victoria 1999-00 to date. Glamorgan 2004. Durham 2005-06. **LOI** (A): 7 (2005-06); HS 4*; BB 3-56 v NZ (Wellington) 2005-06. HS 54* Vic v NSW (Sydney) 2001-02. UK HS 38 Du v Hants (Chester-le-St) 2006. BB 6-59 Vic v Q (Melbourne) 2003-04. UK BB 5-80 Du v Yorks (Chester-le-St) 2005. LO HS 19 Vic v Tas (Melbourne) 2003-04. LO BB 5-48 v Sussex (Chester-le-St) 2005. T20 HS 0. T20 BB 2-18.

LOWE, James Adam (Northallerton C, Yorks), b Bury St Edmunds, Suffolk 4 Nov 1982. 6'2". RHB, WK, occ OB. Durham 2003-06. HS 80 v Hants (Southampton) 2003 – on debut. LO HS 36 v B (Chester-le-Street) 2005.

RELEASED/RETIRED continued on p 38

DURHAM 2006

RESULTS SUMMARY

	Place	*Won*	*Lost*	*Tied*	*Drew*	*No Result*
County Championship (1st Division)	**7th**	4	8		4	
All First-Class Matches		5	9		4	
C & G Trophy (North Conference)	2nd	6	2			1
Pro40 League (1st Division)	8th	2	4	1		1
Twenty20 Cup (North Division)	6th	2	6			

COUNTY CHAMPIONSHIP AVERAGES

BATTING AND FIELDING

Cap		*M*	*I*	*NO*	*HS*	*Runs*	*Avge*	*100*	*50*	*Ct/St*
–	G.T.Park	2	4	2	100*	256	128.00	1	1	–
2005	D.M.Benkenstein	16	29	2	151	1427	52.85	3	7	7
–	J.P.Maher	16	30	2	106	978	34.92	2	4	12/1
–	O.D.Gibson	13	22	4	155	596	33.11	1	2	5
–	P.Mustard	16	27	2	130	816	32.64	2	3	53/1
–	B.W.Harmison	7	13	2	75	335	30.45	–	3	4
2005	G.J.Muchall	14	26	–	219	755	29.03	2	3	10
–	G.M.Scott	7	14	–	77	312	22.28	–	2	4
1998	J.J.B.Lewis	9	16	–	99	355	22.18	–	2	5
2005	G.R.Breese	16	27	–	110	578	21.40	1	1	13
–	G.J.Pratt	6	10	–	52	193	19.30	–	1	7
–	C.D.Thorp	11	20	2	75	285	15.83	–	2	4
–	M.L.Lewis	11	18	9	38	127	14.11	–	–	4
–	G.Onions	15	24	6	40	209	11.61	–	–	3
–	M.M.Iqbal	2	4	–	20	44	11.00	–	–	1
1999	N.Killeen	7	10	2	34	68	8.50	–	–	2
–	J.A.Lowe	3	6	–	25	37	6.16	–	–	4

Also batted: A.M.Davies (1 match – cap 2005) 10, 0; S.J.Harmison (2 – cap 1999) 18, 3*, 8; P.J.Wiseman (2) 4, 6*.

BOWLING

	O	*M*	*R*	*W*	*Avge*	*Best*	*5wI*	*10wM*
C.D.Thorp	298.3	88	883	38	23.23	6- 55	2	1
M.L.Lewis	292.3	67	1031	35	29.45	4- 69	–	–
O.D.Gibson	394.4	77	1458	49	29.75	6-110	1	–
N.Killeen	182.5	48	507	16	31.68	5- 29	1	–
G.Onions	413.5	78	1608	50	32.16	5- 45	1	–
D.M.Benkenstein	141.1	38	536	14	38.28	3- 16	–	–
G.R.Breese	358.3	61	1217	26	46.80	4- 75	–	–

Also bowled: A.M.Davies 8-5-9-1; S.J.Harmison 32-9-95-4; M.M.Iqbal 33-3-200-2; G.M.Scott 31.1-6-151-3; G.J.Muchall 2-0-22-0; P.J.Wiseman 56-11-230-1.

The First-Class Averages (pp 130–146) give the records of Durham players in all first-class matches for the county (Durham's other opponents being Oxford UCCE and West Indies A), with the exception of S.J.Harmison whose full county figures are as above, P.D.Collingwood whose seven first-class appearances were all for England, and:

L.E.Plunkett 1-1-0-28-28-28.00-0-0-0ct. 6.5-1-24-2-12.00-2/24.

Durham abandoned their capping system in 2006

DURHAM RECORDS

FIRST-CLASS CRICKET

Highest Total	For 645-6d		v	Middlesex	Lord's	2002
	V 810-4d		by	Warwicks	Birmingham	1994
Lowest Total	For 67		v	Middlesex	Lord's	1996
	V 56		by	Somerset	Chester-le-St[2]	2003
Highest Innings	For 273	M.L.Love	v	Hampshire	Chester-le-St[2]	2003
	V 501*	B.C.Lara	for	Warwicks	Birmingham	1994

Highest Partnership for each Wicket

1st	334*	S.Hutton/M.A.Roseberry	v	Oxford U	Oxford	1996
2nd	258	J.J.B.Lewis/M.L.Love	v	Notts	Chester-le-St[2]	2001
3rd	205	G.Fowler/S.Hutton	v	Yorkshire	Leeds	1993
4th	250	P.D.Collingwood/D.M.Benkenstein	v	Derbys	Derby	2005
5th	222	D.M.Benkenstein/G.R.Breese	v	Middlesex	Lord's	2006
6th	249	G.J.Muchall/P.Mustard	v	Kent	Canterbury	2006
7th	315	D.M.Benkenstein/O.D.Gibson	v	Yorkshire	Leeds	2006
8th	134	A.C.Cummins/D.A.Graveney	v	Warwicks	Birmingham	1994
9th	127	D.G.C.Ligertwood/S.J.E.Brown	v	Surrey	Stockton	1996
10th	103	M.M.Betts/D.M.Cox	v	Sussex	Hove	1996

Best Bowling	For	9- 64	M.M.Betts	v	Northants	Northampton	1997
(Innings)	V	9- 36	M.S.Kasprowicz	for	Glamorgan	Cardiff	2003
Best Bowling	For	14-177	A.Walker	v	Essex	Chelmsford	1995
(Match)	V	13-110	M.S.Kasprowicz	for	Glamorgan	Chester-le-St[2]	2003

Most Runs – Season	1536	W.Larkins	(av 37.46)	1992
Most Runs – Career	7854	J.J.B.Lewis	(av 31.41)	1997-2006
Most 100s – Season	6	P.D.Collingwood		2005
Most 100s – Career	14	J.E.Morris		1994-99
	14	P.D.Collingwood		1996-2005
Most Wkts – Season	77	S.J.E.Brown	(av 25.87)	1996
Most Wkts – Career	518	S.J.E.Brown	(av 28.30)	1992-2002
Most Career W-K Dismissals	194	M.P.Speight	(189 ct; 5 st)	1997-2001
Most Career Catches in the Field	116	P.D.Collingwood		1996-2005

LIMITED-OVERS CRICKET

Highest Total	**CGT**	326-4		v	Herefords	Chester-le-St[2]	1995
	P40	319-3		v	Worcs	Worcester	2004
	T20	180-4		v	Notts	Chester-le-St[2]	2005
Lowest Total	**CGT**	82		v	Worcs	Chester-le-St[1]	1968
	P40	72		v	Warwicks	Birmingham	2002
	T20	98		v	Yorks	Chester-le-St[2]	2006
Highest Innings	**CGT**	132	M.A.Gough	v	Wales MC	Cardiff	2002
	P40	131*	W.Larkins	v	Hampshire	Portsmouth	1994
	T20	67*	P.Mustard	v	Derbyshire	Chester-le-St[2]	2006
Best Bowling	**CGT**	7-32	S.P.Davis	v	Lancashire	Chester-le-St[1]	1983
	P40	6-31	N.Killeen	v	Derbyshire	Derby	2000
	T20	4- 7	N.Killeen	v	Leics	Leicester	2004

[1] Chester-le-Street CC (Ropery Lane) [2] Riverside Ground

ESSEX

Formation of Present Club: 14 January 1876
Inaugural First-Class Match: 1894
Colours: Blue, Gold and Red
Badge: Three Seaxes above Scroll bearing 'Essex'
County Champions: (6) 1979, 1983, 1984, 1986, 1991, 1992
Gillette/NatWest/C & G Trophy Winners: (2) 1985, 1997
Benson and Hedges Cup Winners: (2) 1979, 1998
Pro 40/National League (Div 1) Winners: (2) 2005, 2006
Sunday League Winners: (3) 1981, 1984, 1985
Twenty20 Cup Winners: (0); best – Semi-Finalist 2006

Chief Executive: David E.East, County Ground, New Writtle Street, Chelmsford CM2 0PG • Tel: 01245 252420 • Fax: 01245 254030 • Email: administration.essex@ecb.co.uk • Web: www.essexcricket.org.uk

First XI Coach/Captain: R.C.Irani. **Vice-Captain**: tba. **Overseas Players**: A.J.Bichel, Danish Kaneria and A.Nel. **2007 Beneficiary:** none. **Head Groundsman**: Stuart Kerrison. **Scorer**: A.E. (Tony) Choat. ‡ New registration. NQ Not qualified for England.

AHMED, Jahid Sheikh (St Peter's HS, Burnham-on-Crouch; East London U), b Chelmsford 20 Feb 1986. 5'11". RHB, RMF. Debut (Essex) 2005. MCC YC 2004. HS 14* v Worcs (Worcester) 2005 – on debut. BB 2-50 v LU (Chelmsford) 2006. LO HS – . LO BB 4-32 v SL (Chelmsford) 2006. T20 HS – . T20 BB 1-25.

NQ**BICHEL, Andrew** John (Laidley HS; Ipswich C, Queensland), b Laidley, Queensland, Australia 27 Aug 1970. RHB, RFM. 5'11". Queensland 1992-93 to date. Worcestershire 2001-02, 2004; cap 2001. Hampshire 2005. Essex debut 2006. **Tests** (A): 19 (1996-97 to 2003-04); HS 71 v WI (Bridgetown) 2002-03; BB 5-60 v WI (Melbourne) 2000-01. **LOI** (A): 67 (1996-97 to 2003-04); HS 64 v NZ (Pt Elizabeth) 2002-03; BB 7-20 v E (Pt Elizabeth) 2002-03. F-c Tours (A): E 1997; SA 1996-97, 2001-02; WI 1998-99, 2002-03; P 2002-03 (in Sharjah); Scot 1998 (Aus A). HS 142 Wo v Northants (Worcester) 2004. 50 wkts (1+3): most – 66 (2001). BB 9-93 (10-131 match) Wo v Glos (Worcester) 2002. LO HS 100 Wo v Glamorgan (Cardiff) 2001 (BHC). LO BB 7-20 (*see LOI*). T20 HS 58*. T20 BB 4-23.

BOPARA, Ravinder Singh (Brampton Manor S; Barking Abbey Sports C), b Newham, London 4 May 1985. 5'8". RHB, RMF. Debut (Essex) 2002; cap 2005. **LOI**: 1 (2006-07); HS 7* and BB 1-19 v A (Sydney) 2006-07. HS 159 v Glamorgan (Cardiff) 2006. BB 5-75 v Surrey (Chelmsford) 2006. LO HS 101* v Somerset (Taunton) 2006 (CGT). LO BB 3-23 v SL (Chelmsford) 2006. T20 HS 83. T20 BB 3-18.

CHAMBERS, Maurice Anthony (Homerton TC; Sir George Monoux C), b Port Antonio, Jamaica 14 Sep 1987. 6'3". RHB, RFM. Debut (Essex) 2005. No f-c appearances 2006. MCC YC 2004. HS 2* and BB 1-73 v Derbys (Chelmsford) 2005 – on debut.

CHOPRA, Varun (Ilford County HS), b Barking 21 Jun 1987. RHB, LB. Debut (Essex) 2006. HS 106 v Glos (Chelmsford) 2006 – on CC debut. LO HS 6 v SL (Chelmsford) 2006. T20 HS 1*.

COOK, Alastair Nathan (Bedford S), b Gloucester 25 Dec 1984. 6'3". LHB, OB. Debut (Essex) 2003; cap 2005. MCC 2004-06. Essex 2nd XI debut 2000 when aged 15y 235d. England U-19 capt 2003-04. YC 2005. **ECB central contract 2007. Tests**: 14 (2005-6 to 2006-07); HS 127 v P (Manchester) 2006. Scored 60 and 104* v I (Nagpur) 2005-06 on debut. First to score four hundreds for England before his 22nd birthday. First to score 1000 runs in the calendar year of his debut for England. **LOI**: 2 (2006): HS 41 v SL (Leeds) 2006. F-c Tours: A 2006-07; WI 2005-06 (Eng A); I 2005-06; SL 2004-05 (Eng A). 1000 runs (2); most – 1466 (2005). HS 195 v Northants (Northampton) 2005. Scored 214 v Australians (Chelmsford) 2005 in 2-day non-f-c match.. BB 3-13 v Northants (Chelmsford) 2005. LO HS 94 v Northants (Northampton) 2005 (NL). T20 HS 9.

NQ**DANISH** Parabha Shanker **KANERIA** (St Patrick's HS; Government Islamia C), b Karachi, Pakistan 16 Dec 1980. 6'1". Cousin of Anil Dalpat (Pakistan) and second Hindu to represent Pakistan. RHB, LBG. Debut (PNSC) 1998-99. Karachi /Whites/Blues 1998-99 to 2004-05. Habib Bank 2000-01 to date. Essex 2004-05; cap 2004. **Tests** (P): 46 (2000-01 to 2006-07); HS 29 v E (Leeds) 2006; BB 7-77 v B (Dhaka) 2001-02. **LOI** (P): 16 (2001-02 to 2006); HS 3*; BB 3-31 v NZ (Dambulla) 2003. F-c Tours (P): E 2006; A 2004-05; WI 2004-05; NZ 2003-04; I 2004-05; SL 2001 (Pak A); B 2001-02; K 2000 (Pak A). HS 47 Karachi Blues v Karachi Whites (Karachi) 2004-05. Ex HS 22 v Northants (Chelmsford) 2005. 50 wkts (1+1); most – 63 (2004). BB 7-39 Karachi Whites v Gujranwala (Karachi) 2000-01. UKBB 7-65 (13-186 match) v Yorks (Chelmsford) 2004. LO HS 16 Habib Bank v KRL (Karachi) 2005-06. LO BB 5-21 Habib Bank v Customs (Karachi) 2005-06. T20 HS 5. T20 BB 4-31.

FLOWER, Andrew (Wainona HS, Harare), b Cape Town, South Africa 28 Apr 1968. 5'10". Elder brother of G.W.Flower. LHB, WK, occ RM/OB. Debut (ZCU President's XI) 1986-87. Zimbabwe B 1987-88. Zimbabwe debut 1988-89. Mashonaland 1993-94 to 2002-03. MCC 1996-2005. Essex debut/cap 2002. S Australia 2003-04. British passport after 2003 season. Qualified for England 2005. *Wisden* 2001. **Tests** (Z): 63 (1992-93 to 2002-03, 20 as captain); HS 232* v I (Nagpur) 2000-01. **LOI** (Z): 213 (1991-92 to 2002-03, 52 as captain); HS 145 v I (Colombo) 2002-03; scored 115* v SL (New Plymouth) on debut. F-c Tours (Z) (C=captain): E 1993, 2000C; A 1994-95C; SA 1999-00; WI 1999-00C; NZ 1995-96C, 1997-98, 2000-01; I 1992-93, 2000-01, 2001-02; P 1993-94C, 1996-97, 1998-99; SL 1996-97, 1997-98, 2001-02; B 2001-02. 1000 runs (5): 1536 (2006). HS 271* v Northants (Northampton) 2006. BB 1-1 Mashonaland v Mashonaland CD (Harare) 1993-94. LO HS 145 (*see LOI*). LO BB (Mashonaland)1-21. T20 HS 83.

NQ**FLOWER, Grant** William (St George's C), b Salisbury, Rhodesia 20 Dec 1970. 5'10". Younger brother of A Flower. RHB, SLA. Debut (Zimbabwe) 1989-90. Mashonaland U-24/Young Mashonaland 1993-94 to 1995-96. Mashonaland 1994-95 to 2003-04. MCC 1996-97. Leicestershire 2002 (one match); cap 2002. Essex debut/cap 2005 (Kolpak registration). **Tests** (Z): 67 (1992-93 to 2003-04); HS 201* v P (Harare) 1994-95 sharing with A.Flower in fourth-wicket partnership of 269, the highest stand between brothers in Test cricket; BB 4-41 (8-104 match) v B (Chittagong) 2001-02. **LOI** (Z): 219 (1992-93 to 2003-04, 1 as captain); HS 142* v B (Bulawayo) 2000-01; BB 4-32 v K (Dhaka) 1998-99. F-c Tours (Z): E 1990, 2000; A 1994-95; SA 1999-00; WI 1999-00; NZ 1995-96, 1997-98, 2000-01; I 1992-93, 2000-01, 2001-02; P 1993-94, 1996-97, 1998-99; SL 1996-97, 1997-98, 2001-02; B 2001-02. HS 243* Mashonaland v Matabeleland (Harare) 1996-97. UK HS 115 v Lancs (Manchester) 2005. BB 7-31 Z v Lahore (Lahore) 1998-99. UK BB 4-66 Le v Warwks (Birmingham) 2002. Ex BB 3-28 v Glos (Bristol) 2006. LO HS 148* Mashonaland v Midlands (Kwekwe) 2002-03. LO BB 4-32 (*see LOI*). T20 HS 4. T20 BB 3-20.

FOSTER, James Savin (Forest S, Snaresbrook; Collingwood C, Durham U), b Whipps Cross 15 Apr 1980. 6'0". RHB, WK. British U 2000-01. Essex debut 2000; cap 2001. Durham UCCE 2001. MCC 2004. **Tests**: 7 (2001-02 to 2002-03); HS 48 v I (Bangalore) 2001-02. **LOI**: 11 (2001-02); HS 13 v I (Bombay) 2001-02. F-c Tours: A 2002-03; WI 2000-01 (Eng A); NZ 2001-02; I 2001-02. 1000 runs (1): 1037 (2004). HS 212 v Leics (Chelmsford) 2004. LO HS 67 v Lancs (Chelmsford) 2006 (P40). T20 HS 62*.

IRANI, Ronald Charles (Smithills CS, Bolton), b Leigh, Lancs 26 Oct 1971. 6'3". RHB, RMF. Lancashire 1990-93. Essex debut/cap 1994; captain 2000 to date; benefit 2003. **Tests**: 3 (1996 to 1999); HS 41 v I (Lord's) 1996; BB 1-22. Took wicket of M.Azharuddin with his fifth ball in Test cricket. **LOI**: 31 (1996 to 2002-03); HS 53 and BB 5-26 v I (Oval) 2002. F-c Tours: NZ 1996-97, 1999-00 (Eng A); P 1995-96 (Eng A); Z 1996-97; B 1999-00 (Eng A). 1000 runs (7); most – 1202 (2005). HS 207* v Northants (Ilford) 2002. 50 wkts (1): 51 (1999). BB 6-71 v Notts (Nottingham) 2002. LO HS 158* v Glamorgan (Chelmsford) 2004 (NL). LO BB 5-26 (*see LOI*). T20 HS 100*.

MIDDLEBROOK, James Daniel (Pudsey Crawshaw S), b Leeds, Yorks 13 May 1977. 6'1". RHB, OB. Yorkshire 1998-2001. Essex debut 2002; cap 2003. HS 115 v Somerset (Taunton) 2004. 50 wkts (1): 56 (2003). BB 6-82 (10-170 match) Y v Hants (Southampton) 2000 – including 4 wickets in 5 balls. Ex BB 6-123 v Kent (Chelmsford) 2003. Hat-trick 2003. LO HS 47 v Worcs (Worcester) 2004 (CGT). LO BB 4-27 v Somerset (Taunton) 2006 (CGT). T20 HS 43. T20 BB 3-25.

NAPIER, Graham Richard (The Gilberd S, Colchester), b Colchester 6 Jan 1980. 5'9½". RHB, RM. Debut (Essex) 1997; cap 2003. MCC 2004. F-c Tour (Eng A): I 2003-04. HS 106* v Notts (Nottingham) 2004. BB 5-56 v Derbys (Derby) 2004. LO HS 79 Essex CB v Lancs CB (Chelmsford) 2000 (NWT). LO BB 6-29 v Worcs (Chelmsford) 2001 (NL). T20 HS 38. T20 BB 3-13.

[NQ]**NEL, Andre** (Dr E.G.Jansen S, Boksburg), b Germiston, Transvaal, South Africa 15 Jul 1977. 6'4". RHB, RFM. Easterns 1996-97 to 2003-04. Northamptonshire 2003; cap 2003. Titans 2004-05. Essex 2005 (one match). **Tests** (SA): 27 (2001-02 to 2006-07); HS 23* v P (Port Elizabeth) 2006-07; BB 6-32 (10-88 match) v WI (Bridgetown) 2004-05. **LOI** (SA): 56 (2000-01 to 2006-07); HS 22 and BB 4-13 v India (Durban) 2006-07. F-c Tours (SA): A 2005-06; WI 2000-01, 2004-05; NZ 2003-04; P 2003-04; SL 2006; Z 2001-02; Ire/Scot 1999 (SA Acad). HS 44 Easterns v FS (Benoni) 2000-01. UK/CC HS 42 Nh v Glamorgan (Cardiff) 2003. Ex HS – and BB 2-12 v Somerset (Colchester) 2005 – on debut. BB 6-25 Easterns v Gauteng (Jo'burg) 2001-02. UK/CC BB 5-47 Nh v Glos (Gloucester) 2003. LO HS 22 (*see LOI*). LO BB 6-27 Easterns v GW (Benoni) 2000-01. T20 HS 12. T20 BB 2-19.

PALLADINO, Antonio Paul (Cardinal Pole SS; Anglia Polytechnic U), b Tower Hamlets, London 29 Jun 1983. 6'0". RHB, RMF. Cambridge UCCE 2003-05. Essex debut 2003. HS 41 v Notts (Nottingham) 2004. BB 6-41 v Kent (Canterbury) 2003. LO HS 16 Essex CB v Essex (Chelmsford) 2003. LO BB 3-32 v Glamorgan (Chelmsford) 2003 (NL). T20 HS – . T20 BB 2-3.

PETTINI, Mark Lewis (Comberton Village C; Hills Road SFC, Cambridge; Cardiff U), b Brighton, Sussex 7 Aug 1983. RHB, RM. 5'10". Debut (Essex) 2001; cap 2006. MCC 2005. 1000 runs (1): 1218 (2006). HS 208* v Derbys (Chelmsford) 2006. LO 92* v Warwks (Birmingham) 2003 (CGT). T20 HS 60.

PHILLIPS, Timothy James (Felsted S; St Hild & St Bede C, Durham U), b Cambridge 13 Mar 1981. 6'1". LHB, SLA. Debut (Essex) 1999, 2001-02, 2005 to date; cap 2006. Durham UCCE 2001-02. HS 89 v Worcs (Worcester) 2005. BB 5-41 v Derbys (Chelmsford) 2006. LO HS 24* v Lancs (Manchester) 2005 (CGT). LO BB 5-34 v Lancs (Chelmsford) 2006 (P40). T20 HS 5*. T20 BB 2-11.

[NQ]**Ten DOESCHATE, Ryan** Neil (Fairbairn C; Cape Town U), b Port Elizabeth, South Africa 30 Jun 1980. 5'10½". RHB, RMF. Debut (Essex) 2003; cap 2006. EU passport – Dutch ancestry. Holland 2005 to date. **LOI** (H): 11 (2006 to 2006-07); HS 109* v Bermuda (Nairobi) 2006-07; BB 4-31 v Canada (Nairobi) 2006-07. F-c Tours (H): SA 2006-07; K 2005-06; Ire 2005; HS 259* and BB 6-20 (9-112 match) Holland v Canada (Pretoria) 2006. Ex HS 105* v LU (Chelmsford) 2006. CC HS 102* v Glamorgan (Cardiff) 2006. Ex BB 5-143 v Surrey (Croydon) 2006. LO HS 109* (*see LOI*). LO BB 4-18 Holland v Papua New Guinea (Belfast) 2005. T20 HS 49*. T20 BB 2-27.

‡**THOMAS,** Stuart **Darren** (Graig CS, Llanelli; Neath Tertiary C), b Morriston, Glamorgan 25 Jan 1975. 6'0". LHB, RFM. Glamorgan 1992-2005; debut v Derbys (Chesterfield) taking 5-80 when aged 17yr 217d; cap 1997; benefit 2006. F-c Tours (Eng A): SA 1995-96 (Gm), 1998-99; NZ 1999-00; Z 1994-95 (Gm), 1998-99. HS 138 v Essex (Chelmsford) 2001. 50 wkts (5); most – 71 (1998). BB 8-50 Eng A v Zim A (Harare) 1998-99 – record Eng A analysis. CC BB 7-33 (10-83 match) v Durham (Cardiff) 2002. LO HS 71* Gm v Surrey (Oval) 2002 (CGT). LO BB 7-16 Gm v Surrey (Swansea) 1998 (SL). T20 HS 43*. T20 BB 3-32.

TUDOR, Alex Jeremy (St Mark's S, Hammersmith; City of Westminster C), b West Brompton, London 23 Oct 1977. 6'5". RHB, RF. Surrey 1995-2004; cap 1999. Essex debut 2005. YC 1999. **Tests**: 10 (1998-99 to 2002-03); HS 99* v NZ (Birmingham) 1999 – record score by an England 'night-watchman'; BB 5-44 v A (Nottingham) 2001. **LOI**: 3 (2002); HS 6; BB 2-30 v I (Oval) 2002. F-c Tours: A 1998-99, 2002-03; SA 1999-00; WI 2000-01 (Eng A); P 2000-01. HS 144 v Derbys (Chelmsford) 2006. BB 7-48 Sy v Lancs (Oval) 2000. Ex BB 5-67 v Somerset (Southend) 2006. LO HS 56 Sy v Lancs (Croydon) 2004 (NL). LO BB 4-26 Sy v Hants (Oval) 2000 (NL).

WESTFIELD, Mervyn Simon (Barking C), b Romford 5 May 1988. 6'0". RHB, RFM. Debut (Essex) 2005. HS 32 v and BB 4-72 v Somerset (Southend) 2006. LO HS 4* (P40). LO BB –

‡**WESTLEY, Thomas** (Linton Village C), b Cambridge 13 March 1989. RHB, OB. Awaiting f-c debut. Cambridgeshire 2005. Essex 2nd XI debut 2004 when aged 15y 88d. LO HS – v SL (Chelmsford) 2006.

RELEASED/RETIRED

(Having made a first-class County appearance in 2006)

[NQ]**ADAMS, Andre** Ryan (Westlake BHS, Auckland), b Mangere, Auckland, New Zealand 17 Jul 1975. 5'9". RHB, RMF. Auckland 1997-98 to date. Essex 2004-06, scoring 124 on debut (*see HS*); cap 2004. Herefordshire 2001. **Tests** (NZ): 1 (2001-02); HS 11 and BB 3-44 v E (Auckland) 2001-02 – on debut. **LOI** (NZ): 48 (2000-01 to 2006-07); HS 45 v P (Rawalpindi) 2001-02; BB 5-22 v I (Queenstown) 2002-03. HS 124 v Leics (Leics) 2004 (91 balls, 7 sixes, 13 fours; 100 off 80 balls) on UK debut. BB 6-25 Auckland v Wellington (Auckland) 2004-05. Ex BB 5-60 v Durham (Southend) 2005. Hat-trick v Somerset (Taunton) 2005. LO HS 90* N Is Selection XI v SL (New Plymouth) 2000-01. LO BB 5-7 Auckland v ND (Auckland) 1999-00. T20 HS 54*. T20 BB 3-27.

GOUGH, D. – *see YORKSHIRE.*

JEFFERSON, W.I. – *see NOTTINGHAMSHIRE.*

A.P.Cowan left the staff having not made a first-class appearance in 2006.

ESSEX 2006

RESULTS SUMMARY

	Place	Won	Lost	Tied	Drew	No Result
County Championship (2nd Division)	**3rd**	7	4		5	
All First-Class Matches		7	4		6	
C & G Trophy (South Conference)	3rd	6	3			
Pro40 League (1st Division)	**1st**	5	2			1
Twenty20 Cup (South Division)	Semi-Finalist	7	3			

COUNTY CHAMPIONSHIP AVERAGES

BATTING AND FIELDING

Cap		*M*	*I*	*NO*	*HS*	*Runs*	*Avge*	*100*	*50*	*Ct/St*
2005	A.N.Cook	3	5	2	132	424	141.33	2	2	5
2002	A.Flower	16	26	5	271*	1424	67.80	6	3	17
1994	R.C.Irani	16	23	5	145	1075	59.72	3	6	1
2004	D.Gough	7	7	4	52*	173	57.66	–	2	1
2006	M.L.Pettini	16	27	2	208*	1125	45.00	3	2	14
2001	J.S.Foster	16	20	3	103	721	42.41	1	6	65/3
-	V.Chopra	8	14	1	106	523	40.23	1	4	6
2005	R.S.Bopara	15	24	3	159	806	38.38	2	3	12
-	A.J.Bichel	8	8	1	75*	265	37.85	–	2	–
2005	G.W.Flower	6	9	–	101	307	34.11	1	2	4
2004	A.R.Adams	8	9	2	75	230	32.85	–	1	4
2003	J.D.Middlebrook	14	16	1	113	488	32.53	1	2	5
-	A.J.Tudor	11	13	1	144	362	30.16	1	1	2
2006	R.N.ten Doeschate	8	11	1	102*	298	29.80	1	1	3
2006	T.J.Phillips	13	16	2	49	335	23.92	–	–	15
-	M.S.Westfield	3	4	2	32	41	20.50	–	–	1
-	A.P.Palladino	5	6	2	7	7	1.75	–	–	4

Also batted: W.I.Jefferson (1 match – cap 2002) 5; G.R.Napier (2 matches – cap 2003) 52, 62, 17*.

BOWLING

	O	*M*	*R*	*W*	*Avge*	*Best*	*5wI*	*10wM*
D.Gough	232.1	46	724	25	28.96	5- 82	1	–
A.J.Bichel	280.5	53	991	32	30.96	6- 38	1	–
A.P.Palladino	150.4	33	489	13	37.61	6- 68	1	–
A.R.Adams	278.1	63	830	21	39.52	4- 72	–	–
R.N.ten Doeschate	229.1	27	1040	25	41.60	5-143	1	–
A.J.Tudor	293.4	53	1195	28	42.67	5- 67	1	–
T.J.Phillips	405.4	60	1533	34	45.08	5- 41	1	–
R.S.Bopara	223.3	38	902	19	47.47	5- 75	1	–
J.D.Middlebrook	510	103	1585	32	49.53	3- 51	–	–
Also bowled:								
G.W.Flower	51.1	13	166	7	23.71	3- 28	–	–
M.S.Westfield	43	5	180	6	30.00	4- 72	–	–

A.N.Cook 2-1-4-0; A.Flower 8-3-20-1; G.R.Napier 37-6-152-1.

The First-Class Averages (pp 130–146) give the records of Essex players in all first-class matches for the county (Essex's other opponents being Loughborough UCCE), with the exception of R.S.Bopara and A.N.Cook whose full county figures are as above.

ESSEX RECORDS

FIRST-CLASS CRICKET

Highest Total	For	761-6d		v	Leics	Chelmsford	1990
	V	803-4d		by	Kent	Brentwood	1934
Lowest Total	For	30		v	Yorkshire	Leyton	1901
	V	14		by	Surrey	Chelmsford	1983
Highest Innings	For	343*	P.A.Perrin	v	Derbyshire	Chesterfield	1904
	V	332	W.H.Ashdown	for	Kent	Brentwood	1934

Highest Partnership for each Wicket

1st	316	G.A.Gooch/P.J.Prichard	v	Kent	Chelmsford	1994
2nd	403	G.A.Gooch/P.J.Prichard	v	Leics	Chelmsford	1990
3rd	347*	M.E.Waugh/N.Hussain	v	Lancashire	Ilford	1992
4th	314	Salim Malik/N.Hussain	v	Surrey	The Oval	1991
5th	316	N.Hussain/M.A.Garnham	v	Leics	Leicester	1991
6th	206	J.W.H.T.Douglas/J.O'Connor	v	Glos	Cheltenham	1923
	206	B.R.Knight/R.A.G.Luckin	v	Middlesex	Brentwood	1962
7th	261	J.W.H.T.Douglas/J.Freeman	v	Lancashire	Leyton	1914
8th	263	D.R.Wilcox/R.M.Taylor	v	Warwicks	Southend	1946
9th	251	J.W.H.T.Douglas/S.N.Hare	v	Derbyshire	Leyton	1921
10th	218	F.H.Vigar/T.P.B.Smith	v	Derbyshire	Chesterfield	1947

Best Bowling	For	10- 32	H.Pickett	v	Leics	Leyton	1895
(Innings)	V	10- 40	E.G.Dennett	for	Glos	Bristol	1906
Best Bowling	For	17-119	W.Mead	v	Hampshire	Southampton	1895
(Match)	V	17- 56	C.W.L.Parker	for	Glos	Gloucester	1925

Most Runs – Season	2559	G.A.Gooch	(av 67.34)	1984
Most Runs – Career	30701	G.A.Gooch	(av 51.77)	1973-97
Most 100s – Season	9	J.O'Connor		1929, 1934
	9	D.J.Insole		1955
Most 100s – Career	94	G.A.Gooch		1973-97
Most Wkts – Season	172	T.P.B.Smith	(av 27.13)	1947
Most Wkts – Career	1610	T.P.B.Smith	(av 26.68)	1929-51
Most Career W-K Dismissals	1231	B.Taylor	(1040 ct; 191 st)	1949-73
Most Career Catches in the Field	519	K.W.R.Fletcher		1962-88

LIMITED-OVERS CRICKET

Highest Total	**CGT**	386-5		v	Wiltshire	Chelmsford	1988
	P40	316-4		v	Glamorgan	Chelmsford	2004
	T20	196-6		v	Sussex	Chelmsford	2006
Lowest Total	**CGT**	57		v	Lancashire	Lord's	1996
	P40	69		v	Derbyshire	Chesterfield	1974
	T20	109		v	Sussex	Hove	2005
Highest Innings	**CGT**	144	G.A.Gooch	v	Hampshire	Chelmsford	1990
	P40	176	G.A.Gooch	v	Glamorgan	Southend	1983
	T20	100*	R.C.Irani	v	Sussex	Hove	2006
Best Bowling	**CGT**	5- 8	J.K.Lever	v	Middlesex	Westcliff	1972
		5- 8	G.A.Gooch	v	Cheshire	Chester	1995
	P40	8-26	K.D.Boyce	v	Lancashire	Manchester	1971
	T20	4-20	S.A.Brant	v	Kent	Maidstone	2004

GLAMORGAN

Formation of Present Club: 6 July 1888
Inaugural First-Class Match: 1921
Colours: Blue and Gold
Badge: Gold Daffodil
County Champions: (3) 1948, 1969, 1997
Gillette/NatWest/C & G Trophy Winners: (0); best – finalist 1977
Benson and Hedges Cup Winners: (0); best – finalist 2000
Pro 40/National League (Div 1) Winners: (2) 2002, 2004
Sunday League Winners: (1) 1993
Twenty20 Cup Winners: (0); best – Semi-Finalist 2004

Chief Executive: Mike J.Fatkin, Sophia Gardens, Cardiff, CF11 9XR • Tel: 029 2040 9380 • Fax: 029 2040 9390 • email: info@glamorgancricket.co.uk • Web: www.glamorgancricket.com

1st XI Coach: A.D.Shaw. **Director of Player Development**: S.L.Watkin. **Captain**: D.L.Hemp. **Vice-Captain**: none. **Overseas Player**: J.P.Maher. **2007 Beneficiary**: none. **Head Groundsman**: Len Smith. **Scorer**: Dr Andrew K.Hignell. ‡ New registration. NQ Not qualified for England.

‡**BRAGG, William** David (Rougemont S, Newport; UWIC), b Newport, Monmouthshire 24 Oct 1986. LHB, WK. Wales MC 2004-06. Awaiting f-c debut. LO HS Wales MC v Notts (Swansea) 2005.

CHERRY, Daniel David (Tonbridge S; U of Wales, Swansea), b Newport, Monmouthshire 7 Feb 1980. 5'9". LHB, RM. Debut (Glamorgan)1998. No f-c appearances 1999-2001. HS 226 v Middx (Southgate) 2005. LO HS 42 v Middx (Lord's) 2005 (NL). LO BB 1-26 (P40). T20 HS 43*. T20 BB 2-6.

COSKER, Dean Andrew (Millfield S), b Weymouth, Dorset 7 Jan 1978. 5'11". RHB, SLA. Debut (Glamorgan) 1996; cap 2000. F-c Tours (Eng A): SA 1998-99, SL 1997-98; Z 1998-99, K 1997-98. HS 52 v Glos (Bristol) 2005. BB 6-140 v Lancs (Colwyn Bay) 1998. LO HS 27* v Somerset (Taunton) 1999 (NL). LO BB 5-54 v Essex (Chelmsford) 2003 (NL). T20 HS 10*. T20 BB 2-20.

CROFT, Robert Damien Bale (St John Lloyd Catholic CS, Llanelli; Neath Tertiary C; W Glamorgan IHE), b Morriston, Swansea 25 May 1970. 5'10½". RHB, OB. Debut (Glamorgan) 1989; cap 1992; benefit 2000; captain 2003 (*part*) to 2006 (*part*). **Tests**: 21 (1996 to 2001); HS 37* v SA (Manchester) 1998; BB 5-95 v NZ (Christchurch) 1996-97. **LOI**: 50 (1996 to 2001); HS 32 v SL (Perth) 1998-99; BB 3-51 v SA (Oval) 1998. F-c Tours: A 1998-99; SA 1993-94 (Eng A), 1995-96 (Gm); WI 1991-92 (Eng A), 1997-98; NZ 1996-97; SL 2000-01, 2003-04; Z 1990-91 (Gm), 1994-95 (Gm), 1996-97. HS 143 v Somerset (Taunton) 1995. 50 wkts (7); most – 76 (1996). BB 8-66 (14-169 match) v Warwks (Swansea) 1992. LO HS 143 v Lincs (Lincoln) 2004 (CGT). LO BB 6-20 v Worcs (Cardiff) 1994 (SL). T20 HS 62*. T20 BB 3-32.

DAVIES, Andrew Philip (Dwr-y-Felin CS; Christ C, Brecon), b Neath 7 Nov 1976. 5'11". LHB, RMF. Debut (Glamorgan) 1995. Wales (MC). No appearances 1997, 2000. HS 41* v Notts (Nottingham) 2005. BB 5-79 v Worcs (Cardiff) 2002. LO HS 24 v Sussex (Hove) 2001 (NL). LO BB 5-19 v Lincs (Sleaford) 2002 (CGT). T20 HS 11. T20 BB 3-17.

GRANT, Richard Neil (Cefn Saeson CS; Neath Port Talbot C), b Neath 5 Jun 1984. 5'10". RHB, RM. Debut (Glamorgan) 2005. HS 44 and BB 1-9 v Essex (Chelmsford) 2006. LO HS 45 v Kent (Cardiff) 2006 (CGT). LO BB 2-21 v West Indies A (Ebbw Vale) 2006. T20 HS 77. T20 BB 4-38.

HARRISON, Adam James (W Monmouth CS), b Newport, Monmouthshire 30 Oct 1985. RHB, RMF. Younger brother of D.S.Harrison; son of S.C.Harrison (Glamorgan 1971-77). MCC 2004. Glamorgan debut 2005. HS 34* and BB 2-65 MCC v Sussex (Lord's) 2004. Gm HS 3. BB 1-54 v Sussex (Swansea) 2005 – on debut. LO HS 6 and BB 1-59 v Hants (Southampton) 2006 (CGT). T20 HS 1*. T20 BB 2-12.

HARRISON, David Stuart (W Monmouth CS; Usk C, Pontypool), b Newport, Monmouthshire 30 Jul 1981. Elder brother of A.J.Harrison; son of S.C.Harrison (Glamorgan 1971-77). 6'4". RHB, RMF. Debut (Glamorgan) 1999; cap 2006. MCC 2005. HS 88 v Essex (Chelmsford) 2004. 50 wkts (1): 57 (2004). BB 5-48 v Somerset (Swansea) 2004. LO HS 37* and LO BB 5-26 v Yorks (Leeds) 2002 (NL). T20 HS 4. T20 BB 2-17.

HEMP, David Lloyd (Olchfa CS; Millfield S; W Glamorgan C; Birmingham U), b Hamilton, Bermuda 8 Nov 1970. UK resident since 1976. 6'0". LHB, RM. Glamorgan 1991-96, 2002 to date; cap 1994; captain 2006 (*part*) to date. Warwickshire 1997-2001; cap 1997. Free State 1997-98. Wales (MC) 1992-93. Bermuda 2006-07. LOI (Bermuda): 12 (2006-07); HS 58 v Holland (Nairobi) 2006-07; BB 1-25). F-c Tours: SA 1995-96 (Gm), 2006-07 (Bermuda); I 1994-95 (Eng A); Z 1994-95 (Gm). 1000 runs (6); most – 1452 (1994); K 2006-07 (Bermuda). HS 247* Bermuda v Holland (Pretoria) 2006-07. CC HS 186* Wa v Worcs (Birmingham) 2001. Gm HS 171* v Kent (Canterbury) 2005. BB 3-23 v South Africa A (Cardiff) 1996. CC BB 2-29 Wa v Glos (Birmingham) 2000. LO HS 121 v Comb U (Cardiff) 1995 (BHC). LO BB 4-32 Wa v Minor C (Lakenham) 1998 (BHC). T20 HS 74.

JONES, Simon Philip (Coedcae CS; Millfield S), b Morriston, Swansea 25 Dec 1978. Son of I.J.Jones (Glamorgan and England 1960-68). 6'3½". LHB, RF. Debut (Glamorgan) 1998; cap 2002. Unavailable 2003 (knee reconstruction). MBE 2005. *Wisden* 2005. **ECB central contract 2007. Tests**: 18 (2002 to 2005); HS 44 v I (Lord's) 2002 – on debut; BB 6-53 v A (Manchester) 2005. **LOI**: 8 (2004-05 to 2005); HS 1; BB 2-43 v Z (Bulawayo) 2004-05 – on debut. F-c Tours: A 2002-03 (*part*); SA 2004-05; WI 2003-04; I 2003-04 (Eng A – *part*). HS 46 v Yorks (Scarborough) 2001. BB 6-45 v Derbys (Cardiff) 2002. LO HS 12* v Notts (Nottingham) 1999 (NL). LO BB 3-19 v Lancs (Manchester) 2005 (NL).

[NQ]**MAHER, James** Patrick (St Augustine's C, Cairns), b Innisfail, Queensland, Australia 27 Feb 1974. LHB, RM. Queensland 1993-94 to date. Glamorgan 2001, 2003; cap 2001. Durham 2005-06. **LOI** (A): 26 (1997-98 to 2003-04); HS 95 v SA (Pretoria) 2001-02. F-c Tour (A): WI 2002-03. 1000 (1+2): most – 1194 (2001-02). HS 223 Q v Vic (Brisbane) 2005-06. Gm HS 217 v Essex (Cardiff) 2001. BB 3-11 Q v WA (Perth) 1995-96. UK BB – . LO HS 187 Q v WA (Brisbane) 2003-04. LO BB 3-29 Gm v Surrey (Croydon) 2003 (NL). T20 HS 59.

O'SHEA, Michael Peter (Barry CS; Millfield S), b Cardiff 24 Oct 1986. 5'11". RHB, OB. England U-15, U-16, U-19. Debut (Glamorgan) 2005; no f-c appearances 2006. Wales MC (2005). HS 24 v Kent (Canterbury) 2005. LO HS 7* (P40).

PENG GILLENDER, **Nicky** (Newcastle upon Tyne RGS), b Newcastle upon Tyne, Northumb 18 Sep 1982. 6'2". RHB, OB. Durham 2000-05; cap 2001. Glamorgan debut 2006. HS 158 Du v Durham UCCE (Chester-le-St) 2003. CC HS 133 Du v Glamorgan (Cardiff) 2003. Scored 98 Du v Surrey (Chester-le-St) on debut. Gm HS 59 v Surrey (Swansea) 2006. LO HS 121 Du v Worcs (Worcester) 2001 (NL). T20 HS 49.

POWELL, Michael John (Crickhowell SS; Pontypool CFE), b Abergavenny, Monmouthshire 3 Feb 1977. 6'1". RHB, OB, occ WK. Debut (Glamorgan) 1997 scoring 200* v OU (Oxford); cap 2000. 1000 runs (5): most – 1327 (2006). HS 299 v Glos (Cheltenham) 2006. BB 2-39 v OU (Oxford) 1999. CC BB – . LO HS 91* v Leics (Cardiff) 2003 (NL). LO BB 1-26 (CGT). T20 HS 68*.

REES, Gareth Peter (Coedcae CS; Bath U), b Swansea 8 Apr 1985. 6'1". LHB, LM. Wales MC 2003-05. Debut (Glamorgan) 2006. HS 57 v Northants (Cardiff) 2006. LO HS 15 Wales MC v Denmark (Abergavenny) 2003 (CGT).

‡SHINGLER, Aaron Craig (Pontardulais CS; Gorseinon TC), b Aldershot, Hants 7 Aug 1987. RHB, RFM. Glamorgan 2nd XI debut aged 16yr 271d. Staff 2006 – awaiting f-c debut. Wales MC 2004-06. LOI for England U-19 v Bangladesh U-19 at Savar 2005-06.

TUDGE, Kyle Daniel (Monmouth S), b Newport 19 Mar 1987. RHB, SLA. Debut (Glamorgan) 2006. MCC YC 2004. Wales MC 2005. HS 4 and BB – v Worcs (Colwyn Bay) 2006. LO HS 4 and BB – Wales MC v Notts (Swansea) 2005 (CGT).

WALLACE, Mark Alexander (Crickhowell HS), b Abergavenny, Monmouthshire 19 Nov 1981. 5'9". LHB, WK. Debut (Glamorgan) 1999; cap 2003. F-c Tour (ECB Acad): SL 2002-03. HS 121 v Durham (Chester-le-St) 2003. LO HS 48 v Suffolk (Bury St Edmunds) 2005 (CGT). T20 HS 35.

WATERS, Huw Thomas (Llantaram CS; Monmouth S), b Cardiff 26 Sep 1986. 6'2". RHB, RMF. Debut (Glamorgan) 2005. Wales MC 2005. HS 34 v Kent (Canterbury) 2005. BB 5-86 v Somerset (Taunton) 2006. LO HS 8.

WATKINS, Ryan Edward (Pontllanfraith CS; Cross Keys TC), b Abergavenny, Monmouthshire 9 Jun 1983. 6'0". LHB, RM. Debut (Glamorgan) 2005. Wales MC 2004-06. HS 87 v Essex (Cardiff) 2006. BB 4-40 v Worcs (Worcester) 2006. LO HS 28* v Notts (Nottingham) 2006 (P40). LO BB 2-25 v Warwks (Colwyn Bay) 2006 P40). T20 HS 6*. T20 BB 2-8.

WHARF, Alexander George (Buttershaw Upper S; Thomas Danby C), b Bradford, Yorks 4 Jun 1975. 6'5". RHB, RMF. Yorkshire 1994-97. Nottinghamshire 1998-99. Glamorgan debut 2000, scoring 100* v OU (Oxford); cap 2000. **LOI**: 13 (2004 to 2004-05): HS 9; BB 4-24 v Z (Harare) 2004-05. HS 113 v Notts (Cardiff) 2005. 50 wkts (1): 52 (2003). BB 6-59 v Glos (Bristol) 2005. LO HS 72 v Lancs (Manchester) 2004 (NL). LO BB 6-5 v Kent (Cardiff) 2004 (NL). T20 HS 19. T20 BB 4-39.

WRIGHT, Ben James (Cowbridge CS), b Preston, Lancs 5 Dec 1987. 5'9". RHB, RM. Debut (Glamorgan) 2006. HS 72 v Glos (Cardiff) 2006 – on debut. LO HS 37 v West Indies A (Ebbw Vale) – on debut.

RELEASED/RETIRED

(Having made a first-class County appearance in 2006)

[NQ]COSGROVE, Mark James, b Elizabeth, South Australia 14 Jun 1984. LHB, RM. South Australia 2002-03 to date. Glamorgan 2006 – scoring 114 v Derbys (Cardiff). **LOI** (A): 3 (2005-06 to 2006-07); HS 74 v B (Fatullah) 2005-06; BB 1-1. HS 233 Gm v Derbys (Derby) 2006. BB 2-22 S Aus v Q (Adelaide) 2006-07. LO HS 121 S Aus v WA (Perth) 2005-06. LO BB 2-21 S Aus v Q (Brisbane) 2005-06. T20 HS 50*. T20 BB 1-22.

RELEASED/RETIRED continued on p 62

GLAMORGAN 2006

RESULTS SUMMARY

	Place	Won	Lost	Tied	Drew	No Result
County Championship (2nd Division)	**8th**	2	7		7	
All First-Class Matches		2	7		7	
C & G Trophy (South Conference)	9th	1	7			1
Pro40 League (1st Division)	7th	2	4†	1		2
† Including Promotion Playoff Match (demoted)						
Twenty20 Cup (Mid/West/Wales Division)	4th	3	4			1

COUNTY CHAMPIONSHIP AVERAGES

BATTING AND FIELDING

Cap		M	I	NO	HS	Runs	Avge	100	50	Ct/St
–	B.B.McCullum	3	6	1	160	306	61.20	1	1	3
2000	M.J.Powell	16	29	3	299	1327	51.03	4	2	7
–	M.J.Cosgrove	10	19	2	233	856	50.35	2	6	5
1994	D.L.Hemp	16	29	1	155	1003	35.82	3	2	18
1992	R.D.B.Croft	16	24	5	72	601	31.63	–	3	9
–	D.D.Cherry	9	17	–	121	532	31.29	1	3	4
2000	A.G.Wharf	10	15	2	86	397	30.53	–	3	9
2003	M.A.Wallace	16	27	4	72	698	30.34	–	5	41/3
–	J.E.C.Franklin	9	15	1	94	346	24.71	–	2	4
–	R.E.Watkins	14	25	2	87	554	24.08	–	2	12
–	N.Peng	8	15	–	59	357	23.80	–	2	10
2006	D.S.Harrison	13	16	3	64	281	21.61	–	1	4
–	G.P.Rees	3	5	1	57	84	21.00	–	1	1
–	R.N.Grant	7	11	–	44	196	17.81	–	–	3
–	A.P.Davies	4	6	3	16	51	17.00	–	–	1
2000	D.A.Cosker	13	16	6	39	168	16.80	–	–	9
–	H.T.Waters	5	7	2	5*	7	1.40	–	–	1

Also batted: (1 match each): A.J.Harrison 3; S.P.Jones (cap 2002) 0, 4*; K.D.Tudge 3*, 4; B.J.Wright 72 (2 ct).

BOWLING

	O	M	R	W	Avge	Best	5wI	10wM
J.E.C.Franklin	251.4	45	950	31	30.64	5-68	1	–
H.T.Waters	111.3	24	380	12	31.66	5-86	1	–
R.D.B.Croft	702.3	125	2112	66	32.00	7-67	3	1
D.S.Harrison	420.1	88	1387	35	39.62	5-76	1	–
D.A.Cosker	502.5	82	1486	33	45.03	4-78	–	–
R.E.Watkins	230.5	36	922	19	48.52	4-40	–	–
A.G.Wharf	262.5	37	983	19	51.73	4-67	–	–
Also bowled:								
M.J.Cosgrove	70	7	234	5	46.80	1- 8	–	–
A.P.Davies	124	24	402	8	50.25	2-28	–	–

D.D.Cherry 0.4-0-4-0; R.N.Grant 25.5-2-128-3; A.J.Harrison 21-3-81-1; S.P.Jones 28-4-96-1; K.D.Tudge 13-1-58-0.

Glamorgan played no fixtures outside the County Championship in 2006. The First-Class Averages (pp 130–146) give the records of their players in all first-class matches for the county.

GLAMORGAN RECORDS

FIRST-CLASS CRICKET

Highest Total	For 718-3d		v	Sussex	Colwyn Bay	2000
	V 712		by	Northants	Northampton	1998
Lowest Total	For 22		v	Lancashire	Liverpool	1924
	V 33		by	Leics	Ebbw Vale	1965
Highest Innings	For 309*	S.P.James	v	Sussex	Colwyn Bay	2000
	V 322*	M.B.Loye	for	Northants	Northampton	1998

Highest Partnership for each Wicket

1st	374	M.T.G.Elliott/S.P.James	v	Sussex	Colwyn Bay	2000
2nd	252	M.P.Maynard/D.L.Hemp	v	Northants	Cardiff	2002
3rd	313	D.E.Davies/W.E.Jones	v	Essex	Brentwood	1948
4th	425*	A.Dale/I.V.A.Richards	v	Middlesex	Cardiff	1993
5th	264	M.Robinson/S.W.Montgomery	v	Hampshire	Bournemouth	1949
6th	230	W.E.Jones/B.L.Muncer	v	Worcs	Worcester	1953
7th	211	P.A.Cottey/O.D.Gibson	v	Leics	Swansea	1996
8th	202	D.Davies/J.J.Hills	v	Sussex	Eastbourne	1928
9th	203*	J.J.Hills/J.C.Clay	v	Worcs	Swansea	1929
10th	143	T.Davies/S.A.B.Daniels	v	Glos	Swansea	1982

Best Bowling	For	10- 51	J.Mercer	v	Worcs	Worcester	1936
(Innings)	V	10- 18	G.Geary	for	Leics	Pontypridd	1929
Best Bowling	For	17-212	J.C.Clay	v	Worcs	Swansea	1937
(Match)	V	16- 96	G.Geary	for	Leics	Pontypridd	1929

Most Runs – Season	2276	H.Morris	(av 55.51)	1990
Most Runs – Career	34056	A.Jones	(av 33.03)	1957-83
Most 100s – Season	10	H.Morris		1990
Most 100s – Career	54	M.P.Maynard		1985-2005
Most Wkts – Season	176	J.C.Clay	(av 17.34)	1937
Most Wkts – Career	2174	D.J.Shepherd	(av 20.95)	1950-72
Most Career W-K Dismissals	933	E.W.Jones	(840 ct; 93 st)	1961-83
Most Career Catches in the Field	656	P.M.Walker		1956-72

LIMITED-OVERS CRICKET

Highest Total	**CGT**	429		v	Surrey	The Oval	2002
	P40	305-6		v	Worcs	Cardiff	2001
	T20	206-6		v	Somerset	Taunton	2006
Lowest Total	**CGT**	76		v	Northants	Northampton	1968
	P40	42		v	Derbyshire	Swansea	1979
	T20	113		v	Warwicks	Birmingham	2003
Highest Innings	**CGT**	162*	I.V.A.Richards	v	Oxfordshire	Swansea	1993
	P40	155*	J.H.Kallis	v	Surrey	Pontypridd	1999
	T20	116*	I.J.Thomas	v	Somerset	Taunton	2004
Best Bowling	**CGT**	5-13	R.J.Shastri	v	Scotland	Edinburgh	1988
	P40	7-16	S.D.Thomas	v	Surrey	Swansea	1998
	T20	4-38	R.N.Grant	v	Worcs	Worcester	2005

GLOUCESTERSHIRE

Formation of Present Club: 1871
Inaugural First-Class Match: 1870
Colours: Blue, Gold, Brown, Silver, Green and Red
Badge: Coat of Arms of the City and County of Bristol
County Champions (since 1890): (0); best – 2nd 1930, 1931, 1947, 1959, 1969, 1986
Gillette/NatWest/C & G Trophy Winners: (5) 1973, 1999, 2000, 2003, 2004
Benson and Hedges Cup Winners: (3) 1977, 1999, 2000
Pro 40/National League (Div 1) Winners: (1) 2000
Sunday League Winners: (0); best – 2nd 1988
Twenty20 Cup Winners: (0); best – Semi-Finalist 2003

Chief Executive: Tom E.M.Richardson, County Ground, Nevil Road, Bristol BS7 9EJ • Tel: 0117 910 8000 • Fax: 0117 924 1193 • Email: info@glosccc.co.uk • Web: www.glosccc.co.uk

Head Coach: M.W.Alleyne. **Captain**: J.Lewis. **Vice-Captain**: No appointment. **Overseas Players**: H.J.H.Marshall, A.A.Noffke, M.J.North and Umar Gul. **2007 Beneficiary**: J.Lewis. **Head Groundsman**: Sean Williams. **Scorer**: Keith T.Gerrish. ‡ New registration. NQ Not qualified for England.

Gloucestershire revised their capping policy in 2004 and now award players with their County Caps when they make their first-class debut.

ADSHEAD, Stephen John (Bridley Moor HS, Redditch), b Worcester 29 Jan 1980. 5'9". RHB, WK. Herefordshire 1999. Leicestershire 2000 (one non-CC match). Worcestershire 2003 (2 matches). Gloucestershire debut/cap 2004. HS 148* v Surrey (Oval) 2005. LO HS 77* Shropshire v Northumb (Oswestry) 2003 (CGT). T20 HS 81.

ALI, Kadeer (Handsworth GS), b Moseley, Birmingham 7 Mar 1983. 6'1". Brother of M.M.Ali (*see WORCESTERSHIRE*), cousin of Kabir Ali (*see WORCESTERSHIRE*). RHB, RM. Worcestershire 2000-04. Gloucestershire debut/cap 2005. F-c Tour (Eng A): I 2003-04. HS 145 v Northants (Northampton) 2006. BB 1-4 (CC). LO HS 66 Worcs CB v Sussex CB (Kidderminster) 2002 (CGT). LO BB 1-4 (Wo – CGT). T20 HS 53.

BANERJEE, Vikram (King Edward's S, Birmingham; Downing C, Cambridge), b Bradford, Yorks 20 Mar 1984. 6'0". LHB, SLA. Cambridge UCCE/U 2004-06; blue 2004-05-06. Gloucestershire debut/cap 2006. HS 29 CU v OU (Cambridge) 2005. GS HS 7. BB 4-150 v Glamorgan (Cardiff) 2006.

BROWN, David Owen (Queen Elizabeth's GS, Blackburn; Collingwood C, Durham), b Burnley, Lancs 8 Dec 1982. Younger brother of M.J.Brown (*see HAMPSHIRE*). RHB, RM. 6'0". Durham UCCE 2003-05. British U 2005. Gloucestershire debut/cap 2006. HS 77 DU v Leics (Leicester) 2005. Gs HS 34 v Glamorgan (Cardiff) 2006. BB 2-48 DU v Northants (Northampton) 2004. Gs BB – . LO HS 63* v Surrey (Bristol) 2006 (CGT) – on debut. T20 HS 36.

BURTON, David Alexander (Sacred Heart RC SS; Lambeth C), b Dulwich, London 23 Aug 1985. 5'11". RHB, RMF. Debut (Gloucestershire); cap 2006. MCC YC 2006. HS 52* and BB – v Glamorgan (Cardiff) 2006.

FISHER, Ian Douglas (Beckfoot GS, Bingley; Thomas Danby C, Leeds), b Bradford, Yorks 31 Mar 1976. 5'10½". LHB, SLA. Yorkshire 1995-96 (Y in Zim) to 2001. Gloucestershire debut 2002; cap 2004. F-c Tour: Z 1995-96 (Y). HS 103* v Essex (Gloucester) 2002. BB 5-30 (10-123 match) v Durham (Bristol) 2003. LO HS 25* v Leics (Cheltenham) 2006 (P40). BB 3-18 v Northants (Northampton) 2004 (NL). T20 HS 9*. T20 BB 4-22.

GIDMAN, Alex Peter Richard (Wycliffe C), b High Wycombe, Bucks 22 Jun 1981. Elder brother of W.R.S.Gidman (*see DURHAM*). 6'3". RHB, RM. Debut (Gloucestershire) 2002; cap 2004. MCC YC 2001. MCC 2004. F-c Tours (Eng A): SL 2004-05. Appointed captain of Eng A tour to India 2003-04 but withdrew because of hand injury. 1000 runs (2); most – 1244 (2006). HS 142 v Surrey (Bristol) 2005. BB 4-47 v Glamorgan (Cardiff) 2005. LO HS 84 v Derbys (Derby) 2006 (P40). LO BB 3-21 v Yorks (Cheltenham) 2006 (P40). T20 HS 61. T20 BB 1-2.

GREENIDGE, Carl Gary (Lodge S and St Michael S, Barbados; Heathcote S, Chingford; W Hatch HS; City of Westminster C), b Basingstoke, Hants 20 Apr 1978. Son of C.Gordon Greenidge (Hampshire, Barbados and West Indies 1970-92). 5'10". RHB, RMF. MCC YC 1998. Surrey 1999-2000. Northamptonshire 2002-04. Gloucestershire debut/cap 2005. HS 46 Nh v Derbys (Derby) 2002. Gs HS 25 v Kent (Maidstone) 2005. 50 wkts (1): 53 (2002). BB 6-40 Nh v Durham (Chester-le-St) 2002. Gs BB 3-50 v Northants (Bristol) 2006. LO HS 20 Nh v Sussex (Northampton) 2002 (NL). LO BB 4-40 v Sussex (Arundel) 2006 (CGT). T20 HS 5*. T20 BB 3-15.

HARDINGES, Mark Andrew (Malvern C; Bath U), b Gloucester 5 Feb 1978. 6'1". RHB, RMF. Debut (Gloucestershire) 1999; cap 2004. British U 2000. HS 172 v OU (Oxford) 2002. CC HS 107* v Essex (Chelmsford) 2006. BB 5-51 v Kent (Maidstone) 2005. LO HS 111* v Lancs (Manchester) 2005 (NL). LO BB 4-19 v Salop (Shrewsbury) 2002 (CGT). T20 HS 94*. T20 BB 3-18.

HODNETT, Grant Phillip (Durban Preparatory HS; Nortwood HS), b Johannesburg, S Africa 17 Aug 1982. 6'4". RHB, LB. Debut (Gloucestershire)/cap 2005; no f-c appearance 2006. HS 49 v Warwks (Birmingham) 2005 – on debut. LO HS 7 v Sussex (Arundel) (CGT) 2006.

KIRBY, Steven Paul (Elton HS; Bury C), b Ainsworth, nr Bolton, Lancs 4 Oct 1977. 6'3½". RHB, RFM. Leicestershire staff 1998 – no f-c appearances. Yorkshire 2001-04, debut as sub for M.J.Hoggard (England duty) taking 7-50; cap 2003. Gloucestershire debut/cap 2005. F-c Tour (Eng A): I 2003-04 (*part*). HS 57 Y v Hants (Leeds) 2002. Gs HS 19* v Derbys (Bristol) 2006. 50 wkts (1): 67 (2003). BB 8-80 (13-154 match) Y v Somerset (Taunton) 2003. Gs BB 5-99 v Northants (Northampton) 2006. LO HS 15 Y v Leics (Leicester) 2003 (NL). LO BB 3-27 Y v Worcs (Scarborough) 2003 (NL). T20 HS 1*. T20 BB 2-15.

LEWIS, Jonathan (Churchfields S, Swindon; Swindon C), b Aylesbury, Bucks 26 Aug 1975. 6'2". RHB, RMF. Debut (Gloucestershire) 1995; cap 1998; captain 2006 to date; benefit 2007. Wiltshire 1993. Northamptonshire staff 1994. **Tests**: 1 (2006); HS 20 and BB 3-68 v SL (Nottingham) 2006. **LOI**: 12 (2005 to 2006-07); HS 9; BB 4-36 v A (Brisbane) 2006-07. F-c Tours (Eng A): WI 2000-01; SL 2004-05. HS 62 v Worcs (Cheltenham) 1999. 50 wkts (6); most – 74 (2003). BB 8-95 v Z (Gloucester) 2000. CC BB 7-38 (10-75 match) v Somerset (Bristol) 2006. Hat-trick 2000. LO HS 40 and LO BB 5-19 v Hants (Southampton) 2005 (NL). T20 HS 43. T20 BB 4-24.

[NQ]**MARSHALL, Hamish** John Hamilton (Mahurangi C, Warkworth; King C, Auckland), b Warkworth, NZ 15 Feb 1979. twin brother of J.A.H.Marshall (ND and NZ 1997-98 to date). 5'9". RHB, RM. N Districts 1998-99 to date. Gloucestershire debut 2006 (scoring 102 v Worcs on UK debut); cap 2006. Buckinghamshire 2003. **Tests** (NZ): 13 (2000-01 to 2005-06); HS 160 v SL (Napier) 2004-05. **LOI** (NZ): 63 (2003-04 to 2006-07); HS 101* v P (Faisalabad) 2003-04. F-c Tours (NZ): SA 2000-01, 2005-06; Z 2005; B 2004-05. 1000 runs (1): 1218 (2006). HS 168 v Leics (Cheltenham) 2006. BB 1-12 (NZ A). Gs BB 1-16. LO HS 111 NZ v Essex (Chelmsford) 2004 LO BB 1-14 (ND). T20 HS 18.

‡[NQ]**NOFFKE, Ashley** Allan b Nambour, Queensland, Australia 30 Apr 1977. RHB, RFM. Debut (Aus Academy in Zim) 1998-99. Queensland 1999-00 to date. Middlesex 2002-03; cap 2003. Durham 2005. F-c Tours (A): E 2001 (*part*); WI 2002-03; Z 1998-99 (Aus Acad). HS 114* Q v S Aus (Brisbane) 2003-04. UK HS 76 M v Worcs (Worcester) 2002. BB 8-24 (12-108 match) M v Derbys (Derby) 2002. LO HS 58 M v Sussex (Lord's) 2002 (BHC). LO BB 4-32 Q v Tasmania (Hobart) 2001-02. T20 HS 11*. T20 BB 3-22.

‡[NQ]**NORTH, Marcus** James (Kent Street Sr HS), b Pakenham, Melbourne, Australia 28 Jul 1979. 6'1". LHB, OB. Debut (Aus Academy in Zim) 1998-99. W Australia 1999-00 to date. Durham 2004. Lancashire 2005. Derbyshire 2006. F-c Tours (Aus A): P 2005-06; Z 1998-99 (Aus Acad). 1000 runs (0+1): 1074 (2003-04). HS 239* WA v Vic (Perth) 2006-07. CC HS 219 Du v Glamorgan (Cardiff) 2004. De HS 161 v Worcs (Chesterfield) 2006. BB 4-16 Du v Durham UCCE (Chester-le-St) 2004 – on DU debut. CC BB 2-45 Du v Yorks (Chester-le-St) 2004. De BB 1-43. LO HS 134* WA v Q (Perth) 2004-05. LO BB 4-26 Durham CB v Bucks (Beaconsfield) 2001 (CGT). T20 HS 59. T20 BB 2-19.

RUDGE, William Douglas (Clifton C), b Southmead, Bristol 15 Jul 1983. 6'4". RHB, RM. Debut (Gloucestershire)/cap 2005. HS 15 v Surrey (Oval) 2005. BB 3-46 v Bangladesh A (Bristol) 2005 – on debut. CC BB 3-75 v Middx (Bristol) 2005. LO HS 4 and BB 2-1 v Sussex (Arundel) 2006 (CGT). T20 HS 1. T20 BB 3-37.

SNELL, Stephen David (Sandown HS), b Winchester, Hampshire 27 Feb 1983. 6'0". RHB, WK. Debut (Gloucestershire)/ cap 2005. No f-c appearances 2006. MCC YC 2002-04. HS 83* v Bangladesh A (Bristol) 2005 – on debut. CC HS 13 v Warwks (Birmingham) 2005. LO HS 17 v Glamorgan (Cardiff) 2005 (NL).

SPEARMAN, Craig Murray, b Auckland, New Zealand 4 Jul 1972. RHB. Auckland 1993-94 to 1994-95. Central Districts 1996-97 to 2003-04. Gloucestershire debut/cap 2002. Qualified for England 2005. **Tests** (NZ): 19 (1995-96 to 2000-01); HS 112 v Z (Auckland) 1995-96. **LOI** (NZ): 51 (1995-96 to 2000-01); HS 86 v Z (Harare) 2000-01. F-c Tours (NZ): SA 2000-01; WI 1995-96; I 1999-00; P 1996-97; SL 1998; Z 1997-98, 2000-01. 1000 runs (3); most – 1462 (2004). HS 341 v Middx (Gloucester) 2004 – record Gloucestershire score. BB 1-37 CD v Wellington (New Plymouth) 1999-00. LO HS 153 v Warwks (Gloucester) 2003 (NL). T20 HS 88.

‡**STAYT, Thomas** Patrick (St Augustine's C, Trowbridge; Exeter U), b Salisbury, Wilts 20 Jan 1986. RHB, RMF. Gloucestershire 2nd XI 2003 to date. Awaiting 1st XI debut.

TAYLOR, Christopher Glyn (Colston's Collegiate S), b Southmead, Bristol 27 Sep 1976. 5'7". RHB, OB. Debut (Gloucestershire) 2000, scoring 104 v Middx – first to score a hundred at Lord's in a Championship match on his first-class debut; cap 2001; captain 2004-05. 1000 runs (1): 1077) 2004. HS 196 v Notts (Nottingham) 2001. BB 3-126 v Northants (Cheltenham) 2000. LO HS 93 v Warwks (Bristol) 2002 (BHC). LO BB 2-5 v Northants (Northampton) 2004 (NL). T20 HS 83.

‡**THOMPSON, Jackson** Gladwin, b Nasik, Maharashtra, India 7 Feb 1986. LHB, LB. Gloucestershire 2nd XI 2002 to date. Awaiting 1st XI debut. LO HS 1 Glos CB v Surrey CB (Bristol) 2002 (CGT).

‡NQ**UMAR GUL** (Peshawar Govt. SS; Peshawar Govt. Superior Science C), b Peshawar, Pakistan 15 Apr 1982. 6'1". RHB, RFM. PIA 2001-02 to 2005-06. Peshawar 2003-04 to 2005-06. Habib Bank 2006-07. **Tests** (P): 14 (2003-04 to 2006-07); HS 26 v WI (Karachi) 2006-07; BB 5-31 v I (Lahore) 2003-04. **LOI** (P): 25 (2002-03 to 2006-07); HS 17* v I (Rawalpindi) 2005-06; BB 5-17 v B (Lahore) 2003-04. F-c Tours (P): E 2006; NZ 2003-04; SL 2005-06. HS 46 Peshawar v Multan (Peshawar) 2005-06. UK HS 13 P v E (Oval) 2006. BB 8-78 Peshawar v Karachi Urban (Peshawar) 2005-06. UK BB 5-123 P v E (Leeds) 2006. LO HS 17* (see LOI). LO BB 5-17 (see LOI). T20 HS 11. T20 BB 4-21.

RELEASED/RETIRED

(Having made a first-class County appearance in 2006)

AVERIS, James Maxwell Michael (Cathedral S, Bristol; Portsmouth U; St Cross C, Oxford), b Bristol 28 May 1974. 5'11". RHB, RMF. Oxford U 1997; blue 1997; rugby blue 1996-97. Gloucestershire 1997-2006; cap 2001. HS 53 v Surrey (Bristol) 2006. BB 6-32 v Northants (Bristol) 2004. LO HS 23* v Lancs (Manchester) 2000 (NL). LO BB 6-23 v Bucks (Ascott Park) 2003 (CGT). T20 HS 10. T20 BB 3-7.

BALL, Martyn Charles John (King Edmund SS; Bath CFE), b Bristol 26 Apr 1970. 5'8". RHB, OB. Gloucestershire 1988-2006; cap 1996; benefit 2002. F-c Tours: I 2001-02; SL 1992-93 (Gs). HS 75 v Somerset (Taunton) 2003. BB 8-46 (14-169 match) v Somerset (Taunton) 1993. LO HS 51 v SL A (Cheltenham) 1999. LO BB 5-33 v Yorks (Leeds) 2003 (NL). T20 HS 27*. T20 BB 3-24.

HARVEY, I.J. – *see DERBYSHIRE.*

WESTON, W.P. – *see DERBYSHIRE.*

WINDOWS, Matthew Guy Newman (Clifton C; Durham U), b Bristol 5 Apr 1973. Son of A.R.Windows (Glos and CU 1960-68). 5'7". RHB, SLA. Gloucestershire 1992-2006; cap 1998; benefit 2006. Combined U 1993-95. F-c Tours (Eng A): SA 1998-99; Z 1998-99. 1000 runs (3); most – 1173 (1998). HS 184 v Warwks (Cheltenham) 1996. BB (Comb U) 1-6. Gs BB – . LO HS 117 v Northants (Cheltenham) 2001 (NL). T20 HS 29.

DURHAM RELEASED/RETIRED (continued from p 21)

MAHER, J.P. – *see GLAMORGAN.*

PRATT, Gary Joseph (Willington Parkside CS), b Bishop Auckland 22 Dec 1981. Younger brother of A.Pratt (Durham 1997-2004). 5'11". LHB, OB. Durham 2000-06. 1000 runs (1): 1055 (2003). HS 150 v Northants (Chester-le-St) 2003. LO HS 101* v Somerset (Taunton) 2003 (NL). T20 HS 62*. Gained fame (without an MBE) as England's 'super sub' in 2005 Ashes series.

TURNER, M.L. – *see SOMERSET*

D.J.Barrick left the staff having not made a first-class appearance in 2006.

GLOUCESTERSHIRE 2006

RESULTS SUMMARY

	Place	*Won*	*Lost*	*Tied*	*Drew*	*No Result*
County Championship (2nd Division)	**7th**	3	6		7	
All First-Class Matches		3	6		7	
C & G Trophy (South Conference)	5th	5	3			1
Pro40 League (2nd Division)	**1st**	6	2			
Twenty20 Cup (Mid/West/Wales Division)	Q-Finalist	6	3			

COUNTY CHAMPIONSHIP AVERAGES

BATTING AND FIELDING

Cap		*M*	*I*	*NO*	*HS*	*Runs*	*Avge*	*100*	*50*	*Ct/St*
2006	H.J.H.Marshall	11	21	1	168	1218	60.90	5	7	6
1999	I.J.Harvey	9	15	5	114	561	56.10	2	2	4
2004	A.P.R.Gidman	16	31	6	120	1244	49.76	4	7	2
2002	C.M.Spearman	16	31	–	192	1370	44.19	6	2	18
2005	Kadeer Ali	11	22	1	145	834	39.71	1	5	6
2004	W.P.C.Weston	13	24	1	130	911	39.60	2	6	7
2004	M.A.Hardinges	11	15	2	107*	444	34.15	2	1	–
2004	S.J.Adshead	16	28	5	79*	687	29.86	–	4	47/2
2004	I.D.Fisher	5	8	2	45	168	28.00	–	-	1
2001	C.G.Taylor	14	27	–	121	705	26.11	1	4	12
1998	J.Lewis	11‡	14	2	57	242	20.16	–	1	3
2001	J.M.M.Averis	4	7	–	53	128	18.28	–	1	–
1998	M.G.N.Windows	5	9	1	48	127	15.87	–	–	2
1996	M.C.J.Ball	10	15	1	58	215	15.35	–	1	1
2005	S.P.Kirby	15	22	11	19*	106	9.63	–	–	3
2005	C.G.Greenidge	5	8	–	20	42	5.25	–	–	3
2006	V.Banerjee	3	5	2	7	12	4.00	–	–	1

Also batted: D.O.Brown (1 match – cap 2006) 34, 22; D.A.Burton (1 – cap 2006) 52*, 1; W.D.Rudge (4 – cap 2005) 1, 8* (1 ct).

BOWLING

	O	*M*	*R*	*W*	*Avge*	*Best*	*5wI*	*10wM*
J.Lewis	322.2	65	1090	48	22.70	7- 38	3	2
I.J.Harvey	142.2	38	378	13	29.07	3- 25	–	–
M.C.J.Ball	307.5	63	930	27	34.44	6-134	1	–
S.P.Kirby	517.4	95	1944	49	39.67	5- 99	1	–
M.A.Hardinges	270.4	58	1011	23	43.95	4-127	–	–
A.P.R.Gidman	232	49	762	17	44.82	3- 38	–	–
J.M.M.Averis	107.4	15	473	10	47.30	4- 75	–	–
I.D.Fisher	201.2	19	755	10	75.50	3-110	–	–
Also bowled:								
V.Banerjee	112	24	400	9	44.44	4-150	–	–
C.G.Greenidge	109.3	13	533	9	59.22	3- 50	–	–

Kadeer Ali 14-2-57-0; D.O.Brown 9-2-30-0; D.A.Burton 20-1-129-0; H.J.H.Marshall 26-7-63-1; W.D.Rudge 59-2-311-2; C.G.Taylor 76-12-267-2.

Gloucestershire played no fixtures outside the County Championship in 2006. The First-Class Averages (pp 130–146) give the records of their players in all first-class matches for the county, with the exception of V.Banerjee and J.Lewis whose full county figures are as above.

‡ Full substitute in five matches (three for W.D.Rudge and one apiece for C.G.Greenidge and M.A.Hardinges).

GLOUCESTERSHIRE RECORDS

FIRST-CLASS CRICKET

Highest Total	For 695-9d		v	Middlesex	Gloucester	2004
	V 774-7d		by	Australians	Bristol	1948
Lowest Total	For 17		v	Australians	Cheltenham	1896
	V 12		by	Northants	Gloucester	1907
Highest Innings	For 341	C.M.Spearman	v	Middlesex	Gloucester	2004
	V 319	C.J.L.Rogers	for	Northants	Northampton	2006

Highest Partnership for each Wicket

1st	395	D.M.Young/R.B.Nicholls	v	Oxford U	Oxford	1962
2nd	256	C.T.M.Pugh/T.W.Graveney	v	Derbyshire	Chesterfield	1960
3rd	336	W.R.Hammond/B.H.Lyon	v	Leics	Leicester	1933
4th	321	W.R.Hammond/W.L.Neale	v	Leics	Gloucester	1937
5th	261	W.G.Grace/W.O.Moberley	v	Yorkshire	Cheltenham	1876
6th	320	G.L.Jessop/J.H.Board	v	Sussex	Hove	1903
7th	248	W.G.Grace/E.L.Thomas	v	Sussex	Hove	1896
8th	239	W.R.Hammond/A.E.Wilson	v	Lancashire	Bristol	1938
9th	193	W.G.Grace/S.A.P.Kitcat	v	Sussex	Bristol	1896
10th	131	W.R.Gouldsworthy/J.G.Bessant	v	Somerset	Bristol	1923

Best Bowling	For	10-40	E.G.Dennett	v	Essex	Bristol	1906
(Innings)	V	10-66	A.A.Mailey	for	Australians	Cheltenham	1921
		10-66	K.Smales	for	Notts	Stroud	1956
Best Bowling	For	17-56	C.W.L.Parker	v	Essex	Gloucester	1925
(Match)	V	15-87	A.J.Conway	for	Worcs	Moreton-in-M	1914

Most Runs – Season	2860	W.R.Hammond	(av 69.75)	1933
Most Runs – Career	33664	W.R.Hammond	(av 57.05)	1920-51
Most 100s – Season	13	W.R.Hammond		1938
Most 100s – Career	113	W.R.Hammond		1920-51
Most Wkts – Season	222	T.W.J.Goddard	(av 16.80)	1937
	222	T.W.J.Goddard	(av 16.37)	1947
Most Wkts – Career	3170	C.W.L.Parker	(av 19.43)	1903-35
Most Career W-K Dismissals	1054	R.C.Russell	(950 ct; 104 st)	1981-2004
Most Career Catches in the Field	719	C.A.Milton		1948-74

LIMITED-OVERS CRICKET

Highest Total	**CGT**	401-7		v	Bucks	Wing	2003
	P40	344-6		v	Northants	Cheltenham	2001
	T20	227-4		v	Somerset	Bristol	2006
Lowest Total	**CGT**	82		v	Notts	Bristol	1987
	P40	49		v	Middlesex	Bristol	1978
	T20	128		v	Glamorgan	Cardiff	2005
Highest Innings	**CGT**	177	A.J.Wright	v	Scotland	Bristol	1997
	P40	153	C.M.Spearman	v	Warwicks	Gloucester	2003
	T20	100*	I.J.Harvey	v	Warwicks	Birmingham	2003
Best Bowling	**CGT**	6-21	C.A.Walsh	v	Kent	Bristol	1990
		6-21	C.A.Walsh	v	Cheshire	Bristol	1992
	P40	6-52	J.N.Shepherd	v	Kent	Bristol	1983
	T20	4-22	I.D.Fisher	v	Somerset	Bristol	2004

HAMPSHIRE

Formation of Present Club: 12 August 1863
Inaugural First-Class Match: 1864
Colours: Blue, Gold and White
Badge: Tudor Rose and Crown
County Champions: (2) 1961, 1973
Gillette/NatWest/C & G Trophy Winners: (2) 1991, 2005
Benson and Hedges Cup Winners: (2) 1988, 1992
Pro 40/National League (Div 1) Winners: (0); best – 3rd 2004
Sunday League Winners: (3) 1975, 1978, 1986
Twenty20 Cup Winners: (0) – best Quarter-Finalist 2004

Chief Executive: Nick S.Pike, The Rose Bowl, Botley Road, West End, Southampton SO30 3XH • Tel: 023 8047 2002 • Fax: 023 8047 2122 • Email: enquiries@rosebowlplc.com • Webs: www.hampshirecricket.com

Director of Cricket: T.M.Tremlett. **First XI Manager/Coach**: V.P.Terry. **Captain**: S.K.Warne. **Vice-Captain**: S.D.Udal. **Overseas Players**: S.R.Clark and S.K.Warne. **2007 Beneficiary**: A.D.Mascarenhas. **Head Groundsman**: Nigel Gray. **Scorer**: A.E. (Tony) Weld. ‡ New registration. [NQ] Not qualified for England.

ADAMS, James Henry Kenneth (Sherborne S; University C, London; Loughborough U), b Winchester 23 Sep 1980. 6'2". LHB, LM. British U 2002-03. Hampshire debut 2002; cap 2006. Loughborough UCCE 2003-4 – scoring 107 v Somerset (Taunton) on debut. Dorset 1998. 1000 runs (1): 1173 (2006). HS 262* v Notts (Nottingham) 2006. BB 2-16 v Durham (Chester-le-St) 2004. LO HS 40 v Glamorgan (Southampton) 2004 (NL). BB – . T20 HS 17*.

‡BALCOMBE, David John (St John's S, Leatherhead; St Hild & St Bede C, Durham), b City of London 24 Dec 1984. 6'4". RHB, RFM. Durham UCCE 2005-06. British U 2006. Awaiting Hampshire f-c debut (one T20 game 2006). HS 73 DU v Leics (Leicester) 2005. BB 5-112 DU v Durham (Durham) 2005. T20 HS 3. T20 BB – .

BENHAM, Christopher Charles (Yately CS; Loughborough U), b Frimley, Surrey 24 Mar 1983. 6'1". RHB, RM/OB. Loughborough UCCE 2004. Hampshire debut 2004. HS 95 v Warwks (Southampton) 2006. LO HS 158 v Glamorgan (Southampton) 2006. T20 HS 59.

BROWN, Michael James (Queen Elizabeth GS, Blackburn; Collingwood C, Durham U), b Burnley, Lancs 9 Feb 1980. 6'0". Elder brother of D.O.Brown (*see GLOUCESTERSHIRE*). RHB, OB. Middlesex 1999-2003. Durham UCCE 2001-02. British U 2001-02. Hampshire debut 2004. HS 133 v LU (Southampton) 2006. CC HS 109* v Glamorgan (Southampton) 2004. LO HS 76 v Glamorgan (Southampton) 2006 (CGT). T20 HS 14.

BRUCE, James Thomas Anthony (Eton C; St Hild & St Bede C, Durham U), b Hammersmith, London 17 Dec 1979. 6'1". RHB, RMF. Durham UCCE 2001-02. Hampshire debut 2003; cap 2006. Cumberland 2001. HS 21* v Glamorgan (Southampton) 2003. BB 5-43 v Notts (Southampton) 2006. LO HS 19* v Essex (Southampton) 2006 (CGT). LO BB 4-18 v Glos (Southampton) 2006 (CGT). T20 HS 12. T20 BB 3-20.

BURROWS, Thomas George (Reading GS; Southampton Solent U), b Wokingham, Berkshire 5 May 1985. 5'8". RHB, WK. Debut (Hampshire) 2005. Berkshire 2001 to 2003. HS 42 v Kent (Canterbury) 2005 – on debut. LO HS 16 v West Indies A (Southampton) 2006. T20 HS – .

CARBERRY, Michael Alexander (St John Rigby Catholic C), b Croydon, Surrey 29 Sep 1980. 6'0". LHB, OB. Surrey 2001-02. Kent 2003-05. Hampshire debut/cap 2006. F-c Tour (Eng A): B 2006-07. HS 153* Sy v CU (Cambridge) 2002. H HS 104 v Middx (Lord's) 2006. CC HS 112 K v Worcs (Canterbury) 2004. BB 2-85 v Durham (Chester-le-St) 2006. LO HS 88 v Surrey (Croydon) 2006 (CGT). LO BB (K) 1-21 (NL). T20 HS 90.

‡NQ**CLARK, Stuart** Rupert, b Sutherland, Sydney, Australia 28 Sep 1975. 6'5½". RHB, RFM. NSW 1997-98 to date. Middlesex 2004-05. **Tests** (A): 9 (2005-06 to 2006-07); HS 39 v E (Brisbane) 2006-07; BB 5-55 (9-89 match) v SA (Cape Town) 2005-06 – on debut. **LOI** (A): 24 (2005-06 to 2006-07); HS 16* v SA (Durban) 2005-06; BB 4-54 v NZ (Sydney) 2006-07. F-c Tours (A): SA 2005-06; P 2005-06 (Aus A); B 2005-06. HS 62 NSW v S Aus (Adelaide) 2006-07. UK HS 34 M v Northants (Northampton) 2004 – on UK debut. BB 8-58 NSW v WA (Perth) 2006-07, including hat-trick. UK BB 5-61 M v Warwks (Lord's) 2005. LO HS 26* M v Sussex (Hove) 2004 (NL). LO BB 4-24 NSW v WA (Perth) 2004-05. T20 HS – . T20 BB 1-35.

CRAWLEY, John Paul (Manchester GS; Trinity C, Cambridge), b Maldon, Essex 21 Sep 1971. Brother of M.A.Crawley (Oxford U, Lancs and Notts 1987-94) and P.M. (Cambridge U 1992). 6'1". RHB, RM, occ WK. Lancashire 1990-2001; cap 1994; captain 1999-2001. Cambridge U 1991-93; blue 1991-92-93; captain 1992-93. Hampshire debut/cap 2002; captain 2003. YC 1994. **Tests**: 37 (1994 to 2002-03); HS 156* v SL (Oval) 1998. **LOI**: 13 (1994-95 to 1998-99); HS 73 v Z (Harare) 1996-97. F-c Tours: A 1994-95, 1998-99, 2002-03; SA 1993-94 (Eng A), 1995-96; WI 1995-96 (La), 1997-98, 2000-01 (Eng A); NZ 1996-97; Z 1996-97. 1000 runs (10); most – 1851 (1998). HS 311* v Notts (Southampton) 2005. BB 1-7. LO HS 114 La v Notts (Manchester) 1995 (BHC). T20 HS 23.

NQ**ERVINE, Sean** Michael (Lomagundi C, Chinhoyi), b Harare, Zimbabwe 6 Dec 1982. Elder brother of C.R.Ervine (Midlands 2003-04 to 2004-05); son of R.M.Ervine (Rhodesia 1977-78); grandson of M.A.Den (Rhodesia 1935-36); nephew of N.B.Ervine (Rhodesia 1977-78) and G.M.Den (Rhodesia and Eastern Province 1963-64 to 1969-70). Irish passport. 6'2". LHB, RM. CFX Academy 2000-01 to 2001. Midlands 2001-02 to 2003-04. Hampshire debut/cap 2005 (Kolpak registration). Western Australia 2006-07. **Tests** (Z): 5 (2003 to 2003-04); HS 86 v B (Harare) 2002-04; BB 4-146 v A (Perth) 2003-04. **LOI** (Z): 42 (2001-02 to 2003-04): HS 100 v I (Adelaide) 2003-04; BB 3-29 v P (Sharjah) 2002-02. F-c Tours: E 2003; A 2003-04. HS 126 Midlands v Manicaland (Mutare) 2002-03. H HS 75 v Glamorgan (Cardiff) 2005. BB 6-82 Midlands v Mashonaland (Kwekwe) 2002-03. H BB 5-60 v Glamorgan (Cardiff) 2005. LO HS 104 v Warwks (Lord's) 2005 (CGT). LO BB 5-50 v Glamorgan (Cardiff) 2005 (CGT). T20 HS 46. T20 BB 3-18.

GRIFFITHS, David Andrew (Sandown HS, IOW), b Newport, IOW 10 Sep 1985. 6'1". LHB, RFM. Debut (Hampshire) 2006. HS 16* and BB – v LU (Southampton) 2006 – on debut. Awaiting CC debut.

NQ**LAMB, Gregory** Arthur (Lomagundi C, Chinhoyi; Guildford C, Surrey), b Harare, Zimbabwe 4 Mar 1980. 5'11". RHB, RM/OB. Debut (ZCU President's XI) 1998-99. ZC/CFX Academy 1998-99 to 1999-00. Mashonaland 2000-01. Hampshire debut 2004. F-c Tour (Zim A): SL 1999-00. HS 100* CFX Academy v Manicaland (Mutare) 1999-00. H HS 94 v Derbys (Derby) 2004 – on UK debut. BB 7-73 CFX Academy v Midlands (Kwekwe) 1999-00. H BB 2-30 v Middx (Southgate) 2005. LO HS 100* v Northants (Southampton) 2005 (NL). LO BB 4-38 v Yorks (Leeds) 2006 (P40). T20 HS 67. T20 BB 4-28.

LATOUF, Kevin John (Millfield S; Barton Peveril C), b Pretoria, South Africa 7 Sep 1985. 5'10". RHB, RM. Debut (Hampshire) 2006. HS 29 v LU (Southampton) 2006 – on debut. Awaiting CC debut. LO HS 25 v Surrey (Oval) 2005 (CGT) on 1st XI debut.

‡LUMB, Michael John (St Stithians C, Johannesburg), b Johannesburg, South Africa 12 Feb 1980. Son of R.G.Lumb (Yorkshire 1970-84); nephew of A.J.S.Smith (SAU and Natal 1972-73 to 1983-84). 6'0". LHB, RM. Yorkshire2000-06; ECB qualified and CC debut 2001; cap 2003. F-c Tour (Eng A): I 2003-04. 1000 runs (1): 1038 (2003). HS 144 Y v Middx (Southgate) 2006. BB 2-10 Y v Kent (Canterbury) 2001. LO HS 92 Y v Glamorgan (Colwyn Bay) 2003 (NL). T20 HS 84*. T20 BB 3-32.

MASCARENHAS, Adrian **Dimitri** (Trinity C, Perth, Australia), b Hammersmith, London 30 Oct 1977. 6'2". Resident in Australia 1979-96. RHB, RMF. Debut (Hampshire) 1996, taking 6-88 v Glamorgan (Southampton); took 16 wickets in first two CC matches; cap 1998; benefit 2007. Dorset 1996. HS 131 v Kent (Canterbury) 2006. 50 wkts (1): 56 (2004). BB 6-25 v Derbys (Southampton) 2004. LO HS 79 v Worcs (Southampton) 1999 (NL) and 79 v Kent (Canterbury) 2004 (NL). LO BB 5-27 v Glos (Southampton) 2002 (NL). T20 HS 52. T20 BB 5-14.

PIETERSEN, Kevin Peter (Maritzburg C; Natal U), b Pietermaritzburg, South Africa 27 Jun 1980. British passport (English mother) – qualified for England Oct 2004. 6'4". RHB, OB. MBE 2005. *Wisden* 2005. Natal/KwaZulu-Natal 1997-98 to 1999-00. Nottinghamshire 2001-04; cap 2002. MCC 2004. Hampshire debut/cap 2005 (no f-c appearances 2006). **Tests**: 23 (2005 to 2006-07); HS 158 v A (Oval) 2005, 158 v SL (Lord's) 2006, and 158 v A (Adelaide) 2006-07; BB 1-11. **LOI**: 40 (2004-05 to 2006-07); HS 116 v SA (Pretoria) 2004-05; scored 454 runs (av 151.33) in 7-match series, including fastest England 100 off 69 balls (E London), v SA 2004-05; BB 1-4. F-c Tours: A 2006-07; I 2003-04 (Eng A), 2005-06; P 2005-06. 1000 runs (3): most – 1546 (2003). HS 254* Nt v Middx (Nottingham) 2002. H HS 126 v Glamorgan (Southampton) 2005. BB 4-31 Nt v DU (Nottingham) 2003. CC BB 3-72 Nt v Hants (Nottingham) 2004. Hants BB – . LO HS 147 Nt v Somerset (Taunton) 2002 (NL). LO BB 3-14 Nt v Middx (Lord's 2004 (NL). T20 HS 67. T20 BB 2-9.

POTHAS, Nic (King Edward VII S; Rand Afrikaans U), b Johannesburg 18 Nov 1973. ECB qualified – EU (Greek) passport. 6'3". RHB, WK. Transvaal 1993-94 to 1996-97. Gauteng 1997-98 to 2000-01. Hampshire debut 2002; cap 2003. **LOI** (SA): 3 (2000-01); HS 24 v P (Singapore) 2000 – on debut. F-c Tours (SA): E 1996 (SA A); WI 2000 (SA A); SL 1998. HS 165 Gauteng v KZ-Natal (Johannesburg) 1998-99. H HS 146* v Worcs (Worcester) 2003. Held 7 catches in an innings v Lancs (Manchester) 2006. LO HS 114* v Glamorgan (Cardiff) 2005 (CGT). T20 HS 59.

‡STOKES, Mitchell Sam Thomas (Cranbourne S; Basingstoke TC), b Basingstoke 27 Mar 1987. 5'8". RHB, OB. Berkshire 2005. Hampshire l-o debut 2005. Awaiting f-c debut. LO HS 36 v West Indies A (Southampton) 2006. T20 HS 62. T20 BB – .

TAYLOR, Billy Victor (Bitterne Park S, Southampton), b Southampton, Hants 11 Jan 1977. Younger brother of J.L.Taylor (Wiltshire 1998 to 2002). 6'3". LHB, RMF. Sussex 1999-2003. Hampshire debut 2004; cap 2006. Wiltshire 1996-99. HS 40 v Essex (Southampton) 2004. BB 6-32 v Middx (Southampton) 2006 (inc hat-trick). LO HS 21* Sx v Notts (Cleethorpes) 1999 (NL). LO BB 5-28 Sx v Middx (Lord's) 2002 (BHC). T20 HS 12*. T20 BB 2-9.

TOMLINSON, James Andrew (Harrow Way S, Andover; Cardiff U), b Winchester 12 Jun 1982. 6'1". LHB, LFM. British U 2002-03. Hampshire debut 2002; no f-c appearances 2005. Wiltshire 2001. HS 23 v I (Southampton) 2002. CC HS 12* v Derbys (Derby) 2004. BB 6-63 v Derbys (Derby) 2003. LO HS 6 (NL). LO BB 4-47 v Glamorgan (Southampton) 2006 (CGT). T20 HS 5. T20 BB 1-20.

TREMLETT, Christopher Timothy (Thornden S, Chandler's Ford; Taunton's C, Southampton), b Southampton 2 Sep 1981. Son of T.M.Tremlett (Hampshire 1976-91); grandson of M.F.Tremlett (Somerset, CD and England 1947-60). 6'7". RHB, RMF. Debut (Hampshire) v NZ A (Portsmouth) 2000, taking wicket of M.H.Richardson with his first ball; cap 2004. **LOI**: 6 (2005 to 2006-07); HS 8; BB 4-32 v B (Nottingham) 2005 – on debut (hat-trick ball hit stump without dislodging bails). F-c Tour (ECB Acad): SL 2002-03. HS 64 v Glos (Southampton) 2005. BB 6-44 v Sussex (Hove) 2005. Hat-trick v Notts (Nottingham) 2005. LO HS 38* v Cheshire (Alderley Edge) 2004 (CGT). LO BB 4-25 v Essex (Southend) 2002 (NL). T20 HS 13. T20 BB 3-20.

UDAL, Shaun David (Cove CS), b Cove, Farnborough 18 Mar 1969. Grandson of G.F.U. Udal (Middx & RAF 1932; Leics 1946); great-great-grandson of J.S.Udal (MCC 1871-75; Fiji 1894-95). 6'2". RHB, OB. Debut (Hampshire) 1989; cap 1992; benefit 2002. **Tests**: 4 (2005-06); HS 33* v P (Faisalabad) 2005-06; BB 4-14 v I (Bombay) 2005-06. **LOI**: 11 (1994 to 2005-06); HS 11* v Z (Brisbane) 1994-95; BB 2-37 v A (Sydney) 1994-95. F-c Tours: A 1994-95; I 2005-06; P 1995-96 (Eng A); 2005-06. HS 117* v Warwks (Southampton) 1997. 50 wkts (7); most – 74 (1993). BB 8-50 v Sussex (Southampton) 1992. LO HS 78 v Surrey (Guildford) 1997 (SL). LO BB 5-43 v Surrey (Oval) 1998 (SL). T20 HS 37. T20 BB 3-21.

NQ**WARNE, Shane** Keith (Hampton HS; Mentone GS), b Upper Ferntree Gully, Melbourne, Australia 13 Sep 1969. 6'0". RHB, LBG. Victoria 1990-91 to 2006-07; captain 1997-98 to 1998-99. Hampshire 2000, 2004 to date; cap 2000; captain 2004 to date. *Wisden* 1993 (also one of *Five Cricketers of the Century*). **Tests** (A): 144 (1991-92 to 2006-07); HS 99 v NZ (Perth) 2001-02; BB 8-71 v E (Brisbane) 1994-95; hat-trick v E (Melbourne) 1994-95. **LOI** (A): 193 (1992-93 to 2002-03, 11 as captain); HS 55 v SA (Pt Elizabeth) 1993-94; BB 5-33 v WI (Sydney) 1996-97. F-c Tours (A): E 1993, 1997, 2001, 2005; SA 1993-94, 1996-97, 2001-02, 2005-06; WI 1994-95, 1998-99; NZ 1992-93, 1999-00; I 1997-98, 2000-01, 2004-05; P 1994-95, 2002-03 (in SL/Sharjah); SL 1992, 1999, 2003-04; Z 1991-92 (Aus B), 1999-00; B 2005-06. HS 107* v Kent (Canterbury) 2005 – maiden 100 in his 321st innings. 50 wkts (6+2); most – 87 (2005). BB 8-71 (*see Tests*). H BB 7-99 v Middx (Southampton) 2006. LO HS 55 (*see LOI*). LO BB 6-42 v Surrey (Croydon) 2006 (CGT). T20 HS 12. T20 BB 1-29.

RELEASED/RETIRED

(Having made a first-class County appearance in 2006)

LOGAN, R.J. – *see NORTHAMPTONSHIRE.*

NQ**McLEAN,** Jonathan ('**Jono**') James (St Stithian's S; Cape Town U), b Johannesburg, South Africa 11 Jul 1980. 6'0". RHB, RM. W Province 2001-02 to 2003-04. SA Acad 2003-04. Hampshire 2005-06. British passport. HS 68 v Glos (Cheltenham) 2005 – on debut. LO HS 36 v Notts (Southampton) 2005 (NL). T20 HS 23.

NQ**THORNELY, Dominic** John (James Fallon HS, Albury), b Albury, NSW, Australia 1 Oct 1978. 6'2". RHB, RM. NSW 2003-04 to date. Surrey 2005. Hampshire 2006; cap 2006. F-c Tour (Aus A): P 2005-06. 1000 (0+1): 1065 (2004-05). HS 261* NSW v WA (Sydney) 2004-05. UK HS 81 Sy v Middx (Lord's) 2005 – on UK debut. H HS 76 v Yorks (Leeds) 2006. BB 3-38 v Sussex (Southampton) 2006. LO HS 107* v Kent (Southampton) 2006 (CGT). LO BB 3-17 v Essex (Southampton) 2006 (CGT). T20 HS 67*. T20 BB 4-22.

HAMPSHIRE 2006

RESULTS SUMMARY

	Place	Won	Lost	Tied	Drew	No Result
County Championship (1st Division)	**3rd**	6	3		7	
All First-Class Matches		6	3		8	
C & G Trophy (South Conference)	4th	5	3			1
Pro40 League (2nd Division)	3rd	6†	2			1
† *Including Promotion Playoff Match (promoted)*						
Twenty20 Cup (South Division)	5th	3	5			

COUNTY CHAMPIONSHIP AVERAGES

BATTING AND FIELDING

Cap		M	I	NO	HS	Runs	Avge	100	50	Ct/St
2002	J.P.Crawley	16	27	1	189	1737	66.80	6	7	8
2003	N.Pothas	15	22	7	122*	973	64.86	4	5	56/2
2006	J.H.K.Adams	16	30	5	262*	1162	46.48	2	4	18
2006	M.A.Carberry	15	28	2	104	938	36.07	2	5	8
2006	D.J.Thornely	15	25	3	76	759	34.50	–	6	12
–	C.C.Benham	8	14	0	95	470	33.57	–	4	9
2000	S.K.Warne	13	17	5	61*	371	30.91	–	2	16
2005	S.M.Ervine	15	22	3	50*	464	24.42	–	1	14
1998	A.D.Mascarenhas	16	24	–	131	474	19.75	1	–	4
–	M.J.Brown	4	7	1	37	96	16.00	–	–	3
1992	S.D.Udal	10	9	1	28	118	14.75	–	–	3
2006	J.T.A.Bruce	13	14	8	17	52	8.66	–	–	2
2004	C.T.Tremlett	9	10	1	23	76	8.44	–	–	–
2006	B.V.Taylor	5	5	2	3	3	1.00	–	–	1

Also batted: T.G.Burrows (1 match) 11, 18 (5 ct); G.A.Lamb (2) 0; 32*, 0 (2 ct); R.J.Logan (2) 0, 4 (1 ct); J.A.Tomlinson (1) 0.

BOWLING

	O	M	R	W	Avge	Best	5wI	10wM
C.T.Tremlett	264.2	51	835	34	24.55	6-89	1	–
A.D.Mascarenhas	429	111	1074	43	24.97	6-65	2	–
D.J.Thornely	199	49	578	22	26.27	3-38	–	–
S.K.Warne	523.4	91	1571	58	27.08	7-99	4	–
B.V.Taylor	108	18	350	12	29.16	6-32	1	–
J.T.A.Bruce	327	67	1109	38	29.18	5-43	1	–
S.M.Ervine	296.1	60	1060	26	40.76	3-57	–	–
S.D.Udal	209	41	646	15	43.06	2-12	–	–

Also bowled: J.H.K.Adams 25.1-4-141-1; C.C.Benham 5-0-37-0; M.A.Carberry 22-0-114-2; J.P.Crawley 5-0-29-0; G.A.Lamb 35-1-135-2; R.J.Logan 36-4-151-3; N.Pothas 19-3-58-1; J.A.Tomlinson 32-8-118-4.

The First-Class Averages (pp 130–146) give the records of Hampshire players in all first-class matches for the county (Hampshire's other opponents being Loughborough UCCE), with the exception of K.P.Pietersen whose seven first-class appearances were all for England.

HAMPSHIRE RECORDS

FIRST-CLASS CRICKET

Highest Total	For 714-5d		v	Notts	Southampton	2005
	V 742		by	Surrey	The Oval	1909
Lowest Total	For 15		v	Warwicks	Birmingham	1922
	V 23		by	Yorkshire	Middlesbrough	1965
Highest Innings	For 316	R.H.Moore	v	Warwicks	Bournemouth	1937
	V 303*	G.A.Hick	for	Worcs	Southampton	1997

Highest Partnership for each Wicket

1st	347	V.P.Terry/C.L.Smith	v	Warwicks	Birmingham	1987
2nd	321	G.Brown/E.I.M.Barrett	v	Glos	Southampton	1920
3rd	344	C.P.Mead/G.Brown	v	Yorkshire	Portsmouth	1927
4th	263	R.E.Marshall/D.A.Livingstone	v	Middlesex	Lord's	1970
5th	235	G.Hill/D.F.Walker	v	Sussex	Portsmouth	1937
6th	411	R.M.Poore/E.G.Wynyard	v	Somerset	Taunton	1899
7th	325	G.Brown/C.H.Abercrombie	v	Essex	Leyton	1913
8th	257	N.Pothas/A.J.Bichel	v	Glos	Cheltenham	2005
9th	230	D.A.Livingstone/A.T.Castell	v	Surrey	Southampton	1962
10th	192	H.A.W.Bowell/W.H.Livsey	v	Worcs	Bournemouth	1921

Best Bowling	For	9- 25	R.M.H.Cottam	v	Lancashire	Manchester	1965
(Innings)	V	10- 46	W.Hickton	for	Lancashire	Manchester	1870
Best Bowling	For	16- 88	J.A.Newman	v	Somerset	Weston-s-Mare	1927
(Match)	V	17-119	W.Mead	for	Essex	Southampton	1895

Most Runs – Season	2854	C.P.Mead	(av 79.27)	1928
Most Runs – Career	48892	C.P.Mead	(av 48.84)	1905-36
Most 100s – Season	12	C.P.Mead		1928
Most 100s – Career	138	C.P.Mead		1905-36
Most Wkts – Season	190	A.S.Kennedy	(av 15.61)	1922
Most Wkts – Career	2669	D.Shackleton	(av 18.23)	1948-69
Most Career W-K Dismissals	700	R.J.Parks	(630 ct/70 st)	1980-92
Most Career Catches in the Field	629	C.P.Mead		1905-36

LIMITED-OVERS CRICKET

Highest Total	**CGT**	371-4		v	Glamorgan	Southampton	1975
	P40	353-8		v	Middlesex	Lord's	2005
	T20	225-2		v	Middlesex	Southampton	2006
Lowest Total	**CGT**	98		v	Lancashire	Manchester	1975
	P40	43		v	Essex	Basingstoke	1972
	T20	95		v	Essex	Chelmsford	2004
Highest Innings	**CGT**	177	C.G.Greenidge	v	Glamorgan	Southampton	1975
	P40	172	C.G.Greenidge	v	Surrey	Southampton	1987
	T20	97*	S.R.Watson	v	Kent	Southampton	2004
Best Bowling	**CGT**	7-30	P.J.Sainsbury	v	Norfolk	Southampton	1965
	P40	6-20	T.E.Jesty	v	Glamorgan	Cardiff	1975
	T20	5-14	A.D.Mascarenhas	v	Sussex	Hove	2004

KENT

Formation of Present Club: 1 March 1859
Substantial Reorganisation: 6 December 1870
Inaugural First-Class Match: 1864
Colours: Maroon and White
Badge: White Horse on a Red Ground
County Champions: (6) 1906, 1909, 1910, 1913, 1970, 1978
Joint Champions: (1) 1977
Gillette/NatWest/C & G Trophy Winners: (2) 1967, 1974
Benson and Hedges Cup Winners: (3) 1973, 1976, 1978
Pro 40/National League (Div 1) Winners: (1) 2001
Sunday League Winners: (4) 1972, 1973, 1976, 1995
Twenty20 Cup Winners: (0); best – Quarter-Finalist 2006

Chief Executive: Paul E.Millman, St Lawrence Ground, Canterbury, CT1 3NZ • Tel: 01227 456886 • Fax: 01227 762168 • Email: kent@ecb.co.uk • Web: www.kentccc.com

First XI Coach: G.Ford. **Captain**: R.W.T.Key. **Vice-Captain**: M.M.Patel. **Overseas Players**: A.J.Hall and Yasir Arafat. **2007 Beneficiary**: none. **Head Groundsman**: Mike Grantham. **Scorer**: Jack C.Foley. ‡ New registration. NQ Not qualified for England.

CHAMBERS, Dominic James (St Edmunds S, Canterbury), b Canterbury 6 Jan 1984. RHB, SLA. Debut (Kent) 2006. Awaiting CC debut. HS 12 v CU (Cambridge) 2006.

COOK, Simon James (Matthew Arnold S), b Oxford 15 Jan 1977. 6'4". RHB, RM. Middlesex 1999-2004; cap 2003. Kent debut 2005. HS 93* M v Notts (Lord's) 2001. K HS 71 v Yorks (Leeds) 2006. BB 8-63 M v Northants (Northampton) 2002. K BB 6-74 v Warwks (Birmingham) 2006. LO HS 67* M v Durham (Lord's) 2003 (NL). LO BB 6-37 M v Leics (Leicester) 2004 (NL). T20 HS 20. T20 BB 3-14.

DENLY, Joseph Liam (Chaucer TC), b Canterbury 16 Mar 1986. 6'0". RHB, LB. Debut (Kent) 2004. HS 115 (& 107*) and BB 2-40 v CU (Cambridge) 2006. CC HS 86 v Warwks (Birmingham) 2006. CC BB 1-8. LO HS 70 v Middx (Lord's) 2006 (CGT). T20 HS 4.

NQ**DEXTER, Neil** John (Northwood HS; Varsity C; U of South Africa), b Johannesburg, S Africa 21 Aug 1984. 6'0". RHB, RM. Debut (Kent) 2005. HS 131* v Notts (Canterbury) 2006. BB 2-40 v Lancs (Manchester) 2006. LO HS 135* v Glamorgan (Cardiff) 2006 (CGT). LO BB 3-17 v Leics (Canterbury) 2006 (P40). T20 HS 36. T20 BB 3-17.

DIXEY, Paul Garrod (King's S, Canterbury), b Canterbury 2 Nov 1987. 5'8". RHB, WK. Debut (Kent) 2005. Awaiting CC debut. HS 24 v Bangladesh A (Canterbury) 2005 – on debut.

NQ**HALL, Andrew** James (Alberton HS), b Alberton, Johannesburg, South Africa 31 Jul 1975. 6'0". RHB, RFM. Transvaal/Gauteng 1995-96 to 2000-01. Easterns 2001-02 to 2003-04. Worcestershire 2003-04. Lions 2004-05 to 2005-06. Kent debut/cap2005. Durham CB 1999. Suffolk 2002. **Tests** (SA): 21 (2001-02 to 2006-07); HS 163 v I (Kanpur) 2004-05; BB 3-1 v SL (Johannesburg) 2002-03. **LOI** (SA): 76 (1998-99 to 2006-07); HS 81 v SL (Galle) 2000-01; BB 4-23 v NZ (Pretoria) 2005-06. F-c Tours (SA): E 2003; WI 2004-05; I 2004-05; SL 2006; Z 1995-96 (Transvaal B). HS 163 (*see Tests*). UK HS 133 K v Glamorgan (Canterbury) 2005. BB 6-77 (11-99 match) Easterns v WP (Port Elizabeth) 2002-03. UK BB 4-32 K v Glamorgan (Canterbury) 2005. LO HS 129* Gauteng v Border (E London) 1999-00. LO BB 4-23 (*see LOI*). T20 HS 59. T20 BB 3-15.

ILES, James Alexander (Maidstone GS), b Chatham 11 Feb 1990. 6'4". RHB, RFM. Debut (Kent) 2006. Awaiting CC debut. HS – and BB 1-27 v CU (Cambridge) 2006.

JONES, Geraint Owen (Harristown State HS, Toowoomba and MacGregor State HS, Brisbane, Australia), b Kundiawa, Papua New Guinea 14 Jul 1976. Welsh parents. 5'10". RHB, WK. Debut (Kent) 2001; cap 2003. MBE 2005. **Tests**: 34 (2003-04 to 2006-07); HS 100 v NZ (Leeds) 2004. **LOI**: 49 (2004 to 2006): HS 80 v Z (Bulawayo) 2004-05. F-c Tours: A 2006-07; SA 2004-05; WI 2003-04; I 2005-06; P 2005-06; SL 2003-04. HS 108* v Essex (Chelmsford) 2003. LO HS 80 (*see LOI*). T20 HS 22.

JONES, Kevin John Francis (Sittingbourne Community C), b Gillingham 9 Sep 1986. 5'11". RHB, RM. Debut (Kent) 2005. No appearances 2006. Awaiting CC and l-o debuts. HS 14 v Bangladesh A (Canterbury) 2005 – on debut.

JOSEPH, Robert **('Robbie')** Hartman (Sutton Vallence S; St Mary's C, Twickenham), b Antigua 20 Jan 1982. Resided in England since 1997. 6'1". RHB, RFM. Debut (First-Class Counties XI v NZ) 2000. Kent debut 2004. HS 29 v Yorks (Canterbury) 2006. BB 5-19 v Bangladesh A (Canterbury) 2005. CC BB 5-57 v Sussex (Canterbury) 2006. LO HS 15 v (Canterbury) 2005 (NL). LO BB 2-21 v Warwks (Canterbury) 2005 (NL).

KEY, Robert William Trevor (Colfe's S), b East Dulwich, London 12 May 1979. 6'1". RHB, RM/OB. Debut (Kent) 1998; cap 2001, captain 2006 to date. MCC 2002-04. *Wisden* 2004. **Tests**: 15 (2002 to 2004-05); HS 221 v WI (Lord's) 2004. **LOI**: 5 (2003); HS 19 v WI (Lord's) 2004. F-c Tours: A 2002-03; SA 1998-99 (Eng A), 2004-05; SL 2002-03 (ECB Acad); Z 1998-99 (Eng A). 1000 runs (4): most – 1896 (2004). HS 221 (*see Tests*). K HS 199 v Surrey (Oval) 2004. LO HS 114 v Notts (Nottingham) 2002 (NL). T20 HS 66*.

KHAN, Amjad (Skolenpa Duevej, Denmark), b Copenhagen, Denmark 14 Oct 1980. 6'0". RHB, RFM. Debut (Kent) 2001. Denmark 1998-2000. Qualified for England Dec 2006. Will miss 2007 season following reconstructive knee surgery. HS 78 v Middx (Lord's) 2003. 50 wkts (2); most – 63 (2002). BB 6-52 v Yorks (Canterbury) 2002. LO HS 65* Denmark v Ire (Harare) 1999-00. LO BB 4-26 v Leics (Leicester) 2003 (NL). T20 HS 15. T20 BB 3-11.

‡[NQ]**McLAREN, Ryan** (Grey C, Bloemfontein), b Kimberley, South Africa 9 Feb 1983. Son of P.McLaren (GW 1977-78 to 1994-95). Nephew of Keith McLaren (GW 1971-72 to 1984-85). Cousin of A.P.McLaren (GW 1998-99 to date). LHB, RMF. Free State 2003-04 to 2004-05. Eagles 2004-05 to date. Joins Kent as Kolpak registration. HS 140 Eagles v Warriors (Bloemfontein) 2005-06. BB 8-38 Eagles v Cape Cobras (Stellenbosch) 2006-07. LO HS 58* Eagles v Dolphins (Durban) 2006-07. LO BB 4-43 Eagles v Lions (Johannesburg) 2005-06. T20 HS 10. T20 BB 2-21.

PATEL, Minal Mahesh (Dartford GS; Erith TC), b Bombay, India 7 Jul 1970. 5'9". RHB, SLA. Debut (Kent) 1989; cap 1994; benefit 2004. No appearances 2003 (back injury). MCC 1999-00, 2004. Central Districts 2005-06. **Tests**: 2 (1996); HS 27 and BB 1-101 v I (Nottingham) 1996. F-c Tours (Eng A): I 1994-95; B 1999-00 (MCC). HS 87 v Glamorgan (Cardiff) 2005. 50 wkts (4); most – 90 (1994). BB 8-96 v Lancs (Canterbury) 1994. LO HS 27* v Somerset (Canterbury) 2001 (CGT). LO BB 3-20 v Somerset (Taunton) 2006 (P40). T20 HS 8. T20 BB 4-26.

SAGGERS, Martin John (Springwood HS, King's Lynn; Huddersfield U), b King's Lynn, Norfolk 23 May 1972. 6'2". RHB, RMF. Durham 1996-98. Kent debut 1999; cap 2001. MCC 2004. Norfolk 1995-96. **Tests**: 3 (2003-04 to 2004); HS 1 and BB 2-29 v B (Chittagong) 2003-04 on debut. F-c Tour: B 2003-04. HS 64 v Worcs (Canterbury) 2004. 50 wkts (4): most – 83 (2002). BB 7-79 v Durham (Chester-le-St) 2000. LO HS 34* Minor C v Leics (Jesmond) 1996 (BHC). LO BB 5-22 v Glos (Canterbury) 2001 (NL). T20 HS 5. T20 BB 2-14.

STEVENS, Darren Ian (Hinckley C), b Leicester 30 Apr 1976. 5'11". RHB, RM. Leicestershire 1997-2004; cap 2002. MCC 2002. Kent debut/cap 2005. F-c Tour (ECB Acad): SL 2002-03. 1000 (1): 1277 (2005). HS 208 v Glamorgan (Canterbury) 2005. BB 4-36 v Yorks (Canterbury) 2006. LO HS 133 Le v Northumb (Jesmond) 2000 (NWT). LO BB 5-32 v Scotland (Edinburgh) 2005 (NL). T20 HS 69. T20 BB 1-13.

TREDWELL, James Cullum (Southlands Community CS, New Romney), b Ashford 27 Feb 1982. 6'0". LHB, OB. Debut (Kent) 2001. MCC 2004. F-c Tour (Eng A): I 2003-04 (capt). HS 61 v Yorks (Leeds) 2002. BB 6-81 (10-165 match) v Sussex (Canterbury) 2006. LO HS 71 Kent CB v Bucks (Maidstone) 2001 (CGT). LO BB 4-16 v Scotland (Canterbury) 2005 (NL). T20 HS 34. T20 BB 4-21.

NQ**VAN JAARSVELD,** Martin (Warmbaths S; Pretoria U), b Klerksdorp, South Africa 18 Jun 1974. 6'2". RHB, OB. N Transvaal/Northerns 1994-95 to 2003-04. Northamptonshire 2004. Titans 2004-05 to date. Kent debut/cap 2005 (Kolpak registration) scoring 118 and 111 v Warwicks (Canterbury) – second player after C.W.G.Bassano (Derbyshire) to score two hundreds on a county debut. **Tests** (SA): 9 (2002-03 to 2004-05); HS 73 v WI (Johannesburg) 2003-04. **LOI** (SA): 11(2002-03 to 2004); HS 45 v E (Birmingham) 2003; BB 1-0. Took wickets with his first and third balls in LOI. F-c Tours (SA): A 2002-03 (SA A); NZ 2003-04; I 2004-05; SL 1998-99 (SA A), 2004; Z 1998-99 (SA Acad). 1000 runs (2+1); most – 1268 (2001-02). HS 262* v Glamorgan (Cardiff) 2005. BB 2-30 SA A v SL A (Potchefstroom) 2003-04. LO HS 123 NT v EP (Pretoria) 1996-97. LO BB 1-0 (*see LOI*). T20 HS 75. T20 BB 2-19.

WALKER, Matthew Jonathan (King's S, Rochester), b Gravesend 2 Jan 1974. Grandson of Jack Walker (Kent 1949). 5'8". LHB, RM. Debut 1992-93 (Z tour); UK Debut 1994; cap 2000. F-c Tour: Z 1992-93 (K). 1000 runs (3); most 1419 (2006). HS 275* v Somerset (Canterbury) 1996. BB 2-21 v Middx (Canterbury) 2004. LO HS 117 v Warwks (Canterbury) 1997 (BHC). LO BB 4-24 v Yorks (Leeds) 2001 (NL). T20 HS 58*.

‡NQ**YASIR ARAFAT** Satti, b Rawalpindi 12 Mar 1982. RHB, RM. Rawalpindi 1997-98 to date. Pakistan Reserves 1999-00. KRL 2000-01 to date. National Bank 2005-06. Sussex debut/cap 2006. Scotland (not f-c) 2004-05. **LOI** (P): 7 (1999-00 to 2006-07); HS 27 v SA (Chandigarh) 2006-07; BB 1-28. F-c Tours (Pak A): SL 2001, 2004-05. HS 100 KRL v DHA (Karachi) 2003-04. UK HS 86 Sx v Yorks (Arundel) 2006 – on UK debut. 50 wkts (0+3); most – 91 (2001-02). BB 7-102 Rawalpindi v Sialkot (Sialkot) 2001-02. UK BB 5-84 Sx v Kent (Hove) 2006. LO HS 87 Rawalpindi v Bahawalpur (Karachi) 2000-01. LO BB 6-24 Pakistan A v England A (Colombo) 2004-05. T20 HS 49. T20 BB 4-21.

RELEASED/RETIRED

(Having made a first-class County appearance in 2006)

CUSDEN, S.M. – *see DERBYSHIRE.*

NQ**BRAVO, Dwayne** John (Tranquillity Govt SS), b Santa Cruz, Trinidad 7 Oct 1983. 5'7". RHB, RFM. Trinidad & Tobago 2001-02 to date. Kent debut 2006. **Tests** (WI): 19 (2004 to 2006-07); HS 113 v A (Hobart) 2005-06; BB 6-55 v E (Manchester) 2004. **LOI** (WI): 59 (2003-04 to 2006-07); HS 112* v E (Ahmedabad) 2006-07; BB 4-39 v I (Madras) 2006-07. F-c Tours (WI): E 2002 (WI A), 2004; A 2005-06; NZ 2005-06; P 2006-07. HS 197 Trinidad v WI B (Couva) 2003-04. BB 6-11 Trinidad v Windward Is (St George's) 2002-03. LO HS 112* (*see LOI*). LO BB 4-34 Trinidad v Barbados (Discovery Bay, Jamaica) 2003-04. T20 HS 19*. T20 BB 2-16.

NINGTON, Matthew John (Northwood BS; UNISA), b Durban, South Africa 16 Oct 1982. 6'1". RHB, RFM. Kent 2004-06. HS 55 v Hants (Canterbury) 2005. BB 3-23 v Bangladesh A (Canterbury) 2005. CC BB 3-48 v Sussex (Canterbury) 2004. LO HS 26* v Glos (Cheltenham) 2004 (NL). LO BB 3-53 v Glamorgan(Canterbury) 2004 (NL). T20 HS 12. T20 BB 4-28.

FERLEY, R.S. – *see NOTTINGHAMSHIRE.*

FULTON, David Paul (The Judd S; Kent U), b Lewisham 15 Nov 1971. 6'2". RHB, SLA, occ WK. Kent 1992-2006; cap 1998; captain 2002-05; benefit 2006. MCC 2002. PCA 2001. 1000 runs (3): most – 1892 (2001). HS 208* v Somerset (Canterbury) 2001. Scored 9 hundreds in 2001, including 208*, 104* and 197 in successive innings. BB 1-37 (not CC). LO HS 82 v Yorks (Leeds) 2001 (NL). T20 HS 15.

[NQ]**HENDERSON, Tyron** (Durban HS), b Durban, South Africa 1 Aug 1974. Grandson of J.K.Henderson (N E Transvaal 1950-51). Great-nephew of W.A.Henderson (N E Transvaal 1937-38 to 1046-47). 6'2". RHB, RFM. Border 1998-99 to 2003-04. Warriors 2004-05 to 2005-06. Kent 2006. Lions 2006-07. Berkshire 2002-03. F-c Tours (SA A): Ire/Scot 1999 (SA Acad); SL 2005-06. HS 81 Border v Gauteng (Johannesburg)1999-00. UK HS 59 K v Hants (Canterbury) 2006. BB 6-56 Border v FS (Bloemfontein) 2000-01. UK BB 5-44 SA Acad v Scotland (Linlithgow) 1999. K BB 4-29 v Lancs (Canterbury) 2006. LO HS 126* Border v GW (Kimberley) 2003-04. LO BB 5-5 Border v WP (E London) 1998-99. T20 HS 85. T20 BB 3-11.

[NQ]**KEMP, Justin** Miles (Queens C; Port Elizabeth U), b Queenstown, Cape Province, South Africa 2 Oct 1977. Son of J.W.Kemp (Border 1975-76 to 1976-77); grandson of J.M.Kemp (Border 1947-48). RHB, RM. E Province 1996-97 to 2002-03. Worcestershire 2003. Northerns 2003-04 to 2004-05. Titans 204-05 to 2006-07. Kent 2005-06; cap 2006. **Tests** (SA): 4 (2000-01 to 2005-06); HS 55 v A (Perth) 2005-06; BB 3-33 v SL (Pretoria) 2000-01 on debut. **LOI** (SA): 66 (2000-01 to 2006-07); HS 100* v I (Cape Town) 2006-07; BB 3-20 v I (Durban) 2001-02. F-c Tours (SA): A 2002-03 (SA A), 2005-06; WI 2000 (SA A), 2000-01; Z 1998-99 (SA Acad). HS 188 EP v North West (Port Elizabeth) 2000-01. CC HS 124* v Yorks (Canterbury) 2006. BB 6-56 EP v Border (Port Elizabeth) 2000-01. CC BB 5-48 Wo v Glamorgan (Cardiff) 2003 – on Worcs debut. K BB 3-53 v Middx (Lord's) 2005. LO HS 107* Northerns v GW (Centurion) 2003-04. LO BB 6-20 EP v FS (Port Elizabeth) 2000-01. T20 HS 85*. T20 BB 3-19.

O'BRIEN, N.J. – *see NORTHAMPTONSHIRE.*

STIFF, D.A. – *see LEICESTERSHIRE.*

KENT 2006

RESULTS SUMMARY

	Place	Won	Lost	Tied	Drew	No Result
County Championship (1st Division)	**5th**	4	4		8	
All First-Class Matches		4	4		9	
C & G Trophy (South Conference)	7th	4	4			1
Pro40 League (2nd Division)	5th	5	3			
Twenty20 Cup (South Division)	Q-Finalist	5	4			

COUNTY CHAMPIONSHIP AVERAGES

BATTING AND FIELDING

Cap		*M*	*I*	*NO*	*HS*	*Runs*	*Avge*	*100*	*50*	*Ct/St*
2005	A.J.Hall	4	5	2	68*	237	79.00	–	2	3
2000	M.J.Walker	16	26	3	197	1419	61.69	5	8	9
2006	J.M.Kemp	6	9	3	124*	369	61.50	2	1	10
2005	M.van Jaarsveld	16	27	2	116	1217	48.68	3	10	36
–	N.J.Dexter	7	10	3	131*	285	40.71	1	–	3
1998	D.P.Fulton	15	26	1	155	969	38.76	2	6	7
2005	D.I.Stevens	16	26	4	126*	845	38.40	2	5	17
–	A.Khan	9	10	7	38	98	32.66	–	–	1
2001	R.W.T.Key	14	25	2	136*	731	31.78	1	2	8
2003	G.O.Jones	7	10	1	60	254	28.22	–	3	12/1
–	D.J.Bravo	5	8	–	76	208	26.00	–	1	–
–	N.J.O'Brien	9	12	1	62	204	18.54	–	1	19/8
–	T.Henderson	6	9	1	59	146	18.25	–	1	2
–	S.J.Cook	11	14	–	71	196	14.00	–	1	1
–	J.C.Tredwell	7	10	1	47	126	14.00	–	–	7
1994	M.M.Patel	13	16	2	61	179	12.78	–	1	4
–	R.H.Joseph	9	12	4	29	63	7.87	–	–	1

Also batted (2 matches each): J.L.Denly 86, 13, 66 (1 ct); R.S.Ferley 14, 22; M.J.Saggers (cap 2001) 2*, 0.

BOWLING

	O	*M*	*R*	*W*	*Avge*	*Best*	*5wI*	*10wM*
A.J.Hall	128.3	34	334	14	23.85	3- 27	–	–
J.M.Kemp	111	16	333	11	30.27	3- 72	–	–
A.Khan	312.1	51	1034	34	30.41	5-100	1	–
S.J.Cook	294	60	925	28	33.03	6- 74	2	–
D.I.Stevens	231.5	39	671	19	35.31	4- 36	–	–
J.C.Tredwell	269.5	43	927	26	35.65	6- 81	1	1
M.M.Patel	389.3	55	1171	32	36.59	4- 83	–	–
R.H.Joseph	244.5	37	897	24	37.37	5- 57	1	–
Also bowled:								
M.J.Saggers	43.1	8	149	5	29.80	3- 38	–	–
R.S.Ferley	112.2	18	342	9	38.00	6-136	1	–
N.J.Dexter	81	14	247	6	41.16	2- 40	–	–
D.J.Bravo	88.1	10	435	8	54.37	6-112	1	–
T.Henderson	144	31	505	9	56.11	4- 29	–	–

J.L.Denly 16-2-44-1; M.van Jaarsveld 29-3-114-1; M.J.Walker 33-6-116-1; D.P.Fulton 1-0-3-0; R.W.T.Key 1-3-0.

The First-Class Averages (pp 130–146) give the records of Kent players in all first-class matches for the county (Kent's other opponents being Cambridge UCCE), with the exception of G.O.Jones and R.W.T.Key whose full county figures are as above.

KENT RECORDS

FIRST-CLASS CRICKET

Highest Total	For 803-4d		v	Essex	Brentwood	1934
	V 676		by	Australians	Canterbury	1921
Lowest Total	For 18		v	Sussex	Gravesend	1867
	V 16		by	Warwicks	Tonbridge	1913
Highest Innings	For 332	W.H.Ashdown	v	Essex	Brentwood	1934
	V 344	W.G.Grace	for	MCC	Canterbury	1876

Highest Partnership for each Wicket

1st	300	N.R.Taylor/M.R.Benson	v	Derbyshire	Canterbury	1991
2nd	366	S.G.Hinks/N.R.Taylor	v	Middlesex	Canterbury	1990
3rd	323	R.W.T.Key/M.van Jaarsveld	v	Surrey	Tunbridge W	2005
4th	368	P.A.de Silva/G.R.Cowdrey	v	Derbyshire	Maidstone	1995
5th	277	F.E.Woolley/L.E.G.Ames	v	New Zealand	Canterbury	1931
6th	315	P.A.de Silva/M.A.Ealham	v	Notts	Nottingham	1995
7th	248	A.P.Day/E.Humphreys	v	Somerset	Taunton	1908
8th	159	M.van Jaarsveld/M.M.Patel	v	Glamorgan	Cardiff	2005
9th	171	M.A.Ealham/P.A.Strang	v	Notts	Nottingham	1997
10th	235	F.E.Woolley/A.Fielder	v	Worcs	Stourbridge	1909

Best Bowling	For	10- 30	C.Blythe	v	Northants	Northampton	1907
(Innings)	V	10- 48	C.H.G.Bland	for	Sussex	Tonbridge	1899
Best Bowling	For	17- 48	C.Blythe	v	Northants	Northampton	1907
(Match)	V	17-106	T.W.J.Goddard	for	Glos	Bristol	1939

Most Runs – Season	2894	F.E.Woolley	(av 59.06)	1928
Most Runs – Career	47868	F.E.Woolley	(av 41.77)	1906-38
Most 100s – Season	10	F.E.Woolley		1928
	10	F.E.Woolley		1934
Most 100s – Career	122	F.E.Woolley		1906-38
Most Wkts – Season	262	A.P.Freeman	(av 14.74)	1933
Most Wkts – Career	3340	A.P.Freeman	(av 17.64)	1914-36
Most Career W-K Dismissals	1253	F.H.Huish	(901 ct/352 st)	1895-1914
Most Career Catches in the Field	773	F.E.Woolley		1906-38

LIMITED-OVERS CRICKET

Highest Total	**CGT**	384-6		v	Berkshire	Finchampstead	1994
	P40	327-6		v	Leics	Canterbury	1993
	T20	186-6		v	Essex	Beckenham	2006
Lowest Total	**CGT**	60		v	Somerset	Taunton	1979
	P40	83		v	Middlesex	Lord's	1984
	T20	91		v	Surrey	The Oval	2006
Highest Innings	**CGT**	136*	C.L.Hooper	v	Berkshire	Finchampstead	1994
	P40	146	A.Symonds	v	Lancs	Tunbridge Wells	2004
	T20	112	A.Symonds	v	Middlesex	Maidstone	2004
Best Bowling	**CGT**	8-31	D.L.Underwood	v	Scotland	Edinburgh	1987
	P40	6- 9	R.A.Woolmer	v	Derbyshire	Chesterfield	1979
	T20	4-21	J.C.Tredwell	v	Middlesex	Beckenham	2006

LANCASHIRE

Formation of Present Club: 12 January 1864
Inaugural First-Class Match: 1865
Colours: Red, Green and Blue
Badge: Red Rose
County Champions (since 1890): (7) 1897, 1904, 1926, 1927, 1928, 1930, 1934
Joint Champions: (1) 1950
Gillette/NatWest/C & G Trophy Winners: (7) 1970, 1971, 1972, 1975, 1990, 1996, 1998
Benson and Hedges Cup Winners: (4) 1984, 1990, 1995, 1996
Pro 40/National League (Div 1) Winners: (1) 1999.
Sunday League Winners: (4) 1969, 1970, 1989, 1998
Twenty20 Cup Winners: (0); best --Finalist 2005

Chief Executive: Jim Cumbes, Old Trafford, Manchester M16 0PX • Tel: 0161 282 4000 • Fax: 0161 282 4100 • Email: enquiries@lccc.co.uk • Web: www.lccc.co.uk

Cricket Manager/First XI Coach: M.Watkinson. **Captain**: M.J.Chilton. **Vice-Captain**: S.G.Law. **Overseas Players**: B.J.Hodge and M.Muralitharan. **2007 Beneficiary**: S.G.Law. **Head Groundsman**: Peter Marron. **Scorer**: Alan West. ‡ New registration. NQ Not qualified for England.

ANDERSON, James Michael (St Theodore RC HS and SFC, Burnley), b Burnley 30 Jul 1982. 6'2". LHB, RFM. Debut (Lancashire) 2002; cap 2003. YC 2003. **Tests**: 16 (2003 to 2006-07); HS 21* v SA (Lord's) 2003; BB 5-73 v Z (Lord's) 2003 on debut. **LOI**: 57 (2002-03 to 2006-07); HS 15 v A (Jaipur) 2006-07; BB 4-25 v Holland (E London) 2002-03. Hat-trick v P (Oval) 2003 – 1st for Eng in 373 LOI. F-c Tours: A 2006-07; SA 2004-05; WI 2003-04, 2005-06 (Eng A) (*part*); I 2005-06 (*part*); SL 2003-04. HS 37* v Durham (Manchester) 2005. 50 wkts (2); most – 60 (2005). BB 6-23 v Hants (Southampton) 2002. Hat-trick (Lancs) 2003. LO HS 15 (*see LOI*). LO BB 4-25 (*see LOI*). T20 HS 16. T20 BB 2-25.

BROWN, Karl Robert (Hesketh Fletcher HS, Atherton), b Bolton 17 May 1988. 5'10". RHB, RMF. Debut (Lancashire) 2006. Awaiting CC debut. HS 32 v DU (Durham) 2006.

CHAPPLE, Glen (West Craven HS; Nelson & Colne C), b Skipton, Yorks 23 Jan 1974. 6'1". RHB, RFM. Debut (Lancashire) 1992; cap 1994; benefit 2004. **LOI**: 1 (2006); HS 14 and BB – v Ire (Belfast) 2006. F-c Tours (Eng A): A 1996-97; WI 1995-96 (La); I 1994-95. HS 155 v Somerset (Manchester) 2001. Scored 100 off 27 balls in contrived circumstances v Glamorgan (Manchester) 1993. 50 wkts (4); most – 55 (1994). BB 6-30 v Somerset (Blackpool) 2002. LO HS 81* v Derbys (Manchester) 2002 (CGT). LO BB 6-18 v Essex (Lord's) 1996 (NWT).T20 HS 55*. T20 BB 2-13.

CHILTON, Mark James (Manchester GS; Durham U), b Sheffield, Yorks 2 Oct 1976. 6'3". RHB, RM. Debut (Lancashire) 1997; cap 2002; captain 2005 to date. British U 1998. 1000 runs (1): 1154 (2003). HS 131 v Kent (Manchester) 2006. BB 1-1 (*twice*). LO HS 115 v Surrey (Croydon) 2004 (NL). LO BB 5-26 Brit U v Sussex (Cambridge) 1997 (BHC). T20 HS 38.

CORK, Dominic Gerald (St Joseph's C, Stoke-on-Trent; Newcastle CFE), b Newcastle-under-Lyme, Staffs 7 Aug 1971. 6'2". RHB, RFM. Derbyshire 1990-2003; cap 1993; captain 1998-2003; benefit 2001. Lancashire debut/cap 2004. *Wisden* 1995. PCA 1995. Staffordshire 1989-90. **Tests**: 37 (1995 to 2002); HS 59 v NZ (Auckland) 1996-97; BB 7-43 v WI (Lord's) 1995 – on debut (record England analysis by Test match debutant); hat-trick v WI (Manchester) 1995 – the first in Test history to occur in the opening over of a day's play. **LOI**: 32 (1992 to 2002-03); HS 31* v NZ (Napier) 1996-97; BB 3-27 v WI (Lord's) 1995. F-c Tours: A 1992-93 (Eng A), 1998-99; SA 1993-94 (Eng A), 1995-96; WI 1991-92 (Eng A); NZ 1996-97; I 1994-95 (Eng A); P 2000-01 (*part*). HS 200* De v Durham (Derby) 2000. La HS 154 v Durham (Manchester) 2006. 50 wkts (7); most – 90 (1995). BB 9-43 (13-93 match) De v Northants (Derby) 1995. Took 8-53 before lunch on his 20th birthday for De v Essex (Derby) 1991. 2 hat-tricks: 1994 and 1995 (*see Tests*). La BB 7-120 v Middx (Lord's) 2004. LO HS 93 De v Derbys CB (Derby) 2000 (NWT). LO BB 6-21 De v Glamorgan (Chesterfield) 1997 (SL). T20 HS 28. T20 BB 4-16.

CROFT, Steven John (Highfield HS, Blackpool; Myerscough C), b Blackpool 11 Oct 1984. 5'10". RHB, RMF. Debut (Lancashire) 2005. Awaiting CC debut. HS 17 v DU (Durham) 2006. LO HS 56 and BB 4-59 v Sussex (Hove) 2006 (P40). T20 HS 31. T20 BB 2-10.

CROSS, Gareth David (Moorside S; Eccles C), b Bury 20 Jun 1984. 5'9". RHB, RMF, WK. Debut (Lancashire) 2005. HS 72 v Kent (Canterbury) 2006. LO HS 21 La CB v Scot (Aberdeen) 2002 (CGT). T20 HS 36.

FLINTOFF, Andrew (Ribbleton Hall HS), b Preston 6 Dec 1977. 6'4". RHB, RF. Debut (Lancashire) 1995; cap 1998; benefit 2006. YC 1998. *Wisden* 2003. PCA 2004, 2005. MBE 2005. BBC Sports Personality of 2005. **ECB central contract 2007. Tests**: 66 (1998 to 2006-07, 11 as captain); HS 167 v WI (Birmingham) 2004; BB 5-58 v WI (Bridgetown) 2003-04. **LOI**: 112 (1998-99 to 2006-07, 14 as captain); HS 123 v WI (Lord's) 2004; BB 4-14 v B (Chittagong) 2003-04. F-c Tours (Eng): A 2002-03 (*part*), 2006-07 (captain); SA 1998-99 (Eng A), 1999-00, 2004-05; WI 2003-04; NZ 2001-02; I 2001-02, 2005-06 (captain); P 2000-01 (*part*), 2005-06; SL 1997-98 (Eng A), 2003-04; Z 1998-99 (Eng A); K 1997-98 (Eng A). HS 167 (*see Tests*). BB 5-24 v Hants (Southampton) 1999. LO HS 143 (off 66 balls) v Essex (Chelmsford) 1999 (NL). LO BB 4-11 v Yorks (Leeds) 2002 (BHC). T20 HS 85. T20 BB 3-4.

NQ**HODGE, Bradley** John (St Bede's C, Mentone; Deakin U), b Sandringham, Victoria, Australia 29 Dec 1974. 5'8". RHB, OB. Victoria 1993-94 to date. Durham 2002. Leicestershire 2003-04; cap 2003; captain 2004 (*part*). Lancashire debut 2005; cap 2006. **Tests** (A): 5 (2005-06); HS 203* v SA (Perth) 2005-06. **LOI** (A): 13 (2005-06 to 1006-07) HS 99* v NZ (Melbourne) 2006-07. F-c Tours (A): I 2004-05; P 2005-06 (Aus A); Z 1998-99 (Aus Acad). 1000 runs (2+3); most 1548 (2004). HS 302* (Leics record) v Notts (Nottingham) 2003. La HS 161 v Middx (Lord's) 2006. BB 4-17 Aus A v WI (Hobart) 2000-01. UK BB 3-21 v Warwks (Birmingham) 2006. LO HS 164 Aus A v SA A (Perth) 2002-03. LO BB 5-28 Aus A v SA A (Canberra) 2002-03. T20 HS 106. T20 BB 4-17.

HOGG, Kyle William (Saddleworth HS), b Birmingham, Warwks 2 Jul 1983. Son of W.Hogg (Lancashire and Warwickshire 1976-83; grandson of S.Ramadhin (Trinidad, Lancashire and West Indies 1949-50 to 1965). 6'4". LHB, RFM. Debut (Lancashire) 2001. Otago 2006-07. F-c Tour (ECB Acad): SL 2002-03. HS 71 Otago v CD (Napier) 2006-07. La HS 70 v Middx (Lord's) 2006. BB 5-48 v Leics (Manchester) 2002 – on CC debut. LO HS 41* v Glamorgan (Manchester) 2005 (NL). LO BB 4-20 v Hants (Southampton) 2002 (NL). T20 HS 25. T20 BB 2-10.

HORTON, Paul James (St Margaret's HS, Liverpool), b Sydney, Australia 20 Sep 1982. 5'10". RHB, RM. UK resident since 1997. Debut (Lancashire) 2003. HS 99 v Essex (Manchester) 2005. LO HS 46 v Bangladesh A (Liverpool) 2005. T20 HS 11.

KEEDY, Gary (Garforth CS), b Wakefield, Yorks 27 Nov 1974. 6'0". LHB, SLA. Yorkshire 1994 (one match). Lancashire debut 1995; cap 2000. F-c Tour: WI 1995-96 (La). HS 57 v Yorks (Leeds) 2002. 50 wkts (3): most – 72 (2004). BB 7-95 (14-227 match) v Glos (Manchester) 2004. LO HS 10* v Essex (Manchester) 2002 (NL). LO BB 5-30 v Sussex (Manchester) 2000 (NL). T20 HS 9*. T20 BB 3-25.

[NQ]**LAW, Stuart** Grant (Craigslea State HS), b Herston, Brisbane, Australia 18 Oct 1968. 6'1". RHB, RM/LB. Queensland 1988-89 to 2003-04; captain 1994-95 to 1996-97, 1999-00 to 2001-02. Essex 1996-2001; cap 1996. Lancashire debut/cap 2002; benefit 2007. *Wisden* 1997. PCA 1999. British Citizenship after 2004 season. **Tests** (A): 1 (1995-96); HS 54* v SL (Perth) 1995-96. **LOI** (A): 54 (1994-95 to 1998-99); HS 110 v Z (Hobart) 1994-95; BB 2-22 v P (Sydney) 1996-97. F-c Tours: E 1995 (Young A); Z 1991-92 (Aus B). 1000 runs (8+2); most – 1833 (1999). HS 263 Ex v Somerset (Chelmsford) 1999. La HS 236* v Warwks (Manchester) 2003. BB 5-39 Q v Tasmania (Brisbane) 1995-96. CC BB 3-27 Ex v Worcs (Chelmsford) 1997. La BB 1-24. LO HS 163 Young A v Surrey (Oval) 1995. LO BB 5-26 Q v SL (Cairns) 1995-96. T20 HS 101.

LOYE, Malachy Bernhard (Moulton S), b Northampton 27 Sep 1972. 6'2". RHB, OB. Northamptonshire 1991-2002; cap 1994. PCA 1998. Lancashire debut 2003 – scoring 126 v Surrey (Oval) and 113 v Notts (Manchester) in his first two innings; cap 2003. Auckland 2006-07. **LOI**: 7 (2006-07); HS 45 v A (Sydney) 2006-07. F-c Tours (Eng A): SA 1993-94, 1998-99; Z 1994-95 (Nh), 1998-99. 1000 runs (6); most – 1296 (2006). HS 322* Nh v Glamorgan (Northampton) 1998 – record Northants score until 2001. La HS 200 v Durham (Chester-le-St) 2005. BB 1-8 v Kent (Blackpool) 2003. LO HS 127 v Durham (Manchester) 2006 (CGT). T20 HS 100.

MAHMOOD, Sajid Iqbal (North C, Bolton), b Bolton 21 Dec 1981. 6'4". RHB, RF. Debut (Lancashire) 2002. **Tests**: 8 (2006 to 2006-07); HS 34 and BB 4-22 v P (Leeds) 2006. **LOI**: 19 (2004 to 2006-07); HS 22* v P (Birmingham) 2006; BB 3-37 v I (Jamshedpur) 2005-06. F-c Tours (Eng A): A 2006-07 (Eng); WI 2005-06; I 2003-04; SL 2004-05. HS 94 v Sussex (Manchester) 2004. BB 5-37 v DU (Durham) 2003. CC BB 5-52 v Sussex (Liverpool) 2006. LO HS 29 v Staffs (Stone) 2004 (CGT). LO BB 4-37 Eng A v West Indies A (Gros Islet) 2005-06. T20 HS 21. T20 BB 1-17.

MARSHALL, Simon James (Birkenhead S; Pembroke C, Cambridge), b Arrowe Park, Wirral, Cheshire 20 Sep 1982. 6'3". RHB, LB. Cambridge U 2002-04; blue 2002-03-04. British U 2004. Lancashire debut 2005. Cheshire 2001-03. Hockey blue. HS 126* CU v OU (Cambridge) 2003. La HS 35* v OU (Oxford) 2005. CC HS 26* v Worcs (Manchester) 2005. BB 6-128 CU v Essex (Cambridge) 2002. La BB 2-23 v OU (Oxford) 2005 – on La debut. CC BB 1-8. LO HS 9. LO BB 3-36 v Durham (Manchester) 2006 (CGT). T20 HS 47. T20 BB 4-20.

MULLANEY, Steven John (St Mary's RC S, Astley), b Warrington, Cheshire 19 Nov 1986. 5'9". RHB, RM. Debut (Lancashire) 2006. Awaiting CC debut. HS 44 v DU (Durham) 2006. LO HS – and BB 1-23 v Worcs (Worcester) 2006 (CGT). T20 HS 5.

[NQ]**MURALITHARAN, Muthiah** (St Anthony's C, Kandy), b Kandy, Sri Lanka 17 Apr 1972. 5'5". RHB, OB. Central Province 1989-90 to 2003-04. Tamil Union 1991-92 to 2003-04. Lancashire 1999 (taking 7-44 and 7-73 v Warwks at Southport on debut), 2001, 2005; cap 1999. Kent 2003; cap 2003. *Wisden* 1998. **Tests** (SL): 109 (1992-93 to 2006-07); HS 67 v I (Kandy) 2001-02; BB 9-51 (13-115 match) v Z (Kandy) 2001-02. **LOI** (SL): 280 (1993-94 to 2006-07); HS 27 v A (Sydney) 2005-06; BB 7-30 v I (Sharjah) 2000-01. F-c Tours (SL): E 1991, 1998, 2002, 2006; A 1995-96, SA 1992-93 (SL U-24), 1994-95, 1997-98, 2000-01, 2002-03; WI 1996-97, 2003; NZ 1994-95, 1996-97; I 1993-94, 1997-98, 2006-07; P 1995-96, 1999-00, 2001-02; Z 1994-95, 1999-00, 2004; B 2005-06. HS 67 (*see Tests*). La HS 24* v Derby (Derby) 2005. 50 wkts (2+3); most – 96 (2003-04). Took 66 wkts in seven CC matches 1999. BB 9-51 (13-115 match) (*see Tests*). La BB 7-39 (11-61 match) v Derbys (Derby) 1999. LO HS 27 (*see LOI*). LO BB 7-30 (*see LOI*). T20 HS 9. T20 BB 4-19.

NEWBY, Oliver James (Ribblesdale HS; Muerscough C), b Blackburn 26 Aug 1984. 6'5". RHB, RMF. Debut (Lancashire) 2003. Nottinghamshire 2005 (whilst on loan). HS 38* Nt v Kent (Nottingham) 2005 – on Notts debut. La HS 19 v Warwks (Birmingham) 2006. BB 4-58 v Notts (Manchester) 2006. LO HS 7* (NL). LO BB 2-37 v Glos (Manchester) 2004 (NL). T20 HS 5. T20 BB 2-34.

SMITH, Thomas Christopher (Parkland HS, Chorley; Runshaw C, Leyland), b Liverpool 26 Dec 1985. 6'3". LHB, RMF. Debut (Lancashire) 2005. F-c Tour (Eng A): B 2006-07. HS 49 v Hants (Southampton) 2006. BB 4-57 v Yorks (Leeds) 2006. LO HS 14* and BB 3-8 v Leics (Manchester) 2006 (CGT). T20 HS 21. T20 BB 2-17.

SUTCLIFFE, Iain John (Leeds GS; Queen's C, Oxford), b Leeds, Yorks 20 Dec 1974. 6'2". LHB, occ LB. Oxford U 1994-96; blue 1995-96; boxing blue 1993-94. Leicestershire 1995-2002; cap 1997. Combined/British U 1995-96. Lancashire debut/cap 2003. F-c Tour (Le): SA 1996-97. 1000 runs (3): most – 1088 (2002). HS 203 Le v Glamorgan (Cardiff) 2001. La HS 159 v Warwks (Blackpool) 2006. BB 2-21 OU v CU (Lord's) 1996. CC BB (Le) 1-7. La BB 1-11. LO HS 105* Le v Notts (Nottingham) 1998 (BHC). T20 HS 4.

SUTTON, Luke David (Millfield S; Durham U), b Keynsham, Somerset 4 Oct 1976. 5'11". RHB, WK. Somerset 1997-98. Derbyshire 2000-05; cap 2002; captain 2004-05. Lancashire debut 2006. HS 151* v Yorks (Manchester) 2006.LO HS 83 De v Lancs (Derby) 2003 (NL). T20 HS 61*.

RELEASED/RETIRED

(Having made a first-class County appearance in 2006)

[NQ]**ASTLE, Nathan** John, b Christchurch, NZ 15 Sep 1971. 5'10". RHB, RM. Canterbury 1991-92 to date. Nottinghamshire 1997. Durham 2005. Lancashire 2006. **Tests** (NZ): 81 (1995-96 to 2006-07); HS 222 v E (Christchurch) 2001-02; BB 3-27 v SL (Wellington) 2004-05. **LOI** (NZ): 223 (1994-95 to 2006-07); HS 145* v USA (Oval) 2004; BB 4-43 v P (Chandigarh) 1996-97. F-c Tours (NZ): E 1999, 2004; A 1997-98, 2001-02, 2004-05; SA 2000-01, 2005-06; WI 1995-96, 2002; I 1999-00, 2003-04; P 1996-97; SL 1998; Z 1997-98, 2000-01, 2005-06; B 2004-05. HS 223 NZ v Q (Brisbane) 2001-02. CC HS 100 Nt v Warwks (Nottingham) 1997 and 100 Nt v Essex (Worksop) 1997. La HS 86 and BB 1-9 v Hants (Southampton) 2006. BB 6-22 C v Otago (Christchurch) 1996-97. CC BB 5-46 Nt v Glos (Bristol) 1997. LO HS 145* (*see LOI*). LO BB 4-14 Canterbury v Otago (Oamaru) 1995-96. T20 HS 75*. T20 BB 3-20.

[NQ]**KARTIK, M.** – *see MIDDLESEX.*

A.R.Crook left the staff without making a first-class appearance in 2006.

LANCASHIRE 2006

RESULTS SUMMARY

	Place	Won	Lost	Tied	Drew	No Result
County Championship (1st Division)	**2nd**	6	1		9	
All First-Class Matches		6	1		10	
C & G Trophy (North Conference)	Finalist	7	2			1
Pro40 League (1st Division)	6th	2	3			3
Twenty20 Cup (North Division)	4th	3	5			

COUNTY CHAMPIONSHIP AVERAGES

BATTING AND FIELDING

Cap		*M*	*I*	*NO*	*HS*	*Runs*	*Avge*	*100*	*50*	*Ct/St*
2006	B.J.Hodge	5	6	1	161	372	74.40	2	–	4
2003	M.B.Loye	16	24	2	148*	1296	58.90	6	6	6
2002	S.G.Law	16	23	3	130	1103	55.15	4	6	16
–	L.D.Sutton	13	16	3	151*	666	51.23	2	2	38/3
–	K.W.Hogg	7	7	1	70	249	41.50	–	2	1
–	N.J.Astle	8	12	–	86	429	35.75	–	3	3
2003	I.J.Sutcliffe	16	25	3	159	774	35.18	2	2	10
–	P.J.Horton	3	5	1	79	132	33.00	–	1	3
1994	G.Chapple	14	19	1	82	580	32.22	–	3	6
2002	M.J.Chilton	16	25	1	131	766	31.91	1	4	13
–	G.D.Cross	3	5	–	72	155	31.00	-	2	13/2
2004	D.G.Cork	14	17	2	154	354	23.60	1	1	11
–	T.C.Smith	15	18	5	49	234	18.00	–	–	14
–	O.J.Newby	6	6	1	19	50	10.00	–	–	–
–	S.I.Mahmood	4	5	–	22	36	7.20	–	–	1
2000	G.Keedy	14	15	9	11*	42	7.00	–	–	3

Also batted: J.M.Anderson (1 match – cap 2003) 7* (1 ct); A.Flintoff (1 – cap 1998) 4, 37 (2 ct); M.Kartik (3) 2*, 40 (1 ct); S.J.Marshall (1) 3, 3.

BOWLING

	O	*M*	*R*	*W*	*Avge*	*Best*	*5wI*	*10wM*
S.I.Mahmood	131.4	24	427	21	20.33	5-52	1	–
D.G.Cork	389.1	86	1071	42	25.50	6-53	1	–
G.Chapple	425.2	117	1124	41	27.41	6-35	1	–
O.J.Newby	116.3	17	463	16	28.93	4-58	–	–
G.Keedy	538.2	84	1595	54	29.53	6-81	1	–
T.C.Smith	383	107	1073	35	30.65	4-57	–	–
K.W.Hogg	170	47	484	13	37.23	2-35	–	–

Also bowled: B.J.Hodge 35-6-97-5; M.Kartik 92-22-234-6; J.M.Anderson 10-2-38-0; N.J.Astle 58.3-12-178-4; M.J.Chilton 18.3-3-52-2; A.Flintoff 23-4-56-2; S.G.Law 12-0-50-1; S.J.Marshall 29.3-4-115-1; I.J.Sutcliffe 1-0-1-0.

The First-Class Averages (pp 130–146) give the records of Lancashire players in all first-class matches for the county (Lancashire's other opponents being Durham UCCE), with the exception of A.Flintoff and S.I.Mahmood whose full county figures are as above.

LANCASHIRE RECORDS

FIRST-CLASS CRICKET

Highest Total	For 863		v	Surrey	The Oval	1990
	V 707-9d		by	Surrey	The Oval	1990
Lowest Total	For 25		v	Derbyshire	Manchester	1871
	V 22		by	Glamorgan	Liverpool	1924
Highest Innings	For 424	A.C.MacLaren	v	Somerset	Taunton	1895
	V 315*	T.W.Hayward	for	Surrey	The Oval	1898

Highest Partnership for each Wicket

1st	368	A.C.MacLaren/R.H.Spooner	v	Glos	Liverpool	1903
2nd	371	F.B.Watson/G.E.Tyldesley	v	Surrey	Manchester	1928
3rd	364	M.A.Atherton/N.H.Fairbrother	v	Surrey	The Oval	1990
4th	358	S.P.Titchard/G.D.Lloyd	v	Essex	Chelmsford	1996
5th	360	S.G.Law/C.L.Hooper	v	Warwicks	Birmingham	2003
6th	278	J.Iddon/H.R.W.Butterworth	v	Sussex	Manchester	1932
7th	248	G.D.Lloyd/I.D.Austin	v	Yorkshire	Leeds	1997
8th	158	J.Lyon/R.M.Ratcliffe	v	Warwicks	Manchester	1979
9th	142	L.O.S.Poidevin/A.Kermode	v	Sussex	Eastbourne	1907
10th	173	J.Briggs/R.Pilling	v	Surrey	Liverpool	1885

Best Bowling	For	10-46	W.Hickton	v	Hampshire	Manchester	1870
(Innings)	V	10-40	G.O.B.Allen	for	Middlesex	Lord's	1929
Best Bowling	For	17-91	H.Dean	v	Yorkshire	Liverpool	1913
(Match)	V	16-65	G.Giffen	for	Australians	Manchester	1886

Most Runs – Season	2633	J.T.Tyldesley	(av 56.02)	1901
Most Runs – Career	34222	G.E.Tyldesley	(av 45.20)	1909-36
Most 100s – Season	11	C.Hallows		1928
Most 100s – Career	90	G.E.Tyldesley		1909-36
Most Wkts – Season	198	E.A.McDonald	(av 18.55)	1925
Most Wkts – Career	1816	J.B.Statham	(av 15.12)	1950-68
Most Career W-K Dismissals	925	G.Duckworth	(635 ct/290 st)	1923-38
	919	W.K.Hegg	(825 ct/94 st)	1986-2005
Most Career Catches in the Field	556	K.J.Grieves		1949-64

LIMITED-OVERS CRICKET

Highest Total	**CGT**	381-3		v	Herts	Radlett	1999
	P40	310-7		v	Somerset	Taunton	2003
	T20	217-4		v	Surrey	The Oval	2005
Lowest Total	**CGT**	59		v	Worcs	Worcester	1963
	P40	68		v	Yorkshire	Leeds	2000
		68		v	Surrey	The Oval	2002
	T20	91		v	Derbyshire	Manchester	2003
Highest Innings	**CGT**	162*	A.R.Crook	v	Bucks	Wormsley	2005
	P40	143	A.Flintoff	v	Essex	Chelmsford	1999
	T20	101	S.G.Law	v	Yorkshire	Manchester	2005
Best Bowling	**CGT**	6-18	G.Chapple	v	Essex	Lord's	1996
	P40	6-25	G.Chapple	v	Yorkshire	Leeds	1998
	T20	4-16	D.G.Cork	v	Notts	Manchester	2006

LEICESTERSHIRE

Formation of Present Club: 25 March 1879
Inaugural First-Class Match: 1894
Colours: Dark Green and Scarlet
Badge: Gold Running Fox on Green Ground
County Champions: (3) 1975, 1996, 1998
Gillette/NatWest/C & G Trophy Winners: (0); best – finalist 1992, 2001
Benson and Hedges Cup Winners: (3) 1972, 1975, 1985
Pro 40/National League (Div 1) Winners: (0); best – 2nd 2001
Sunday League Champions: (2) 1974, 1977
Twenty20 Cup Winners: (2) 2004, 2006

Chief Executive: Paul Maylard-Mason, County Ground, Grace Road, Leicester LE2 8AD • Tel: 0871 282 1879 • Fax: 0871 282 1873 • Email: enquiries@leicestershireccc.co.uk • Web: www.leicestershireccc.co.uk

Senior Coach: Tim Boon. **Head Coach/Academy Director**: Phil Whitticase. **Captain**: J.N.Snape. **Vice-Captain**: tba. **Overseas Players**: Mansoor Amjad and D.Mongia. **2007 Beneficiary**: P.A.Nixon. **Head Groundsman**: Andy Whiteman. **Scorer**: Graham A.York. ‡ New registration. [NQ] Not qualified for England.

[NQ]**ACKERMAN, Hylton** Deon ('HD') (Rondebosch BHS), b Cape Town, South Africa 14 Feb 1973. 5'11". Son of H.M.Ackerman (Border, NE Transvaal, Northants, Natal, W Province 1963-64 to 1981-82). RHB, RM. W Province 1993-94 to 2002-03. Gauteng 2003-04. Lions 2004-05. Leicestershire debut/captain/cap 2005 (Kolpak registration). Cape Cobras 2005-06. Warriors 2006-07. Tests (SA): 4 (1997-98): HS 57 v P (Durban) 1997-98 – on debut. F-c Tours (SA): E 1996 (SA A); A 1995-96 (WP); SL 1995 (SA U-24), 1998; Z 1996-97 (WP). 1000 runs (2+1); most – 1808 (2006). HS 309* v Glamorgan (Cardiff) 2006. LO HS 114* v Sussex (Hove) 2005 (NL). T20 HS 87.

ALLENBY, James (Christ Church GS, Perth), b Perth, W Australia 12 Sep 1982. 6'0". RHB, RM. Debut (Leicestershire) 2006. Western Australia 2006-07. HS 103* v Essex (Leicester) 2006. BB – . LO HS 43* v Worcs (Leicester) 2006 (P40). LO BB 4-19 v Warwks (Leicester) 2006 (CGT). T20 HS 64. T20 BB 2-22.

BOYCE, Matthew Andrew Golding (Oakham S; Nottingham U), b Cheltenham, Glos 13 Aug 1985. 5'9". LHB, RM. Debut (Leicestershire) 2006. Awaiting CC debut. HS 6 v P (Leicester) 2006.

BROAD, Stuart Christopher John (Oakham S), b Nottingham 24 Jun 1986. 6'6". LHB, RFM. Son of B.C.Broad (Glos, Notts, OFS and England 1979-94). Debut (Leicestershire) 2005. **LOI**: 5 (2006); HS 8*; BB 3-57 v P (Southampton) 2006. F-c Tours (Eng A): WI 2005-06; B 2006-07. HS 65* v Derbys (Leicester) 2006. BB 5-83 v Glos (Leicester) 2006. LO HS 11* v Kent (Canterbury) 2006 (P40). LO BB 3-57 (*see LOI*). T20 HS – . T20 BB 3-13.

CUMMINS, Ryan Anthony Gilbert (Wallington CGS; Loughborough U), b Sutton, Surrey 14 Apr 1984. 6'4". RHB, RM. Loughborough UCCE 2003-05. Leicestershire debut 2005. HS 26 LU v Sussex (Hove) 2005. Le HS 13 v Worcs (Worcester) 2006. BB 4-46 v West Indies A (Leicester) 2006. CC BB 3-32 v Lancs (Leicester) 2005. LO HS 2 (CGT). LO BB 2-14 v Durham (Chester-le-St) 2006 (CGT). T20 HS – . T20 BB – .

‡**GURNEY, Harry** Frederick, b Nottingham 25 Oct 1986. RHB, LMF. Bradford/Leeds UCCE 2006 (not f-c). Leics 2nd XI 2006. Joined Leicestershire staff 2006 – awaiting 1st XI debut.

HARRISON, Paul William (Forest S and Collyer's C, Horsham; Loughborough U), b Cuckfield, Sussex 22 May 1984. 6'2". RHB, RM, WK. Loughborough UCCE 2004-06. Warwickshire 2005 (one non-CC match). British U 2006. Leicestershire debut 2006. HS 54 LU v Notts (Nottingham) 2005. Le HS 5. LO HS 61 v Yorks (Scarborough) 2006 (P40). T20 HS 18.

NQ**HENDERSON, Claude** William (Worcester HS), b Worcester, Cape Province South Africa 14 Jun 1972. Elder brother of J.M.Henderson (Boland, Transvaal, North West, Free Ste and Eagles 1994-95 to 2005-06). 6'1½". RHB, SLA. Boland 1990-91 to 1997-98. W Province 1998-99 to 2003-04. Leicestershire debut/cap 2004 (first Kolpak registration). Lions 2006-07. **Tests** (SA): 7 (2001-02 to 2002-03); HS 30 and BB 4-116 v A (Adelaide) 2001-02. **LOI** (SA): 4 (2001-02); HS – ; BB 4-17 v Z (Harare) 2001-02. F-c Tours (SA): A 2001-02; SL 1998 (SA A); Z 2001-02. HS 71 WP v KZ-Natal (Cape Town) 2003-04. Le HS 63 v Glamorgan (Leicester 2004) – on UK debut. BB 7-57 Boland v EP (Paarl) 1994-95. Le BB 7-74 v Durham (Leicester) 2004. LO HS 45 Lions v Eagles (Johannesburg) 2006-07. LO BB 6-29 Boland v Easterns (Paarl) 1997-98. T20 HS 9*. T20 BB 3-26.

NQ**MANSOOR AMJAD** (Quaid HS, Sialkot), b Sialkot, Pakistan 14 Dec 1987. 6'0". RHB, LBG. Zarai Taraqiati Bank 2003-04 to 2004-05. Sialkot 2004-05 to date. National Bank 2005-06. Leicestershire debut 2006. F-c Tours (Pak A): I 2006-07 (Sialkot); Z 2005; K 2004.HS 122* NBP v Sialkot (Multan) 2005-06. Le HS 27 and BB – v Glos (Cheltenham) 2006. BB 6-19 Pak A v Zim A (Harare) 2005. LO HS 52* NBP v PTC (Rawalpindi) 2005-06. LO BB 5-37 NBP v Service Industries (Faisalabad) 2005-06. T20 HS 23. T20 BB 2-28.

MASTERS, David Daniel (Fort Luton HS; Mid Kent CHE), b Chatham, Kent 22 Apr 1978. Son of K.D.Masters (Kent 1983-84). 6'4". RHB, RMF. Kent 2000-02. Leicestershire debut 2003. HS 119 v Sussex (Hove) 2003. BB 6-27 K v Durham (Tunbridge Wells) 2000. Le BB 6-74 v Durham (Chester-le-St) 2005. LO HS 39 v Glos (Cheltenham) 2006 (P40). LO BB 5-20 K v Durham (Maidstone) 2002 (NL). T20 HS 7. T20 BB 3-7.

MAUNDERS, John Kenneth (Ashford HS; Spelthorne C), b Ashford, Middx 4 Apr 1981. 5'10". LHB, RM. Middlesex 1999 (one non-CC match); 2nd XI debut aged 16y 19d. Leicestershire debut 2003. HS 180 v Glos (Cheltenham) 2006. BB 4-15 v Worcs (Worcester) 2006. LO HS 49 M v Glamorgan (Cardiff) 2001 (NL). LO BB 2-16 v Warwks (Birmingham) 2005 (CGT). T20 HS 10.

NAIK, Jigar Kumar Hakumatrai (Rushey Mead SS; Gateway SFC; Nottingham Trent U; Loughborough U), b Leicester 10 Aug 1984. 6'2". RHB, OB. Debut (Leicestershire) 2006. HS 13 and BB 1-55 v West Indies A (Leicester) 2006. CC HS 1. CC BB – . LO HS 1 Leics CB v Kent CB (Maidstone) 2002 (CGT).

NEW, Thomas James (Quarrydale S), b Sutton in Ashfield, Notts 18 Jan 1985. 5'10". LHB, WK. Debut (Leicestershire) 2004. HS 89 v Derbys (Leicester) 2005. LO HS 68 v Northants (Oakham) 2006 (CGT).

NIXON, Paul Andrew (Ullswater HS, Penrith), b Carlisle, Cumberland 21 Oct 1970. 6'0". LHB, WK. Leicestershire 1989-99, 2003 to date; cap 1994; benefit 2007. MCC 1999-00. Kent 2000-02; cap 2000. Cumberland 1987. **LOI**: 10 (2006-07); HS 49 v NZ (Perth) 2006-07. F-c Tours: SA 1996-97 (Le); I 1994-95 (Eng A); P 2000-01; B 1999-00 (MCC). 1000 runs (1): 1046 (1994). HS 144* v Northants (Northampton) 2006. LO HS 101 v SL A (Galle) 1998-99. T20 HS 57*.

ROBINSON, Darren David John (Tabor HS, Braintree; Chelmsford CFE), b Braintree, Essex 2 Mar 1973. 5'10½". RHB, RMF. Essex 1993-2003; cap 1997. Leicestershire debut 2004. 1000 runs (3): most – 1474 (2002). HS 200 Ex v NZ (Chelmsford) 1999. CC HS 175 Ex v Glos (Gloucester) 2002. Le HS 154 v Yorks (Leicester 2004). BB 1-7 (Ex). LO HS 137* Ex v Sussex (Hove) 1998 (BHC). LO BB (Ex)1-7 (SL). T20 HS 41.

ROSENBERG, Marc Christopher (Kearnsey C, Durban; Loughborough U), b Johannesburg, South Africa 10 Feb 1982. RHB, RM. Loughborough UCCE 2004. North West 2004-05. Leicestershire debut 2006. Awaiting CC debut. HS 86 North West v GW (Potchefstroom) 2004-05. UK HS 33* v West Indies A (Leicester) 2006. BB 1-27 LU v Somerset (Taunton) 2004. Le BB – . LO HS 26 North West v GW (Potchefstroom) 2004-05. LO BB 3-17 North West v WP (Cape Town) 2004-05.

ROWE, Daniel Thomas (Archbishop McGrath S; Glamorgan U), b Bridgend, Glamorgan 22 Mar 1984. 6'0". RHB, RM. Debut (Leicestershire) 2006. Cardiff UCCE 2004-06 (not f-c). Awaiting CC debut. HS 0 and BB 1-22 v West Indies A (Leicester) 2006. LO HS – and 1-26 v Derbys (Leicester) 2006 (P40).

SADLER, John Leonard (St Thomas A'Beckett S, Sandal), b Dewsbury, Yorks 19 Nov 1981. 5'11". LHB, LBG. Debut (Leicestershire) 2003. 1000 runs (1): 1024 (2006). HS 145 v Surrey (Leicester) 2003 and 145 v Sussex (Hove) 2003. BB 1-22 (not CC). LO HS 88 v Yorks (Leeds) 2004 (NL). T20 HS 73.

SNAPE, Jeremy Nicholas (Denstone C; Durham U), b Stoke-on-Trent, Staffs 27 Apr 1973. 5'8½". RHB, OB. Northamptonshire 1992-97. Combined U 1993-94. Gloucestershire 1999-2002; cap 1999. Leicestershire debut 2003; cap 2006; captain 2006 to date. **LOI**: 10 (2001-02 to 2002-03); HS 38 v I (Madras) 2001-02; BB 3-43 v Z (Bulawayo) 2001-02. F-c Tour: Z 1994-95 (Nh). HS 131 Gs v Sussex (Cheltenham) 2001. Le HS 90 v Derbys (Leicester) 2006. BB 5-65 Nh v Durham (Northampton) 1995. Le BB 3-108 v Surrey (Leicester) 2003. LO HS 104* Gs v Notts (Nottingham) 2001 (NL). LO BB 5-32 Nh v Leics (Northampton) 1997 (BHC). T20 HS 47*. T20 BB 4-22.

‡STIFF, David Alexander (Batley GS; Wakefield C), b Dewsbury, Yorks 20 Oct 1984. RHB, RFM. Kent 2004-06. HS 18 and CC BB 2-58 K v Lancs (Tunbridge W) 2004. BB 3-88 K v NZ (Canterbury) 2004. LO HS – and BB 1-27 Yorks CB v Glos CB (Bristol) 2001 (CGT).

WALKER, Nicholas Guy Eades (Haileybury Imperial Service C), b Enfield, Middlesex 7 Aug 1984. 6'2". RHB, RFM. Derbyshire 2004-2005. Leicestershire debut 2006. Hertfordshire 2001-03. HS 80 off 57 balls (4 sixes, 11 fours), the record score by a Derbyshire No. 11, adding 103 for 10th wicket with M.A.Sheikh, and took 5-68 v Somerset (Derby) 2004. BB 5-59 and Le HS 21 v Somerset (Leicester) 2006. LO HS 43 De v Scot (Derby) 2004 (NL). LO BB 4-26 v Somerset (Leicester) 2006 (P40). T20 HS 16*. T20 BB 3-19.

RELEASED/RETIRED

(Registered players who made a first-class appearance in 2006)

CLARK, Steven George (Worksop C; Loughborough U), b Doncaster, Yorks 17 Nov 1982. 6'1". RHB, RMF. Loughborough UCCE 2005. Leicestershire 2006. HS 47* LU v Notts (Nottingham) 2005. Le HS 23* and BB 1-29 v Somerset (Taunton) 2006 – on Le debut. BB 5-29 LU v Worcs (Kidderminster) 2005. LO HS 52 Yorks CB v Northants CB (Northampton) 2002 (CGT). LO BB 1-31 (Yorks CB – CGT).

NQ**GRIFFITH, Adam** Richard, b Launceston, Tasmania 11 Feb 1978. 6'6". RHB, RFM. Tasmania 2002-03 to date. Leicestershire debut 2006. HS 47 Tas v Vic (Melbourne) 2006-07. Le HS 41* v Glos (Leicester) 2006 – on debut. BB 7-54 Tas v Vic (Hobart) 2004-05. Le BB 3-34 v Glamorgan (Cardiff) 2006. LO HS 33 Aus A v Z (Perth) 2003-04. LO BB 4-36 Tas v Vic (Melbourne) 2005-06. T20 HS 6. T20 BB 3-14.

HABIB, Aftab (Millfield S; Taunton S), b Reading, Berks 7 Feb 1972. Cousin of Zahid Sadiq (Surrey and Derbys 1988-90). 5'11". RHB, RM. Middlesex 1992 (one match). Leicestershire 1995-2001, 2005-06; cap 1998. Essex 2002-04; cap 2002. Berkshire 1995. Canterbury (l-o) 1997-98. **Tests**: 2 (1999); HS 19 v NZ (Lord's) 1999. F-c Tours (Eng A): WI 2000-01 (*part*); NZ 1999-00; B 1999-00. 1000 runs (2); most – 1055 (1999). HS 215 v Worcs (Leicester) 1996. BB (Ex) 1-10. Le BB – . LO HS 111 v Durham (Chester-le-St) 1997 (BHC). LO BB 2-5 v Ire (Dublin) 1999. T20 HS 16*.

LIDDLE, C.J. – *see SUSSEX.*

MADDY, D.L. – *see WARWICKSHIRE.*

NQ**MOHAMMAD ASIF**, b Sheikhupura, Pakistan 20 Dec 1982. LHB, RFM. Sheikhupura 2000-01 to 2001-02. Khan Research Labs 2001-02 to 2003-04. Quetta 2003-04. Sialkot 2004-05 to date. National Bank 2004-05 to 2005-06. Leicestershire 2006. **Tests** (P): 9 (2004-05 to 2006-07); HS 12* v A (Sydney) 2004-05 – on debut; BB 6-44 (11-71 match) v SL (Kandy) 2005-06. **LOI** (P): 22 (2005-06 to 2006-07); HS 6; BB 3-28 v E (Cardiff) 2006. F-c Tours (P): E 2006; A 2004-05; SA 2006-07; I 2006-07 (Sialkot); SL 2004-05 (Pak A), 2005-06; Z 2004-05 (Pak A). HS 42 KRL v Allied Bank (Karachi) 2002-03. 50 wkts (0+1): 54 (2005-06). BB 7-35 Sialkot v Multan (Multan) 2004-05. LO HS 12* Pakistan A v Sri Lanka A (Colombo) 2004-05. LO BB 4-30 KRL v Rawalpindi (Rawalpindi) 2001-02. T20 HS 1*. T20 BB 5-11.

NQ**MONGIA, Dinesh**, b Chandigarh, India 17 Apr 1977. LHB, SLA. Punjab 1995-96 to date. North Zone 1998-99 to 2005-06. Lancashire 2004. Leicestershire 2005-06; cap 2005. Staffordshire 2004. **LOI** (I): 55 (2000-01 to 2006-07); HS 159* v Z (Gauhati) 2001-02; BB 3-31 v Z (Mohali) 2001-02. F-c Tours (I): E 2002; WI 2001-02; SL 2001. 1000 runs (0+1): 1041 (2000-01). HS 308* Punjab v Jammu & Kashmir (Jullundur) 2000-01. UK HS 164 v Essex (Chelmsford) 2006. BB 4-34 Punjab v Kerala (Palghat) 2003-04. UK BB 2-8 v Worcs (Leicester) 2005. LO HS 159* (*see LOI*). LO BB 5-44 Punjab v Himachal Pradesh (Delhi) 2005-06. T20 HS 50. T20 BB 3-19.

A.Sheriyar left the staff without making a first-class appearance in 2006.

GLAMORGAN RELEASED/RETIRED (continued from p 32)

NQ**FRANKLIN, James** Edward Charles (Wellington C; Victoria U), b Wellington, New Zealand 7 Nov 1980. 6'4½". LHB, LFM. Wellington 1998-99 to date. Gloucestershire 2004; cap 2004. Glamorgan 2006. **Tests** (NZ): 21 (2000-01 to 2006-07); HS 122* v SA (Cape Town) 2006-07; BB 6-119 v A (Auckland) 2004-05. Hat-trick v B (Dhaka) 2004-05. **LOI** (NZ): 56 (2000-01 to 2006-07); HS 45* v SL (Queenstown) 2006-07; BB 5-42 v E (Chester-le-St) 2004. F-c Tours (NZ): E 2004; A 2004-05; SA 2004-05 (NZ A), 2005-06; Z 2005; B 2004-05. HS 208 Wellington v Auckland (Wellington) 2005-06. UK HS 94 Gm v Glos (Cheltenham) 2006. BB 7-30 Wellington v CD (Wellington) 2005-06. UK BB 7-60 Gs v Lancs (Cheltenham) 2004 – on UK debut. Gm BB 5-68 v Surrey (Oval) 2006. LO HS 76 Wellington v Otago (Wellington) 2004-05. LO BB 5-42 (see LOI). T20 HS 69*. T20 BB 3-23.

NQ**McCULLUM, Brendon** Barrie (Kings HS, Dunedin), b Dunedin, New Zealand 27 Sep 1981. Brother of N.L. (Otago 1999-00 to date); son of S.J.McCullum (Otago 1976-77 to 1990-91). 5'6". RHB, WK. Otago 1999-00 to 2002-03. Canterbury 2003-04 to date. Glamorgan 2006. **Tests** (NZ): 25 (2003-04 to 2006-07); HS 143 v B (Dhaka) 2004-05. **LOI** (NZ): 104 (2001-02 to 2006-07); HS 86* v A (Hamilton) 2006-07. F-c Tours (NZ): E 2004; A 2004-05; SA 2005-06; Z 2005; B 2004-05. HS 160 Gm v Leics (Cardiff) 2006 – on Gm debut. LO HS 86* (*see* LOI). T20 HS 63.

S.D.Thomas (*see ESSEX*) left the staff having not made a first-class appearance in 2006.

LEICESTERSHIRE 2006

RESULTS SUMMARY

	Place	Won	Lost	Tied	Drew	No Result
County Championship (2nd Division)	**4th**	5	4		7	
All First-Class Matches		5	5		8	1
C & G Trophy (North Conference)	6th	4	4			1
Pro40 League (2nd Division)	6th	3	5			
Twenty20 Cup (North Division)	**Winners**	9	2			

COUNTY CHAMPIONSHIP AVERAGES

BATTING AND FIELDING

Cap		*M*	*I*	*NO*	*HS*	*Runs*	*Avge*	*100*	*50*	*Ct/St*
2005	H.D.Ackerman	14	26	4	309*	1804	82.00	4	14	14
1994	P.A.Nixon	16	23	8	144*	895	59.66	2	6	43/3
–	D.Mongia	10	16	2	165	657	46.92	2	2	2
–	J.L.Sadler	14	24	5	128*	881	46.36	1	6	15
–	J.K.Maunders	16	29	1	180	959	34.25	1	6	9
2004	C.W.Henderson	15	20	5	62*	499	33.26	–	1	6
–	D.D.J.Robinson	12	23	1	106	691	31.40	1	3	10
1996	D.L.Maddy	10	17	1	97	434	27.12	–	3	14
–	J.N.Snape	7	9	1	90	209	26.12	–	1	3
–	T.J.New	4	8	–	52	198	24.75	–	2	1
–	A.R.Griffith	5	6	2	41*	84	21.00	–	–	–
–	S.C.J.Broad	12	15	2	65*	211	16.23	–	1	6
–	D.D.Masters	14	16	1	52	219	14.60	–	1	6
–	R.A.G.Cummins	5	5	3	13	24	12.00	–	–	2
–	Mohammad Asif	7	8	2	21	58	9.66	–	–	4
–	N.G.E.Walker	4	4	–	21	27	6.75	–	–	2

Also batted: J.Allenby (1 match) 103*, 68*; S.G.Clark (2) 12, 23*, 0; A.Habib (1 – cap 1998) 4 (1 ct); C.J.Liddle (4) 1*, 0, 1 (2 ct); Mansoor Amjad (1) 27, 25 (1 ct); J.K.H.Naik (2) 1 (2 ct).

BOWLING

	O	*M*	*R*	*W*	*Avge*	*Best*	*5wI*	*10wM*
S.C.J.Broad	360.2	67	1381	44	31.38	5-83	4	–
Mohammad Asif	240.1	45	788	25	31.52	5-56	2	–
N.G.E.Walker	121.1	25	406	11	36.90	5-59	1	–
D.D.Masters	465.5	129	1232	32	38.50	4-89	–	–
C.W.Henderson	550.4	97	1773	44	40.29	5-69	2	–
D.L.Maddy	168.3	38	548	11	49.81	3-70	–	–
A.R.Griffith	182.4	32	621	11	56.45	3-34	–	–
Also bowled:								
J.K.Maunders	68.2	9	219	6	36.50	4-15	–	–
C.J.Liddle	89.4	15	366	9	40.66	3-42	–	–
R.A.G.Cummins	99	14	416	9	46.22	3-36	–	–
D.Mongia	155.1	46	393	8	49.12	2-62	–	–

J.Allenby 8-2-23-0; S.G.Clark 12-1-69-2; Mansoor Amjad 24-1-102-0; J.K.H.Naik 21-3-112-0; P.A.Nixon 5-0-69-0; D.D.J.Robinson 4.4-0-117-0; J.N.Snape 43.5-6-136-3.

The First-Class Averages (pp 130–146) give the records of Leicestershire players in all first-class matches for the county (Leicestershire's other opponents being the Pakistanis, West Indies A and an abandoned match against Loughborough UCCE), with the exception of S.C.J.Broad and Mohammad Asif whose full county figures are as above, and:

P.W.Harrison 1-2-0-5-5-2.50-0-0-2ct. Did not bowl.

LEICESTERSHIRE RECORDS

FIRST-CLASS CRICKET

Highest Total	For 701-4d		v	Worcs	Worcester	1906
	V 761-6d		by	Essex	Chelmsford	1990
Lowest Total	For 25		v	Kent	Leicester	1912
	V 24		by	Glamorgan	Leicester	1971
	24		by	Oxford U	Oxford	1985
Highest Innings	For 309*	H.D.Ackerman	v	Glamorgan	Cardiff	2006
	V 341	G.H.Hirst	for	Yorkshire	Leicester	1905

Highest Partnership for each Wicket

1st	390	B.Dudleston/J.F.Steele	v	Derbyshire	Leicester	1979
2nd	289*	J.C.Balderstone/D.I.Gower	v	Essex	Leicester	1981
3rd	436*	D.L.Maddy/B.J.Hodge	v	L'boro UCCE	Leicester	2003
4th	290*	P.Willey/T.J.Boon	v	Warwicks	Leicester	1984
5th	322	B.F.Smith/P.V.Simmons	v	Notts	Worksop	1998
6th	284	P.V.Simmons/P.A.Nixon	v	Durham	Chester-le-St	1996
7th	219*	J.D.R.Benson/P.Whitticase	v	Hampshire	Bournemouth	1991
8th	172	P.A.Nixon/D.J.Millns	v	Lancashire	Manchester	1996
9th	160	W.W.Odell/R.T.Crawford	v	Worcs	Leicester	1902
10th	228	R.Illingworth/K.Higgs	v	Northants	Leicester	1977

Best Bowling	For	10- 18	G.Geary	v	Glamorgan	Pontypridd	1929
(Innings)	V	10- 32	H.Pickett	for	Essex	Leyton	1895
Best Bowling	For	16- 96	G.Geary	v	Glamorgan	Pontypridd	1929
(Match)	V	16-102	C.Blythe	for	Kent	Leicester	1909

Most Runs – Season	2446	L.G.Berry	(av 52.04)	1937
Most Runs – Career	30143	L.G.Berry	(av 30.32)	1924-51
Most 100s – Season	7	L.G.Berry		1937
	7	W.Watson		1959
	7	B.F.Davison		1982
Most 100s – Career	45	L.G.Berry		1924-51
Most Wkts – Season	170	J.E.Walsh	(av 18.96)	1948
Most Wkts – Career	2130	W.E.Astill	(av 23.19)	1906-39
Most Career W-K Dismissals	903	R.W.Tolchard	(794 ct/109 st)	1965-83
Most Career Catches in the Field	427	M.R.Hallam		1950-70

LIMITED-OVERS CRICKET

Highest Total	**CGT**	406-5		v	Berkshire	Leicester	1996
	P40	344-4		v	Durham	Chester-le-St	1996
	T20	221-3		v	Yorkshire	Leeds	2004
Lowest Total	**CGT**	56		v	Northants	Leicester	1964
	P40	36		v	Sussex	Leicester	1973
	T20	137		v	Derbyshire	Derby	2005
Highest Innings	**CGT**	201	V.J.Wells	v	Berkshire	Leicester	1996
	P40	154*	B.J.Hodge	v	Sussex	Horsham	2004
	T20	111	D.L.Maddy	v	Yorkshire	Leeds	2004
Best Bowling	**CGT**	6-16	C.M.Willoughby	v	Somerset	Leicester	2005
	P40	6-17	K.Higgs	v	Glamorgan	Leicester	1973
	T20	4-22	C.E.Dagnall	v	Notts	Leicester	2004
		4-22	J.N.Snape	v	Essex	Nottingham	2006

MIDDLESEX

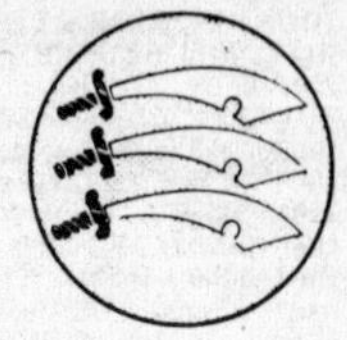

Formation of Present Club: 2 February 1864
Inaugural First-Class Match: 1864
Colours: Blue
Badge: Three Seaxes
County Champions (since 1890): (10) 1903, 1920, 1921, 1947, 1976, 1980, 1982, 1985, 1990, 1993
Joint Champions: (2) 1949, 1977
Gillette/NatWest/C & G Trophy Winners: (4) 1977, 1980, 1984, 1988
Benson and Hedges Cup Winners: (2) 1983, 1986
Pro 40/National League (Div 1) Winners: (0); best – 1st (Div 2) 2004
Sunday League Winners: (1) 1992
Twenty20 Cup Winners: (0); best – Quarter-Finalist 2005

Secretary: Vincent J.Codrington, Lord's Cricket Ground, London NW8 8QN • Tel: 020 7289 1300 • Fax: 020 7289 5831 • Email: enquiries@middlesexccc.com • Web: www.middlesexccc.com

Director of Cricket: John E.Emburey. **Head Coach**: Richard A.Pybus. **Assistant Coach**: Jason C.Pooley. **Captain**: E.T.Smith. **Vice-Captain**: no appointment. **Overseas Players**: M.Kartik and W.P.U.C.J.Vaas. **2007 Beneficiary**: D.C.Nash. **Head Groundsman**: Mick Hunt. **Scorer**: Don K.Shelley. ‡ New registration. [NQ] Not qualified for England.

COMPTON, Nicholas Richard Denis (Harrow S), b Durban, South Africa 26 Jun 1983. 6'1". Son of R.Compton (Natal 1978-79 to 1980-81). Grandson of D.C.S.Compton (Middlesex, England, Holkar, Europeans, Commonwealth and Cavaliers 1936-1964); great-nephew of L.H.Compton (Middlesex 1938-56). RHB, OB. Debut (Middlesex) 2004; cap 2006. F-c Tour (Eng A): B 2006-07. 1000 runs (1): 1315 (2006). HS 190 v Durham (Lord's) 2006. BB 1-94. LO HS 86* v Lancs (Shenley) 2002 (NL). T20 HS 50*.

DALRYMPLE, James William Murray (Radley C; St Peter's C, Oxford), b Nairobi, Kenya 21 Jan 1981. 5'11". RHB, OB. Oxford UCCE 2001-02; captain 2002; blue 2001-02. British U 2001-02. Middlesex debut 2001; cap 2004. **LOI**: 24 (2006 to 2006-07); HS 67 v SL (Lord's) 2006; BB 2-5 v I (Jaipur) 2006-07. HS 244 v Surrey (Oval) 2004. BB 5-49 OU v CU (Cambridge) 2003. M BB 4-53 v Hants (Southgate) 2005. LO HS 107 v Glamorgan (Lord's) 2004 (CGT). LO BB 4-14 v Essex (Southgate) 2001 (NL). T20 HS 39. T20 BB 2-22.

FINN, Steven Thomas (Parmiter's S, Garston), b Watford, Herts 4 Apr 1989. 6'5½". RHB, RMF. Debut (Middlesex) 2005. Awaiting CC debut. No f-c appearances 2006. HS – and BB 1-16 v CU (Cambridge) 2005.

GODLEMAN, Billy Ashley (Islington Green S), b Islington, London 11 Feb 1989. 6'3". LHB, LB. Debut (Middlesex) 2005. Awaiting CC debut. No f-c appearances 2006. HS 69* v CU (Cambridge) 2005. T20 HS 41.

HUTTON, Benjamin Leonard (Radley C; Durham U), b Johannesburg, South Africa 29 Jan 1977. Elder son of R.A.Hutton (Yorkshire, CU, Transvaal & England 1962 to 1975-76); grandson of Sir Leonard (Yorkshire and England 1934-60); elder brother of O.R.Hutton (OU 2004); nephew of J.L.Hutton (MCC 1973-74). 6'2". LHB, RMF. British U 1998-99. Middlesex debut 1999; cap 2003; captain 2005-06. 1000 runs (2); most – 1129 (2004). HS 152 v Kent (Lord's) 2005. BB 4-37 v SL (Shenley) 2002. CC BB 3-14 v Northants (Lord's) 2004. LO HS 77 v Durham (Chester-le-St) 2001 (NL). LO BB 5-45 v Derbys (Southgate) 2001 (NL). T20 HS 27*. T20 BB 2-21.

JOHNSON, Richard Leonard (Sunbury Manor S; S Pelthorne C), b Chertsey, Surrey 29 Dec 1974. 6'2". RHB, RFM. Middlesex 1992-2000; cap 1995. MCC 1999-00. Somerset 2001-06; cap 2001; benefit 2006. **Tests**: 3 (2003 to 2003-04); HS 26 v SL (Galle) 2003-04; BB 6-33 v Z (Chester-le-St) 2003 on debut, including wickets with his third and fourth balls. Hit first ball in Test cricket for four. **LOI**: 10 (2003 to 2003-04); HS 10 v SA (Manchester) 2003; BB 3-22 v B (Dhaka) 2003-04. Took wicket with his second ball in LOI. F-c Tours: I 1994-95 (Eng A – *part*), 2001-02; SL 2003-04, B 1999-00 (MCC); 2003-04. HS 118 Sm v Glos (Bristol) 2003 (100 off 75 balls). Won Walter Lawrence Trophy 2004 for 63-ball hundred Sm v Durham (Chester-le-St). M HS 69 v Essex (Chelmsford) 2000. 50 wkts (4); most – 62 (2001). BB 10-45 v Derbys (Derby) 1994 (second youngest to take all ten wickets in any f-c match). LO HS 53 Sm v Derbys (Derby) 2003 (NL). LO BB 5-50 v Kent (Lord's) 1997 (NWT). T20 HS 10. T20 BB 3-21.

JOYCE, Edmund Christopher (Presentation C, Bray, Co Wicklow; Trinity C, Dublin), b Dublin, Ireland 22 Sep 1978. 5'11". Brother of four Ireland cricketers: Augustine (2000), Dominick (2004-06), Cecilia (2001-06) and Isobel, her twin (1999-2006). LHB, RM. Ireland 1997-98. Middlesex debut 1999; cap 2002. Qualified for England 2005. MCC 2006. **LOI**: 12 (2006 to 2006-07); HS 107 v A (Sydney) 2006-07. F-c Tour (Eng A): WI 2005-06. 1000 runs (5); most 1668 (2005). HS 211 v Warwks (Birmingham) 2006. BB 2-34 v CU (Cambridge) 2004. CC BB 1-4. LO HS 115* Ireland v UAE (Belfast) 2005. LO BB 2-10 v Notts (Nottingham) 2003 (NL). T20 HS 31.

‡[NQ]**KARTIK, Murali,** b Madras, India 11 Sep 1976. LHB, SLA. Railways 1996-97 to date. Central Zone 1997-98 to date. Lancashire 2005-06. **Tests** (I): 8 (1999-00 to 2004-05); HS 43 v B (Dhaka) 2000-01; BB 4-44 v A (Bombay) 2004-05. **LOI** (I): 31 (1999-00 to 2005-06); HS 32* v A (Perth) 2003-04; BB 3-36 v A (Jodhpur) 2002-03. F-c Tours (Ind A): E 2003; A 2003-04 (Ind); SA 2001-02; WI 1999-00, 2002-03; P 1997-98; SL 2002; B 2000-01 (Ind). HS 96 Railways v Rest of India (Delhi) 2005-06. La HS 40 v Hants (Southampton) 2006. BB 9-70 Rest of India v Bombay (Bombay) 2000-01. La BB 5-75 (10-168 match) v Essex (Chelmsford) 2005. LO HS 37* Central Zone v South Zone (Poona) 2004-05. LO BB 5-29 India Seniors v India B (Chandigarh) 2005-06.

KEEGAN, Chad Blake (Durban HS), b Sandton, near Johannesburg, South Africa 30 Jul 1979. 6'1". RHB, RFM. Debut (Middlesex) 2001; cap 2003. MCC YC 2000. Qualified for England March 2005. HS 44 v Surrey (Oval) 2004. 50 wkts (1): 63 (2003). BB 6-114 v Leics (Southgate) 2003. LO HS 50 v Notts (Lord's) 2003 (NL). LO BB 6-33 v Notts (Nottingham) 2005 (NL). T20 HS 42. T20 BB 3-34.

[NQ]**MORGAN, Eoin** Joseph Gerard, b Dublin, Ireland 10 Sep 1986. LHB, RM. British passport. Ireland 2004-to date. Middlesex debut 2006. LOI (Ire): 6 (2006 to 2006-07); HS 115 v Canada (Nairobi) 2006-07. F-c Tours (Ire): Namibia 2005-06; UAE 2006-07. HS 209* Ire v UAE (Abu Dhabi) 2006-07. M HS 38 v Durham (Lord's) 2006. BB – . LO HS 115 (see LOI). LO BB – . T20 HS 66.

‡**MURTAGH, Timothy** James (John Fisher S; St Mary's C), b Lambeth, London 2 Aug 1981. Elder brother of C.P.Murtagh (*see SURREY*); nephew of A.J.Murtagh (Hampshire and E Province 1973-77). 6'0". LHB, RFM. British U 2000-03. Surrey 2001-06. HS 74* Sy v Middx (Oval) 2004 and 74* Sy v Warwks (Croydon) 2005. BB 6-86 Brit U v P (Nottingham) 2001. CC BB 5-39 Sy v Leics (Oval) 2002. LO HS 31* Sy v Durham (Oval) 2005 (NL). LO BB 4-14 Sy v Derbys (Derby) 2005 (NL). T20 HS 24*. T20 BB 6-24.

NASH, David Charles (Sunbury Manor S; Malvern C), b Chertsey, Surrey 19 Jan 1978. 5'8". RHB, occ LB, WK. Debut (Middlesex) 1997; cap 2000; benefit 2007. F-c Tour (Eng A): SL 1997-98 HS 114 v Somerset (Lord's) 1998. BB 1-8. LO HS 67 v Sussex (Lord's) 2002 (BHC).

PEPLOE, Christopher Thomas (Twyford C of E HS; Surrey U, Roehampton), b Hammersmith, London 26 Apr 1981. 6'4". LHB, SLA. MCC YC 2002-03. Debut (Middlesex) 2003. HS 46 v Lancs (Lord's) 2006. BB 4-31 v Yorks (Southgate) 2006. LO HS 14* v Hants (Southampton) 2005 (NL). LO BB 4-38 v Glamorgan (Cardiff) 2005 (NL). T20 HS 7. T20 BB 3-35.

RICHARDSON, Alan (Alleyne's HS; Stafford CFE; Durham U), b Newcastle-under-Lyme, Staffs 6 May 1975. 6'2". RHB, RMF. Derbyshire 1995 (one match). Warwickshire 1999-2004, cap 2002. Middlesex debut/cap 2005, taking 7-113 v Notts (Lord's) on debut. Staffordshire 1996-98. HS 91 Wa v Hants (Birmingham) 2002 – adding 214 for 10th wicket with N.V.Knight. M HS 25 v Notts (Nottingham) 2005. 50 wkts (1): 57 (2005). BB 8-46 Wa v Sussex (Birmingham) 2002. M BB 7-113 (*see above*). LO HS 21* v Lancs (Lord's) 2005 (NL). LO BB 5-35 Wa v Staffs (Stone) 2002 (CGT). T20 HS 6*. T20 BB 3-13.

SCOTT, Ben James Matthew (Whitton S, Richmond; Richmond C), b Isleworth, Middx 4 Aug 1981. 5'8". RHB, WK. Surrey 2003. Middlesex debut 2004. MCC YC 2000. HS 101* v Northants (Lord's) 2004. LO HS 73* v Surrey (Southgate) 2006 (CGT). T20 HS 32*.

SHAH, Owais Alam (Isleworth & Syon S), b Karachi, Pakistan 22 Oct 1978. 6'0". RHB, OB. Debut (Middlesex) 1996; cap 2000; captain 2004 (*part*). MCC 2002-05. YC 2001. **Tests**: 1 (2005-06); HS 88 v I (Bombay) 2005-06 – HS by England player appearing in only one Test. **LOI**: 18 (2001 to 2005-06); HS 62 v P (Lord's) 2001. F-c Tours (Eng A): A 1996-97; WI 2005-06 (*part*); I 2005-06 (Eng – *part*); SL 1997-98, 2004-05. 1000 runs (6); most 1728 (2005). HS 203 v Derbys (Southgate) 2001. BB 3-33 v Glos (Bristol) 1999. LO HS 134 v Sussex (Arundel) 1999 (NL). LO BB 2-2 v Glamorgan(Cardiff) 1998 (BHC). T20 HS 79. T20 BB 1-10.

SILVERWOOD, Christopher Eric Wilfred (Garforth CS), b Pontefract, Yorks 5 Mar 1975. 6'1". RHB, RFM. Yorkshire 1993-2005; cap 1996; benefit 2004. MCC 1996. Middlesex debut/cap 2006. YC 1996. **Tests**: 6 (1996-97 to 2002-03); HS 10 v A (Perth) 2002-03; BB 5-91 v SA (Cape Town) 1999-00. **LOI**: 7 (1996-97 to 2001-02); HS 12 v NZ (Auckland) 1996-97; BB 3-43 v Z (Bulawayo) 2001-02. F-c Tours: A 2002-03 (*part*); SA 1999-00 (*part*); WI 1997-98, 2000-01 (Eng A); NZ 1996-97; Z 1995-96 (Y), 1996-97. HS 80 Y v Durham (Chester-le-St) 2005. M HS 50 v Sussex (Horsham) 2006. 50 wkts (3); most – 63 (2006). BB 7-93 (12-148 match) Y v Kent (Leeds) 1997. M BB 6-51 v Yorks (Southgate) 2006. LO HS 61 Y v Northants (Northampton) 2002 (CGT). LO BB 5-28 Y v Scot (Leeds) 1996 (BHC). T20 HS 13*. T20 BB 2-22.

SMITH, Edward Thomas (Tonbridge S; Peterhouse, Cambridge), b Pembury, Kent 19 Jul 1977. 6'2". RHB, RM. Cambridge U 1996-98, scoring 101 v Glamorgan (Cambridge) on debut; blue 1996-97 (*injured 1998*). Kent 1996-2004; cap 2001. Middlesex debut/cap 2005; captain 2006. British U 1998. **Tests**: 3 (2003); HS 64 v SA (Nottingham) 2003 on debut. F-c Tour (Eng A): I 2003-04. 1000 runs (7: most – 1534 (2003). Scored 135, 0, 149, 113, 203 and 108 in successive f-c innings 2003. HS 213 K v Warwks (Canterbury) 2003. M HS 166 v Warwks (Lord's) 2006. BB 1-60 (off 5 overs) v Sussex (Southgate) 2006. LO HS 122 K v Glamorgan(Maidstone) 2003 (NL). T20 HS 85.

STRAUSS, Andrew John (Radley C; Durham U), b Johannesburg, South Africa 2 Mar 1977. 5'11". LHB, LM. Debut (Middlesex) 1998; cap 2001; captain 2002 (*part*) to 2004 (*part*). MCC 2002. Oxfordshire 1996. *Wisden* 2004. MBE 2005. **ECB central contract 2007**. **Tests**: 36 (2004 to 2006-07, 4 as captain); HS 147 v SA (Johannesburg) 2004-05. Scored 112 & 83 (run out) v NZ (Lord's) on debut and 126 & 94* v SA (Pt Elizabeth) 2004-05 on his debut overseas. **LOI**: 74 (2003-04 to 2006-07, 13 as captain); HS 152 v B (Nottingham) 2005. F-c Tours: A 2006-07; SA 2004-05; I 2005-06; P 2005-06. 1000 runs (3); most – 1529 (2003). HS 176 v Durham (Lord's) 2001. BB 1-27 v Notts (Lord's) 2003. LO HS 152 (*see LOI*). T20 HS 60.

‡[NQ]**VAAS**, Warnakulasuriya Patabendige Ushantha **Chaminda** Joseph, b Mattumagala 27 Jan 1974. LHB, LFM. Colts 1990-91 to date. Hampshire 2003. Worcestershire 2005. **Tests**: 96 (1994-95 to 2006-07); HS 74* v Z (Colombo) 2001-02; BB 7-71 (14-191 match) v WI (Colombo) 2001-02. **LOI**: 289 (1993-94 to 2006-07, 1 as captain); HS 50* v P (Sharjah) 2000-01; BB 8-19 v Z (Colombo) 2001-02, including the first of two LOI hat tricks. F-c Tours (SL): E 2002, 2006; A 1995-96, 2004; SA 1994-95, 1997-98, 2000-01, 2002-03; WI 2003; NZ 1994-95, 1996-97, 2004-05, 2006-07; I 1993-94, 1997-98, 2005-06; P 1995-96, 1999-00, 2001-02, 2004-05; Z 1994-95, 1999-00, 2004; B 1998-99 (v P). HS 134 Colts v Burgher (Colombo) 2004-05. UK HS 50* SL v British U (Northampton) 2002 and 50* SL v Eng (Lord's) 2006. CC HS 45 Wo v Derbys (Worcester) 2005. 50 wkts (0+2); most 62 (2001-02). BB 7-54 W Province v S Province (Colombo) 2004-05. UK BB 4-34 SL v British U (Cambridge) 2006. CC BB 4-82 H v Derbys (Southampton) 2003 – on CC debut. LO HS 62* Colts v Sinhalese (Colombo) 1999-00. LO BB 8-19 (*see LOI*). T20 HS 12. T20 BB 1-28.

WHELAN, Christopher David (St Margaret's HS), b Liverpool, Lancs 8 May 1986. 6'2". RHB, RMF. Debut (Middlesex) 2005. HS 9* and CC BB 2-54 v Hants (Southampton) 2005. No f-c appearances 2006. BB 2-34 v CU (Cambridge) 2005. LO HS 6 (NL). BB 1-43 (P40).

WRIGHT, Christopher Julian Clement (Eggars S, Alton; Anglia Ruskin U), b Chipping Norton, Oxon 14 Jul 1985. 6'3". RHB, RFM. UCCE 2004-05. Middlesex debut 2004. Tamil Union 2005-06. HS 76 CU v Essex (Cambridge) 2005. M HS 42 v Kent (Lord's) 2006. BB 2-33 v OU (Oxford) 2006. LO HS 18 Tamil Union v Air Force (Colombo) 2005-06. LO BB 3-21 Tamil Union v Singha (Colombo) 2005-06. T20 HS 1*. T20 BB 2-24.

RELEASED/RETIRED

(Having made a first-class County appearance in 2006)

ALI, Syed **Mohammad** Bukhari (Punjab C of Commerce), b Bahawalpur, Pakistan 8 Nov 1973. 6'0". Nephew of Taslim Arif (Karachi, Sind, National Bank and Pakistan 1967-68 to 1988-89). British passport. RHB, LFM. Railways 1993-94. Lahore 1993-94. United Bank 1994-95. Islamabad 1994-95. ADBP 1995-96 to 1998-99. Rawalpindi 1995-96. Bahawalpur 1998-99. 55 f-c matches in Pakistan before his UK debut in 2002. Derbyshire 2002-04. Middlesex 2006. HS 92 Bahawalpur v Lahore (Rahim Yar Khan) 1998-99. CC HS 53 De v Durham (Derby) 2002 – on debut. M HS 23* v Sussex (Horsham) 2006. 50 wkts (0+1): 56 (1993-94). BB 6-37 Railways v National Bank (Faisalabad) 1993-94. CC BB 4-75 De v Glamorgan (Cardiff) 2004. M BB 2-15 v OU (Oxford) 2006 – on debut. LO HS 19 De v Lancs (Manchester) 2002 (CGT). LO BB 4-34 Railways v United Bank (Karachi) 1993-94. T 20 HS 0*. T20 BB 3-24.

BETTS, Melvyn Morris (Fyndoune CS, Sacriston), b Sacriston, Co Durham 26 Mar 1975. 5'10". RHB, RFM. Durham 1993-2000; cap 1998. Warwickshire 2001-03; cap 2001. Middlesex 2004-06. F-c Tour (Eng A): Z 1998-99. HS 73 Wa v Lancs (Birmingham) 2003. M HS 36* v Sussex (Hove) 2005. BB 9-64 (Durham record; 13-143 match) v Northants (Northampton) 1997. M BB 5-89 v Worcs (Worcester) 2004. LO HS 21 Du v Hants (Chester-le-St) 1997 (SL). LO BB 4-15 v Wales MC (Lamphey) 2004 (CGT). T20 HS 13*. T20 BB 2-51.

[NQ]**LOUW, Johann** (Fraserburg HS; Port Elizabeth U), b Cape Town, South Africa 12 Apr 1979. 6'2". RHB, RFM. Griqualand West 2000-01 to 2002-03. Eastern Province 2003-04. Northamptonshire 2004-05 (Kolpak registration). Dolphins 2004-05 to date. Eagles 2005-06. Middlesex 2006. HS 124 EP v Boland (Pt Elizabeth) 2003-04. UK HS 64 Nh v Somerset (Taunton) 2005. M HS 42 v Notts (Lord's) 2006. 50 wkts (1): 60 (2004). BB 6-51 Nh v Essex (Northampton) 2005. M BB 5-117 v Hants (Southampton) 2006. LO HS 72 GW v Northerns (Kimberley) 2000-01. LO BB 5-27 Nh v Warwks (Northampton) 2004 (NL). T20 HS 17. T20 BB 4-18.

RELEASED/RETIRED continued on p 86

MIDDLESEX 2006

RESULTS SUMMARY

	Place	Won	Lost	Tied	Drew	No Result
County Championship (1st Division)	**9th**	1	7		8	
All First-Class Matches		1	7		9	
C & G Trophy (South Conference)	2nd	6	2			1
Pro40 League (1st Division)	9th	2	6			
Twenty20 Cup (South Division)	6th	1	7			

COUNTY CHAMPIONSHIP AVERAGES

BATTING AND FIELDING

Cap		M	I	NO	HS	Runs	Avge	100	50	Ct/St
2002	E.C.Joyce	11	20	1	211	1077	56.68	3	5	9
2006	N.R.D.Compton	16	29	3	190	1207	46.42	5	4	7
2000	D.C.Nash	8	14	4	68*	460	46.00	–	4	13/2
2006	S.B.Styris	10	17	1	133	679	42.43	1	5	14
2000	O.A.Shah	15	28	–	126	1038	37.07	2	7	12
2005	E.T.Smith	16	30	1	166	1075	37.06	4	2	12
1993	P.N.Weekes	7	13	4	128*	332	36.88	1	–	–
2004	J.W.M.Dalrymple	10‡	17	–	71	557	32.76	–	4	3
–	C.J.C.Wright	4	7	3	42	122	30.50	–	–	–
2003	B.L.Hutton	10	18	1	105	459	27.00	1	1	16
–	S.M.B.Ali	4	8	4	23*	87	21.75	–	–	3
–	C.T.Peploe	10	14	1	46	204	15.69	–	–	2
2006	C.E.W.Silverwood	15	24	6	50	271	15.05	–	1	4
–	B.J.M.Scott	8	13	–	49	195	15.00	–	–	22/1
–	J.Louw	16	26	5	42	303	14.42	–	–	1
–	E.J.G.Morgan	6	11	–	38	144	13.09	–	–	1/1
2003	C.B.Keegan	7	10	1	34*	111	12.33	–	–	3
–	M.M.Betts	2	4	–	7	18	4.50	–	–	1

Also batted (1 match each): A.Richardson (cap 2005) 9, 0*; A.J.Strauss (cap 2001) 0, 141 (2 ct).

BOWLING

	O	M	R	W	Avge	Best	5wI	10wM
C.E.W.Silverwood	485.2	93	1539	61	25.22	6- 51	4	–
S.B.Styris	198.3	37	670	18	37.22	6- 71	1	–
C.B.Keegan	200.4	43	736	19	38.73	5- 90	1	–
J.W.M.Dalrymple	310.4	47	949	24	39.54	3- 29	–	–
J.Louw	514.4	93	1825	39	46.79	5-117	1	–
C.T.Peploe	282.2	55	944	12	78.66	4- 31	–	–
Also bowled:								
S.M.B.Ali	102.3	13	424	7	60.57	2- 56	–	–
C.J.C.Wright	90	8	469	5	93.80	2-100	–	–

M.M.Betts 26-4-88-4; N.R.D.Compton 7-0-103-1; B.L.Hutton 51.4-6-238-2; E.C.Joyce 13-0-102-1; D.C.Nash 4.5-0-53-1; A.Richardson 40-10-121-4; O.A.Shah 15.4-1-98-0; E.T.Smith 5-0-60-1; P.N.Weekes 102.3-9-319-4.

The First-Class Averages (pp 130–146) give the records of Middlesex players in all first-class matches for the county (their other opponents being Oxford UCCE), with the exception of O.A.Shah and A.J.Strauss whose full county figures are as above, and:

J.W.M.Dalrymple 11-18-0-96-653-36.27-0-5-5ct. 319.4-47-976-25-39.04-3/29.

E.C.Joyce 12-21-1-211-1162-58.10-3-6-10ct. 19-3-120-1-120.00-1/21.

‡ Full substitute for C.T.Peploe v Durham at Lord's.

MIDDLESEX RECORDS

FIRST-CLASS CRICKET

Highest Total	For 642-3d		v	Hampshire	Southampton	1923
	V 734-5d		by	Lancashire	Manchester	2003
Lowest Total	For 20		v	MCC	Lord's	1864
	V 31		by	Glos	Bristol	1924
Highest Innings	For 331*	J.D.B.Robertson	v	Worcs	Worcester	1949
	V 341	C.M.Spearman	for	Glos	Gloucester	2004

Highest Partnership for each Wicket

1st	372	M.W.Gatting/J.L.Langer	v	Essex	Southgate	1998
2nd	380	F.A.Tarrant/J.W.Hearne	v	Lancashire	Lord's	1914
3rd	424*	W.J.Edrich/D.C.S.Compton	v	Somerset	Lord's	1948
4th	325	J.W.Hearne/E.H.Hendren	v	Hampshire	Lord's	1919
5th	338	R.S.Lucas/T.C.O'Brien	v	Sussex	Hove	1895
6th	270	J.D.Carr/P.N.Weekes	v	Glos	Lord's	1994
7th	271*	E.H.Hendren/F.T.Mann	v	Notts	Nottingham	1925
8th	182*	M.H.C.Doll/H.R.Murrell	v	Notts	Lord's	1913
9th	160*	E.H.Hendren/T.J.Durston	v	Essex	Leyton	1927
10th	230	R.W.Nicholls/W.Roche	v	Kent	Lord's	1899

Best Bowling (Innings)	For	10- 40	G.O.B.Allen	v	Lancashire	Lord's	1929
	V	9- 38	R.C.R-Glasgow†	for	Somerset	Lord's	1924
Best Bowling (Match)	For	16-114	G.Burton	v	Yorkshire	Sheffield	1888
		16-114	J.T.Hearne	v	Lancashire	Manchester	1898
	V	16-109	C.W.L.Parker	for	Glos	Cheltenham	1930

Most Runs – Season	2669	E.H.Hendren	(av 83.41)	1923
Most Runs – Career	40302	E.H.Hendren	(av 48.81)	1907-37
Most 100s – Season	13	D.C.S.Compton		1947
Most 100s – Career	119	E.H.Hendren		1907-37
Most Wkts – Season	158	F.J.Titmus	(av 14.63)	1955
Most Wkts – Career	2361	F.J.Titmus	(av 21.27)	1949-82
Most Career W-K Dismissals	1223	J.T.Murray	(1024 ct/199 st)	1952-75
Most Career Catches in the Field	561	E.H.Hendren		1907-37

LIMITED-OVERS CRICKET

Highest Total	**CGT**	304-7		v	Surrey	The Oval	1995
		304-8		v	Cornwall	St Austell	1995
	P40	337-5		v	Somerset	Southgate	2003
	T20	210-6		v	Hampshire	Southampton	2005
Lowest Total	**CGT**	41		v	Essex	Westcliff	1972
	P40	23		v	Yorkshire	Leeds	1974
	T20	108		v	Sussex	Richmond	2006
Highest Innings	**CGT**	158	G.D.Barlow	v	Lancashire	Lord's	1984
	P40	147*	M.R.Ramprakash	v	Worcs	Lord's	1990
	T20	85	E.T.Smith	v	Kent	Beckenham	2005
Best Bowling	**CGT**	6-15	W.W.Daniel	v	Sussex	Hove	1980
	P40	6- 6	R.W.Hooker	v	Surrey	Lord's	1969
	T20	4-18	J.Louw	v	Hampshire	Southgate	2006

† R.C.Robertson-Glasgow

NORTHAMPTONSHIRE

Formation of Present Club: 31 July 1878
Inaugural First-Class Match: 1905
Colours: Maroon
Badge: Tudor Rose
County Champions: (0); best – 2nd 1912, 1957, 1965, 1976
Gillette/NatWest/C & G Trophy Winners: (2) 1976, 1992
Benson and Hedges Cup Winners: (1) 1980
Pro 40/National League (Div 1) Winners: (0); best – 2nd 2006
Sunday League Winners: (0); best – 3rd 1991
Twenty20 Cup Winners: (0); best – Quarter-Finalist 2005, 2006

Chief Executive: Mark J.Tagg, County Ground, Wantage Road, Northampton, NN1 4TJ • Tel: 01604 514455 • Fax: 01604 609288 • Email: post@nccc.co.uk • Web: www.nccc.co.uk

First XI Coach: David J.Capel. **Captain**: D.J.G.Sales. **Vice-Captain**: none. **Overseas Players**: C.J.L.Rogers and J.J.van der Wath. **2007 Beneficiary**: D.J.G.Sales. **Head Groundsman**: Paul Marshall. **Scorer**: A.C. (Tony) Kingston. ‡ New registration. [NQ] Not qualified for England.

AFZAAL, Usman (Manvers Pierrepont CS; S Notts C), b Rawalpindi, Pakistan 9 Jun 1977. 6'0". LHB, SLA. Nottinghamshire 1995-2003; cap 2000. MCC 2002. Northamptonshire debut 2004; cap 2005. **Tests**: 3 (2001); HS 54 v A (Oval) 2001; BB 1-49. F-c Tours: SA 1996-97 (Nt); WI 2000-01 (Eng A); NZ 2001-02. 1000 runs (6): most – 1365 (2004). HS 168* v Essex (Northampton) 2005. BB 4-101 Nt v Glos (Nottingham) 1998. Nh BB 3-65 v Kent (Northampton) 2004. LO HS 122* v Middx (Northampton) 2005 (NL). LO BB 3-4 v Cambs (Northampton) 2004 (CGT). T20 HS 64*. T20 BB 2-15.

BROWN, Jason Fred (St Margaret Ward HS & SFC), b Newcastle-under-Lyme, Staffs 10 Oct 1974. 6'0". RHB, OB. Debut (Northamptonshire) 1996; cap 2000. Staffordshire 1994-95. F-c Tours: WI 2000-01 (*part*) (Eng A); SL 2000-01 (*no f-c*). HS 38 v Hants (Northampton) 2003. 50 wkts (3): most – 66 (2003). BB 7-69 v Durham (Chester-le-St) 2003. LO HS 16 v Lancs (Manchester) 2002 (NL). LO BB 5-19 v Cambs (Northampton) 2004 (CGT). T20 HS 6*. T20 BB 5-27.

‡**BROWNING, Richard** James (Wolverhampton GS), b Wolverhampton, Staffs 9 Oct 1987. 6'3". RHB, RMF. Derbyshire (l-o only) 2006. Awaiting f-c debut. LO HS 2 De v Worcs (Worcester) 2006 (P40).

COVERDALE, Paul Stephen (Wellingborough S; Loughborough U), b Harrogate, Yorks 24 Jul 1983. Son of S.P.Coverdale (Yorkshire, Cambridge U and Northamptonshire 1973-80, 1987; Northants Secretary-Manager/Chief Executive 1985-2004). 5'10". RHB, RM. Joined Northamptonshire staff 2004. Awaiting f-c debut. LO HS 19 Northants CB v Leics CB (Barwell) 2001. LO BB 1-21 (CGT).

‡[NQ]**CROOK, Andrew** Richard (Rostrevor C), b Modbury, S Australia 14 Oct 1980. 6'4". Elder brother of S.P.Crook. RHB, OB. British passport. S Australia 1998-99 (one match). Lancashire 2004-05. Aus Academy 1999-2000. HS 88 La v OU (Oxford) 2005. BB 3-71 and CC HS 43 La v Essex (Manchester) 2005. LO HS 162* La v Bucks (Wormsley) 2005 (Lancs CGT record). LO BB 3-32 La v Hants (Manchester) 2005. T20 HS 15. T20 BB 2-25.

NQ**CROOK, Steven** Paul (Rostrevor C; Magill U), b Modbury, S Australia 28 May 1983. Younger brother of A.R.Crook. 5'11". RHB, RFM. British passport. Lancashire 2003-05. Northamptonshire debut 2005 (whilst on loan from Lancashire). Aus Academy 2001-02. HS 97 v Yorks (Northampton) 2005. BB 3-46 v Leics (Northampton) 2006. 3-54 v Durham (Chester-le-St) 2005. LO HS 23 v Glamorgan (Cardiff) 2006 (P40). LO BB 4-20 v Sussex (Northampton) 2006 (P40). T20 HS 27.

‡**DAWSON, Richard** Kevin James (Batley GS; Exeter U), b Doncaster, Yorks 4 Aug 1980. 6'3". RHB, OB. British U 2000. Yorkshire 2001-06; cap 2004. MCC 2002. Devon 1999-2000. **Tests**: 7 (2001-02 to 2002-03); HS 19* v A (Perth) 2002-03; BB 4-134 v I (Chandigarh) 2001-02 – on debut. F-c Tours: A 2002-03; NZ 2001-02; I 2001-02; SL 2002-03 (ECB Acad), 2004-05 (Eng A). HS 87 Y v Kent (Canterbury) 2002. BB 6-82 Y v Glamorgan (Scarborough) 2001. LO HS 41 Y v Leics (Scarborough) 2002 (NL). LO BB 4-13 Y v Derbys (Derby) 2002 (BHC). T20 HS 22. T20 BB 3-24.

NQ**KLUSENER, Lance** (Durban HS), b Durban, South Africa 4 Sep 1971. 5'10". LHB, RM/OB. Natal/KwaZulu-Natal 1993-94 to 2003-04. Nottinghamshire 2002. Middlesex 2004. Dolphins 2004-05 to date. Northamptonshire debut/cap 2006 (Kolpak Registration). *Wisden* 1999. **Tests** (SA): 49 (1996-97 to 2004); HS 174 v E (Pt Elizabeth) 1999-00; BB 8-64 v I (Calcutta) 1996-97 – on debut. **LOI** (SA): 171 (1995-96 to 2004); HS 103* v NZ (Auckland) 1998-99; BB 6-49 v SL (Lahore) 1997-98. F-c Tours (SA): E 1996 (SA A), 1998; A 1997-98, 2001-02; WI 2000-01; NZ 1998-99; I 1996-97, 1999-00; P 1997-98; SL 1995 (SA U-24), 2000, 2004; Z 1999-00, 2001-02. 1000 runs (1): 1251 (2006 – inc 6 hundreds). HS 174 (*see Tests*). CC HS 147* v Somerset (Northampton) 2006. BB 8-34 Natal v WP (Durban) 1995-96. CC BB 6-69 v Leics (Oakham) 2006. LO HS 142* SA v Northants (Northampton) 1998. LO BB 6-49 (*see LOI*). T20 HS 72*. T20 BB 2-13.

LOGAN, Richard James (Wolverhampton GS), b Stone, Staffs 28 Jan 1980. 6'1". RHB, RMF. Northamptonshire 1999-2000. Nottinghamshire 2001-04. Hampshire 2005-06. HS 37* Nt v Hants (Nottingham) 2001. BB 6-93 Nt v Derbys (Nottingham) 2001. LO HS 28* H v Northants (Northampton) 2005 (NL). LO BB 5-24 Nt v Suffolk (Mildenhall) 2001 (CGT). T20 HS 11*. T20 BB 5-26.

‡**LUCAS, David** Scott (Djanogly CTC, Nottingham), b Nottingham 19 Aug 1978. 6'2". RHB, LMF. Nottinghamshire 1999-2002. Yorkshire 2005. Lincolnshire 2006. HS 49 Nt v DU (Nottingham) 2002. CC HS 46* Nt v Middx (Nottingham) 2000. BB 5-49 Y v Bangladesh A (Leeds) 2005. CC BB 5-104 Nt v Essex (Nottingham) 1999. LO HS 32 v Derbys (Derby) 2005 (NL). LO BB 4-27 Nt v Derbys (Derby) 2000 (NL).

‡NQ**O'BRIEN, Niall** John (Marian C, Dublin), b Dublin, Ireland 8 Nov 1981. 5'6". LHB, WK. Irish passport. Kent 2004-06. Ireland 2006-07. HS 176 Ireland v UAE (Windhoek) 2005. UK HS 69 K v Warwks (Birmingham) 2004. BB 1-4 K v CU (Cambridge) 2006. LOI (Ire): 7 (2006-07); HS 53 v Holland (Ayr) 2006-07. LO HS 53 (*see LOI*). T20 HS 12.

PANESAR, Mudhsuden Singh ('***Monty***') (Stopsley HS; Bedford Modern S; Loughborough U), b Luton, Beds 25 Apr 1982. 6'0". LHB, SLA. Debut (Northamptonshire) 2001; cap 2006. British U 2002-05. Loughborough U 2004. MCC 2006. Bedfordshire 1998-99. **ECB central contract 2007. Tests**: 13 (2005-06 to 2006-07); HS 26 v SL (Nottingham) 2006; BB 5-72 v P (Manchester) 2006. **LOI**: 9 (2006-07); HS 6 v NZ (Adelaide) 2006-07; BB 2-35 v NZ (Perth) 2006-07. F-c Tours: A 2006-07; I 2005-06; SL 2002-03 (ECB Acad). HS 39* v Worcs (Northampton) 2005. BB 7-181 v Essex (Chelmsford) 2005. 50 wkts (2); most – 71 (2006). LO HS 16* v Essex (Colchester) 2002 (NL). LO BB 5-20 ECB Acad v SL Acad XI (Colombo) 2002-03. T20 HS 2. T20 BB 2-22.

PETERS, Stephen David (Coopers Coborn & Co S), b Harold Wood, Essex 10 Dec 1978. 5'11". RHB, occ LB. Essex 1996-2001, scoring 110 and 12* v CU (Cambridge) on debut. Worcestershire 2002-05. Northamptonshire debut 2006. 1000 runs (2); most – 1177 (2003). HS 178 v Essex (Northampton) 2006. BB1-19 Ex v OU (Chelmsford) 1999. LO HS 84* v Glamorgan (Cardiff) 2006 (P40). T20 HS 26*.

NQ**ROGERS, Christopher** John Llewellyn (Wesley C, Perth; Curtin U, Perth), b St George, Sydney, Australia 31 Aug 1977. Son of W.J.Rogers (NSW 1968-69 to 1969-70). 5'10". LHB, LBG. W Australia 1998-99 to date. Derbyshire 2004. Leicestershire 2005. Northamptonshire debut 2006. Shropshire 2003. HS 319 v Glos (Northampton) 2006. LO HS 117* WA v Q (Perth) 2003-04. T20 HS 35.

SALES, David John Grimwood (Caterham S; Cumnor House S), b Carshalton, Surrey 3 Dec 1977. 6'0". RHB, RM. Debut (Northamptonshire) 1996 v Worcs (Kidderminster) scoring 0 and 210* – record Championship score on f-c debut; youngest (18yr 237d) to score 200 in a Championship match; cap 1999; captain 2004 to date; benefit 2007. Wellington 2001-02. F-c Tours (Eng A): NZ 1999-00; SL 1997-98; K 1997-98; B 1999-00. Sustained severe knee injury prior to start of England A tour of WI 2000-01 – no f-c appearances 2001. 1000 runs (4); most – 1291 (1999). HS 303* v Essex (Northampton) 1999 – youngest Englishman (21y 240d) to score a f-c 300. BB 4-25 v SL A (Northampton) 1999. CC BB 2-7 v Yorks (Scarborough) 1999. LO HS 161 v Yorks (Northampton) 2006 (CGT). T20 HS 78*. T20 BB 1-10.

‡NQ**VAN DER WATH, Johannes** Jacobus (Ermelo HS), b Newcastle, Natal, South Africa 10 Jan 1978. RHB, RFM. Easterns 1996-97. Free State 1997-98 to 2003-04. Eagles 2004-05 to date. Sussex 2005. **LOI** (SA): 8 (2005-06 to 2006-07); HS 37* v A (Sydney) 2005-06; BB 2-21 v SA (Melbourne) 2005-06 – on debut. F-c Tour (SA A): SL 2005-06. HS 113* FS v KZ-Natal (Bloemfontein) 2001-02. UK HS 34 Sx v Warwks (Hove) 2005. BB 6-27 Eagles v Dolphins (Durban) 2006-07. UK BB 3-21 Sx v B (Hove) 2005. CC BB 2-113 Sx v Notts (Nottingham) 2005. LO HS 91 FS v GW (Bloemfontein) 2000-01. LO BB 4-31 SA A v NZ (Potchefstroom) 2005-06. T20 HS 35. T20 BB 2-11.

NQ**WESSELS,** Mattheus Hendrik (**'Riki'**) (Woodridge C, Pt Elizabeth; Northants U), b Marogudoore, Queensland, Australia 12 Nov 1985. Left Australia when 2 months old. Son of K.C.Wessels (OFS, Sussex, WP, NT, Q, EP, GW, Australia and South Africa 1973-74 to 1999-00). 5'11". RHB, WK. MCC 2004. Northamptonshire debut 2005 (Kolpak registration). HS 107 v Durham (Chester-le-St) 2005. LO HS 80 v Glamorgan (Northampton) 2005 (NL). T20 HS 49*.

WHITE, Graeme Geoffrey (Stowe S), b Milton Keynes, Beds 18 Apr 1987. 5'11". RHB, SLA. Debut (Northamptonshire) 2006. HS 37 v Derbys (Northampton) 2006 – on debut. BB – .

WHITE, Robert Allan (Stowe S; Durham U; Loughborough U), b Chelmsford, Essex 15 Oct 1979. 5'11". RHB, LB. Debut (Northamptonshire) 2000. Loughborough UCCE 2003. British U 2003. HS 277 and BB 2-30 v Glos (Northampton) 2002 – highest maiden f-c hundred in UK; included 107 before lunch on first day. LO HS 101 v Glamorgan (Northampton) 2004 (NL). LO BB 2-18 v Sussex (Northampton) 2002 (NL). T20 HS 66.

WIGLEY, David Harry (St Mary's RCS, Menstom, Ilkley; Loughborough U), b Bradford, Yorks 26 Oct 1981. 6'4". RHB, RFM. Yorkshire 2002 (one match). Loughborough UCCE 2003-04. British U 2004. Worcestershire 2003, 2005. Northamptonshire debut 2006. HS 28 v Surrey (Oval) 2006. BB 5-77 v P (Northampton) 2006. CC BB 4-68 Wo v Derbys (Derby) 2005. LO HS 9 v Worcs (Worcester) 2006 (CGT). LO BB 4-37 Wo v Leics (Worcester) 2004 (NL). T20 HS 1. T20 BB 1-8.

RELEASED/RETIRED continued on p 80

NORTHAMPTONSHIRE 2006

RESULTS SUMMARY

	Place	Won	Lost	Tied	Drew	No Result
County Championship (2nd Division)	**6th**	3	5		8	
All First-Class Matches		4	6		8	
C & G Trophy (North Conference)	10th	1	8			2
Pro40 League (1st Division)	2nd	5	2			1
Twenty20 Cup (Mid/West/Wales Division)	Q-Finalist	5	3	1		

COUNTY CHAMPIONSHIP AVERAGES

BATTING AND FIELDING

Cap		*M*	*I*	*NO*	*HS*	*Runs*	*Avge*	*100*	*50*	*Ct/St*
–	C.J.L.Rogers	13	22	2	319	1352	67.60	4	5	11
2006	L.Klusener	16	26	7	147*	1251	65.84	6	3	9
1999	D.J.G.Sales	16	26	1	225	1204	48.16	2	5	12
2005	U.Afzaal	16	28	4	151	1110	46.25	3	5	5
–	S.D.Peters	14	26	2	178	893	37.20	2	4	7
–	B.M.Shafayat	16	28	2	118	855	32.88	2	5	20/3
–	M.J.Nicholson	15	20	4	106*	454	28.37	1	1	6
2005	B.J.Phillips	15	22	2	75	463	23.15	–	4	6
–	M.H.Wessels	8	14	2	59*	270	22.50	–	1	23/1
–	S.P.Crook	7	8	1	44	114	16.28	–	–	5
–	R.A.White	7	10	1	48*	117	13.00	–	–	3
–	D.H.Wigley	6	8	2	28	53	8.83	–	–	2
2006	M.S.Panesar	8	10	2	34	62	7.75	–	–	1
2000	J.F.Brown	13	17	5	20*	80	6.66	–	–	2
–	S.C.Ganguly	3	5	–	9	19	3.80	–	–	–

Also batted: C.Pietersen (1 match) 12, 39*; G.G.White (2) 37, 0, 0.

BOWLING

	O	*M*	*R*	*W*	*Avge*	*Best*	*5wI*	*10wM*
M.S.Panesar	414.4	106	1098	42	26.14	5- 32	4	1
M.J.Nicholson	474.5	113	1471	46	31.97	7- 62	2	–
B.J.Phillips	328.2	76	955	26	36.73	3- 10	–	–
L.Klusener	206.3	41	699	19	36.78	6- 69	1	–
S.P.Crook	155.1	7	726	15	48.40	3- 46	–	–
J.F.Brown	542	110	1632	33	49.45	5- 82	1	–
Also bowled:								
U.Afzaal	111.3	16	419	6	69.83	3- 75	–	–
D.H.Wigley	127.2	15	605	8	75.62	2-104	–	–

S.C.Ganguly 36-8-112-2; C.Pietersen 39-4-137-1; C.J.L.Rogers 21-5-71-1; D.J.G.Sales 2-0-2-0; B.M.Shafayat 10-0-55-0; G.G.White 26-1-79-0; R.A.White 48-3-227-3.

The First-Class Averages (pp 130–146) give the records of Northamptonshire players in all first-class matches for the county (Northamptonshire's other opponents being Cambridge UCCE and the Pakistanis), with the exception of:

M.S.Panesar 9-11-3-34-93-11.62-0-0-1ct. 444.4-117-1171-43-27.23-5/32-4-1.

NORTHAMPTONSHIRE RECORDS

FIRST-CLASS CRICKET

Highest Total	For 781-7d		v	Notts	Northampton	1995
	V 673-8d		by	Yorkshire	Leeds	2003
Lowest Total	For 12		v	Glos	Gloucester	1907
	V 33		by	Lancashire	Northampton	1977
Highest Innings	For 331*	M.E.K.Hussey	v	Somerset	Taunton	2003
	V 333	K.S.Duleepsinhji	for	Sussex	Hove	1930

Highest Partnership for each Wicket

1st	375	R.A.White/M.J.Powell	v	Glos	Northampton	2002
2nd	344	G.Cook/R.J.Boyd-Moss	v	Lancashire	Northampton	1986
3rd	393	A.Fordham/A.J.Lamb	v	Yorkshire	Leeds	1990
4th	370	R.T.Virgin/P.Willey	v	Somerset	Northampton	1976
5th	401	M.B.Loye/D.Ripley	v	Glamorgan	Northampton	1998
6th	376	R.Subba Row/A.Lightfoot	v	Surrey	The Oval	1958
7th	293	D.J.G.Sales/D.Ripley	v	Essex	Northampton	1999
8th	164	D.Ripley/N.G.B.Cook	v	Lancashire	Manchester	1987
9th	156	R.Subba Row/S.Starkie	v	Lancashire	Northampton	1955
10th	148	B.W.Bellamy/J.V.Murdin	v	Glamorgan	Northampton	1925

Best Bowling	For	10-127	V.W.C.Jupp	v	Kent	Tunbridge W	1932
(Innings)	V	10- 30	C.Blythe	for	Kent	Northampton	1907
Best Bowling	For	15- 31	G.E.Tribe	v	Yorkshire	Northampton	1958
(Match)	V	17- 48	C.Blythe	for	Kent	Northampton	1907

Most Runs – Season	2198	D.Brookes	(av 51.11)	1952
Most Runs – Career	28980	D.Brookes	(av 36.13)	1934-59
Most 100s – Season	8	R.A.Haywood		1921
Most 100s – Career	67	D.Brookes		1934-59
Most Wkts – Season	175	G.E.Tribe	(av 18.70)	1955
Most Wkts – Career	1102	E.W.Clark	(av 21.26)	1922-47
Most Career W-K Dismissals	810	K.V.Andrew	(653 ct/157 st)	1953-66
Most Career Catches in the Field	469	D.S.Steele		1963-84

LIMITED-OVERS CRICKET

Highest Total	**CGT**	360-2		v	Staffs	Northampton	1990
	P40	319-7		v	Scotland	Northampton	2003
	T20	224-5		v	Glos	Milton Keynes	2005
Lowest Total	**CGT**	62		v	Leics	Leicester	1974
	P40	41		v	Middlesex	Northampton	1972
	T20	128-5		v	Glos	Bristol	2003
Highest Innings	**CGT**	161	D.J.G.Sales	v	Yorkshire	Northampton	2006
	P40	172*	W.Larkins	v	Warwicks	Luton	1983
	T20	88	M.E.K.Hussey	v	Somerset	Northampton	2003
Best Bowling	**CGT**	7-10	C.Pietersen	v	Denmark	Brondby	2005
	P40	7-39	A.Hodgson	v	Somerset	Northampton	1976
	T20	5-27	J.F.Brown	v	Somerset	Northampton	2003

NOTTINGHAMSHIRE

Formation of Present Club: March/April 1841
Substantial Reorganisation: 11 December 1866
Inaugural First-Class Match: 1864
Colours: Green and Gold
Badge: Badge of City of Nottingham
County Champions (since 1890): (5) 1907, 1929, 1981, 1987, 2005
Gillette/NatWest/C & G Trophy Winners: (1) 1987
Benson and Hedges Cup Winners: (1) 1989
Pro 40/National League (Div 1) Winners: (0); best – 5th 2001, 2005
Sunday League Winners: (1) 1991
Twenty20 Cup Winners: (0); best – Finalist 2006

Chief Executive: Derek Brewer, Trent Bridge, Nottingham NG2 6AG • Tel: 0115 982 3000 • Fax: 0115 945 5730 • Email: administration@nottsccc.co.uk • Webs: www.nottsccc.co.uk • www.trentbridge.co.uk

Director of Cricket: Mike Newell. **Club Coach**: Paul Johnson. **Captain**: S.P.Fleming. **Vice-Captain**: tba. **Overseas Players**: S.P.Fleming and D.J.Hussey. **2007 Beneficiary**: P.J.Franks. **Head Groundsman**: Steve Birks. **Scorers**: Gordon Stringfellow (home), L. Brian Hewes (away). ‡ New registration. NQ Not qualified for England.

ALLEYNE, David (Enfield GS; Hertford Regional C; City & Islington C), b York 17 Apr 1976. 5'11". RHB, WK. Middlesex 2001-02. Nottinghamshire debut 2004. HS 109* v Warwks (Nottingham) 2006. LO HS 58 M v Notts (Nottingham) 2000 (NL). T20 HS 24*.

CLOUGH, Gareth David (Pudsey Grangefield S), b Leeds, Yorks 23 May 1978. 6'0". RHB, RM. Yorkshire 1998. Nottinghamshire debut 2001. No f-c appearances 2004. HS 55 v Ind A (Nottingham) 2003. CC HS 33 Y v Glamorgan (Cardiff) 1998 – on debut. BB 3-69 v Glos (Nottingham) 2001. LO HS 42* v Durham (Nottingham) 2003 (NL). LO BB 6-25 v Sussex (Nottingham) 2006 (P40). T20 HS 40*. T20 BB 2-17.

EALHAM, Mark Alan (Stour Valley SS, Chartham), b Willesborough, Ashford, Kent 27 Aug 1969. Son of A.G.E.Ealham (Kent 1966-82). 5'9". RHB, RMF. Kent 1989-2003; cap 1992; benefit 2003. Nottinghamshire debut/cap 2004. Lawrence Trophy (fastest f-c hundred of 2006 – 45 balls v MCC at Lord's). **Tests**: 8 (1996 to 1998); HS 53* v A (Birmingham) 1997; BB 4-21 v I (Nottingham) 1996. **LOI**: 64 (1996 to 2001); HS 45 v WI (Bridgetown) 1997-98; BB 5-15 v Z (Kimberley) 1999-00 – Eng record (then). F-c Tours: A 1996-97 (Eng A); SA 1999-00 (*part*); SL 1997-98; Z 1992-93 (K); K 1997-98. 1000 runs (1): 1055 (1997). HS 153* K v Northants (Canterbury) 2001. Nt HS 139 v Leics (Leicester) 2004. BB 8-36 (10-74 match) K v Warwks (Birmingham) 1996. 50 wkts (1): 56 (2005). Nt BB 5-31 v Glos (Nottingham) 2005. LO HS 112 K v Derbys (Maidstone) 1995 (off 44 balls – SL record). LO BB 6-53 K v Hants (Basingstoke) 1993 (SL). T20 HS 91. T20 BB 2-22.

‡FERLEY, Robert Steven (King Edward VII HS; Sutton Valence S; Grey C, Durham U), b Norwich, Norfolk 4 Feb 1982. 5'8". RHB, SLA. Durham UCCE 2001-03. British U 2001-03. Kent 2003-06. Norfolk 1998. HS 78* DU v Durham (Chester-le-St) 2003. BB 6-136 K v Middx (Canterbury) 2006. LO HS 42 K v Lancs (Manchester) 2004 (NL). LO BB 4-33 K v Yorks (Scarborough) 2006 (P40). T20 HS 16*. T20 BB 1-9.

NQ**FLEMING, Stephen** Paul (Cashmere HS, Canterbury; Christchurch C of Ed), b Christchurch, New Zealand 1 Apr 1973. 6'3". LHB, RSM. Canterbury 1991-92 to 1999-00. Middlesex 2001; cap 2001. Wellington 2001-02 to date. Yorkshire 2003. Nottinghamshire debut/cap 2005; captain 2005 to date. **Tests** (NZ): 104 (1993-94 to 2006-07, 80 as captain); HS 274* v SL (Colombo) 2002-03. **LOI** (NZ): 269 (1993-94 to 2006-07, 205 as captain); HS 134* v SA (Johannesburg) 2002-03; BB 1-8. F-c Tours (NZ) (C=captain): E 1994, 1999C, 2004C; A 1997-98C, 2001-02C, 2004-05C; SA 1993-94 (Cant), 1994-95, 2000-01C, 2005-06C; WI 1995-96, 2002C; I 1995-96, 1999-00C, 2003-04C; P 1996-97, 2002C; SL 1998C, 2003C; Z 1997-98C, 2000-01C, 2005C; B 2004-05C. 1000 runs (1): 1091 (2001). HS 274* (*see Tests*). UK HS 238 v Surrey (Oval) 2005. LO HS 139* Y v Warwks (Leeds) 2003 (NL). LO BB (NZ) 1-3. T20 HS 64*.

FOOTITT, Mark Harold Alan (Carlton le Willows S; West Notts C), b Nottingham 25 Nov 1985. 6'2". RHB, LFM. Debut (Nottinghamshire) 2005. MCC 2006. HS 19* v Hants (Southampton) 2005. BB 5-45 v WI A (Nottingham) 2006. CC BB 4-45 v Glamorgan (Nottingham) 2005 – on debut. LO HS (Nt CB) – . T20 HS – .

FRANKS, Paul John (Southwell Minster CS), b Mansfield 3 Feb 1979. 6'2". LHB, RMF. Debut (Nottinghamshire) 1996; cap 1999; benefit 2007. Canterbury 2002-03. YC 2000. **LOI**: 1 (2000); HS 4 v WI (Nottingham) 2000. F-c Tours (Eng A): SA 1998-99; WI 2000-01; NZ 1999-00; SL 2004-05; B 1999-00. HS 123* v Leics (Leicester) 2003. 50 wkts (2); most – 63 (1999). BB 7-56 v Middx (Lord's) 2000. Hat-trick 1997. LO HS 84* v Lincs (Lincoln) 2003 (CGT). LO BB 6-27 v Durham (Chester-le-St) 2000 (NL). T20 HS 29*. T20 BB 2-19.

GALLIAN, Jason Edward Riche (Pittwater House S, Sydney; Keble C, Oxford), b Manly, Sydney, Australia 25 Jun 1971. Qualified for England 1994. 6'0". RHB, RM. Lancashire 1990-97, taking wicket of D.A.Hagan (OU) with his first ball; cap 1994. Oxford U 1992-93; blue 1992-93; captain 1993. Combined U 1992-93. Nottinghamshire debut/cap 1998; captain 1998 (part) to 2004; benefit 2005. Captained Australia YC v England YC 1989-90, scoring 158* in 1st 'Test'. **Tests**: 3 (1995 to 1995-96); HS 28 v SA (Pt Elizabeth) 1995-96. F-c Tours: A 1996-97 (Eng A); WI 1995-96 (La); SA 1995-96 (part); I 1994-95 (Eng A); P 1995-96 (Eng A). 1000 runs (6); most – 1220 (2005). HS 312 La v Derbys (Manchester) 1996 (record score at Old Trafford). Nt HS 199 v Sussex (Nottingham) 2005. BB 6-115 La v Surrey (Southport) 1996. Nt BB 2-28 v Warwks (Nottingham) 1999. LO HS 134 La v Notts (Manchester) 1995 (BHC). LO BB 5-15 La v Minor C (Leek) 1995 (BHC). T20 HS 62.

HARRIS, Andrew James (Hadfield CS; Glossopdale Community C), b Ashton-under-Lyne, Lancs 26 Jun 1973. 6'1". RHB, RM. Derbyshire 1994-99; cap 1996. Nottinghamshire debut/cap 2000. F-c Tour (Eng A): A 1996-97. HS 41* v Northants (Northampton) 2002. Dismissed 'Timed Out' v DU (Nottingham) 2003 – third instance in f-c cricket. 50 wkts (2); most – 67 (2002). BB 7-54 (11-122 match) v Northants (Nottingham) 2002. LO HS 34 v Durham (Nottingham) 2006 (CGT). LO BB 5-35 v Hants (Nottingham) 2000 (NL). T20 HS 6. T20 BB 2-13.

NQ**HUSSEY, David** John, b Morley, Perth, Australia 15 Jul 1977. Younger brother of M.E.K.Hussey (WA, Northants, Glos, Durham and Australia 1994-95 to date). RHB, OB. Victoria 2002-03 to date. Nottinghamshire debut/cap 2004, scoring 107* v Oxford UCCE (Oxford) – UK debut. 1000 runs (3); most – 1315 (2004). HS 232* v Warwks (Nottingham) 2005. Scored 170, 116 and 140 in successive innings 2004. BB 4-105 v Hants (Nottingham) 2005. LO HS 130 Vic v Q (Brisbane) 2005-06. LO BB 3-48 Sussex CB v Glos (Horsham) 2001 (CGT). T20 HS 86. T20 BB 2-22.

‡**JEFFERSON, William** Ingleby (Beeston Hall S, Norfolk; Oundle S; St Hild & St Bede C, Durham U), b Derby 25 Oct 1979. Son of R.I.Jefferson (Cambridge U and Surrey 1961-66); grandson of J.Jefferson (Army 1919, Comb Services 1922). 6'10½". RHB, RMF. British U 2000-02. Essex 2000-06; cap 2002. Durham UCCE 2001-02. Scored 50 and 65 in first two l-o innings. F-c Tour (Eng A): B 2006-07. 1000 runs (1): 1555 (2004). HS 222 Ex v Hants (Southampton) 2004. BB 1-16 (Ex – CC). LO HS 132 Ex v Essex CB (Chelmsford) 2003 (CGT). BB 2-9 Ex v Worcs (Worcester) 2005 (NL). T20 HS 51.

‡**MIERKALNS, Joshua** Aleck (Arnold Hill S), b Nottingham 11 Sep 1985. 6'0". RHB, RM. Debut (Nottinghamshire) 2006. HS 18 v West Indies A (Nottingham) 2006. Awaiting CC debut. LO HS 4 v Durham (Chester-le-St) 2006 (P40). T20 HS 4.

NOON, Wayne Michael (Caistor S), b Grimsby, Lincs 5 Feb 1971. 5'9". RHB, WK. Northamptonshire 1989-92. Nottinghamshire debut 1994; cap 1995; benefit 2003. Canterbury 1994-95. Worcs 2nd XI debut when aged 15yr 199d. F-c Tours: SA 1991-92 (Nh), 1996-97 (Nt). No f-c appearances 2004-05-06. HS 83 v Northants (Northampton) 1997. LO HS 46 v Warwks (Birmingham) 1998 (BHC). T20 HS 12.

PATEL, Samit Rohit (Worksop C), b Leicester 30 Nov 1984. 5'8". RHB, SLA. Debut (Nottinghamshire) 2002. No f-c appearances 2004. Notts 2nd XI debut 1999 when aged 14yr 274d. HS 173 v DU (Durham) 2006. CC HS 156 v Middx (Lord's) 2006. BB 3-73 v Kent (Nottingham) 2005. LO HS 93* v Scot (Nottingham) 2006 (CGT). LO BB 3-40 v Durham (Chester-le-St) 2006 (P40). T20 HS 65. T20 BB 3-11.

READ, Christopher Mark Wells (Torquay GS; Bath U), b Paignton, Devon 10 Aug 1978. 5'8". RHB, WK. Gloucestershire (l-o only) 1997. Debut 1997-98 for England A in Kenya. Nottinghamshire debut 1998; cap 1999. MCC 2002. Devon 1995-97. **Tests**: 15 (1999 to 2006-07); HS 55 v P (Leeds) 2006. Made six dismissals twice in successive innings 2006-07 to establish an Ashes record. **LOI**: 36 (1999-00 to 2006-07); HS 30* v SA (Manchester) 2003. F-c Tours: A 2006-07; SA 1998-99 (Eng A), 1999-00; WI 2000-01 (Eng A), 2003-04, 2005-06 (Eng A); SL 1997-98 (Eng A), 2002-03 (ECB Acad), 2003-04; Z 1998-99 (Eng A); B 2003-04; K 1997-98 (Eng A). HS 160 v Warwks (Nottingham) 1999. LO HS 135 v Durham (Nottingham) 2006 (CGT). T20 HS 48*.

SHAFAYAT, Bilal Mustapha (Greenwood Dale; Nottingham Bluecoat SFC), b Nottingham 10 Jul 1984. 5'7". RHB, RMF. Nottinghamshire 2001-04. National Bank of Pakistan 2004-05. Northamptonshire 2005-06. Captained Eng U-19 tour of Australia 2002-03. F-c Tour (Eng A): I 2003-04. 1000 runs (1): 1058 (2005). HS 161 Nh v Derbys (Derby) 2005. Nt HS 105 and BB 1-22 v DU (Nottingham) 2003. BB 2-25 Nh v P (Northampton) 2006. CC BB – . LO HS 97* Nh v Glos (Stowe) 2005 (NL). LO BB 4-33 Nh v Worcs (Worcester) 2005 (NL). T20 HS 40. T20 BB 2-13.

SHRECK, Charles Edward (Truro S), b Truro, Cornwall 6 Jan 1978. 6'7". RHB, RFM. Debut (Nottinghamshire) 2003; cap 2006. No appearances 2005 (injured). Wellington 2005-06. Cornwall 1997-2002. HS 19 v Essex (Chelmsford) 2003. BB 8-31 (12-129 match) v Middx (Nottingham) 2006. Hat-trick v Middx (Lord's) 2006. LO HS 9* Wellington v CD (Palmerston N) 2005-06. LO BB 5-19 Cornwall v Worcs (Truro) 2002 (CGT). Took 5-35 v Worcs (Nottingham) 2002 (NL) – on 1st XI debut. T20 HS 1*. T20 BB 3-33.

SIDEBOTTOM, Ryan Jay (King James's GS, Almondbury), b Huddersfield, Yorks 15 Jan 1978. Son of A.Sidebottom (Yorks, OFS and England 1973-91). 6'3". LHB, LFM. Yorkshire 1997-2003; cap 2000. Nottinghamshire debut/cap 2004. **Tests**: 1 (2001); HS 4 v P (Lord's) 2001. **LOI**: 2 (2001-02); HS 2*; BB 1-42 (twice). F-c Tour (Eng A): WI 2000-01. HS 54 Y v Glamorgan (Cardiff) 1998. Nt HS 33 v Durham (Chester-le-St) 2006. 50 wkts (2); most – 50 (2005, 2006). BB 7-97 Y v Derbys (Leeds) 2003. Nt BB 5-22 v Kent (Nottingham) 2006. LO HS 32 v Middx (Nottingham) 2005 (NL). LO BB 6-40 Y v Glamorgan(Cardiff) 1998 (SL). T20 HS 12*. T20 BB 3-20.

SWANN, Graeme Peter (Sponne SS, Towcester), b Northampton 24 Mar 1979. Son of R.Swann (Northumberland 1969-72; Bedfordshire 1988-95); younger brother of A.J.Swann (Northamptonshire and Lancashire 1996-2004). 6'0". RHB, OB. Northamptonshire 1998-2004; cap 1999. Nottinghamshire debut 2005. MCC 2005. Bedfordshire 1996. **LOI**: 1 (1999-00); dnb v SA (Bloemfontein) 1999-00. F-c Tours (Eng A): SA 1998-99, 1999-00 (Eng); WI 2000-01 (*part*); SL 2004-05; Z 1998-99. HS 183 Nh v Glos (Bristol) 2002 – including 114 before lunch on third day. Nt HS 85 v Kent (Canterbury) 2006. 50 wkts (1): 57 (1999). BB 7-33 Nh v Derbys (Northampton) 2003. Nt BB 6-57 v Warwks (Birmingham) 2005. LO HS 83 Nh v Leics (Northampton) 2001 (NL). LO BB 5-35 Nh v Durham (Chester-le-St) 1999 (NL). T20 HS 62. T20 BB 3-16.

‡**WAGH, Mark** Anant (King Edward's S, Birmingham; Keble C, Oxford), b Birmingham, Warwks 20 Oct 1976. 6'2". RHB, OB. Oxford U 1996-98; blue 1996-97-98; captain 1997. Warwickshire 1997-2006; cap 2000. British U 1996-1998. Mashonaland A 1998-99. 1000 runs (4); most – 1277 (2001). HS 315 Wa v Middx (Lord's) 2001. BB 7-222 Wa v Lancs (Birmingham) 2003. LO HS 102* Wa v Kent (Birmingham) 2004 (NL). LO BB 4-35 Wa v Glamorgan(Birmingham) 2004 (NL). T20 HS 56. T20 BB 2-16.

RELEASED/RETIRED

(Having made a first-class County appearance in 2006)

BICKNELL, Darren John (Robert Haining County SS; Guildford TC), b Guildford, Surrey 24 Jun 1967. Elder brother of M.P.Bicknell (Surrey and England 1986-2006). 6'4". LHB, SLA. Surrey 1987-99; cap 1990; benefit 1999. Nottinghamshire 2000-06; cap 2000. Lawrence Trophy 1989. F-c Tours (Eng A): WI 1991-92; P 1990-91; SL 1990-91; Z 1989-90. 1000 runs (9); most – 1888 (1991). HS 235* Sy v Notts (Nottingham) 1994. Nt HS 180* v Warwks (Birmingham) 2000 – sharing unbroken 1st wkt stand of 406 with G.E.Welton. BB 3-7 Sy v Sussex (Guildford) 1996. Nt BB 3-33 v Essex (Nottingham) 2004. LO HS 135* Sy v Yorks (Oval) 1989 (NWT). LO BB (Sy) 1-11 (SL). T20 HS 10.

McMAHON, Paul Joseph (Trinity RC CS, Nottingham; Wadham C, Oxford), b Wigan, Lancs 12 Mar 1983. 6'2". RHB, OB. Nottinghamshire 2002-06. Oxford UCCE 2003-04-05; captain 2004-05; blue 2003-04-05. British U 2004. HS 99 OU v CU (Oxford) 2004. Nt HS 30 v Middlesex (Lord's) 2003. BB 5-30 OU v CU (Cambridge) 2005. Nt BB 4-59 v Essex (Chelmsford) 2003. LO HS 8 (P40). T20 HS – . T20 BB 1-22.

SMITH, W.R. – *see DURHAM.*

SINGH, Anurag (King Edward's, Birmingham; Gonville & Caius C, Cambridge), b Kanpur, India 9 Sep 1975. 5'11½". RHB, OB. Warwickshire 1995-2000. Cambridge U 1996-98; blue 1996-97-98; captain 1997-98. British U 1996-98; captain 1998). Worcestershire 2001-03. Nottinghamshire 2004-06. 1000 runs (2); most – 1167 (2002). HS 187 Wo v Glos (Bristol) 2002. Nt HS 131 v LU (Nottingham) 2005. LO HS 123 Brit U v Somerset (Taunton) 1996 (BHC). T20 HS 35.

[NQ]**SMITH, Gregory** James (Pretoria BHS; Pretoria Technikon), b Pretoria, South Africa 30 Oct 1971. ECB qualified – British passport. 6'4". RHB, LFM. N Transvaal/Northerns 1993-94 to 2001-02. Nottinghamshire 2001-06; cap 2001. F-c Tour (SA A): E 1996. HS 68 NT v WP (Pretoria) 1995-96. Nt HS 44* v Sussex (Nottingham) 2001. 50 wkts (3): most – 51 (2003, 2005). BB 8-53 (11-74 match) v Essex (Nottingham) 2002. LO HS 20 v Glamorgan (Nottingham) 2006 (P40). LO BB 5-11 NT v GW (Kimberley) 1995-96. T20 HS 11*. T20 BB 1-17.

WARREN, Russell John (Kingsthorpe Upper S), b Northampton 10 Sep 1971. 6'1". RHB, OB, WK. Northamptonshire 1992-2002; cap 1995. Nottinghamshire 2003-06; cap 2004. 1000 runs (1): 1303 (2001). HS 201* Nh v Glamorgan(Northampton) 1996. Nt HS 134 v Leics (Nottingham) 2004. LO HS 100* Nh v Ire (Northampton) 1994 (NWT). T20 HS 26.

NORTHAMPTON RELEASED/RETIRED (continued from p 73)

(Having made a first-class County appearance in 2006)

[NQ]**GANGULY, Sourav** Chandidas (St Xavier's Collegiate S), b Calcutta, India 8 Jul 1972. Younger brother of Snehasish C. Ganguly (Bengal 1986-87 to 1996-97). 5'11". LHB, RM. Bengal 1989-90 to date. East Zone 1990-91 to 2005-06. Lancashire 2000. Glamorgan 2005. Northamptonshire 2006. **Tests** (I): 91 (1996 to 2006-07, 49 as captain); HS 173 v SL (Bombay) 1997-98; BB 3-28 v A (Calcutta) 1997-98. **LOI** (I): 285 (1991-92 to 2006-07, 146 as captain); HS 183 v SL (Taunton) 1999; BB 5-16 v P (Toronto) 1997-98. F-c Tours (I) (C=captain): E 1996, 2002C; A 1991-92, 1999-00, 2003-04C; SA 1996-97, 2001-02C, 2006-07; WI 1996-97, 2001-02C; NZ 1998-99, 2002-03C; P 2003-04C, 2005-06; SL 1997, 1998-99, 2001C; Z 1998-99; 2001C, 2005-06C; B 2000-01C, 2004-05C. HS 200* Bengal v Tripura (Calcutta) 1993-94 and 200* Bengal v Bihar (Calcutta) 1994-95. UK HS 142 Gm v Kent (Cardiff) 2005. Nh HS 9. BB 6-46 Bengal v Orissa (Calcutta) 2000-01. UK BB 3-10 Ind v Hants (Southampton) 2002. CC BB 3-68 Gm v Notts (Nottingham) 2005. Nh BB 1-19. LO HS 183 (*see LOI*). LO BB 5-16 (*see LOI*). T20 HS 73. T20 BB 3-27.

PHILLIPS, B.J. – *see SOMERSET.*

[NQ]**NICHOLSON, M.J.** – *see SURREY.*

[NQ]**PIETERSEN, Charl** (Northern Cape HS, Kimberley), b Kimberley, South Africa 6 Jan 1983. Elder brother of R.Pietersen (Griqualand West 2005-06). 5'8". LHB, LMF. Griqualand West 2001-02 to 2006-07. Northamptonshire 2005-06 (Kolpak registration). HS 54 GW v Northerns (Kimberley) 2006-07. UK HS 39* Nh v Surrey (Northampton) 2006. BB 6-43 GW v Boland (Kimberley) 2002-03. UK BB 3-74 Nh v B (Northampton) 2005. CC BB 1-31. LO HS 26* GW v Easterns (Benoni) 2006-07. LO BB 7-10 Nh v Denmark (Brondby) 2005 (Nh CGT record). T20 HS 3*. T20 BB 3-35.

SHAFAYAT, B. – *see NOTTINGHAMSHIRE.*

M.J.Phythian and A.R.White left the staff without making a f-c appearance for the County in 2006.

NOTTINGHAMSHIRE 2006

RESULTS SUMMARY

	Place	Won	Lost	Tied	Drew	No Result
County Championship (1st Division)	**8th**	4	7		5	
All First-Class Matches		6	7		6	
C & G Trophy (North Conference)	4th	4	2			3
Pro40 League (1st Division)	4th	4	3			1
Twenty20 Cup (North Division)	Finalist	8	3			

COUNTY CHAMPIONSHIP AVERAGES

BATTING AND FIELDING

Cap		*M*	*I*	*NO*	*HS*	*Runs*	*Avge*	*100*	*50*	*Ct/St*
2004	D.J.Hussey	16	26	4	164	1103	50.13	5	1	12
2005	S.P.Fleming	13	22	2	192	992	49.60	2	8	17
–	S.R.Patel	6	10	1	156	373	41.44	1	1	3
–	D.Alleyne	10	18	1	109*	537	31.58	1	4	26/5
2000	D.J.Bicknell	15	25	–	95	723	28.92	–	4	2
–	G.P.Swann	13	19	1	85	510	28.33	–	3	5
1999	C.M.W.Read	9	14	2	102*	329	27.41	1	2	27
2004	M.A.Ealham	16	24	2	101*	595	27.04	1	4	11
–	W.R.Smith	11	17	–	141	437	25.70	1	1	7
2004	R.J.Warren	3	5	–	93	109	21.80	–	1	1
1998	J.E.R.Gallian	12	21	–	114	438	20.85	1	2	16
1999	P.J.Franks	11	17	1	64	282	17.62	–	2	–
2004	R.J.Sidebottom	13	20	5	33	200	13.33	–	–	5
2000	A.J.Harris	12	17	2	28*	119	7.93	–	–	2
2001	G.J.Smith	4	4	–	17	19	4.75	–	–	1
2006	C.E.Shreck	11	15	10	5*	11	2.20	–	–	4

Also batted (1 match): M.H.A.Footitt 0*.

BOWLING

	O	*M*	*R*	*W*	*Avge*	*Best*	*5wI*	*10wM*
M.A.Ealham	335.4	93	896	42	21.33	5-59	2	–
C.E.Shreck	416.4	83	1505	54	27.87	8-31	4	2
R.J.Sidebottom	444.5	122	1181	41	28.80	5-22	1	–
A.J.Harris	330.5	66	1099	36	30.52	5-53	1	–
G.P.Swann	401.5	85	1107	24	46.12	4-54	–	–
P.J.Franks	228.5	38	876	12	73.00	2-24	–	–
Also bowled:								
D.J.Hussey	44	3	231	5	46.20	2-66	–	–

M.H.A.Footitt 11-0-62-0; S.R.Patel 44.1-11-129-2; G.J.Smith 78.2-18-253-2.

The First-Class Averages (pp 130–146) give the records of Nottinghamshire players in all first-class matches for the county (Nottinghamshire's other opponents being the MCC, Durham UCCE and West Indies A), with the exception of:

M.H.A.Footitt 2-1-1-0*-0 ∞ 0-0-0ct. 23-1-107-5-21.40-5/45-1-0.
C.M.W.Read 10-16-3-110*-451-34.69-2-2-32ct-0st. Did not bowl.

NOTTINGHAMSHIRE RECORDS

FIRST-CLASS CRICKET

Highest Total	For 739-7d		v	Leics	Nottingham	1903
	V 781-7d		by	Northants	Northampton	1995
Lowest Total	For 13		v	Yorkshire	Nottingham	1901
	V 16		by	Derbyshire	Nottingham	1879
	16		by	Surrey	The Oval	1880
Highest Innings	For 312*	W.W.Keeton	v	Middlesex	The Oval	1939
	V 345	C.G.Macartney	for	Australians	Nottingham	1921

Highest Partnership for each Wicket

1st	406*	D.J.Bicknell/G.E.Welton	v	Warwicks	Birmingham	2000
2nd	398	A.Shrewsbury/W.Gunn	v	Sussex	Nottingham	1890
3rd	369	W.Gunn/J.R.Gunn	v	Leics	Nottingham	1903
4th	361	A.O.Jones/J.R.Gunn	v	Essex	Leyton	1905
5th	266	A.Shrewsbury/W.Gunn	v	Sussex	Hove	1884
6th	372*	K.P.Pietersen/J.E.Morris	v	Derbyshire	Derby	2001
7th	301	C.C.Lewis/B.N.French	v	Durham	Chester-le-St	1993
8th	220	G.F.H.Heane/R.Winrow	v	Somerset	Nottingham	1935
9th	170	J.C.Adams/K.P.Evans	v	Somerset	Taunton	1994
10th	152	E.B.Alletson/W.Riley	v	Sussex	Hove	1911
	152	U.Afzaal/A.J.Harris	v	Worcs	Nottingham	2000

Best Bowling	For	10-66	K.Smales	v	Glos	Stroud	1956
(Innings)	V	10-10	H.Verity	for	Yorkshire	Leeds	1932
Best Bowling	For	17-89	F.C.Matthews	v	Northants	Nottingham	1923
(Match)	V	17-89	W.G.Grace	for	Glos	Cheltenham	1877

Most Runs – Season	2620	W.W.Whysall	(av 53.46)	1929
Most Runs – Career	31592	G.Gunn	(av 35.69)	1902-32
Most 100s – Season	9	W.W.Whysall		1928
	9	M.J.Harris		1971
	9	B.C.Broad		1990
Most 100s – Career	65	J.Hardstaff jr		1930-55
Most Wkts – Season	181	B.Dooland	(av 14.96)	1954
Most Wkts – Career	1653	T.G.Wass	(av 20.34)	1896-1920
Most Career W-K Dismissals	957	T.W.Oates	(733 ct/224 st)	1897-1925
Most Career Catches in the Field	466	A.O.Jones		1892-1914

LIMITED-OVERS CRICKET

Highest Total	**CGT**	344-6		v	Northumb	Jesmond	1994
	P40	329-6		v	Derbyshire	Nottingham	1993
	T20	213-6		v	Northants	Nottingham	2006
Lowest Total	**CGT**	123		v	Yorkshire	Scarborough	1969
	P40	66		v	Yorkshire	Bradford	1969
	T20	91		v	Lancashire	Manchester	2006
Highest Innings	**CGT**	149*	D.W.Randall	v	Devon	Torquay	1988
	P40	167*	P.Johnson	v	Kent	Nottingham	1993
	T20	91	M.A.Ealham	v	Yorkshire	Nottingham	2004
Best Bowling	**CGT**	6-10	K.P.Evans	v	Northumb	Jesmond	1994
	P40	6-12	R.J.Hadlee	v	Lancashire	Nottingham	1980
	T20	5-26	R.J.Logan	v	Lancashire	Nottingham	2003

SOMERSET

Formation of Present Club: 18 August 1875
Inaugural First-Class Match: 1882
Colours: Black, White and Maroon
Badge: Somerset Dragon
County Champions: (0); best – 2nd (Div 1) 2001
Gillette/NatWest/C & G Trophy Winners: (3) 1979, 1983, 2001
Benson and Hedges Cup Winners: (2) 1981, 1982
Pro 40/National League (Div 1) Winners: (0); best – 4th 2001
Sunday League Winners: (1) 1979
Twenty20 Cup Winners: (1) 2005

Chief Executive: Richard A.Gould, County Ground, Taunton TA1 1JT • Tel: 01823 272946 • Fax: 01823 332395 • Email: enquiries@somersetcountycc.co.uk • Web: www.somersetcountycc.co.uk

Director of Cricket: Brian C.Rose. **Captain**: J.L.Langer. **Vice-Captain**: tba. **Overseas Players**: J.L.Langer and C.L.White. **2007 Beneficiary**: none. **Head Groundsman**: Phil Frost. **Scorer**: Gerald A.Stickley. ‡ New registration. NQ Not qualified for England.

ANDREW, Gareth Mark (Ansford Community S; Richard Huish C), b Yeovil 27 Dec 1983. 6'0". LHB, RMF. Debut (Somerset) 2003. No f-c appearances 2006. Somerset 2nd XI debut 1999 when aged 15y 247d. HS 44 and BB 4-63 v SL A (Taunton) 2004. CC HS 32 v Lancs (Taunton) 2005. CC BB 4-134 v Derbys (Taunton) 2005. LO HS 33 v Leics (Leicester) 2006 (P40). LO BB 4-48 v Scot (Taunton) 2004 (NL). T20 HS 12. T20 BB 4-22.

BLACKWELL, Ian David (Brookfield Community S), b Chesterfield, Derbys 10 Jun 1978. 6'2". LHB, SLA. Derbyshire 1997-99. Somerset debut 2000; cap 2001; captain 2006 (*part*). **Tests**: 1 (2005-06): HS 4 v I (Nagpur) 2005-06. **LOI**: 34 (2002-03 to 2005-06); HS 82 v I (Colombo) 2002-03; BB 3-26 v A (Adelaide) 2002-03. F-c Tour: I 2005-06. 1000 runs (2); most – 1256 (2005). HS 247* v Derbys (Taunton) 2003 – off 156 balls and including 204 off 98 balls in reduced post-lunch session. Won Walter Lawrence Trophy 2005 for 67-ball hundred v Derbys (Taunton). BB 7-90 v Glamorgan (Taunton) 2004 and 7-90 v Notts (Nottingham) 2004. LO HS 134* v Sussex (Taunton) 2005 (NL). LO BB 5-26 v Derbys (Taunton) 2005 (NL). T20 HS 82. T20 BB 4-26.

CADDICK, Andrew Richard (Papanui HS), b Christchurch, NZ 21 Nov 1968. Son of English emigrants – qualified for England 1992. 6'5". RHB, RFM. Debut (Somerset) 1991; cap 1992; benefit 1999. Represented NZ in 1987-88 Youth World Cup. *Wisden* 2000. **Tests**: 62 (1993 to 2002-03); HS 49* v A (Birmingham) 2001; BB 7-46 v SA (Durban) 1999-00. **LOI**: 54 (1993 to 2002-03); HS 36 v A (Oval) 2001; BB 4-19 v SA (Johannesburg) 1999-00. F-c Tours: A 1992-93 (Eng A), 2002-03; SA 1999-00; WI 1993-94, 1997-98; NZ 1996-97, 2001-02; P 2000-01; SL 2000-01; Z 1996-97. HS 92 v Worcs (Worcester) 1995. 50 wkts (11) inc 100 (1): 105 (1998). BB 9-32 (12-120 match) v Lancs (Taunton) 1993. LO HS 39 v Hants (Taunton) 1996 (SL). LO BB 6-30 v Glos (Taunton) 1992 (NWT). T20 HS 0. T20 BB 2-12.

NQ**CULLEN, Daniel** James, b Woodville, Adelaide, Australia 10 Apr 1984. RHB, OB. S Australia 2004-05 to date. Somerset debut 2006. **Tests** (A): 1 (2005-06); HS – and BB 1-25 v B (Chittagong) 2005-06. **LOI** (A): 5 (2005-06 to 2006-07); HS 2*; BB 2-25 v B (Fatullah) 2005-06. F-c Tours (A): P 2005-06 (Aus A); B 2005-06. HS 42 S Aus v Tas (Hobart) 2004-05. BB 5-38 S Aus v WA (Perth) 2004-05. LO HS 27* S Aus v Tas (Launceston) 2006-07. LO BB 3-28 S Aus v Vic (Melbourne) 2005-06. T20 HS 10. T20 BB 3-23.

DURSTON, Wesley John (Millfield S; University C, Worcester), b Taunton 6 Oct 1980. 5'10". RHB, OB. Debut (Somerset) 2002. HS 146* v Derbys (Derby) 2005. BB 3-23 v SL A (Taunton) 2004. CC BB 2-31 v Surrey (Bath) 2006. LO HS 62* v Yorks (Taunton) 2006 (P40). LO BB 3-44 v Surrey (Taunton) 2006 (P40). T20 HS 34. T20 BB 3-25.

EDWARDS, Neil James (Cape Cornwall CS; Richard Huish C), b Treliske, Cornwall 14 Oct 1983. 6'3". LHB, RM. Debut (Somerset) 2002. Cornwall 2000-06. HS 160 v Hants (Taunton) 2003. BB 1-16. LO HS 65 v Yorks (Taunton) 2006 (P40). T20 HS 1.

FRANCIS, John Daniel (King Edward VI S, Southampton; Durham U; Loughborough U), b Bromley, Kent 13 Nov 1980. Younger brother of S.R.G.Francis (*see SOMERSET DEPARTURES*). LHB, SLA. Hampshire 2001-03. British U 2002-03. Loughborough UCCE 2003. Somerset debut 2004. 1000 (1): 1062 (2005). HS 125* v Yorks (Leeds) 2005 – carrying bat. BB (H) 1-1. Sm BB 1-4. LO HS 103* H v Northants (Southampton) 2002 (NL). T20 HS 49.

GAZZARD, Carl Matthew (Mounts Bay CS, Penzance; Richard Huish C), b Penzance, Cornwall 15 Apr 1982. 6'0". RHB, WK. Debut (Somerset) 2002. Cornwall 1998-2005. HS 74 v Worcs (Worcester) 2005. LO HS 157 v Derbys (Derby) 2004 (NL). T20 HS 39.

HILDRETH James Charles (Millfield S), b Milton Keynes, Bucks 9 Sep 1984. 5'10", RHB, RMF. Debut (Somerset) 2003. HS 227* v Northants (Taunton) 2006. BB 2-39 v Hants (Taunton) 2004. LO HS 122 v Derbys (Derby) 2006 (P40). LO BB 1-20 v Glos (Taunton) 2006 (CGT). T20 HS 71. T20 BB 3-24.

JONES, Philip **Steffan** (Stradey CS, Llanelli; Neath TC; Loughborough U; Homerton C, Cambridge), b Llanelli, Carms, Wales 9 Feb 1974. 6'2". RHB, RMF. Cambridge U 1997; blue 1997. Somerset 1997-2003; cap 2001. Northamptonshire 2004-05. Wales MC 1994-95. HS 105 v NZ (Taunton) 1999. CC HS Sm v Northants (Taunton) 2003. 50 wkts (2): 59 (2001, 2006). BB 6-25 De v Glamorgan (Cardiff) 2006. Sm BB 6-110 (match 10-156) v Warwks (Birmingham) 2002. LO HS 27 v Northants (Northampton) 2000 (NL). LO BB 6-56 Nh v Ire (Clontarf) 2004 (CGT). T20 HS 24*. T20 BB 3-26.

‡**KIESWETTER, Craig** (Diocesan C; Millfield S), b Johannesburg, South Africa 18 Nov 1987. 6'1". RHB, WK. Represented South Africa in U-19 World Cup 2006.

NQ**LANGER, Justin** Lee (Aquinas C; U of WA), b Perth, Australia 21 Nov 1970. Nephew of R.S.Langer (W Australia 1973-74 to 1981-82). 5'8". LHB, RM. W Australia 1991-92 to date. Middlesex 1998-2000; cap 1998; captain 2000. Somerset debut 2006; captain 2007. *Wisden* 2000. **Tests** (A): 104 (1992-93 to 2005-06); HS 250 v E (Melbourne) 2002-03. **LOI**: 8 (1993-94 to 1997); HS 36 v I (Sharjah) 1993-94. F-c Tours (A): E 1995 (Young A), 1997, 2001, 2005; SA 1996-97, 2001-02, 2005-06; WI 1994-95, 1998-99, 2002-03; NZ 1992-93, 1999-00, 2004-05; I 2000-01, 2004-05; P 1994-95, 1998-99, 2002-03 (*in UAE*); SL 1999, 2002-03, 2003-04; Z 1999-00. 1000 runs (3+6); most – 1472 (2000). HS 342 v Surrey (Guildford) 2006 – Somerset record f-c score. BB 2-17 Aus A v SA A (Brisbane) 1997-98. UK BB 1-10 M v Northants (Northampton) 1998. LO HS 146 WA v S Aus (Perth) 1999-00 (MM). LO BB 3-51 v Surrey (Guildford) 1998 (SL). T20 HS 97.

LETT, Robin Jonathan (Millfield S; Oxford Brookes U), b Westminster, London 23 Dec 1986. 6'2". RHB, RM. Debut (Somerset) 2006. HS 50 v Glamorgan (Taunton) 2006 – on debut.

MUNDAY, Michael Kenneth (Truro S, Cornwall; Corpus Christi C, Oxford), b Nottingham 22 Oct 1984. 5'7½". RHB, LB. Oxford U 2003-06; blue 2003-04-05-06. Somerset debut 2005. Cornwall 2001 to date. HS 17* and BB 6-77 (11-143 match) OU v CU (Oxford) 2006. Sm HS 5*. Sm BB 3-83 v Essex (Southend) 2006. LO HS – and BB 1-39 Cornwall v Sussex (Truro) 2001 (CGT).

PARSONS, Keith Alan (The Castle S, Taunton; Richard Huish C), b Taunton 2 May 1973. Identical twin brother of K.J.Parsons (Somerset staff 1992-94). 6'1". RHB, RM. Debut (Somerset) 1992; cap 1999; benefit 2004. HS 193* v WI (Taunton) 2000. CC HS 153 v Essex (Taunton) 2006. BB 5-13 v Lancs (Taunton) 2000. LO HS 121 v Worcs (Taunton) 2002 (CGT). LO BB 5-39 v Derbys (Derby) 2004 (NL). T20 HS 57*. T20 BB 3-12.

‡**PHILLIPS, Ben** James (Langley Park S and SFC, Beckenham), b Lewisham, London 30 Sep 1974. 6'6". RHB, RFM. Kent 1996-98. Northamptonshire 2002-06; cap 2005. HS 100* K v Lancs (Manchester) 1997. BB 6-29 Nh v CU (Cambridge) 2006. CC BB 5-47 K v Sussex (Horsham) 1997. LO HS 44* Nh v Kent (Canterbury) 2004 (NL). LO BB 4-25 K v Northants (Canterbury) 2000 (NL). T20 HS 41*. T20 BB 4-18.

‡**SPURWAY, Samuel** Harold Patrick (Richard Huish C), b Taunton 13 Mar 1987. 6'0". LHB, WK. Debut (Somerset) 2006. HS 83 v Northants (Taunton) 2006. LO HS 31 v Leics (Leicester) 2006 (P40). T20 HS 15*.

SUPPIAH, Arul Vivasvan (Exeter U), b Kuala Lumpur, Malaysia 30 Aug 1983. Son of R.Suppiah (Kuala Lumpur). Brother of R.V.Suppiah (Malaysia 1997-98 to 2006; f-c 2004). 6'0". RHB, SLA. Somerset debut (Somerset) 2002. Malaysia 2000-01 to 2005 (not f-c). Devon 2003-05. HS 123 v Derbys (Derby) 2005. BB 3-46 v WI A (Taunton) 2002. CC BB 2-36 v Leics (Leicester) 2004. LO HS 79 v Derbys (Derby) 2005 (NL). LO BB 4-39 v Surrey (Oval) 2006 (CGT). T20 HS 18*. T20 BB 2-14.

TREGO, Peter David (Wyvern CS, W-s-M), b Weston-super-Mare 12 Jun 1981. 6'0". RHB, RMF. Somerset 2000-02, 2006; 2nd XI debut 1997 when aged 16y 20d. Kent 2003. Middlesex 2005. HS 140 v West Indies A (Taunton) 2002. CC HS 135 v Derbys (Taunton) 2006. BB 6-59 M v Notts (Nottingham) 2005. Sm BB 4-84 v Yorks (Scarborough) 2000. LO HS 31* and BB 4-39 K v Leics (Canterbury) 2003 (NL). T20 HS 47. T20 BB 2-17.

TRESCOTHICK, Marcus Edward (Sir Bernard Lovell S), b Keynsham 25 Dec 1975. 6'2". LHB, RM. Debut (Somerset) 1993; cap 1999; joint captain 2002. PCA 2000. *Wisden* 2004. MBE 2005. **ECB central contract 2007**. **Tests**: 76 (2000 to 2006, 2 as captain); HS 219 v SA (Oval) 2003; BB 1-34. **LOI**: 123 (2000 to 2006, 10 as captain); HS 137 v P (Lord's) 2001; BB 2-7 v Z (Manchester) 2000. F-c Tours: A 2002-03; SA 2004-05; WI 2003-04; NZ 1999-00 (Eng A), 2001-02; I 2001-02, 2005-06; P 2000-01, 2005-06; SL 2000-01, 2003-04; B 1999-00 (Eng A), 2003-04. HS 219 (*see Tests*). Sm HS 190 v Middx (Taunton) 1999. BB 4-36 (inc hat-trick) v Young A (Taunton) 1995. CC BB 4-82 v Yorks (Leeds) 1998. Hat-trick 1995. LO HS 158 v Kent (Canterbury) 2006 (CGT). LO BB 4-50 v Northants (Northampton) 2000 (NL). T20 HS 72.

‡**TURNER, Mark** Leif (Thornhill CS), b Sunderland 23 Oct 1984. 5'11". RHB, RMF. Durham 2005-06. HS 18 and CC BB 1-47 Du v Essex (Chester-le-St) 2005 – on debut. BB 2-51 Du v Oxford UCCE (Oxford) 2006. T20 HS – . T20 BB – .

NQ**WHITE, Cameron** Leon, b Bairnsdale, Victoria, Australia 18 Aug 1983. 6'1½". RHB, LBG. Victoria 2000-01 to date. Somerset debut/cap 2006; captain 2006 (*part*). **LOI** (A): 16 (2005-06 to 2006-07); HS 45 v NZ (Hobart) 2006-07; BB 1-5. HS 260* v Derbys (Derby) 2006 – world record score in the fourth innings of a f-c match. BB 6-66 Vic v WA (Perth) 2002-03. LO HS 126* Vic v NSW (Canberra) 2006-07. LO BB 4-15 Vic v Tas (Melbourne) 2004-05. T20 HS 141*. T20 BB 3-8.

‡NQ**WILLOUGHBY, Charl** Myles (Wynberg BHS; Stellenbosch U), b Cape Town, South Africa 3 Dec 1974. 6'2". LHB, LMF. Boland 1994-95 to 1999-00. W Province 2000-01 to 2003-04. MCC 2001, 2004. WP-Boland 2004-05. Leicestershire 2005 (Kolpak registration). Cape Cobras 2005-06 to date. Somerset debut 2006 (Kolpak). Berkshire 2000. **Tests** (SA): 2 (2003); HS – ; BB 1-47 v B (Chittagong) 2002-03 – on debut. **LOI** (SA): 3 (1999-00 to 2003); HS 0; BB 2-39 v P (Sharjah) 1999-00 – on debut. F-c Tours (SA): E 2003; WI 2000 (SA A); Z 1998-99 (SA Acad), 2004 (SA A); B 2003. HS 47 v Worcs (Taunton) 2006. 50 wkts (1+2); most – 66 (2006). BB 7-44 v Glos (Taunton) 2006. LO HS 12* v Middx (Bath) 2006 (CGT). LO BB 6-16 Le v Somerset (Leicester) 2005 (NL). T20 HS 11. T20 BB 4-9.

WOOD, Matthew James (Exmouth Community C; Exeter U), b Exeter, Devon 30 Sep 1980. 5'11". RHB, OB. Debut (Somerset) 2001; cap 2005. 2nd XI debut 1997 when aged 16y 345d. Devon 1998-2004. 1000 (1): 1058 (2005). HS 297 v Yorks (Taunton) 2005. LO HS 129 v Yorks (Taunton) 2005 (NL). T20 HS 94.

WOODMAN, Robert James (Castle School; Taunton; Richard Huish S), b Taunton 12 Oct 1986. 5'11". LHB, LMF. Debut (Somerset) 2005. No 1st XI appearances 2006. Devon 2006. HS 46* v Worcs (Worcester) 2005 – on debut. BB 1-78. LO HS – . LO BB 1-38 (NL). T20 HS 1*. T20 BB 2-37.

RELEASED/RETIRED

(Registered players who made a first-class County appearance in 2006)

FRANCIS, Simon Richard George (Yardley Court, Tonbridge; King Edward VI S, Southampton; Durham U), b Bromley, Kent 15 Aug 1978. Elder brother of J.D.Francis. 6'2". RHB, RMF. Hampshire 1997-2000. British U 1998-99. Somerset 2002-06. F-c Tour (Eng A): I 2003-04. HS 44 v Yorks (Taunton) 2003. BB 5-42 v Glamorgan (Taunton) 2004. Hat-trick 2003. LO HS 33* v Derbys (Taunton) 2003 (NL). LO BB 8-66 v Derbys (Derby) 2004 (CGT) – record l-o Sm analysis. T20 HS 9*. T20 BB 2-22.

JOHNSON, R.L. – *see MIDDLESEX.*

M.Parsons left the staff without making a first-class appearance in 2006.

MIDDLESEX RELEASED/RETIRED (continued from p 68)

SAVILL, Thomas Edward (Bilborough C; Homerton C, Cambridge), b Sheffield, Yorks 16 May 1983. 6'6". RHB, RFM. Cambridge UCCE 2002-06, blue 2003-04-05-06. Nottinghamshire 2002 – no CC appearance. Middlesex summer contract 2003-05 – no 1st XI appearances. HS 59 CU v CU (Cambridge) 2005. BB 4-62 CU v Northants (Cambridge) 2006. LO HS 35* Notts CB v Oxon (Oxford) 2001 (CGT). LO BB 1-45 (Notts CB – CGT).

NQ**STYRIS, Scott** Bernard (Hamilton BHS), b Brisbane, Australia 10 Jul 1975. 5'10". RHB, RMF. Northern Districts 1994-95 to 2004-05. Middlesex 2005-06; cap 2006. Auckland 2005-06. **Tests** (NZ): 27 (2002 to 2005-6); HS 170 v SA (Auckland) 2003-04; BB 3-28 v I (Wellington) 2002-03. **LOI** (NZ): 123 (1999-00 to 2006-07); HS 141 v SL (Bloemfontein) 2002-03; BB 6-25 v WI (Pt-of-Spain) 2002. F-c Tours (NZ): E 2000 (NZ A), 2004; A 2004-05; SA 2000-01, 2005-06; WI 2002; I 2003-04; SL 2002-03; Z 2005; B 2004-05. HS 212* ND v Otago (Hamilton) 2001-02. UK HS 133 and BB 6-71 v Lancs (Lord's) 2006. BB 6-32 ND v Otago (Gisborne) 1999-00. LO HS 141 (*see LOI*). LO BB 6-25 (*see LOI*). T20 HS 73*. T20 BB 3-25.

WEEKES, Paul Nicholas (Homerton House SS, Hackney), b Hackney, London 8 Jul 1969. 5'10". LHB, OB. Middlesex 1990-2006; cap 1993; benefit 2002. F-c Tour (Eng A): I 1994-95. 1000 runs (2); most – 1218 (1996). HS 171* v Somerset (Uxbridge) 1996. BB 8-39 v Glamorgan (Lord's) 1996. LO HS 143* v Cornwall (St Austell) 1995 (NWT). LO BB 4-17 v Kent (Lord's) 2001 (BHC). T20 HS 56. T20 BB 3-29.

C.M.P.Jones, A.P.Nambiar and A.D.Poynter left the staff without making a f-c appearance in 2006.

SOMERSET 2006

RESULTS SUMMARY

	Place	Won	Lost	Tied	Drew	No Result
County Championship (2nd Division)	**9th**	3	9		4	
All First-Class Matches		3	9		4	
C & G Trophy (South Conference)	6th	4	4			1
Pro40 League (2nd Division)	7th	2	6			
Twenty20 Cup (Mid/West/Wales Division)	5th	2	5	1		

COUNTY CHAMPIONSHIP AVERAGES

BATTING AND FIELDING

Cap		M	I	NO	HS	Runs	Avge	100	50	Ct/St
2006	C.L.White	12	22	2	260*	1190	59.50	5	3	6
–	S.H.P.Spurway	3	4	–	83	164	41.00	–	1	7
–	D.J.Cullen	4	6	4	24*	81	40.50	–	–	1
1999	K.A.Parsons	10	15	2	153	511	39.30	1	2	9
–	W.J.Durston	13	23	3	89	765	38.25	–	7	15
–	J.C.Hildreth	14	24	1	227*	798	34.69	1	3	11
1999	M.E.Trescothick	3	6	–	154	187	31.16	1	–	5
–	N.J.Edwards	7	10	–	77	309	30.90	–	2	4
–	P.D.Trego	12	20	–	135	596	29.80	3	2	5
–	A.V.Suppiah	12	19	–	99	563	29.63	–	4	6
2005	M.J.Wood	16	27	–	73	622	23.03	–	5	8
–	S.R.G.Francis	3	5	1	38	85	21.25	–	–	1
2001	R.L.Johnson	8	12	1	51	211	19.18	–	1	2
1992	A.R.Caddick	16	25	5	68	341	17.05	–	1	5
–	R.J.Lett	3	4	–	50	65	16.25	–	1	–
–	C.M.Gazzard	13	22	2	35	305	15.25	–	–	32
–	J.D.Francis	5	9	–	41	131	14.55	–	–	5
–	C.M.Willoughby	15	22	9	47	127	9.76	–	–	2
–	M.K.Munday	3	4	1	5*	9	3.00	–	–	–

Also batted (2 matches each): I.D.Blackwell (cap 2001) 49, 43; J.L.Langer 18, 30, 342 (1 ct).

BOWLING

	O	M	R	W	Avge	Best	5wI	10wM
C.M.Willoughby	498.3	121	1687	66	25.56	7- 44	3	–
K.A.Parsons	95	16	337	11	30.63	3- 33	–	–
R.L.Johnson	195.4	28	717	22	32.59	5- 37	1	–
A.R.Caddick	612.3	111	2282	63	36.22	5- 40	4	–
W.J.Durston	112.3	14	416	10	41.60	2- 31	–	–
C.L.White	186.5	19	723	15	48.20	5-148	1	–
P.D.Trego	242.5	34	965	19	50.78	3- 87	–	–
Also bowled:								
D.J.Cullen	119	17	381	7	54.42	5-137	1	–

I.D.Blackwell 46-7-139-3; N.J.Edwards 3-1-12-0; J.D.Francis 1-0-9-0; S.R.G.Francis 55-13-237-4; J.C.Hildreth 5-0-27-0; M.K.Munday 59-2-262-3; A.V.Suppiah 91-9-385-2.

Somerset played no fixtures outside the County Championship in 2006. The First-Class Averages (pp 130–146) give the records of their players in all first-class matches for the county, with the exception of M.K.Munday and M.E.Trescothick whose full county figures are as above.

SOMERSET RECORDS

FIRST-CLASS CRICKET

Highest Total	For 705-9d		v	Hampshire	Taunton	2003
	V 811		by	Surrey	The Oval	1899
Lowest Total	For 25		v	Glos	Bristol	1947
	V 22		by	Glos	Bristol	1920
Highest Innings	For 342	J.L.Langer	v	Surrey	Guildford	2006
	V 424	A.C.MacLaren	for	Lancashire	Taunton	1895

Highest Partnership for each Wicket

1st	346	H.T.Hewett/L.C.H.Palairet	v	Yorkshire	Taunton	1892
2nd	290	J.C.W.MacBryan/M.D.Lyon	v	Derbyshire	Burton upon T	1924
3rd	319	P.M.Roebuck/M.D.Crowe	v	Leics	Taunton	1984
4th	310	P.W.Denning/I.T.Botham	v	Glos	Taunton	1980
5th	320	J.D.Francis/I.D.Blackwell	v	Durham UCCE	Taunton	2005
6th	265	W.E.Alley/K.E.Palmer	v	Northants	Northampton	1961
7th	279	R.J.Harden/G.D.Rose	v	Sussex	Taunton	1997
8th	172	I.V.A.Richards/I.T.Botham	v	Leics	Leicester	1983
	172	A.R.K.Pierson/P.S.Jones	v	N Zealanders	Taunton	1999
9th	183	C.H.M.Greetham/H.W.Stephenson	v	Leics	Weston-s-Mare	1963
	183	C.J.Tavaré/N.A.Mallender	v	Sussex	Hove	1990
10th	163	I.D.Blackwell/N.A.M.McLean	v	Derbyshire	Taunton	2003

Best Bowling	For	10- 49	E.J.Tyler	v	Surrey	Taunton	1895
(Innings)	V	10- 35	A.Drake	for	Yorkshire	Weston-s-Mare	1914
Best Bowling	For	16- 83	J.C.White	v	Worcs	Bath	1919
(Match)	V	17-137	W.Brearley	for	Lancashire	Manchester	1905

Most Runs – Season	2761	W.E.Alley	(av 58.74)	1961
Most Runs – Career	21142	H.Gimblett	(av 36.96)	1935-54
Most 100s – Season	11	S.J.Cook		1991
Most 100s – Career	49	H.Gimblett		1935-54
Most Wkts – Season	169	A.W.Wellard	(av 19.24)	1938
Most Wkts – Career	2166	J.C.White	(av 18.02)	1909-37
Most Career W-K Dismissals	1007	H.W.Stephenson	(698 ct/309 st)	1948-64
Most Career Catches in the Field	381	J.C.White		1909-37

LIMITED-OVERS CRICKET

Highest Total	**CGT**	413-4		v	Devon	Torquay	1990
	P40	377-9		v	Sussex	Hove	2003
	T20	250-3		v	Glos	Taunton	2006
Lowest Total	**CGT**	58		v	Middlesex	Southgate	2000
	P40	58		v	Essex	Chelmsford	1977
	T20	119-9		v	Glos	Taunton	2003
Highest Innings	**CGT**	162*	C.J.Tavaré	v	Devon	Torquay	1990
	P40	175*	I.T.Botham	v	Northants	Wellingborough	1986
	T20	141*	C.L.White	v	Worcs	Worcester	2006
Best Bowling	**CGT**	8-66	S.R.G.Francis	v	Derbyshire	Derby	2004
	P40	6-24	I.V.A.Richards	v	Lancashire	Manchester	1983
	T20	4-15	A.W.Laraman	v	Worcs	Taunton	2004

SURREY

Formation of Present Club: 22 August 1845
Inaugural First-Class Match: 1864
Colours: Chocolate
Badge: Prince of Wales' Feathers
County Champions (since 1890): (18) 1890, 1891, 1892, 1894, 1895, 1899, 1914, 1952, 1953, 1954, 1955, 1956, 1957, 1958, 1971, 1999, 2000, 2002
Joint Champions: (1) 1950
Gillette/NatWest/C & G Trophy Winners: (1) 1982
Benson and Hedges Cup Winners: (3) 1974, 1997, 2001
Pro 40/National League (Div 1) Winners: (1) 2003
Sunday League Winners: (1) 1996
Twenty20 Cup Winners: (1) 2003

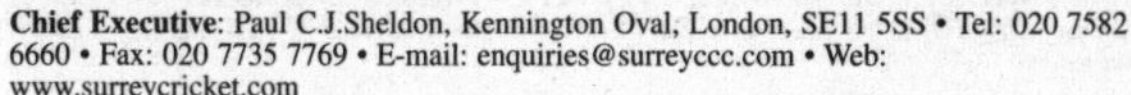

Chief Executive: Paul C.J.Sheldon, Kennington Oval, London, SE11 5SS • Tel: 020 7582 6660 • Fax: 020 7735 7769 • E-mail: enquiries@surreyccc.com • Web: www.surreycricket.com

First XI Coach: Alan R.Butcher. **Captain**: M.A.Butcher. **Vice-Captain**: R.Clarke. **Overseas Players**: Azhar Mahmood and M.J.Nicholson. **2007 Beneficiary**: I.D.K.Salisbury. **Head Groundsman**: W.H. (Bill) Gordon. **Scorer**: Keith R.Booth. ‡ New registration. [NQ] Not qualified for England.

[NQ]**AZHAR MAHMOOD** SAGAR (F.G. No. 1 HS, Islamabad), b Rawalpindi, Pakistan 28 Feb 1975. 5'11". RHB, RFM. Islamabad 1993-94 to 1997-98, 2001-02 to date. United Bank 1995-96 to 1996-97. Rawalpindi 1998-99 to 2004-05. PIA 2001-02. Surrey debut 2002; cap 2004. Habib Bank 2006-07. **Tests** (P): 21 (1997-98 to 2001); HS 136 v SA (Johannesburg) 1997-98; BB 4-50 v E (Lord's) 2001. Scored 128* and 50* v SA (Rawalpindi) 1997-98 on debut. **LOI** (P): 142 (1996-97 to 2006-07); HS 67 v I (Adelaide) 1999-00; BB 6-18 v WI (Sharjah) 1999-00. F-c Tours (P): E 1997 (Pak A), 2001; A 1999-00; SA 1997-98; I 1998-99; SL 2000; Z 1997-98. HS 204* v Middx (Oval) 2005. 50 wkts (0+1): 59 (1996-97). BB 8-61 v Lancs (Oval) 2002. LO HS 101* v Glamorgan (Oval) 2006 (CGT). LO BB 6-18 (*see LOI*). T20 HS 65*. T20 BB 4-20.

BATTY, Jonathan Neil (Wheatley Park S, Oxon; Repton S; Durham U; Keble C, Oxford), b Chesterfield, Derbys 18 Apr 1974. 5'10". RHB, WK. Minor C 1996. Comb U 1994-95. Oxford U 1996; blue 1996. Surrey debut 1997; cap 2001; captain 2004. Oxfordshire 1993-96. 1000 runs (1): 1025 (2006). HS 168* v Essex (Chelmsford) 2003. BB 1-21 v Lancs (Manchester) 2000. LO HS 158* v Hants (Oval) 2005 (CGT). T20 HS 59.

BENNING, James Graham Edward (Beacon S; Chesham S; Caterham S), b Mill Hill, N London 4 May 1983. 6'0". RHB, RM. Debut (Surrey) 2003. Buckinghamshire 2000-01. HS 128 v OU (Oxford) 2004. CC HS 112 v Glos (Oval) 2006. BB 3-57 v Kent (Tunbridge Wells) 2005. LO HS 189* v Glos (Bristol) 2006 (CGT). LO BB 4-43 v Leics (Oval) 2003 (NL). T20 HS 88. T20 BB 1-7.

BROWN, Alistair Duncan (Caterham S), b Beckenham, Kent 11 Feb 1970. 5'10". RHB, OB, occ WK. Debut (Surrey) 1992; cap 1994; benefit 2002. Lawrence Trophy 1998. **LOI**: 16 (1996 to 2001); HS 118 v I (Manchester) 1996. 1000 runs (8); most – 1382 (1993). HS 295* v Leics (Oakham) 2000 – record score (all levels) in Rutland. BB 3-25 v Somerset (Guildford) 2006. LO HS 268 v Glamorgan(Oval) 2002 (CGT) – world record l-o score (160 balls, 12 sixes, 30 fours). LO BB 3-39 v Notts (Nottingham) 2000 (NL). T20 HS 83.

BUTCHER, Mark Alan (Trinity S; Archbishop Tenison's S, Croydon), b Croydon 23 Aug 1972. Son of A.R.Butcher (Surrey, Glamorgan and England 1972-92, 1998); brother of G.P.Butcher (Glamorgan and; Surrey 1994-2001); nephew of I.P.Butcher (Leics and Glos 1980-90) and M.S.Butcher (Surrey 1982). 5'11". LHB, RM/OB. Debut (Surrey) 1992; cap 1996; captain 2005 to date; benefit 2005. **Tests**: 71 (1997 to 2004-05, 1 as captain); HS 173* v A (Leeds) 2001; BB 4-42 v A (Birmingham) 2001. F-c Tours: A 1996-97 (Eng A), 1998-99, 2002-03; SA 1999-00, 2004-05; WI 1997-98, 2003-04; NZ 2001-02; I 2001-02; SL 2003-04; B 2003-04. 1000 runs (8); most – 1604 (1996). HS 259 v Leics (Leicester) 1999. BB 5-86 v Lancs (Manchester) 2000. LO HS 104 v Yorks (Oval) 2003 (NL). LO BB 3-23 v Sussex (Oval) 1992 (SL). T20 HS 60.

CLARKE, Rikki (Broadwater SS; Godalming C), b Orsett, Essex 29 Sep 1981. 6'4". RHB, RFM. Debut (Surrey) 2002 – scoring 107* v CU (Cambridge); cap 2005. MCC 2006. YC 2002. **Tests**: 2 (2003-04); HS 55 and BB 2-7 v B (Chittagong) 2003-04. **LOI**: 20 (2003 to 2006); HS 39 v P (Lord's) 2006; BB 2-28 v B (Dhaka) 2003-04. F-c Tours: WI 2003-04, 2005-06; SL 2002-03 (ECB Acad), 2004-05; B 2003-04. 1000 runs (1): 1027 (2006). HS 214 v Somerset (Guildford) 2006. BB 4-21 v Leics (Leicester) 2003. LO HS 98* v Derbys (Derby) 2002 (NL). LO BB 4-49 v Warwks (Birmingham) 2005 (NL). T20 HS79*. T20 BB 3-11.

CLINTON, Richard Selvey (Colfes S), b Sidcup, Kent 1 Sep 1981. Son of G.S.Clinton (Kent and Surrey 1974-90). 6'3". LHB, RM. Kent staff 1999-2000 – no f-c appearances. Essex 2001-02. Loughborough U. 2004-06. Surrey debut 2004. British U 2006. HS 108* LU v Essex (Chelmsford) 2006. Sy HS 105 v Kent (Tunbridge Wells) 2005. BB 2-30 Ex v A (Chelmsford) 2001. CC BB – . LO HS 56 Ex v Durham (Ilford) 2001 (NL). LO BB 2-16 v Staffs (Leek) 2005 (CGT).

NQ**DERNBACH, Jade** Winston (St John the Baptist S), b Johannesburg, South Africa 3 Mar 1986. 6'1½". RHB, RMF. Italian passport. UK resident since 1998. Debut (Surrey) 2003, when aged 17. HS 9 and BB 3-67 v Glos Bristol) 2006. LO HS 21 v Warwks (Birmingham) 2005 (NL). LO BB 4-36 v Scot (Oval) 2005 (NL). T20 HS 1. T20 BB 1-19.

DOSHI, Nayan Dilip (King Alfred S, London), b Nottingham 6 Oct 1978. Son of D.R.Doshi (Bengal, Notts, Warwks, Saurashtra, and India 1968-69 to 1986). 6'4". RHB, SLA. Saurashtra 2001-02 to date. Surrey debut 2004; cap 2006. Buckinghamshire 2001. 50 wkts (1): 51 (2006). HS 37 Saurashtra v Vidarbha (Rajkot) 2005-06. Sy HS 33 v Notts (Oval) 2005. BB 7-110 (10-183 match) v Sussex (Hove) 2004. LO HS 38* Saurashtra v Baroda (Bombay) 2001-02. LO BB 5-30 v Derbys (Chesterfield) 2006 (P40). T20 HS 1*. T20 BB 4-22.

HAMILTON-BROWN, Rory James (Millfield S), b St John's Wood, London 3 Sep 1987. 6'0". RHB, OB. Debut (Surrey) 2005. Awaiting CC debut. No f-c appearances 2006. HS 9 v Bangladesh A (Oval) 2005. LO HS 20 v Sussex (Guildford) 2005 (NL).

‡**MILLER, Daniel** James (Ewell Castle S; Kingston-upon-Thames C; Loughborough U), b Hammersmith, London 12 Jun 1983. 6'5". LHB, RMF. Loughborough UCCE 2006. Awaiting Surrey f-c debut. HS 0* and BB 1-11 LU v Essex (Chelmsford) 2006. LO HS 1 v Northants (Croydon) 2002 (NL).

NQ**MOHAMMAD AKRAM** AWAN (Modern SS; Gordon C, Rawalpindi), b Islamabad, Pakistan 10 Sep 1972. 6'2". RHB, RFM. Rawalpindi 1992-93 to 1998-99, 2001-02 to 2002-03. Allied Bank 1996-97 to 2000-01. Northamptonshire 1997. Essex 2003. Sussex 2004; cap 2004. Surrey debut 2005; cap 2006. **Tests** (P): 9 (1995-96 to 2001-02); HS 10* and BB 5-138 v A (Perth) 1999-00. **LOI** (P): 23 (1995-96 to 2000-01; HS 7*; BB 2-28 v I (Toronto) 1997. F-c Tours (P): E 1996; A 1995-96; 1999-00; SA 1997-98; WI 1999-00; NZ 2000-01. HS 35* Sx v Warwks (Birmingham) 2004. Sy HS 27* v Notts (Oval) 2005. BB 8-49 (10-142 match) Ex v Surrey (Oval) 2003. Sy BB 6-34 v Glos (Oval) 2006. LO HS 33 Allied Bank v Faisalabad (Faisalabad) 1998-99. LO BB 4-19 Nh v Surrey (Northampton) 1997 (SL). T20 HS 7*. T20 BB 2-22.

NEWMAN, Scott Alexander (Trinity S, Croydon; Coulsdon C; Brighton U), b Epsom 3 Nov 1979. 6'2". LHB, RM. Debut (Surrey) 2002 – scoring 99 v Hants (Oval) 2002; cap 2005. F-c Tour (Eng A): I 2003-04. 1000 runs (3); most – 1404 (2006). HS 219 (and 117) v Glamorgan (Oval) 2005. LO HS 106 v Essex (Oval) 2004 (NL). T20 HS 59.

‡[NQ]**NICHOLSON, Matthew** James (Knox GS; Edith Cowan U, Perth), b St Leonards, Sydney, Australia 2 Oct 1974. 6'6". RHB, RFM. W Australia.1996-97 to 2002-03. NSW 2003-04 to date. Missed entire 1997-98 season (salmonella poisoning, glandular fever, Ross River fever, chronic fatigue syndrome). Registered as an overseas player by Sussex for 2005 but was unable to take up his contract because of injury. Northamptonshire 2006. **Tests** (A): 1 (1998-99); HS 9 and BB 3-56 v E (Melbourne) 1998-99. F-c Tour (A): Z 1999-00. HS 106* Nh v Derbys (Northampton) 2006. BB 7-62 Nh v Glos (Northampton) 2006. LO HS 25 NSW v Q (Sydney 2003-04. LO BB 3-23 Nh v Middx (Northampton) 2006 (P40). T20 HS 8. T20 BB 3-12.

ORMOND, James (St Thomas More S, Nuneaton), b Walsgrave, Coventry, Warwks 20 Aug 1977. 6'3". RHB, RFM. Leicestershire 1995-2001; cap 1999. Surrey debut 2002; cap 2003. **Tests**: 2 (2001 to 2001-02); HS 18 v A (Oval) 2001; BB 1-70. F-c Tours: NZ 2001-02; I 2001-02; SL 1997-98 (Eng A); K 1997-98 (Eng A). HS 57 v Glos (Bristol) 2004. 50 wkts (4); most – 52 (1999, 2004). BB 7-63 v Glamorgan (Cardiff) 2005. Hat-trick (4 wkts in 6 balls) 2003. LO HS 32 v Somerset (Taunton) 2005 (NL). LO BB 4-12 Le v Middx (Leicester) 1998 (SL). T20 HS 6. T20 BB 5-26.

RAMPRAKASH, Mark Ravin (Gayton HS; Harrow Weald SFC), b Bushey, Herts 5 Sep 1969. 5'9". RHB, OB. Middlesex 1987-2000; cap 1990; captain 1997-99. Surrey debut 2001 – scoring 146 v Kent (Oval); cap 2002. YC 1991. PCA 2006. **Tests**: 52 (1991 to 2001-02); HS 154 v WI (Bridgetown) 1997-98; BB 1-2. **LOI**: 18 (1991 to 2001-02); HS 51 v WI (Pt-of-Spain) 1997-98; BB 3-28 v Z (Harare) 2001-02. F-c Tours: A 1994-95 (*part*), 1998-99; SA 1995-96; WI 1991-92 (Eng A), 1993-94, 1997-98; NZ 1991-92, 2001-02; I 1994-95 (Eng A), 2001-02; P 1990-91 (Eng A); SL 1990-91 (Eng A). 1000 runs (16 inc 2000 (2): 2258 (1995), 2278 (2006). Averaged 103.54 in f-c matches, the second-highest average by any batsman scoring 1000 runs in a season (105.28 in CC) 2006, setting world records by scoring 2000 runs in only 20 innings, posting scores of at least 150 in five successive matches and reaching double figures in each of his 24 innings. HS 301* v Northants (Oval) 2006. BB 3-32 M v Glamorgan (Lord's) 1998. Sy BB 2-35 v Northants (Northampton) 2004. LO HS 147* M v Worcs (Lord's) 1990 (SL). LO BB 5-38 M v Leics (Lord's) 1993 (SL). T20 HS 85.

SAKER, Neil Clifford (Raynes Park HS; Nescot C), b Tooting, London 20 Sep 1984. 6'4". RHB, RFM. Debut (Surrey) 2003. No f-c appearance 2004. HS 58* v Essex (Colchester) 2006. BB 4-79 v Somerset (Bath) 2006. LO HS 22 v Glos (Bristol) 2006 (CGT). LO BB 4-43 v Kent (Canterbury) 2005 (NL).

SALISBURY, Ian David Kenneth (Moulton CS), b Northampton 21 Jan 1970. 5'11". RHB, LBG. Sussex 1989-96; cap 1991. Surrey debut 1997; cap 1998; benefit 2007. MCC YC 1988. YC 1992. *Wisden* 1992. **Tests**: 15 (1992 to 2000-01); HS 50 v P (Manchester) 1992; BB 4-163 v WI (Georgetown) 1993-94. **LOI**: 4 (1992-93 to 1993-94); HS 5; BB 3-41 v WI (Pt-of-Spain) 1993-94. F-c Tours: WI 1991-92 (Eng A), 1993-94; I 1992-93; 1994-95 (Eng A); P 1990-91 (Eng A), 1995-96 (Eng A), 2000-01; SL 1990-91 (Eng A). HS 101* v Leics (Oval) 2003. 50 wkts (7); most – 87 (1992). BB 8-60 (12-91 match) v Somerset (Oval) 2000. LO HS 59* v Glamorgan(Oval) 2004 (NL). LO BB 5-30 Sx v Leics (Leicester) 1992 (SL). T20 HS 20. T20 BB 2-6.

SCHOFIELD, Christopher Paul (Wardle HS), b Birch Hill, Rochdale 6 Oct 1978. 6'2". LHB, LBG. Lancashire 1998-2004; cap 2002. Surrey debut 2006. **Tests**: 2 (2000); HS 57 v Z (Nottingham) 2000. F-c Tours (Eng A): WI 2000-01; NZ 1999-00; B 1999-00. HS 99 La v Warwks (Manchester) 2004. Sy HS 95 and BB 3-78 v Glos (Bristol) 2006. BB 6-120 Eng A v Bangladesh (Chittagong) 1999-00. CC BB 5-66 La v Durham (Manchester) 1999. LO HS 69* La v Ind A (Blackpool) 2003 and 69* v Surrey (Manchester) 2004 (NL). LO BB 5-31 La v Derbys (Manchester) 2001 (NL). T20 HS 27. T20 BB 2-9.

NQ**WALTERS, Stewart** Jonathan (Guildford GS, Perth, WA), b Mornington, Victoria, Australia 25 Jun 1983. 6'1". RHB, RM. Debut (Surrey) 2006. HS 67 v Glos (Bristol) 2006. BB 1-9 v Derbys (Derby) 2006. LO HS 32* v Sussex (Hove) 2005 (NL). LO BB 1-38 (CGT). T20 HS 9*. T20 BB – .

RELEASED/RETIRED

(Having made a first-class County appearance in 2006)

BICKNELL, Martin Paul (Robert Haining County SS), b Guildford 14 Jan 1969. Younger brother of D.J.Bicknell (Surrey and Notts 1987-2006). 6'3". RHB, RFM. Surrey 1986-2006; cap 1989; benefit 1997; Testimonial 2006. *Wisden* 2000. **Tests**: 4 (1993 to 2003); HS 15 v SA (Leeds) 2003; BB 4-84 v SA (Oval) 2003. **LOI**: 7 (1990-91); HS 31* v A (Perth) 1990-91; BB 3-55 v NZ (Christchurch) 1990-91. F-c Tours: A 1990-91; SA 1993-94 (Eng A); Z 1989-90 (Eng A). HS 141 v Essex (Chelmsford) 2003. 50 wkts (11); most – 72 (2001). BB 9-45 v CU (Oval) 1988. CC BB 9-47 (16-119 match) v Leics (Guildford) 2000. Took his 1000th f-c wicket 2004. LO HS 66* v Northants (Oval) 1991 (NWT). LO BB 7-30 v Glamorgan(Oval) 1999 (NL). T20 HS 10*. T20 BB 2-11.

NQ**KUMBLE, Anil** (National HS; R.V. Engineering C, Bangalore), b Bangalore, India 17 Oct 1970. 6'1½". RHB, LBG. Karnataka 1989-90 to 2005-06. South Zone 1990-91 to date. Northamptonshire 1995; cap 1995. Leicestershire 2000. Surrey 2006. *Wisden* 1995. **Tests** (I): 113 (1990 to 2006-07); HS 88 v SA (Calcutta) 1996-97; BB 10-74 (14-149 match) v P (Delhi) 1998-99. **LOI** (I): 268 (1989-90 to 2006-07, 1 as captain); HS 26 v A (Perth) 1999-00; BB 6-12 v WI (Calcutta) 1993-94. F-c Tours (I): E 1990, 1996, 2002; A 1999-00, 2003-04; SA 1992-93, 1996-97, 2001-02, 2006-07; WI 1996-97, 2001-02, 2006; NZ 1993-94, 1998-99; P 2003-04, 2005-06; SL 1993, 1997, 1998-99; Z 1992-93, 1998-99, 2005-06; B 2004-05. HS 154* Karnataka v Kerala (Bijapur) 1991-92. 50 wkts (1+2) inc 100 (1): 105 (1995). CC HS 56 Le v Kent (Canterbury) 2000. Sy HS 8. BB 10-74 (*see Tests*). CC BB 8-100 (11-183) Sy v Northants (Oval) 2006. LO HS 30* Karnataka v Wills XI (Bangalore) 1994-95. LO BB 6-12 (*see LOI*). T20 HS 8. T20 BB 2-20.

MURTAGH, T.J. – *see MIDDLESEX.*

S.P.Pope left the staff without making a first-class appearance in 2006.

SURREY 2006

RESULTS SUMMARY

	Place	Won	Lost	Tied	Drew	No Result
County Championship (2nd Division)	**1st**	10	2		4	
All First-Class Matches		10	2		5	
C & G Trophy (South Conference)	8th	2	6			1
Pro40 League (2nd Division)	4th	5	2			1
Twenty20 Cup (South Division)	Semi-Finalist	6	4			

COUNTY CHAMPIONSHIP AVERAGES

BATTING AND FIELDING

Cap		*M*	*I*	*NO*	*HS*	*Runs*	*Avge*	*100*	*50*	*Ct/St*
2002	M.R.Ramprakash	14	23	2	301*	2211	105.28	8	8	13
2005	R.Clarke	11	18	3	214	970	64.66	3	3	12
1996	M.A.Butcher	16	28	4	151	1418	59.08	5	8	17
1994	A.D.Brown	15	26	4	215	1177	53.50	5	3	8
2005	S.A.Newman	16	27	–	143	1171	43.37	1	9	13
1989	M.P.Bicknell	4	6	2	59	156	39.00	–	1	2
2004	Azhar Mahmood	13	20	4	101	600	37.50	1	2	18
2001	J.N.Batty	16	27	–	133	935	34.62	2	6	44/9
–	J.G.E.Benning	7	12	1	112	366	33.27	1	2	4
2003	J.Ormond	3	4	2	41*	62	31.00	–	–	–
–	S.J.Walters	3	6	–	67	166	27.66	–	1	3
–	N.C.Saker	7	10	1	58*	192	21.33	–	1	4
1998	I.D.K.Salisbury	15	18	3	74	316	21.06	–	2	11
2006	N.D.Doshi	13	12	7	32	94	18.80	–	–	3
2006	Mohammad Akram	13	11	4	21*	64	9.14	–	–	3

Also batted: R.S.Clinton (1 match)11, 12; J.W.Dernbach (2) 9, 4*, 0*; A.Kumble (3) 6*, 8(4 ct); T.J.Murtagh (2) 4, 37*, 41* (1 ct); C.P.Schofield (2) 3, 16, 95(2 ct).

BOWLING

	O	*M*	*R*	*W*	*Avge*	*Best*	*5wI*	*10wM*
A.Kumble	140	27	418	19	22.00	8-100	2	1
I.D.K.Salisbury	544.2	99	1662	59	28.16	5- 46	1	–
N.D.Doshi	449.5	82	1415	50	28.30	6- 91	1	1
Mohammad Akram	345	64	1254	36	34.83	6- 34	1	–
Azhar Mahmood	336.4	69	1161	31	37.45	5- 69	1	–
R.Clarke	188	34	738	18	41.00	4- 45	–	–
N.C.Saker	146.4	16	657	14	46.92	4- 79	–	–
Also bowled:								
T.J.Murtagh	56	14	183	7	26.14	3- 48	–	–
J.Ormond	74	19	202	6	33.66	3- 39	–	–
C.P.Schofield	73.2	10	296	8	37.00	3- 78	–	–
M.P.Bicknell	101	26	303	7	43.28	5- 93	1	–

J.G.E.Benning 38-4-213-3; A.D.Brown 23.5-2-74-3; M.A.Butcher 5-0-8-1; J.W.Dernbach 44.2-9-165-4; S.J.Walters 26-7-69-2.

The First-Class Averages (pp 130–146) give the records of Surrey players in all first-class matches for the county (Surrey's other opponents being Durham UCCE), with the exception of R.Clarke and R.S.Clinton whose full county figures are as above.

SURREY RECORDS

FIRST-CLASS CRICKET

Highest Total	For 811		v	Somerset	The Oval	1899
	V 863		by	Lancashire	The Oval	1990
Lowest Total	For 14		v	Essex	Chelmsford	1983
	V 16		by	MCC	Lord's	1872
Highest Innings	For 357*	R.Abel	v	Somerset	The Oval	1899
	V 366	N.H.Fairbrother	for	Lancashire	The Oval	1990

Highest Partnership for each Wicket

1st	428	J.B.Hobbs/A.Sandham	v	Oxford U	The Oval	1926
2nd	371	J.B.Hobbs/E.G.Hayes	v	Hampshire	The Oval	1909
3rd	413	D.J.Bicknell/D.M.Ward	v	Kent	Canterbury	1990
4th	448	R.Abel/T.W.Hayward	v	Yorkshire	The Oval	1899
5th	318	M.R.Ramprakash/Azhar Mahmood	v	Middlesex	The Oval	2005
6th	298	A.Sandham/H.S.Harrison	v	Sussex	The Oval	1913
7th	262	C.J.Richards/K.T.Medlycott	v	Kent	The Oval	1987
8th	205	I.A.Greig/M.P.Bicknell	v	Lancashire	The Oval	1990
9th	168	E.R.T.Holmes/E.W.J.Brooks	v	Hampshire	The Oval	1936
10th	173	A.Ducat/A.Sandham	v	Essex	Leyton	1921

Best Bowling	For	10-43	T.Rushby	v	Somerset	Taunton	1921
(Innings)	V	10-28	W.P.Howell	for	Australians	The Oval	1899
Best Bowling	For	16-83	G.A.R.Lock	v	Kent	Blackheath	1956
(Match)	V	15-57	W.P.Howell	for	Australians	The Oval	1899

Most Runs – Season	3246	T.W.Hayward	(av 72.13)	1906
Most Runs – Career	43554	J.B.Hobbs	(av 49.72)	1905-34
Most 100s – Season	13	T.W.Hayward		1906
	13	J.B.Hobbs		1925
Most 100s – Career	144	J.B.Hobbs		1905-34
Most Wkts – Season	252	T.Richardson	(av 13.94)	1895
Most Wkts – Career	1775	T.Richardson	(av 17.87)	1892-1904
Most Career W-K Dismissals	1221	H.Strudwick	(1035 ct/186 st)	1902-27
Most Career Catches in the Field	605	M.J.Stewart		1954-72

LIMITED-OVERS CRICKET

Highest Total	**CGT**	438-5		v	Glamorgan	The Oval	2002
	P40	375-4		v	Yorkshire	Scarborough	1994
	T20	224-5		v	Glos	Bristol	2006
Lowest Total	**CGT**	74		v	Kent	The Oval	1967
	P40	64		v	Worcs	Worcester	1978
	T20	118		v	Hampshire	The Oval	2005
Highest Innings	**CGT**	268	A.D.Brown	v	Glamorgan	The Oval	2002
	P40	203	A.D.Brown	v	Hampshire	Guildford	1997
	T20	88	J.G.E.Benning	v	Kent	The Oval	2006
Best Bowling	**CGT**	7-33	R.D.Jackman	v	Yorkshire	Harrogate	1970
	P40	7-30	M.P.Bicknell	v	Glamorgan	The Oval	1999
	T20	6-24	T.J.Murtagh	v	Middlesex	Lord's	2005

SUSSEX

Formation of Present Club: 1 March 1839
Substantial Reorganisation: August 1857
Inaugural First-Class Match: 1864
Colours: Dark Blue, Light Blue and Gold
Badge: County Arms of Six Martlets
County Champions: (2) 2003, 2006
Gillette/NatWest/C & G Trophy Winners: (5) 1963, 1964, 1978, 1986, 2006
Benson and Hedges Cup Winners: (0); best – semi-finalist 1982, 1999
Pro 40/National League (Div 1) Winners: (0); best – 3rd 2006
Pro 40/National League (Div 2) Winners: (2) 1999, 2005
Sunday League Winners: (1) 1982
Twenty20 Cup Winners: (0); best – 2nd in Group 2003

Chief Executive: Gus Mackay, County Ground, Eaton Road, Hove BN3 3AN • Tel: 01273 827100 • Fax: 01273 771549 • Email: info@sussexcricket.co.uk • Web: www.sussexcricket.co.uk

Professional Cricket Manager: M.A.Robinson. **Club Coach**: M.J.G.Davis. **Captain**: C.J.Adams. **Vice-Captain**: No appointment. **Overseas Players**: Mushtaq Ahmed and Rana Naved-ul-Hasan. **2007 Beneficiary**: R.R.Montgomerie. **Head Groundsman**: Lawrence Gosling. **Scorer**: M.J. (Mike) Charman. ‡ New registration. NQ Not qualified for England.

ADAMS, Christopher John (Repton S), b Whitwell, Derbyshire 6 May 1970. 6'0". RHB, RM/OB. Derbyshire 1988-97; cap 1992. Sussex debut/cap 1998; captain 1998 to date; benefit 2003. *Wisden* 2003. **Tests**: 5 (1999-00); HS 31 v SA (Cape Town) 1999-00; BB 1-42. **LOI**: 5 (1998 to 1999-00); HS 42 v SA (Cape Town) 1999-00. F-c Tour: SA 1999-00. 1000 runs (8); most – 1742 (1996). HS 239 De v Hants (Southampton) 1996. Sx HS 217 v Lancs (Manchester) 2002. BB 4-28 v Durham (Chester-le-St) 2001. LO HS 163 v Middx (Arundel) 1999 (NL). LO BB 5-16 v Middx (Hove) 1998 (SL). T20 HS 63.

NQ**GOODWIN, Murray** William (Newton Moore HS, Bunbury, WA), b Salisbury, Rhodesia 11 Dec 1972. Younger brother of D.G.Goodwin (Zimbabwe 1986-97 to 1989-90). 5'9". Emigrated to Australia in Nov 1986. Gained Australian citizenship in Sep 1997. Kolpak registration 2005 to date. RHB, LB. W Australia 1994-95 to 1996-97, 2000-01 to 2005-06. Mashonaland 1997-98 to 1998-99. Sussex debut/cap 2001. Holland 1997. **Tests** (Z): 19 (1997-98 to 2000); HS 166* v P (Bulawayo) 1997-98. **LOI** (Z): 71 (1997-98 to 2000); HS 112* v WI (Chester-le-St) 2000; BB 1-12. F-c Tours (Z): E 2000, SA 1999-00; WI 1999-00; NZ 1997-98; P 1998-99; SL 1997-98. 1000 runs (5+1); most – 1654 (2001). HS 335* (Sussex record) v Leics (Hove) 2003. BB 2-23 Z v Lahore City (Lahore) 1998-99. Sx BB – . LO HS 167 WA v NSW (Perth) 2000-01 (MC). LO BB 1-9 Mashonaland v Eng A (Harare) 1998-99. T20 HS 67*.

HODD, Andrew John (Bexhill C), b Chichester, Sussex 12 Jan 1984. RHB, WK. Sussex 2003 (1 match), 2006. Surrey 2005 (one match). HS 57* (and 55*) Sy v Bangladesh A (Oval) 2005. Sx/CC HS 18 v Warwks (Hove) 2006. LO HS 9 Sy v Somerset (Taunton) 2005 (NL). T20 HS – .

HOPKINSON, Carl Daniel (Brighton C), b Brighton 14 Sep 1981. 5'11". RHB, RM. Debut (Sussex) 2002. HS 74 v Notts (Hove) 2006. BB 1-20. CC BB 1-35. LO HS 69* v Hants (Hove) 2006 (CGT). LO BB 3-19 v Scot (Edinburgh) 2003 (NL). T20 HS 22*.

KIRTLEY, Robert James (Clifton C), b Eastbourne 10 Jan 1975. 6'0". RHB, RFM. Debut (Sussex) 1995; cap 1998; benefit 2006. Mashonaland 1996-97. **Tests**: 4 (2003 to 2003-04); HS 12 v SL (Colombo) 2003-04; BB 6-34 v SA (Nottingham) 2003 on debut. **LOI**: 11 (2001-02 to 2004-05); HS 1 (*twice*); BB 2-33 v Z (Harare) 2001-02 on debut, and 2-33 v B (Dhaka) 2003-04. F-c Tours (Eng A): NZ 1999-00; SL 2003-04 (Eng); B 1999-00. HS 59 v Durham (Eastbourne) 1998. 50 wkts (7); most – 75 (2001). BB 7-21 v Hants (Southampton) 1999. Took 5-53 (7-88 match) for Mashonaland v Eng XI (Harare) 1996-97. LO HS 30* v Middx (Lord's) 2003 (CGT). LO BB 5-27 v Lancs (Lord's) 2006 (CGT Final). T20 HS 2. T20 BB 2-8.

LEWRY, Jason David (Durrington HS, Worthing), b Worthing 2 Apr 1971. 6'2". LHB, LFM. Debut (Sussex) 1994; cap 1996; benefit 2002. F-c Tour: Z 1998-99 (Eng A). HS 72 v Surrey (Oval) 2004. 50 wkts (5); most – 62 (1998). BB 8-106 v Leics (Hove) 2003. 2 hat-tricks (1998, 2001). LO HS 16* v Yorks (Arundel) 2004 (NL). LO BB 4-29 v Somerset (Bath) 1995 (SL). T20 HS 8*. T20 BB 3-34.

‡LIDDLE, Christopher John (Nunthorpe CS), b Middlesbrough, Yorks 1 Feb 1984. 6'5". RHB, LFM. Leicestershire 2005-06. HS 4*. CC HS 1* and BB 3-42 v Somerset (Leicester) 2006. LO HS 1 and BB – Le v Hants (Leicester) 2006 (P40).

MARTIN-JENKINS, Robin Simon Christopher (Radley C; Durham U), b Guildford, Surrey 28 Oct 1975. Son of C.D.A.Martin-Jenkins (*Times* Chief Cricket Correspondent/ BBC Commentator). 6'5". RHB, RFM. Debut (Sussex) 1995; cap 2000. British U 1996. 1000 runs (1): 1008 (2002). HS 205* v Somerset (Taunton) 2002. BB 7-51 v Leics (Horsham) 2002. LO HS 68* v Northants (Hove) 2003 (NL). LO BB 4-22 v Kent (Canterbury) 2002 (BHC). T20 HS 56*. T20 BB 4-20.

MONTGOMERIE, Richard Robert (Rugby S; Worcester C, Oxford), b Rugby, Warwks 3 Jul 1971. 5'10½". RHB, OB. Oxford U 1991-94; blue 1991-92-93-94; captain 1994; half blues for rackets and real tennis. Northamptonshire 1991-98; cap 1995. Sussex debut/cap 1999; benefit 2007. F-c Tour: Z 1994-95 (Nh). 1000 runs (5); most – 1704 (2001). HS 196 v Hants (Hove) 2002. BB 1-0. LO HS 132* v Somerset (Hove) 2005 (NL). T20 HS 20

[NQ]**MUSHTAQ AHMED** (Mahmoodia HS, Sahiwal), b Sahiwal, Pakistan 28 Jun 1970. 5'5". RHB, LBG. Multan 1986-87, 1988-89, 1990-91. United Bank 1987-88 to 1995-96. Islamabad 1994-95. Lahore 1996-97, 2000-01. Peshawar 1998-99. National Bank 2001-02 to 2004-05. WAPDA 2005-06 to date. Somerset 1993-95, 1997-98; cap 1993. Surrey 2002 (2 matches). Sussex debut/cap 2003. *Wisden* 1996. PCA 2003. **Tests** (P): 52 (1989-90 to 2003-04); HS 59 v SA (Rawalpindi) 1997-98; BB 7-56 (10-171 match) v NZ (Christchurch) 1995-96. **LOI** (P): 144 (1988-89 to 2003-04); HS 34* v SA (Colombo) 2000-01; BB 5-36 v I (Toronto) 1996-97. F-c Tours (P): E 1992, 1996; A 1989-90, 1991-92, 1992-93, 1995-96, 1996-97, 1999-00; SA 1997-98; WI 1992-93, 1999-00; NZ 1992-93, 1993-94, 1995-96, 2000-01; I 1998-99; SL 1994-95, 1996-97, 2000-01; Z 1997-98. HS 90* v Kent (Hove) 2005. 50 wkts (8+2) inc 100 (2): 103 (2003), 102 (2006). Took 1000th f-c wicket during 2004 season. BB 9-48 (13-132 match) v Notts (Nottingham) 2006. LO HS 41 Sm v Durham (Taunton) 1998 (SL). LO BB 7-24 Sm v Ire (Taunton) 1997 (BHC). T20 HS 16. T20 BB 5-11.

NASH, Christopher David (Collyers SFC; Loughborough U), b Cuckfield 19 May 1983. 5'11". RHB, OB. Debut (Sussex) 2002 – no f-c appearances 2003-04. Loughborough UCCE 2003-04. British U 2004. HS 67 v Hants (Hove) 2006. BB (LU) 1-5. Sx BB 1-63. LO HS 82 v Warwks (Hove) 2006 (P40). T20 HS 20.

[NQ]**NAVED-UL-HASAN, Rana**, b Sheikhupura, Pakistan 28 Feb 1978. RHB, RMF. Debut Pakistan A v England A (Multan) 1995-96. Lahore 1999-00. Customs 2000-01. Sheikhupura 2000-01 to 2001-02. Allied Bank 2001-02. WAPDA 2002-03 to date. Sialkot 2003-04 to 2005-06. Sussex debut/cap 2005. Herefordshire 2002. **Tests** (P): 9 (2004-05 to 2006-07); HS 42* v E (Lahore) 2005-06; BB 3-30 v E (Faisalabad) 2005-06. **LOI** (P): 60 (2002-03 to 2006-07); HS 29 v A (Melbourne) 2004-05; BB 6-27 v I (Jamshedpur) 2004-05. F-c Tours (P): A 2004-05; SA 2006-07; WI 2004-05; I 2004-05. HS 139 v Middx (Lord's) 2005. 50 wkts (1+3); most – 91 (2000-01). BB 7-49 Sheikhupura v Sialkot (Muridke) 2001-02. Sx BB 7-62 (11-148 match) v Yorks (Leeds) 2006. LO HS 70* Lahore v Habib Bank (Sheikhupura) 1999-00. LO BB 6-27 (***see LOI***). T20 HS 40*. T20 BB 3-9.

PRIOR, Matthew James (Brighton C), b Johannesburg, South Africa 26 Feb 82. 6'2". RHB, WK. Debut (Sussex) 2001; cap 2003. **LOI**: 12 (2004-05 to 2005-06); HS 45 v P (Lahore) 2005-06. F-c Tours (Eng A): I 2003-04; SL 2004-05; B 2006-07. 1000 runs (2); most – 1158 (2004). HS 201* v LU (Hove) 2004. CC HS 153* v Essex (Colchester) 2003. LO HS 144 v Warwks (Hove) 2005 (NL). T20 HS 73.

RAYNER, Oliver Philip (St Bede's S, Sussex), b Fallingbostel, W Germany, 1 Nov 1985. 6'5".RHB, OB. Debut (Sussex) 2006, scoring 101 v SL (Hove) – first hundred in debut for Sussex since 1920. HS 101 (*see above*). CC HS 23 and BB 3-89 v Kent (Hove) 2006. LO HS 61 v Lancs (Hove) 2006 (P40). LO BB1-25 (P40). T20 HS 11. T20 BB – .

[NQ]**SAQLAIN MUSHTAQ** (Govt Muslim League HS, M.A.O. College, Lahore), b Lahore, Pakistan 29 Dec 1976. If British passport application in April 2007 is successful he will be eligible to play for Sussex as an European Union player. Brother of Sibtain Mushtaq (Lahore 1988-89). 5'11". RHB, OB. Islamabad 1994-95 to 1997-98. PIA 1994-95 to 2003-04. Lahore 2003-04. Surrey 1997-2005; cap 1998. Ireland (not f-c) 2006. *Wisden* 1999. **Tests** (P): 49 (1995-96 to 2003-04); HS 101* v NZ (Christchurch) 2000-01; BB 8-164 v E (Lahore) 2000-01 (all eight wickets to fall). **LOI** (P): 169 (1995-96 to 2003-04); HS 37* v A (Brisbane) 1999-00; BB 5-20 v E (Rawalpindi) 2000-01, 2 hat-tricks. F-c Tours (P): E 1996, 2001; A 1995-96, 1996-97, 1999-00; SA 1997-98, 2002-03; WI 1999-00; NZ 2000-01; I 1998-99, SL 1996-97, 2002-03; Z 1997-98, 2002-03; B 1998-99, 2001-02. HS 101* (*see Tests*). UK HS 78 P v Northants (Northampton) 1996 – on UK debut. CC HS 69 Sy v Middx (Lord's) 2003. 50 wkts (5+1); most – 66 (2000). BB 8-65 (11-107 match) Sy v Derbys (Oval) 1988. Took 7-11 (including 7-5 in 34 balls) Sy v Derbys (Oval) 2000. Three hat-tricks, all for Surrey, 1997 and 1999 (2). LO HS 38* v Yorks (Leeds) 2001 (NL). LO BB 5-20 (*see LOI*). T20 HS 5. T20 BB 2-35.

‡**SMITH, Thomas** Michael John (Sussex Downs C), b Eastbourne 22 Aug 1987. RHB, SLA. Sussex staff 2006. LO HS – and BB 2-45 v Durham (Chester-le-St) 2006 (P40).

‡**THORNELY, Michael** Alistair (Brighton C), b Camden, London 19 Oct 1987. RHB, RM. Sussex 2nd XI debut 2005. Awaiting f-c debut.

WRIGHT, Luke James (Belvoir HS; Ratcliffe C; Loughborough U), b Grantham, Lincs 7 Mar 1985. 5'11". Younger brother of A.S.Wright (Leicestershire 2001-02). RHB, RM. Leicestershire 2003 (one f-c match). Sussex debut 2004. HS 100 v LU (Hove) 2004 – on Sx debut. CC HS 59 v Middx (Horsham) 2006. BB 3-33 v Surrey (Hove) 2005. LO HS 35 v Surrey (Guildford) 2005 (NL). LO BB 4-12 v Middx (Hove) 2004 (NL). T20 HS 26*. T20 BB 3-17.

YARDY, Michael Howard (William Parker S, Hastings), b Pembury, Kent 27 Nov 1980. 6'0". LHB, LM/SLA. Debut (Sussex) 2000; cap 2005. LOI: 5 (2006 to 2006-07); HS 12* v P (Birmingham) 2006; BB 3-24 v P (Nottingham) 2006 – on debut. F-c Tour (Eng A): B 2006-07 (capt). 1000 (1): 1520 (2005). HS 257 (record Sussex score v touring team) and BB 5-83 v B (Hove) 2005. CC HS 179 v Middx (Lord's) 2005. CC BB 2-62 v Glamorgan (Swansea) 2005. LO HS 98* v Surrey (Oval) 2006 (CGT). LO BB 6-27 v Warwks (Birmingham) 2005 (NL). T20 HS 68*. T20 BB 2-15.

RELEASED/RETIRED continued on p 104

SUSSEX 2006

RESULTS SUMMARY

	Place	Won	Lost	Tied	Drew	No Result
County Championship (1st Division)	**1st**	9	2		5	
All First-Class Matches		9	2		6	
C & G Trophy (South Conference)	**Winners**	8	2			
Pro40 League (1st Division)	3rd	5	3			
Twenty20 Cup (South Division)	4th	4	4			

COUNTY CHAMPIONSHIP AVERAGES

BATTING AND FIELDING

Cap		*M*	*I*	*NO*	*HS*	*Runs*	*Avge*	*100*	*50*	*Ct/St*
2001	M.W.Goodwin	16	27	1	235	1649	63.42	6	7	4
2005	M.H.Yardy	12	20	2	159*	914	50.77	3	4	9
1998	C.J.Adams	16	25	1	155	1218	50.75	3	7	28
2003	M.J.Prior	14	22	2	124	934	46.70	3	4	34/11
2006	Yasir Arafat	8	12	3	86	390	43.33	–	2	1
–	C.D.Nash	3	5	–	67	173	34.60	–	1	–
2000	R.S.C.Martin-Jenkins	14	21	3	91	592	32.88	–	3	1
1999	R.R.Montgomerie	16	27	–	100	878	32.51	1	7	17
–	C.D.Hopkinson	16	27	–	74	691	25.59	–	6	10
–	L.J.Wright	10	16	2	59	313	22.35	–	3	6
1998	R.J.Kirtley	7	9	4	36	90	18.00	–	–	1
2005	Naved-ul-Hasan	6	8	–	64	134	16.75	–	1	1
2003	Mushtaq Ahmed	15	19	5	42*	222	15.85	–	–	2
1996	J.D.Lewry	16	19	11	27*	89	11.12	–	–	10
–	O.P.Rayner	4	5	1	23	32	8.00	–	–	6

Also batted: A.J.Hodd (2) 18, 8, 3 (7 ct); D.J.Spencer (1) 16 (1 ct).

BOWLING

	O	*M*	*R*	*W*	*Avge*	*Best*	*5wI*	*10wM*
Naved-ul-Hasan	165.2	37	585	35	16.71	7-62	3	1
Mushtaq Ahmed	623.5	118	2031	102	19.91	9-48	11	4
J.D.Lewry	494.2	117	1321	57	23.17	6-68	2	–
Yasir Arafat	271.1	48	1019	41	24.85	5-84	2	–
R.S.C.Martin-Jenkins	216.1	72	489	14	34.92	4-78	–	–
L.J.Wright	153	29	514	14	36.71	3-39	–	–
R.J.Kirtley	204.4	48	643	16	40.18	3-82	–	–
Also bowled:								
O.P.Rayner	68	21	233	6	38.83	3-89	–	–

C.J.Adams 1-0-2-0; C.D.Hopkinson 5-1-31-0; C.D.Nash 8-3-24-0; D.J.Spencer 13-1-70-1; M.H.Yardy 46-4-159-2.

The First-Class Averages (pp 130–146) give the records of Sussex players in all first-class matches for the county (Sussex's other opponents being the Sri Lankans).

SUSSEX RECORDS

FIRST-CLASS CRICKET

Highest Total	For 705-8d		v	Surrey	Hastings	1902
	V 726		by	Notts	Nottingham	1895
Lowest Total	For 19		v	Surrey	Godalming	1830
	19		v	Notts	Hove	1873
	V 18		by	Kent	Gravesend	1867
Highest Innings	For 335*	M.W.Goodwin	v	Leics	Hove	2003
	V 322	E.Paynter	for	Lancashire	Hove	1937

Highest Partnership for each Wicket

1st	490	E.H.Bowley/J.G.Langridge	v	Middlesex	Hove	1933
2nd	385	E.H.Bowley/M.W.Tate	v	Northants	Hove	1921
3rd	385*	M.H.Yardy/M.W.Goodwin	v	Warwicks	Hove	2006
4th	326*	J.Langridge/G.Cox	v	Yorkshire	Leeds	1949
5th	297	J.H.Parks/H.W.Parks	v	Hampshire	Portsmouth	1937
6th	255	K.S.Duleepsinhji/M.W.Tate	v	Northants	Hove	1930
7th	344	K.S.Ranjitsinhji/W.Newham	v	Essex	Leyton	1902
8th	291	R.S.C.Martin-Jenkins/M.J.G.Davis	v	Somerset	Taunton	2002
9th	178	H.W.Parks/A.F.Wensley	v	Derbyshire	Horsham	1930
10th	156	G.R.Cox/H.R.Butt	v	Cambridge U	Cambridge	1908

Best Bowling	For	10- 48	C.H.G.Bland	v	Kent	Tonbridge	1899
(Innings)	V	9- 11	A.P.Freeman	for	Kent	Hove	1922
Best Bowling	For	17-106	G.R.Cox	v	Warwicks	Horsham	1926
(Match)	V	17- 67	A.P.Freeman	for	Kent	Hove	1922

Most Runs – Season	2850	J.G.Langridge	(av 64.77)	1949
Most Runs – Career	34152	J.G.Langridge	(av 37.69)	1928-55
Most 100s – Season	12	J.G.Langridge		1949
Most 100s – Career	76	J.G.Langridge		1928-55
Most Wkts – Season	198	M.W.Tate	(av 13.47)	1925
Most Wkts – Career	2211	M.W.Tate	(av 17.41)	1912-37
Most Career W-K Dismissals	1176	H.R.Butt	(911 ct/265 st)	1890-1912
Most Career Catches in the Field	779	J.G.Langridge		1928-55

LIMITED-OVERS CRICKET

Highest Total	**CGT**	384-9		v	Ireland	Belfast	1996
	P40	323-5		v	Leics	Horsham	2004
	T20	180-6		v	Essex	Hove	2003
Lowest Total	**CGT**	49		v	Derbyshire	Chesterfield	1969
	P40	59		v	Glamorgan	Hove	1996
	T20	67		v	Hampshire	Hove	2004
Highest Innings	**CGT**	158*	M.W.Goodwin	v	Essex	Chelmsford	2006
	P40	163	C.J.Adams	v	Middlesex	Arundel	1999
	T20	73	M.J.Prior	v	Essex	Hove	2006
Best Bowling	**CGT**	6- 9	A.I.C.Dodemaide	v	Ireland	Downpatrick	1990
	P40	7-41	A.N.Jones	v	Notts	Nottingham	1986
	T20	5-11	Mushtaq Ahmed	v	Essex	Hove	2005

WARWICKSHIRE

Formation of Present Club: 8 April 1882
Substantial Reorganisation: 19 January 1884
Inaugural First-Class Match: 1894
Colours: Dark Blue, Gold and Silver
Badge: Bear and Ragged Staff
County Champions: (6) 1911, 1951, 1972, 1994, 1995, 2004
Gillette/NatWest/C & G Trophy Winners: (5) 1966, 1968, 1989, 1993, 1995
Benson and Hedges Cup Winners: (2) 1994, 2002
Pro 40/National League (Div 1) Winners: (0); best – 3rd 2001, 2002
Sunday League Winners: (3) 1980, 1994, 1997
Twenty20 Cup Winners: (0); best – Finalist 2003

Chief Executive: Colin Povey, County Ground, Edgbaston, Birmingham, B5 7QU • Tel: 0121 446 4422 • Fax: 0121 446 4544 • Email: info@edgbaston.com • Web: www.edgbaston.com

Director of Coaching/First XI Coach: Mark J.Greatbatch. **Captain**: H.H.Streak. **Vice-Captain**: D.R.Brown. **Overseas Player**: P.L.Harris, K.C.Sangakkara and D.W.Steyn. **2007 Beneficiary**: S.J.Rouse. **Head Groundsman**: Steve Rouse. **Scorer**: David E.Wainwright. ‡ New registration. NQ Not qualified for England.

AMBROSE, Timothy Raymond (Merewether HS, NSW; TAFE C), b Newcastle, NSW, Australia 1 Dec 1982. ECB qualified – British/EU passport. 5'7". RHB, WK. Sussex 2001-05; cap 2003. Warwickshire debut 2006. HS 149 Sx v Yorks (Leeds) 2002. LO HS 95 Sx v Bucks (Beaconsfield) 2002 (CGT). T20 HS 54*.

ANYON, James Edward (Garstang HS; Preston C; Loughborough U), b Lancaster, Lancs 5 May 1983. 6'1". LHB, RFM. Loughborough U 2003-04. Warwickshire debut 2005. Cumberland 2003. HS 21 LU v Leics (Leicester) 2003. Wa HS 18* v Lancs (Birmingham) 2006. BB 5-83 v Notts (Birmingham) 2006. LO HS 12 v Worcs (Birmingham) 2006 (CGT). LO BB 3-41 v Scot (Birmingham) 2006 (CGT). T20 HS 8*. T20 BB 3-6.

BELL, Ian Ronald (Princethorpe C), b Walsgrave-on-Sowe 11 Apr 1982. 5'9". RHB, RM. Debut (Warwickshire) 1999; cap 2001. MCC 2004. YC 2004. MBE 2005. **ECB central contract 2007. Tests**: 23 (2004 to 2006-07); HS 162* (inc 105* before lunch 2nd day) v B (Chester-le-St) 2005; BB 1-33. **LOI**: 36 (2004-05 to 2006-07; HS 88 v P (Cardiff) 2006; BB 3-9 v Z (Bulawayo) 2004-05 – taking a wicket with his third ball in LOI. F-c Tours: A 2006-07; WI 2000-01 (Eng A – *part*); I 2005-06; P 2005-06; SL 2002-03 (ECB Acad), 2004-05. 1000 runs (2); most – 1714 (2004). Scored 480 runs (avge 80.00) in April 2005 – record f-c UK aggregate before May. HS 262* v Sussex (Horsham) 2004. BB 4-4 v Middx (Lord's) 2004. LO HS 137 v Yorks (Birmingham) 2005 (NL). LO BB 5-41 v Essex (Chelmsford) 2003 (NL). T20 HS 66*. T20 BB 1-12.

BROWN, Douglas Robert (Alloa Academy; W London IHE), b Stirling, Scotland 29 Oct 1969. 6'2". RHB, RFM. Scotland 1989, 2006 to 2006-07. Warwickshire debut 1991-92 (SA tour); cap 1995; benefit 2005. Wellington 1995-96. **LOI** (E): 9 (1997-98); HS 21 v WI (Bridgetown) 1997-98; BB 2-28 v WI (Sharjah) 1997-98. LOI (Scot): 13 (2006 to 2006-07); HS 50*v Canada (Nairobi) 2006-07; BB 3-37 v K (Mombasa) 2006-07. F-c Tours (Wa): SA 1991-92, 1994-95; SL 1997-98 (Eng A). 1000 runs (1): 1028 (2003). HS 203 v Sussex (Hove) 2000. 50 wkts (4); most – 81 (1997). BB 8-89 (11-154 match) F-C Counties XI v Pak A (Chelmsford) 1997. Wa BB 7-66 v Durham (Chester-le-St) 1999. LO HS 108 v Essex (Birmingham) 2003 (CGT). LO BB 5-31 v Worcs (Worcester) 1997 (BHC). T20 HS 37. T20 BB 3-21.

CARTER, Neil Miller (Hottentots Holland HS; Cape Technicon), b Cape Town, South Africa 29 Jan 1975. British passport. 6'2". LHB, LFM. Boland 1999-00 to 2000-01. Warwickshire debut 2001; cap 2005. HS 103 v Sussex (Hove) 2002 – completed maiden hundred off 67 balls. BB 6-63 Boland v GW (Kimberley) 2000-01 and 6-63 v Sussex (Birmingham) 2006. LO HS 135 v Scot (Birmingham) 2006 (CGT). LO BB 5-31 v Durham (Birmingham) 2002 (NL). T20 HS 47. T20 BB 5-19.

DAGGETT, Lee Martin (Woodhey HS, and Holy Cross C, Bury; John Snow C, Durham) b Bury, Lancs 1 Oct 1982. 6'0". RHB, RFM. Durham UCCE 2003-05. British U 2004. Warwickshire debut 2006. HS 12* v Lancs (Blackpool) 2006. BB 8-94 DU v Durham (Chester-le-St) 2004. Wa BB 6-30 v Durham (Birmingham) 2006. LO HS 5* (twice – CGT, P40). LO BB 2-33 v Essex (Birmingham) 2006 (P40).

GILES, Ashley Fraser (George Abbot S, Guildford), b Chertsey, Surrey 19 Mar 1973. 6'3". RHB, SLA. Debut (Warwickshire) 1993; cap 1996; benefit 2006. No f-c appearances 2006 (injured). *Wisden* 2004. MBE 2005. **ECB central contract 2007. Tests**: 54 (1998 to 2006-07): HS 59 v A (Oval) 2005; BB 5-57 v WI (Birmingham) 2004. **LOI**: 62 (1997 to 2005); HS 41 v SA (Pretoria) 2004-05; BB 5-57 v I (Delhi) 2001-02. F-c Tours: A 1996-97 (Eng A), 2002-03 (*part*), 2006-07 (*part*); SA 2004-05; WI 2003-04; NZ 2001-02; I 2001-02; P 2000-01, 2005-06; SL 1997-98 (Eng A), 2000-01, 2003-04; B 2003-04; K 1997-98 (Eng A). HS 128* v Sussex (Hove) 2000. 50 wkts (2); most – 64 (1996). BB 8-90 (12-135 match) v Northants (Northampton) 2000. LO HS 107 v Derbys (Birmingham) 2000 (NWT). LO BB 5-21 v Norfolk (Birmingham) 1997 (NWT). T20 HS 0*. T20 BB 2-21.

NQ**GROENEWALD, Timothy** Duncan (Maritzburg C; South Africa U), b Pietermaritzburg, South Africa 10 Jan 1984. 6'0". RHB, RFM. Debut (Warwickshire) 2006. HS 76 v Durham (Chester-le-St) 2006. BB 2-36 v Yorks (Birmingham) 2006 – on CC debut. LO HS 9* (CGT). LO BB 2-42 v Essex (Birmingham) 2006 (P40). T20 HS – . T20 BB – .

NQ**HARRIS, Paul** Lee (Fish Hoek HS; Cape Town CFE), b Salisbury, Rhodesia 2 Nov 1978. RHB, SLA. W Province 1998-99 to 2001-02. Northerns 2002-03 to 2005-06. Titans 2004-05 to date. Warwickshire debut 2006. **Tests** (SA): 4 (2006-07); HS 11* v I (Cape Town) 2006-07 – on debut; BB 4-46 v P (Pretoria) 2006-07. HS 47 Northerns v North West (Potchefstroom) 2005-06. Wa HS 32 v Yorks (Scarborough) 2006. 50 wkts (1): 50 (2005-06). BB 6-54 Titans v Cobras (Benoni) 2005-06. Wa BB 6-80 v Hants (Southampton) 2006. LO HS 10 Northerns v GW (Pretoria) 2003-04. LO BB 3-33 v Essex (Birmingham) 2006 (P40). T20 HS 3. T20 BB 2-23.

‡**JAMES, Nicholas** Alexander (King Edward VI S, Aston), b Sandwell 17 Sep 1986. 5'9". LHB, SLA. Staffordshire 2006. Awaiting f-c debut. LO HS 30 v Worcs (Birmingham) 2006 (CGT) on Wa debut. LO BB 2-34 v Notts (Birmingham) 2006 (CGT).

LOUDON, Alexander Guy Rushworth (Wellesley House; Eton C; Collingwood C, Durham U), b Westminster, London 6 Sep 1980. Younger brother of H.J.H.Loudon (Durham UCCE 2001). 6'3". RHB, OB. Durham UCCE 2001-03; captain 2003. Kent 2003-04. Warwickshire debut 2005; cap 2006. MCC 2006. **LOI**: 1 (2006); HS 0 v SL (Chester-le-St) 2006. F-c Tours (Eng A): WI 2005-06; B 2006-07. HS 172 DU (record) v Durham (Chester-le-St) 2003. Wa HS 95* v Middx (Lord's) 2005. BB 6-47 K v Middx (Canterbury) 2004. Wa BB 6-66 v Glos (Birmingham) 2005. LO HS 73* v Kent (Canterbury) 2005 (NL). LO BB 4-48 K v Essex (Colchester) 2004 (NL). T20 HS 27. T20 BB 5-33.

MADDY, Darren Lee (Wreake Valley C), b Leicester 23 May 1974. 5'9". RHB, RM/OB. Leicestershire 1994-2006; cap 1996; benefit 2006. **Tests**: 3 (1999 to 1999-00); HS 24 v SA (Durban) 1999-00. **LOI**: 8 (1998 to 1999-00); HS 53 v Z (Harare) 1999-00. F-c Tours (Eng A): SA 1996-97 (Le), 1998-99, 1999-00 (Eng); SL 1997-98; Z 1998-99; K 1997-98. 1000 runs (4); most – 1187 (2002). HS 229* Le v LU (Leicester) 2003. CC HS 162 Le v Durham (Darlington) 1998. BB 5-37 Le v Hants (Southampton) 2002. LO HS 167* Le v Scot (Edinburgh) 2006 (CGT). LO BB 4-16 Le v Somerset (Taunton) 2000 (NL). T20 HS 111. T20 BB 2-10.

PARKER, Luke Charles (Finham Park S; Oxford Brookes U), b Coventry 27 Sep 1983. 6'0". RHB, RM. Oxford UCCE 2004-06. British U 2005-06. Warwickshire debut 2005. MCC 2006. HS 140 OU v Durham (Oxford) 2006. Wa HS 73 v Notts (Birmingham) 2006. BB 2-37 v Glos (Oxford) 2005. LO HS 17 Warwks CB v Cumb (Millom) 2001.

POONIA, Navdeep Singh (Moseley Park S; Wolverhampton U), b Govan, Glasgow, Scotland 11 May 1986. 6'3". RHB, RM. Debut (Warwickshire) 2006 – awaiting CC debut. Scotland 2006 to date (no f-c appearances). **LOI** (Scot): 8 (2006 to 2006-07); HS 67 v Canada (Mombasa) 2006-07. HS 35 v West Indies A (Birmingham) 2006. LO HS 67 (*see LOI*). T20 HS 19.

POWELL, Michael James (Lawrence Sheriff S, Rugby), b Bolton, Lancs 5 Apr 1975. 5'11". RHB, RM. Debut (Warwickshire) 1996; cap 1999; captain 2001-03. Griqualand West 2001-02. MCC 2004. Otago 2005-06. F-c Tour (Eng A): WI 2000-01. 1000 runs (1): 1046 (2000). HS 236 v OU (Oxford) 2001. CC HS 146 v Glamorgan (Birmingham) 2005. BB 2-16 v OU (Oxford) 1998. CC BB 2-29 v Somerset (Taunton) 2002. LO HS 101* v Northants (Birmingham) 2002 (BHC). LO BB 5-40 v Kent (Canterbury) 2002 (CGT). T20 HS 44*.

‡NQ**SANGAKKARA, Kumar** Chokshanada (Trinity C, Kandy; Colombo U), b Matale, Sri Lanka 27 Oct 1977. 5'11". LHB, OB, WK. Nondescripts 1997-98 to date. Central Province 2003-04 to 2004-05. **Tests** (SL): 64 (2000 to 2006-07); HS 287 v SA (Colombo SSC) 2006-07 – sharing in world record f-c partnership for any wicket of 624 with D.P.M.D.Jayawardena. **LOI** (SL): 182 (2000 to 2006-07); HS 138* v F-c Tours (SL): E 2002, 2006; A 2004; SA 1999-00 (SL A), 2000-01, 2002-03; WI 2003; NZ 2004-05, 2006-07; I 2005-06; P 2001-02, 2004-05; Z 2003-04; B 2005-06. 1000 runs (0+1): 1191 (2003-04). HS 287 (*see Tests*). BB 1-13 SL v Zim A (Harare) 2004. LO HS 156* SL A v Zim A (Moratuwa) 1999-00. T20 HS 93.

SHANTRY, Adam John (Priory S; Shrewsbury SFC), b Bristol 13 Nov 1982. 6'2½". Son of B.K.Shantry (Gloucestershire 1978-79). LHB, LFM. Northamptonshire 2003-04. Warwickshire debut 2006 (no CC appearance). Shropshire 2001. HS 38* Nh v Somerset (Northampton) 2003 – on CC debut (also took CC BB 3-8 including 3 wkts in 5 balls). BB 5-49 (and Wa HS 4*) v West Indies A (Birmingham) 2006. LO HS 15 Nh CB v Yorks CB (Northampton) 2002 (CGT). LO BB 5-37 Nh v NZ (Northampton) 2004. T20 HS – . T20 BB – .

NQ**STREAK, Heath** Hilton (Falcon C), b Bulawayo, Rhodesia 16 Mar 1974. 6'1". Son of D.H.Streak (Rhodesia 1976-77 to 1978-79, Matabeleland 1995-96). RHB, RFM. Debut for Zimbabwe B v Kent (Harare) 1992-93. Matabeleland 1993-94 to 2003-04. Hampshire 1995. Warwickshire debut 2004; cap 2005; captain 2006 to date. **Tests** (Z): 65 (1993-94 to 2005-06, 21 as captain); HS 127* v WI (Harare) 2003-04; BB 6-73 v I (Harare) 2005-06. **LOI** (Z): 187 (1993-94 to 2005, 68 as captain; HS 79* v NZ (Auckland) 2000-01; BB 5-32 v I (Bulawayo) 1996-97. F-c Tours (Z) (C=captain): E 1993, 2000, 2003C; A 1994-95, 2003-04C; SA 2004-05; WI 1999-00; NZ 1995-96, 1997-98, 2000-01C; I 2000-01C, 2001-02; P 1993-94, 1998-99; SL 1996, 1997-98, 2001-02; B 2001-02C. HS 131 Matabeleland – v Mashonaland CD (Bulawayo) 1995-96 and 131 v Midlands (Bulawayo) 2003-04. Wa HS 68* v Yorks (Scarborough) 2006. Wa BB 7-80 (13-158 match) v Northants (Birmingham) 2004 – on Wa debut. 50 wkts (1): 53 (1995). BB 7-55 Matabeleland – v Mashonaland (Bulawayo) 2003-04. LO HS 90* Matabeleland v Manicaland (Bulawayo) 2003-04. LO BB 5-32 (*see LOI*). T20 HS 59. T20 BB 3-21.

[NQ]**STEYN, Dale** Willem (Hans Merensky HS, Phalaborwa), b Phalaborwa, N Province, South Africa 27 Jun 1983. RHB, RF. Northerns 2003-04 to 2005-06. Titans 2004-05 to date. Essex 2005. **Tests** (SA): 11 (2004-05 to 2006-07); HS 13 and BB 5-47 v NZ (Pretoria) 2006. **LOI** (SA): 2 (2005-06); HS – ; BB 1-58. F-c Tours (SA): SL 2005-06 (SA A), 2006. HS 82 Ex v Durham (Chester-le-St) 2005. 50 wkts (0+1): 69 (2005-06). BB 5-27 Titans v Warriors (Benoni) 2005-06. UK BB 3-69 Ex v Leics (Chelmsford) 2005 – on UK debut. LO HS 6*. LO BB 5-20 SA A v SL A (Colombo) 2005-06. T20 HS 1. T20 BB 2-10.

TAHIR, Naqaash (Moseley S; Spring Hill C), b Birmingham 14 Nov 1983. 5'10", RHB, RFM. Debut (Warwickshire) 2004. HS 49 v Worcs (Worcester) 2004. BB 7-107 v Lancs (Blackpool) 2006. LO HS 1* (NL). LO BB 1-23 (NL).

TROTT, Ian **Jonathan** Leonard (Rondebosch BHC; Stellenbosch U), b Cape Town, South Africa 22 Apr 1981. 6'0". Stepbrother of K.C.Jackson (WP and Boland 1988-89 to 2001-02). RHB, RM. Boland 2000-01. W Province 2001-02. EU/British passport. Warwickshire debut 2003 scoring 134 v Sussex (Birmingham); cap 2005. Otago 2005-06. 1000 runs (3); most – 1170 (2004). HS 210 v Sussex (Birmingham) 2005. BB 7-39 v Kent (Canterbury) 2003. LO HS 112* v Somerset (Taunton) 2005 (NL). LO BB 4-55 v Hants (Lord's) 2005 (CGT). T20 HS 75*. T20 BB 2-19.

TROUGHTON, Jamie Oliver (**'*Jim*'**) (Trinity S; Leamington Spa; Birmingham U), b Camden, London 2 Mar 1979. Great-grandson of H.T.Crichton (Warwicks 1908). 5'11". LHB, SLA. Debut (Warwickshire) 2001; cap 2002. **LOI**: 6 (2003); HS 20 v P (Lord's) 2003. F-c Tour (ECB Acad): SL 2002-03. 1000 runs (1): 1067 (2002). HS 131* v Hants (Southampton) 2002. BB 3-1 v CU (Cambridge) 2004. CC BB 2-26 v Lancs (Birmingham) 2006. LO HS 115* and BB 4-23 Warwks CB v Cumb (Millom) 2001 (CGT). T20 HS 51. T20 BB 2-10.

WESTWOOD, Ian James (Wheelers Lane S; Solihull SFC), b Birmingham 13 Jul 1982. 5'7½". LHB, OB. Debut (Warwickshire) 2003. HS 178 v West Indies A (Birmingham) 2006. CC HS 106 v Glamorgan (Colwyn Bay) 2005. BB 2-46 v Kent (Birmingham) 2006. LO HS 55 and BB 1-28 Warwks CB v Cambs (March) 2001 (CGT). T20 HS 19*.

WOAKES, Christopher Roger (Barr Beacon Language C), b Birmingham 2 March 1989. RHB, RM. Debut (Warwickshire) 2006. Awaiting CC debut. Herefordshire 2006. HS 4 and BB 2-64 v West Indies A (Birmingham) 2006.

RELEASED/RETIRED

(Having made a first-class County appearance in 2006)

ALI, M.M. – *see WORCESTERSHIRE.*

FROST, Tony (James Brinkley HS; Stoke-on-Trent C), b Stoke-on-Trent, Staffs 17 Nov 1975. 5'11". RHB, WK. Warwickshire 1997-2006; cap 1999. HS 135* v Sussex (Horsham) 2004. LO HS 47 v Beds (Luton) (CGT). T20 HS 33*.

KLOKKER, Frederik Andreas (Hindsholm S), b Odense, Denmark 13 Mar 1983. LHB, WK. Warwickshire (1 match) 2006. Denmark (not f-c) 1999-00 to 2005. MCC YC 2002-05. HS 40 Wa v Sussex (Hove) 2006. LO HS 138* Denmark v USA (Armagh) 2005.

KNIGHT, Nicholas Verity (Felsted S; Loughborough U), b Watford, Herts 28 Nov 1969. 6'0". LHB, occ RM. Essex 1991-94; cap 1994. Warwickshire 1994-95 (SA tour) to 2006; cap 1995; captain 2004-05; benefit 2004. **Tests**: 17 (1995 to 2001); HS 113 v P (Leeds) 1996. **LOI**: 100 (1996 to 2002-03); HS 125* v P (Nottingham) 1996. F-c Tours: SA 1994-95 (Wa), 1999-00 (*part*); NZ 1996-97; I 1994-95 (Eng A); SL 1997-98 (Eng A – captain); P 1995-96 (Eng A); Z 1996-97; K 1997-98 (Eng A – captain). 1000 runs (7); most – 1520 (2002). HS 303* v Middx (Lord's) 2004. BB 1-61. LO HS 151 v Somerset (Birmingham) 1995 (NWT). LO BB 1-14 (SL). T20 HS 89.

NQVETTORI, Daniel Luca (St Paul's Collegiate, Hamilton), b Epsom, Auckland, New Zealand 27 Jan 1979. Nephew of A.J.Hill (CD 1975-76 to 1976-77). 6'3". LHB, SLA. N Districts 1996-97 to date. Nottinghamshire 2003. Warwickshire 2006 (1 match – injured). **Tests** (NZ): 72 (1996-97 to 2006-07); HS 137* v P (Hamilton) 2003-04; BB 7-87 (12-149 match) v A (Auckland) 1999-00. **LOI** (NZ): 185 (1996-97 to 2006-07, 11 as captain); HS 83 v A (Christchurch) 2004-05; BB 5-30 v WI (Lord's) 2004. F-c Tours (NZ): E 1999, 2004; A 1997-98, 2001-02, 2004-05; SA 1997-98 (NZ Acad), 2005-06; WI 2002; I 1999-00, 2003-04; P 2002; SL 1998, 2003; Z 1997-98, 2000-01, 2005; B 2004-05. HS 137* (*see Tests*). CC HS 27 Wa v Middx (Lord's) 2006. BB 7-87 (*see Tests*). CC BB 4-74 Nt v Kent (Maidstone) 2003. Wa BB – . LO HS 138 ND v Auckland (Auckland) 2004-05. LO BB 5-30 (*see LOI*). T20 HS 5. T20 BB – .

WAGH, M.A. – *see NOTTINGHAMSHIRE.*

N.A.Warren left the staff without making a first-class appearance in 2006.

SUSSEX RELEASED/RETIRED (continued from p 97)

RELEASED/RETIRED

(Having made a first-class County appearance in 2006)

HEATHER, Sean Andrew (Chichester HS), b Chichester 5 Feb 1982. 6'0". RHB, RM. Sussex 2005-06. No CC appearances. HS 7 v B (Hove) 2005. LO HS 11 v Middx (Lord's) 2006 (P40). T20 HS 8. T20 BB 3-16.

LINLEY, Timothy Edward (St Mary's RC CS, Menston; Notre Dame SFC; Oxford Brookes U), b Leeds 23 Mar 1982. 6'2". RHB, RFM. Oxford UCCE 2003-05. British U 2004. Sussex 2006 (1 match). No CC appearances. HS 42 OU v Derbys (Oxford) 2005. BB 3-44 OU v Surrey (Oxford) 2004. Sx HS 0 and BB 1-56 v Sri Lankans (Hove) 2006.

SPENCER, Duncan John (Gosnells HS, W Australia), b Nelson, Lancs 5 Apr 1972. 5'8". RHB, RF. Kent 1993-94. W Australia 1993-94. Sussex 2006. HS 75 K v Z (Canterbury) 1993. Sx HS 17 v SL (Hove) 2006. CC HS 16 and Sx BB 1-70 v Warwks (Hove) 2006. BB 4-31 K v Leics (Leicester) 1994. LO HS 17* K v Northants (Canterbury) 1993 (SL). LO BB 4-35 WA v NSW (Perth) 2000-01.

TURK, Neil Richard Keith (Sackville S, E Grinstead; Exeter U), b Cuckfield 28 Apr 1983. 6'0". LHB, RM. Sussex 2006 (1 match). HS 24 v SL (Hove) 2006. LO HS 36 v Essex (Chelmsford) 2002 (NL).

NQYASIR ARAFAT Satti – *see KENT.*

WARWICKSHIRE 2006

RESULTS SUMMARY

	Place	*Won*	*Lost*	*Tied*	*Drew*	*No Result*
County Championship (1st Division)	**4th**	6	5		5	
All First-Class Matches		7	5		6	
C & G Trophy (North Conference)	9th	2	6			1
Pro40 League (1st Division)	5th	3	4			1
Twenty20 Cup (Mid/West/Wales Division)	3rd	4	3			1

COUNTY CHAMPIONSHIP AVERAGES

BATTING AND FIELDING

Cap		*M*	*I*	*NO*	*HS*	*Runs*	*Avge*	*100*	*50*	*Ct/St*
1999	T.Frost	6	11	5	96	377	62.83	-	3	15
2005	I.J.L.Trott	16	28	2	177*	1073	41.26	3	3	20
1995	N.V.Knight	16	29	1	126	991	35.39	2	5	21
–	T.R.Ambrose	9	14	1	133	443	34.07	1	3	30/4
2001	I.R.Bell	4	7	–	79	214	30.57	–	2	2
–	I.J.Westwood	11	20	2	81	519	28.83	–	4	5
2000	M.A.Wagh	12	23	2	128	600	28.57	2	1	1
2005	H.H.Streak	14	23	5	68*	485	26.94	–	2	5
1999	M.J.Powell	5	9	1	42	195	24.37	–	–	4
2002	J.O.Troughton	9	16	–	103	364	22.75	1	2	3
–	M.M.Ali	5	8	–	68	172	21.50	–	2	2
2006	A.G.R.Loudon	13	21	–	73	448	21.33	–	4	7
–	T.D.Groenewald	4	7	1	76	125	20.83	–	1	–
1995	D.R.Brown	10	18	1	69	335	19.70	–	2	4
–	L.C.Parker	3	6	-	73	110	18.33	–	1	3
2005	N.M.Carter	12	20	4	36	250	15.62	–	–	1
–	P.L.Harris	8	11	1	32	140	14.00	–	–	3
–	L.M.Daggett	5	9	4	12*	37	7.40	–	–	1
–	J.E.Anyon	10	17	6	18*	60	5.45	–	–	3

Also batted: F.A.Klokker (1) 40 (3 ct); N.Tahir (2) 21, 7 (1 ct); D.L.Vettori (1) 27.

BOWLING

	O	*M*	*R*	*W*	*Avge*	*Best*	*5wI*	*10wM*
L.M.Daggett	115.4	25	405	16	25.31	6- 30	1	–
N.Tahir	65.5	11	256	10	25.60	7-107	1	–
P.L.Harris	347.2	91	905	31	29.19	6- 80	4	–
D.R.Brown	307.3	68	914	31	29.48	4- 45	–	–
H.H.Streak	430.4	95	1335	40	33.37	6- 73	2	–
J.E.Anyon	320.2	63	953	27	35.29	5- 83	1	–
N.M.Carter	369.2	69	1353	34	39.79	6- 63	1	–
A.G.R.Loudon	329.2	44	1007	25	40.28	5- 49	2	–
Also bowled:								
I.R.Bell	30	5	111	5	22.20	2- 59	–	–
J.O.Troughton	93.3	17	336	7	48.00	2- 26	–	–

M.M.Ali 73.3-13-318-2; T.D.Groenewald 77-12-286-3; N.V.Knight 9-0-41-0; M.J.Powell 19-0-80-0; I.J.L.Trott 3-0-28-1; D.L.Vettori 31-4-92-0; M.A.Wagh 3-0-14-0; I.J.Westwood 23-3-58-2.

The First-Class Averages (pp 130–146) give the records of Warwickshire's players in all first-class matches for the county (Warwickshire's other opponents being Cambridge UCCE and West Indies A), with the exception of I.R.Bell whose full county figures are as above, and:

A.G.R.Loudon 14-22-0-73-458-20.81-0-4-9ct. 339.2-49-1023-29-35.27-5/49-2-0.

L.C.Parker 4-7-0-73-140-20.00-0-1-4ct. Did not bowl.

WARWICKSHIRE RECORDS

FIRST-CLASS CRICKET

Highest Total	For	810-4d		v	Durham	Birmingham	1994
	V	887		by	Yorkshire	Birmingham	1896
Lowest Total	For	16		v	Kent	Tonbridge	1913
	V	15		by	Hampshire	Birmingham	1922
Highest Innings	For	501*	B.C.Lara	v	Durham	Birmingham	1994
	V	322	I.V.A.Richards	for	Somerset	Taunton	1985

Highest Partnership for each Wicket

1st	377*	N.F.Horner/K.Ibadulla	v	Surrey	The Oval	1960
2nd	465*	J.A.Jameson/R.B.Kanhai	v	Glos	Birmingham	1974
3rd	327	S.P.Kinneir/W.G.Quaife	v	Lancashire	Birmingham	1901
4th	470	A.I.Kallicharran/G.W.Humpage	v	Lancashire	Southport	1982
5th	322*	B.C.Lara/K.J.Piper	v	Durham	Birmingham	1994
6th	220	H.E.Dollery/J.Buckingham	v	Derbyshire	Derby	1938
7th	289*	I.R.Bell/T.Frost	v	Sussex	Horsham	2004
8th	228	A.J.W.Croom/R.E.S.Wyatt	v	Worcs	Dudley	1925
9th	154	G.W.Stephens/A.J.W.Croom	v	Derbyshire	Birmingham	1925
10th	214	N.V.Knight/A.Richardson	v	Hampshire	Birmingham	2002

Best Bowling	For	10-41	J.D.Bannister	v	Comb Servs	Birmingham	1959
(Innings)	V	10-36	H.Verity	for	Yorkshire	Leeds	1931
Best Bowling	For	15-76	S.Hargreave	v	Surrey	The Oval	1903
(Match)	V	17-92	A.P.Freeman	for	Kent	Folkestone	1932

Most Runs – Season	2417	M.J.K.Smith	(av 60.42)	1959
Most Runs – Career	35146	D.L.Amiss	(av 41.64)	1960-87
Most 100s – Season	9	A.I.Kallicharran		1984
	9	B.C.Lara		1994
Most 100s – Career	78	D.L.Amiss		1960-87
Most Wkts – Season	180	W.E.Hollies	(av 15.13)	1946
Most Wkts – Career	2201	W.E.Hollies	(av 20.45)	1932-57
Most Career W-K Dismissals	800	E.J.Smith	(662 ct/138 st)	1904-30
Most Career Catches in the Field	422	M.J.K.Smith		1956-75

LIMITED-OVERS CRICKET

Highest Total	**CGT**	392-5		v	Oxfordshire	Birmingham	1984
	P40	310-5		v	Lancs	Birmingham	2004
	T20	205-7		v	Glamorgan	Swansea	2005
		205-2		v	Northants	Birmingham	2005
Lowest Total	**CGT**	98		v	Leics	Leicester	1998
	P40	59		v	Yorks	Leeds	2001
	T20	115		v	Surrey	Nottingham	2003
Highest Innings	**CGT**	206	A.I.Kallicharran	v	Oxfordshire	Birmingham	1984
	P40	137	I.R.Bell	v	Yorkshire	Birmingham	2005
	T20	89	N.V.Knight	v	Worcestershire	Worcester	2003
Best Bowling	**CGT**	6-32	K.Ibadulla	v	Hampshire	Birmingham	1965
		6-32	A.I.Kallicharran	v	Oxfordshire	Birmingham	1984
	P40	6-15	A.A.Donald	v	Yorkshire	Birmingham	1995
	T20	5-19	N.M.Carter	v	Worcestershire	Birmingham	2005

WORCESTERSHIRE

Formation of Present Club: 11 March 1865
Inaugural First-Class Match: 1899
Colours: Dark Green and Black
Badge: Shield Argent a Fess between three Pears Sable
County Championships: (5) 1964, 1965, 1974, 1988, 1989
Gillette/NatWest/C & G Trophy Winners: (1) 1994
Benson and Hedges Cup Winners: (1) 1991
Pro 40/National League (Div 1) Winners: (0); best – 2nd 1999, 2002
Sunday League Winners: (3) 1971, 1987, 1988
Twenty20 Cup Winners: (0); best – Quarter-Finalist 2004

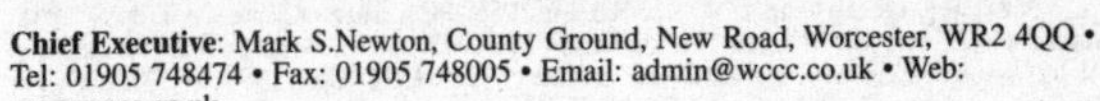

Chief Executive: Mark S.Newton, County Ground, New Road, Worcester, WR2 4QQ • Tel: 01905 748474 • Fax: 01905 748005 • Email: admin@wccc.co.uk • Web: www.wccc.co.uk

Director of Cricket/First XI Coach: Steve J.Rhodes. **Captain**: V.S.Solanki. **Vice-Captain**: G.J.Batty. **Overseas Players**: D.E.Bollinger and P.A.Jaques. **2007 Beneficiary**: V.S.Solanki. **Head Groundsman**: Tim Packwood. **Scorer**: Neil D.Smith. ‡ New registration. [NQ]Not qualified for England.

Worcestershire revised their capping policy in 2002 and now award players with their County Colours when they make their Championship debut.

ALI, Kabir (Moseley CS and SFC), b Moseley, Birmingham 24 Nov 1980. 6'0". Cousin of Kadeer Ali (*see GLOUCESTERSHIRE*) and M.M.Ali (*see below*). RHB, RMF. Debut (Worcestershire) 1999. Rajasthan 2006-07. **Tests**: 1 (2003); HS 9 and BB 3-80 v SA (Leeds) 2003 – on debut. **LOI**: 14 (2003 to 2006); HS 39* v P (Rawalpindi) 2005-06; BB 4-45 v I (Delhi) 2005-06. F-c Tours (Eng A): WI 2005-06; SL 2002-03 (ECB Acad). HS 84* v Durham (Stockton) 2003. 50 wkts (3); most – 71 (2002). BB 8-53 (*before lunch first day*) v Yorks (Scarborough) 2003. LO HS 92 v Essex (Worcester) 2003 (NL). LO BB 5-36 v Yorks (Leeds) 2002 (NL). T20 HS 49. T20 BB 2-25.

‡ALI, Moeen Munir (Moseley S), b Birmingham 18 Jun 1987. Brother of Kadeer Ali (*see GLOUCESTERSHIRE*) and cousin of Kabir Ali (*see above*). 6'0". LHB, OB. Warwickshire 2005-06 having joined staff when aged 15. HS 68 Wa v Notts (Nottingham) 2006 – on CC debut – and 68 Wa v Durham (Chester-le-St) 2006. BB 2-50 Wa v Lancs (Birmingham) 2006. LO HS 64 Wa v Northants (Birmingham) 2006 (P40). LO BB 1-9 Wa v Derbys (Derby) 2006 (CGT).

BATTY, Gareth Jon (Bingley GS), b Bradford, Yorks 13 Oct 1977. Younger brother of J.D.Batty (Yorkshire and Somerset 1989-96). 5'11". RHB, OB. Yorkshire 1997. Surrey 1999-2001. Worcestershire debut 2002. **Tests**: 7 (2003-04 to 2005); HS 38 v SL (Kandy) 2003-04; BB 3-55 v SL (Galle) 2003-04. Took wicket with his third ball in Test cricket. **LOI**: 7 (2002-03 to 2005-06); HS 3; BB 2-40 v WI (Gros Islet) 2003-04. F-c Tours: WI 2003-04, 2005-06; SL 2002-03 (ECB Acad); SL 2003-04; B 2003-04. HS 133 v Surrey (Oval) 2004. 50 wkts (2); most – 60 (2003). BB 7-52 (10-113 match) v Northants (Northampton) 2004. LO HS 83* Sy v Yorks (Oval) 2001 (NL). LO BB 4-27 v Leics (Leicester) 2006 (CGT). T20 HS 87. T20 BB 3-38.

‡[NQ]**BOLLINGER, Douglas** Erwin, b Baulkham Hills, Sydney, Australia 24 Jul 1981. LHB, LFM. New South Wales 2002-03 to date. HS 31* NSW v Q (Brisbane) 2006-07. BB 4-44 NSW v Vic (Sydney) 2006-07. LO HS 6* NSW v Tas (Sydney) 2006-07. LO BB 4-24 NSW v S Aus (Canberra) 2004-05. T20 HS – . T20 BB – .

DAVIES, Steven Michael (King Charles I S, Kidderminster), b Bromsgrove 17 Jun 1986. 5'10". LHB, WK. Debut (Worcestershire) 2005. 2nd XI debut 2001 when 15yr 8d. MCC 2006. F-c Tour (Eng A): B 2006-07. 1000 runs (1): 1052 (2006). HS 192 v Glos (Bristol) 2006. LO HS 52 v Derbys (Worcester) 2006 (P40). T20 HS 27.

HICK, Graeme Ashley (Prince Edward HS, Salisbury), b Salisbury, Rhodesia 23 May 1966. 6'3". RHB, OB. Zimbabwe 1983-84 to 1985-86. Worcestershire debut 1984; cap 1986; benefit 1999; captain 2000-02; Testimonial 2006. N Districts 1987-88 to 1988-89. MCC 1988-1991. Queensland 1990-91. *Wisden* 1986. PCA 1988. Lawrence Trophy 1988. **Tests**: 65 (1991 to 2000-01); HS 178 v I (Bombay) 1992-93; BB 4-126 v NZ (Wellington) 1991-92. Took wicket with his third ball in Test cricket. **LOI**: 120 (1991 to 2000-01); HS 126* v SL (Adelaide) 1998-99; BB 5-33 v Z (Harare) 1999-00. F-c Tours: E 1985 (Z); A 1994-95, 1998-99 (*part*); SA 1995-96, 1999-00 (*part*); WI 1993-94; NZ 1991-92; I 1992-93; P 2000-01; SL 1983-84 (Z), 1992-93, 2000-01; Z 1990-91 (Wo), 1996-97 (Wo). 1000 runs (19+1), inc 2000 (3): 2004 (1986), 2713 (1988), 2347 (1990); youngest to score 2000 (1986). Scored 1019 runs before June 1988, including a record 410 runs in April. Fewest innings for 10,000 runs in county cricket (179). Youngest (24) to score 50 f-c hundreds. Second-youngest (32) to score 100 f-c hundreds. Scored 645 runs without being dismissed (UK record) in 1990. 100th f-c hundred for Worcestershire 2006. HS 405* (Worcs record and then second highest in UK f-c matches) v Somerset (Taunton) 1988. BB 5-18 v Leics (Worcester) 1995. LO HS 172* v Devon (Worcester) 1987 (NWT). LO BB 5-19 Eng v Pak A (Lahore) 1998-99. T20 HS 116*.

[NQ]**JAQUES, Philip** Anthony (Fig Tree HS, Wollongong; Australian C of PE, Homebush), b Wollongong, NSW, Australia 3 May 1979. 6'1". LHB, SLC. British passport (English parents). NSW 2000-01 to date. Northamptonshire 2003; cap 2003. Yorkshire 2004-05; cap 2005. Worcestershire debut 2006. **Tests** (A): 2 (2005-06); HS 66 v B (Chittagong) 2005-06. **LOI** (A): 6 (2005-06 to 2006-07); HS 94 v SA (Melbourne) 2005-06. 1000 runs (4+1); most – 1409 (2003). HS 244 v Essex (Chelmsford) 2006. First to score 200s for (243 v Hants 2004) and against Yorkshire (222 for Northants 2003). LO HS 158* NSW v S Aus (Adelaide) 2005-06. T20 HS 92.

‡**KERVEZEE, Alexei** Nicolaas, b Walvis Bay, Namibia 11 Sep 1989. RHB, OB. Holland 2005-06. **LOI** (H): 10 (2006 to 2006-07); HS 49 v Canada (Potchefstroom) 2006-07. HS 46* v Ireland (Belfast) 2005. LO HS 49 (*see LOI*).

KHALID, Shaftab Ahmed (Dormers Wells HS; W Thames C; Middlesex U), b Lahore, Pakistan 6 Oct 1982. 5'11". RHB, OB. Debut (Worcestershire) 2003 – no 1st XI appearances 2006. F-c Tour (Eng A): I 2003-04. HS 20 v LU (Worcester) 2005. CC HS 13 v Glamorgan (Worcester) 2003 – on CC debut. BB 4-131 v Northants (Northampton) 2003. LO HS 9* (CGT). LO BB 2-40 v Essex (Worcester) 2003 (NL). T20 HS – .

MALIK Muhammad **Nadeem**, (Wilford Meadows CS; Bilborough C), b Nottingham 6 Oct 1982. 6'5". RHB, RFM. Nottinghamshire 2001-03. Worcestershire debut 2004. Notts 2nd XI debut 1999 when aged 16y 337d. HS 39* v NZ (Worcester) 2004. CC HS 35 v Glamorgan (Colwyn Bay) 2006. BB 5-57 Nt v Derbys (Nottingham) 2001. Wo BB 5-71 v Leics (Leicester) 2005. LO HS 11 Nt v Worcs (Nottingham) 2002 (NL). LO BB 4-42 v Sussex (Worcester) 2004 (NL). T20 HS 3*. T20 BB 3-23.

MASON, Matthew Sean (Mazenod C, Lesmurdie, WA), b Claremont, Perth, Australia 20 Mar 1974. British passport. 6'5". RHB, RFM. W Australia 1996-97 to 1997-98. Worcestershire debut 2002. HS 63 v Warwks (Worcester) 2004. 50 wkts (3); most – 53 (2003, 2005). BB 8-45 (10-117) v Glos (Worcester) 2006. LO HS 25 v Durham (Worcester) 2004 (NL). LO BB 4-34 v Surrey (Guildford) 2003 (NL). T20 HS 8*. T20 BB 3-42.

MITCHELL, Daryl Keith Henry (Prince Henry's HS; University C, Worcester), b Badsey, near Evesham 25 Nov 1983. 5'10". RHB, RM. Debut (Worcestershire) 2005. HS 134* v Glamorgan (Colwyn Bay) 2006. BB 1-59 v Essex (Worcester) 2005. LO HS 7 v West Indies A (Worcester) 2006. T20 HS 4. T20 BB 2-26.

MOORE, Stephen Colin (St Stithian's C, Johannesburg; Exeter U), b Johannesburg, South Africa 4 Nov 1980. 6'1". RHB, RM. Debut (Worcestershire) 2003. 1000 runs (2); most – 1399 (2005). HS 246 v Derbys (Worcester) 2005. BB 1-13 v Lancs (Worcester) 2004. LO HS 105 v Leics (Leicester) 2006 (P40). LO BB 1-1 (NL). T20 HS 53.

NQ**PRICE, Raymond** William (Watershed C), b Salisbury, Rhodesia 12 Jun 1976. 6'2". RHB, SLA. Mashonaland CD 1995-96. Zimbabwe Academy 1998-99 to 1999-2000. Midlands 1999-00 to 2003-04. Worcestershire debut 2004; Kolpak registration 2005 to date. **Tests** (Z): 18 (1999-00 to 2003-04); HS 36 v A (Perth) 2003-04; BB 6-73 (10-161 match) v WI (Harare) 2003-04. **LOI** (Z): 26 (2002-03 to 2003-04); HS 20* v B (Harare) 2003-04;BB 2-16 v WI (Bulawayo) 2003-04. F-c Tours (Z): E 2003; A 2003-04; I 2001-02; SL 1999-00 (Zim A); K 2001-02 (Zim A). HS 117* Midlands v Manicaland (Mutare) 2003-04. Wo HS 76 * v Lancs (Worcester) 2004. BB 8-35 Midlands v CFX Academy) Kwekwe) 2001-02. Wo BB 4-38 v Northants (Northampton) 2006. LO HS 47 v West Indies A (Worcester) 2006. LO BB 4-21 v Notts (Worcester) 2005 (NL). T20 HS 10. T20 BB 2-13.

SILLENCE, Roger John (Highbury SS; Salisbury Art C), b Salisbury, Wilts 29 Jun 1977. 6'3". RHB, RMF. Gloucestershire 2001-05, taking 5-97 v Sussex (Hove) on debut; cap 2004. Worcestershire debut 2006. Wiltshire 1997-2000. HS 101 Gs v Derbys (Bristol) 2002. Wo HS 64 v Northants (Northampton) 2006. BB 7-96 v Somerset (Taunton) 2006. LO HS 94 v West Indies A (Worcester) 2006. LO BB 4-35 Gs v WI A (Cheltenham) 2002. T20 HS 22*. T20 BB 2-27.

SMITH, Benjamin Francis (Kibworth HS), b Corby, Northants 3 Apr 1972. 5'9". RHB, RM. Leicestershire 1990-2001; cap 1995. MCC 1999-2000. Central Districts 2001-01 to 2001-02. Worcestershire debut 2002; captain 2003 to 2004 (*part*). F-c Tour (Le): SA 1996-97. 1000 runs (7); most – 1546 (2005). HS 204 Le v Surrey (Oval) 1998. Wo HS 203 v Somerset (Taunton) 2006. BB (Le) 1-5. Wo BB 1-39. LO HS 115 Le v Somerset (Weston-s-M) 1995 (SL). LO BB 1-2 (CGT). T20 HS 105.

SOLANKI, Vikram Singh (Regis S, Wolverhampton), b Udaipur, India 1 Apr 1976. 6'0". RHB, OB. Debut (Worcestershire) 1995; cap 1998; captain 2005 to date; benefit 2007. Rajasthan 2006-07. F-c Tours (Eng A): SA 1998-99, 1999-00 (Eng – *part*); WI 2000-01, 2005-06; NZ 1999-00; SL 2004-05; Z 1996-97 (Wo), 1998-99; B 1999-00. **LOI**: 51 (1999-00 to 2006); HS 106 v SA (Oval) 2003; BB 1-17. 1000 runs (3); most – 1339 (1999). HS 222 v Glos (Bristol) 2006. BB 5-40 v Middx (Lord's) 2004. LO HS 164* v Worcs CB (Worcester) 2003 (CGT). LO BB 4-14 v Somerset (Taunton) 2006 (P40). T20 HS 92. T20 BB 1-25.

WEDGE, Stuart Andrew (Codsall Community HS), b Wolverhampton, Staffs 24 Oct 1985. 5'10". LHB, LMF. Debut (Worcestershire) 2005. HS 0*. CC HS – . BB 5-112 v Essex (Worcester) 2005 – on CC debut. LO HS – . LO BB 2-31 v Yorks (Worcester) 2006 (CGT). T20 HS – . T20 BB – .

RELEASED/RETIRED continued on p 116

WORCESTERSHIRE 2006

RESULTS SUMMARY

	Place	*Won*	*Lost*	*Tied*	*Drew*	*No Result*
County Championship (2nd Division)	**2nd**	8	4		4	
All First-Class Matches		8	4		4	
C & G Trophy (North Conference)	3rd	5	3			1
Pro40 League (2nd Division)	2nd	6	2			
Twenty20 Cup (Mid/West/Wales Division)	6th	2	6			

COUNTY CHAMPIONSHIP AVERAGES

BATTING AND FIELDING

Cap		*M*	*I*	*NO*	*HS*	*Runs*	*Avge*	*100*	*50*	*Ct/St*
2006[c]	P.A.Jaques	8	15	2	244	1148	88.30	3	7	8
1986	G.A.Hick	14	23	2	182	1023	48.71	4	3	36
2005[c]	D.K.H.Mitchell	4	8	2	134*	282	47.00	1	2	3
2006[c]	L.Vincent	6	11	1	141	469	46.90	2	1	5
2002[c]	G.J.Batty	15	24	8	112*	744	46.50	1	3	14
1998	V.S.Solanki	16	29	2	222	1252	46.37	4	4	12
2005[c]	S.M.Davies	16	27	1	192	1004	38.61	3	3	58/5
2002[c]	B.F.Smith	16	27	2	203	915	36.60	2	3	23
2003[c]	S.C.Moore	16	30	2	97	960	34.28	–	9	6
2006[c]	R.J.Sillence	13	19	1	64	487	27.05	–	3	5
2004[c]	R.W.Price	8	10	3	56	106	15.14	–	1	3
2002[c]	M.S.Mason	10	11	5	29*	85	14.16	–	–	2
2002[c]	Kabir Ali	11	16	2	38*	168	12.00	–	–	1
2004[c]	M.N.Malik	6	1	3	35	68	11.33	–	–	–
2006[c]	Z.Khan	16	21	6	30*	161	10.73	–	–	4

Also played: S.A.Wedge (2‡ matches – 2005[c]) did not bat.

BOWLING

	O	*M*	*R*	*W*	*Avge*	*Best*	*5wI*	*10wM*
M.S.Mason	296.1	71	910	41	22.19	8- 45	3	1
Kabir Ali	337.1	68	1161	40	29.02	7- 43	3	–
Z.Khan	618.4	132	2268	78	29.07	9-138	5	2
M.N.Malik	137	30	536	17	31.52	3- 49	–	–
G.J.Batty	496.1	112	1439	43	33.46	6-119	1	–
R.J.Sillence	220.4	35	792	23	34.43	7- 96	1	–
R.W.Price	279.4	54	813	15	54.20	4- 38	–	–
Also bowled:								
V.S.Solanki	52.3	8	165	5	33.00	2- 16	–	–

P.A.Jaques 0.2-0-15-0; S.C.Moore 10-1-108-1; B.F.Smith 5-0-48-1; L.Vincent 22-2-76-1; S.A.Wedge 27-3-108-4.

Worcestershire played no fixtures outside the County Championship in 2006. The First-Class Averages (pp 130–146) give the records of their players in all first-class matches for the county, with the exception of S.M. Davies whose full county figures are as above.

‡ Full substitute for Kabir Ali v Essex at Chelmsford.

2006[c] Denotes awarded Worcestershire 1st XI colours, a system which replaced capping in 2002.

WORCESTERSHIRE RECORDS

FIRST-CLASS CRICKET

Highest Total	For	696-8d		v	Somerset	Worcester	2005
	V	701-4d		by	Leics	Worcester	1906
Lowest Total	For	24		v	Yorkshire	Huddersfield	1903
	V	30		by	Hampshire	Worcester	1903
Highest Innings	For	405*	G.A.Hick	v	Somerset	Taunton	1988
	V	331*	J.D.B.Robertson	for	Middlesex	Worcester	1949

Highest Partnership for each Wicket

1st	309	F.L.Bowley/H.K.Foster	v	Derbyshire	Derby	1901
2nd	300	W.P.C.Weston/G.A.Hick	v	Indians	Worcester	1996
3rd	438*	G.A.Hick/T.M.Moody	v	Hampshire	Southampton	1997
4th	330	B.F.Smith/G.A.Hick	v	Somerset	Taunton	2006
5th	393	E.G.Arnold/W.B.Burns	v	Warwicks	Birmingham	1909
6th	265	G.A.Hick/S.J.Rhodes	v	Somerset	Taunton	1988
7th	256	D.A.Leatherdale/S.J.Rhodes	v	Notts	Nottingham	2002
8th	184	S.J.Rhodes/S.R.Lampitt	v	Derbyshire	Kidderminster	1991
9th	181	J.A.Cuffe/R.D.Burrows	v	Glos	Worcester	1907
10th	119	W.B.Burns/G.A.Wilson	v	Somerset	Worcester	1906

Best Bowling	For	9- 23	C.F.Root	v	Lancashire	Worcester	1931
(Innings)	V	10- 51	J.Mercer	for	Glamorgan	Worcester	1936
Best Bowling	For	15- 87	A.J.Conway	v	Glos	Moreton-in-M	1914
(Match)	V	17-212	J.C.Clay	for	Glamorgan	Swansea	1937

Most Runs – Season	2654	H.H.I.Gibbons	(av 52.03)	1934
Most Runs – Career	34490	D.Kenyon	(av 34.18)	1946-67
Most 100s – Season	10	G.M.Turner		1970
	10	G.A.Hick		1988
Most 100s – Career	102	G.A.Hick		1984-2006
Most Wkts – Season	207	C.F.Root	(av 17.52)	1925
Most Wkts – Career	2143	R.T.D.Perks	(av 23.73)	1930-55
Most Career W-K Dismissals	1095	S.J.Rhodes	(991 ct/104 st)	1985-2004
Most Career Catches in the Field	487	G.A.Hick		1984-2006

LIMITED-OVERS CRICKET

Highest Total	**CGT**	404-3		v	Devon	Worcester	1987
	P40	307-4		v	Derbyshire	Worcester	1975
	T20	223-9		v	Glamorgan	Worcester	2005
Lowest Total	**CGT**	98		v	Durham	Chester-le-St	1968
	P40	86		v	Yorkshire	Leeds	1969
	T20	86		v	Northants	Worcester	2006
Highest Innings	**CGT**	180*	T.M.Moody	v	Surrey	The Oval	1994
	P40	160	T.M.Moody	v	Kent	Worcester	1991
	T20	116*	G.A.Hicks	v	Northants	Luton	2004
Best Bowling	**CGT**	7-19	N.V.Radford	v	Beds	Bedford	1991
	P40	6-16	Shoaib Akhtar	v	Glos	Worcester	2005
	T20	3-21	M.Hayward	v	Somerset	Worcester	2003

YORKSHIRE

Formation of Present Club: 8 January 1863
Substantial Reorganisation: 10 December 1891
Inaugural First-Class Match: 1864
Colours: Dark Blue, Light Blue and Gold
Badge: White Rose
County Championships (since 1890): (30) 1893, 1896, 1898, 1900, 1901, 1902, 1905, 1908, 1912, 1919, 1922, 1923, 1924, 1925, 1931, 1932, 1933, 1935, 1937, 1938, 1939, 1946, 1959, 1960, 1962, 1963, 1966, 1967, 1968, 2001
Joint Champions: (1) 1949
Gillette/NatWest/C & G Trophy Winners: (3) 1965, 1969, 2002
Benson and Hedges Cup Winners: (1) 1987
Pro 40/National League (Div 1) Winners: (0); best – 2nd 2000
Sunday League Winners: (1) 1983
Twenty20 Cup Winners: (0); best – 2nd in Group 2003

Chief Executive: Stewart M.Regan, Headingley Cricket Ground, Leeds, LS6 3BU • Tel: 0113 278 7394 • Fax: 0113 278 4099 • Email: cricket@yorkshireccc.org.uk • Web: www.yorkshireccc.org.uk

Director of Cricket: Martyn D.Moxon. **Captain**: D.Gough. **Vice-Captain**: none. **Overseas Players**: M.T.G.Elliott, J.N.Gillespie and Younis Khan. **2007 Beneficiary**: none. **Head Groundsman**: Andy Fogarty. **Scorer**: John T.Potter. ‡ New registration. NQNot qualified for England.

BRESNAN, Timothy Thomas (Castleford HS and TC; Pontefract New C), b Pontefract 28 Feb 1985. 6'0". RHB, RMF. Debut (Yorkshire) 2003; cap 2006. MCC 2006. **LOI**: 4 (2006); HS 20 v SL (Manchester) 2006; BB 1-38 v SL (Oval) 2006. F-c Tour (Eng A): B 2006-07. HS 94 v MCC v Notts (Lord's) 2006. Y HS 91 v Hants (Leeds) 2006. BB 5-42 v Worcs (Worcester) 2005. LO HS 61 v Leics (Leeds) 2003 (NL). BB 4-25 v Somerset (Leeds) 2005 (NL). T20 HS 42. T20 BB 3-21.

BROPHY, Gerard Louis (Christian Brothers C, Boksburg; Witwatersrand TC), b Welkom, Orange Free State, South Africa 26 Nov 1975. 5'11". British/EU passport. Qualified for England 2006. RHB, WK. Transvaal/Gauteng 1996-97 to 1998-99. Free State 1999-00 to 2000-01. Northamptonshire 2002-05. Yorkshire debut 2006. F-c Tour (SA Acad): Z 1998. HS 185 SA Academy v Zim President's XI (Harare) 1998-99. UK HS 181 Nh v Sussex (Hove) 2004. Y HS 97 v Warwks (Scarborough) 2006. LO HS Nh 57* v NZ (Northampton) 2004. T20 HS 57.

NQ**ELLIOTT, Matthew** Thomas Gray (Kyabram Secondary C; La Trobe U), b Chelsea, Victoria, Australia 28 Sep 1971. 6'3". LHB, LM/SLC. Victoria 1992-93 to 2004-05. Glamorgan 2000, 2004-05; cap 2000. Yorkshire 2002. S Australia 2005-06 to date. *Wisden* 1997. **Tests** (A): 21 (1996-97 to 2004); HS 199 v E (Leeds) 1997. **LOI** (A): 1 (1997); HS 1 v E (Lord's) 1997. F-c Tours (A): E 1995 (Young A), 1997; SA 1996-97; WI 1998-99. 1000 runs (3+5); most – 1429 (2003-04). HS 203 v Tasmania (Melbourne) 1995-96. UK HS 199 (*see Tests*). CC HS 177 Gm v Sussex (Colwyn Bay) 2000. Y HS 127 v Warwks (Birmingham) 2002. BB 3-68 Vic Q (Melbourne) 2004-05. UK BB 1-23. Y BB 1-64. LO HS 156 v Dorset (Bournemouth) 2000 (NWT). T20 HS 52*.

GALE, Andrew William (Whitcliffe Mount S; Heckmondwike GS), b Dewsbury 28 Nov 1983. 6'2". LHB, LB. Debut (Yorkshire) 2004, 2006. HS 149 v Warwks (Scarborough) 2006. LO HS 70* v Somerset (Scarborough) 2004 (NL). T20 HS 50.

NQ**GILLESPIE, Jason** Neil (Cabra C, Adelaide), b Darlinghurst, Sydney, Australia 19 April 1975. 6'5". RHB, RFM. S Australia 1994-95 to date. Yorkshire debut 2006. *Wisden* 2001. **Tests** (A): 71 (1996-97 to 2005-06); HS 201* v B (Chittagong) 2005-06 (probably his final Test innings); BB 7-37 v E (Leeds) 1997. **LOI** (A); 97 (1996 to 2005); HS 44* v WI (Adelaide) 2004-05; BB 5-22 v P (Nairobi) 2002. F-c Tours (A): E 1997, 2001, 2005; SA 1996-97, 2001-02: WI 1998-99, 2002-03; NZ 2004-05; I 2000-01, 2004-05; P 2002-03 (in SL); SL 1999, 2003-04; B 2005-06; Scot/Ire 1998 (Aus A). HS 201* (*see Tests*). Y HS 45 v Lancs (Leeds) 2006. 50 wkts (1): 51 (1995-96). BB 8-50 S Aus v NSW (Sydney) 2001-02. Y BB 6-37 v Durham (Chester-le-St) 2006. LO HS 44* (*see LOI*). LO BB 5-22 (*see LOI*). T20 HS 24. T20 BB 1-49.

GOUGH, Darren (Priory CS, Lundwood), b Monk Bretton, Barnsley 18 Sep 1970. 5'11". RHB, RFM. Yorkshire 1989-2003; cap 1993; benefit 2001; captain 2007. Essex 2004-06; cap 2004. *Wisden* 1998. **Tests**: 58 (1994 to 2003); HS 65 v NZ (Manchester) 1994 – on debut; BB 6-42 v SA (Leeds) 1998; hat-trick v A (Sydney) 1998-99 – first for E v A since 1899. **LOI**: 158 (1994 to 2006); HS 46* v A (Chester-le-St) 2005; BB 5-44 v Z (Sydney) 1994-95 and 5-44 v A (Lord's) 1997. Took wickets with his sixth balls in both Tests and LOI. F-c Tours: A 1994-95, 1998-99; SA 1991-92 (Y), 1992-93 (Y), 1993-94 (Eng A), 1995-96, 1999-00; NZ 1996-97; P 2000-01; SL 2000-01; Z 1996-97. HS 121 Y v Warwks (Leeds) 1996. 50 wkts (5); most – 67 (1996). BB 7-28 (10-80 match) v Lancs (Leeds) 1995 (not CC). CC BB 7-42 (10-96 match) v Somerset (Taunton) 1993. 2 hat-tricks (1995, 1998-99); took 4 wkts in 5 balls v Kent (Leeds) 1995. LO HS 72* v Leics (Leicester) 1991 (SL). LO BB 7-27 v Ire (Leeds) 1997 (NWT). T20 HS 37. T20 BB 3-16.

GUY, Simon Mark (Wickersley CS), b Rotherham 17 Nov 1978. 5'7". RHB, WK. Debut (Yorkshire) 2000. HS 52* v Durham (Leeds) 2006. LO HS 40 v Leics (Leeds) 2005 (NL).

HOGGARD, Matthew James (Grangefield S, Pudsey), b Leeds 31 Dec 1976. 6'2". RHB, RFM. Debut (Yorkshire) 1996; cap 2000. Free State 1998-99 to 1999-00. MCC 2004. MBE 2005. *Wisden* 2005. **ECB central contract 2007. Tests**: 62 (2000 to 2006-07); HS 38 v WI (Oval) 2004; BB 7-61 (12-205 match) v SA (Johannesburg) 2004-05; hat-trick v WI (Bridgetown) 2003-04. **LOI**: 26 (2001-02 to 2005-06); HS 7; BB 5-49 v Z (Harare) 2001-02. F-c Tours: A 2002-03, 2006-07; SA 2004-05; WI 2003-04; NZ 2001-02; I 2001-02, 2005-06; P 2000-01, 2005-06; SL 2000-01, 2003-04; B 2003-04. HS 89* v Glamorgan (Leeds) 2004. 50 wkts (2); most – 50 (2000, 2005). BB 7-49 v Somerset (Leeds) 2003. Hat-trick 2003-04. LO HS 7* (*twice*). LO BB 5-28 v Leics (Leicester) 2000 (NL). T20 HS 18. T20 BB 3-23.

NQ**KRUIS,** Gideon ('**Deon**') Jacobus (St Albans C, Pretoria; Pretoria U), b Pretoria, South Africa 9 May 1974. 6'3". RHB, RFM. N Transvaal 1993-94 to 1996-97. N Griqualand West 1997-98 to 2003-04. MCC 2000-01. Eagles 2004-05. Yorkshire debut 2005; cap 2006. Kolpak registration. HS 59 GW v B (Kimberley) 2000-01. Y HS 37* v Durham (Chester-le-St) 2005. 50 wkts (1): 64 (2005). BB 7-58 GW v Northerns (Pretoria) 1997-98. Y BB 5-59 v Northants (Leeds) 2005. LO HS 31* v Surrey (Oval) 2006 (P40). LO BB 4-26 GW v Boland (Kimberley) 1999-00. T20 HS 1. T20 BB 2-15.

LAWSON, Mark Anthony Kenneth (Castle Hall Language C, Mirfield), b Leeds 24 Oct 1985. 5'8". RHB, LB. Debut (Yorkshire) 2004. HS 44 v Hants (Southampton) 2006. BB 6-88 v Middx (Scarborough) 2006. LO HS 20 v Warwks (Birmingham) 2005 (NL). LO BB 2-50 v Hants (Leeds) 2006 (P40). T20 HS 4*. T20 BB 2-34.

LEE, James Edward (Immanuel Community C), b Sheffield 23 Dec 1988. 6'1". LHB, RMF. Debut (Yorkshire) 2006. HS 21* and BB – v Yorks (Manchester) 2006 – on debut. No l-o appearances.

McGRATH, Anthony (Yorkshire Martyrs Collegiate S), b Bradford 6 Oct 1975. 6'2". RHB, RM. Debut (Yorkshire) 1995; cap 1999; captain 2003. MCC 1999-00. **Tests**: 4 (2003); HS 81 v Z (Chester-le-St) 2003; BB 3-16 v Z (Lord's) 2003 on debut. **LOI**: 14 (2003 to 2004); HS 52 v SA (Manchester) 2003; BB 1-13. F-c Tours (Eng A): A 1996-97; P 1995-96; Z 1995-96 (Y); B 1999-00 (MCC). 1000 runs (2); most – 1425 (2005). HS 174 and BB 5-39 v Derbys (Derby) 2004. LO HS 148 v Somerset (Taunton) 2006 (P40). LO BB 4-41 v Surrey (Leeds) 2003 (NL). T20 HS 58*. T20 BB 3-27.

PATTERSON, Steven Andrew (Malet Lambert CS; St Mary's C, Hull), b Hull 3 Oct 1983. RHB, RMF. Debut (Yorkshire) 2005. HS 46 v Lancs (Manchester) 2006. BB 1-25 v Warwks (Scarborough) 2006 – on CC debut. LO HS 25* v Worcs (Leeds) 2006 (P40). LO BB 3-11 Yorks CB v Northants CB (Northampton) 2002.

PYRAH, Richard Michael (Ossett S; Wakefield C), b Dewsbury 1 Nov 1982. 6'0". RHB, RM. Debut (Yorkshire) 2004. No f-c appearances 2006. HS 78 v Worcs (Worcester) 2005. BB 1-4. CC BB 1-9. LO HS 42 v Durham (Scarborough) 2004 (NL). LO BB 5-50 Yorks CB v Somerset (Scarborough) 2002 (CGT). T20 HS 33*.

RASHID, Adil, b Bradford 17 Feb 1988. RHB, LB. Debut (Yorkshire) 2006. F-c Tour (Eng A): B 2006-07. Match double (114, 48, 8-157 and 2-45) for Eng U-19 v Ind U-19 (Taunton) 2006. HS 63 v Notts (Leeds) 2006. BB 6-67 v Warwks (Scarborough) 2006 – on debut. LO HS 28 and BB 2-63 v Surrey (Oval) 2006 (P40) – on l-o debut.

‡[NQ]**RUDOLPH**, Jacobus Andries ('**Jacques**') (Afrikaanse Hoer Seunskool), b Springs, Transvaal, South Africa 4 May 1981. 5'11". LHB, LBG. Northerns 1999-00 to 2003-04. Titans 2004-05. Eagles 2005-06 to date. Joins Yorkshire 2007. Kolpak registration. **Tests** (SA): 35 (2003 to 2006); HS 222* v B (Chittagong) 2003 – on debut; BB 1-1 v E (Leeds) 2003. **LOI** (SA): 43 (2003 to 2005-06); HS 81 v B (Dhaka) 2003. F-c Tours (SA): E 2003; A 2001-02, 2005-06; WI 2004-05; NZ 2003-04; I 2004-05; SL 2004, 2005-06, 2006; B 2003. HS 222* (*see Tests*). UK HS 92 SA v Kent (Canterbury) 2003. BB 5-87 Northerns B v GW B (Pretoria) 1998-99. UK BB 1-1 (*see Tests*). LO HS 134* SA A v Kenya (Laudium) 2001-02. LO BB 4-40 SA A v NZ A (Colombo) 2005-06. T20 HS 71. T20 BB 3-16.

SAYERS, Joseph John (St Mary's RC CS, Menston; Worcester C, Oxford) b Leeds 5 Nov 1983. 6'0". LHB, OB. Oxford U 2002-04; blue 2002-03-04. Yorkshire debut 2004. HS 147 OU v CU (Oxford) 2004. Y HS 122* v Middx (Scarborough) 2006. BB – . LO HS 62 v Glos (Leeds) 2003 (NL). LO BB 1-31 (NL). T20 HS 12.

SHAHZAD, Ajmal (Woodhouse Grove S; Bradford U), Huddersfield 27 Jul 1985. 6'0". RHB, RMF. Debut (Yorkshire) 2006 (first British-born Asian to play for Yorkshire). HS 2 and BB – v Middx (Scarborough) 2006 – on debut. LO HS 11* v Leics (Leicester) 2006 (CGT). LO BB 3-30 v Kent (Scarborough) 2006 (P40). T20 HS 2*. T20 BB 2-22.

THORNICROFT, Nicholas David (Easingwold S), b York 23 Jan 1985. 5'11". LHB, RMF. Debut 2002-04. Essex 2005 (on loan). No Yorkshire f-c appearances since 2004. HS 30 v Notts (Leeds) 2004. BB 2-27 v Durham (Chester-le-St) 2004. LO HS 20 v Surrey (Oval) 2006 (P40). LO BB 5-42 v Glos (Leeds) 2003 (NL). T20 HS 0*. T20 BB –

VAUGHAN, Michael Paul (Silverdale CS, Sheffield), b Salford, Lancs 29 Oct 1974. 6'2". RHB, OB. Debut (Yorkshire) 1993; cap 1995; benefit 2005. *Wisden* 2002. PCA 2002. OBE 2005. **ECB central contract 2007. Tests**: 64 (1999-00 to 2005-06, 33 as captain); HS 197 and BB 2-71 v I (Nottingham) 2002. Scored Eng record 1,481 runs (avge 61.70) with six hundreds in 2002. **LOI**: 77 (2000-01 to 2006-07, 51 as captain); HS 90* v Z (Bulawayo) 2004-05; BB 4-22 v SL (Manchester) 2002. F-c Tours (C=captain): A 1996-97 (Eng A), 2002-03; SA 1998-99C (Eng A), 1999-00, 2004-05C; WI 2003-04C; NZ 2001-02; I 1994-95 (Eng A), 2001-02; P 2000-01, 2005-06; SL 2000-01, 2003-04C; Z 1995-96 (Y), 1998-99C (Eng A); B 2003-04C. 1000 runs (4); most – 1244 (1995). HS 197 (*see Tests*). Y HS 183 v Glamorgan (Cardiff) 1996. BB 4-39 v OU (Oxford) 1994. CC BB 4-47 v Somerset (Leeds) 2001. LO HS 125* v Somerset (Taunton) 2001 (BHC). LO BB 4-22 (*see LOI*). T20 HS 27.

WAINWRIGHT, David John (Hemsworth HS and SFC; Loughborough U); b Pontefract 21 Mar 1985. LHB, SLA. Debut (Yorkshire) 2004 (no 1st XI appearances 2006). Loughborough UCCE 2005-06. British U 2006. HS 62 v Bangladesh A (Leeds) 2005. CC HS 5. BB 4-48 LU v Worcs (Worcester) 2005. Y BB 3-22 v Bangladesh A (Leeds) 2005. CC BB 1-86. LO HS – (NL).

WHITE, Craig (Flora Hill HS, Bendigo, Australia; Bendigo HS), b Morley 16 Dec 1969. Brother-in-law of D.S.Lehmann (S Australia, Victoria, Yorkshire and Australia 1987-88 to 2006-07). 6'0". RHB, RFM/OB. Debut (Yorkshire) 1990; cap 1993; benefit 2002; captain 2004-06. Victoria 1990-91 (2 matches). **Tests**: 30 (1994 to 2002-03); HS 121 v I (Ahmedabad) 2001-02; BB 5-32 v WI (Oval) 2000. **LOI**: 51 (1994-95 to 2002 03); HS 57* v A (Melbourne) 2002-03; BB 5-21 v Z (Bulawayo) 1999-00. F-c Tours: A 1994-95, 1996-97 (Eng A), 2002-03; SA 1991-92 (Y), 1992-93 (Y); NZ 1996-97, 2001-02; I 2001-02; P 1995-96 (Eng A), 2000-01; SL 2000-01; Z 1996-97 (*part*). HS 186 v Lancs (Manchester) 2001. BB 8-55 v Glos (Gloucester) 1998 – inc hat-trick. Hat-trick 1998. LO HS 148 v Leics (Leicester) 1997 (SL). LO BB 5-19 v Somerset (Scarborough) 2002 (NL). T20 HS 55. T20 BB 1-22.

WOOD, Matthew James (Shelley HS & SFC), b Huddersfield 6 Apr 1977. 5'9". RHB, OB. Debut (Yorkshire) 1997; cap 2001. MCC 1999-00. F-c Tour (MCC): B 1999-00. 1000 runs (4): most – 1432 (2003). HS 207 v Somerset (Taunton) 2003. BB 1-4 v Somerset (Leeds) 2003. LO HS 160 v Devon (Exmouth) 2004 (CGT). LO BB 3-45 v Cambs (March) 2003 (CGT). T20 HS 96*. T20 BB 1-11.

‡[NQ]**YOUNIS KHAN**, Mohammad, b Mardan (Shah Latif SS, Karachi; All Hadeed GHS, Karachi), North-West Frontier Province, Pakistan 29 Nov 1977. 5'11½". RHB, RM/LB. Peshawar 1998-99 to 2004-05. Habib Bank 1999-00 to date. Nottinghamshire 2005. **Tests** (P): 53 (1999-00 to 2006-07, 2 as captain); HS 267 v I (Bangalore) 2004-05; BB 1-24. **LOI** (P): 148 (1999-00 to 2006-07, 6 as captain); HS 144 v Hong Kong (Colombo) 2004; BB 1-24. F-c Tours (P): E 2001, 2006; A 2004-05; SA 2002-03, 2006-07; WI 1999-00, 2004-05; NZ 2000-01; I 2004-05; SL 2000, 2002-03, 2005-06; Z 2002-03; B 2001-02. 1000 runs (0+1): 1315 (1999-00). HS 267 (*see Tests*). UK HS 173 P v E (Leeds) 2006. CC HS 53 Nt v Glamorgan (Cardiff) 2005. BB 3-24 Habib Bank v Faisalabad (Faisalabad) 1999-00). UK BB 2-21 Nt v Warwks (Nottingham) 2005. HS LO: 144(*see LOI*). LO BB 3-5 v Glos (Cheltenham) 2005 (NL). T20 HS 35.

RELEASED/RETIRED

(Having made a first-class County appearance in 2006)

BLAIN, John Angus Rae (Penicuik HS; Jewel & Esk Valley C), b Edinburgh, Scotland 4 Jan 1979. 6'1". RHB, RMF. Scotland 1996-2006. Northamptonshire 1997-2003. Yorkshire 2004-06. **LOI** (Scot): 18 (1999 to 2006-07); HS 30* v Canada (Mombasa) 2006-07. BB 4-37 v B (Edinburgh) 1999. HS 53 Scot v Ire (Aberdeen) 2006. CC HS 34 Nh v Surrey (Northampton) 2001. Y HS 28* v Notts (Nottingham) 2004 and 28* v Derbys (Leeds) 2004. BB 6-42 Nh v Kent (Canterbury) 2001. Y BB 4-38 v Derbys (Leeds) 2004. LO HS 30* (*see LOI*). LO BB 5-24 Nh v Derbys (Derby) 1997 (SL).

CLAYDON, M.E. – *see DURHAM.*

DAWSON, R.J. – *see NORTHAMPTONSHIRE.*

NQ**LEHMANN, Darren** Scott (Gawler HS), b Gawler, S Australia 5 Feb 1970. Brother-in-law of C.White (*see YORKSHIRE*). 5'10". LHB, SLA. S Australia 1987-88 to 1989-90, 1993-94 to date; captain 1998-99 to date. Victoria 1990-91 to 1992-93. Yorkshire 1997-98, 2000, 2002, 2004, 2006; cap 1997; captain 2002. *Wisden* 2000. Lawrence Trophy 2000. **Tests** (A): 27 (1997-98 to 2004-05); HS 177 v B (Cairns) 2003; BB 3-42 v SL (Colombo) 2003-04. **LOI** (A): 117 (1996 to 2004-05); HS 119 v SL (Perth) 2002-03; BB 4-7 v Z (Harare) 2004. F-c Tours (A): E 1991 (Vic); SA 2001-02; WI 2002-03; I 1997-98, 2004-05; P 1998-99; SL 2003-04. 1000 runs (5+6); most – 1706 (2006). HS 339 v Durham (Leeds) 2006 – record score at Headingley – his final f-c innings in UK. BB 4-35 v Essex (Chelmsford) 2004. LO HS 191 v Notts (Scarborough) 2001 (NL). LO BB 4-7 (*see LOI*). T20 HS 48. T20 BB 3-19.

LUMB, M.J. – *see HAMPSHIRE.*

R.J.Blakey left the staff without making a f-c appearance in 2006.

WORCESTERSHIRE RELEASED/RETIRED (continued from p 109)

(Having made a first-class County appearance in 2006)

NQ**KHAN, Zaheer** (KTS HS; RBNB C), b Shrirampur, Maharashtra, India 7 Oct 1978. 6'2". RHB, LFM. Baroda 1999-00 to 2005-06. West Zone 1999-00 to date. Surrey 2004. Worcestershire 2006. Bombay 2006-07. **Tests** (I): 45 (2000-01 to 2006-07); HS 75 v B (Dhaka) 2004-05 – record score by No. 11 in Tests; BB 5-29 v NZ (Hamilton) 2002-03. **LOI** (I): 113 (2000-01 to 2006-07); HS 34* v NZ (Wellington) 2002-03; BB 5-42 v SL (Margao) 2006-07. F-c Tours (I): E 2002; A 2003-04; SA 2001-02, 2006-07; WI 2001-02; NZ 2002-03; P 2003-04 (*part*), 2005-06; SL 2001; Z 2001, 2005-06; B 2000-01, 2004-05. HS 75 (*see Tests*). UK HS 30* Wo v Somerset (Worcester) 2006 – on Wo debut. 50 wkts (1): 78 (2006). BB 9-138 (11-260 match) Wo v Essex (Chelmsford) 2006. LO HS 42 Wo v Kent (Worcester) 2006 (P40). LO BB 5-42 (*see LOI*). T20 HS – . T20 BB 2-15.

NQ**VINCENT, Lou** (Westlake BHS; Adelaide HS),b Warkworth, Auckland, New Zealand 11 Nov 1978. 5'9". RHB, RM/OB, WK. Auckland 1997-98 to date. NZ Academy 1998-99. North Island 1999-00. Worcestershire 2006. Suffolk 2005. **Tests** (NZ): 22 (2001-02 to 2005); HS 224 v SL (Wellington) 2004-05. Scored 104 and 54 v A (Perth) 2001-02 on debut. **LOI** (NZ): 94 (2000-01 to 2006-07); HS 172 v Z (Bulawayo) 2005-06. F-c Tours (NZ): A 2001-02; SA 2004-05 (NZ A); WI 2002; I 2003-04; P 2002; Z 2005-06. HS 224 (*see Tests*). BB 2-37 Auckland v Wellington (Auckland) 1999-00. LO HS 172 (*see LOI*). LO BB 2-25 Auckland v Otago (Queenstown) 2006-07. T20 HS 47. T20 BB 3-28.

YORKSHIRE 2006

RESULTS SUMMARY

	Place	Won	Lost	Tied	Drew	No Result
County Championship (1st Division)	**6th**	3	6		7	
All First-Class Matches		3	6		7	
C & G Trophy (North Conference)	7th	3	4			2
Pro40 League (2nd Division)	9th	1	6			1
Twenty20 Cup (North Division)	Q-Finalist	4	4			1

COUNTY CHAMPIONSHIP AVERAGES

BATTING AND FIELDING

Cap		*M*	*I*	*NO*	*HS*	*Runs*	*Avge*	*100*	*50*	*Ct/St*
1997	D.S.Lehmann	15	23	1	339	1706	77.54	6	3	1
1999	A.McGrath	15	24	3	140*	1293	61.57	4	9	18
2003	M.J.Lumb	16	25	2	144	963	41.86	2	7	10
1993	C.White	15	23	1	147	859	39.04	3	3	5
–	J.J.Sayers	13	21	3	122*	590	32.77	1	3	7
1995	M.P.Vaughan	3	6	–	99	178	29.66	–	2	–
–	S.M.Guy	6	8	2	52*	150	25.00	–	1	15/5
–	J.N.Gillespie	14	21	6	45	370	24.66	–	–	1
–	A.W.Gale	5	9	–	149	219	24.33	1	–	2
–	A.Rashid	5	6	–	63	115	19.16	–	1	2
2006	T.T.Bresnan	10	14	1	91	249	19.15	–	1	4
2001	M.J.Wood	6	10	–	92	177	17.70	–	1	6
–	G.L.Brophy	10	16	–	97	251	15.68	–	1	26/3
–	M.A.K.Lawson	7	10	2	44	124	15.50	–	–	5
–	S.A.Patterson	5	7	1	46	85	14.16	–	–	1
2006	G.J.Kruis	13	17	9	28*	85	10.62	–	–	2
2004	R.K.J.Dawson	8	13	1	56	127	10.58	–	1	2
2000	M.J.Hoggard	3	5	1	7	12	3.00	–	–	1

Also batted: J.A.R.Blain (3 matches) 12, 10, 2 (2 ct); M.E.Claydon (2) 38, 0; J.E.Lee (1) 1, 21*; A.Shahzad (1) 2.

BOWLING

	O	*M*	*R*	*W*	*Avge*	*Best*	*5wI*	*10wM*
A.Rashid	180.2	21	629	25	25.16	6- 67	1	–
T.T.Bresnan	258.3	47	828	27	30.66	5- 58	1	–
J.N.Gillespie	434.3	103	1210	36	33.61	6- 37	1	–
M.A.K.Lawson	207	3	897	26	34.50	6- 88	2	–
G.J.Kruis	381	65	1342	38	35.31	5- 67	2	–
A.McGrath	216	28	734	18	40.77	4- 62	–	–
Also bowled:								
M.J.Hoggard	97	18	304	8	38.00	3- 63	–	–
D.S.Lehmann	146.3	8	472	9	52.44	2- 40	–	–
J.A.R.Blain	59	3	287	5	57.40	2- 72	–	–
R.K.J.Dawson	196	20	701	8	87.62	4-151	–	–

M.E.Claydon 43-6-171-2; J.E.Lee 9-0-36-0; M.J.Lumb 1-0-6-0; S.A.Patterson 62.4-13-203-2; J.J.Sayers 2-0-7-0; A.Shahzad 12-1-45-0; C.White 32.2-4-75-4.

Yorkshire played no fixtures outside the County Championship in 2006. The First-Class Averages (pp 130–146) give the records of their players in all first-class matches for the county, with the exception of T.T.Bresnan and M.J.Hoggard whose full county figures are as above, and D.J.Wainwright whose three first-class appearances were for Loughborough UCCE and British Universities.

YORKSHIRE RECORDS

FIRST-CLASS CRICKET

Highest Total	For 887		v	Warwicks	Birmingham	1896
	V 681-7d		by	Leics	Bradford	1996
Lowest Total	For 23		v	Hampshire	Middlesbrough	1965
	V 13		by	Notts	Nottingham	1901
Highest Innings	For 341	G.H.Hirst	v	Leics	Leicester	1905
	V 318*	W.G.Grace	for	Glos	Cheltenham	1876

Highest Partnership for each Wicket

1st	555	P.Holmes/H.Sutcliffe	v	Essex	Leyton	1932
2nd	346	W.Barber/M.Leyland	v	Middlesex	Sheffield	1932
3rd	323*	H.Sutcliffe/M.Leyland	v	Glamorgan	Huddersfield	1928
4th	358	D.S.Lehmann/M.J.Lumb	v	Durham	Leeds	2006
5th	340	E.Wainwright/G.H.Hirst	v	Surrey	The Oval	1899
6th	276	M.Leyland/E.Robinson	v	Glamorgan	Swansea	1926
7th	254	W.Rhodes/D.C.F.Burton	v	Hampshire	Dewsbury	1919
8th	292	R.Peel/Lord Hawke	v	Warwicks	Birmingham	1896
9th	192	G.H.Hirst/S.Haigh	v	Surrey	Bradford	1898
10th	149	G.Boycott/G.B.Stevenson	v	Warwicks	Birmingham	1982

Best Bowling	For	10-10	H.Verity	v	Notts	Leeds	1932
(Innings)	V	10-37	C.V.Grimmett	for	Australians	Sheffield	1930
Best Bowling	For	17-91	H.Verity	v	Essex	Leyton	1933
(Match)	V	17-91	H.Dean	for	Lancashire	Liverpool	1913

Most Runs – Season	2883	H.Sutcliffe	(av 80.08)	1932
Most Runs – Career	38558	H.Sutcliffe	(av 50.20)	1919-45
Most 100s – Season	12	H.Sutcliffe		1932
Most 100s – Career	112	H.Sutcliffe		1919-45
Most Wkts – Season	240	W.Rhodes	(av 12.72)	1900
Most Wkts – Career	3598	W.Rhodes	(av 16.01)	1898-1930
Most Career W-K Dismissals	1186	D.Hunter	(863 ct/323 st)	1888-1909
Most Career Catches in the Field	665	J.Tunnicliffe		1891-1907

LIMITED-OVERS CRICKET

Highest Total	**CGT**	411-6		v	Devon	Exmouth	2004
	P40	352-6		v	Notts	Scarborough	2001
	T20	211-6		v	Leics	Leeds	2004
Lowest Total	**CGT**	76		v	Surrey	Harrogate	1970
	P40	54		v	Essex	Leeds	2003
	T20	97		v	Lancashire	Manchester	2005
Highest Innings	**CGT**	160	M.J.Wood	v	Devon	Exmouth	2004
	P40	191	D.S.Lehmann	v	Notts	Scarborough	2001
	T20	109	I.J.Harvey	v	Derbyshire	Leeds	2005
Best Bowling	**CGT**	7-27	D.Gough	v	Ireland	Leeds	1997
	P40	7-15	R.A.Hutton	v	Worcs	Leeds	1969
	T20	3-18	A.K.D.Gray	v	Lancashire	Leeds	2004

FIRST-CLASS UMPIRES 2006

† New appointment See page 11 for key to abbreviations.

BAILEY, Robert John (Biddulph HS), b Biddulph, Staffs 28 Oct 1963. RHB, OB. Northamptonshire 1982-99; cap 1985; benefit 1993; captain 1996-97. Derbyshire 2000-01; cap 2000. Staffordshire 1980. YC 1984. **Tests:** 4 (1988 to 1989-90); HS 43 v WI (Oval) 1988. **LOI:** 4 (1984-85 to 1989-90); HS 43* v SL (Oval) 1988. Tours: SA 1991-92 (Nh); WI 1989-90; Z 1994-95 (Nh). 1000 runs (13); most – 1987 (1990). HS 224* Nh v Glamorgan (Swansea) 1986. BB 5-54 Nh v Notts (Northampton) 1993. F-c career: 374 matches; 21844 runs @ 40.52, 47 hundreds; 121 wickets @ 42.51; 272 ct. Appointed 2006.

BAINTON, Neil Laurence, b Romford, Essex 2 October 1970. No f-c appearances. Appointed 2006.

BENSON, Mark Richard (Sutton Valence S), b Shoreham, Sussex 6 Jul 1958. LHB, OB. Kent 1980-95; cap 1981; captain 1991-96 (did not play in 1996); benefit 1991. **Tests:** 1 (1986); HS 30 v I (Birmingham) 1986. **LOI**: 1 (1986; HS 24). 1000 runs (11); most – 1725 (1987). HS 257 K v Hants (Southampton) 1991. BB 2-55 K v Surrey (Dartford) 1986. F-c career: 292 matches; 18387 runs @ 40.23, 48 hundreds; 5 wickets @ 98.60; 140 ct. Appointed 2000. Umpired 15 Tests (2004-05 to 2006-07) and 38 LOI (2004 to 2006-07). ICC International Panel 2004-06. **ICC Elite panel 2006 to date.**

BURGESS, Graham Iefvion (Millfield S), b Glastonbury, Somerset 5 May 1943. RHB, RM. Somerset 1966-79; cap 1968; testimonial 1977. HS 129 Sm v Glos (Taunton) 1973. BB 7-43 (13-75 match) Sm v OU (Oxford) 1975. F-c career: 252 matches; 7129 runs @ 18.90, 2 hundreds; 474 wickets @ 28.57. Appointed 1991.

COWLEY, Nigel Geoffrey (Dutchy Manor SS, Mere), b Shaftesbury, Dorset 1 Mar 1953. RHB, OB. Dorset 1972. Hampshire 1974-89; cap 1978; benefit 1988. Glamorgan 1990. 1000 runs (1): 1042 (1984). HS 109* H v Somerset (Taunton) 1977. BB 6-48 H v Leics (Southampton) 1982. F-c career: 271 matches; 7309 runs @ 23.35, 2 hundreds; 437 wickets @ 34.04. Appointed 2000.

DUDLESTON, Barry (Stockport S), b Bebington, Cheshire 16 Jul 1945. RHB, SLA. Leicestershire 1966-80; cap 1969; benefit 1980. Gloucestershire 1981-83. Rhodesia 1976-77 to 1979-80. 1000 runs (8); most – 1374 (1970). HS 202 Le v Derbys (Leicester) 1979. BB 4-6 Le v Surrey (Leicester) 1972. F-c career: 295 matches; 14747 runs @ 32.48, 32 hundreds; 47 wickets @ 29.04. Appointed 1984. Umpired 2 Tests (1991 to 1992) and 4 LOI (1992 to 2001).

EVANS, Jeffery Howard, b Llanelli, Carms 7 Aug 1954. No f-c appearances. Appointed 2001.

GOULD, Ian James (Westgate SS, Slough), b Taplow, Bucks 19 Aug 1957. LHB, WK. Middlesex 1975 to 1980-81, 1996; cap 1977. Auckland 1979-80. Sussex 1981-90; cap 1981; captain 1987; benefit 1990. MCC YC. **LOI:** 18 (1982-83 to 1983; HS 42). Tours: A 1982-83; P 1980-81 (Int); Z 1980-81 (M). HS 128 M v Worcs (Worcester) 1978. BB 3-10 Sx v Surrey (Oval) 1989. Middlesex coach 1991-2000. Reappeared in one match (v OU) 1996. F-c career: 298 matches; 8756 runs @ 26.05, 4 hundreds; 7 wickets @ 52.14; 603 dismissals (536 ct, 67 st). Appointed 2002. Umpired 8 LOI (2006-07).

HARRIS, Michael John ('***Pasty***') (Gerrans S, nr Truro), b St Just-in-Roseland, Cornwall 25 May 1944. RHB, LB, WK. Middlesex 1964-68; cap 1967. Nottinghamshire 1969-82; cap 1970; benefit 1977. E Province 1971-72. Wellington 1975-76. 1000 runs (11); most – 2238 (1971). Equalled Notts record with 9 hundreds in 1971. HS 201* Nt v Glamorgan (Nottingham) 1973. BB 4-16 Nt v Warwks (Nottingham) 1969. F-c career: 344 matches; 19196 runs @ 36.70, 41 hundreds; 79 wickets @ 43.78; 302 dismissals (288 ct, 14 st). Appointed 1998.

HARTLEY, Peter John (Greenhead GS; Bradford C), b Keighley, Yorks 18 Apr 1960. RHB, RMF. Warwickshire 1982. Yorkshire 1985-97; cap 1987; benefit 1996. Hampshire 1998-2000; cap 1998. Tours (Y): SA 1991-92; WI 1986-87; Z 1995-96. HS 127* Y v Lancs (Manchester) 1988. 50 wkts (7); most – 81 (1995). BB 9-41 (inc hat-trick, 4 wkts in 5 balls and 5 in 9; 11-68 match) Y v Derbys (Chesterfield) 1995. Hat-trick 1995. F-c career: 232 matches; 4321 runs @ 19.91, 2 hundreds; 683 wickets @ 30.21. Appointed 2003. **ICC International Panel (Third Umpire) 2006 to date.**

HOLDER, John Wakefield (Combermere S), b St George, Barbados 19 Mar 1945. RHB, RFM. Hampshire 1968-72. HS 33 H v Sussex (Hove) 1971. BB 7-79 H v Glos (Gloucester) 1972. Hat-trick 1972. F-c career: 47 matches; 374 runs @ 10.68; 139 wickets @ 24.56. Appointed 1983. Umpired 11 Tests (1988 to 2001) and 19 LOI (1988 to 2001).

HOLDER, Vanburn Alonza (Richmond SM), b Deans Village, St Michael, Barbados 8 Oct 1945. RHB, RFM. Barbados 1966-67 to 1977-78. Worcestershire 1968-80; cap 1970; benefit 1979. Shropshire 1981. **Tests** (WI): 40 (1969 to 1978-79); 682 runs @ 14.20, HS 42 v NZ (P-o-S) 1971-72; 109 wkts @ 33.27, BB 6-28 v A (P-o-S) 1977-78. **LOI** (WI): 12. Tours (WI): E 1969, 1973, 1976; A 1975-76; I 1974-75, 1978-79; P 1973-74 (RW), 1974-75; SL 1974-75, 1978-79. HS 122 Barbados v Trinidad (Bridgetown) 1973-74. BB 7-40 Wo v Glamorgan (Cardiff) 1974. F-c career: 311 matches; 3559 runs @ 13.03, 1 hundred; 947 wickets @ 24.48. Appointed 1992.

ILLINGWORTH, Richard Keith (Salts GS), b Bradford, Yorks 23 Aug 1963. RHB, SLA. Worcestershire 1982-2000; cap 1986; benefit 1997. Natal 1988-89. Derbyshire 2001. Wiltshire 2005. **Tests:** 9 (1991 to 1995-96); HS 28 v SA (Pt Elizabeth) 1995-96; BB 4-96 v WI (Nottingham) 1995. Took wicket of P.V.Simmons with his first ball in Tests – v WI (Nottingham) 1991. **LOI:** 25 (1991 to 1995-96); HS 14 v P (Melbourne) 1991-92; BB 3-33 v Z (Albury) 1991-92. Tours: SA 1995-96; NZ 1991-92; P 1990-91 (Eng A); SL 1990-91 (Eng A); Z 1989-90 (Eng A), 1990-91 (Wo), 1993-94 (Wo), 1996-97 (Wo). HS 120* Wo v Warwks (Worcester) 1987 – as night-watchman. Scored 106 for England A v Z (Harare) 1989-90 – also as night-watchman. 50 wkts (5); most – 75 (1990). BB 7-50 Wo v OU (Oxford) 1985. F-c career: 376 matches; 7027 runs @ 22.45, 4 hundreds; 831 wickets @ 31.54; 161 ct. Appointed 2006.

JESTY, Trevor Edward (Privet County SS, Gosport), b Gosport, Hants 2 Jun 1948. RHB, RM. Hampshire 1966-84; cap 1971; benefit 1982. Surrey 1985-87; cap 1985; captain 1985. Lancashire 1987-88 to 1991; cap 1989. Border 1973-74. GW 1974-75 to 1980-81. Canterbury 1979-80. *Wisden* 1982. **LOI:** 10. Tours: WI 1987-88 (La), 1982-83 (Int); Z 1988-89 (La). 1000 runs (10); most – 1645 (1982). HS 248 H v CU (Cambridge) 1984. Scored 122* La v OU (Oxford) 1991 in his final f-c innings. 50 wkts (2); most – 52 (1981). BB 7-75 H v Worcs (Southampton) 1976. F-c career: 490 matches; 21916 runs @ 32.71, 35 hundreds; 585 wickets @ 27.47. Appointed 1994.

JONES, Allan Arthur (St John's C, Horsham), b Horley, Surrey 9 Dec 1947. RHB, RFM. Sussex 1966-69. Somerset 1970-75; cap 1972. Middlesex 1976-79; cap 1976. Glamorgan 1980-81. Northern Transvaal 1972-73. Orange Free State 1976-77. HS 33 M v Kent (Canterbury) 1978. BB 9-51 Sm v Sussex (Hove) 1972. F-c career: 214 matches; 799 runs @ 5.39; 549 wickets @ 28.07. Appointed 1985. Umpired 1 LOI (1996).

KETTLEBOROUGH, Richard Allan (Worksop C), b Sheffield, Yorks 15 Mar 1973. LHB, RM. Yorkshire 1994-97. Middlesex 1998-99. Tour: Z 1995-96 (Y). HS 108 Y v Essex (Leeds) 1996. BB 2-26 Y v Notts (Scarborough) 1996. F-c career: 33 matches; 1258 runs @ 25.16, 1 hundred; 3 wickets @ 81.00; 20 ct. Appointed 2006.

LEADBEATER, Barrie (Harehills SS), b Harehills, Leeds, Yorks 14 Aug 1943. RHB, RM. Yorkshire 1966-79; cap 1969; joint benefit with G.A.Cope 1980. Tour: WI 1969-70 (DN). HS 140* Y v Hants (Portsmouth) 1976. BB 1-1. F-c career: 147 matches; 5373 runs @ 25.34, 1 hundred; 1 wicket @ 5.00. Appointed 1981. Umpired 5 LOI (1983 to 2000).

LLONG, Nigel James (Ashford North S), b Ashford, Kent 11 Feb 1969. LHB, OB. Kent 1990-98; cap 1993. Tour: Z 1992-93 (K). HS 130 K v Hants (Canterbury) 1996. BB 5-21 K v Middx (Canterbury) 1996. F-c career: 68 matches; 3024 runs @ 31.17, 6 hundreds; 35 wickets @ 35.97. Appointed 2002. Umpired 6 LOI (2006 to 2006-07). **ICC International Panel 2004 to date.**

LLOYDS, Jeremy William (Blundell's S), b Penang, Malaya 17 Nov 1954. LHB, OB. Somerset 1979-84; cap 1982. Gloucestershire 1985-91; cap 1985. Orange Free State

1983-84 to 1987-88, Tour (Glos): SL 1986-87. 1000 runs (3); most – 1295 (1986). HS 132* Sm v Northants (Northampton) 1982. BB 7-88 Sm v Essex (Chelmsford) 1982. F-c career: 267 matches; 10679 runs @ 31.04, 10 hundreds; 333 wickets @ 38.86; 229 ct. Appointed 1998. Umpired 5 Tests (2003-04 to 2004-05) and 18 LOI (2000 to 2005-06). **ICC International Panel 2003-06.**

MALLENDER, Neil Alan (Beverley GS), b Kirk Sandall, Yorks 13 Aug 1961. RHB, RFM. Northamptonshire 1980-86 and 1995-96; cap 1984. Somerset 1987-94; cap 1987; benefit 1994. Otago 1983-84 to 1992-93; captain 1990-91 to 1992-93. **Tests:** 2 (1992); 8 runs @ 2.66, HS 4; 10 wkts @ 21.50, BB 5-50 v P (Leeds) 1992 – on debut. Tour: Z 1994-95 (Nh). HS 100* Otago v CD (Palmerston N) 1991-92. UK HS 87* Sm v Sussex (Hove) 1990. 50 wkts (6); most – 56 (1983). BB 7-27 Otago v Auckland (Auckland) 1984-85. UK BB 7-41 Nh v Derbys (Northampton) 1982. F-c career: 345 matches; 4709 runs @ 17.18, 1 hundred; 937 wickets @ 26.31; 111 ct. Appointed 1999. Umpired 3 Tests (2003-04) and 22 LOI (2001 to 2003-04), including 2002-03 World Cup. **ICC Elite Panel 2004**.

PALMER, Roy (Southbroom SM, Devizes), b Devizes, Wilts 12 Jul 1942. RHB, RFM. Younger brother of K.E.Palmer, MBE (Somerset and England 1955-69). Somerset 1965-70. HS 84 Sm v Leics (Taunton) 1967. BB 6-45 Sm v Middx (Lord's) 1967. F-c career: 74 matches; 1037 runs @ 13.29; 172 wickets @ 31.62. Appointed 1980. Umpired 2 Tests (1992 to 1993) and 8 LOI (1983 to 1995).

†**ROBINSON,** Robert **Timothy** (Dunstable GS; High Pavement SFC; Sheffield U), b Sutton in Ashfield 21 Nov 1958. RHB, RM. Nottinghamshire 1978-99; cap 1983; captain 1988-95; benefit 1992. *Wisden* 1985. **Tests:** 29 (1984-85 to 1989); HS 175 v A (Leeds) 1985. **LOI**: 26 (1984-85 to 1988); HS 83 v P (Sharjah) 1986-87. Tours: A 1987-88; SA 1989-90 (Eng XI), 1996-97 (Nt); NZ 1987-88; WI 1985-86; I/SL 1984-85; P 1987-88. 1000 runs (14) inc 2000 (1): 2032 (1984). HS 220* v Yorks (Nottingham) 1990. BB 1-22. F-c career: 425 matches; 27571 runs @ 42.15, 63 hundreds; 4 wickets @ 72.25; 257 ct. Appointed 2007.

SHARP, George (Elwick Road SS, Hartlepool), b West Hartlepool, Co Durham 12 Mar 1950. RHB, WK, occ LM. Northamptonshire 1968-85; cap 1973; benefit 1982. HS 98 Nh v Yorks (Northampton) 1983. BB 1-47. F-c career: 306 matches; 6254 runs @ 19.85; 1 wicket @ 70.00; 655 dismissals (565 ct, 90 st). Appointed 1992. Umpired 15 Tests (1996 to 2001-02) and 31 LOI (1995-96 to 2001-02). **ICC International Panel 1996 to 2001-02.**

STEELE, John Frederick (Endon SS), b Brown Edge, Staffs 23 Jul 1946. RHB, SLA. Brother of D.S. (Northants, Derbys and England 1963-84). Leicestershire 1970-83; cap 1971; benefit 1983. Glamorgan 1984-86; cap 1984. Natal 1973-74 to 1977-78. Staffordshire 1965-69. Tour: SA 1974-75 (DHR). 1000 runs (6); most – 1347 (1972). HS 195 Le v Derbys (Leicester) 1971. BB 7-29 Natal B v GW (Umzinto) 1973-74 and 7-29 Le v Glos (Leicester) 1980. F-c career: 379 matches; 15054 runs @ 28.95, 21 hundreds; 584 wickets @ 27.04; 413 ct. Appointed 1997.

WILLEY Peter (Seaham SS), b Sedgefield, Co Durham 6 Dec 1949. RHB, OB. Northamptonshire 1966-83; cap 1971; benefit 1981. Leicestershire 1984-91; cap 1984; captain 1987. E Province 1982-83 to 1984-85. Northumberland 1992. **Tests:** 26 (1976 to 1986); 1184 runs @ 26.90, HS 102* v WI (St John's) 1980-81; 7 wkts @ 65.14, BB 2-73 v WI (Lord's) 1980. **LOI:** 26. Tours: A 1979-80; SA 1972-73 (DHR), 1981-82 (SAB); WI 1980-81, 1985-86; I 1979-80; SL 1977-78 (DHR). 1000 runs (10); most – 1783 (1982). HS 227 Nh v Somerset (Northampton) 1976. 50 wkts (3); most – 52 (1979). BB 7-37 Nh v OU (Oxford) 1975. F-c career: 559 matches; 24361 runs @ 30.56, 44 hundreds; 756 wickets @ 30.95. Appointed 1993. Umpired 25 Tests (1995-96 to 2003-04) and 34 LOI (1996 to 2003), including 1999 and 2002-03 World Cups. **ICC International Panel 1996 to 2001-02 and 2003-04.**

RESERVE FIRST-CLASS LIST: Martin J.Bodenham, †Keith Coburn, Nicholas G.B.Cook, Stephen A.Garratt, Michael A.Gough, †David J.Millns, Terence J.Urben.

Test Match and LOI statistics to 1 May and 11 February 2007 (inclusive) respectively.

INTERNATIONAL UMPIRES AND REFEREES 2007

ELITE PANEL OF UMPIRES 2007

The Elite Panel of ICC Umpires and Referees was introduced in April 2002 to raise standards and guarantee impartial adjudication. Two umpires from this panel stand in Test matches while one officiates with a home umpire from the Supplementary International Panel in limited-overs internationals.

Full Names	*Birthdate*	*Birthplace*	*Tests*	*Debut*	*LOI*	*Debut*
ALIM Sarwar DAR	06.06.68	Jhang, Pakistan	37	2003-04	73	1999-00
ASAD RAUF	12.05.56	Lahore, Pakistan	9	2004-05	37	1999-00
BENSON, Mark Richard	06.07.58	Shoreham, England	15	2004-05	38	2004
BOWDEN, Brent Fraser	11.04.63	Auckland, New Zealand	39	1999-00	102	1994-95
BUCKNOR, Stephen Anthony	31.05.46	Montego Bay, Jamaica	117	1988-89	153	1988-89
DOCTROVE, Billy Raymond	03.07.55	Marigot, Dominica	11	1997-98	57	1997-98
HAIR, Darrell Bruce	30.09.52	Mudgee, Australia	76	1991-92	129	1991-92
HARPER, Daryl John	23.10.61	Adelaide, Australia	63	1998-99	133	1993-94
KOERTZEN, Rudolf Eric ('Rudi')	26.03.49	Knysna, South Africa	79	1992-93	158	1992-93
TAUFEL, Simon James Arthur	21.01.71	Sydney, Australia	40	2000-01	103	1998-99

ELITE PANEL OF REFEREES 2007

Full Names	*Birthdate*	*Birthplace*	*Tests*	*Debut*	*LOI*	*Debut*
BROAD, Brian Christopher	29.09.57	Bristol, England	23	2003-04	80	2003-04
CROWE, Jeffrey John	14.09.58	Auckland, New Zealand	18	2004-05	64	2003-04
HURST. Alan George	15.07.50	Melbourne, Australia	11	2004-05	32	2004-05
LLOYD, Clive Hubert	31.08.44	Georgetown, Guyana	53	1992-93	127	1992-93
MADUGALLE, Ranjan Senerath	22.04.59	Kandy, Sri Lanka	93	1993-94	193	1993-94
MAHANAMA, Roshan Siriwardena	31.05.66	Colombo, Sri Lanka	13	2004	63	2004
PROCTER, Michael John	15.09.46	Durban, South Africa	41	2001-02	119	2001-02
SRINATH, Javagal	31.08.69	Mysore, India	4	2006	10	2006-07

INTERNATIONAL UMPIRES PANEL 2007

Nominated by their respective cricket boards, members from this panel officiate in home LOI and supplement the Elite panel for Test matches. Specialist third umpires have been selected to undertake adjudication involving television replays. The number of Test matches/LOI in which they have stood is shown in brackets.

			Third Umpire
Australia	S.J.Davis (9/57)	P.D.Parker (8/52)	R.L.Parry (-/4)
Bangladesh	Nadir Shah (-/12)	Enamal Haque (-/3)	Ziaul Islam (-/-)
England	I.J.Gould (-/8)	N.J.Llong (-/6)	P.J.Hartley (-/-)
India	A.M.Saheba (-/7)	S.L.Shastri (-/11)	G.A.Pratapkumar (-/2)
New Zealand	G.A.Baxter (-/11)	A.L.Hill (4/36)	E.A.Watkin (2/21)
Pakistan	Nadeem Ghauri (5/31)	Zamir Haider (-/1)	Riazuddin (12/12)
South Africa	I.L.Howell (7/53)	B.G.Jerling (4/48)	K.H.Hurter (-/5)
Sri Lanka	E.A.R.de Silva (33/61)	T.H.Wijewardene (4/34)	P.Manuel (11/43)
West Indies	C.R.Duncan (2/10)	N.Malcolm (-/-)	C.E.Mack (-/1), G.E.Greaves (-/-)
Zimbabwe	K.C.Barbour (4/38)	R.B.Tiffin (38/93)	I.D.Robinson (28/90)

ASSOCIATE AND AFFILIATE INTERNATIONAL UMPIRES PANEL

The number of LOI in which they have stood is shown in brackets.

Paul K.Baldwin (Germany – 3), Roger Dill (Bermuda – 14), Jeff J.Luck (Namibia – 3), Subhash R.Modi (Kenya – 10), Buddi B.Pradhan (Nepal – 7), Shahul Hamid (Indonesia – 5).

Test Match and LOI statistics to 1 May and 11 February 2007 (inclusive) respectively.

UNIVERSITY FIRST-CLASS REGISTER 2006

‡ Represented British Universities v Sri Lankans

CAMBRIDGE († Blue 2006)

Full Names	*Birthdate*	*Birthplace*	*College*	*Bat/Bowl*	*F-C Debut*
†AUSTIN, Matthew Lorenzo	31.01.85	Colchester	Emmanuel	RHB	2006
†BANERJEE, Vikram	20.03.84	Bradford	Downing	LHB/SLA	2004
†BARTHOLOMEW, Ian David	08.02.83	Hemel Hempstead	Christ's	LHB	2006
BOTT, Mark Daniel	13.05.86	Nottingham	(Anglia RU)	RHB/LB	2006
BUCKHAM, Craig Thomas	09.08.83	Ashford (Kent)	(Anglia RU)	RHB/LB	2004
†CELLIERS, Grant	13.12.78	Ermelo, SA	Jesus	RHB/RM	2001-02
†CHERVAK, James Alexander	07.04.85	Harrogate	Jesus	RHB/LB	2005
FRIEDLANDER, Matthew James	01.08.79	Durban, S Africa	(Anglia RU)	RHB/RFM	2003-04
†HEYWOOD, James John Neville	24.09.82	Eastbourne	Homerton	RHB/WK	2003
HUNTINGTON, Christopher James	29.03.87	Cambridge	(Anglia RU)	LHB/RSM	2006
†JACKLIN, Benjamin David	26.04.84	Leeds	Magdalene	RHB/RM	2005
JAMES, Gareth David	01.12.84	Walthamstow	(Anglia RU)	RHB/LB	2004
JOGIA, Kunal Ashokkumar	18.09.84	Leicester	(Anglia RU)	RHB/RSM	2006
†KEMP, Robin Andrew	29.09.84	Luton	St John's	RHB/RM	2005
LEE, Nicholas Trevor	16.10.83	Dartford	(Anglia RU)	RHB/LB	2004
†MASSEY, Ian Robert	10.09.85	Hereford	Queens	RHB/OB	2006
MOHAMMAD AMIN	19.10.84	Gujranwala, Pakistan	(Anglia RU)	RHB/RMF	2005
OWEN, Frederick Gerard	25.09.85	Chester	Corpus Christi	RHB	2006
†SAVILL, Thomas Edward	16.05.83	Sheffield	Homerton	RHB/RFM	2002
SHARIF, Zoheb Khalid	22.02.83	Leytonstone	(Anglia RU)	LHB/LB	2001
†SMITH, Brendan Mitchell	24.09.85	Basildon	(Anglia RU)	LHB/LFM	2006

DURHAM

Full Names	*Birthdate*	*Birthplace*	*College*	*Bat/Bowl*	*F-C Debut*
‡BALCOMBE, David John	24.12.84	City of London	St Hild & St Bede	RHB/RFM	2005
BARTRAM, Thomas Stephen	11.02.86	York	St Cuthbert's Society	RHB/RMF	2006
BEGG, Christian George	19.05.86	Johannesburg, SA	St Aidan's	LHB/SLA	2006
DOBSON, William Thomas	11.03.86	Oxford	St Aidan's	RHB/RMF	2006
HODSON, William Greig	06.11.82	Wakefield	St Cuthbert's Society	RHB/OB	2006
JONES, Martin Craig	08.11.85	Bristol	St Hild & St Bede	RHB/RMF	2006
‡LAMB, Nicholas John	09.11.85	St Albans	Collingwood	RHB/RMF	2005
‡MORRIS, James Calum	17.01.85	Welwyn Gdn City	University	RHB/LB	2005
MUMTAZ HABIBULLAH	01.01.87	Kabul, Afghanistan	Trevelyan	RHB/RMF	2006
PARRY, Sean Jonathan Pryce	01.06.87	Hong Kong Island	St Mary's	RHB/RM	2006
PHYTHIAN, Mark John	26.04.85	Peterborough	University	RHB/WK	2005
PROWTING, Nicholas Roger	26.10.85	Chelmsford	Van Mildert	RHB/RM	2006
SHILVOCK, Daniel James Francis	22.11.83	Birmingham	St Hild & St Bede	RHB/LB	2005
WAKE, Cameron John	28.06.85	Kettering	St Hild & St Bede	RHB/RMF	2006
WOOD, James Robert	08.09.85	Cape Town, SA	Van Mildert	RHB	2005

LOUGHBOROUGH

Full Names	*Birthdate*	*Birthplace*	*Bat/Bowl*	*F-C Debut*
‡BRATHWAITE, Ruel Marlon Ricardo	06.09.85	Bridgetown, Barbados	RHB/RFM	2006
‡CLINTON, Richard Selvey	01.09.81	Sidcup	LHB/RM	2001
FOSTER, Edward John	21.01.85	Shrewsbury	LHB/RM	2005
GIFFORD, William McLean	10.10.85	Sutton Coldfield	RHB/RM	2005
‡HARRISON, Paul William	22.05.84	Cuckfield	RHB/WK	2004
HOLT, David Robert	29.12.81	Hammersmith, London	RHB	2005
KING, Richard Eric	03.01.84	Hitchin, Herts	RHB/LMF	2003
MILLER, Daniel James	12.06.83	Hammersmith, London	LHB/RFM	2006
MORRIS, Richard Kyle	26.09.87	Newbury	RHB/RMF	2006
MURTAGH, Christopher Paul	14.10.84	Lambeth, London	RHB/LB	2005
‡SHIRAZI, Damien Cyrus	23.03.83	Neath	LHB/RM	2004
‡WAINWRIGHT, David John	21.03.85	Pontefract	LHB/SLA	2004

OXFORD († Blue 2006)

Full Names	*Birthdate*	*Birthplace*	*College*	*Bat/Bowl*	*F-C Debut*
ANWAR, Omar Sohail	01.07.83	Harrow	(Brookes U)	RHB	2003
BRADSHAW, Duncan Philip	19.02.86	Harare, Zimbabwe	(Brookes U)	RHB/RFM	2006
†CLINTON, Paul James Selvey	30.08.83	Dartford	Keble	RHB/RM	2004
†DUNBAR, Peter Raymond	18.09.84	Harrow	Balliol	RHB/RM	2006
†GERARD, Darren Charles	17.04.84	Barnet	St Edmund Hall	RHB/RM	2006
†HILLYARD, Nicholas James	24.02.81	Edinburgh	Linacre	RHB/OB	2006
HOOPER, John Harry Patrick	14.01.86	Tooting Bec	(Brookes U)	LHB/LM	2006
†HOBBISS, Michael Holland	17.08.85	Manchester	Worcester	RHB/RM	2006
KALAM, Tarique	20.03.87	Cape Town, SA	(Brookes U)	RHB/RMF	2006
‡KNAPPETT, Joshua Philip Thomas	15.04.85	Westminster	(Brookes U)	RHB/WK	2004
MORETON, Stephen John Patrick	09.09.84	Birmingham	(Brookes U)	RHB/LB	2005
†MORSE, Edward James	30.01.86	Stevenage	St Edmund Hall	RHB/RM	2005
†MUNDAY, Michael Kenneth	22.10.84	Nottingham	Corpus Christi	RHB/LB	2003
†OBEROI, Salil	07.12.83	Delhi, India	Merton	RHB, OB	2002-03
‡PARKER, Luke Charles	27.09.83	Coventry	(Brookes U)	RHB/RM	2004
‡RICHARDS, Mali Alexander	02.09.83	Taunton	(Brookes U)	LHB/RM	2004
†SADLER, Oliver James	02.04.87	Newcastle-u-Lyme	Oriel	RHB/SLA	2006
†STEARN, Christopher Paul	11.07.80	Luton	Worcester	RHB/RM	2005
WILSHAW, Peter James	15.07.87	Newcastle-u-Lyme	(Brookes U)	RHB/RM	2006
†WOODS, Nicholas James	02.01.86	Bolton	Queens	RHB/LB	2005
YOUNG, Peter James William	14.09.86	Hammersmith	(Brookes U)	LHB/RM	2006

TOURING TEAMS FIRST-CLASS REGISTER 2006

PAKISTAN

Full Names	*Birthdate*	*Birthplace*	*Team*	*Type*	*F-C Debut*
ABDUL RAZZAQ	01.12.79	Lahore	Lahore	RHB/RFM	1996-97
ARSHAD KHAN	22.03.71	Peshawar	Peshawar	RHB/OB	1988-89
DANISH KANERIA	16.12.80	Karachi	Habib Bank	RHB/LB	1998-99
FAISAL IQBAL	30.12.81	Karachi	Karachi	RHB/RM	1998-99
IFTIKHAR ANJUM	01.12.80	Khanewal	Islamabad	RHB/RM	1999-00
IMRAN FARHAT	20.05.82	Lahore	Lahore	LHB/LB	1998-99
INZAMAM-UL-HAQ	03.03.70	Multan	Multan	RHB/SLA	1985-86
JANNISAR KHAN	06.10.81	Peshawar	Peshawar	RHB/RM	1996-97
KAMRAN AKMAL	13.01.82	Lahore	Lahore	RHB/WK	1997-98
MOHAMMAD ASIF	20.12.82	Sheikhupura	KRL	LHB/RFM	2000-01
MOHAMMAD SAMI	24.02.81	Karachi	Karachi	RHB/RFM	1999-00
MOHAMMAD HAFEEZ	17.10.80	Sargodha	Sui Gas	RHB/OB	1998-99
SALMAN BUTT	07.10.84	Lahore	Lahore	LHB/OB	2000-01
SAMIULLAH KHAN	04.08.82	Mianwali	Sui Gas	RHB/LMF	2002-03
SHAHID AFRIDI	01.03.80	Khyber Agency	Karachi	RHB/LBG	1995-96
SHAHID NAZIR	04.12.77	Faisalabad	Habib Bank	RHB/RFM	1995-96
SHOAIB MALIK	01.02.82	Sialkot	Sialkot	RHB/OB	1997
TAUFIQ UMAR	20.06.81	Lahore	Habib Bank	LHB/OB	1998-99
UMAR GUL	14.04.84	Peshawar	Habib Bank	RHB/RFM	2001-02
YOUNIS KHAN	29.11.77	Mardan, NWFP	Habib Bank	RHB/LB	1998-99
YOUSUF YOUHANA, Mohd	27.08.74	Lahore	Lahore	RHB/OB	1996-97

FOR SRI LANKA TOURING TEAM REGISTER SEE PAGE 213

FOR WEST INDIES A TOURING TEAM REGISTER SEE PAGE 210

THE 2006 FIRST-CLASS SEASON STATISTICAL HIGHLIGHTS

FIRST TO INDIVIDUAL TARGETS

1000 RUNS	M.R.Ramprakash	Surrey	22 June
2000 RUNS	M.R.Ramprakash	Surrey	9 August
100 WICKETS	Mushtaq Ahmed	Sussex	22 September

TEAM HIGHLIGHTS

HIGHEST INNINGS TOTALS

717	Surrey v Somerset	Guildford
688-8d	Somerset v Surrey	Guildford
677-7d	Yorkshire v Durham	Leeds
669-5d	Surrey v Northamptonshire	The Oval
668-7d	Surrey v Leicestershire	The Oval
660-5d	Northamptonshire v Essex	Northampton
650-7d	Worcestershire v Essex	Chelmsford
647-7d	Glamorgan v Gloucestershire	Cheltenham
642-9d	Nottinghamshire v Middlesex	Lord's
639-8d	Essex v Glamorgan	Cardiff
639-8d	Surrey v Gloucestershire	The Oval
628	Northamptonshire v Gloucestershire	Northampton
625-8d	Somerset v Northamptonshire	Taunton
620	Essex v Northamptonshire	Northampton
618	Worcestershire v Somerset	Taunton
603-6d	Kent v Middlesex	Canterbury
600-6d	Kent v Nottinghamshire	Canterbury

HIGHEST FOURTH INNINGS TOTALS

498	Somerset (set 579) v Derbyshire	Derby
470-9	Surrey (set 501) v Gloucestershire	Bristol
433	Yorkshire (set 500) v Warwickshire	Birmingham
404-5	Hampshire (set 404) v Yorkshire	Leeds

LOWEST INNINGS TOTALS († *One batsman absent hurt*)

46	Durham UCCE v Nottinghamshire	Durham
49†	Middlesex v Nottinghamshire	Nottingham
56	Glamorgan v Northamptonshire	Northampton
67	Northamptonshire v Worcestershire	Worcester
80	Durham v Sussex	Chester-le-St
98	Middlesex v Hampshire	Southampton

MATCH AGGREGATES OF 1500 RUNS

1609-26	Northamptonshire (628, 35-0) v Gloucestershire (350, 596-6d)	Northampton
1560-32	Sussex (507, 379-3d) v Middlesex (466, 208-9)	Southgate
1546-37	Gloucestershire (459, 329-8d) v Surrey (288, 470-9)	Bristol
1540-28	Worcestershire (650-7d, 121-1) v Essex (283, 486)	Chelmsford

BATSMEN'S MATCHES (Qualification: 1200 runs, average 70 per wicket)

84.81 (1357-16)	Northamptonshire (660-5d, 77-1) v Essex (620)	Northampton
78.05 (1405-18)	Somerset (688-8d) v Surrey (717)	Guildford

MOST FIFTIES IN AN INNINGS

7	Sri Lanka (537-9) v England (1st Test)	Lord's
6	Sussex (560-5d) v Nottinghamshire	Nottingham

ELEVEN BOWLERS IN AN INNINGS

Hampshire v Middlesex (309-4d)	Lord's

MOST EXTRAS IN AN INNINGS

	B	LB	W	NB		
78	10	21	5	42	Glamorgan (597) v Gloucestershire	Cardiff
66	19	10	1	36	Leicestershire (515) v Derbyshire	Leicester
62	31	20	1	10	England A (595-9d) v Pakistanis	Canterbury
62	23	15	4	20	Yorkshire (536) v Warwickshire	Scarborough
61	5	20	9	27	Essex (422-3d) v Loughborough UCCE	Chelmsford
61	7	10	8	36	Essex (548) v Gloucestershire	Bristol

Under ECB regulations, Test matches excluded, two penalty extras were scored for each no-ball.

BATTING HIGHLIGHTS

TRIPLE HUNDREDS († *County record*)

H.D.Ackerman	309*†	Leicestershire v Glamorgan	Cardiff
J.L.Langer	342†	Somerset v Surrey	Guildford
D.S.Lehmann	339	Yorkshire v Durham	Leeds
M.R.Ramprakash	301*	Surrey v Northamptonshire	The Oval
C.J.L.Rogers	319	Northamptonshire v Gloucestershire	Northampton

DOUBLE HUNDREDS

H.D.Ackerman		216	Leicestershire v Northamptonshire	Northampton
J.H.K.Adams		262*	Hampshire v Nottinghamshire	Nottingham
A.D.Brown		215	Surrey v Leicestershire	The Oval
R.Clarke		214	Surrey v Somerset	Guildford
M.J.Cosgrove		233	Glamorgan v Derbyshire	Derby
A.Flower		271*	Essex v Northamptonshire	Northampton
M.W.Goodwin	(2)	214*	Sussex v Warwickshire	Hove
		235	Sussex v Yorkshire	Arundel
J.C.Hildreth		227*	Somerset v Northamptonshire	Taunton
P.A.Jaques	(2)	244	Worcestershire v Essex	Chelmsford
		202	Worcestershire v Northamptonshire	Worcester
E.C.Joyce		211	Middlesex v Warwickshire	Birmingham
Md Yousuf Youhana		202	Pakistan v England (1st Test)	Lord's
G.J.Muchall		219	Durham v Kent	Canterbury
M.L.Pettini		208*	Essex v Derbyshire	Chelmsford
M.J.Powell	(2)	202	Glamorgan v Essex	Chelmsford
		299	Glamorgan v Gloucestershire	Cheltenham
			Highest score for Glamorgan in England.	
M.R.Ramprakash		292	Surrey v Gloucestershire	The Oval
C.J.L.Rogers		222*	Northamptonshire v Somerset	Taunton
D.J.G.Sales		225	Northamptonshire v Essex	Northampton
B.F.Smith		203	Worcestershire v Somerset	Taunton
V.S.Solanki		222	Worcestershire v Gloucestershire	Bristol
C.L.White		260*	Somerset v Derbyshire	Derby
			World record first-class score in the fourth innings.	

HUNDREDS IN THREE CONSECUTIVE INNINGS

M.B.Loye (Lancashire)	148*	v Sussex	Hove
	100	v Yorkshire	Manchester
	107	v Middlesex	Manchester
M.R.Ramprakash (Surrey)	155	v Northamptonshire	Northampton
	167	v Somerset	Guildford
	301*	v Northamptonshire	The Oval

HUNDRED IN EACH INNINGS OF A MATCH

M.A.Butcher	151	108	Surrey v Glamorgan	The Oval
J.P.Crawley	106	116	Hampshire v Nottinghamshire	Southampton
J.L.Denly	115	107*	Kent v Cambridge UCCE	Cambridge
G.A.Hick	104	105*	Worcestershire v Essex	Worcester
C.J.L.Rogers	128	222*	Northamptonshire v Somerset	Taunton
C.M.Spearman	140	137	Gloucestershire v Northamptonshire	Northampton

HUNDRED ON FIRST-CLASS DEBUT

B.W.Harmison	110	Durham v Oxford UCCE	Oxford

He scored 105 for Durham v West Indies A at Chester-le-Street in his second match.

O.P.Rayner	101	Sussex v Sri Lankans	Hove

First instance for Sussex since 1920.

HUNDRED ON FIRST-CLASS DEBUT IN BRITAIN

M.J.Cosgrove	114	Glamorgan v Derbyshire	Cardiff
H.J.H.Marshall	102	Gloucestershire v Derbyshire	Bristol

FASTEST HUNDRED (WALTER LAWRENCE TROPHY)

M.A.Ealham (112*)	45 balls	Nottinghamshire v MCC	Lord's

M.L.Pettini (27 balls) and M.W.Goodwin (32 balls) scored faster hundreds but in contrived circumstances to accelerate a declaration.

HUNDRED BEFORE LUNCH

		Day		
C.M.Spearman	0*-100	1	Gloucestershire v Surrey	Bristol
L.Vincent	0-104*	1	Worcestershire v Essex	Worcester

MOST SIXES IN AN INNINGS

11	M.W.Goodwin (156)	Sussex v Middlesex	Southgate
11	M.L.Pettini (114*)	Essex v Leicestershire	Leicester

200 RUNS FROM BOUNDARIES IN AN INNINGS

Runs	*6s*	*4s*			
226	3	52	D.S.Lehmann (339)	Yorkshire v Durham	Leeds
212	2	50	C.J.L.Rogers (319)	Northamptonshire v Gloucestershire	Northampton

CARRYING BAT THROUGH COMPLETED INNINGS (*One man absent*)

N.R.D.Compton	105*	Middlesex (230) v Nottinghamshire	Lord's
J.J.Sayers	122*	Yorkshire (326) v Middlesex	Scarborough

LONGEST INNINGS

Min	*Balls*			
667	479	M.J.Powell (299)	Glamorgan v Gloucestershire	Cheltenham
624	471	A.Flower (271*)	Essex v Northamptonshire	Northampton
618	416	J.L.Langer (342)	Somerset v Surrey	Guildford

FIRST-WICKET PARTNERSHIP OF 100 IN EACH INNINGS

252/184*	N.J.Dexter/J.L.Denly	Kent v Cambridge UCCE	Cambridge
109/171	P.A.Jaques/S.C.Moore	Worcestershire v Surrey	The Oval
153/151	S.D.Peters/C.J.L.Rogers	Northamptonshire v Somerset	Taunton

OTHER NOTABLE PARTNERSHIPS († *County record*)

First Wicket

281*	D.P.Fulton/R.W.T.Key	Kent v Hampshire	Canterbury
252	N.J.Dexter/J.L.Denly	Kent v Cambridge UCCE	Cambridge

Second Wicket

281	J.N.Batty/M.R.Ramprakash	Surrey v Northamptonshire	Northampton
276	J.H.K.Adams/J.P.Crawley	Hampshire v Nottinghamshire	Nottingham
253	C.M.Spearman/H.J.H.Marshall	Gloucestershire v Worcestershire	Bristol

Third Wicket

385*†	M.H.Yardy/M.W.Goodwin	Sussex v Warwickshire	Hove
363	Younis Khan/Md Yousuf Youhana	Pakistan v England (3rd Test)	Leeds
353	M.R.Ramprakash/M.A.Butcher	Surrey v Northamptonshire	The Oval
339	R.S.Bopara/A.Flower	Essex v Glamorgan	Cardiff
288	W.R.Smith/S.P.Fleming	Nottinghamshire v Middlesex	Lord's
254	Kadeer Ali/H.J.H.Marshall	Gloucestershire v Northamptonshire	Northampton

Fourth Wicket

358†	D.S.Lehmann/M.J.Lumb	Yorkshire v Durham	Leeds
330†	B.F.Smith/G.A.Hick	Worcestershire v Somerset	Taunton
278	A.Flower/R.C.Irani	Essex v Somerset	Taunton
254	M.W.Goodwin/C.J.Adams	Sussex v Yorkshire	Arundel

Fifth Wicket

345	V.S.Solanki/S.M.Davies	Worcestershire v Gloucestershire	Bristol
243*	J.L.Sadler/J.Allenby	Leicestershire v Essex	Leicester
231	D.J.G.Sales/L.Klusener	Northamptonshire v Essex	Northampton
229	D.S.Lehmann/C.White	Yorkshire v Kent	Canterbury
226	A.D.Brown/R.Clarke	Surrey v Leicestershire	The Oval
222†	D.M.Benkenstein/G.R.Breese	Durham v Middlesex	Lord's

Sixth Wicket

249†	G.J.Muchall/P.Mustard	Durham v Kent	Canterbury
238*	T.T.Samaraweera/C.K.Kapugedera	Sri Lankans v Sussex	Hove
226	D.J.Hussey/M.A.Ealham	Nottinghamshire v Lancashire	Nottingham

Seventh Wicket

315	D.M.Benkenstein/O.D.Gibson	Durham v Yorkshire	Leeds
202	K.A.Parsons/P.D.Trego	Somerset v Essex	Taunton

Tenth Wicket

127*	C.M.W.Read/S.C.J.Broad	England A v Pakistanis	Canterbury

BOWLING HIGHLIGHTS

EIGHT OR MORE WICKETS IN AN INNINGS

Z.Khan	9-138	Worcestershire v Essex	Chelmsford
A.Kumble	8-100	Surrey v Northamptonshire	The Oval
M.S.Mason	8-45	Worcestershire v Gloucestershire	Worcester
M.Muralitharan	8-70	Sri Lanka v England (3rd Test)	Nottingham
Mushtaq Ahmed	9-48	Sussex v Nottinghamshire	Nottingham
C.E.Shreck	8-31	Nottinghamshire v Middlesex	Nottingham

TEN OR MORE WICKETS IN A MATCH

R.D.B.Croft		13-187	Glamorgan v Gloucestershire	Cheltenham
N.D.Doshi		10-159	Surrey v Worcestershire	The Oval
S.J.Harmison		11-76	England v Pakistan (2nd Test)	Manchester
Z.Khan	(2)	10-140	Worcestershire v Somerset	Worcester
		11-260	Worcestershire v Essex	Chelmsford
A.Kumble		11-183	Surrey v Northamptonshire	The Oval
J.Lewis	(2)	10-75	Gloucestershire v Somerset	Bristol
		10-170	Gloucestershire v Worcestershire	Worcester
M.S.Mason		10-117	Worcestershire v Gloucestershire	Worcester
M.K.Munday		11-143	Oxford U v Cambridge U	Oxford
M.Muralitharan	(2)	10-115	Sri Lanka v England (2nd Test)	Birmingham
		11-132	Sri Lanka v England (3rd Test)	Nottingham
Mushtaq Ahmed	(4)	10-37	Sussex v Durham	Chester-le-St

		10-202	Sussex v Middlesex	Horsham
		13-132	Sussex v Kent	Canterbury
		13-108	Sussex v Nottinghamshire	Nottingham
Naved-ul-Hasan		11-148	Sussex v Yorkshire	Leeds
M.S.Panesar		10-177	Northamptonshire v Worcestershire	Northampton
C.E.Shreck	(2)	12-129	Nottinghamshire v Middlesex	Nottingham
		10-131	Nottinghamshire v Durham	Chester-le-St
C.D.Thorp		11-97	Durham v Hampshire	Southampton
J.C.Tredwell		10-165	Kent v Sussex	Canterbury

HAT-TRICKS

C.E.Shreck	Nottinghamshire v Middlesex	Lord's
B.V.Taylor	Hampshire v Middlesex	Southampton

200 RUNS CONCEDED IN AN INNINGS

C.W.Henderson	54.2-5-235-2	Leicestershire v Surrey	The Oval
M.S.Panesar	58-10-211-3	Northamptonshire v Worcestershire	Worcester
C.T.Peploe	50-4-205-2	Middlesex v Kent	Canterbury

60 OVERS IN AN INNINGS

M.C.J.Ball	60-19-113-2	Gloucestershire v Glamorgan	Cheltenham

NO-BALLED FOR THROWING

S.K.Warne	Hampshire v Lancashire	Southampton

An act of protest against Lancashire's failure to declare – called once.

MATCH DOUBLE (100 RUNS AND 10 WICKETS)

C.D.Thorp	75, 28; 6-55, 5-42	Durham v Hampshire	Southampton

SIX OR MORE WICKET-KEEPING DISMISSALS IN AN INNINGS

S.M.Davies	6 ct	Worcestershire v Leicestershire	Worcester
P.Mustard	6 ct	Durham v Hampshire	Southampton
N.Pothas (2)	7 ct	Hampshire v Lancashire	Manchester
	5 ct, 1 st	Hampshire v Sussex	Hove

NINE OR MORE WICKET-KEEPING DISMISSALS IN A MATCH

D.Alleyne	7 ct, 2 st	Nottinghamshire v Warwickshire Also scored 57 and 109*.	Nottingham
P.Mustard	6 ct	Durham v Hampshire	Southampton
D.J.Pipe	8 ct, 1 st	Derbyshire v Worcestershire	Worcester

NO BYES CONCEDED IN TOTAL OF 550 OR MORE

717	C.M.Gazzard	Somerset v Surrey	Guildford
660-5d	J.S.Foster	Essex v Northamptonshire	Northampton
650-7d	J.S.Foster	Essex v Worcestershire	Chelmsford
580-3d	L.J.Goddard	Derbyshire v Essex	Chelmsford
560-5d	D.Alleyne	Nottinghamshire v Sussex	Nottingham

FIVE CATCHES IN AN INNINGS IN THE FIELD

Azhar Mahmood	Surrey v Worcestershire	The Oval
R.E.Watkins	Glamorgan v Gloucestershire	Cheltenham

2006 FIRST-CLASS AVERAGES

These averages involve the 505 cricketers who appeared in the 175 first-class matches played by 31 teams in the British Isles during the 2006 season.

'*Cap*' denotes the season in which the player was awarded a 1st XI cap by the county he represented in 2006. For Worcestershire players, 2006^{C} denotes the award of county colours in 2006. Gloucestershire now cap players on first-class debut.

Team abbreviations: BU – British Universities; CU – Cambridge University/Cambridge UCCE; De – Derbyshire; Du – Durham; DU – Durham UCCE; E – England; EA – England A; Ex – Essex; Gm – Glamorgan; Gs – Gloucestershire; H – Hampshire; K – Kent; La – Lancashire; Le – Leicestershire; LU – Loughborough UCCE; M – Middlesex; MCC – Marylebone Cricket Club; Nh – Northamptonshire; Nt – Nottinghamshire; OU – Oxford University/Oxford UCCE; P – Pakistan (is); SL – Sri Lanka (ans); Sm – Somerset; Sy – Surrey; Sx – Sussex; Wa – Warwickshire; WIA – West Indies A; Wo – Worcestershire; Y – Yorkshire. † Left-handed batsman.

BATTING AND FIELDING

	Cap	*M*	*I*	*NO*	*HS*	*Runs*	*Avge*	*100*	*50*	*Ct/St*
Abdul Razzaq (P)	–	3	5	1	37	106	26.50	–	–	1
Ackerman, H.D.(Le)	2005	15	28	4	309*	1808	75.33	4	14	14
Adams, A.R.(Ex)	2004	8	9	2	75	230	32.85	–	1	4
Adams, C.J.(Sx)	1998	16	25	1	155	1218	50.75	3	7	28
† Adams, J.H.K.(H)	2006	17	31	5	262*	1173	45.11	2	4	18
Adnan, M.Hassan (De)	2004	18	29	2	117	893	33.07	1	5	4
Adshead, S.J. (Gs)	2004	16	28	5	79*	687	29.86	–	4	47/2
† Afzaal, U. (Nh)	2005	18	32	6	151	1315	50.57	4	6	6
Ahmed, J.S.(Ex)	–	1	–	–	–	–	–	–	–	1
Ali, Kabir(Wo)	2002^{c}	11	16	2	38*	168	12.00	–	–	1
Ali, Kadeer(Gs)	2005	11	22	1	145	834	39.71	1	5	6
† Ali, M.M.(Wa)	–	6	9	–	68	177	19.66	–	2	2
Ali, S.M.H.(M)	–	5	8	4	23*	87	21.75	–	–	3
Allenby, J.(Le)	–	2	4	2	103*	239	119.50	1	1	2
Alleyne, D.(Nt)	–	12	20	1	109*	543	28.57	1	4	29/5
Ambrose, T.R.(Wa)	–	9	14	1	133	443	34.07	1	3	30/4
† Anderson, J.M.(La)	2003	1	1	1	7*	7	–	–	–	1
Anwar, O.S.(OU)	–	3	6	1	34	138	27.60	–	–	–
† Anyon, J.E.(Wa)	–	11	17	6	18*	60	5.45	–	–	3
Arshad Khan (P)	–	1	1	–	23	23	23.00	–	–	–
Astle, N.J.(La)	–	8	12	–	86	429	35.75	–	3	3
Austin, M.L.(CU)	–	1	2	–	23	35	17.50	–	–	–
Averis, J.M.M.(Gs)	2001	4	7	–	53	128	18.28	–	1	–
Azhar Mahmood(Sy)	2004	13	20	4	101	600	37.50	1	2	18
Balcombe, D.J.(DU/BU)	–	4	6	1	15	38	7.60	–	–	1
Ball, M.C.J.(Gs)	1996	10	15	1	58	215	15.35	–	1	16
Bandara, C.M.(SL)	–	1	1	–	2	2	2.00	–	–	–
† Banerjee, V.(CU/Gs)	2006	7	11	3	28	72	9.00	–	–	2
Banks, O.A.C.(WIA)	–	1	1	–	23	23	23.00	–	–	1
† Bartholomew, I.D.(CU)	–	1	2	–	42	60	30.00	–	–	–
Bartram, T.S.(DU)	–	2	2	1	2*	4	4.00	–	–	–
Batty, G.J.(Wo)	2002^{c}	15	24	8	112*	744	46.50	1	3	14
Batty, J.N.(Sy)	2001	17	29	–	133	1025	35.34	2	7	44/9
† Begg, C.G.(DU)	–	2	3	–	2	4	1.33	–	–	2
Bell, I.R.(Wa/E/EA)	2001	9	16	4	119	713	59.41	3	4	4
Benham, C.C.(H)	–	9	15	–	95	504	33.60	–	4	9

F-C	Cap	M	I	NO	HS	Runs	Avge	100	50	Ct/St
Benkenstein, D.M.(Du)	2005	17	31	2	151	1500	51.72	3	7	8
Benning, J.G.E.(Sy)	–	8	13	2	122*	488	44.36	2	2	4
Best, T.L.(WIA)	–	2	3	–	18	19	6.33	–	–	–
Betts, M.M.(M)	–	2	4	–	7	18	4.50	–	–	1
Bichel, A.J.(Ex)	–	8	8	1	75*	265	37.85	–	2	–
† Bicknell, D.J.(Nt)	2000	18	29	–	95	851	29.34	–	4	2
Bicknell, M.P.(Sy)	1989	4	6	2	59	156	39.00	–	1	2
† Birt, T.R.(De)	–	14	24	2	181	1059	48.13	3	6	7
† Blackwell, I.D.(Sm)	2001	2	2	–	49	92	46.00	–	–	–
Blain, J.A.R.(Y)	–	3	3	–	12	24	8.00	–	–	2
Bopara, R.S.(Ex/MCC/EA)	2005	18	28	3	159	882	35.28	2	3	14
Borrington, P.M.(De)	–	1	2	–	38	56	28.00	–	–	–
† Botha, A.G.(De)	2004	12	21	2	100	470	24.73	1	4	14
Bott, M.D.(CU)	–	1	2	–	20	26	13.00	–	–	1
† Boyce, M.A.G.(Le)	–	1	2	–	6	10	5.00	–	–	–
Bradshaw, D.P.(OU)	–	1	2	–	20	26	13.00	–	–	–
Brathwaite, R.M.R.(LU/BU)	–	3	3	2	24*	41	41.00	–	–	–
Bravo, D.J.(K)	–	5	8	–	76	208	26.00	–	1	–
Breese, G.R.(Du)	–	17	29	–	110	623	21.48	1	1	14
Bresnan, T.T.(Y/MCC/EA)	2006	12	17	1	94	387	24.18	–	2	4
Bridge, G.D.(Du)	–	1	2	–	43	48	24.00	–	–	–
† Broad, S.C.J.(Le/EA)	–	14	17	4	65*	279	21.46	–	2	6
Brophy, G.L.(Y)	–	10	16	–	97	251	15.68	–	1	26/3
Brown, A.D.(Sy)	1994	16	27	4	215	1264	54.95	5	4	9
Brown, D.O.(Gs)	2006	1	2	–	34	56	28.00	–	–	–
Brown, D.R.(Wa)	1995	11	19	1	69	368	20.44	–	2	4
Brown, J.F.(Nh)	2000	15	19	5	20*	85	6.07	–	–	3
† Brown, K.R.(La)	–	1	2	–	32	34	17.00	–	–	–
Brown, M.J.(H)	–	5	8	1	133	229	32.71	1	–	3
† Browne, P.A.(WIA)	–	4	5	1	55*	118	29.50	–	1	9/1
Bruce, J.T.A.(H)	2006	13	14	8	17	52	8.66	–	–	2
Buckham, C.T.(CU)	–	1	–	–	–	–	–	–	–	–
Burrows, T.G.(H)	–	2	3	–	20	49	16.33	–	–	5
Burton, D.A.(Gs)	2006	1	2	1	52*	53	53.00	–	1	–
† Butcher, M.A.(Sy)	1996	17	29	4	151	1465	58.60	5	8	17
Caddick, A.R.(Sm)	1992	16	25	5	68	341	17.05	–	1	5
† Carberry, M.A.(H)	2006	15	28	2	104	938	36.07	2	5	8
† Carter, N.M.(Wa)	2005	13	20	4	36	250	15.62	–	–	1
Celliers, G.(CU)	–	2	4	1	61*	129	43.00	–	1	5
Chambers, D.J.(K)	–	1	1	–	12	12	12.00	–	–	1
Chapple, G.(La)	1994	14	19	1	82	580	32.22	–	3	6
† Chattergoon, S.(WIA)	–	2	4	–	30	57	14.25	–	–	3
† Cherry, D.D.(Gm)	–	9	17	–	121	532	31.29	1	3	4
Chervak, J.A.(CU)	–	1	2	–	89	92	46.00	–	1	–
Chilton, M.J.(La)	2002	16	25	1	131	766	31.91	1	4	13
† Chopra, V.(Ex)	–	9	16	1	106	569	37.93	1	4	7
Clark, S.G.(Le)	–	3	5	1	23*	45	11.25	–	–	1
Clarke, R.(Sy/MCC/EA)	2005	13	21	3	214	1027	57.05	3	3	14
† Claydon, M.E.(Y)	–	2	2	–	38	38	19.00	–	–	–
Clinton, P.J.S.(OU)	–	1	1	–	10	10	10.00	–	–	2
† Clinton, R.S.(LU/BU/Sy)	–	4	7	2	108*	236	47.20	1	–	1
Clough, G.D.(Nt)	–	1	–	–	–	–	–	–	–	1
† Coetzer, K.J.(Du)	–	1	2	–	63	98	49.00	–	1	–
Collingwood, P.D.(E)	1998	7	12	1	186	460	41.81	1	1	10

F-C	Cap	M	I	NO	HS	Runs	Avge	100	50	Ct/St
Compton, N.R.D.(M)	2006	17	31	3	190	1313	46.89	6	4	7
† Cook, A.N.(Ex/E/MCC/EA)	2005	13	23	5	132	1159	64.38	4	6	15
Cook, S.J.(K)	–	11	14	–	71	196	14.00	–	1	1
Cork, D.G.(La)	2004	14	17	2	154	354	23.60	1	1	11
† Cosgrove, M.J.(Gm)	–	10	19	2	233	856	50.35	2	6	5
Cosker, D.A.(Gm)	2000	13	16	6	39	168	16.80	–	–	9
Crawley, J.P.(H)	2002	16	27	1	189	1737	66.80	6	7	8
Croft, R.D.B.(Gm)	1992	16	24	5	72	601	31.63	–	3	9
Croft, S.J.(La)	–	1	1	–	17	17	17.00	–	–	1
Crook, S.P.(Nh)	–	8	10	2	44	138	17.25	–	–	5
Cross, G.D.(La)	–	4	6	–	72	162	27.00	–	2	13/4
Cullen, D.J.(Sm)	–	4	6	4	24*	81	40.50	–	–	1
Cummins, R.A.G.(Le)	–	7	8	4	13	38	9.50	–	–	2
Cusden, S.M.J.(K)	–	1	–	–	–	–	–	–	–	–
Daggett, L.M.(Wa)	–	5	9	4	12*	37	7.40	–	–	1
Dalrymple, J.W.M.(M/EA)	2004	12	19	–	96	654	34.42	–	5	6
Danish Kaneria (P)	–	6	7	3	29	49	12.25	–	–	–
Davies, A.M.(Du)	2005	2	2	–	10	10	5.00	–	–	2
† Davies, A.P.(Gm)	–	4	6	3	16	51	17.00	–	–	1
† Davies, S.M.(Wo/MCC)	2005[c]	17	29	1	192	1052	37.57	3	3	63/5
Dawson, R.K.J.(Y)	2004	8	13	1	56	127	10.58	–	1	2
† Dean, K.J.(De)	1998	5	5	2	18	19	6.33	–	–	–
Denly, J.L.(K)	–	3	5	1	115	387	96.75	2	2	1
Dennington, M.J.(K)	–	1	1	1	2*	2	–	–	–	–
Dernbach, J.W.(Sy)	–	2	3	2	9	13	13.00	–	–	–
Dexter, N.J.(K)	–	8	12	4	131*	463	57.87	2	1	3
Dilshan, T.M.(SL)	–	6	12	–	69	331	27.58	–	2	6
† Di Venuto, M.J.(De)	2000	14	23	1	161*	1198	54.45	3	7	19
Dixey, P.G.(K)	–	1	1	–	0	0	0.00	–	–	3
Dobson, W.T.(DU)	–	2	3	2	13	15	15.00	–	–	1
Doshi, N.D.(Sy)	2006	14	13	8	32	106	21.20	–	–	3
Dunbar, P.R.(OU)	–	1	2	–	46	50	25.00	–	–	–
Durston, W.J.(Sm)	–	13	23	3	89	765	38.25	–	7	15
Ealham, M.A.(Nt)	2004	17	26	3	112*	732	31.82	2	4	13
† Edwards, N.J.(Sm)	–	7	10	–	77	309	30.90	–	2	4
† Ervine, S.M.(H)	2005	15	22	3	50*	464	24.42	–	1	14
Faisal Iqbal (P)	–	7	11	3	82	288	36.00	–	2	6
Ferley, R.S.(K)	–	3	3	–	22	36	12.00	–	–	–
† Fisher, I.D.(Gs)	2004	5	8	2	45	168	28.00	–	–	1
† Fleming, S.P.(Nt)	2005	13	22	2	192	992	49.60	2	8	17
Flintoff, A.(La/E)	1998	4	7	2	37	88	17.60	–	–	6
† Flower, A.(Ex)	2002	17	27	6	271*	1536	73.14	7	3	18
Flower, G.W.(Ex)	2005	7	11	–	101	364	33.09	1	3	7
Footitt, M.H.A.(Nt/MCC)	–	3	3	3	5*	5	–	–	–	–
† Foster, E.J.(LU)	–	2	2	–	105	105	52.50	1	–	1
Foster, J.S.(Ex)	2001	17	21	4	103	822	48.35	2	6	65/3
† Francis, J.D.(Sm)	–	5	9	–	41	131	14.55	–	–	5
Francis, S.R.G.(Sm)	–	3	5	1	38	85	21.25	–	–	1
† Franklin, J.E.C.(Gm)	–	9	15	1	94	346	24.71	–	2	4
† Franks, P.J.(Nt)	1999	14	20	3	64	376	22.11	–	3	1
Friedlander, M.J.(CU)	–	3	5	–	16	37	7.40	–	–	1
† Frost, T.(Wa)	1999	8	13	5	96	431	53.87	–	4	20
Fulton, D.P.(K)	1998	15	26	1	155	969	38.76	2	6	7
† Gale, A.W.(Y)	–	5	9	–	149	219	24.33	1	–	2

F-C	Cap	M	I	NO	HS	Runs	Avge	100	50	Ct/St
Gallian, J.E.R.(Nt)	1998	14	24	–	171	679	28.29	2	3	17
† Ganguly, S.C.(Nh)	–	4	6	1	9	24	4.80	–	–	–
Gazzard, C.M.(Sm)	–	13	22	2	35	305	15.25	–	–	32
Gerard, D.C.(OU)	–	1	–	–	–	–	–	–	–	1
Gibson, O.D.(Du)	–	13	22	4	155	596	33.11	1	2	5
Gidman, A.P.R.(Gs)	2004	16	31	6	120	1244	49.76	4	7	2
Gifford, W.M.(LU)	–	2	2	–	0	0	0.00	–	–	–
Gillespie, J.N.(Y)	–	14	21	6	45	370	24.66	–	–	1
Goddard, L.J.(De)	–	4	6	2	91	209	52.25	–	1	8
Goodwin, M.W.(Sx)	2001	16	27	1	235	1649	63.42	6	7	4
Gough, D.(Ex)	2004	7	7	4	52*	173	57.66	–	2	1
Grant, R.N.(Gm)	–	7	11	–	44	196	17.81	–	–	3
Gray, A.K.D.(De)	–	8	11	2	29	162	18.00	–	–	–
Greenidge, C.G.(Gs)	2005	5	8	–	20	42	5.25	–	–	3
Griffith, A.R.(Le)	–	5	6	2	41*	84	21.00	–	–	–
† Griffiths, D.A.(H)	–	1	1	1	16*	16	–	–	–	–
Groenewald, T.D.(Wa)	–	6	9	2	76	157	22.42	–	1	1
Guy, S.M.(Y)	–	6	8	2	52*	150	25.00	–	1	15/5
Habib, A.(Le)	1998	1	1	–	4	4	4.00	–	–	1
Hall, A.J.(K)	2005	4	5	2	68*	237	79.00	–	2	3
Hardinges, M.A.(Gs)	2004	11	15	2	107*	444	34.15	2	1	–
† Harmison, B.W.(Du)	–	9	17	2	110	563	37.53	2	3	5
Harmison, S.J.(Du/E)	1999	6	8	2	36	105	17.50	–	–	1
Harris, A.J.(Nt)	2000	13	17	2	28*	119	7.93	–	–	2
Harris, P.L.(Wa)	–	8	11	1	32	140	14.00	–	–	3
Harrison, A.J.(Gm)	–	1	1	–	3	3	3.00	–	–	–
Harrison, D.S.(Gm)	2006	13	16	3	64	281	21.61	–	1	4
Harrison, P.W.(LU/BU/Le)	–	3	6	1	28*	77	15.40	–	–	6
Harvey, I.J.(Gs)	1999	9	15	5	114	561	56.10	2	2	4
Heather, S.A.(Sx)	–	1	1	–	0	0	0.00	–	–	1
† Hemp, D.L.(Gm)	1994	16	29	1	155	1003	35.82	3	2	18
Henderson, C.W.(Le)	–	17	24	6	62*	545	30.27	–	1	7
Henderson, T.(K)	–	6	9	1	59	146	18.25	–	1	2
Heywood, J.J.N.(CU)	–	4	6	–	27	35	5.83	–	–	6
Hick, G.A.(Wo)	1986	14	23	2	182	1023	48.71	4	3	36
Hildreth, J.C.(Sm)	–	14	24	1	227*	798	34.69	1	3	11
Hillyard, N.J.(OU)	–	1	1	–	79	79	79.00	–	1	–
† Hinds, R.O.(WIA)	–	2	2	–	27	27	13.50	–	–	3
Hobbiss, M.H.(OU)	–	1	1	1	78*	78	–	–	1	–
Hodd, A.J.(Sx)	–	3	4	–	18	29	7.25	–	–	8
Hodge, B.J.(La)	2006	6	7	2	161	505	101.00	3	–	4
Hodson, W.G.(DU)	–	1	2	–	29	29	14.50	–	–	1
† Hogg, K.W.(La)	–	8	8	1	70	254	36.28	–	2	1
Hoggard, M.J.(Y/E/EA)	2000	11	16	2	13	81	5.78	–	–	3
Holt, D.R.(LU)	–	1	–	–	–	–	–	–	–	–
† Hooper, J.H.P.(OU)	–	1	1	1	3*	3	–	–	–	–
Hopkinson, C.D.(Sx)	–	17	28	–	74	723	25.82	–	6	10
Horton, P.J.(La)	–	4	7	2	79	227	45.40	–	2	3
Hunter, I.D.(De)	–	14	13	6	48	102	14.57	–	–	6
† Huntingdon, C.J.(CU)	–	2	3	–	29	37	12.33	–	–	–
Hussey, D.J.(Nt)	2004	17	28	4	164	1143	47.62	5	1	14
† Hutton, B.L.(M)	2003	11	20	1	105	583	30.68	2	1	16
Iftikhar Anjum (P)	–	1	1	1	33*	33	–	–	–	2
Iles, J.A.(K)	–	1	–	–	–	–	–	–	–	–

F-C	Cap	M	I	NO	HS	Runs	Avge	100	50	Ct/St
† Imran Farhat (P)	–	6	11	–	91	416	37.81	–	3	7
Inzamam-ul-Haq (P)	–	5	9	2	69	252	36.00	–	2	–
Iqbal, M.M.(Du)	–	4	8	3	20	53	10.60	–	–	2
Irani, R.C.(Ex)	1994	16	23	5	145	1075	59.72	3	6	1
Jacklin, B.D.(CU)	–	1	2	1	19*	23	23.00	–	–	–
James, G.D.(CU)	–	3	5	–	36	95	19.00	–	–	1
Jannisar Khan (P)	–	1	1	–	31	31	31.00	–	–	–
† Jaques, P.A.(Wo)	2006c	8	15	2	244	1148	88.30	3	7	8
† Jayasuriya, S.T.(SL)	–	1	2	–	4	8	4.00	–	–	–
Jayawardena, D.P.M.D.(SL)	–	6	11	–	119	317	28.81	1	1	9
Jayawardena, H.A.P.W.(SL)	–	3	3	2	52*	75	75.00	–	1	9/2
Jefferson, W.I.(Ex)	2002	1	1	–	5	5	5.00	–	–	–
Jogia, K.A.(CU)	–	2	3	–	20	24	8.00	–	–	2
Johnson, R.L.(Sm)	2001	8	12	1	51	211	19.18	–	1	2
Jones, G.O.(K/E)	2003	12	17	2	60	336	22.40	–	3	39/3
Jones, M.C.(DU)	–	1	1	–	1	1	1.00	–	–	–
Jones, P.S.(De)	–	17	21	6	34*	227	15.13	–	–	4
† Jones, S.P.(Gm)	2002	1	2	1	4*	4	4.00	–	–	–
Joseph, R.H.(K)	–	9	12	4	29	63	7.87	–	–	1
Joseph, S.C.(WIA)	–	4	6	1	29	111	22.20	–	–	2
† Joyce, E.C.(M/MCC/EA)	2002	14	24	1	211	1215	52.82	3	6	10
Kalam, T.(OU)	–	3	3	–	8	14	4.66	–	–	1
Kamran Akmal (P)	–	7	9	1	62*	202	25.25	–	2	21/3
Kapugedara, C.K.(SL)	–	6	11	2	134*	400	44.44	1	1	1
† Kartik, M.(La)	–	3	2	1	40	42	42.00	–	–	1
† Keedy, G.(La)	2000	15	16	10	11*	45	7.50	–	–	4
Keegan, C.B.(M)	2003	7	10	1	34*	111	12.33	–	–	3
† Kelly, R.(WIA)	–	3	4	1	9	25	8.33	–	–	–
Kemp, J.M.(K)	2006	6	9	3	124*	369	61.50	2	1	10
Kemp, R.A.(CU)	–	1	2	–	5	6	3.00	–	–	–
Key, R.W.T.(K/EA)	2001	16	29	3	136*	956	36.76	2	3	10
Khan, A.(K)	–	9	10	7	38	98	32.66	–	–	1
Khan, Z.(Wo)	2006c	16	21	6	30*	161	10.73	–	–	4
Killeen, N.(Du)	1999	9	12	3	34	72	8.00	–	–	2
King, R.E.(LU)	–	2	2	–	30	30	15.00	–	–	–
Kirby, S.P.(Gs)	2005	15	22	11	19*	106	9.63	–	–	3
Kirtley, R.J.(Sx)	1998	8	10	5	36	118	23.60	–	–	2
† Klokker, F.A.(Wa)	–	1	1	–	40	40	40.00	–	–	3
† Klusener, L.(Nh)	2006	16	26	7	147*	1251	65.84	6	3	9
Knappett, J.P.T.(OU/BU)	–	4	8	1	100*	230	32.85	1	1	9/2
† Knight, N.V.(Wa)	1995	17	30	1	126	1070	36.89	2	6	22
Kruis, G.J.(Y)	2006	13	17	9	28*	85	10.62	–	–	2
Kulasekara, M.D.N.(SL)	–	5	7	3	64	104	26.00	–	1	–
Kumble, A.(Sy)	–	3	2	1	8	14	14.00	–	–	4
Lamb, G.A.(H)	–	3	4	1	32*	61	20.33	–	–	2
Lamb, N.J.(DU/BU)	–	4	7	1	62	105	17.50	–	1	–
† Langer, J.L.(Sm)	–	2	3	–	342	390	130.00	1	–	1
Latouf, K.J.(H)	–	1	1	–	29	29	29.00	–	–	–
Law, S.G.(La)	2002	16	23	3	130	1103	55.15	4	6	16
Lawson, M.A.K.(Y)	–	7	10	2	44	124	15.50	–	–	5
† Lee, J.E.(Y)	–	1	2	1	21*	22	22.00	–	–	1
Lee, N.T.(CU)	–	3	5	–	43	75	15.00	–	–	1
† Lehmann, D.S.(Y)	1997	15	23	1	339	1706	77.54	6	3	1
Lett, R.J.(Sm)	–	3	4	–	50	65	16.25	–	1	–

F-C	*Cap*	*M*	*I*	*NO*	*HS*	*Runs*	*Avge*	*100*	*50*	*Ct/St*
Lewis, J.(Gs/E/EA)	1998	13	17	2	57	269	17.93	–	1	4
Lewis, J.J.B.(Du)	1998	9	16	–	99	355	22.18	–	2	5
Lewis, M.L.(Du)	–	11	18	9	38	127	14.11	–	–	4
† Lewry, J.D.(Sx)	1996	16	19	11	27*	89	11.12	–	–	10
Liddle, C.J.(Le)	–	6	6	3	4*	6	2.00	–	–	2
Linley, T.E.(Sx)	–	1	1	–	0	0	0.00	–	–	–
Logan, R.J.(H)	–	3	3	–	4	8	2.66	–	–	1
Loudon, A.G.R.(Wa/MCC/EA)	2006	17	26	–	123	681	26.19	1	5	12
Louw, J.(M)	–	17	27	5	42	314	14.27	–	–	1
Lowe, J.A.(Du)	–	5	10	–	30	130	13.00	–	–	4
Loye, M.B.(La)	2003	16	24	2	148*	1296	58.90	6	6	6
† Lumb, M.J.(Y)	2003	16	25	2	144	963	41.86	2	7	10
† Lungley, T.(De)	–	1	1	1	27*	27	–	–	–	1
McCullum, B.B.(Gm)	–	3	6	1	160	306	61.20	1	1	3
McGrath, A.(Y)	1999	15	24	3	140*	1293	61.57	4	9	18
McLean, J.J.(H)	–	1	1	–	60	60	60.00	–	1	–
McMahon, P.J.(Nt)	–	1	–	–	–	–	–	–	–	–
Maddy, D.L.(Le)	1996	11	19	1	97	538	29.88	–	4	16
Maharoof, M.F.(SL)	–	5	9	–	59	185	20.55	–	1	–
† Maher, J.P.(Du)	–	16	30	2	106	978	34.92	2	4	12/1
Mahmood, S.I.(La/E)	–	9	10	1	34	99	11.00	–	–	1
Malik, M.N.(Wo)	2004[c]	6	9	3	35	68	11.33	–	–	–
Malinga, S.L.(SL)	–	5	6	–	26	71	11.83	–	–	–
Mansoor Amjad (Le)	–	1	2	–	27	52	26.00	–	–	1
Marshall, H.J.H.(Gs)	2006	11	21	1	168	1218	60.90	5	7	6
Marshall, S.J.(La)	–	2	3	–	34	40	13.33	–	–	–
Martin-Jenkins, R.S.C.(Sx)	2000	14	21	3	91	592	32.88	–	3	1
Mascarenhas, A.D.(H)	1998	16	24	–	131	474	19.75	1	–	4
Mason, M.S.(Wo)	2002[c]	10	11	5	29*	85	14.16	–	–	2
Massey, I.R.(CU)	–	2	4	–	46	110	27.50	–	–	–
Masters, D.D.(Le)	–	14	16	1	52	219	14.60	–	1	6
† Maunders, J.K.(Le)	–	16	29	1	180	959	34.25	1	6	9
Middlebrook, J.D.(Ex)	2003	15	17	1	113	494	30.87	1	2	6
Mierkalns, J.A.(Nt)	–	1	1	–	18	18	18.00	–	–	–
† Miller, D.J.(LU)	–	2	1	1	0*	0	–	–	–	–
Mitchell, D.K.H.(Wo)	2005[c]	4	8	2	134*	282	47.00	1	2	3
Mohammad Akram (Sy)	2006	14	11	4	21*	64	9.14	–	–	3
Mohammad Amin (CU)	–	3	3	2	25*	41	41.00	–	–	1
† Mohammad Asif (Le/P)	–	9	9	2	21	58	8.28	–	–	4
Mohammad Hafeez (P)	–	1	1	–	95	95	95.00	–	1	1
Mohammad Sami (P)	–	5	6	1	28*	48	9.60	–	–	3
† Mohammed, D.(WIA)	–	3	4	–	19	44	11.00	–	–	2
Mohammed, J.(WIA)	–	1	2	–	5	9	4.50	–	–	1
† Mongia, D.(Le)	–	11	18	3	165	800	53.33	3	2	2
Montgomerie, R.R.(Sx)	1999	17	28	–	100	905	32.32	1	7	17
Moore, S.C.(Wo)	2003[c]	16	30	2	97	960	34.28	–	9	6
Moreton S.J.P.(OU)	–	3	6	–	63	134	22.33	–	1	1
† Morgan, E.J.G.(M)	–	6	11	–	38	144	13.09	–	–	1/1
Morris, J.C.(DU/BU)	–	4	7	–	81	151	21.57	–	1	2
Morris, R.K.(LU)	–	2	2	–	7	8	4.00	–	–	1
Morse, E.J.(OU)	–	3	2	2	0*	0	–	–	–	3
Morton, R.S.(WIA)	–	4	6	1	105	322	64.40	1	2	5
† Mubarak, J.(SL)	–	3	6	1	33	69	13.80	–	–	2
Muchall, G.J.(Du)	2005	15	28	–	219	778	27.78	2	3	11

F-C	Cap	M	I	NO	HS	Runs	Avge	100	50	Ct/St
Mullaney, S.J.(La)	–	1	1	–	44	44	44.00	–	–	1
Mumtaz Habib (DU)	–	2	3	–	10	12	4.00	–	–	–
Munday, M.K.(OU/Sm)	–	7	8	3	17*	42	8.40	–	–	3
Muralitharan, M.(SL)	–	4	6	3	33	37	12.33	–	–	–
Murtagh, C.P.(LU)	–	2	2	–	27	46	23.00	–	–	–
† Murtagh, T.J.(Sy)	–	3	3	2	41*	82	82.00	–	–	2
Mushtaq Ahmed (Sx)	2003	15	19	5	42*	222	15.85	–	–	2
† Mustard, P.(Du)	–	16	27	2	130	816	32.64	2	3	53/1
Naik, J.K.H.(Le)	–	3	2	–	13	14	7.00	–	–	2
Napier, G.R.(Ex)	2003	3	3	1	62	131	65.50	–	2	1
Nash, C.D.(Sx)	–	4	6	–	67	184	30.66	–	1	–
Nash, D.C.(M)	2000	8	14	4	68*	460	46.00	–	4	13/2
Naved-ul-Hasan (Sx)	2005	6	8	–	64	134	16.75	–	1	1
Needham, J.(De)	–	1	2	–	29	29	14.50	–	–	–
† New, T.J.(Le)	–	6	12	–	85	414	34.50	–	5	2
Newby, O.J.(La)	–	7	7	2	19	51	10.20	–	–	1
† Newman, S.A.(Sy)	2005	17	29	1	144*	1404	50.14	2	10	13
Nicholson, M.J.(Nh)	–	15	20	4	106*	454	28.37	1	1	6
† Nixon, P.A.(Le)	1994	16	23	8	144*	895	59.66	2	6	43/3
† North, M.J.(De)	–	3	6	1	161	465	93.00	2	2	6
Oberoi, S.(OU)	–	3	6	1	115	188	37.60	1	–	4
† O'Brien, N.J.(K)	–	10	13	1	62	241	20.08	–	1	19/8
Onions, G.(Du)	–	16	26	6	40	232	11.60	–	–	3
Ormond, J.(Sy)	2003	4	4	2	41*	62	31.00	–	–	–
Owen, F.G.(CU)	–	1	2	–	1	1	0.50	–	–	–
Palladino, A.P.(Ex)	–	6	6	2	7	7	1.75	–	–	5
† Panesar, M.S.(Nh/E/MCC)	2006	17	21	8	34	136	10.46	–	–	3
Park, G.T.(Du)	–	4	8	4	100*	316	79.00	1	1	4
Parker, L.C.(MCC/OU/BU/Wa)	–	8	15	–	140	431	28.73	1	2	4
Parry, S.J.P.(DU)	–	1	2	–	36	66	33.00	–	–	–
Parsons, K.A.(Sm)	1999	10	15	2	153	511	39.30	1	2	9
Patel, M.M.(K)	1994	13	16	2	61	179	12.78	–	1	4
Patel, S.R.(Nt)	–	8	12	2	173	612	61.20	2	2	3
Patterson, S.A.(Y)	–	5	7	1	46	85	14.16	–	–	1
Peng, N.(Gm)	–	8	15	–	59	357	23.80	–	2	10
† Peploe, C.T.(M)	–	10	14	1	46	204	15.69	–	–	2
Peters, S.D.(Nh)	–	16	30	2	178	1122	40.07	3	5	11
Pettini, M.L.(Ex)	2006	17	29	3	208*	1218	46.84	3	3	15
Phillips, B.J.(Nh)	2005	17	25	2	75	515	22.39	–	4	6
† Phillips, T.J.(Ex)	2006	14	17	2	49	336	22.40	–	–	16
Phythian, M.J.(DU)	–	3	5	2	62*	92	30.66	–	1	8/1
† Pietersen, C.(Nh)	–	3	4	2	39*	91	45.50	–	–	–
Pietersen, K.P.(E)	2005	7	12	–	158	707	58.91	3	1	7
Pipe, D.J.(De)	–	14	20	4	89	515	32.18	–	3	43/7
Plunkett, L.E.(Du/E/EA)	–	6	7	1	28	103	17.16	–	–	2
Poonia, N.S.(Wa)	–	1	1	–	35	35	35.00	–	–	–
Pothas, N.(H)	2003	15	22	7	122*	973	64.86	4	5	56/2
Powell, D.B.(WIA)	–	3	4	2	62	125	62.50	–	1	1
Powell, M.J.(Gm)	2000	16	29	3	299	1327	51.03	4	2	7
Powell, M.J.(Wa)	1999	6	11	1	56	256	25.60	–	1	4
Pratt, G.J.(Du)	–	6	10	–	52	193	19.30	–	1	7
Price, R.W.(Wo)	2004[c]	8	10	3	56	106	15.14	–	1	3
Prior, M.J.(Sx)	2003	14	22	2	124	934	46.70	3	4	34/11
Prowting, N.R.(DU)	–	3	5	–	27	60	12.00	–	–	1

F-C	Cap	M	I	NO	HS	Runs	Avge	100	50	Ct/St
Ramprakash, M.R.(Sy)	2002	15	24	2	301*	2278	103.54	8	9	13
Rashid, A.(Y)	–	5	6	–	63	115	19.16	–	1	2
Rayner, O.P.(Sx)	–	5	6	1	101	133	26.60	1	–	6
Read, C.M.W.(Nt/E/EA)	1999	14	21	4	150*	727	42.76	3	3	44/1
† Rees, G.P.(Gm)	–	3	5	1	57	84	21.00	–	1	1
† Richards, M.A.(OU/BU)	–	4	8	2	39*	92	15.33	–	–	4
Richardson, A.(M)	2005	1	2	1	9	9	9.00	–	–	–
† Richardson, A.P.(WIA)	–	3	3	1	4	7	3.50	–	–	1
Robinson, D.D.J.(Le)	–	13	25	1	106	738	30.75	1	3	10
† Rogers, C.J.L.(Nh)	–	14	24	2	319	1360	61.81	4	5	12
Rosenburg, M.C.(Le)	–	1	2	1	33*	48	48.00	–	–	1
Rowe, D.T.(Le)	–	1	1	–	0	0	0.00	–	–	1
Rudge, W.D.(Gs)	2005	4	2	1	8*	9	9.00	–	–	1
† Sadler, J.L.(Le)	–	15	26	5	128*	1024	48.76	1	8	15
Sadler, O.J.(OU)	–	1	2	1	22	39	39.00	–	–	–
Saggers, M.J.(K)	2001	2	2	1	2*	2	2.00	–	–	–
Saker, N.C.(Sy)	–	7	10	1	58*	192	21.33	–	1	4
Sales, D.J.G.(Nh)	1999	17	27	1	225	1219	46.88	2	5	13
Salisbury, I.D.K.(Sy)	1998	16	19	4	74	363	24.20	–	2	11
† Salman Butt (P)	–	5	10	–	84	323	32.30	–	4	3
Samaraweera, T.T.(SL)	–	5	9	1	114	267	33.37	2	–	4
Samiullah Khan (P)	–	1	–	–	–	–	–	–	–	1
Sammy, D.J.G.(WIA)	–	3	4	–	17	37	9.25	–	–	1
† Sangakkara, K.C.(SL)	–	6	12	1	66	347	31.54	–	2	9/1
Savill, T.E.(CU)	–	3	5	–	56	157	31.40	–	2	2
† Sayers, J.J.(Y)	–	13	21	3	122*	590	32.77	1	3	7
† Schofield, C.P.(Sy)	–	2	3	–	95	114	38.00	–	1	2
Scott, B.J.M.(M)	–	9	15	2	49	248	19.07	–	–	28/2
Scott, G.M.(Du)	–	9	18	–	133	551	30.61	1	3	7
Shafayat, B.M.(Nh)	–	17	30	2	118	887	31.67	2	5	20/3
Shah, O.A.(M/EA)	2000	17	30	–	126	1079	35.96	2	7	14
Shahid Afridi(P)	–	3	4	–	17	62	15.50	–	–	–
Shahid Nazir (P)	–	4	4	1	17	47	15.66	–	–	1
Shahzad, A.(Y)	–	1	1	–	2	2	2.00	–	–	–
† Shantry, A.J.(Wa)	–	1	1	1	4*	4	–	–	–	–
† Sharif, Z.K.(CU)	–	3	5	3	140*	292	146.00	2	–	–
† Sheikh, M.A.(De)	–	9	13	3	51*	270	27.00	–	1	1
Shilvock, D.J.F.(DU)	–	1	1	–	15	15	15.00	–	–	–
† Shirazi, D.C.(LU/BU)	–	3	5	1	46*	139	34.75	–	–	2
Shoaib Malik (P)	–	1	2	1	110*	128	128.00	1	–	1
Shreck, C.E.(Nt)	2006	12	16	10	5*	11	1.83	–	–	4
† Sidebottom, R.J.(Nt)	2004	15	22	6	33	222	13.87	–	–	7
Sillence, R.J.(Wo)	2006[c]	13	19	1	64	487	27.05	–	3	5
Silverwood, C.E.W.(M)	2006	16	24	6	50	271	15.05	–	1	4
Simmons, L.M.P.(WIA)	–	3	4	–	100	151	37.75	1	–	2
Singh, A.(Nt)	–	1	1	–	0	0	0.00	–	–	–
Smith, B.F.(Wo)	2002[c]	16	27	2	203	915	36.60	2	3	23
† Smith, B.M.(CU)	–	2	1	–	0	0	0.00	–	–	–
Smith, D.R.(WIA)	–	3	3	–	66	120	40.00	–	1	2
† Smith, D.S.(WIA)	–	3	4	–	51	125	31.25	–	1	2
Smith, E.T.(M)	2005	17	31	1	166	1209	40.30	5	2	12
Smith, G.J.(Nt)	2001	6	6	–	17	21	3.50	–	–	1
Smith, G.M.(De)	–	5	9	1	86	227	28.37	–	1	4
† Smith, T.C.(La)	–	15	18	5	49	234	18.00	–	–	14

F-C	Cap	M	I	NO	HS	Runs	Avge	100	50	Ct/St
Smith, W.R.(Nt)	–	14	21	–	141	575	27.38	1	2	8
Snape, J.N.(Le)	–	8	11	1	90	219	21.90	–	1	3
Solanki, V.S.(Wo)	1998	16	29	2	222	1252	46.37	4	4	12
Spearman, C.M.(Gs)	2002	16	31	–	192	1370	44.19	6	2	18
Spencer, D.J.(Sx)	–	2	2	–	17	33	16.50	–	–	1
† Spurway, S.H.P.(Sm)	–	3	4	–	83	164	41.00	–	1	7
Stearn, C.P.(OU)	–	1	1	–	38	38	38.00	–	–	–
Stephenson, J.P.(MCC)	–	1	2	–	1	1	0.50	–	–	–
Stevens, D.I.(K)	2005	17	27	4	126*	897	39.00	2	6	18
Stiff, D.A.(K)	–	1	–	–	–	–	–	–	–	–
† Strauss, A.J.(M/E)	2001	8	14	–	141	741	52.92	3	2	11
Streak, H.H.(Wa)	2005	15	24	6	68*	513	28.50	–	2	5
† Stubbings, S.D.(De)	2001	18	32	1	124	1056	34.06	2	6	12
Styris, S.B.(M)	2006	10	17	1	133	679	42.43	1	5	14
Suppiah, A.V.(Sm)	–	12	19	–	99	563	29.63	–	4	6
† Sutcliffe, I.J.(La)	2003	17	27	4	159	847	36.82	2	3	11
Sutton, L.D.(La)	–	13	16	3	151*	666	51.23	2	2	38/3
Swann, G.P.(Nt)	–	15	21	1	85	546	27.30	–	3	9
Tahir, N.(Wa)	–	3	3	1	21	36	18.00	–	–	1
† Taufiq Umar (P)	–	2	4	–	29	49	12.25	–	–	1
† Taylor, B.V.(H)	2006	6	6	3	3	5	1.66	–	–	1
Taylor, C.G.(Gs)	2001	14	27	–	121	705	26.11	1	4	12
Taylor, C.R.(De)	–	15	26	–	121	908	34.92	3	4	10
Ten Doeschate, R.N.(Ex)	2006	9	12	2	105*	403	40.30	2	1	4
† Tharanga, W.U.(SL)	–	7	13	–	140	449	34.53	2	1	2
Thornely, D.J.(H)	2006	15	25	3	76	759	34.50	–	6	12
Thorp, C.D.(Du)	–	12	21	2	75	326	17.15	–	2	4
† Tomlinson, J.A.(H)	–	2	2	–	3	3	1.50	–	–	–
† Tredwell, J.C.(K)	–	7	10	1	47	126	14.00	–	–	7
Trego, P.D.(Sm)	–	12	20	–	135	596	29.80	3	2	5
Tremlett, C.T.(H)	2004	9	10	1	23	76	8.44	–	–	–
† Trescothick, M.E.(Sm/E)	1999	10	18	–	154	510	28.33	2	1	19
Trott, I.J.L.(Wa)	2005	17	29	2	177*	1128	41.77	3	4	20
† Troughton, J.O.(Wa)	2002	10	18	1	103	390	22.94	1	2	4
Tudge, K.D.(Gm)	–	1	2	1	4	7	7.00	–	–	–
Tudor, A.J.(Ex)	–	11	13	1	144	362	30.16	1	1	2
† Turk, N.R.K.(Sx)	–	1	1	–	24	24	24.00	–	–	–
Turner, M.L.(Du)	–	1	–	–	–	–	–	–	–	–
Udal, S.D.(H)	1992	10	9	1	28	118	14.75	–	–	3
Umar Gul (P)	–	6	7	1	13	34	5.66	–	–	2
† Vaas, W.P.U.C.J.(SL)	–	5	10	5	50*	248	49.60	–	1	–
† Vandort, M.G.(SL)	–	6	12	1	105	264	24.00	1	1	2
Van Jaarsveld, M.(K)	2005	16	27	2	116	1217	48.68	3	10	36
Vaughan, M.P.(Y)	1995	3	6	–	99	178	29.66	–	2	–
† Vettori, D.L.(Wa)	–	1	1	–	27	27	27.00	–	–	–
Vincent, L.(Wo)	2006[c]	6	11	1	141	469	46.90	2	1	5
Wagg, G.G.(De)	–	9	14	1	94	317	24.38	–	1	3
Wagh, M.A.(Wa)	2000	13	24	2	128	648	29.45	2	1	2
† Wainwright, D.J.(LU/BU)	–	3	4	–	40	70	17.50	–	–	2
Wake, C.J.(DU)	–	3	5	–	34	47	9.40	–	–	1
† Walker, M.J.(K)	2000	16	26	3	197	1419	61.69	5	8	9
Walker, N.G.E.(Le)	–	5	6	–	21	38	6.33	–	–	2
† Wallace, M.A.(Gm)	2003	16	27	4	72	698	30.34	–	5	41/3
Walters, S.J.(Sy)	–	3	6	–	67	166	27.66	–	1	3

F-C	Cap	M	I	NO	HS	Runs	Avge	100	50	Ct/St
Warne, S.K.(H)	2000	13	17	5	61*	371	30.91	–	2	16
Warren, R.J.(Nt)	2004	5	8	–	93	140	17.50	–	1	3
Waters, H.T.(Gm)	–	5	7	2	5*	7	1.40	–	–	1
† Watkins, R.E.(Gm)	–	14	25	2	87	554	24.08	–	2	12
† Wedge, S.A.(Wo)	2005c	2	–	–	–	–	–	–	–	–
† Weekes, P.N.(M)	1993	8	15	4	128*	348	31.63	1	–	–
Welch, G.(De)	2001	15	23	5	94	353	19.61	–	2	8
Wessels, M.H.(Nh)	–	10	17	2	62	353	23.53	–	2	27/1
Westfield, M.S.(Ex)	–	3	4	2	32	41	20.50	–	–	1
† Weston, W.P.C.(Gs)	2004	13	24	1	130	911	39.60	2	6	7
† Westwood, I.J.(Wa)	–	13	23	3	178	850	42.50	2	4	5
Wharf, A.G.(Gm)	2000	10	15	2	86	397	30.53	–	3	9
White, C.(Y)	1993	15	23	1	147	859	39.04	3	3	5
White, C.L.(Sm)	2006	12	22	2	260*	1190	59.50	5	3	6
White, G.G.(Nh)	–	2	3	–	37	37	12.33	–	–	–
White, R.A.(Nh)	–	9	14	1	141	288	22.15	1	–	4
White, W.A.(De)	–	1	2	2	19*	37	–	–	–	–
Wigley, D.H.(Nh)	–	8	10	2	28	73	9.12	–	–	5
† Willoughby, C.M.(Sm)	–	15	22	9	47	127	9.76	–	–	2
Wilshaw, P.J.(OU)	–	3	5	–	63	217	43.40	–	3	3
Windows, M.G.N.(Gs)	1998	5	9	1	48	127	15.87	–	–	2
Wiseman, P.J.(Du)	–	2	2	1	6*	10	10.00	–	–	–
Woakes, C.R.(Wa)	–	1	1	–	4	4	4.00	–	–	3
Wood, J.R.(DU)	–	3	5	–	31	65	13.00	–	–	–/1
Wood, M.J.(Sm)	2005	16	27	–	73	622	23.03	–	5	8
Wood, M.J.(Y)	2001	6	10	–	92	177	17.70	–	1	6
Woods, N.J.(OU)	–	2	2	1	22*	30	30.00	–	–	2
Wright, B.J.(Gm)	–	1	1	–	72	72	72.00	–	1	2
Wright, C.J.C.(M)	–	5	8	3	42	133	26.60	–	–	–
Wright, L.J.(Sx)	–	11	17	2	59	313	20.86	–	3	7
† Yardy, M.H.(Sx)	2005	12	20	2	159*	914	50.77	3	4	9
Yasir Arafat (Sx)	2006	8	12	3	86	390	43.33	–	2	1
† Young, P.J.W.(OU)	–	3	4	1	40	95	31.66	–	–	1
Younis Khan (P)	–	5	9	2	173	459	65.57	1	3	6
Yousuf Youhana, Mohd (P)	–	5	9	1	202	666	83.25	3	–	1
† Zoysa, D.N.T.(SL)	–	3	1	–	32	32	32.00	–	–	–

BOWLING

See BATTING and FIELDING section for details of matches, caps and teams

	Cat	O	M	R	W	Avge	Best	5wI	10wM
Abdul Razzaq	RFM	79.5	15	268	6	44.66	2-72	–	–
Adams, A.R.	RMF	278.1	63	830	21	39.52	4-72	–	–
Adams, C.J.	RM/OB	1	0	2	0				
Adams, J.H.K.	LM	25.1	4	141	1	141.00	1-46	–	–
Adnan, M.Hassan	OB	9	0	37	1	37.00	1- 4	–	–
Afzaal, U.	SLA	119.5	16	471	7	67.28	3-75	–	–
Ahmed, J.S.	RMF	21	4	76	2	38.00	2-50	–	–
Ali, Kabir	RMF	337.1	68	1161	40	29.02	7-43	3	–
Ali, Kadeer	RM	14	2	57	0				
Ali, M.M.	OB	74.2	13	318	3	106.00	2-50	–	–
Ali, S.M.H.	LFM	115.2	17	453	10	45.30	2-15	–	–
Allenby, J.	RM	8	2	23	0				
Anderson, J.M.	RFM	10	2	38	0				

F-C	Cat	O	M	R	W	Avge	Best	5wI	10wM
Anyon, J.E.	RFM	342.2	71	1011	31	32.61	5- 83	1	–
Arshad Khan	OB	29.3	8	96	2	48.00	2- 31	–	–
Astle, N.J.	RM	58.3	12	178	4	44.50	1- 9	–	–
Averis, J.M.M.	RMF	107.4	15	473	10	47.30	4- 75	–	–
Azhar Mahmood	RFM	336.4	69	1161	31	37.45	5- 69	1	–
Balcombe, D.J.	RFM	104.2	16	450	9	50.00	3- 67	–	–
Ball, M.C.J.	OB	307.5	63	930	27	34.44	6-134	1	–
Bandara, C.M.	LBG	24	8	48	3	16.00	2- 25	–	–
Banerjee, V.	SLA	229.5	41	801	14	57.21	4-150	–	–
Banks, O.A.C.	OB	28	4	93	3	31.00	3- 36	–	–
Bartram, T.S.	RMF	32	7	145	3	48.33	2- 84	–	–
Batty, G.J.	OB	496.1	112	1439	43	33.46	6-119	1	–
Bell, I.R.	RM	35	10	111	5	22.20	2- 59	–	–
Benham, C.C.	RM/OB	5	0	37	0				
Benkenstein, D.M.	RM/OB	146.1	38	552	14	39.42	3- 16	–	–
Benning, J.G.E.	RM	42	4	237	3	79.00	2- 58	–	–
Best, T.L.	RF	42	10	146	6	24.33	3- 27	–	–
Betts, M.M.	RFM	26	4	88	4	22.00	2- 29	–	–
Bichel, A.J.	RFM	280.5	53	991	32	30.96	6- 38	1	–
Bicknell, M.P.	RFM	101	26	303	7	43.28	5- 93	1	–
Birt, T.R.	RM	25.1	2	119	2	59.50	1- 24	–	–
Blackwell, I.D.	SLA	46	7	139	3	46.33	2- 63	–	–
Blain, J.A.R.	RMF	59	3	287	5	57.40	2- 72	–	–
Bopara, R.S.	RMF	258.3	43	1035	23	45.00	5- 75	1	–
Botha, A.G.	SLA	332.3	74	1124	29	38.75	6-117	1	–
Bradshaw, D.P.	RFM	11	2	45	0				
Brathwaite, R.M.R.	RFM	84	9	351	6	58.50	3- 61	–	–
Bravo, D.J.	RFM	88.1	10	435	8	54.37	6-112	1	–
Breese, G.R.	OB	371.3	61	1297	27	48.03	4- 75	–	–
Bresnan, T.T.	RMF	317.3	62	1058	33	32.06	5- 58	1	–
Bridge, G.D.	SLA	16	5	73	1	73.00	1- 73	–	–
Broad, S.C.J.	RFM	402.5	80	1491	48	31.06	5- 83	4	–
Brown, A.D.	LB	23.5	2	74	3	24.66	3- 25	–	–
Brown, D.O.	RM	9	2	30	0				
Brown, D.R.	RFM	324.3	73	940	33	28.48	4- 45	–	–
Brown, J.F.	OB	594	129	1765	35	50.42	5- 82	1	–
Bruce, J.T.A.	RMF	327	67	1109	38	29.18	5- 43	1	–
Buckham, C.T.	LB	7	0	47	0				
Burton, D.A.	RMF	20	1	129	0				
Butcher, M.A.	RM/OB	5	0	8	1	8.00	1- 8	–	–
Caddick, A.R.	RFM	612.3	111	2282	63	36.22	5- 40	4	–
Carberry, M.A.	OB	22	0	114	2	57.00	2- 85	–	–
Carter, N.M.	LFM	392.2	77	1392	34	40.94	6- 63	1	–
Celliers, G.	RM	13	2	63	0				
Chapple, G.	RFM	425.2	117	1124	41	27.41	6- 35	1	–
Chattergoon, S.	LB	1	0	1	0				
Cherry, D.D.	RM	0.4	0	4	0				
Chilton, M.J.	RM	18.3	3	52	2	26.00	1- 1	–	–
Clark, S.G.	RMF	12	1	69	2	34.50	1- 29	–	–
Clarke, R.	RFM	234.4	45	911	22	41.40	4- 45	–	–
Claydon, M.E.	RMF	43	6	171	2	85.50	1- 42	–	–
Clough, G.D.	RM	13	4	56	2	28.00	2- 56	–	–
Coetzer, K.J.	RM	3	0	19	0				
Collingwood, P.D.	RMF	39	6	134	1	134.00	1- 33	–	–

F-C	Cat	O	M	R	W	Avge	Best	5wI	10wM
Compton, N.R.D.	OB	7	0	103	1	103.00	1- 94	–	–
Cook, A.N.	OB	4	1	8	0				
Cook, S.J.	RM	294	60	925	28	33.03	6- 74	2	–
Cork, D.G.	RFM	389.1	86	1071	42	25.50	6- 53	1	–
Cosgrove, M.J.	RM	70	7	234	5	46.80	1- 8	–	–
Cosker, D.A.	SLA	502.5	82	1486	33	45.03	4- 78	–	–
Crawley, J.P.	RM	5	0	29	0				
Croft, R.D.B.	OB	702.3	125	2112	66	32.00	7- 67	3	1
Crook, S.P.	RFM	175.1	13	782	17	46.00	3- 46	–	–
Cullen, D.J.	OB	119	17	381	7	54.42	5-137	1	–
Cummins, R.A.G.	RM	145	20	593	13	45.61	4- 46	–	–
Cusden, S.M.J.	RFM	18	1	83	2	41.50	2- 62	–	–
Daggett, L.M.	RFM	115.4	25	405	16	25.31	6- 30	1	–
Dalrymple, J.W.M.	OB	355.4	57	1084	29	37.37	4- 61	–	–
Danish Kaneria	LBG	307	47	924	23	40.17	4- 32	–	–
Davies, A.M.	RMF	32	12	99	2	49.50	1- 9	–	–
Davies, A.P.	RMF	124	24	402	8	50.25	2- 28	–	–
Dawson, R.K.J.	OB	196	20	701	8	87.62	4-151	–	–
Dean, K.J.	LMF	89.5	17	364	6	60.66	2- 32	–	–
Denly, J.L.	LB	36	8	104	4	26.00	2- 40	–	–
Dennington, M.J.	RFM	26	8	50	3	16.66	2- 21	–	–
Dernbach, J.W.	RMF	44.2	9	165	4	41.25	3- 67	–	–
Dexter, N.J.	RM	89	14	281	6	46.83	2- 40	–	–
Dilshan, T.M.	OB	23	7	86	3	28.66	2- 16	–	–
Dobson, W.T.	RMF	32	5	126	1	126.00	1- 67	–	–
Doshi, N.D.	SLA	468.5	90	1434	51	28.11	6- 91	1	1
Durston, W.J.	OB	112.3	14	416	10	41.60	2- 31	–	–
Ealham, M.A.	RMF	359.4	104	956	46	20.78	5- 59	2	–
Edwards, N.J.	RM	3	1	12	0				
Ervine, S.M.	RM	296.1	60	1060	26	40.76	3- 57	–	–
Ferley, R.S.	SLA	122.2	19	378	9	42.00	6-136	1	–
Fisher, I.D.	SLA	201.2	19	755	10	75.50	3-110	–	–
Flintoff, A.	RF	151.5	27	410	14	29.28	3- 52	–	–
Flower, A.	RM	8	3	20	1	20.00	1- 20	–	–
Flower, G.W.	SLA	58.1	16	190	8	23.75	3- 28	–	–
Footitt, M.H.A.	LFM	50	5	220	7	31.42	5- 45	1	–
Francis, J.D.	SLA	1	0	9	0				
Francis, S.R.G.	RMF	55	13	237	4	59.25	3- 61	–	–
Franklin, J.E.C.	LFM	251.4	45	950	31	30.64	5- 68	1	–
Franks, P.J.	RMF	279.1	43	1071	18	59.50	2- 24	–	–
Friedlander, M.J.	RFM	44.4	4	216	5	43.20	2- 56	–	–
Fulton, D.P.	SLA	1	0	3	0				
Ganguly, S.C.	RM	42	9	131	3	43.66	1- 19	–	–
Gerard, D.C.	RMF	22.5	9	62	2	31.00	2- 25	–	–
Gibson, O.D.	RFM	394.4	77	1458	49	29.75	6-110	1	–
Gidman, A.P.R.	RM	232	49	762	17	44.82	3- 38	–	–
Gillespie, J.N.	RFM	434.3	103	1210	36	33.61	6- 37	1	–
Gough, D.	RFM	232.1	46	724	25	28.96	5- 82	1	–
Grant, R.N.	RM	25.5	2	128	3	42.66	1- 9	–	–
Gray, A.K.D.	OB	191.4	37	635	14	45.35	3-106	–	–
Greenidge, C.G.	RMF	109.3	13	533	9	59.22	3- 50	–	–
Griffith, A.R.	RFM	182.4	32	621	11	56.45	3- 34	–	–
Griffiths, D.A.	RFM	6	2	29	0				
Groenewald, T.D.	RFM	117	22	396	6	66.00	2- 36	–	–

F-C	Cat	O	M	R	W	Avge	Best	5wI	10wM
Hall, A.J.	RFM	128.3	34	334	14	23.85	3- 27	–	–
Hardinges, M.A.	RMF	270.4	58	1011	23	43.95	4-127	–	–
Harmison, S.J.	RF	183.3	38	637	24	26.54	6- 19	2	1
Harris, A.J.	RM	345.5	70	1151	38	30.28	5- 53	1	–
Harris, P.L.	SLA	347.2	91	905	31	29.19	6- 80	4	–
Harrison, A.J.	RMF	21	3	81	1	81.00	1- 81	–	–
Harrison, D.S.	RMF	420.1	88	1387	35	39.62	5- 76	1	–
Harvey, I.J.	RMF	142.2	38	378	13	29.07	3- 25	–	–
Henderson, C.W.	SLA	620.4	108	2054	49	41.91	5- 69	2	–
Henderson, T.	RFM	144	31	505	9	56.11	4- 29	–	–
Hildreth, J.C.	RMF	5	0	27	0				
Hinds, R.O.	SLA	60	20	155	2	77.50	2- 40	–	–
Hobbiss, M.H.	RM	9	2	31	0				
Hodge, B.J.	OB	35	6	97	5	19.40	3- 21	–	–
Hodson, W.G.	OB	16	3	59	0				
Hogg, K.W.	RFM	194	54	528	15	35.20	2- 33	–	–
Hoggard, M.J.	RFM	371	70	1146	33	34.72	4- 27	–	–
Hopkinson, C.D.	RM	9.4	2	48	0				
Hunter, I.D.	RMF	369	79	1328	36	36.88	4- 22	–	–
Hussey, D.J.	OB	45	3	236	6	39.33	2- 66	–	–
Hutton, B.L.	RMF	58.4	6	263	3	87.66	2- 20	–	–
Iftikhar Anjum	RM	16	1	75	2	37.50	2- 19	–	–
Iles, J.A.	RFM	13	6	37	1	37.00	1- 27	–	–
Imran Farhat	LB	57	8	166	5	33.20	2- 8	–	–
Iqbal, M.M.	LB	81.1	6	417	9	46.33	4- 36	–	–
Jacklin, B.D.	RM	39.4	10	98	0				
James, G.D.	LB	2	0	7	0				
Jannisar Khan	RM	9	1	36	1	36.00	1- 28	–	–
Jaques, P.A.	SLC	0.2	0	15	0				
Jayasuriya, S.T.	SLA	33.5	7	73	3	24.33	2- 19	–	–
Jayawardena, D.P.M.D.	RM	4	1	9	0				
Jogia, K.A.	RSM	1	1	0	0				
Johnson, R.L.	RFM	195.4	28	717	22	32.59	5- 37	1	–
Jones, M.C.	RMF	16	1	75	0				
Jones, P.S.	RMF	524.1	108	1871	59	31.71	6- 25	1	–
Jones, S.P.	RF	28	4	96	1	96.00	1- 96	–	–
Joseph, R.H.	RFM	244.5	37	897	24	37.37	5- 57	1	–
Joyce, E.C.	RM	22	3	132	1	132.00	1- 21	–	–
Kalam, T.	RFM	64	10	255	2	127.50	1- 29	–	–
Kapugedara, C.K.	RMF	15	3	46	0				
Kartik, M.	SLA	92	22	234	6	39.00	3- 89	–	–
Keedy, G.	SLA	566.2	88	1660	61	27.21	6- 40	2	–
Keegan, C.B.	RFM	200.4	43	736	19	38.73	5- 90	1	–
Kelly, R.	RFM	38.2	8	139	2	69.50	2- 21	–	–
Kemp, J.M.	RMF	111	16	333	11	30.27	3- 72	–	–
Kemp, R.A.	RM	26	3	80	1	80.00	1- 80	–	–
Key, R.W.T.	RM/OB	5	2	10	0				
Khan, A.	RFM	312.1	51	1034	34	30.41	5-100	1	–
Khan, Z.	LFM	618.4	132	2268	78	29.07	9-138	5	2
Killeen, N.	RMF	234	55	671	19	35.31	5- 29	1	–
King, R.E.	LMF	37	7	153	6	25.50	3- 49	–	–
Kirby, S.P.	RFM	517.4	95	1944	49	39.67	5- 99	1	–
Kirtley, R.J.	RFM	236.4	53	748	18	41.55	3- 82	–	–
Klusener, L.	RM/OB	206.3	41	699	19	36.78	6- 69	1	–

F-C	Cat	O	M	R	W	Avge	Best	5wI	10wM
Knight, N.V.	RM	9	0	41	0				
Kruis, G.J.	RFM	381	65	1342	38	35.31	5- 67	2	–
Kulasekara, M.D.N.	RFM	102	20	344	9	38.22	4- 83	–	–
Kumble, A.	LBG	140	27	418	19	22.00	8-100	2	1
Lamb, G.A.	RM/OB	35	1	135	2	67.50	2- 95	–	–
Lamb, N.J.	RMF	99.3	22	381	6	63.50	4- 92	–	–
Law, S.G.	RM/LB	12	0	50	1	50.00	1- 24	–	–
Lawson, M.A.K.	LB	207	3	897	26	34.50	6- 88	2	–
Lee, J.E.	RMF	9	0	36	0				
Lehmann, D.S.	SLA	146.3	8	472	9	52.44	2- 40	–	–
Lewis, J.	RMF	394.2	82	1302	60	21.70	7- 38	4	2
Lewis, M.L.	RFM	292.3	67	1031	35	29.45	4- 69	–	–
Lewry, J.D.	LFM	494.2	117	1321	57	23.17	6- 68	2	–
Liddle, C.J.	LFM	126.4	24	478	11	43.45	3- 42	–	–
Linley, T.E.	RMF	27	7	56	1	56.00	1- 56	–	–
Logan, R.J.	RMF	43	5	178	3	59.33	2- 71	–	–
Loudon, A.G.R.	OB	357.3	50	1097	32	34.28	5- 49	2	–
Louw, J.	RFM	535.4	100	1890	43	43.95	5-117	1	–
Lumb, M.J.	RM	1	0	6	0				
Lungley, T.	RM	16	4	88	2	44.00	2- 59	–	–
McGrath, A.	RM	216	28	734	18	40.77	4- 62	–	–
McMahon, P.J.	OB	1	0	6	0				
Maddy, D.L.	RM/OB	174.3	39	564	11	51.27	3- 70	–	–
Maharoof, M.F.	RM	89.3	19	358	6	59.66	3- 41	–	–
Mahmood, S.I.	RF	268.4	45	925	36	25.69	5- 52	1	–
Malik, M.N.	RFM	137	30	536	17	31.52	3- 49	–	–
Malinga, S.L.	RFM	124.3	15	436	13	33.53	5- 79	1	–
Mansoor Amjad	LBG	24	1	102	0				
Marshall, H.J.H.	RM	26	7	63	1	63.00	1- 16	–	–
Marshall, S.J.	LB	58.3	17	163	4	40.75	2- 27	–	–
Martin-Jenkins, R.S.C.	RFM	216.1	72	489	14	34.92	4- 78	–	–
Mascarenhas, A.D.	RMF	429	111	1074	43	24.97	6- 65	2	–
Mason, M.S.	RFM	296.1	71	910	41	22.19	8- 45	3	1
Masters, D.D.	RMF	465.5	129	1232	32	38.50	4- 89	–	–
Maunders, J.K.	RM	68.2	9	219	6	36.50	4- 15	–	–
Middlebrook, J.D.	OB	563.3	122	1706	41	41.60	5- 70	1	–
Miller, D.J.	RMF	46	9	150	2	75.00	1- 11	–	–
Mohammad Akram	RFM	365	72	1294	42	30.80	6- 34	2	–
Mohammad Amin	RMF	89	16	377	7	53.85	3- 66	–	–
Mohammad Asif	RFM	299.1	55	996	30	33.20	5- 56	2	–
Mohammad Hafeez	OB	4	1	13	0				
Mohammad Sami	RFM	163.3	20	673	15	44.86	3- 53	–	–
Mohammed, D.	SLC	55	12	193	5	38.60	2-102	–	–
Mongia, D.	SLA	160.1	46	417	8	52.12	2- 62	–	–
Moore, S.C.	RM	10	1	108	1	108.00	1- 61	–	–
Moreton, S.J.P.	LB	50.5	7	216	8	27.00	2- 24	–	–
Morris, J.C.	LB	69	5	323	4	80.75	1- 37	–	–
Morris, R.K.	RFM	31	1	166	3	55.33	2- 58	–	–
Morse, E.J.	RM	70	12	268	3	89.33	2- 49	–	–
Mubarak, J.	OB	1	0	8	0				
Muchall, G.J.	RM	3	0	26	0				
Mullaney, S.J.	RM	10	0	36	0				
Mumtaz Habib	RMF	52	7	186	4	46.50	3- 92	–	–
Munday, M.K.	LB	179.5	27	658	20	32.90	6- 77	2	1

F-C	Cat	O	M	R	W	Avge	Best	5wI	10wM
Muralitharan, M.	OB	189.2	45	507	28	18.10	8-70	2	2
Murtagh, T.J.	RFM	67	18	223	7	31.85	3-48	–	–
Mushtaq Ahmed	LBG	623.5	118	2031	102	19.91	9-48	11	4
Naik, J.K.H.	OB	37	6	167	1	167.00	1-55	–	–
Napier, G.R.	RM	56	9	203	1	203.00	1- 6	–	–
Nash, C.D.	OB	25	4	87	1	87.00	1-63	–	–
Nash, D.C.	LB	4.5	0	53	1	53.00	1-53	–	–
Naved-ul-Hasan	RMF	165.2	37	585	35	16.71	7-62	3	1
Needham, J.	OB	15	1	88	0				
Newby, O.J.	RMF	138.3	20	523	19	27.52	4-58	–	–
Nicholson, M.J.	RFM	474.5	113	1471	46	31.97	7-62	2	–
Nixon, P.A.	(WK)	5	0	69	0				
North, M.J.	OB	42	8	91	1	91.00	1-43	–	–
Oberoi, S.	OB	23	3	82	0				
O'Brien, N.J.	(WK)	0.3	0	4	1	4.00	1- 4	–	–
Onions, G.	RMF	440.2	85	1704	54	31.55	5-45	1	–
Ormond, J.	RFM	93	24	229	6	38.16	3-39	–	–
Palladino, A.P.	RMF	165.4	36	547	13	42.07	6-68	1	–
Panesar, M.S.	SLA	759	195	2029	71	28.57	5-32	6	1
Parker, L.C.	RM	33.4	4	114	2	57.00	1-21	–	–
Parsons, K.A.	RM	95	16	337	11	30.63	3-33	–	–
Patel, M.M.	SLA	389.3	55	1171	32	36.59	4-83	–	–
Patel, S.R.	SLA	49.1	11	158	2	79.00	1-22	–	–
Patterson, S.A.	RMF	62.4	13	203	2	101.50	1-25	–	–
Peploe, C.T.	SLA	282.2	55	944	12	78.66	4-31	–	–
Phillips, B.J.	RFM	374.2	89	1081	34	31.79	6-29	1	–
Phillips, T.J.	SLA	429.4	67	1615	37	43.64	5-41	1	–
Pietersen, C.	LMF	51.4	4	212	2	106.00	1-39	–	–
Pietersen, K.P.	OB	14	1	76	1	76.00	1-11	–	–
Plunkett, L.E.	RFM	162.2	30	516	19	27.15	3-17	–	–
Pothas, N.	(WK)	19	3	58	1	58.00	1-16	–	–
Powell, D.B.	RFM	73	24	208	6	34.66	2-31	–	–
Powell, M.J.(Wa)	RM	19	0	80	0				
Price, R.W.	SLA	279.4	54	813	15	54.20	4-38	–	–
Prowting, N.R.	RM	4	0	39	0				
Rashid, A.	LB	180.2	21	629	25	25.16	6-67	1	–
Rayner, O.P.	OB	98	26	348	6	58.00	3-89	–	–
Read, C.M.W.	(WK)	3	1	8	0				
Richards, M.A.	RMF	106	11	433	10	43.30	3-62	–	–
Richardson, A.	RMF	40	10	121	4	30.25	4-50	–	–
Richardson, A.P.	RFM	45.2	7	181	6	30.16	3-54	–	–
Robinson, D.D.J.	RMF	4.4	0	117	0				
Rogers, C.J.L.	LBG	21	5	71	1	71.00	1-16	–	–
Rowe, D.T.	RM	9	4	22	1	22.00	1-22	–	–
Rudge, W.D.	RM	59	2	311	2	155.50	1-99	–	–
Saggers, M.J.	RMF	43.1	8	149	5	29.80	3-38	–	–
Saker, N.C.	RFM	146.4	16	657	14	46.92	4-79	–	–
Sales, D.J.G.	RM	2	0	2	0				
Salisbury, I.D.K.	LBG	577.3	106	1732	62	27.93	5-46	1	–
Salman Butt	OB	25.1	2	102	0				
Samaraweera, T.T.	OB	7	0	31	0				
Samiullah Khan	LMF	15.3	2	59	2	29.50	2-35	–	–
Sammy, D.J.G	RM	62	24	163	10	16.30	5-85	1	–
Sangakkara, K.C.	OB	5	1	20	0				

F-C	Cat	O	M	R	W	Avge	Best	5wI	10wM
Savill, T.E.	RFM	97.3	17	345	10	34.50	4- 62	–	–
Sayers, J.J.	OB	2	0	7	0				
Schofield, C.P.	LBG	73.2	10	296	8	37.00	3- 78	–	–
Scott, G.M.	OB	44.1	6	237	3	79.00	2- 39	–	–
Shafayat, B.M.	RMF	17.2	0	86	2	43.00	2- 25	–	–
Shah, O.A.	OB	20.4	4	106	0				
Shahid Afridi	LBG	70.3	1	269	5	53.80	2- 21	–	–
Shahid Nazir	RFM	97	20	348	9	38.66	3- 32	–	–
Shahzad, A.	RMF	12	1	45	0				
Shantry, A.J.	LFM	24	11	65	7	9.28	5- 49	1	–
Sharif, Z.K.	LB	40	8	156	3	52.00	2- 19	–	–
Sheikh, M.A.	RM	218.5	62	650	15	43.33	5- 65	1	–
Shilvock, D.J.F.	LB	1	0	10	0				
Shirazi, D.C.	RM	6	0	33	1	33.00	1- 33	–	–
Shoaib Malik	OB	5	1	10	0				
Shreck, C.E.	RFM	426	89	1512	61	24.78	8- 31	5	2
Sidebottom, R.J.	LFM	485.5	134	1307	50	26.14	5- 22	1	–
Sillence, R.J.	RMF	220.4	35	792	23	34.43	7- 96	1	–
Silverwood, C.E.W.	RFM	504.2	95	1591	63	25.25	6- 51	4	–
Smith, B.F.	RM	5	0	48	1	48.00	1- 39	–	–
Smith, B.M.	LFM	51	8	222	5	44.40	4-102	–	–
Smith, D.R.	RM	59.4	19	201	7	28.71	3- 17	–	–
Smith, D.S.	OB	3	1	12	0				
Smith, E.T.	RM	5	0	60	1	60.00	1- 60	–	–
Smith, G.J.	LFM	135.2	27	467	12	38.91	4- 75	–	–
Smith, G.M.	OB/RM	46.5	6	182	2	91.00	1- 18	–	–
Smith, T.C.	RMF	383	107	1073	35	30.65	4- 57	–	–
Snape, J.N.	OB	53.1	7	183	3	61.00	2- 27	–	–
Solanki, V.S.	OB	52.3	8	165	5	33.00	2- 16	–	–
Spencer, D.J.	RF	38	4	155	2	77.50	1- 70	–	–
Stephenson, J.P.	RM	10.4	3	34	3	11.33	3- 6	–	–
Stevens, D.I.	RM	235.5	39	688	19	36.21	4- 36	–	–
Stiff, D.A.	RFM	15.3	2	75	1	75.00	1- 53	–	–
Streak, H.H.	RFM	446.4	100	1374	41	33.51	6- 73	2	–
Stubbings, S.D.	OB	1	0	2	0				
Styris, S.B.	RMF	198.3	37	670	18	37.22	6- 71	1	–
Suppiah, A.V.	SLA	91	9	385	2	192.50	1- 13	–	–
Sutcliffe, I.J.	LB	1	0	1	0				
Swann, G.P.	OB	439.5	95	1247	28	44.53	4- 54	–	–
Tahir, N.	RFM	98	19	375	13	28.84	7-107	1	–
Taufiq Umar	OB	2	0	8	0				
Taylor, B.V.	RMF	116.3	22	364	12	30.33	6- 32	1	–
Taylor, C.G.	OB	76	12	267	2	133.50	2- 75	–	–
Ten Doeschate, R.N.	RMF	249.1	31	1115	28	39.82	5-143	1	–
Thornely, D.J.	RM	199	49	578	22	26.27	3- 38	–	–
Thorp, C.D.	RMF	327.3	94	968	39	24.82	6- 55	2	1
Tomlinson, J.A.	LFM	39	10	146	4	36.50	2- 54	–	–
Tredwell, J.C.	OB	269.5	43	927	26	35.65	6- 81	1	1
Trego, P.D.	RMF	242.5	34	965	19	50.78	3- 87	–	–
Tremlett, C.T.	RMF	264.2	51	835	34	24.55	6- 89	1	–
Trott, I.J.L.	RM	3	0	28	1	28.00	1- 22	–	–
Troughton, J.O.	SLA	97.1	17	351	9	39.00	2- 15	–	–
Tudge, K.D.	SLA	13	1	58	0				
Tudor, A.J.	RF	293.4	53	1195	28	42.67	5- 67	1	–

F-C	Cat	O	M	R	W	Avge	Best	5wI	10wM
Turk, N.R.K.	RM	3	0	9	0				
Turner, M.L.	RMF	23	0	86	2	43.00	2- 51	–	–
Udal, S.D.	OB	209	41	646	15	43.06	2- 12	–	–
Umar Gul	RFM	215.2	30	816	24	34.00	5-123	1	–
Vaas, W.P.U.C.J.	LFM	142	36	352	12	29.33	4- 34	–	–
Van Jaarsveld, M.	OB	29	3	114	1	114.00	1- 37	–	–
Vettori, D.L.	SLA	31	4	92	0				
Vincent, L.	RM/OB	22	2	76	1	76.00	1- 12	–	–
Wagg, G.G.	LM	213.2	34	904	24	37.66	6- 38	1	–
Wagh, M.A.	OB	3	0	14	0				
Wainwright, D.J.	SLA	65.5	7	271	2	135.50	1- 45	–	–
Wake, C.J.	RMF	11	0	90	2	45.00	1- 24	–	–
Walker, M.J.	RM	33	6	116	1	116.00	1- 18	–	–
Walker, N.G.E.	RFM	152.1	30	498	14	35.57	5- 59	1	–
Walters, S.J.	RM	26	7	69	2	34.50	1- 9	–	–
Warne, S.K.	LBG	523.4	91	1571	58	27.08	7- 99	4	–
Waters, H.T.	RMF	111.3	24	380	12	31.66	5- 86	1	–
Watkins, R.E.	RM	230.5	36	922	19	48.52	4- 40	–	–
Wedge, S.A.	LMF	27	3	108	4	27.00	3- 11	–	–
Weekes, P.N.	OB	108.3	9	338	5	67.60	1- 19	–	–
Welch, G.	RM	391.3	98	1198	36	33.27	4- 33	–	–
Westfield, M.S.	RFM	43	5	180	6	30.00	4- 72	–	–
Westwood, I.J.	OB	23	3	58	2	29.00	2- 46	–	–
Wharf, A.G.	RMF	262.5	37	983	19	51.73	4- 67	–	–
White, C.	RFM/OB	32.2	4	75	4	18.75	2- 11	–	–
White, C.L.	LBG	186.5	19	723	15	48.20	5-148	1	–
White, G.G.	SLA	26	1	79	0				
White, R.A.	LB	48	3	227	3	75.66	2- 57	–	–
White, W.A.	RMF	21	4	83	6	13.83	4- 35	–	–
Wigley, D.H.	RFM	185	30	796	18	44.22	5- 77	1	–
Willoughby, C.M.	LMF	498.5	121	1687	66	25.56	7- 44	3	–
Wiseman, P.J.	OB	56	11	230	1	230.00	1-127	–	–
Woakes, C.R.	RM	23	2	102	3	34.00	2- 64	–	–
Woods, N.J.	SLA	68	18	211	6	35.16	3- 46	–	–
Wright, C.J.C.	RFM	103	11	506	7	72.28	2- 33	–	–
Wright, L.J.	RM	178	36	582	15	38.80	3- 39	–	–
Yardy, M.H.	LM/SLA	46	4	159	2	79.50	1- 37	–	–
Yasir Arafat	RM	271.1	48	1019	41	24.85	5- 84	2	–
Young, P.J.W.	RM	40	3	147	1	147.00	1- 71	–	–
Zoysa, D.N.T.	LFM	63.4	18	143	9	15.88	4- 38	–	–

COUNTY CHAMPIONSHIP 2006
LONDON VICTORIA FINAL TABLES

DIVISION 1

	P	*W*	*L*	*T*	*D*	*Bonus Points Bat*	*Bowl*	*Deduct Points*	*Total Points*
1 **SUSSEX** (3)	16	9	2	–	5	49	47	–	242
2 Lancashire (-)	16	6	1	–	9	58	46	–	224
3 Hampshire (2)	16	6	3	–	7	48	48	1.0	207
4 Warwickshire (4)	16	6	5	–	5	42	43	–	189
5 Kent (5)	16	4	4	–	8	43	44	–	175
6 Yorkshire (-)	16	3	6	–	7	43	41	–	154
7 Durham (-)	16	4	8	–	4	39	43	0.5	153.5
8 Nottinghamshire (1)	16	4	7	–	5	40	37	–	153
9 Middlesex (6)	16	1	7	–	8	47	42	1.5	133.5

DIVISION 2

	P	*W*	*L*	*T*	*D*	*Bonus Points Bat*	*Bowl*	*Deduct Points*	*Total Points*
1 SURREY (-)	16	10	2	–	4	62	44	–	262
2 Worcestershire (6)	16	8	4	–	4	58	43	–	229
3 Essex (5)	16	7	4	–	5	62	40	–	220
4 Leicestershire (7)	16	5	4	–	7	47	41	0.5	185.5
5 Derbyshire (9)	16	4	4	–	8	51	41	1.5	178.5
6 Northamptonshire (4)	16	3	5	–	8	52	37	–	163
7 Gloucestershire (-)	16	3	6	–	7	51	36	1.5	155.5
8 Glamorgan (-)	16	2	7	–	7	51	41	1.5	146.5
9 Somerset (8)	16	3	9	–	4	43	40	1.0	140

2005 final positions for that division are shown in brackets.

SCORING OF CHAMPIONSHIP POINTS 2006

(a) For a win, 14 points, plus any points scored in the first innings.

(b) In a tie, each side to score seven points, plus any points scored in the first innings.

(c) In a drawn match, each side to score four points, plus any points scored in the first innings (see also paragraph (f) below).

(d) If the scores are equal in a drawn match, the side batting in the fourth innings to score seven points plus any points scored in the first innings, and the opposing side to score four points plus any points scored in the first innings.

(e) **First Innings Points** (awarded only for performances **in the first 130 overs** of each first innings and retained whatever the result of the match).
- A maximum of five batting points to be available as under:-
  200 to 249 runs – 1 point; 250 to 299 runs – 2 points; 300 to 349 runs – 3 points;
  350 to 399 runs – 4 points; 400 runs or over – 5 points.
- A maximum of three bowling points to be available as under:-
  3 to 5 wickets taken – 1 point; 6 to 8 wickets taken – 2 points; 9 to 10 wickets taken – 3 points.

(f) If play starts when fewer than eight hours' playing time remains (in which event a one innings match shall be played as provided for in First-Class Playing Condition 18), no first innings points shall be scored. The side winning on the one innings to score 14 points. In a tie, each side to score seven points. In a drawn match, each side to score four points. If the scores are equal in a drawn match, the side batting in the second innings to score seven points and the opposing side to score four points.

(g) If a match is abandoned without a ball being bowled, each side to score four points.

(h) The side which has the highest aggregate of points gained at the end of the season shall be the Champion County of their respective Division. Should any sides in the Championship table be equal on points, the following tie-breakers will be applied in the order stated: most wins, least losses, team achieving most points in contests between teams level on points, most wickets taken, most runs scored. At the end of the season, the top two teams from the Second Division will be promoted and the bottom two teams from the First Division will be relegated.

COUNTY CHAMPIONS

The English County Championship was not officially constituted until December 1889. Prior to that date there was no generally accepted method of awarding the title; although the 'least matches lost' method existed, it was not consistently applied. Rules governing playing qualifications were agreed in 1873 and the first unofficial points system 15 years later.

Research has produced a list of champions dating back to 1826, but at least seven different versions exist for the period from 1864 to 1889 (see *The Wisden Book of Cricket Records*). Only from 1890 can any authorised list of county champions commence.

That first official Championship was contested between eight counties: Gloucestershire, Kent, Lancashire, Middlesex, Nottinghamshire, Surrey, Sussex and Yorkshire. The remaining counties were admitted in the following seasons: 1891 – Somerset, 1895 – Derbyshire, Essex, Hampshire, Leicestershire and Warwickshire, 1899 – Worcestershire, 1905 – Northamptonshire, 1921 – Glamorgan, and 1992 – Durham.

The Championship pennant was introduced by the 1951 champions, Warwickshire, and the Lord's Taverners' Trophy was first presented in 1973. The first sponsors, Schweppes (1977 to 1983), were succeeded by Britannic Assurance (1984 to 1998), PPP Healthcare (1999-2000), CricInfo (2001), Frizzell (2002 to 2005) and Liverpool Victoria (2006). Based on their previous season's positions, the 18 counties were separated into two divisions in 2001. From 2001 to 2005 the bottom three Division 1 teams were relegated and the top three Division 2 sides promoted. This was reduced to two teams from the end of the 2006 season.

1890	Surrey
1891	Surrey
1892	Surrey
1893	Yorkshire
1894	Surrey
1895	Surrey
1896	Yorkshire
1897	Lancashire
1898	Yorkshire
1899	Surrey
1900	Yorkshire
1901	Yorkshire
1902	Yorkshire
1903	Middlesex
1904	Lancashire
1905	Yorkshire
1906	Kent
1907	Nottinghamshire
1908	Yorkshire
1909	Kent
1910	Kent
1911	Warwickshire
1912	Yorkshire
1913	Kent
1914	Surrey
1919	Yorkshire
1920	Middlesex
1921	Middlesex
1922	Yorkshire
1923	Yorkshire
1924	Yorkshire
1925	Yorkshire
1926	Lancashire
1927	Lancashire
1928	Lancashire
1929	Nottinghamshire
1930	Lancashire
1931	Yorkshire
1932	Yorkshire
1933	Yorkshire
1934	Lancashire
1935	Yorkshire
1936	Derbyshire
1937	Yorkshire
1938	Yorkshire
1939	Yorkshire
1946	Yorkshire
1947	Middlesex
1948	Glamorgan
1949	Middlesex Yorkshire
1950	Lancashire Surrey
1951	Warwickshire
1952	Surrey
1953	Surrey
1954	Surrey
1955	Surrey
1956	Surrey
1957	Surrey
1958	Surrey
1959	Yorkshire
1960	Yorkshire
1961	Hampshire
1962	Yorkshire
1963	Yorkshire
1964	Worcestershire
1965	Worcestershire
1966	Yorkshire
1967	Yorkshire
1968	Yorkshire
1969	Glamorgan
1970	Kent
1971	Surrey
1972	Warwickshire
1973	Hampshire
1974	Worcestershire
1975	Leicestershire
1976	Middlesex
1977	Kent Middlesex
1978	Kent
1979	Essex
1980	Middlesex
1981	Nottinghamshire
1982	Middlesex
1983	Essex
1984	Essex
1985	Middlesex
1986	Essex
1987	Nottinghamshire
1988	Worcestershire
1989	Worcestershire
1990	Middlesex
1991	Essex
1992	Essex
1993	Middlesex
1994	Warwickshire
1995	Warwickshire
1996	Leicestershire
1997	Glamorgan
1998	Leicestershire
1999	Surrey
2000	Surrey
2001	Yorkshire
2002	Surrey
2003	Sussex
2004	Warwickshire
2005	Nottinghamshire
2006	Sussex

COUNTY CHAMPIONSHIP RESULTS 2006

DIVISION 1

	DURHAM	HANTS	KENT	LANCS	MIDDX	NOTTS	SUSSEX	WARWKS	YORKS
DURHAM	–	C-le-St H 174	Stockton K 95	C-le-St La 128	C-le-St Du 135	C-le-St Nt 6w	C-le-St Sx I/39	C-le-St Du 7w	C-le-St Y 145
HANTS	So'ton Du 227	–	So'ton Drawn	So'ton Drawn	So'ton H 10w	So'ton H 299	So'ton Sx 94	So'ton Wa 2w	So'ton H 10w
KENT	Cant Du I/56	Cant Drawn	–	Cant K 2w	Cant Drawn	Cant Drawn	Cant Sx 2w	Tun W K 9w	Cant Drawn
LANCS	Man Drawn	Man Drawn	Man La 6w	–	Man Drawn	Man Drawn	L'pool La 9w	B'pool Drawn	Man Drawn
MIDDX	Lord's Drawn	Lord's Drawn	Lord's K 7w	Lord's La 10w	–	Lord's Nt I/25	Southgate Drawn	Lord's Drawn	Southgate M 8w
NOTTS	N'ham Drawn	N'ham Drawn	N'ham Nt I/85	N'ham La 5w	N'ham Nt I/33	–	N'ham Sx I/245	N'ham Wa 60	N'ham Drawn
SUSSEX	Hove Sx I/133	Hove Drawn	Hove Drawn	Hove Drawn	Horsham Sx 224	Hove Sx 41	–	Hove Drawn	Arundel Sx I/25
WARWKS	B'ham Wa 18	B'ham H 193	B'ham Drawn	B'ham La 7w	B'ham Drawn	B'ham Wa 59	B'ham Wa 13	–	B'ham Wa 66
YORKS	Leeds Drawn	Leeds H 5w	Leeds Drawn	Leeds Drawn	Scar Drawn	Leeds Y 68	Leeds Sx 5w	Scar Y I/96	–

DIVISION 2

	DERBYS	ESSEX	GLAM	GLOS	LEICS	N'HANTS	SOM'T	SURREY	WORCS
DERBYS	–	Derby Ex 8w	Derby Gm 6w	Derby Drawn	Derby Drawn	Derby Drawn	Derby De 80	Derby Sy 5w	Ch'field Drawn
ESSEX	Chelms Ex I/178	–	Chelms Drawn	Chelms Drawn	Chelms Le 8w	Chelms Drawn	Southend Ex 211	Colchester Ex I/2	Chelms Wo 9w
GLAM	Cardiff De 28	Cardiff Ex I/30	–	Cardiff Drawn	Cardiff Drawn	Cardiff Nh 9w	Swansea Sm 6w	Swansea Drawn	Col Bay Wo 311
GLOS	Bristol Drawn	Bristol Ex 7w	Chelt Gm 10w	–	Chelt Le 4w	Bristol Gs 6w	Bristol Gs I/7	Bristol Drawn	Bristol Drawn
LEICS	Leics Drawn	Leics Le 5w	Leics Drawn	Leics Gs 7w	–	Oakham Drawn	Leics Le 190	Leics Sy 99	Leics Le 3w
N'HANTS	No'ton Drawn	No'ton Drawn	No'ton Nh 168	No'ton Drawn	No'ton Drawn	–	No'ton Nh I/46	No'ton Sy 229	No'ton Wo 5w
SOM'T	Taunton De 344	Taunton Ex 3w	Taunton Drawn	Taunton Sm I/76	Taunton Drawn	Taunton Drawn	–	Bath Sy 4w	Taunton Wo 10w
SURREY	Oval Drawn	Croydon Sy 6w	Oval Sy 218	Oval Sy I/297	Oval Sy I/158	Oval Sy 7w	Guildford Drawn	–	Oval Wo 2w
WORCS	Worcs De 35	Worcs Drawn	Worcs Drawn	Worcs Wo 58	Worcs Wo 192	Worcs Wo I/222	Worcs Sm 227	Worcs Sy I/107	–

COUNTY CHAMPIONSHIP RESULTS 2007

KEEP YOUR OWN RECORD (see page 149)

DIVISION 1

	DURHAM	HANTS	KENT	LANCS	SURREY	SUSSEX	WARWKS	WORCS	YORKS
DURHAM	–	C-le-St	C-le-St	C-le-St	C-le-St	C-le-St	C-le-St	C-le-St	C-le-St
HANTS	tba	–	So'ton	So'ton	So'ton	So'ton	So'ton	So'ton	So'ton
KENT	Cant	Cant	–	Cant	Cant	Cant	Cant	Cant	Tun W
LANCS	B'pool	Man	Man	–	Man	Man	Man	L'pool	Man
SURREY	Oval	Oval	Croydon	Oval	–	Oval	Oval	Guildford	Oval
SUSSEX	Hove	Arundel	Hove	Hove	Hove	–	Hove	Hove	Hove
WARWKS	B'ham	B'ham	B'ham	B'ham	B'ham	B'ham	–	B'ham	B'ham
WORCS	Worcs	Worcs	Worcs	Worcs	Worcs	Worcs	Worcs	–	Worcs
YORKS	Leeds	Leeds	Scar	Leeds	Leeds	Leeds	Scar	Leeds	–

DIVISION 2

	DERBYS	ESSEX	GLAM	GLOS	LEICS	MIDDX	N'HANTS	NOTTS	SOM'T
DERBYS	–	Derby	Derby	Derby	Derby	Derby	Derby	Derby	Ch'field
ESSEX	Chelms	–	Chelms	Southend	Colchester	Chelms	Chelms	Chelms	Chelms
GLAM	Cardiff	tba	–	Cardiff	tba	tba	Col Bay	tba	Cardiff
GLOS	Chelt	Chelt	Bristol	–	Bristol	Bristol	Glos	Bristol	Bristol
LEICS	Leics	Leics	Leics	Leics	–	Leics	Leics	Oakham	Leics
MIDDX	Southgate	Lord's	Lord's	Lord's	Southgate	–	Lord's	Lord's	Lord's
N'HANTS	No'ton	No'ton	No'ton	No'ton	No'ton	No'ton	–	No'ton	No'ton
NOTTS	N'ham	N'ham	N'ham	N'ham	N'ham	N'ham	N'ham	–	N'ham
SOM'T	Taunton	Taunton	Taunton	Taunton	Taunton	Taunton	Taunton	Taunton	–

NATWEST LIMITED-OVERS INTERNATIONALS 2006

ENGLAND v SRI LANKA

Lord's, London, 17 June. Toss: England. **SRI LANKA** won by 20 runs. Sri Lanka 257-9 (50; W.U.Tharanga 120; S.J.Harmison 3-52). England 237-9 (50; M.E.Trescothick 67; J.W.M.Dalrymple 67; S.L.Malinga 3-26, C.R.D.Fernando 3-51). Award: W.U.Tharanga.

Kennington Oval, London 20 June. Toss: Sri Lanka. **SRI LANKA** won by 46 runs. Sri Lanka 319-8 (50; S.T.Jayasuriya 122, D.P.M.D.Jayawardena 66, K.C.Sangakkara 51; S.J.Harmison 3-31). England 273 (46.4; K.P.Pietersen 73, P.D.Collingwood 56; S.T.Jayasuriya 3-51). Award: S.T.Jayasuriya.

Riverside, Chester-le-Street 24 June. Toss: England. **SRI LANKA** won by eight wickets. England 261-7)50; I.R.Bell 77). Sri Lanka 265-2 (42.2; D.P.M.D.Jayawardena 126*, K.C.Sangakkara 58*). Award: D.P.M.D.Jayawardena.

Old Trafford, Manchester 28 June. Toss: Sri Lanka. **SRI LANKA** won by 33 runs. Sri Lanka 318-7 (50; W.U.Tharanga 60, D.P.M.D.Jayawardena 100, M.F.Maharoof 58*). England 285 (48.4; A.J.Strauss 45, M.E.Trescothick 44). Award: D.P.M.D.Jayawardena.

Headingley, Leeds 1 July. Toss: England. **SRI LANKA** won by eight wickets. England 321-7 (50; M.E.Trescothick 121; S.L.Malinga 4-44). Sri Lanka 324-2 (37.3; W.U.Tharanga 109, S.T.Jayasuriya 152). Award: S.T.Jayasuriya. Series award: S.T.Jayasuriya.

TWENTY20 INTERNATIONAL

Rose Bowl, Southampton, 15 June (floodlit). Toss: Sri Lanka. **SRI LANKA** won by 2 runs. Sri Lanka 163 (20; S.T.Jayasuriya 41; P.D.Collingwood 4-22). England 161-5 (20; M.E.Trescothick 72; S.T.Jayasuriya 2-32). Award: S.T.Jayasuriya.

ENGLAND v PAKISTAN

Sophia Gardens, Cardiff, 30 August (floodlit). Toss: Pakistan. **No result**. England 202 (49.2; I.R.Bell 88; Shoaib Akhtar 3-45, Mohammad Asif 3-28). Pakistan (set 159 off 32 overs) 46-1 (7). No award.

Lord's, London, 2 September. Toss: Pakistan. **PAKISTAN** won by seven wickets. England 166 (39.1; Shoaib Akhtar 4-28). Pakistan 169-3 (36.4; Younis Khan 55). Award: Shoaib Akhtar.

Rose Bowl, Southampton, 5 September (floodlit). Toss: Pakistan. **PAKISTAN** won by two wickets. England 271-9 (50; A.J.Strauss 50, P.D.Collingwood 61, J.W.M.Dalrymple 62; Naved-ul-Hasan 4-57). Pakistan 274-8 (48.5; Younis Khan 101, Mohammad Younis Youhana 60; S.C.J.Broad 3-57). Award: Younis Khan.

Trent Bridge, Nottingham, 8 September (floodlit). Toss: Pakistan. **ENGLAND** won by eight wickets. Pakistan 235-8 (50; Abdul Razzaq 75*; M.H.Yardy 3-24). England 237-2 (46.2; A.J.Strauss 78, I.R.Bell 86*). Award: I.R.Bell.

Edgbaston, Birmingham, 10 September. Toss: England. **ENGLAND** won by three wickets. Pakistan 154-9 (50; Younis Khan 47). England 155-7 (31). Award: Sajid Mahmood. Series award: Younis Khan.

TWENTY20 INTERNATIONAL

County Ground, Bristol, 28 August. Toss: England. **PAKISTAN** won by five wickets. England 144-7 (20; M.E.Trescothick 53; Abdul Razzaq 3-30). Pakistan 148-5 (17.5; Mohammad Hafeez 46). Award: Shahid Afridi.

2006 C & G TROPHY FINAL

LANCASHIRE v SUSSEX

At Lord's, London on 26 August.
Result: **SUSSEX** won by 15 runs.
Toss: Lancashire. Award: R.J.Kirtley

	SUSSEX		**Runs**	**Balls**	**4/6**	**Fall**
	R.R.Montgomerie	run out	1	7	–	1- 4
†	M.J.Prior	c Mahmood b Hogg	23	32	3	2- 27
*	C.J.Adams	c Astle b Mahmood	6	19	1	3- 38
	M.W.Goodwin	c Sutton b Chapple	7	23	–	4- 46
	M.H.Yardy	lbw b Kartik	37	96	1	8-145
	C.D.Hopkinson	run out	1	6	–	5- 52
	R.S.C.Martin-Jenkins	c Sutton b Chapple	15	19	2	6- 78
	Yasir Arafat	c Sutton b Mahmood	37	43	5	7-134
	L.J.Wright	st Sutton b Kartik	19	19	2	9-164
	Mushtaq Ahmed	b Mahmood	8	11	–	10-172
	R.J.Kirtley	not out	4	9	–	
	Extras	(LB 1, W 11, NB 2)	14			
	Total	(47.1 overs; 200 minutes)	**172**			

	LANCASHIRE		**Runs**	**Balls**	**4/6**	**Fall**
	M.B.Loye	lbw b Kirtley	12	13	–/1	1- 23
*	M.J.Chilton	st Prior b Mushtaq	20	59	1	5- 67
	N.J.Astle	lbw b Kirtley	3	6	–	2- 27
	S.G.Law	lbw b Kirtley	0	1	–	3- 27
†	L.D.Sutton	c Arafat b Wright	13	36	2	4- 51
	G.Chapple	c Montgomerie b Mushtaq	17	30	3	6- 72
	K.W.Hogg	c Montgomerie b Wright	28	69	2	7-130
	D.G.Cork	not out	35	53	2	
	T.C.Smith	lbw b Kirtley	10	14	1	8-151
	S.I.Mahmood	b Arafat	2	3	–	9-156
	M.Kartik	lbw b Kirtley	0	1	–	10-157
	Extras	(LB 10, W 5, NB 2)	17			
	Total	(47.2 overs; 197 minutes)	**157**			

LANCASHIRE	**O**	**M**	**R**	**W**	**SUSSEX**	**O**	**M**	**R**	**W**
Cork	8	0	30	0	Kirtley	8.2	1	27	5
Hogg	8	1	31	1	Yasir Arafat	9	2	24	1
Mahmood	8.1	1	16	3	Martin-Jenkins	9	2	26	0
Chapple	9	0	36	2	Wright	6	0	33	2
Kartik	8	1	28	2	Mushtaq Ahmed	10	1	19	2
Smith	6	0	30	0	Yardy	5	0	18	0

Scores after 15 overs: Sussex 46-3; Lancashire 49-3.

Umpires: J.W.Lloyds and N.A.Mallender.

CHELTENHAM & GLOUCESTER TROPHY

PRINCIPAL RECORDS 1963-2006

(Including Gillette Cup and NatWest Trophy Matches)

Highest Total	438-5		Surrey v Glamorgan	The Oval	2002
Highest Total in a Final	322-5		Warwicks v Sussex	Lord's	1993
Highest Total Batting Second	429		Glamorgan v Surrey	The Oval	2002
Highest Total to Win Batting Second	359-8		Hampshire v Surrey	The Oval	2005
Lowest Total	39		Ireland v Sussex	Hove	1985
Lowest Total in a Final	57		Essex v Lancashire	Lord's	1996
Lowest Total to Win Batting First	98		Worcs v Durham	Chester-le-St	1968
Highest Score	268	A.D.Brown	Surrey v Glamorgan	The Oval	2002
Fastest Hundred	36 balls	G.D.Rose	Somerset v Devon	Torquay	1990
Most Hundreds	8	R.A.Smith	Hampshire		1985-03
	8	N.V.Knight	Essex/Warwickshire		1992-06
Most Runs	2547	(av 48.98)	G.A.Gooch	Essex	1973-96

Highest Partnership for each Wicket

1st	311	A.J.Wright/N.J.Trainor	Glos v Scotland	Bristol	1997
2nd	286	I.S.Anderson/A.Hill	Derbys v Cornwall	Derby	1986
3rd	309*	T.S.Curtis/T.M.Moody	Worcs v Surrey	The Oval	1994
4th	234*	D.Lloyd/C.H.Lloyd	Lancashire v Glos	Manchester	1978
5th	166	M.A.Lynch/G.R.J.Roope	Surrey v Durham	The Oval	1982
6th	226	N.J.Llong/M.V.Fleming	Kent v Cheshire	Bowdon	1999
7th	170	D.R.Brown/A.F.Giles	Warwicks v Essex	Birmingham	2003
8th	112	A.L.Penberthy/J.E.Emburey	Northants v Lancs	Manchester	1996
9th	155	C.M.W.Read/A.J.Harris	Notts v Durham	Nottingham	2006
10th	81	S.Turner/R.E.East	Essex v Yorkshire	Leeds	1982

Best Bowling	8-21	M.A.Holding	Derbys v Sussex	Hove	1988
Most Wickets	88	(av 14.35)	A.A.Donald	Warwks/Worcs	1987-02

Most Wicket-Keeping Dismissals in an Innings

8 (8ct)	D.J.Pipe	Worcs v Herts	Hertford	2001

Most Match Wins: 98 – Lancashire.

Most Cup/Trophy Wins: 7 – Lancashire

GILLETTE CUP WINNERS

1963	Sussex	1970	Lancashire	1977	Middlesex
1964	Sussex	1971	Lancashire	1978	Sussex
1965	Yorkshire	1972	Lancashire	1979	Somerset
1966	Warwickshire	1973	Gloucestershire	1980	Middlesex
1967	Kent	1974	Kent		
1968	Warwickshire	1975	Lancashire		
1969	Yorkshire	1976	Northamptonshire		

NATWEST TROPHY WINNERS

1981	Derbyshire	1988	Middlesex	1995	Warwickshire
1982	Surrey	1989	Warwickshire	1996	Lancashire
1983	Somerset	1990	Lancashire	1997	Essex
1984	Middlesex	1991	Hampshire	1998	Lancashire
1985	Essex	1992	Northamptonshire	1999	Gloucestershire
1986	Sussex	1993	Warwickshire	2000	Gloucestershire
1987	Nottinghamshire	1994	Worcestershire		

CHELTENHAM & GLOUCESTER TROPHY WINNERS

2001	Somerset	2003	Gloucestershire	2005	Hampshire
2002	Yorkshire	2004	Gloucestershire	2006	Sussex

CHELTENHAM & GLOUCESTER

TROPHY 2006

After following virtually the same knock-out format since its inauguration as the Gillette Cup in 1963, this competition was drastically revamped for the 2006 season. The Minor Counties were omitted and the 18 first-class counties, joined by Ireland and Scotland, were divided into two leagues or conferences. The winner of each league contested the final at Lord's. A semi-final stage has been added for the 2007 competition. Friends Provident take over the sponsorship for the next three seasons.

SOUTH CONFERENCE

	P	*W*	*L*	*T*	*NR*	*Pts*	*RR*
1 SUSSEX	9	7	2	–	–	14	0.45
2 Middlesex	9	6	2	–	1	13	0.40
3 Essex	9	6	3	–	–	12	0.84
4 Hampshire	9	5	3	–	1	11	1.12
5 Gloucestershire	9	5	3	–	1	11	0.41
6 Somerset	9	4	4	–	1	9	0.01
7 Kent	9	4	4	–	1	9	0.01
8 Surrey	9	2	6	–	1	5	–1.08
9 Glamorgan	9	1	7	–	1	3	–1.18
10 Ireland	9	1	7	–	1	3	–1.26

NORTH CONFERENCE

	P	*W*	*L*	*T*	*NR*	*Pts*	*NRR*
1 LANCASHIRE	9	7	1	–	1	15	1.10
2 Durham	9	6	2	–	1	13	–0.03
3 Worcestershire	9	5	3	–	1	11	0.27
4 Nottinghamshire	9	4	2	–	3	11	0.53
5 Derbyshire	9	5	4	–	–	10	–0.21
6 Leicestershire	9	4	4	–	1	9	–0.03
7 Yorkshire	9	3	4	–	2	8	–0.27
8 Scotland	9	3	6	–	–	6	–0.55
9 Warwickshire	9	2	6	–	1	5	–0.35
10 Northamptonshire	9	1	8	–	–	2	–0.54

IRELAND

C & G TROPHY REGISTER 2006

Full Names	*Birthdate*	*Birthplace*	*Bat/Bowl*	*F-C Debut*
BOTHA, Andre Cornelius	12.09.75	Johannesburg, S Africa	LHB/RM	1998-99
BRAY, Jeremy Paul	30.11.73	Sydney, Australia	LHB	2004
GILLESPIE, Peter Gerard	11.05.74	Strabane	RHB/RM	1996
JOHNSTON, David Trent	29.04.74	Wollongong, Australia	RHB/RFM	1998-99
JOYCE, Dominick Ignatius	14.06.81	Dublin	RHB	2004
LANGFORD-SMITH, David	07.12.76	Sydney, Australia	RHB/RFM	2006
McCALLAN, William Kyle	27.08.75	Carrickfergus	RHB/OB	1996
McCOUBREY, Adrian George Agustus Mathew	03.04.80	Ballymena	RHB/RFM	1999
MOONEY, John Francis	10.02.82	Dublin	LHB/RM	2004
MOONEY, Paul John Kevin	15.10.76	Dublin	RHB/RM	1998
MORGAN, Eoin Joseph Gerard	10.09.86	Dublin	LHB/RM	2004
O'BRIEN, Kevin Joseph	04.03.84	Dublin	RHB/RMF	2006
PORTERFIELD, William Thomas Stuart	06.09.84	Londonderry	LHB	2006
SAQLAIN MUSHTAQ	29.12.76	Lahore, Pakistan	RHB/OB	1994-95
SHAHID AFRIDI	01.03.80	Khyber Agency, Pakistan	RHB/LBG	1995-96
WILSON, Gary Craig	05.02.86	Dundonald	RHB	2005
WHITE, Andrew Roland	03.07.80	Newtownards, Co Down	RHB/OB	2004

SCOTLAND

C & G TROPHY REGISTER 2006

Full Names	*Birthdate*	*Birthplace*	*Bat/Bowl*	*F-C Debut*
COETZER, Kyle James	14.04.84	Aberdeen	RHB/RMF	2004
HAMILTON, Gavin Mark	16.09.74	Broxburn	LHB/RMF	1993
HOFFMAN, Paul Jacob Christopher	14.01.70	Rockhampton, Australia	RHB/RMF	2004
LOCKHART, Douglas Ross	19.01.76	Glasgow	RHB/WK	1996
LYONS, Ross Thomas	08.12.84	Greenock	LHB/SLA	2006
McCALLUM, Neil Francis Ian	22.11.77	Edinburgh	RHB	2006
MacRAE, Neil John	25.03.72	Liverpool	RHB/LB	1999
MORAN, Ian Anthony	16.08.79	Sydney, Australia	RHB, RFM	–
NEL, Johann Dewald	06.06.80	Klerksdorp, S Africa	RHB/RMF	2004
RICHARDS, Corey John	25.08.75	Camden, NSW, Australia	RHB/RM	1995-96
SMITH, Colin John Ogilvie	27.09.72	Aberdeen	RHB/WK	1999
STANGER, Ian Michael	05.10.71	Glasgow	RHB/RMF	1997
WATSON, Ryan Robert	12.11.76	Salisbury, Rhodesia	RHB/RM	2004
WATTS, David Fraser	05.06.79	King's Lynn, Norfolk	RHB/RM	1999
WRIGHT, Craig McIntyre	28.04.74	Paisley	RHB/RMF	1997

BENSON AND HEDGES CUP

PRINCIPAL RECORDS 1972-2002

Highest Total	388-7		Essex v Scotland	Chelmsford	1992
Highest Total Batting Second	318-5		Lancashire v Leics	Manchester	1995
Lowest Total	50		Hampshire v Yorks	Leeds	1991
Largest Victory (Runs)	172		Essex v Scotland	Chelmsford	1992
Highest Score	198*	G.A.Gooch	Essex v Sussex	Hove	1982
Fastest Hundred	62 min	M.A.Nash	Glamorgan v Hants	Swansea	1976
Highest Partnership for each Wicket					
1st	252	V.P.Terry/C.L.Smith	Hants v Combined U	Southampton	1990
2nd	285*	C.G.Greenidge/D.R.Turner	Hants v Minor C (S)	Amersham	1973
3rd	271	C.J.Adams/M.G.Bevan	Sussex v Essex	Chelmsford	2000
4th	207	R.C.Russell/A.J.Wright	Glos v British U	Bristol	1998
5th	160	A.J.Lamb/D.J.Capel	Northants v Leics	Northampton	1986
6th	167*	M.G.Bevan/R.J.Blakey	Yorkshire v Lancs	Manchester	1996
7th	149*	J.D.Love/C.M.Old	Yorks v Scotland	Bradford	1981
8th	112	D.C.Nash/A.A.Noffke	Middlesex v Sussex	Lord's	2002
9th	83	P.G.Newman/M.A.Holding	Derbyshire v Notts	Nottingham	1985
10th	80*	D.L.Bairstow/M.Johnson	Yorkshire v Derbys	Derby	1981
Best Bowling	7-12	W.W.Daniel	Middx v Minor C (E)	Ipswich	1978
	7-22	J.R.Thomson	Middx v Hampshire	Lord's	1981
	7-24	Mushtaq Ahmed	Somerset v Ireland	Taunton	1997
	7-32	R.G.D.Willis	Warwicks v Yorks	Birmingham	1981
Four Wickets in Four Balls		S.M.Pollock	Warwicks v Leics	Birmingham	1996
Most Wicket-Keeping Dismissals in an Innings					
	8 (8ct)	D.J.S.Taylor	Somerset v Combined U	Taunton	1982
Most Catches in an Innings					
	5	V.J.Marks	Combined U v Kent	Oxford	1976

BENSON AND HEDGES CUP WINNERS

1972	Leicestershire	1983	Middlesex	1994	Warwickshire
1973	Kent	1984	Lancashire	1995	Lancashire
1974	Surrey	1985	Leicestershire	1996	Lancashire
1975	Leicestershire	1986	Middlesex	1997	Surrey
1976	Kent	1987	Yorkshire	1998	Essex
1977	Gloucestershire	1988	Hampshire	1999	Gloucestershire
1978	Kent	1989	Nottinghamshire	2000	Gloucestershire
1979	Essex	1990	Lancashire	2001	Surrey
1980	Northamptonshire	1991	Worcestershire	2002	Warwickshire
1981	Somerset	1992	Hampshire		
1982	Somerset	1993	Derbyshire		

NATWEST PRO 40 LEAGUE 2006

This competition, with each county playing its divisional opponents once instead of twice, replaced the Totesport National League, with Scotland omitted. The bottom two First Division teams were relegated and replaced by the top two from the Second Division for 2007. A play-off for a 2007 First Division place was introduced between the team finishing third in the Second Division (given a home tie) and the one finishing seventh in the First Division.

FIRST DIVISION	*P*	*W*	*L*	*T*	*NR*	*Pts*	*NRR*
1 ESSEX (1)	8	5	2	–	1	11	1.23
2 Northamptonshire (3)	8	5	2	–	1	11	–0.03
3 Sussex (-)	8	5	3	–	–	10	0.14
4 Nottinghamshire (5)	8	4	3	–	1	9	0.06
5 Warwickshire (-)	8	3	4	–	1	7	–0.16
6 Lancashire (6)	8	2	3	–	3	7	0.41
7 Glamorgan (4)	8	2	3	1	2	7	–0.48
8 Durham (-)	8	2	4	1	1	6	–0.30
9 Middlesex (2)	8	2	6	–	–	4	–0.78

SECOND DIVISION	*P*	*W*	*L*	*T*	*NR*	*Pts*	*NRR*
1 Gloucestershire (-)	8	6	2	–	–	12	0.28
2 Worcestershire (-)	8	6	2	–	–	12	1.03
3 Hampshire (-)	8	5	2	–	1	11	0.55
4 Surrey (7)	8	5	2	–	1	11	0.33
5 Kent (8)	8	5	3	–	–	10	0.77
6 Leicestershire (4)	8	3	5	–	–	6	0.10
7 Somerset (6)	8	2	6	–	–	4	–0.84
8 Derbyshire (5)	8	1	6	–	1	3	–0.86
9 Yorkshire (9)	8	1	6	–	1	3	–1.46

Win = 2 points. Tie (T)/No Result (NR) = 1 point. Positions of counties finishing equal on points are decided by most wins or, if equal, by which team gained most points in the match played between them. If still equal the side with higher net run-rate will take precedence (NRR – overall run-rate in all matches, i.e. total runs scored times 100 divided by balls received, minus the run-rate of its opponents in those same matches).

Horizontal rules segregate the counties relegated and promoted for the 2007 competition. 2005 final positions for that division are shown in brackets.

PLAY-OFF MATCH

At the Rose Bowl, Southampton on 24 September. HAMPSHIRE beat Glamorgan by 151 runs. Hampshire 265-9 (40 overs; C.C.Benham 158, A.P.Davies 3-53). Glamorgan 114 (25.2 overs; S.M.Ervine 4-24, J.T.A.Bruce 3-48). Award: C.C.Benham who completed his 100 off 79 balls.

HIGHEST BATTING AGGREGATE	– Div 1	360	(av 60.00)	O.A.Shah	Middlesex
	– Div 2	354	(av 50.57)	C.G.Taylor	Gloucestershire
HIGHEST BOWLING AGGREGATE	– Div 1	17	(av 12.41)	A.J.Bichel	Essex
	– Div 2	19	(av 17.42)	N.D.Doshi	Surrey

PRO 40/NATIONAL/SUNDAY LEAGUE CHAMPIONS

1969	Lancashire	1982	Sussex	1995	Kent
1970	Lancashire	1983	Yorkshire	1996	Surrey
1971	Worcestershire	1984	Essex	1997	Warwickshire
1972	Kent	1985	Essex	1998	Lancashire
1973	Kent	1986	Hampshire	1999	Lancashire
1974	Leicestershire	1987	Worcestershire	2000	Gloucestershire
1975	Hampshire	1988	Worcestershire	2001	Kent
1976	Kent	1989	Lancashire	2002	Glamorgan
1977	Leicestershire	1990	Derbyshire	2003	Surrey
1978	Hampshire	1991	Nottinghamshire	2004	Glamorgan
1979	Somerset	1992	Middlesex	2005	Essex
1980	Warwickshire	1993	Glamorgan	2006	Essex
1981	Essex	1994	Warwickshire		

PRO 40/NATIONAL/SUNDAY LEAGUE 1969-2006

PRINCIPAL RECORDS

Highest Total		377-9		Somerset v Sussex	Hove	2003
Highest Total Batting Second		323-5		Sussex v Leics	Horsham	2004
Lowest Total		23		Middlesex v Yorks	Leeds	1974
Largest Victory (Runs)		220		Somerset v Glamorgan	Neath	1990
Highest Scores		203	A.D.Brown	Surrey v Hampshire	Guildford	1997
		191	D.S.Lehmann	Yorks v Notts	Scarborough	2001
		176	G.A.Gooch	Essex v Glamorgan	Southend	1983
		175*	I.T.Botham	Somerset v Northants	Wellingborough	1986
Fastest Hundred		44 balls	M.A.Ealham	Kent v Derbyshire	Maidstone	1995
Most Sixes (Inns)		13	I.T.Botham	Somerset v Northants	Wellingborough	1986
Highest Partnership for each Wicket						
1st	239		G.A.Gooch/B.R.Hardie	Essex v Notts	Nottingham	1985
2nd	273		G.A.Gooch/K.S.McEwan	Essex v Notts	Nottingham	1983
3rd	228*		M.W.Goodwin/C.J.Adams	Sussex v Middlesex	Hove	2003
4th	219		C.G.Greenidge/C.L.Smith	Hampshire v Surrey	Southampton	1987
5th	221*		R.R.Sarwan/M.A.Hardinges	Glos v Lancashire	Manchester	2005
6th	167		C.L.Cairns/C.M.W.Read	Notts v Sussex	Nottingham	2003
7th	164		J.N.Snape/M.A.Hardinges	Glos v Notts	Nottingham	2001
8th	116*		N.D.Burns/P.A.J.DeFreitas	Leics v Northants	Leicester	2001
9th	105		D.G.Moir/R.W.Taylor	Derbyshire v Kent	Derby	1984
10th	82		G.Chapple/P.J.Martin	Lancashire v Worcs	Manchester	1996
Best Bowling		8-26	K.D.Boyce	Essex v Lancashire	Manchester	1971
		7-15	R.A.Hutton	Yorkshire v Worcs	Leeds	1969
		7-16	S.D.Thomas	Glamorgan v Surrey	Swansea	1998
		7-30	M.P.Bicknell	Surrey v Glamorgan	The Oval	1999
		7-39	A.Hodgson	Northants v Somerset	Northampton	1976
		7-41	A.N.Jones	Sussex v Notts	Nottingham	1986
Four Wkts in Four Balls			A.Ward	Derbyshire v Sussex	Derby	1970
			V.C.Drakes	Notts v Derbys	Nottingham	1999
Most Economical Analysis						
	8-8-0-0		B.A.Langford	Somerset v Essex	Yeovil	1969
Most Expensive Analysis						
	9-0-99-1		M.R.Strong	Northants v Glos	Cheltenham	2001
Most Wicket-Keeping Dismissals in an Innings						
	7 (6ct, 1st)		R.W.Taylor	Derbyshire v Lancs	Manchester	1975
Most Catches in an Innings by a Fielder						
	5		J.M.Rice	Hampshire v Warwicks	Southampton	1978

TWENTY 20 CUP 2006

GROUP TABLES

	MIDLANDS/WALES/WEST	P	W	L	T	NR	Pts	NRR
1	GLOUCESTERSHIRE	8	6	2	–	–	12	–0.39
2	NORTHAMPTONSHIRE	8	5	2	1	–	11	0.24
3	Warwickshire	8	4	3	–	1	9	0.46
4	Glamorgan	8	3	4	–	1	7	–0.16
5	Somerset	8	2	5	1	–	5	0.28
6	Worcestershire	8	2	6	–	–	4	–0.46

	NORTH	P	W	L	T	NR	Pts	NRR
1	LEICESTERSHIRE	8	6	2	–	–	12	1.45
2	NOTTINGHAMSHIRE	8	6	2	–	–	12	0.55
3	YORKSHIRE	8	4	3	–	1	9	0.74
4	Lancashire	8	3	5	–	–	6	0.03
5	Derbyshire	8	2	5	–	1	5	–1.33
6	Durham	8	2	6	–	–	4	–1.48

	SOUTH	P	W	L	T	NR	Pts	NRR
1	ESSEX	8	6	2	–	–	12	0.53
2	SURREY	8	5	3	–	–	10	1.45
3	KENT	8	5	3	–	–	10	–0.29
4	Sussex	8	4	4	–	–	8	–0.14
5	Hampshire	8	3	5	–	–	6	0.00
6	Middlesex	8	1	7	–	–	2	–1.61

QUARTER-FINALS: ESSEX beat Yorkshire by 5 wickets at Chelmsford
LEICESTERSHIRE beat Kent by 9 wickets at Leicester
NOTTINGHAMSHIRE beat Northamptonshire by 63 runs at Nottingham
SURREY beat Gloucestershire by 80 runs at Bristol

SEMI-FINALS: LEICESTERSHIRE beat Essex by 23 runs at Nottingham
NOTTINGHAMSHIRE beat Surrey by 37 runs at Nottingham

LEADING AVERAGES 2006

BATTING		*M*	*I*	*NO*	*HS*	*Runs*	*Avge*	*100*	*50*	*R/100b*
J.L.Langer	Somerset	8	8	1	97	464	66.28	–	4	161.1
H.D.Ackerman	Leicestershire	11	11	–	87	409	37.18	–	5	118.8
C.L.White	Somerset	8	8	2	141*	403	67.16	2	1	180.7
D.J.Hussey	Nottinghamshire	11	10	3	71	394	56.28	–	2	149.8
R.C.Irani	Essex	10	10	2	100*	338	42.25	1	3	146.3
S.P.Fleming	Nottinghamshire	10	10	1	64*	336	37.33	–	3	115.4
J.G.E.Benning	Surrey	10	10	1	88	326	36.22	–	4	155.9

BOWLING		*O*	*M*	*R*	*W*	*Avge*	*BB*	*4w*	*R/Over*
N.D.Doshi	Surrey	35	0	243	21	11.57	4-22	3	6.94
A.R.Griffith	Leicestershire	35.5	0	228	18	12.66	3-14	–	6.42
Yasir Arafat	Sussex	29.4	1	223	16	13.93	4-21	2	7.51
M.M.Patel	Kent	32.4	0	257	15	17.13	4-26	1	7.86
S.C.J.Broad	Leicestershire	36	0	179	14	12.78	3-13	–	4.97
M.L.Lewis	Durham	29	0	199	14	14.21	4-19	1	6.86
A.J.Bichel	Essex	40	0	324	14	23.14	4-23	1	8.10

TWENTY20 CUP FINAL 2006

NOTTINGHAMSHIRE v LEICESTERSHIRE

At Trent Bridge, Nottingham, on 12 August.
Result: **LEICESTERSHIRE** won by 4 runs
Toss: Leicestershire. Award: D.L.Maddy.

LEICESTERSHIRE		Runs	Balls	4/6	Fall
H.D.Ackerman	b Sidebottom	11	11	1	1- 26
D.L.Maddy	not out	86	61	6/4	
J.Allenby	run out	64	41	5/3	2-159
P.W.Harrison	not out	10	7	–	
* J.N.Snape					
J.L.Sadler					
† P.A.Nixon					
C.W.Henderson					
D.D.Masters					
S.C.J.Broad					
R.A.G.Cummins					
Extras	(LB6)	6			
Total	(20 overs; 2 wickets)	**177**			

NOTTINGHAMSHIRE		Runs	Balls	4/6	Fall
G.P.Swann	lbw b Maddy	14	18	1	1- 51
* S.P.Fleming	c Cummins b Snape	53	39	8	2-108
D.J.Hussey	c Snape b Broad	37	23	5/1	3-109
† C.M.W.Read	c Broad b Henderson	2	6	–	4-122
S.R.Patel	run out	27	17	5	6-160
M.A.Ealham	c Maddy b Allenby	16	7	2/1	5-151
P.J.Franks	run out	11	6	–/1	7-164
G.D.Clough	c Maddy b Allenby	0	1	–	8-165
W.R.Smith	not out	9	3	–/1	
R.J.Sidebottom	not out	0	–	–	
C.E.Shreck					
Extras	(LB 3, W 1)	4			
Total	(20 overs; 8 wickets)	**173**			

NOTTINGHAMSHIRE	O	M	R	W	**LEICESTERSHIRE**	O	M	R	W
Sidebottom	4	0	23	1	Broad	4	0	18	1
Shreck	4	0	33	0	Cummins	3	0	40	0
Swann	4	0	30	0	Masters	2	0	18	0
Ealham	4	0	47	0	Maddy	2	0	16	1
Clough	2	0	15	0	Henderson	4	0	34	1
Franks	2	0	23	0	Snape	3	0	21	1
					Allenby	2	0	23	2

Umpires: P.J.Hartley and A.A.Jones

TWENTY 20 CUP WINNERS

2003 Surrey
2004 Leicestershire
2005 Somerset
2006 Leicestershire

TWENTY20 CUP RECORDS 2003-06

Highest Total	250-3		Somerset v Glos	Taunton	2006
Lowest Total	67		Sussex v Hampshire	Hove	2004
Hundreds	141*	C.L.White	Somerset v Worcs	Worcester	2006
	116*	G.A.Hick	Worcs v Northants	Luton	2004
	116*	I.J.Thomas	Glamorgan v Somerset	Taunton	2004
	116*	C.L.White	Somerset v Glos	Taunton	2006
	112	A.Symonds	Kent v Middlesex	Maidstone	2004
	111	D.L.Maddy	Leics v Yorks	Leeds	2004
	109	I.J.Harvey	Yorkshire v Derbys	Leeds	2005
	108*	I.J.Harvey	Yorkshire v Lancs	Leeds	2004
	105	B.F.Smith	Worcs v Glamorgan	Worcester	2005
	105	G.C.Smith	Somerset v Northants	Taunton	2005
	101	S.G.Law	Lancs v Yorkshire	Manchester	2005
	100*	I.J.Harvey	Glos v Warwicks	Birmingham	2003
	100*	R.C.Irani	Essex v Sussex	Hove	2006
	100	M.B.Loye	Lancs v Durham	Manchester	2005

Highest Partnership for each Wicket

1st	167	B.J.Hodge/D.L.Maddy	Leics v Yorkshire	Leeds	2004
2nd	186	J.L.Langer/C.L.White	Somerset v Glos	Taunton	2006
3rd	120	M.J.Wood/C.M.Gazzard	Somerset v Worcs	Taunton	2005
4th	139	M.R.Ramprakash/R.Clarke	Surrey v Glos	Bristol	2006
5th	117	M.van Jaarsveld/M.J.Walker	Kent v Leics	Leicester	2006
6th	98*	R.W.T.Key/M.J.Walker	Kent v Middlesex	Beckenham	2006
7th	63	J.S.Foster/A.R.Adams	Essex v Middlesex	Southgate	2005
8th	68	M.W.Alleyne/J.Lewis	Glos v Glamorgan	Cardiff	2005
9th	59*	G.Chapple/P.J.Martin	Lancs v Leics	Leicester	2003
10th	59	H.H.Streak/J.E.Anyon	Warwicks v Worcs	Birmingham	2005

Five Wickets	6-24	T.J.Murtagh	Surrey v Middlesex	Lord's	2005
	5-11	Mushtaq Ahmed	Sussex v Essex	Hove	2005
	5-14	A.D.Mascarenhas	Hampshire v Sussex	Hove	2004
	5-19	N.N.Carter	Warwicks v Worcs	Birmingham	2005
	5-21	A.J.Hollioake	Surrey v Hampshire	Southampton	2003
	5-24	C.O.Obuya	Warwicks v Glamorgan	Birmingham	2003
	5-26	R.J.Logan	Notts v Lancs	Nottingham	2003
	5-26	J.Ormond	Surrey v Middlesex	The Oval	2003
	5-27	J.F.Brown	Northants v Somerset	Northampton	2003
	5-33	A.G.R.Loudon	Warwicks v Glamorgan	Swansea	2005
	5-34	A.J.Hollioake	Surrey v Hampshire	The Oval	2004
Hat-Tricks		J.E.Anyon	Warwicks v Somerset	Birmingham	2005
		D.G.Cork	Lancs v Notts	Manchester	2004
		A.D.Mascarenhas	Hampshire v Sussex	Hove	2004

Most Economical Analyses

4-1-6-2	J.Louw	Northants v Warwicks	Birmingham	2004
4-0-6-1	M.W.Alleyne	Glos v Worcs	Worcester	2005
4-1-7-1	R.S.C.Martin-Jenkins	Sussex v Hampshire	Hove	2004
4-1-7-4	N.Killeen	Durham v Leics	Leicester	2004

Most Expensive Analyses

4-0-65-2	M.J.Hoggard	Yorkshire v Lancs	Leeds	2005
4-0-63-1	R.J.Kirtley	Sussex v Surrey	Hove	2004
4-0-61-0	A.P.Davies	Glamorgan v Glos	Bristol	2006
4-0-60-0	S.P.Kirby	Yorks v Lancs	Leeds	2004
4-0-60-1	J.E.Anyon	Warwicks v Glos	Birmingham	2006

MINOR COUNTIES CHAMPIONSHIP

FINAL TABLES 2006

EASTERN DIVISION

	P	W	L	D	Bonus Points Bat	Bonus Points Bowl	Total Points	Net Runs/Wkt
BUCKINGHAMSHIRE (6)	6	5	–	1	12	18	114	13.69
Suffolk (1)	6	4	–	2	15	20	107	9.62
Lincolnshire (8)	6	3	1	2	18	18	92	7.41
Norfolk (3)	6	3	1	2	15	18	89	7.86
Bedfordshire (10)	6	2	3	1*	10	19	67	–0.22
Staffordshire (5)	6	2	3	1*	10	17	65	0.51
Cambridgeshire (2)	6	1	2	3*	12	20	62	–5.19
Northumberland (4)	6	1	4	1	11	13	42†	–12.45
Hertfordshire (9)	6	–	3	3*	10	14	40	–4.50
Cumberland (7)	6	–	4	2*	9	15	34	–17.81

WESTERN DIVISION

	P	W	L	D	Bonus Points Bat	Bonus Points Bowl	Total Points	Net Runs/Wkt
DEVON (2)	6	6	–	–	20	20	136	12.16
Dorset (10)	6	4	1	1	17	24	109	10.56
Wiltshire (9)	6	2	1	3	21	23	86†	9.37
Shropshire (6)	6	2	1	3	18	19	81	2.18
Cornwall (4)	6	2	1	3	14	23	81	–5.70
Cheshire (1)	6	2	2	2	14	19	73	1.46
Wales (7)	6	1	2	3	9	21	58	0.75
Oxfordshire (5)	6	–	3	3	9	24	45	–4.20
Berkshire (3)	6	–	3	3	10	20	42	–21.58
Herefordshire (8)	6	–	5	1	16	21	41	–9.87

* Includes 6 points for match reduced to single innings with no bonus points (2 matches for Hertfordshire). Win = 16 points. Draw/Tie = 4 points. 2005 final positions are shown in brackets. † 2 points deducted for a slow over rate.

2006 CHAMPIONSHIP FINAL

At The Maer Ground, Exmouth, on 10, 11, 12 September. Toss: Devon. **DEVON beat BUCKINGHAMSHIRE by 180 runs.** Devon 302 (N.D.Hancock 95, D.G.Court 53*; D.J.Spencer 4-71) and 293-3 dec (N.D.Hancock 139*, C.M.Mole 88*). Buckinghamshire 288-8 closed (70 overs; A.D.Hales 92) and 127 (A.Jones 7-32).

2006 MCCA KNOCK-OUT TROPHY FINAL

At Lord's, London, on 16 August. Toss: Northumberland. **NORTHUMBERLAND beat DORSET by eight wickets**. Dorset 207-9 (50 overs; G.R.Treagus 87, T.Webley 47; S.Humble 3-41, J.B.Windows 3-41). Northumberland 209-2 (34.4 overs; D.J.Barrick 97*, A.Worthy 57).

MINOR COUNTIES RECORDS

Highest Total	621		Surrey II v Devon	The Oval	1928
Lowest Total	14		Cheshire v Staffs	Stoke	1909
Highest Score	282	E.Garnett	Berkshire v Wiltshire	Reading	1908
Most Runs – Season	1212	A.F.Brazier	Surrey II		1949
Record Partnership:					
2nd wkt	388*	T.H.Clark/A.F.Brazier	Surrey II v Sussex II	The Oval	1949
Best Bowling – Innings	10- 11	S.Turner	Cambs v Cumberland	Penrith	1987
– Match	18-100	N.W.Harding	Kent II v Wiltshire	Swindon	1937
Most Wickets – Season	119	S.F.Barnes	Staffordshire		1906

MINOR COUNTIES CHAMPIONS

1895	Norfolk / Durham / Worcestershire
1896	Worcestershire
1897	Worcestershire
1898	Worcestershire
1899	Northamptonshire / Buckinghamshire
1900	Glamorgan / Durham / Northamptonshire
1901	Durham
1902	Wiltshire
1903	Northamptonshire
1904	Northamptonshire
1905	Norfolk
1906	Staffordshire
1907	Lancashire II
1908	Staffordshire
1909	Wiltshire
1910	Norfolk
1911	Staffordshire
1912	*In abeyance*
1913	Norfolk
1920	Staffordshire
1921	Staffordshire
1922	Buckinghamshire
1923	Buckinghamshire
1924	Berkshire
1925	Buckinghamshire
1926	Durham
1927	Staffordshire
1928	Berkshire
1929	Oxfordshire
1930	Durham
1931	Leicestershire II
1932	Buckinghamshire
1933	*Undecided*
1934	Lancashire II
1935	Middlesex II
1936	Hertfordshire
1937	Lancashire II
1938	Buckinghamshire
1939	Surrey II
1946	Suffolk
1947	Yorkshire II
1948	Lancashire II
1949	Lancashire II
1950	Surrey II
1951	Kent II
1952	Buckinghamshire
1953	Berkshire
1954	Surrey II
1955	Surrey II
1956	Kent II
1957	Yorkshire II
1958	Yorkshire II
1959	Warwickshire II
1960	Lancashire II
1961	Somerset II
1962	Warwickshire II
1963	Cambridgeshire
1964	Lancashire II
1965	Somerset II
1966	Lincolnshire
1967	Cheshire
1968	Yorkshire II
1969	Buckinghamshire
1970	Bedfordshire
1971	Yorkshire II
1972	Bedfordshire
1973	Shropshire
1974	Oxfordshire
1975	Hertfordshire
1976	Durham
1977	Suffolk
1978	Devon
1979	Suffolk
1980	Durham
1981	Durham
1982	Oxfordshire
1983	Hertfordshire
1984	Durham
1985	Cheshire
1986	Cumberland
1987	Buckinghamshire
1988	Cheshire
1989	Oxfordshire
1990	Hertfordshire
1991	Staffordshire
1992	Staffordshire
1993	Staffordshire
1994	Devon
1995	Devon
1996	Devon
1997	Devon
1998	Staffordshire
1999	Cumberland
2000	Dorset
2001	Cheshire / Lincolnshire
2002	Herefordshire / Norfolk
2003	Lincolnshire
2004	Bedfordshire / Devon
2005	Cheshire / Suffolk
2006	Devon

LEADING CHAMPIONSHIP AGGEGATES 2006

BATTING

		M	I	NO	HS	Runs	Avge	100	50
N.D.Hancock	Devon	7	13	3	155*	799	79.90	4	3
V.Atri	Lincolnshire	6	11	1	153	714	71.40	3	4
C.A.Smith	Oxfordshire	5	10	0	166	649	64.90	2	3
A.J.Hall	Cheshire	6	11	0	156	635	57.72	3	1
C.J.Rogers	Norfolk	6	11	3	137	618	77.25	2	3
B.Parker	Northumberland	5	10	1	105*	561	62.33	2	4
N.J.Ferraby	Cambridgeshire	6	11	0	146	531	48.27	1	4
G.P.Rees	Wales	6	12	1	135	529	48.09	1	4
D.M.Ward	Hertfordshire	6	10	1	139	516	57.33	2	2
M.C.Dobson	Lincolnshire	6	11	2	96*	487	54.11	–	4
J.C.Harrison	Buckinghamshire	7	13	2	102	473	43.00	1	2
A.D.Hales	Buckinghamshire	5	10	1	92	470	52.22	–	5
R.I.Dawson	Devon	7	13	2	126*	461	41.90	1	3
N.R.C.Dumelow	Cheshire	6	11	0	156	461	41.90	2	1
T.B.Huggins	Suffolk	6	11	1	121*	459	45.90	1	3
S.G.Cordingley	Hertfordshire	4	7	0	155	434	62.00	2	2
J.D.Whitney	Shropshire	6	10	0	164	419	41.90	1	2
M.H.Steed	Bedfordshire	6	10	2	117	418	52.25	1	1
D.J.Cowley	Dorset	6	10	2	108	417	52.12	1	4
W.D.Bragg	Wales	6	12	2	86*	410	41.00	–	4
P.J.Dennett	Wiltshire	5	8	0	126	409	51.12	1	3
J.T.Ralph	Shropshire	5	8	1	109	407	58.14	2	1
R.J.Foan	Devon	6	10	0	150	400	40.00	1	1

BOWLING

		O	M	R	W	Avge	BB	5w	10w
A.J.Procter	Devon	323.4	86	902	43	20.97	7- 62	4	1
C.Brown	Norfolk	261	53	778	35	22.22	7-120	2	–
C.P.Schofield	Suffolk	159.1	40	472	32	14.75	8-112	3	2
T.G.Sharp	Cornwall	200.2	36	666	32	20.81	5- 93	2	–
P.J.Sampson	Buckinghamshire	179	32	601	31	19.38	5- 53	1	–
P.R.Sawyer	Buckinghamshire	189.4	24	666	27	24.66	6- 17	1	–
A.C.McGarry	Suffolk	207	58	598	27	22.14	6- 76	2	–
J.S.Miles	Lincolnshire	178	41	529	26	20.34	5- 63	1	–
S.Rashid	Staffordshire	182.1	26	608	26	23.38	5- 57	3	1
A.J.Syddall	Cambridgeshire	168.5	43	550	24	22.91	5- 48	2	–
I.R.Slegg	Norfolk	183	38	512	24	21.33	4- 35	–	–
N.R.C.Dumelow	Cheshire	191	49	559	23	24.30	7-114	2	–
J.Hibberd	Wiltshire	101.3	28	283	22	12.86	4- 9	–	–
J.E.Bishop	Suffolk	151	35	541	22	24.59	6- 33	2	1
T.S.Anning	Devon	165.2	40	494	22	22.45	5- 14	2	–
B.J.Frazer	Hertfordshire	177.1	35	669	21	31.85	7-142	1	–
K.A.Arnold	Oxfordshire	202.2	44	580	21	27.61	3- 53	–	–
A.R.Roberts	Bedfordshire	127.1	30	362	20	18.10	5- 45	2	1
M.D.Ford	Dorset	131.5	39	411	20	20.55	4- 32	–	–
L.C.Ryan	Oxfordshire	145.5	30	543	20	27.15	5- 84	1	–
M.Robinson	Shropshire	173.4	34	599	20	29.95	5- 86	1	–
J.M.Golding	Wiltshire	113.4	26	320	19	16.84	5- 17	1	–
T.C.Hicks	Dorset	142.1	29	441	19	23.21	4- 69	–	–
R.D.Bedbrook	Wiltshire	166.1	37	528	19	27.78	5- 39	1	–
Ajaz Akhtar	Cambridgeshire	143.1	46	346	18	19.22	4- 32	–	–
R.C.Kitzinger	Dorset	143.1	44	407	18	22.61	4- 41	–	–
M.J.Metcalfe	Dorset	164.1	56	425	18	23.61	6- 37	1	–

SECOND XI CHAMPIONSHIP 2006
FINAL TABLE

		P	W	L	D	Deduct	Bonus Points Bat	Bonus Points Bowl	Total Points	Avge
1	KENT (1)	6	4	1	1	–	22	19	101	16.83
2	Sussex (13)	9	4	–	5	–	25	33	134	14.89
3	Yorkshire (10)	14	6	4	4	–	49	43	192	13.71
4	Surrey (7)	15	5	2	8	5.5	47	54	197.5	13.17
5	Durham (5)	12	4	1	7	2	39	33	154	12.83
6	Warwickshire (19)	12	4	4	4	–	34	43	149	12.42
7	Lancashire (4)	12	5	2	5*	–	22	35	147	12.25
8	Gloucestershire (2)	8	3	2	3	–	15	28	97	12.13
9	Derbyshire (11)	10	4	2	4*	–	23	25	120	12.00
10	Somerset (8)	6	2	2	2	–	20	15	71	11.83
11	Leicestershire (9)	10	3	1	6*	3.5	27	27	116.5	11.65
12	Hampshire (3)	10	3	4	3*	5	30	31	110	11.00
13	Glamorgan (18)	6	1	1	4	–	16	14	60	10.00
14	Middlesex (16)	10	1	4	5	2.5	32	32	95.5	9.55
15	Nottinghamshire (12)	9	2	5	2*	–	20	25	81	9.00
16	Essex (6)	9	1	5	3	–	25	29	80	8.89
17	MCC Young Cricketers (14)	12	1	4	7*	–	25	29	96	8.00
18	Northamptonshire (14)	9	1	8	–	–	28	30	72	8.00
19	Worcestershire (16)	7	–	2	5	0.5	17	15	51.5	7.36

Win = 14 points, plus any first-innings points. Draw = 4 points, plus any first-innings points.
* Including one match abandoned without a ball bowled (4 points).
2005 final positions are shown in brackets.

SECOND XI CHAMPIONS

1959	Gloucestershire	1975	Surrey	1991	Yorkshire
1960	Northamptonshire	1976	Kent	1992	Surrey
1961	Kent	1977	Yorkshire	1993	Middlesex
1962	Worcestershire	1978	Sussex	1994	Somerset
1963	Worcestershire	1979	Warwickshire	1995	Hampshire
1964	Lancashire	1980	Glamorgan	1996	Warwickshire
1965	Glamorgan	1981	Hampshire	1997	Lancashire
1966	Surrey	1982	Worcestershire	1998	Northamptonshire
1967	Hampshire	1983	Leicestershire	1999	Middlesex
1968	Surrey	1984	Yorkshire	2000	Middlesex
1969	Kent	1985	Nottinghamshire	2001	Hampshire
1970	Kent	1986	Lancashire	2002	Kent
1971	Hampshire	1987	Kent/Yorkshire	2003	Yorkshire
1972	Nottinghamshire	1988	Surrey	2004	Somerset
1973	Essex	1989	Middlesex	2005	Kent
1974	Middlesex	1990	Sussex	2006	Kent

SECOND XI TROPHY 2006

Semi-Finals: WARWICKSHIRE beat HAMPSHIRE by one wicket at Southampton. YORKSHIRE beat NOTTINGHAMSHIRE by nine wickets at Stamford Bridge.

Final: WARWICKSHIRE 326 (50 overs; N.S.Poonia 101, J.O.Troughton 80, M.M.Ali 63; G.Norton 5-54, M.A.K.Lawson 3-64) beat YORKSHIRE 233 (40 overs; D.J.Wainwright 70*, S.M.Guy 64; N.Tahir 4-35, I.J.Westwood 3-59) by 93 runs at Leeds.

YOUNG CRICKETER OF THE YEAR

This annual award, made by The Cricket Writers' Club, which celebrated its 60th anniversary in 2006, is currently restricted to players qualified for England, Andrew Symonds meeting that requirement at the time of his award, and under the age of 23 on 1st May. In 1986 their ballot resulted in a dead heat. Up to 1 April 2007 their selections have gained a tally of 1,912 international Test match caps (shown in brackets).

1950	R.Tattersall (16)	1979	P.W.G.Parker (1)
1951	P.B.H.May (66)	1980	G.R.Dilley (41)
1952	F.S.Trueman (67)	1981	M.W.Gatting (79)
1953	M.C.Cowdrey (114)	1982	N.G.Cowans (19)
1954	P.J.Loader (13)	1983	N.A.Foster (29)
1955	K.F.Barrington (82)	1984	R.J.Bailey (4)
1956	B.Taylor	1985	D.V.Lawrence (5)
1957	M.J.Stewart (8)	1986	A.A.Metcalfe
1958	A.C.D.Ingleby-Mackenzie		J.J.Whitaker (1)
1959	G.Pullar (28)	1987	R.J.Blakey (2)
1960	D.A.Allen (39)	1988	M.P.Maynard (4)
1961	P.H.Parfitt (37)	1989	N.Hussain (96)
1962	P.J.Sharpe (12)	1990	M.A.Atherton (115)
1963	G.Boycott (108)	1991	M.R.Ramprakash (52)
1964	J.M.Brearley (39)	1992	I.D.K.Salisbury (15)
1965	A.P.E.Knott (95)	1993	M.N.Lathwell (2)
1966	D.L.Underwood (86)	1994	J.P.Crawley (37)
1967	A.W.Greig (58)	1995	A.Symonds (13-Australia)
1968	R.M.H.Cottam (4)	1996	C.E.W.Silverwood (6)
1969	A.Ward (5)	1997	B.C.Hollioake (2)
1970	C.M.Old (46)	1998	A.Flintoff (66)
1971	J.Whitehouse	1999	A.J.Tudor (10)
1972	D.R.Owen-Thomas	2000	P.J.Franks
1973	M.Hendrick (30)	2001	O.A.Shah (1)
1974	P.H.Edmonds (51)	2002	R.Clarke (2)
1975	A.Kennedy	2003	J.M.Anderson (16)
1976	G.Miller (34)	2004	I.R.Bell (23)
1977	I.T.Botham (102)	2005	A.N.Cook (14)
1978	D.I.Gower (117)	2006	S.C.J.Broad

THE PROFESSIONAL CRICKETERS' ASSOCIATION

PLAYER OF THE YEAR

Founded in 1967, the Professional Cricketers' Association introduced this award, decided by their membership, in 1970. Since 1998 it has been presented at their Annual Awards Dinner at the Royal Albert Hall. Only John Lever and Andrew Flintoff won the award in successive years.

1970	M.J.Procter	1982	M.D.Marshall	1995	D.G.Cork
	J.D.Bond	1983	K.S.McEwan	1996	P.V.Simmons
1971	L.R.Gibbs	1984	R.J.Hadlee	1997	S.P.James
1972	A.M.E.Roberts	1985	N.V.Radford	1998	M.B.Loye
1973	P.G.Lee	1986	C.A.Walsh	1999	S.G.Law
1974	B.Stead	1987	R.J.Hadlee	2000	M.E.Trescothick
1975	Zaheer Abbas	1988	G.A.Hick	2001	D.P.Fulton
1976	P.G.Lee	1989	S.J.Cook	2002	M.P.Vaughan
1977	M.J.Procter	1990	G.A.Gooch	2003	Mushtaq Ahmed
1978	J.K.Lever	1991	Waqar Younis	2004	A.Flintoff
1979	J.K.Lever	1992	C.A.Walsh	2005	A.Flintoff
1980	R.D.Jackman	1993	S.L.Watkin	2006	M.R.Ramprakash
1981	R.J.Hadlee	1994	B.C.Lara		

FIRST–CLASS CAREER RECORDS

Compiled by **Philip Bailey**

The following career records are for all players who appeared in first-class cricket during the 2006 season, and are complete to the end of that season. Some players who did not appear in 2006 but may do so in 2007 are included.

BATTING AND FIELDING

'1000' denotes instances of scoring 1000 runs in a season. Where these have been achieved outside the British Isles they are shown after a plus sign.

	M	*I*	*NO*	*HS*	*Runs*	*Avge*	*100*	*50*	*1000*	*Ct/St*
Abdul Razzaq	101	157	24	203*	4487	33.73	8	21	–	23
Ackerman, H.D.	154	256	26	309*	10408	45.25	26	62	2+1	121
Adams, A.R.	68	88	6	124	1958	23.87	2	9	–	44
Adams, C.J.	306	499	36	239	18031	38.94	45	88	8	364
Adams, J.H.K.	53	95	10	262*	2743	32.27	3	12	1	37
Adnan, M.H.	116	192	22	191	6812	40.07	10	46	1	62
Adshead, S.J.	52	89	16	148*	2318	31.75	1	14	–	133/12
Afzaal, U.	182	314	34	168*	10559	37.71	26	51	6	87
Ahmed, J.S.	2	1	1	14*	14	–	–	–	–	1
Ali, Kabir	81	111	19	84*	1719	18.68	–	7	–	22
Ali, Kadeer	49	90	4	145	2138	24.86	1	14	–	24
Ali, M.M.	7	10	–	68	234	23.40	–	3	–	4
Ali, S.M.B.	89	120	30	92	1334	14.82	–	5	–	29
Allenby, J.	2	4	2	103*	239	119.50	1	1	–	2
Alleyne, D.	22	33	4	109*	849	29.27	1	4	–	57/5
Ambrose, T.R.	56	90	6	149	2765	32.91	3	18	–	106/14
Amjad Khan	57	65	23	78	824	19.61	–	3	–	9
Anderson, J.M.	53	62	31	37*	318	10.25	–	–	–	20
Andrew, G.M.	11	14	1	44	163	12.53	–	–	–	5
Anwar, O.S.	13	18	1	99	402	23.64	–	2	–	2
Anyon, J.E.	22	32	14	21	112	6.22	–	–	–	8
Arshad Khan	171	222	34	79*	2348	12.48	–	6	–	80
Astle, N.J.	167	265	23	223	9165	37.87	19	49	–	128
Austin, M.L.	1	2	–	23	35	17.50	–	–	–	–
Averis, J.M.M.	70	93	17	53	984	12.94	–	1	–	14
Azhar Mahmood	132	205	26	204*	5566	31.09	6	29	–	116
Balcombe, D.J.	7	9	1	73	127	15.87	–	1	–	2
Ball, M.C.J.	193	295	54	75	4633	19.22	–	16	–	233
Bandara, C.M.	100	135	29	79	1966	18.54	–	8	–	62
Banerjee, V.	9	15	3	29	139	11.58	–	–	–	2
Banks, O.A.C.	51	78	14	90	1474	23.03	–	8	–	30
Bartholomew, I.D.	1	2	–	42	60	30.00	–	–	–	–
Bartram, T.S.	2	2	1	2*	4	4.00	–	–	–	–
Batty, G.J.	93	144	27	133	3152	26.94	2	15	–	68
Batty, J.N.	144	218	27	168*	6270	32.82	12	31	1	378/51
Begg, C.G.	2	3	–	2	4	1.33	–	–	–	2
Bell, I.R.	100	172	17	262*	6756	43.58	17	35	2	61
Benham, C.C.	18	31	1	95	823	27.43	–	5	–	14
Benkenstein, D.M.	157	234	28	259	9575	46.48	24	48	2	113
Benning, J.G.E.	20	34	3	128	1165	37.58	4	5	–	8
Best, T.L.	48	61	13	42*	582	12.12	–	–	–	13
Betts, M.M.	117	168	37	73	1897	14.48	–	5	–	38
Bichel, A.J.	166	214	21	142	4954	25.66	6	21	–	79

F-C	M	I	NO	HS	Runs	Avge	100	50	1000	Ct/St
Bicknell, D.J.	324	560	43	235*	19931	38.55	46	91	9	107
Bicknell, M.P.	292	358	87	141	6740	24.87	3	26	–	103
Birt, T.R.	34	62	3	181	2382	40.37	6	13	1	15
Blackwell, I.D.	115	177	13	247*	6372	38.85	16	29	2	45
Blain, J.A.R.	38	43	16	53	353	13.07	–	1	–	10
Bopara, R.S.	48	79	13	159	2246	34.03	3	8	–	35
Borrington, P.M.	3	4	–	38	88	22.00	–	–	–	–
Botha, A.G.	84	137	21	156*	2889	24.90	3	12	–	62
Bott, M.D.	1	2	–	20	26	13.00	–	–	–	1
Boyce, M.A.G.	1	2	–	6	10	5.00	–	–	–	–
Bradshaw, D.P.	1	2	–	20	26	13.00	–	–	–	–
Brathwaite, R.M.R.	3	3	2	24*	41	41.00	–	–	–	–
Bravo, D.J.	66	122	6	197	3490	30.08	7	17	–	47
Breese, G.R.	105	168	18	165*	3941	26.27	3	25	–	85
Bresnan, T.T.	41	56	7	94	950	19.38	–	6	–	12
Bridge, G.D.	40	66	12	52	966	17.88	–	3	–	20
Broad, S.C.J.	25	31	8	65*	387	16.82	–	2	–	8
Brophy, G.L.	63	102	14	185	2759	31.35	5	13	–	151/10
Brown, A.D.	231	365	39	295*	14428	44.25	44	57	8	235/1
Brown, D.O.	11	18	–	77	498	27.66	–	4	–	7
Brown, D.R.	209	319	41	203	8511	30.61	10	44	1	130
Brown, J.F.	105	123	51	38	508	7.05	–	–	–	21
Brown, K.R.	1	2	–	32	34	17.00	–	–	–	–
Brown, M.J.	46	81	8	133	2121	29.05	3	13	–	40
Browne, P.A.	38	67	4	83	1451	23.03	–	8	–	75/5
Bruce, J.T.A.	35	39	16	21*	159	6.91	–	–	–	10
Buckham, C.T.	3	3	2	8	14	14.00	–	–	–	2
Burrows, T.G.	3	5	–	42	104	20.80	–	–	–	10
Burton, D.A.	1	2	1	52*	53	53.00	–	1	–	–
Butcher, M.A.	255	439	34	259	16346	40.36	34	90	8	235
Caddick, A.R.	244	328	63	92	3957	14.93	–	8	–	83
Cairns, C.L.	217	341	38	158	10702	35.32	13	71	1	78
Carberry, M.A.	50	87	8	153*	2982	37.74	6	16	–	24
Carter, N.M.	71	96	19	103	1451	18.84	1	3	–	20
Celliers, G.	12	23	2	61*	325	15.47	–	2	–	11
Chambers, D.J.	1	1	–	12	12	12.00	–	–	–	1
Chapple, G.	204	281	54	155	5685	25.04	6	25	–	68
Chattergoon, S.	42	72	3	143	2256	32.69	3	12	–	31
Cherry, D.D.	33	59	1	226	1626	28.03	3	4	–	9
Chervak, J.A.	2	4	–	89	166	41.50	–	1	–	1
Chilton, M.J.	129	209	14	131	6349	32.55	16	23	1	103
Chopra, V.	9	16	1	106	569	37.93	1	4	–	7
Clark, S.G.	6	8	2	47*	102	17.00	–	–	–	2
Clarke, R.	66	108	12	214	3900	40.62	10	15	1	77
Claydon, M.E.	3	2	–	38	38	19.00	–	–	–	–
Clinton, P.J.S.	6	7	–	24	67	9.57	–	–	–	2
Clinton, R.S.	39	68	5	108*	1837	29.15	4	9	–	23
Clough, G.D.	11	15	2	55	147	11.30	–	1	–	4
Coetzer, K.J.	9	15	3	133*	456	38.00	1	2	–	–
Collingwood, P.D.	132	231	17	190	7446	34.79	16	35	2	138
Compton, N.R.D.	22	40	7	190	1521	46.09	6	5	1	10
Cook, A.N.	52	92	11	195	3915	48.33	11	22	2	56
Cook, S.J.	91	119	13	93*	1736	16.37	–	4	–	27
Cork, D.G.	265	390	50	200*	8636	25.40	8	50	–	196
Cosgrove, M.J.	36	66	4	233	2624	42.32	6	17	–	28
Cosker, D.A.	134	166	54	52	1487	13.27	–	1	–	92

F-C	M	I	NO	HS	Runs	Avge	100	50	1000	Ct/St
Crawley, J.P.	319	527	51	311*	22771	47.83	52	123	10	207/1
Croft, R.D.B.	334	495	90	143	10722	26.47	6	48	–	159
Croft, S.J.	2	2	–	17	23	11.50	–	–	–	1
Crook, A.R.	5	7	–	88	200	28.57	–	1	–	4
Crook, S.P.	19	22	4	97	610	33.88	–	4	–	7
Cross, G.D.	6	9	–	72	200	22.22	–	2	–	22/6
Cullen, D.J.	26	34	14	42	334	16.70	–	–	–	7
Cummins, R.A.G.	15	16	8	26	73	9.12	–	–	–	3
Cusden, S.M.J.	6	7	5	12*	28	14.00	–	–	–	2
Daggett, L.M.	14	20	10	12*	58	5.80	–	–	–	1
Dalrymple, J.W.M.	63	105	10	244	3422	36.02	5	18	–	35
Danish Kaneria	99	120	61	47	511	8.66	–	–	–	32
Davies, A.M.	43	65	23	62	488	11.61	–	1	–	9
Davies, A.P.	34	46	11	41*	487	13.91	–	–	–	8
Davies, S.M.	28	48	2	192	1679	36.50	4	5	1	74/8
Dawson, R.K.J.	88	132	15	87	2496	21.33	–	11	–	46
Dean, K.J.	105	141	44	54*	1130	11.64	–	2	–	20
Denly, J.L.	5	8	1	115	401	57.28	2	2	–	1
Dennington, M.J.	12	18	4	55	271	19.35	–	3	–	5
Dernbach, J.W.	6	7	4	9	18	6.00	–	–	–	1
Dexter, N.J.	11	18	5	131*	639	49.15	2	3	–	7
Dilshan, T.M.	160	259	18	200*	8957	37.16	20	39	0+2	289/27
Di Venuto, M.J.	231	409	20	230	16745	43.04	36	101	6	261
Dixey, P.G.	2	3	1	24	40	20.00	–	–	–	6
Dobson, W.T.	2	3	2	13	15	15.00	–	–	–	1
Doshi, N.D.	47	61	15	37	451	9.80	–	–	–	7
Dunbar, P.R.	1	2	–	46	50	25.00	–	–	–	–
Durston, W.J.	25	43	6	146*	1303	35.21	1	8	–	33
Ealham, M.A.	240	369	55	153*	10227	32.57	12	63	1	127
Edwards, N.J.	24	41	–	160	1306	31.85	1	5	–	17
Elliott, M.T.G.	194	357	27	203	16312	49.43	50	77	3+5	213
Ervine, S.M.	61	98	10	126	2795	31.76	4	16	–	58
Faisal Iqbal	103	159	17	200	6080	42.81	13	33	0+1	79/1
Ferley, R.S.	26	34	7	78*	502	18.59	–	2	–	8
Fisher, I.D.	75	112	19	103*	2130	22.90	1	7	–	26
Fleming, S.P.	224	368	31	274*	14759	43.79	31	86	1	299
Flintoff, A.	154	242	17	167	7914	35.17	15	46	–	164
Flower, A.	223	372	69	271*	16379	54.05	49	75	5	361/21
Flower, G.W.	168	289	22	243*	10068	37.70	21	57	–	151
Footitt, M.H.A.	5	6	4	19*	40	20.00	–	–	–	1
Foster, E.J.	3	4	1	105	210	70.00	1	1	–	1
Foster, J.S.	106	154	21	212	4588	34.49	8	22	1	276/28
Francis, J.D.	54	96	8	125*	2638	29.97	6	14	1	32
Francis, S.R.G.	58	77	33	44	509	11.56	–	–	–	18
Franklin, J.E.C.	85	125	19	208	2921	27.55	3	12	–	27
Franks, P.J.	135	197	40	123*	4157	26.47	3	20	–	44
Friedlander, M.J.	9	14	–	81	201	14.35	–	1	–	3
Frost, T.	92	134	21	135*	3178	28.12	3	16	–	225/16
Fulton, D.P.	200	352	20	208*	12125	36.52	28	53	3	266
Gale, A.W.	9	16	–	149	297	18.56	1	–	–	4
Gallian, J.E.R.	218	374	35	312	13233	39.03	34	63	6	191
Ganguly, S.C.	207	320	38	200*	12277	43.53	25	71	–	149
Gazzard, C.M.	27	42	6	74	732	20.33	–	1	–	58/1
Gerard, D.C.	1	–	–	–	–	–	–	–	–	1
Gibson, O.D.	162	244	34	155	5026	23.93	2	25	–	62
Gidman, A.P.R.	68	121	13	142	4111	38.06	8	26	2	42

F-C	M	I	NO	HS	Runs	Avge	100	50	1000	Ct/St
Gifford, W.M.	5	7	1	33	78	13.00	–	–	–	3
Gillespie, J.N.	143	189	48	201*	2552	18.09	1	6	–	56
Goddard, L.J.	9	12	4	91	265	33.12	–	1	–	17
Godleman, B.A.	1	1	1	69*	69	–	–	1	–	–
Goodwin, M.W.	194	339	24	335*	15148	48.08	46	65	5+1	116
Gough, D.	226	300	58	121	4240	17.52	1	19	–	45
Grant, R.N.	11	18	1	44	299	17.58	–	–	–	4
Gray, A.K.D.	34	50	10	104	1048	26.20	1	3	–	25
Greenidge, C.G.	41	49	7	46	348	8.28	–	–	–	15
Griffith, A.R.	35	55	14	41*	441	10.75	–	–	–	5
Griffiths, D.A.	1	1	1	16*	16	–	–	–	–	–
Groenewald, T.D.	6	9	2	76	157	22.42	–	1	–	1
Guy, S.M.	32	45	6	52*	612	15.69	–	1	–	86/12
Habib, A.	159	241	29	215	8873	41.85	21	46	2	80
Hall, A.J.	115	169	23	163	4999	34.23	5	34	–	83
Hamilton-Brown, R.J.	1	2	–	9	14	7.00	–	–	–	1
Hardinges, M.A.	35	52	6	172	1175	25.54	3	3	–	16
Harmison, B.W.	9	17	2	110	563	37.53	2	3	–	5
Harmison, S.J.	130	179	49	42	1258	9.67	–	–	–	22
Harris, A.J.	117	158	39	41*	1030	8.65	–	–	–	34
Harris, P.L.	40	49	9	47	625	15.62	–	–	–	17
Harrison, A.J.	3	3	1	34*	37	18.50	–	–	–	–
Harrison, D.S.	68	98	14	88	1341	15.96	–	4	–	24
Harrison, P.W.	10	16	4	54	297	24.75	–	1	–	15
Harvey, I.J.	163	269	28	209*	8120	33.69	13	46	–	110
Heather, S.A.	2	2	–	7	7	3.50	–	–	–	1
Hemp, D.L.	236	402	37	247*	13319	36.49	26	71	6	162
Henderson, C.W.	163	220	54	71	3031	18.25	–	8	–	63
Henderson, T.	73	117	16	81	1749	17.31	–	6	–	23
Heywood, J.J.N.	8	12	2	27	65	6.50	–	–	–	12
Hick, G.A.	500	829	80	405*	39460	52.68	132	150	19+1	668
Hildreth, J.C.	44	75	7	227*	2504	36.82	5	14	–	38
Hillyard, N.J.	1	1	–	79	79	79.00	–	1	–	–
Hinds, R.O.	77	125	15	168	4117	37.42	5	25	–	58
Hobbiss, M.H.	1	1	1	78*	78	–	–	1	–	–
Hodd, A.J.	5	6	2	57*	141	35.25	–	2	–	11
Hodge, B.J.	184	324	31	302*	13970	47.67	43	50	2+3	108
Hodnett, G.P.	1	2	–	49	59	29.50	–	–	–	1
Hodson, W.G.	1	2	–	29	29	14.50	–	–	–	1
Hogg, K.W.	29	37	2	70	702	20.05	–	5	–	10
Hoggard, M.J.	142	184	58	89*	1112	8.82	–	2	–	43
Holt, D.R.	2	1	–	5	5	5.00	–	–	–	1
Hooper, J.H.P.	1	1	1	3*	3	–	–	–	–	–
Hopkinson, C.D.	28	46	1	74	1126	25.02	–	9	–	15
Horton, P.J.	12	18	3	99	601	40.06	–	4	–	6/1
Hunter, I.D.	49	67	16	65	897	17.58	–	2	–	15
Huntington, C.J.	2	3	–	29	37	12.33	–	–	–	–
Hussey, D.J.	83	126	15	232*	5641	50.81	21	21	3	91
Hutton, B.L.	106	182	15	152	5516	33.02	17	18	2	132
Iftikhar Anjum	72	114	26	78	1498	17.02	–	4	–	43
Iles, J.A.	1	–	–	–	–	–	–	–	–	–
Imran Farhat	102	174	11	242	6845	41.99	15	29	0+1	102
Inzamam–ul–Haq	234	374	55	329	16337	51.21	45	84	0+2	165
Iqbal, M.M.	4	8	3	20	53	10.60	–	–	–	2
Irani, R.C.	228	367	47	207*	13007	40.64	26	72	7	75
Jacklin, B.D.	2	4	2	19*	27	13.50	–	–	–	–

F-C	M	I	NO	HS	Runs	Avge	100	50	1000	Ct/St
James, G.D.	11	20	1	44	307	16.15	–	–	–	4
Jannisar Khan	44	65	8	159	1484	26.03	2	7	–	25
Jaques, P.A.	86	151	8	244	8357	58.44	24	40	4+1	71
Jayasuriya, S.T.	246	388	33	340	14083	39.67	29	67	0+1	156
Jayawardena, D.P.M.D.	160	252	19	374	11774	50.53	33	55	0+2	196
Jayawardena, H.A.P.W.	123	189	22	143	3970	23.77	3	16	–	294/54
Jefferson, W.I.	67	120	11	222	4300	39.44	11	17	1	58
Jogia, K.A.	2	3	–	20	24	8.00	–	–	–	2
Johnson, R.L.	162	223	28	118	3497	17.93	2	8	–	62
Jones, G.O.	73	107	13	108*	2964	31.53	4	18	–	223/15
Jones, M.C.	1	1	–	1	1	1.00	–	–	–	–
Jones, P.S.	100	120	30	105	1549	17.21	1	4	–	21
Jones, S.P.	75	90	30	46	716	11.93	–	–	–	17
Joseph, R.H.	19	25	9	29	152	9.50	–	–	–	5
Joseph, S.C.	78	136	9	211*	3984	31.37	8	17	–	75
Joyce, E.C.	94	158	14	211	6815	47.32	17	37	5	79
Kalam, T.	3	3	–	8	14	4.66	–	–	–	1
Kamran Akmal	110	170	22	174	4587	30.99	8	19	–	356/35
Kapugedera, C.K.	12	20	5	134*	645	43.00	1	4	–	3
Kartik, M.	94	110	13	96	1861	19.18	–	11	–	54
Katich, S.M.	148	253	34	228*	10846	49.52	29	57	2+3	139
Keedy, G.	147	167	88	57	861	10.89	–	1	–	41
Keegan, C.B.	47	57	6	44	607	11.90	–	–	–	14
Kelly, R.	23	37	4	93	777	23.54	–	6	–	13
Kemp, J.M.	87	141	17	188	4594	37.04	10	22	–	99
Kemp, R.A.	2	4	–	5	7	1.75	–	–	–	–
Kervezee, A.N.	5	6	2	46*	107	26.75	–	–	–	1
Key, R.W.T.	160	278	15	221	10650	40.49	30	42	4	100
Khan, Z.	95	121	27	75	1371	14.58	–	2	–	29
Killeen, N.	98	143	30	48	1297	11.47	–	–	–	25
King, R.E.	6	7	–	30	49	7.00	–	–	–	–
Kirby, S.P.	76	106	36	57	553	7.90	–	1	–	16
Kirtley, R.J.	158	218	73	59	1878	12.95	–	3	–	52
Klokker, F.A.	1	1	–	40	40	40.00	–	–	–	3
Klusener, L.	160	225	49	174	6982	39.67	16	32	1	87
Knappett, J.P.T.	10	16	2	100*	507	36.21	1	3	–	21/3
Knight, N.V.	240	409	43	303*	16172	44.18	40	77	7	292
Kruis, G.J.	105	151	45	59	1491	14.06	–	2	–	41
Kulasekara, M.D.N.	50	67	19	95	949	19.77	–	3	–	15
Kumble, A.	216	277	56	154*	5045	22.82	6	16	–	106
Lamb, G.A.	29	44	5	100*	903	23.15	1	5	–	24
Lamb, N.J.	6	10	1	62	136	15.11	–	1	–	–
Langer, J.L.	291	511	48	342	23511	50.77	72	90	3+6	242
Latouf, K.J.	1	1	–	29	29	29.00	–	–	–	–
Law, S.G.	338	554	61	263	25060	50.83	75	115	8+2	378
Lawson, M.A.K.	13	19	4	44	188	12.53	–	–	–	6
Lee, J.E.	1	2	1	21*	22	22.00	–	–	–	–
Lee, N.T.	4	7	–	43	90	12.85	–	–	–	1
Lehmann, D.S.	273	459	32	339	24865	58.23	80	107	5+6	139
Lett, R.J.	3	4	–	50	65	16.25	–	1	–	–
Lewis, J.	158	222	47	62	2513	14.36	–	5	–	38
Lewis, J.J.B.	205	365	26	210*	10821	31.92	16	66	4	117
Lewis, M.L.	75	104	31	54*	672	9.20	–	1	–	35
Lewry, J.D.	152	205	53	72	1609	10.58	–	2	–	41
Liddle, C.J.	7	6	3	4*	6	2.00	–	–	–	2
Linley, T.E.	8	8	–	42	75	9.37	–	–	–	1

F-C	M	I	NO	HS	Runs	Avge	100	50	1000	Ct/St
Logan, R.J.	46	64	13	37*	494	9.68	–	–	–	15
Loudon, A.G.R.	58	95	5	172	2724	30.26	2	17	–	41
Louw, J.	77	113	17	124	1798	18.72	1	7	–	27
Love, M.L.	196	342	32	300*	15611	50.35	40	72	2+3	248
Lowe, J.A.	9	18	–	80	341	18.94	–	1	–	6
Loye, M.B.	212	336	29	322*	12839	41.82	38	52	6	104
Lucas, D.S.	23	28	8	49	436	21.80	–	–	–	3
Lumb, M.J.	81	141	12	144	4286	33.22	8	25	1	48
Lungley, T.	23	36	6	47	424	14.13	–	–	–	8
McCullum, B.B.	55	90	5	160	2815	33.11	6	14	–	130/11
McGrath, A.	170	290	23	174	9816	36.76	22	46	2	122
McLaren, R.	23	35	4	140	1019	32.87	1	6	–	14
McLean, J.J.	13	18	1	68	464	27.29	–	5	–	11
McMahon, P.J.	18	21	3	99	340	18.88	–	2	–	11
Maddy, D.L.	214	350	21	229*	10673	32.44	19	53	4	228
Maharoof, M.F.	31	44	5	72	828	21.23	–	4	–	12
Maher, J.P.	178	318	30	223	11972	41.56	25	58	1+2	181/3
Mahmood, S.I.	40	50	7	94	655	15.23	–	2	–	7
Malan, D.J.	4	7	–	64	158	22.57	–	1	–	2
Malik, M.N.	37	48	17	39*	276	8.90	–	–	–	3
Malinga, S.L.	64	80	35	30	377	8.37	–	–	–	21
Mansoor Amjad	35	51	4	122*	1415	30.10	2	7	–	19
Marshall, H.J.H.	75	125	8	168	3913	33.44	8	19	1	37
Marshall, S.J.	18	29	6	126*	773	33.60	1	3	–	4
Martin-Jenkins, R.S.C.	130	201	25	205*	5357	30.43	3	27	1	34
Mascarenhas, A.D.	146	220	24	131	4769	24.33	7	16	–	58
Mason, M.S.	68	87	23	63	924	14.43	–	3	–	13
Massey, I.R.	2	4	–	46	110	27.50	–	–	–	–
Masters, D.D.	78	94	20	119	953	12.87	1	2	–	26
Maunders, J.K.	56	102	3	180	2969	29.98	5	14	–	26
Middlebrook, J.D.	104	148	16	115	3212	24.33	3	12	–	47
Mierkalns, J.A.	1	1	–	18	18	18.00	–	–	–	–
Miller, D.J.	2	1	1	0*	0	–	–	–	–	–
Mitchell, D.K.H.	10	18	4	134*	478	34.14	1	4	–	9
Mohammad Akram	122	149	43	35*	927	8.74	–	–	–	30
Mohammad Amin	4	4	2	25*	42	21.00	–	–	–	1
Mohammad Asif	64	85	34	42	426	8.35	–	–	–	26
Mohammad Hafeez	80	134	5	180	4250	32.94	8	22	–	64
Mohammad Sami	75	98	32	49	905	13.71	–	–	–	27
Md Yousuf Youhana	109	179	16	223	8008	49.12	23	40	–	74
Mohammed, D.	49	76	11	52	1018	15.66	–	3	–	29
Mohammed, J.	4	8	1	124*	214	30.57	1	–	–	4
Mongia, D.	118	179	19	308*	8004	50.02	27	28	0+1	118
Montgomerie, R.R.	234	404	32	196	13208	35.50	27	73	5	217
Moore, S.C.	53	96	10	246	3460	40.23	5	19	2	26
Moreton, S.J.P.	6	11	–	74	273	24.81	–	2	–	2
Morgan, E.J.G.	10	19	–	151	438	23.05	1	1	–	4/1
Morris, J.C.	5	9	–	81	185	20.55	–	1	–	3
Morris, R.K.	2	2	–	7	8	4.00	–	–	–	1
Morse, E.J.	5	4	3	7*	7	7.00	–	–	–	3
Morton, R.S.	59	97	6	114	3185	35.00	7	20	–	71
Mubarak, J.	78	137	12	169	3606	28.84	3	20	–	74
Muchall, G.J.	79	143	6	219	4009	29.26	7	19	–	51
Mullaney, S.J.	1	1	–	44	44	44.00	–	–	–	1
Mumtaz Habib	2	3	–	10	12	4.00	–	–	–	–
Munday, M.K.	19	16	8	17*	58	7.25	–	–	–	8

F-C	M	I	NO	HS	Runs	Avge	100	50	1000	Ct/St
Muralitharan, M.	199	245	71	67	1968	11.31	–	1	–	109
Murtagh, C.P.	5	7	2	37*	98	19.60	–	–	–	2
Murtagh, T.J.	38	53	22	74*	933	30.09	–	6	–	17
Mushtaq Ahmed	285	357	50	90*	4871	15.86	–	19	–	112
Mustard, P.	50	79	4	130	2103	28.04	2	9	–	151/7
Naik, J.K.H.	3	2	–	13	14	7.00	–	–	–	2
Napier, G.R.	68	98	18	106*	2429	30.36	2	16	–	30
Nash, C.D.	13	19	2	67	547	32.17	–	5	–	5
Nash, D.C.	124	178	37	114	4755	33.72	7	24	–	252/21
Naved-ul-Hasan	82	118	14	139	2452	23.57	2	8	–	44
Needham, J.	2	4	1	29	36	12.00	–	–	–	–
Nel, A.	83	93	32	44	844	13.83	–	–	–	30
New, T.J.	18	30	4	89	837	32.19	–	8	–	20/2
Newby, O.J.	11	11	4	38*	100	14.28	–	–	–	1
Newman, S.A.	58	101	3	219	4449	45.39	10	25	3	45
Nicholson, M.J.	86	125	24	106*	2114	20.93	2	4	–	46
Nixon, P.A.	297	437	99	144*	11122	32.90	16	52	1	786/65
Noffke, A.A.	77	96	19	114*	1893	24.58	1	6	–	31
North, M.J.	85	150	16	219	5800	43.28	14	33	0+1	60
Oberoi, S.	10	17	1	247	745	46.56	2	2	–	9
O'Brien, N.J.	41	59	10	176	1461	29.81	2	7	–	111/19
Onions, G.	28	42	13	40	321	11.06	–	–	–	6
Ormond, J.	123	148	36	57	1744	15.57	–	2	–	26
O'Shea, M.P.	3	5	–	24	52	10.40	–	–	–	1
Owen, F.G.	1	2	–	1	1	0.50	–	–	–	–
Paget, C.D.	4	4	2	7	7	3.50	–	–	–	–
Palladino, A.P.	23	24	10	41	178	12.71	–	–	–	10
Panesar, M.S.	49	62	26	39*	304	8.44	–	–	–	13
Park, G.T.	13	21	6	100*	647	43.13	1	2	–	19
Parker, L.C.	20	33	3	140	903	30.10	1	4	–	10
Parry, S.J.P.	1	2	–	36	66	33.00	–	–	–	–
Parsons, K.A.	130	209	23	193*	5324	28.62	6	28	–	115
Patel, M.M.	207	276	51	87	3878	17.23	–	16	–	101
Patel, S.R.	13	19	2	173	738	43.41	2	3	–	4
Patterson, S.A.	6	7	1	46	85	14.16	–	–	–	2
Peng, N.	76	131	2	158	3089	23.94	4	14	–	45
Peploe, C.T.	27	38	6	46	504	15.75	–	–	–	9
Peters, S.D.	132	223	19	178	6400	31.37	12	32	2	97
Pettini, M.L.	28	48	5	208*	1734	40.32	3	8	1	24
Phillips, B.J.	80	114	17	100*	2009	20.71	1	11	–	19
Phillips, T.J.	34	46	7	89	840	21.53	–	2	–	23
Phythian, M.J.	5	6	2	62*	92	23.00	–	1	–	14/1
Pietersen, C.	21	32	9	45	418	18.17	–	–	–	4
Pietersen, K.P.	98	161	13	254*	7584	51.24	26	31	3	91
Pipe, D.J.	45	67	9	104*	1296	22.34	1	5	–	124/14
Plunkett, L.E.	40	60	14	74*	887	19.28	–	2	–	13
Poonia, N.S.	1	1	–	35	35	35.00	–	–	–	–
Pope, S.P.	5	8	3	17*	65	13.00	–	–	–	10/1
Pothas, N.	161	249	43	165	8075	39.19	19	40	–	454/38
Powell, D.B.	63	87	14	62	983	13.46	–	3	–	19
Powell, M.J. (Gm)	154	262	23	299	9445	39.51	21	44	5	94
Powell, M.J. (Wa)	134	224	11	236	6857	32.19	12	37	1	97
Pratt, G.J.	53	94	1	150	2410	25.91	1	15	1	39
Price, R.W.	79	124	23	117*	1608	15.92	1	7	–	28
Prior, M.J.	102	160	15	201*	5676	39.14	14	29	2	224/18
Prowting, N.R.	3	5	–	27	60	12.00	–	–	–	1

F-C	M	I	NO	HS	Runs	Avge	100	50	1000	Ct/St
Pyrah, R.M.	6	10	1	78	236	26.22	–	1	–	1
Ramprakash, M.R.	386	636	79	301*	28633	51.40	87	130	16	222
Rashid, A.	5	6	–	63	115	19.16	–	1	–	2
Rayner, O.P.	5	6	1	101	133	26.60	1	–	–	6
Read, C.M.W.	171	258	40	160	6790	31.14	9	37	–	495/23
Rees, G.P.	3	5	1	57	84	21.00	–	1	–	1
Richards, M.A.	8	12	2	43	154	15.40	–	–	–	7
Richardson, A.	78	80	31	91	538	10.97	–	1	–	20
Richardson, A.P.	25	38	11	31*	194	7.18	–	–	–	11
Robinson, D.D.J.	181	320	15	200	10082	33.05	21	49	3	152
Rogers, C.J.L.	79	143	9	319	6360	47.46	17	30	1	75
Rosenberg, M.C.	6	10	1	86	255	28.33	–	1	–	1
Rowe, D.T.	1	1	–	0	0	0.00	–	–	–	1
Rudge, W.D.	9	10	2	15	44	5.50	–	–	–	3
Sadler, J.L.	42	72	12	145	2326	38.76	3	15	1	31
Sadler, O.J.	1	2	1	22	39	39.00	–	–	–	–
Saggers, M.J.	95	119	32	64	1010	11.60	–	2	–	26
Saker, N.C.	10	14	1	58*	198	15.23	–	1	–	4
Sales, D.J.G.	155	243	20	303*	8937	40.07	17	46	4	130
Salisbury, I.D.K.	305	391	79	101*	6445	20.65	2	23	–	195
Salman Butt	47	82	3	206	2745	34.74	7	13	–	16
Samaraweera, T.T.	166	220	46	206	7422	42.65	15	44	0+1	135
Samiullah Khan	33	38	14	17*	121	5.04	–	–	–	9
Sammy, D.J.G.	29	51	5	87	1005	21.84	–	8	–	43
Sangakkara, K.C.	135	214	14	287	8098	40.49	14	43	0+1	289/33
Savill, T.E.	17	24	4	59	363	18.15	–	3	–	12
Sayers, J.J.	39	65	5	147	2095	34.91	5	11	–	21
Schofield, C.P.	70	98	14	99	2537	30.20	–	21	–	42
Scott, B.J.M.	34	54	12	101*	1005	23.92	1	4	–	86/11
Scott, G.M.	17	33	2	133	891	28.74	1	4	–	10
Shafayat, B.M.	61	106	3	161	3277	31.81	6	18	1	51/4
Shah, O.A.	168	284	23	203	10778	41.29	28	58	6	129
Shahid Afridi	89	151	4	164	4686	31.87	11	22	–	55
Shahid Nazir	111	137	28	60*	1371	12.57	–	2	–	31
Shahzad, A.	1	1	–	2	2	2.00	–	–	–	–
Shantry, A.J.	6	7	5	38*	66	33.00	–	–	–	2
Sharif, Z.K.	12	19	5	140*	614	43.85	2	3	–	3
Sheikh, M.A.	47	66	16	58*	1238	24.76	–	4	–	5
Sheriyar, A.	152	165	65	21	829	8.29	–	–	–	22
Shilvock, D.J.F.	2	1	–	15	15	15.00	–	–	–	–
Shirazi, D.C.	4	5	1	46*	139	34.75	–	–	–	2
Shoaib Malik	67	101	13	148*	2468	28.04	6	10	–	31
Shreck, C.E.	34	40	21	19	78	4.10	–	–	–	8
Sidebottom, R.J.	100	126	36	54	1024	11.37	–	1	–	39
Sillence, R.J.	26	37	1	101	866	24.05	1	4	–	8
Silverwood, C.E.W.	164	221	44	80	2782	15.71	–	9	–	38
Simmons, L.M.P.	39	68	6	200	1883	30.37	3	10	–	47/4
Singh, A.	108	176	7	187	5437	32.17	11	24	2	42
Smith, B.F.	282	441	50	204	16235	41.52	40	77	7	173
Smith, B.M.	2	1	–	0	0	0.00	–	–	–	–
Smith, D.R.	51	83	5	114	2154	27.61	5	6	–	48
Smith, D.S.	87	158	5	181	5604	36.62	12	29	0+1	76
Smith, E.T.	168	290	15	213	11173	40.62	29	46	7	73
Smith, G.J.	147	179	56	68	1619	13.16	–	2	–	30
Smith, G.M.	14	27	2	86	538	21.52	–	3	–	5
Smith, T.C.P.	16	19	5	49	234	16.71	–	–	–	15

F-C	M	I	NO	HS	Runs	Avge	100	50	1000	Ct/St
Smith, W.R.	29	44	3	156	1123	27.39	2	3	–	18
Snape, J.N.	121	180	31	131	4194	28.14	3	23	–	74
Snell, S.D.	2	4	1	83*	141	47.00	–	1	–	4
Solanki, V.S.	202	332	23	222	11260	36.44	20	61	3	231
Spearman, C.M.	179	325	15	341	11954	38.56	28	51	3	171
Spencer, D.J.	16	18	2	75	233	14.56	–	1	–	10
Spurway, S.H.P.	3	4	–	83	164	41.00	–	1	–	7
Stearn, C.P.	2	2	1	38	71	71.00	–	–	–	1
Stephenson, J.P.	304	512	56	202*	14773	32.39	25	78	5	182
Stevens, D.I.	113	188	13	208	5716	32.66	10	35	1	95
Steyn, D.W.	35	44	12	82	317	9.90	–	1	–	7
Stiff, D.A.	8	6	3	18	57	19.00	–	–	–	1
Strauss, A.J.	121	215	12	176	8544	42.08	22	37	3	89
Streak, H.H.	164	249	45	131	5406	26.50	6	25	–	58
Stubbings, S.D.	106	191	8	151	5879	32.12	10	33	3	48
Styris, S.B.	109	179	18	212*	5181	32.18	9	26	–	88
Suppiah, A.V.	24	40	–	123	1069	26.72	1	6	–	9
Sutcliffe, I.J.	179	285	26	203	9097	35.12	15	49	3	102
Sutton, L.D.	100	170	23	151*	4764	32.40	7	16	–	219/10
Swann, G.P.	141	202	11	183	4932	25.82	4	23	–	94
Tahir, N.	20	22	9	49	281	21.61	–	–	–	2
Taufeeq Umar	85	148	5	176	5355	37.44	10	31	–	86
Taylor, B.V.	53	68	26	40	431	10.26	–	–	–	6
Taylor, C.G.	82	148	7	196	4602	32.63	11	16	1	55
Taylor, C.R.	31	53	3	121	1324	26.48	3	6	–	18
Ten Doeschate, R.N.	20	24	4	259*	1326	66.30	6	3	–	9
Tharanga, W.U.	43	74	1	165	2227	30.50	4	11	–	41
Thomas, S.D.	169	234	44	138	3977	20.93	2	18	–	56
Thornely, D.J.	47	78	7	261*	3038	42.78	6	19	0+1	28
Thornicroft, N.D.	7	12	5	30	54	7.71	–	–	–	1
Thorp, C.D.	23	35	2	75	441	13.36	–	2	–	9
Tomlinson, J.A.	17	26	11	23	76	5.06	–	–	–	5
Tredwell, J.C.	39	55	7	61	953	19.85	–	3	–	41
Trego, P.D.	34	52	4	140	1364	28.41	4	5	–	13
Tremlett, C.T.	61	80	22	64	1015	17.50	–	2	–	16
Trescothick, M.E.	207	360	18	219	12227	35.75	24	63	–	240
Trott, I.J.L.	83	145	14	210	5297	40.43	11	29	3	84
Troughton, J.O.	65	104	8	131*	3567	37.15	10	20	1	29
Tudge, K.D.	1	2	1	4	7	7.00	–	–	–	–
Tudor, A.J.	106	135	28	144	2489	23.26	2	8	–	31
Turk, N.R.K.	1	1	–	24	24	24.00	–	–	–	–
Turner, M.L.	3	2	1	18	19	19.00	–	–	–	–
Udal, S.D.	255	359	67	117*	6727	23.03	1	28	–	116
Umar Gul	35	38	6	46	349	10.90	–	–	–	10
Vaas, W.P.U.C.J.	163	219	44	134	4064	23.22	3	16	–	49
Van der Wath, J.J.	53	83	14	113*	1734	25.13	2	10	–	20
Vandort, M.G.	91	149	13	226	4942	36.33	10	24	–	78
Van Jaarsveld, M.	152	259	24	262*	10453	44.48	28	50	2+1	203
Vaughan, M.P.	230	407	25	197	14549	38.08	39	61	4	106
Vettori, D.L.	115	157	22	137*	3289	24.36	3	17	–	53
Vincent, L.	80	128	9	224	4442	37.32	10	27	–	100
Wagg, G.G.	19	29	3	94	601	23.11	–	3	–	5
Wagh, M.A.	140	234	20	315	8077	37.74	20	34	4	71
Wainwright, D.J.	9	11	2	62	228	25.33	–	1	–	6
Wake, C.J.	3	5	–	34	47	9.40	–	–	–	1
Walker, M.J.	165	273	31	275*	8941	36.94	22	38	3	115

F-C	M	I	NO	HS	Runs	Avge	100	50	1000	Ct/St
Walker, N.G.E.	23	29	6	80	415	18.04	–	3	–	9
Wallace, M.A.	102	168	16	121	4240	27.89	4	23	–	273/16
Walters, S.J.	3	6	–	67	166	27.66	–	1	–	3
Warne, S.K.	278	379	47	107*	6342	19.10	2	24	–	239
Warren, R.J.	146	238	26	201*	7776	36.67	15	41	1	128/5
Waters, H.T.	12	20	9	34	48	4.36	–	–	–	1
Watkins, R.E.	19	34	2	87	685	21.40	–	2	–	12
Wedge, S.A.	4	2	2	0*	0	–	–	–	–	–
Weekes, P.N.	236	372	55	171*	11060	34.88	20	55	2	210
Welch, G.	171	265	43	115*	5075	22.86	2	21	–	73
Wessels, M.H.	25	42	5	107	1001	27.05	3	4	–	54/6
Westfield, M.S.	4	6	2	32	41	10.25	–	–	–	1
Weston, W.P.C.	228	402	34	205	12591	34.21	24	64	4	128
Westwood, I.J.	26	48	7	178	1534	37.41	3	7	–	11
Wharf, A.G.	96	144	22	113	2607	21.36	3	12	–	53
Whelan, C.D.	2	2	1	9*	10	10.00	–	–	–	–
White, A.R.	8	10	3	152*	334	47.71	1	1	–	5
White, C.	265	420	57	186	11949	32.91	20	60	–	163
White, C.L.	62	102	11	260*	3249	35.70	6	14	1	63
White, G.G.	2	3	–	37	37	12.33	–	–	–	–
White, R.A.	42	72	4	277	1944	28.58	2	8	–	24
White, W.A.	3	4	2	19*	45	22.50	–	–	–	–
Wigley, D.H.	19	23	7	28	175	10.93	–	–	–	9
Willoughby, C.M.	135	159	65	47	481	5.11	–	–	–	32
Wilshaw, P.J.	3	5	–	63	217	43.40	–	3	–	3
Windows, M.G.N.	170	302	21	184	9103	32.39	16	47	3	92
Wiseman, P.J.	157	213	44	130	3487	20.63	2	13	–	72
Woakes, C.R.	1	1	–	4	4	4.00	–	–	–	3
Wood, J.R.	4	7	–	31	94	13.42	–	–	–	0/1
Wood, M.J. (Sm)	74	129	6	297	4320	35.12	9	27	1	25
Wood, M.J. (Y)	128	223	20	207	6797	33.48	16	30	4	113
Woods, N.J.	6	8	2	26	131	21.83	–	–	–	3
Wright, B.J.	1	1	–	72	72	72.00	–	1	–	2
Wright, C.J.C.	16	23	3	76	429	21.45	–	2	–	5
Wright, L.J.	21	30	3	100	568	21.03	1	3	–	13
Yardy, M.H.	70	120	13	257	4184	39.10	9	18	1	54
Yasir Arafat	98	152	22	100	3485	26.80	1	20	–	33
Young, P.J.W.	3	4	1	40	95	31.66	–	–	–	1
Younis Khan	101	163	17	267	7465	51.13	24	31	0+1	106
Zoysa, D.N.T.	96	115	21	66	1341	14.26	–	4	–	17

BOWLING

'50wS' denotes instances of taking 50 or more wickets in a season. Where these have been achieved outside the British Isles they are shown after a plus sign.

	Runs	Wkts	Avge	Best	5wI	10wM	50wS
Abdul Razzaq	9613	295	32.58	7- 51	10	2	–
Ackerman, H.D.	57	0					
Adams, A.R.	6422	246	26.10	6- 25	9	1	–
Adams, C.J.	1913	41	46.65	4- 28	–	–	–
Adams, J.H.K.	390	7	55.71	2- 16	–	–	–
Adnan, M.H.	318	4	79.50	1- 4	–	–	–
Afzaal, U.	4108	78	52.66	4-101	–	–	–
Ahmed, J.S.	217	3	72.33	2- 50	–	–	–
Ali, Kabir	8424	299	28.17	8- 53	13	2	3

F-C	Runs	Wkts	Avge	Best	5wI	10wM	50wS
Ali, Kadeer	289	3	96.33	1- 4	–	–	–
Ali, M.M.	333	3	111.00	2- 50	–	–	–
Ali, S.M.B.	9060	274	33.06	6- 37	11	2	0+1
Allenby, J.	23	0					
Ambrose, T.R.	1	0					
Amjad Khan	6192	190	32.58	6- 52	6	–	2
Anderson, J.M.	5189	190	27.31	6- 23	8	1	2
Andrew, G.M.	989	28	35.32	4- 63	–	–	–
Anwar, O.S.	1	0					
Anyon, J.E.	1930	50	38.60	5- 83	1	–	–
Arshad Khan	13182	562	23.45	8- 80	29	6	0+2
Astle, N.J.	4787	149	32.12	6- 22	2	–	–
Averis, J.M.M.	6746	156	43.24	6- 32	5	–	–
Azhar Mahmood	11666	443	26.33	8- 61	16	3	0+1
Balcombe, D.J.	841	17	49.47	5-112	1	–	–
Ball, M.C.J.	14682	389	37.74	8- 46	13	1	–
Bandara, C.M.	6647	255	26.06	8- 49	9	2	–
Banerjee, V.	1089	16	68.06	4-150	–	–	–
Banks, O.A.C.	5601	150	37.34	7- 70	6	1	–
Bartram, T.S.	145	3	48.33	2- 84	–	–	–
Batty, G.J.	8887	280	31.73	7- 52	10	1	2
Batty, J.N.	61	1	61.00	1- 21	–	–	–
Bell, I.R.	1478	47	31.44	4- 4	–	–	–
Benham, C.C.	37	0					
Benkenstein, D.M.	2771	82	33.79	4- 16	–	–	–
Benning, J.G.E.	703	11	63.90	3- 57	–	–	–
Best, T.L.	4104	153	26.82	7- 33	6	1	–
Betts, M.M.	10723	347	30.90	9- 64	14	2	–
Bichel, A.J.	17839	680	26.23	9- 93	32	6	1+3
Bicknell, D.J.	1015	29	35.00	3- 7	–	–	–
Bicknell, M.P.	26589	1061	25.06	9- 45	44	4	11
Birt, T.R.	119	2	59.50	1- 24	–	–	–
Blackwell, I.D.	8238	188	43.81	7- 90	7	–	–
Blain, J.A.R.	3887	102	38.10	6- 42	2	–	–
Bopara, R.S.	2298	46	49.95	5- 75	1	–	–
Botha, A.G.	7084	205	34.55	8- 53	5	1	–
Bradshaw, D.P.	45	0					
Brathwaite, R.M.R.	351	6	58.50	3- 61	–	–	–
Bravo, D.J.	3319	110	30.17	6- 11	6	–	–
Breese, G.R.	7898	268	29.47	7- 60	12	3	–
Bresnan, T.T.	3445	104	33.12	5- 42	2	–	–
Bridge, G.D.	3141	89	35.29	6- 84	1	–	–
Broad, S.C.J.	2402	80	30.02	5- 83	4	–	–
Brophy, G.L.	1	0					
Brown, A.D.	592	5	118.40	3- 25	–	–	–
Brown, D.O.	679	10	67.90	2- 48	–	–	–
Brown, D.R.	16177	567	28.53	8- 89	21	4	4
Brown, J.F.	11975	374	32.01	7- 69	21	5	3
Browne, P.A.	0	0					
Bruce, J.T.A.	3026	85	35.60	5- 43	1	–	–
Buckham, C.T.	187	0					
Burton, D.A.	129	0					
Butcher, M.A.	4209	125	33.67	5- 86	1	–	–
Caddick, A.R.	28082	1070	26.24	9- 32	73	16	11

F-C	Runs	Wkts	Avge	Best	5wI	10wM	50wS
Cairns, C.L.	18322	647	28.31	8- 47	30	6	3
Carberry, M.A.	365	5	73.00	2- 85	–	–	–
Carter, N.M.	6864	179	38.34	6- 63	5	–	–
Celliers, G.	182	2	91.00	1- 31	–	–	–
Chapple, G.	17325	604	28.68	6- 30	24	1	4
Chattergoon, S.	106	6	17.66	4- 9	–	–	–
Cherry, D.D.	13	0					
Chilton, M.J.	651	10	65.10	1- 1	–	–	–
Clark, S.G.	323	13	24.84	5- 29	1	–	–
Clarke, R.	3952	95	41.60	4- 21	–	–	–
Claydon, M.E.	263	3	87.66	1- 27	–	–	–
Clinton, R.S.	152	2	76.00	2- 30	–	–	–
Clough, G.D.	684	12	57.00	3- 69	–	–	–
Coetzer, K.J.	22	0					
Collingwood, P.D.	4021	100	40.21	5- 52	1	–	–
Compton, N.R.D.	103	1	103.00	1- 94	–	–	–
Cook, A.N.	111	3	37.00	3- 13	–	–	–
Cook, S.J.	7582	237	31.99	8- 63	8	–	–
Cork, D.G.	22266	845	26.35	9- 43	32	5	7
Cosgrove, M.J.	579	13	44.53	1- 0	–	–	–
Cosker, D.A.	12302	318	38.68	6-140	2	–	–
Crawley, J.P.	261	2	130.50	1- 7	–	–	–
Croft, R.D.B.	34324	948	36.20	8- 66	41	8	8
Croft, S.J.	49	0					
Crook, A.R.	509	7	72.71	3- 71	–	–	–
Crook, S.P.	1532	29	52.82	3- 46	–	–	–
Cullen, D.J.	3347	83	40.32	5- 38	4	–	–
Cummins, R.A.G.	1404	29	48.41	4- 46	–	–	–
Cusden, S.M.J.	594	18	33.00	4- 68	–	–	–
Daggett, L.M.	1212	33	36.72	8- 94	2	–	–
Dalrymple, J.W.M.	4681	108	43.34	5- 49	1	–	–
Danish Kaneria	12586	467	26.95	7- 39	33	5	1+1
Davies, A.M.	3298	148	22.28	6- 32	7	–	1
Davies, A.P.	2858	66	43.30	5- 79	1	–	–
Dawson, R.K.J.	7646	181	42.24	6- 82	5	–	–
Dean, K.J.	9549	364	26.23	8- 52	15	4	2
Denly, J.L.	104	4	26.00	2- 40	–	–	–
Dennington, M.J.	624	19	32.84	3- 23	–	–	–
Dernbach, J.W.	500	9	55.55	3- 67	–	–	–
Dexter, N.J.	442	8	55.25	2- 40	–	–	–
Dilshan, T.M.	1207	40	30.17	5- 49	1	–	–
Di Venuto, M.J.	480	5	96.00	1- 0	–	–	–
Dobson, W.T.	126	1	126.00	1- 67	–	–	–
Doshi, N.D.	4261	123	34.64	7-110	5	3	1
Durston, W.J.	1170	24	48.75	3- 23	–	–	–
Ealham, M.A.	15206	553	27.49	8- 36	22	1	1
Edwards, N.J.	193	2	96.50	1- 16	–	–	–
Elliott, M.T.G.	754	13	58.00	3- 68	–	–	–
Ervine, S.M.	4611	123	37.48	6- 82	5	–	–
Faisal Iqbal	98	1	98.00	1- 6	–	–	–
Ferley, R.S.	2268	54	42.00	6-136	1	–	–
Fisher, I.D.	6553	155	42.27	5- 30	7	1	–
Fleming, S.P.	129	0					
Flintoff, A.	8799	280	31.42	5- 24	3	–	–

F-C	*Runs*	*Wkts*	*Avge*	*Best*	*5wI*	*10wM*	*50wS*
Flower, A.	270	7	38.57	1- 1	–	–	–
Flower, G.W.	5450	162	33.64	7- 31	3	–	–
Footitt, M.H.A.	480	13	36.92	5- 45	1	–	–
Foster, J.S.	6	0					
Francis, J.D.	164	4	41.00	1- 1	–	–	–
Francis, S.R.G.	5521	135	40.89	5- 42	3	–	–
Franklin, J.E.C.	7334	299	24.52	7- 30	11	1	–
Franks, P.J.	11406	363	31.42	7- 56	11	–	2
Friedlander, M.J.	713	15	47.53	3- 67	–	–	–
Frost, T.	15	0					
Fulton, D.P.	120	1	120.00	1- 37	–	–	–
Gallian, J.E.R.	4099	95	43.14	6-115	1	–	–
Ganguly, S.C.	5505	148	37.19	6- 46	4	–	–
Gerard, D.C.	62	2	31.00	2- 25	–	–	–
Gibson, O.D.	16659	579	28.77	7- 55	24	5	2
Gidman, A.P.R.	3025	65	46.53	4- 47	–	–	–
Gillespie, J.N.	12936	508	25.46	8- 50	19	1	0+1
Goodwin, M.W.	357	7	51.00	2- 23	–	–	–
Gough, D.	21813	809	26.96	7- 28	30	3	5
Grant, R.N.	146	3	48.66	1- 9	–	–	–
Gray, A.K.D.	2559	56	45.69	4-128	–	–	–
Greenidge, C.G.	4220	112	37.67	6- 40	4	–	1
Griffith, A.R.	4323	133	32.50	7- 54	7	1	–
Griffiths, D.A.	29	0					
Groenewald, T.D.	396	6	66.00	2- 36	–	–	–
Guy, S.M.	8	0					
Habib, A.	80	1	80.00	1- 10	–	–	–
Hall, A.J.	9186	352	26.09	6- 77	12	1	–
Hardinges, M.A.	2663	69	38.59	5- 51	1	–	–
Harmison, S.J.	13162	453	29.05	7- 12	15	1	3
Harris, A.J.	11955	387	30.89	7- 54	16	3	2
Harris, P.L.	4039	140	28.85	6- 54	9	–	0+1
Harrison, A.J.	243	5	48.60	2- 65	–	–	–
Harrison, D.S.	6200	170	36.47	5- 48	6	–	1
Harvey, I.J.	11577	423	27.36	8-101	15	2	–
Hemp, D.L.	813	17	47.82	3- 23	–	–	–
Henderson, C.W.	17501	556	31.47	7- 57	18	–	–
Henderson, T.	5922	212	27.93	6- 56	6	–	–
Hick, G.A.	10308	232	44.43	5- 18	5	1	–
Hildreth, J.C.	176	2	88.00	2- 39	–	–	–
Hinds, R.O.	3321	115	28.87	9- 68	2	1	–
Hobbiss, M.H.	31	0					
Hodge, B.J.	2737	68	40.25	4- 17	–	–	–
Hodson, W.G.	59	0					
Hogg, K.W.	2037	54	37.72	5- 48	1	–	–
Hoggard, M.J.	13803	504	27.38	7- 49	15	1	2
Hopkinson, C.D.	167	2	83.50	1- 20	–	–	–
Hunter, I.D.	4780	118	40.50	5- 63	1	–	–
Hussey, D.J.	1010	19	53.15	4-105	–	–	–
Hutton, B.L.	2211	35	63.17	4- 37	–	–	–
Iftikhar Anjum	7152	300	23.84	7- 59	20	3	0+4
Iles, J.A.	37	1	37.00	1- 27	–	–	–
Imran Farhat	2317	82	28.25	7- 31	2	–	–
Inzamam–ul–Haq	1295	39	33.20	5- 80	2	–	–

F-C	Runs	Wkts	Avge	Best	5wI	10wM	50wS
Iqbal, M.M.	417	9	46.33	4- 36	–	–	–
Irani, R.C.	10007	339	29.51	6- 71	9	–	1
Jacklin, B.D.	185	0					
James, G.D.	7	0					
Jannisar Khan	2201	73	30.15	5- 44	2	–	–
Jaques, P.A.	87	0					
Jayasuriya, S.T.	6258	191	32.76	5- 34	2	–	–
Jayawardena, D.P.M.D.	1531	50	30.62	5- 72	1	–	–
Jefferson, W.I.	60	1	60.00	1- 16	–	–	–
Jogia, K.A.	0	0					
Johnson, R.L.	14710	522	28.18	10- 45	20	3	4
Jones, G.O.	4	0					
Jones, M.C.	75	0					
Jones, P.S.	10050	266	37.78	6- 25	6	1	2
Jones, S.P.	6900	217	31.79	6- 45	11	1	–
Joseph, R.H.	1780	53	33.58	5- 19	2	–	–
Joseph, S.C.	203	4	50.75	2- 13	–	–	–
Joyce, E.C.	913	10	91.30	2- 34	–	–	–
Kalam, T.	255	2	127.50	1- 29	–	–	–
Kapugedera, C.K.	72	0					
Kartik, M.	8173	322	25.38	9- 70	19	3	–
Katich, S.M.	2986	78	38.28	7-130	3	–	–
Keedy, G.	14300	457	31.29	7- 95	22	5	3
Keegan, C.B.	4887	140	34.90	6-114	6	–	1
Kelly, R.	1556	62	25.09	6- 31	2	–	–
Kemp, J.M.	4726	176	26.85	6- 56	5	–	–
Kemp, R.A.	166	3	55.33	2- 86	–	–	–
Kervezee, A.N.	11	0					
Key, R.W.T.	59	0					
Khan, Z.	10732	381	28.16	9-138	23	7	1
Killeen, N.	8033	248	32.39	7- 70	8	–	1
King, R.E.	498	8	62.25	3- 49	–	–	–
Kirby, S.P.	8345	278	30.01	8- 80	10	3	1
Kirtley, R.J.	15725	594	26.47	7- 21	29	4	7
Klusener, L.	12790	452	28.29	8- 34	18	4	–
Knight, N.V.	271	1	271.00	1- 61	–	–	–
Kruis, G.J.	10676	354	30.15	7- 58	18	1	1
Kulasekara, M.D.N.	3784	157	24.10	6- 71	6	1	0+1
Kumble, A.	25771	1024	25.16	10- 74	69	19	1+2
Lamb, G.A.	854	31	27.54	7- 73	1	–	–
Lamb, N.J.	488	9	54.22	4- 92	–	–	–
Langer, J.L.	204	5	40.80	2- 17	–	–	–
Law, S.G.	4215	83	50.78	5- 39	1	–	–
Lawson, M.A.K.	1577	42	37.54	6- 88	4	–	–
Lee, J.E.	36	0					
Lehmann, D.S.	4219	117	36.05	4- 35	–	–	–
Lewis, J.	15200	574	26.48	8- 95	30	5	6
Lewis, J.J.B.	121	1	121.00	1- 73	–	–	–
Lewis, M.L.	7458	261	28.57	6- 59	7	–	–
Lewry, J.D.	14048	537	26.16	8-106	31	4	5
Liddle, C.J.	523	11	47.54	3- 42	–	–	–
Linley, T.E.	536	14	38.28	3- 44	–	–	–
Logan, R.J.	4473	117	38.23	6- 93	4	–	–
Loudon, A.G.R.	3732	100	37.32	6- 47	6	–	–

F-C	Runs	Wkts	Avge	Best	5wI	10wM	50wS
Louw, J.	7453	218	34.18	6- 51	7	–	1
Love, M.L.	11	1	11.00	1- 5	–	–	–
Loye, M.B.	61	1	61.00	1- 8	–	–	–
Lucas, D.S.	1993	60	33.21	5- 49	2	–	–
Lumb, M.J.	212	6	35.33	2- 10	–	–	–
Lungley, T.	1742	49	35.55	4-101	–	–	–
McGrath, A.	3223	95	33.92	5- 39	1	–	–
McLaren, R.	1849	60	30.81	6- 96	3	–	–
McMahon, P.J.	1587	44	36.06	5- 30	1	–	–
Maddy, D.L.	5734	173	33.14	5- 37	4	–	–
Maharoof, M.F.	2114	69	30.63	4- 12	–	–	–
Maher, J.P.	504	10	50.40	3- 11	–	–	–
Mahmood, S.I.	3450	115	30.00	5- 37	3	–	–
Malan, D.J.	152	3	50.66	1- 22	–	–	–
Malik, M.N.	3522	112	31.44	5- 57	4	–	–
Malinga, S.L.	5967	193	30.91	6- 17	5	–	–
Mansoor Amjad	3025	105	28.80	6- 19	5	–	–
Marshall, H.J.H.	176	3	58.66	1- 12	–	–	–
Marshall, S.J.	1892	28	67.57	6-128	1	–	–
Martin-Jenkins, R.S.C.	9044	263	34:38	7- 51	5	–	–
Mascarenhas, A.D.	9742	349	27.91	6- 25	14	–	1
Mason, M.S.	5984	225	26.59	8- 45	8	1	3
Masters, D.D.	6553	195	33.60	6- 27	5	–	–
Maunders, J.K.	725	22	32.95	4- 15	–	–	–
Middlebrook, J.D.	9755	250	39.02	6- 82	7	1	1
Miller, D.J.	150	2	75.00	1- 11	–	–	–
Mitchell, D.K.H.	99	1	99.00	1- 59	–	–	–
Mohammad Akram	11727	410	28.60	8- 49	18	1	–
Mohammad Amin	489	9	54.33	3- 66	–	–	–
Mohammad Asif	6347	259	24.50	7- 35	15	5	0+1
Mohammad Hafeez	2356	78	30.20	8- 57	3	1	–
Mohammad Sami	8099	258	31.39	8- 64	14	2	–
Mohd Yousuf Youhana	24	0					
Mohammed, D.	4462	173	25.79	7- 48	6	2	0+1
Mongia, D.	1611	45	35.80	4- 34	–	–	–
Montgomerie, R.R.	147	2	73.50	1- 0	–	–	–
Moore, S.C.	279	5	55.80	1- 13	–	–	–
Moreton, S.J.P.	297	8	37.12	2- 24	–	–	–
Morgan, E.J.G.	14	0					
Morris, J.C.	355	7	50.71	2- 29	–	–	–
Morris, R.K.	166	3	55.33	2- 58	–	–	–
Morse, E.J.	426	10	42.60	4- 78	–	–	–
Morton, R.S.	261	8	32.62	3- 17	–	–	–
Mubarak, J.	970	17	57.05	2- 0	–	–	–
Muchall, G.J.	615	15	41.00	3- 26	–	–	–
Mullaney, S.J.	36	0					
Mumtaz Habib	186	4	46.50	3- 92	–	–	–
Munday, M.K.	1580	52	30.38	6- 77	3	1	–
Muralitharan, M.	22297	1180	18.89	9- 51	103	30	2+3
Murtagh, T.J.	2818	76	37.07	6- 86	3	–	–
Mushtaq Ahmed	32785	1281	25.59	9- 48	93	28	8+2
Naik, J.K.H.	181	1	181.00	1- 55	–	–	–
Napier, G.R.	5399	132	40.90	5- 56	2	–	–
Nash, C.D.	544	6	90.66	1- 5	–	–	–

F-C	Runs	Wkts	Avge	Best	5wI	10wM	50wS
Nash, D.C.	105	2	52.50	1- 8	–	–	–
Naved–ul–Hasan	8870	388	22.86	7- 49	23	4	1+3
Needham, J.	156	2	78.00	2- 42	–	–	–
Nel, A.	7582	295	25.70	6- 25	12	1	–
Newby, O.J.	935	27	34.62	4- 58	–	–	–
Newman, S.A.	22	0					
Nicholson, M.J.	8783	302	29.08	7- 62	10	–	–
Nixon, P.A.	91	0					
Noffke, A.A.	7657	247	31.00	8- 24	9	1	–
North, M.J.	1977	43	45.97	4- 16	–	–	–
Oberoi, S.	143	3	47.66	3- 49	–	–	–
O'Brien, N.J.	4	1	4.00	1- 4	–	–	–
Onions, G.	2606	67	38.89	5- 45	1	–	1
Ormond, J.	12278	423	29.02	7- 63	20	1	4
Paget, C.D.	206	3	68.66	3- 63	–	–	–
Palladino, A.P.	1992	40	49.80	6- 41	2	–	–
Panesar, M.S.	5428	185	29.34	7-181	11	2	2
Park, G.T.	261	0					
Parker, L.C.	258	6	43.00	2- 37	–	–	–
Parsons, K.A.	4646	106	43.83	5- 13	2	–	–
Patel, M.M.	19202	629	30.52	8- 96	30	9	4
Patel, S.R.	386	8	48.25	3- 73	–	–	–
Patterson, S.A.	256	2	128.00	1- 25	–	–	–
Peng, N.	2	0					
Peploe, C.T.	2729	49	55.69	4- 31	–	–	–
Peters, S.D.	31	1	31.00	1- 19	–	–	–
Phillips, B.J.	5339	176	30.33	6- 29	4	–	–
Phillips, T.J.	3641	75	48.54	5- 41	1	–	–
Pietersen, C.	1816	42	43.23	6- 43	1	–	–
Pietersen, K.P.	2681	56	47.87	4- 31	–	–	–
Plunkett, L.E.	3917	123	31.84	6- 74	4	–	1
Pothas, N.	63	1	63.00	1- 16	–	–	–
Powell, D.B.	5405	184	29.37	6- 49	6	–	–
Powell, M.J. (Gm)	132	2	66.00	2- 39	–	–	–
Powell, M.J. (Wa)	744	11	67.63	2- 16	–	–	–
Pratt, G.J.	19	0					
Price, R.W.	8983	270	33.27	8- 35	15	3	–
Prowting, N.R.	39	0					
Pyrah, R.M.	36	3	12.00	1- 4	–	–	–
Ramprakash, M.R.	2178	34	64.05	3- 32	–	–	–
Rashid, A.	629	25	25.16	6- 67	1	–	–
Rayner, O.P.	348	6	58.00	3- 89	–	–	–
Read, C.M.W.	33	0					
Richards, M.A.	629	11	57.18	3- 62	–	–	–
Richardson, A.	6978	227	30.74	8- 46	7	1	1
Richardson, A.P.	2070	84	24.64	5- 32	3	–	–
Robinson, D.D.J.	399	1	399.00	1- 7	–	–	–
Rogers, C.J.L.	106	1	106.00	1- 16	–	–	–
Rosenberg, M.C.	69	2	34.50	1- 27	–	–	–
Rowe, D.T.	22	1	22.00	1- 22	–	–	–
Rudge, W.D.	816	16	51.00	3- 46	–	–	–
Sadler, J.L.	98	1	98.00	1- 22	–	–	–
Saggers, M.J.	8669	352	24.62	7- 79	16	–	4
Saker, N.C.	929	16	58.06	4- 79	–	–	–

F-C	Runs	Wkts	Avge	Best	5wI	10wM	50wS
Sales, D.J.G.	171	9	19.00	4- 25	–	–	–
Salisbury, I.D.K.	27255	842	32.36	8- 60	35	6	7
Salman Butt	354	4	88.50	4- 82	–	–	–
Samaraweera, T.T.	8102	346	23.41	6- 55	15	2	0+1
Samiullah Khan	2744	140	19.60	6- 41	5	1	0+1
Sammy, D.J.G.	1444	61	23.67	6- 50	4	–	–
Sangakkara, K.C.	66	1	66.00	1- 13	–	–	–
Savill, T.E.	1832	36	50.88	4- 62	–	–	–
Sayers, J.J.	54	0					
Schofield, C.P.	5643	179	31.52	6-120	4	–	–
Scott, G.M.	296	3	98.66	2- 39	–	–	–
Shafayat, B.M.	339	3	113.00	2- 25	–	–	–
Shah, O.A.	1098	21	52.28	3- 33	–	–	–
Shahid Afridi	5614	189	29.70	6-101	6	–	–
Shahid Nazir	8424	414	20.34	7- 39	18	1	0+2
Shahzad, A.	45	0					
Shantry, A.J.	328	17	19.29	5- 49	1	–	–
Sharif, Z.K.	796	14	56.85	4- 98	–	–	–
Sheikh, M.A.	3484	90	38.71	5- 65	1	–	–
Sheriyar, A.	15085	503	29.99	7-130	23	3	4
Shilvock, D.J.F.	124	3	41.33	2- 77	–	–	–
Shirazi, D.C.	33	1	33.00	1- 33	–	–	–
Shoaib Malik	4749	162	29.31	7- 81	5	1	–
Shreck, C.E.	3657	130	28.13	8- 31	10	2	1
Sidebottom, R.J.	7727	309	25.00	7- 97	11	1	2
Sillence, R.J.	2028	57	35.57	7- 96	3	–	–
Silverwood, C.E.W.	14359	533	26.93	7- 93	24	1	3
Simmons, L.M.P.	94	6	15.66	3- 6	–	–	–
Singh, A.	124	0					
Smith, B.F.	439	4	109.75	1- 5	–	–	–
Smith, B.M.	222	5	44.40	4-102	–	–	–
Smith, D.R.	1877	62	30.27	4- 45	–	–	–
Smith, D.S.	124	2	62.00	1- 2	–	–	–
Smith, E.T.	119	1	119.00	1- 60	–	–	–
Smith, G.J.	12700	457	27.78	8- 53	17	2	3
Smith, G.M.	433	8	54.12	2- 60	–	–	–
Smith, T.C.P.	1119	36	31.08	4- 57	–	–	–
Smith, W.R.	448	6	74.66	3- 34	–	–	–
Snape, J.N.	5583	113	49.40	5- 65	1	–	–
Solanki, V.S.	3771	83	45.43	5- 40	4	1	–
Spearman, C.M.	55	1	55.00	1- 37	–	–	–
Spencer, D.J.	1412	36	39.22	4- 31	–	–	–
Stephenson, J.P.	12890	396	32.55	7- 44	11	1	–
Stevens, D.I.	1756	42	41.80	4- 36	–	–	–
Steyn, D.W.	3989	132	30.21	5- 27	6	1	0+1
Stiff, D.A.	579	10	57.90	3- 88	–	–	–
Strauss, A.J.	58	1	58.00	1- 27	–	–	–
Streak, H.H.	13563	486	27.90	7- 55	17	2	1
Stubbings, S.D.	79	0					
Styris, S.B.	5998	199	30.14	6- 32	9	1	–
Suppiah, A.V.	780	12	65.00	3- 46	–	–	–
Sutcliffe, I.J.	330	9	36.66	2- 21	–	–	–
Swann, G.P.	11751	355	33.10	7- 33	14	2	1
Tahir, N.	1479	52	28.44	7-107	1	–	–

F-C	Runs	Wkts	Avge	Best	5wI	10wM	50wS
Taufeeq Umar	365	12	30.41	3- 33	–	–	–
Taylor, B.V.	4483	135	33.20	6- 32	4	–	–
Taylor, C.G.	532	6	88.66	3-126	–	–	–
Ten Doeschate, R.N.	1854	52	35.65	6- 20	2	–	–
Thomas, S.D.	16023	504	31.79	8- 50	18	1	5
Thornely, D.J.	1246	31	40.19	3- 38	–	–	–
Thornicroft, N.D.	543	11	49.36	2- 27	–	–	–
Thorp, C.D.	1726	53	32.56	6- 55	2	1	–
Tomlinson, J.A.	1731	34	50.91	6- 63	1	–	–
Tredwell, J.C.	3752	91	41.23	6- 81	2	1	–
Trego, P.D.	2813	64	43.95	6- 59	1	–	–
Tremlett, C.T.	5601	214	26.17	6- 44	6	–	–
Trescothick, M.E.	1541	36	42.80	4- 36	–	–	–
Trott, I.J.L.	1173	32	36.65	7- 39	1	–	–
Troughton, J.O.	1115	20	55.75	3- 1	–	–	–
Tudge, K.D.	58	0					
Tudor, A.J.	9268	316	29.32	7- 48	14	–	–
Turk, N.R.K.	9	0					
Turner, M.L.	252	4	63.00	2- 51	–	–	–
Udal, S.D.	23180	710	32.64	8- 50	33	4	7
Umar Gul	4102	162	25.32	8- 78	11	1	0+1
Vaas, W.P.U.C.J.	14378	583	24.66	7- 54	25	3	0+2
Van der Wath, J.J.	4413	153	28.84	6- 37	8	–	–
Vandort, M.G.	53	1	53.00	1- 46	–	–	–
Van Jaarsveld, M.	664	14	47.42	2- 30	–	–	–
Vaughan, M.P.	5142	114	45.10	4- 39	–	–	–
Vettori, D.L.	11963	365	32.77	7- 87	22	2	–
Vincent, L.	456	6	76.00	2- 37	–	–	–
Wagg, G.G.	1630	47	34.68	6- 38	1	–	–
Wagh, M.A.	4567	98	46.60	7-222	2	–	–
Wainwright, D.J.	692	20	34.60	4- 48	–	–	–
Wake, C.J.	90	2	45.00	1- 24	–	–	–
Walker, M.J.	1071	20	53.55	2- 21	–	–	–
Walker, N.G.E.	2057	49	41.97	5- 59	2	–	–
Walters, S.J.	69	2	34.50	1- 9	–	–	–
Warne, S.K.	31855	1236	25.77	8- 71	62	11	6+2
Warren, R.J.	0	0					
Waters, H.T.	712	23	30.95	5- 86	1	–	–
Watkins, R.E.	1047	22	47.59	4- 40	–	–	–
Wedge, S.A.	319	9	35.44	5-112	1	–	–
Weekes, P.N.	12759	304	41.97	8- 39	5	–	–
Welch, G.	15034	477	31.51	6- 30	17	1	4
Westfield, M.S.	270	7	38.57	4- 72	–	–	–
Weston, W.P.C.	658	5	131.60	2- 39	–	–	–
Westwood, I.J.	145	3	48.33	2- 46	–	–	–
Wharf, A.G.	8783	236	37.21	6- 59	5	1	1
Whelan, C.D.	182	7	26.00	2- 34	–	–	–
White, A.R.	327	8	40.87	3- 24	–	–	–
White, C.	11249	395	28.47	8- 55	11	–	–
White, C.L.	4683	124	37.76	6- 66	2	1	–
White, G.G.	79	0					
White, R.A.	612	12	51.00	2- 30	–	–	–
White, W.A.	363	11	33.00	4- 35	–	–	–
Wigley, D.H.	1922	46	41.78	5- 77	1	–	–

F-C	Runs	Wkts	Avge	Best	5wI	10wM	50wS
Willoughby, C.M.	12739	510	24.97	7- 44	20	3	1+2
Windows, M.G.N.	131	2	65.50	1- 6	–	–	–
Wiseman, P.J.	14158	417	33.95	9- 13	17	4	–
Woakes, C.R.	102	3	34.00	2- 64	–	–	–
Wood, M.J. (Sm)	68	0					
Wood, M.J. (Y)	39	2	19.50	1- 4	–	–	–
Woods, N.J.	366	6	61.00	3- 46	–	–	–
Wright, C.J.C.	1517	20	75.85	2- 33	–	–	–
Wright, L.J.	1110	29	38.27	3- 33	–	–	–
Yardy, M.H.	1056	15	70.40	5- 83	1	–	–
Yasir Arafat	9305	412	22.58	7-102	23	2	0+3
Young, P.J.W.	147	1	147.00	1- 71	–	–	–
Younis Khan	662	12	55.16	3- 24	–	–	–
Zoysa, D.N.T.	6056	254	23.84	7- 58	5	–	–

LIMITED-OVERS 'LIST A' CAREER RECORDS

Compiled by **Philip Bailey**

The following career records, to the end of the 2006 season, include all players currently registered with first-class counties. These records are restricted to performances in limited-overs matches of 'List A' status as defined by the Association of Cricket Statisticians and Historians now incorporated by ICC into their Classification of Cricket. The following matches qualify for List A status and are included in the figures that follow: Limited-Overs Internationals; Other International matches (e.g. Commonwealth Games, 'A' team internationals); Premier domestic limited-overs tournaments in Test status countries; Official tourist matches against the main first-class teams.

The following matches do NOT qualify for inclusion: World Cup warm-up games; Tourist matches against first-class teams outside the major domestic competitions (e.g. Universities, Minor Counties etc.); Festival, pre-season friendly games and Twenty20 Cup matches.

Editor's note: I have deducted from Philip's match totals for A.R.Adams, S.P.Fleming and H.J.H.Marshall the LOI scheduled between New Zealand and West Indies at Southampton on 8 July 2004. Although the ICC ruled that this should count as a match because the toss was made, Law 16 clearly states that the umpire's call of 'play' heralds the start of a match and not the toss.

	M	Runs	Avge	HS	100	50	Wkts	Avge	Best	Ct/St
Ackerman, H.D.	160	4289	32.74	114*	1	30	0	–	–	57
Adams, A.R.	110	1127	19.10	90*	–	1	144	27.84	5- 7	27
Adams, C.J.	346	10950	40.25	163	20	68	32	38.03	5-16	161
Adams, J.H.K.	8	107	13.37	40	–	–	0	–	–	4
Adnan, M.Hassan	69	1789	31.38	113*	2	13	6	27.00	2-13	26
Adshead, S.J.	55	796	20.41	77*	–	3	–	–	–	65/25
Afzaal, U.	149	4232	36.17	122*	4	29	39	24.79	3- 4	38
Ahmed, J.S.	4	–	–	–	–	–	10	17.00	4-32	–
Ali, Kabir	130	911	15.70	92	–	3	187	25.49	5-36	23
Ali, Kadeer	27	641	24.65	66	–	5	1	59.00	1- 4	2
Ali, M.M.	9	173	24.71	64	–	2	1	115.00	1- 9	1
Allenby, J.	14	144	18.00	43*	–	–	8	30.37	4-19	6
Alleyne, D.	38	321	11.06	58	–	1	–	–	–	29/7
Ambrose, T.R.	61	1220	23.92	95	–	6	–	–	–	68/8
Amjad Khan	51	265	12.04	65*	–	1	56	32.46	4-26	13

L-O	M	Runs	Avge	HS	100	50	Wkts	Avge	Best	Ct/St
Anderson, J.M.	88	149	10.64	13*	–	–	133	24.75	4-25	16
Andrew, G.M.	41	172	10.11	33	–	–	40	34.00	4-48	12
Anyon, J.E.	26	13	2.60	12	–	–	24	35.66	3-41	4
Azhar Mahmood	244	3176	21.17	101*	2	11	256	32.45	6-18	73
Ball, M.C.J.	282	1776	13.98	51	–	1	288	30.47	5-33	137
Ballance, G.S.	3	127	42.33	73	–	1	–	–	–	1
Barrick, D.J.	1	24	–	24*	–	–	0	–	–	1
Batty, G.J.	133	1452	16.68	83*	–	4	121	32.41	4-27	51
Batty, J.N.	148	2054	21.62	158*	1	10	–	–	–	138/25
Bell, I.R.	112	3490	37.12	137	2	29	33	34.48	5-41	35
Benham, C.C.	12	487	48.70	158	2	3	–	–	–	4
Benkenstein,D.M.	212	4872	34.30	107*	1	27	68	26.67	4-16	75
Benning, J.G.E.	47	1546	35.13	189*	1	12	26	33.34	4-43	11
Betts, M.M.	97	368	9.68	21	–	–	118	29.88	4-15	16
Bichel, A.J.	217	2280	20.00	100	1	5	293	26.05	7-20	69
Birt, T.R.	38	1141	30.02	145	2	6	5	17.00	2-15	14
Blackwell, I.D.	194	4294	26.83	134*	3	25	141	36.29	5-26	48
Blain, J.A.R.	56	158	9.87	29	–	–	78	25.71	5-24	14
Bopara, R.S.	60	1202	29.31	101*	1	7	38	29.23	3-23	18
Botha, A.G.	94	1061	20.80	60*	–	2	94	29.27	5-60	41
Breese, G.R.	86	929	18.58	52*	–	2	87	28.33	4-24	42
Bresnan, T.T.	90	769	17.08	61	–	1	78	39.20	4-25	28
Bridge, G.D.	49	332	15.09	50*	–	1	55	27.96	4-20	8
Broad, S.C.J.	12	31	31.00	11*	–	–	12	41.00	3-57	2
Brophy, G.L.	67	941	21.88	57*	–	4	–	–	–	58/13
Brown, A.D.	354	10287	31.84	268	18	47	12	36.50	3-39	122
Brown, D.O.	2	77	77.00	63*	–	1	0	–	–	–
Brown, D.R.	300	4678	23.15	108	1	22	357	26.34	5-31	73
Brown, J.F.	129	107	5.63	16	–	–	119	37.19	5-19	26
Brown, M.J.	8	227	28.37	76	–	1	–	–	–	3
Browning, R.J.	1	2	2.00	2	–	–	0	–	–	–
Bruce, J.T.A.	21	59	11.80	19*	–	–	33	18.75	4-18	7
Burrows, T.G.	3	18	9.00	16	–	–	–	–	–	3/2
Butcher, M.A.	174	3732	29.38	104	1	22	49	45.10	3-23	55
Caddick, A.R.	252	801	10.68	39	–	–	329	26.36	6-30	41
Cairns, C.L.	425	10364	32.59	143	9	55	455	27.93	6-12	118
Carberry, M.A.	64	1368	24.42	88	–	12	1	41.00	1-21	22
Carter, N.M.	120	1633	18.77	135	1	4	166	25.46	5-31	12
Chapple, G.	244	1736	17.01	81*	–	8	273	28.94	6-18	54
Cherry, D.D.	22	312	15.60	42	–	–	1	91.00	1-26	5
Chilton, M.J.	147	3679	30.40	115	4	18	41	24.19	5-26	46
Chopra, V.	2	7	3.50	6	–	–	–	–	–	–
Clarke, R.	104	1944	24.60	98*	–	9	65	38.44	4-49	40
Claydon, M.E.	7	15	7.50	9	–	–	8	36.62	2-41	–
Clinton, R.S.	18	189	15.75	56	–	1	2	29.00	2-16	3
Clough, G.D.	86	585	17.20	42*	–	–	79	31.45	6-25	27
Coetzer, K.J.	10	86	10.75	30	–	–	0	–	–	3
Collingwood,P.D.	257	6300	31.81	118*	4	37	150	34.44	6-31	125
Compton, N.R.D.	28	449	23.63	86*	–	3	0	–	–	9
Cook, A.N.	25	626	29.80	94	–	3	0	–	–	11
Cook, S.J.	135	1028	17.13	67*	–	2	166	28.37	6-37	18
Cork, D.G.	273	3872	21.27	93	–	19	338	27.20	6-21	103
Cosker, D.A.	151	357	8.30	27*	–	–	156	33.39	5-54	59
Crawley, J.P.	286	7945	31.65	114	7	49	0	–	–	85/4
Croft, R.D.B.	374	6127	24.02	143	4	31	384	32.46	6-20	89
Croft, S.J.	10	151	21.57	56	–	1	8	24.87	4-59	7

L-O	M	Runs	Avge	HS	100	50	Wkts	Avge	Best	Ct/St
Crook, A.R.	16	361	30.08	162*	1	–	10	31.90	3-32	4
Crook, S.P.	19	146	11.23	23	–	–	13	44.15	4-20	4
Cross, G.D.	9	87	14.50	21	–	–	–	–	–	6/5
Cummins, R.A.G.	11	3	1.50	2	–	–	15	19.46	2-14	3
Cusden, S.M.J.	6	5	2.50	3	–	–	4	48.25	1-29	–
Daggett, L.M.	7	14	–	5*	–	–	7	35.85	2-33	–
Dalrymple, J.W.M.	95	2012	30.48	107	2	12	74	32.98	4-14	40
Danish Kaneria	92	130	5.90	16	–	–	138	23.28	5-21	18
Davies, A.M.	63	164	7.45	31*	–	–	60	29.53	4-13	9
Davies, A.P.	98	265	13.94	24	–	–	141	26.26	5-19	13
Davies, S.M.	32	374	17.00	52	–	1	–	–	–	31/10
Dawson, R.K.J.	100	478	9.75	41	–	–	105	28.93	4-13	35
Dean, K.J.	137	239	7.96	16*	–	–	156	29.56	5-32	24
Denly, J.L.	11	193	21.44	70	–	1	–	–	–	2
Dernbach, J.W.	19	29	4.83	21	–	–	26	27.03	4-36	6
Dexter, N.J.	17	442	31.57	135*	1	1	10	22.60	3-17	3
Di Venuto, M.J.	244	7617	34.15	173*	13	38	5	36.20	1-10	92
Doshi, N.D.	55	190	10.00	38*	–	–	52	41.07	5-30	13
Durston, W.J.	38	677	32.23	62*	–	5	18	36.22	3-44	9
Ealham, M.A.	385	6061	24.43	112	1	26	432	27.08	6-53	104
Edwards, N.J.	5	113	22.60	65	–	1	–	–	–	1
Elliott, M.T.G.	140	5125	43.80	156	13	30	–	–	–	55
Ervine, S.M.	102	2113	28.55	104	3	7	108	31.51	5-50	22
Ferley, R.S.	32	226	17.38	42	–	–	41	27.17	4-33	12
Fisher, I.D.	54	194	9.23	25*	–	–	58	26.25	3-18	17
Fleming, S.P.	417	12430	34.43	139*	19	73	2	15.50	1- 3	199
Flintoff, A.	236	5748	30.41	143	6	30	224	23.00	4-11	90
Flower, A.	380	12511	38.97	145	12	97	1	103.00	1-21	254/48
Flower, G.W.	314	9313	33.98	148*	11	59	176	34.55	4-32	125
Footitt, M.H.A.	1	–	–	–	–	–	0	–	–	–
Foster, J.S.	102	1241	22.56	67	–	3	–	–	–	127/27
Francis, J.D.	65	1745	34.21	103*	1	12	–	–	–	15
Francis, S.R.G.	70	240	12.63	33*	–	–	77	34.33	8-66	16
Franks, P.J.	135	1527	21.20	84*	–	4	159	26.88	6-27	20
Gallian, J.E.R.	209	5855	30.81	134	8	36	55	32.87	5-15	71
Gazzard, C.M.	52	924	23.10	157	1	4	–	–	–	48/6
Gibson, O.D.	194	2428	20.93	102*	1	5	276	24.82	5-19	55
Gidman, A.P.R.	86	1656	24.35	84	–	8	28	42.42	3-21	31
Gifford, W.M.	1	1	1.00	1	–	–	–	–	–	–
Gilbert, C.R.	4	31	7.75	13	–	–	6	27.16	3-33	1
Gillespie, J.N.	149	490	12.56	44*	–	–	210	26.72	5-22	20
Goddard, L.J.	6	69	23.00	36	–	–	–	–	–	8
Goodwin, M.W.	275	8333	35.01	167	11	52	7	43.71	1- 9	91
Gough, D.	390	1979	13.64	72*	–	2	554	24.35	7-27	64
Grant, R.N.	30	516	20.64	45	–	–	6	45.50	2-21	6
Gray, A.K.D.	49	189	11.11	30*	–	–	47	29.44	4-34	13
Greenidge, C.G.	54	101	7.21	20	–	–	63	34.41	4-40	15
Groenewald, T.D.	5	9	4.50	9*	–	–	2	69.00	2-42	1
Guy, S.M.	19	195	17.72	40	–	–	–	–	–	18/7
Hall, A.J.	214	4268	30.48	129*	4	23	237	27.33	4-23	60
Hamilton-Brown, R.J.	4	43	14.33	20	–	–	–	–	–	–
Hardinges, M.A.	59	772	17.15	111*	1	3	50	35.68	4-19	23
Harmison, B.W.	8	142	17.75	57	–	1	1	51.00	1-51	5
Harmison, S.J.	101	139	6.04	17	–	–	131	31.38	5-33	15
Harris, A.J.	133	211	7.03	34	–	–	175	28.22	5-35	27
Harrison, A.J.	1	6	6.00	6	–	–	1	59.00	1-59	1

L-O	M	Runs	Avge	HS	100	50	Wkts	Avge	Best	Ct/St
Harrison, D.S.	58	357	14.28	37*	–	–	68	27.20	5-26	6
Harrison, P.W.	3	98	32.66	61	–	1	–	–	–	3
Harvey, I.J.	302	5906	24.71	112	2	27	445	22.18	5-19	81
Heather, S.A.	2	15	7.50	11	–	–	–	–	–	2
Hemp, D.L.	243	4997	26.86	121	5	25	11	16.18	4-32	88
Henderson, C.W.	176	775	17.22	32	–	–	220	24.90	6-29	44
Hick, G.A.	625	21180	41.12	172*	39	134	225	29.55	5-19	277
Hildreth, J.C.	62	1469	29.97	122	1	6	2	58.50	1-20	18
Hodd, A.J.	3	13	4.33	9	–	–	–	–	–	3
Hodge, B.J.	171	5674	38.33	164	12	30	30	37.46	5-28	65
Hodnett, G.P.	1	7	7.00	7	–	–	–	–	–	–
Hogg, K.W.	78	544	17.00	41*	–	–	78	27.80	4-20	14
Hoggard, M.J.	120	61	3.58	7*	–	–	172	24.23	5-28	14
Hopkinson, C.D.	65	987	21.93	69*	–	6	14	36.14	3-19	32
Horton, P.J.	10	143	20.42	46	–	–	–	–	–	–
Hunter, I.D.	72	274	7.82	39	–	–	76	33.65	4-29	14
Hussey, D.J.	89	2643	39.44	130	4	13	9	47.88	3-48	44
Hutton, B.L.	118	1577	19.96	77	–	7	51	31.19	5-45	59
Iqbal, M.M.	1	–	–	–	–	–	0	–	–	–
Irani, R.C.	310	7498	30.47	158*	7	43	309	25.22	5-26	81
James, G.D.	2	52	52.00	51*	–	1	–	–	–	–
James, N.A.	3	44	22.00	30	–	–	4	24.00	2-34	1
Jaques, P.A.	90	3677	45.39	158*	9	21	0	–	–	24
Jefferson, W.I.	65	2152	35.86	132	4	11	2	4.50	2- 9	31
Johnson, R.L.	190	1107	11.77	53	–	1	207	32.88	5-50	23
Jones, G.O.	103	1761	24.12	80	–	7	–	–	–	122/18
Jones, P.S.	151	472	11.51	27	–	–	206	28.66	6-56	28
Jones, S.P.	23	32	10.66	12*	–	–	18	46.88	3-19	2
Joseph, R.H.	14	23	11.50	15	–	–	15	27.73	2-21	2
Joyce, E.C.	120	3407	35.86	115*	3	23	2	90.50	2-10	45
Kartik, M.	113	313	10.09	37*	–	–	138	31.56	5-29	36
Katich, S.M.	178	5858	39.05	136*	7	45	24	31.91	3-21	84
Keedy, G.	34	21	5.25	10*	–	–	32	34.28	5-30	2
Keegan, C.B.	82	594	16.97	50	–	1	129	23.33	6-33	19
Kervezee, A.N.	6	145	29.00	47	–	–	0	–	–	4
Key, R.W.T.	140	3638	29.33	114	1	26	–	–	–	21
Khan, Z.	156	703	13.26	42	–	–	226	27.64	4-19	39
Killeen, N.	196	635	9.47	32	–	–	269	24.03	6-31	36
King, R.E.	3	2	1.00	2	–	–	2	46.00	2-39	1
Kirby, S.P.	37	43	4.30	15	–	–	31	45.29	3-27	7
Kirtley, R.J.	200	352	9.02	30*	–	–	298	22.76	5-27	57
Klokker, F.A.	12	241	26.77	138*	1	1	–	–	–	14/3
Klusener, L.	289	5893	39.28	142*	3	31	312	30.18	6-49	76
Kruis, G.J.	103	404	12.24	31*	–	–	121	31.34	4-26	26
Lamb, G.A.	44	814	23.94	100*	1	4	17	25.88	4-38	26
Langer, J.L.	182	6039	38.46	146	9	42	7	30.71	3-51	86/2
Latouf, K.J.	10	76	10.85	25	–	–	–	–	–	6
Law, S.G.	373	11301	34.66	163	20	60	90	35.17	5-26	149
Lawson, M.A.K.	4	30	7.50	20	–	–	3	47.00	2-50	1
Lewis, J.	161	599	10.69	40	–	–	210	26.58	5-19	30
Lewis, J.J.B.	237	4747	27.43	102	1	22	0	–	–	41
Lewry, J.D.	76	217	7.48	16*	–	–	100	27.12	4-29	13
Liddle, C.J.	1	1	1.00	1	–	–	0	–	–	1
Logan, R.J.	56	202	11.22	28*	–	–	61	34.75	5-24	19
Loudon, A.G.R.	59	1031	21.93	73*	–	7	35	38.60	4-48	21
Love, M.L.	155	4545	33.41	127*	5	21	0	–	–	68

L-O	M	Runs	Avge	HS	100	50	Wkts	Avge	Best	Ct/St
Lowe, J.A.	1	36	36.00	36	–	–	–	–	–	–
Loye, M.B.	261	7904	35.28	127	10	52	–	–	–	61
Lucas, D.S.	35	109	10.90	32	–	–	44	31.50	4-27	4
Lumb, M.J.	108	2649	28.18	92	–	18	0	–	–	32
Lungley, T.	57	353	13.57	45	–	–	61	29.70	4-28	15
Lyth, A.	1	23	23.00	23	–	–	–	–	–	1
McCullum, B.B.	120	1646	20.83	58	–	7	–	–	–	138/9
McGrath, A.	230	5704	30.83	148	4	32	61	34.57	4-41	73
McLaren, R.	26	337	30.63	55	–	1	18	35.11	4-43	10
Maddy, D.L.	295	7388	30.40	167*	9	44	176	28.56	4-16	111
Mahmood, S.I.	73	275	8.59	29	–	–	105	25.24	4-37	7
Malan, D.J.	5	90	18.00	42	–	–	0	–	–	–
Malik, M.N.	47	83	11.85	11	–	–	45	36.44	4-42	7
Mansoor Amjad	54	587	17.78	52*	–	1	71	29.70	5-37	15
Marshall, H.J.H.	159	3661	27.73	111	3	24	1	72.00	1-14	65
Marshall, S.J.	16	25	4.16	9	–	–	10	56.40	3-36	7
Martin-Jenkins, R.S.C.	181	1643	14.53	68*	–	3	191	29.16	4-22	41
Mascarenhas, A.D.	181	2991	23.00	79	–	18	222	24.14	5-27	46
Mason, M.S.	70	153	7.65	25	–	–	84	27.51	4-34	14
Masters, D.D.	79	340	13.07	39	–	–	65	38.33	5-20	8
Maunders, J.K.	22	314	14.95	49	–	–	4	20.50	2-16	6
Middlebrook, J.D.	108	911	18.59	47	–	–	94	31.69	4-27	32
Mierkalns, J.A.	1	4	4.00	4	–	–	–	–	–	–
Miller, D.J.	1	1	1.00	1	–	–	0	–	–	–
Mitchell, D.K.H.	4	13	3.25	7	–	–	4	16.75	4-42	2
Mohammad Akram	119	231	7.70	33	–	–	131	32.05	4-19	23
Mongia, D.	178	4910	34.82	159*	10	21	101	24.90	5-44	78
Montgomerie,R.R.	189	5939	36.21	132*	7	40	0	–	–	49
Moore, S.C.	55	1554	31.71	105*	2	9	1	42.00	1- 1	12
Morgan, E.J.G.	27	653	32.65	99	–	5	0	–	–	7
Morris, J.C.	2	17	17.00	17	–	–	0	–	–	–
Muchall, G.J.	65	1472	30.04	101*	1	7	1	137.00	1-15	12
Mullaney, S.J.	1	–	–	–	–	–	1	23.00	1-23	–
Munday, M.K.	1	–	–	–	–	–	1	39.00	1-39	–
Muralitharan, M.	352	631	6.31	27	–	–	528	22.39	7-30	131
Murtagh, C.P.	2	34	–	30*	–	–	–	–	–	2
Murtagh, T.J.	66	350	12.50	31*	–	–	80	32.72	4-14	18
Mushtaq Ahmed	371	1597	11.40	41	–	–	453	28.37	7-24	58
Mustard, P.	57	663	17.44	84	–	2	–	–	–	60/11
Naik, J.K.H.	2	1	1.00	1	–	–	0	–	–	–
Napier, G.R.	124	1384	17.51	79	–	7	114	24.38	6-29	31
Nash, C.D.	7	205	29.28	82	–	1	0	–	–	1
Nash, D.C.	112	1321	20.64	67	–	5	–	–	–	88/15
Naved-ul-Hasan	111	1162	21.51	70*	–	4	180	25.03	6-27	34
Needham, J.	11	60	20.00	14	–	–	6	56.16	1-29	2
Nel, A.	144	234	10.63	21*	–	–	204	24.18	6-27	34
Nelson, M.A.G.	2	13	–	13*	–	–	0	–	–	–
New, T.J.	17	425	26.56	68	–	2	–	–	–	1
Newby, O.J.	7	16	16.00	7*	–	–	6	51.33	2-37	2
Newman, S.A.	47	929	21.11	106	1	3	–	–	–	10
Nicholson, M.J.	51	244	10.60	25	–	–	54	37.59	3-23	15
Nixon, P.A.	341	5722	24.98	101	1	24	0	–	–	359/85
Noffke, A.A.	76	348	13.92	58	–	1	81	34.70	4-32	20
North, M.J.	86	2340	32.05	134*	4	16	36	29.25	4-26	27
O'Brien, N.J.	38	318	18.70	53	–	1	–	–	–	29/13
Onions, G.	21	28	5.60	11	–	–	20	33.50	3-39	1

L-O	M	Runs	Avge	HS	100	50	Wkts	Avge	Best	Ct/St
Ormond, J.	115	356	9.12	32	–	–	142	26.93	4-12	23
O'Shea, M.P.	2	7	7.00	7*	–	–	0	–	–	2
Paget, C.D.	1	–	–	–	–	–	1	61.00	1-61	–
Palladino, A.P.	14	17	5.66	16	–	–	18	25.77	3-32	1
Panesar, M.S.	11	50	16.66	16*	–	–	11	30.63	5-20	3
Park, G.T.	3	39	19.50	32	–	–	–	–	–	3
Parker, L.C.	4	40	13.33	17	–	–	0	–	–	2
Parsons, K.A.	239	5099	30.17	121	2	28	143	35.57	5-39	98
Patel, M.M.	84	269	9.96	27*	–	–	88	30.69	3-20	24
Patel, S.R.	42	834	32.07	93*	–	4	25	29.16	3-40	4
Patterson, S.A.	14	69	69.00	25*	–	–	13	41.76	3-11	3
Peng, N.	99	2340	25.16	121	3	12	–	–	–	20
Peploe, C.T.	16	30	4.28	14*	–	–	26	19.96	4-38	6
Peters, S.D.	122	2026	19.29	84*	–	10	–	–	–	33
Pettini, M.L.	53	1023	24.95	92*	–	9	–	–	–	16
Phillips, B.J.	92	802	18.65	44*	–	–	99	30.38	4-25	23
Phillips, T.J.	23	101	16.83	24*	–	–	31	21.74	5-34	8
Pietersen, C.	23	51	12.75	14*	–	–	27	31.70	7-10	4
Pietersen, K.P.	140	4597	45.06	147	8	28	35	50.11	3-14	61
Pipe, D.J.	43	479	19.16	56	–	2	–	–	–	36/13
Plunkett, L.E.	45	354	18.63	56	–	1	52	34.55	4-28	9
Poonia, N.S.	11	277	25.18	59	–	1	–	–	–	2
Pope, S.P.	6	27	5.40	15	–	–	–	–	–	11/1
Pothas, N.	191	3741	35.62	114*	2	21	–	–	–	176/42
Powell, M.J.(Gm)	175	4094	28.04	91*	–	23	1	26.00	1-26	70
Powell, M.J.(Wa)	109	1961	25.46	101*	1	5	25	29.08	5-40	53
Pratt, G.J.	78	1749	31.80	101*	1	11	–	–	–	31
Price, R.W.	92	326	9.31	47	–	–	89	33.53	4-21	19
Prior, M.J.	130	2756	24.17	144	3	14	–	–	–	93/21
Pyrah, R.M.	19	328	19.29	42	–	–	12	26.58	5-50	7
Ramprakash, M.R.	368	11739	39.13	147*	12	77	46	29.43	5-38	124
Rankin, W.B.	3	5	5.00	5*	–	–	2	38.50	1-25	–
Rashid, A.	2	28	14.00	28	–	–	3	32.33	2-63	–
Rayner, O.P.	5	94	47.00	61	–	1	3	56.33	1-25	–
Read, C.M.W.	205	3333	27.54	135	2	8	–	–	–	213/46
Redfern, D.J.	1	6	6.00	6	–	–	–	–	–	–
Rees, G.P.	3	38	12.66	15	–	–	–	–	–	1
Richardson, A.	57	102	10.20	21*	–	–	53	36.37	5-35	11
Robinson, D.D.J.	190	4399	26.34	137*	4	21	1	26.00	1- 7	51
Rogers, C.J.L.	61	1725	31.94	117*	1	11	2	13.00	2-22	33
Rowe, D.T.	1	–	–	–	–	–	1	26.00	1-26	1
Rudge, W.D.	4	8	4.00	4	–	–	3	43.66	2- 1	–
Sadler, J.L.	59	997	20.77	88	–	3	–	–	–	13
Saggers, M.J.	112	293	9.45	34*	–	–	149	26.04	5-22	22
Saker, N.C.	15	48	16.00	22	–	–	14	43.57	4-43	2
Sales, D.J.G.	203	5265	31.71	161	3	33	0	–	–	91
Salisbury,I.D.K.	249	1569	13.52	59*	–	1	247	32.80	5-30	89
Sayers, J.J.	12	232	23.20	62	–	2	1	71.00	1-31	–
Schofield, C.P.	93	1078	22.00	69*	–	3	88	25.68	5-31	24
Scott, B.J.M.	56	400	19.04	73*	–	2	–	–	–	48/16
Scott, G.M.	14	424	38.54	100	1	2	7	24.57	2-24	4
Shafayat, B.M.	78	1466	21.88	97*	–	6	20	33.00	4-33	29/2
Shah, O.A.	223	5995	32.58	134	10	34	11	33.90	2- 2	79
Shahzad, A.	4	18	6.00	11*	–	–	5	27.20	3-30	–
Shantry, A.J.	7	25	8.33	15	–	–	10	16.70	5-37	5
Sheikh, M.A.	109	469	11.72	50*	–	1	110	29.70	4-17	18

L-O	M	Runs	Avge	HS	100	50	Wkts	Avge	Best	Ct/St
Shirazi, D.C.	4	117	39.00	101	1	–	–	–	–	–
Shreck, C.E.	21	28	14.00	9*	–	–	31	25.96	5-19	5
Sidebottom, R.J.	134	341	11.00	32	–	–	138	29.66	6-40	30
Sillence, R.J.	20	359	29.91	94	–	2	19	26.52	4-35	6
Silverwood, C.E.W.	190	979	13.59	61	–	4	248	24.37	5-28	29
Singh, A.	116	3031	28.06	123	1	20	–	–	–	29
Smith, B.F.	350	8788	30.19	115	2	56	2	52.50	1- 2	125
Smith, E.T.	112	3146	31.46	122	2	22	–	–	–	24
Smith, G.M.	14	281	21.61	57	–	2	5	57.20	2-44	8
Smith, T.C.	12	36	12.00	14*	–	–	13	25.53	3- 8	3
Smith, T.M.J.	1	–	–	–	–	–	2	22.50	2-45	1
Smith, W.R.	29	584	24.33	95*	–	5	–	–	–	8
Snape, J.N.	259	3559	23.11	104*	1	11	210	29.15	5-32	91
Snell, S.D.	10	31	3.87	17	–	–	–	–	–	16
Solanki, V.S.	302	7541	29.92	164*	11	41	24	33.45	4-14	114
Spearman, C.M.	258	7078	28.42	153	7	43	0	–	–	96
Spencer, D.J.	20	79	9.87	17*	–	–	23	29.56	4-35	5
Spurway, S.H.P.	4	31	15.50	31	–	–	–	–	–	4/2
Stevens, D.I.	162	4062	28.60	133	3	27	30	34.43	5-32	68
Steyn, D.W.	27	14	2.80	6*	–	–	36	25.00	5-20	3
Stiff, D.A.	1	–	–	–	–	–	1	27.00	1-27	–
Stokes, M.S.T.	4	49	16.33	36	–	–	0	–	–	2
Strauss, A.J.	162	4353	30.44	152	4	29	0	–	–	39
Streak, H.H.	294	4008	26.02	90*	–	14	369	28.55	5-32	72
Stubbings, S.D.	102	2326	25.84	110	1	12	–	–	–	16
Suppiah, A.V.	34	821	25.65	79	–	5	25	30.60	4-39	13
Sutcliffe, I.J.	122	3220	29.54	105*	4	20	–	–	–	27
Sutton, L.D.	121	1698	20.21	83	–	6	–	–	–	134/14
Swann, G.P.	158	2194	19.58	83	–	11	152	28.73	5-35	44
Tahir, N.	7	2	2.00	1*	–	–	2	84.50	1-23	1
Taylor, B.V.	111	177	6.55	21*	–	–	142	24.94	5-28	20
Taylor, C.G.	113	1976	22.97	93	–	11	6	21.50	2- 5	40/1
Taylor, C.R.	17	621	51.75	111*	2	2	–	–	–	7
Ten Doeschate, R.N.	40	826	51.62	89*	–	5	30	20.73	4-18	14
Thomas, S.D.	140	1273	16.53	71*	–	1	171	27.29	7-16	25
Thornicroft, N.D.	14	52	17.33	20	–	–	16	35.18	5-42	2
Thorp, C.D.	27	215	19.54	52	–	1	33	28.75	6-17	3
Tomlinson, J.A.	18	15	2.14	6	–	–	16	36.75	4-47	2
Tredwell, J.C.	87	808	17.56	71	–	2	82	32.01	4-16	42
Trego, P.D.	45	351	11.70	31*	–	–	38	31.36	4-39	8
Tremlett, C.T.	81	328	9.64	38*	–	–	124	21.99	4-25	16
Trescothick, M.E.	273	8856	37.21	158	23	39	57	28.70	4-50	104
Trott, I.J.L.	102	2924	38.98	112*	4	19	34	24.05	4-55	34
Troughton, J.O.	86	1977	28.65	115*	2	10	23	24.78	4-23	32
Tudge, K.D.	1	4	4.00	4	–	–	0	–	–	–
Tudor, A.J.	72	428	12.58	56	–	1	103	23.64	4-26	21
Turk, N.R.K.	3	64	21.33	36	–	–	0	–	–	–
Udal, S.D.	357	2504	15.65	78	–	8	405	29.83	5-43	117
Umar Gul	52	70	8.75	17*	–	–	67	29.79	5-17	6
Vaas, W.P.U.C.J.	325	2300	15.33	62*	–	3	415	26.50	8-19	68
Van der Wath,J.J.	96	1467	26.19	91	–	9	124	26.26	4-31	23
Van Jaarsveld,M.	192	5861	38.81	123	8	38	14	47.00	1- 0	107
Vaughan, M.P.	258	6527	29.13	125*	3	41	73	32.46	4-22	77
Wagg, G.G.	37	396	15.84	45	–	–	33	34.39	4-50	10
Wagh, M.A.	69	1500	25.00	102*	1	9	25	34.48	4-35	12
Wainwright, D.J.	2	–	–	–	–	–	0	–	–	–

L-O	M	Runs	Avge	HS	100	50	Wkts	Avge	Best	Ct/St
Walker, M.J.	235	5221	28.53	117	3	32	30	24.66	4-24	63
Walker, N.G.E.	20	118	9.07	43	–	–	16	24.25	4-26	8
Wallace, M.A.	99	973	16.21	48	–	–	–	–	–	105/23
Walters, S.J.	15	191	21.22	32*	–	–	1	83.00	1-38	5
Warne, S.K.	297	1819	11.81	55	–	1	452	24.53	6-42	119
Warren, R.J.	177	3363	24.54	100*	1	15	–	–	–	135/11
Waters, H.T.	2	8	8.00	8	–	–	0	–	–	–
Watkins, R.E.	14	120	13.33	28*	–	–	11	42.18	2-25	1
Wedge, S.A.	1	–	–	–	–	–	2	15.50	2-31	1
Weekes, P.N.	323	7632	30.77	143*	9	46	329	29.23	4-17	138
Welch, G.	224	2582	19.86	82	–	8	197	35.57	6-31	32
Wessels, M.H.	26	404	22.44	80	–	1	–	–	–	23
Westfield, M.S.	2	6	–	4*	–	–	0	–	–	1
Westley, T.	1	–	–	–	–	–	–	–	–	–
Weston, W.P.C.	192	4116	25.09	134	4	21	1	2.00	1- 2	44
Westwood, I.J.	13	186	31.00	55	–	1	2	69.50	1-28	2
Wharf, A.G.	129	1207	17.49	72	–	1	151	30.33	6- 5	37
Whelan, C.D.	2	6	3.00	6	–	–	1	83.00	1-43	–
White, A.R.	20	311	20.73	45	–	–	10	36.30	3-17	6
White, C.	341	6933	26.56	148	5	28	337	25.02	5-19	95
White, C.L.	66	1401	31.13	109*	2	7	52	35.40	4-15	28
White, R.A.	40	719	19.43	101	1	3	2	23.00	2-18	8
White, W.A.	2	–	–	–	–	–	2	50.50	1-38	–
Wigley, D.H.	14	14	2.00	9	–	–	10	53.40	4-37	2
Willoughby, C.M.	165	112	5.09	12*	–	–	206	26.95	6-16	23
Wilshaw, P.J.	2	20	10.00	20	–	–	–	–	–	2
Windows, M.G.N.	225	4936	26.97	117	3	25	0	–	–	74
Wiseman, P.J.	113	953	15.37	65*	–	2	72	44.15	4-45	28
Wood, M.J. (Sm)	73	1935	29.76	129	2	13	–	–	–	12
Wood, M.J. (Y)	145	3271	27.25	160	5	14	3	25.33	3-45	57
Wright, B.J.	1	37	37.00	37	–	–	–	–	–	–
Wright, C.J.C.	16	44	7.33	18	–	–	11	47.45	3-21	3
Wright, L.J.	57	439	14.63	35	–	–	50	34.34	4-12	18
Yardy, M.H.	101	1562	20.55	98*	–	8	59	31.40	6-27	41
Yasir Arafat	141	1701	21.53	87	–	6	219	24.46	6-24	29
Younis Khan	167	4529	33.05	144	3	31	16	24.12	3- 5	88

SCORING OF EXTRAS 2007

The variable penalties involved in scoring no-balls and wides in our international and county cricket remain unchanged from last season:

COMPETITION	NO-BALL PENALTY	WIDE PENALTY
Test Matches Limited-Overs Internationals	1 + other runs scored	1 + other runs scored
County Championship Second XI Championship	2 + other runs scored	1 + other runs scored
Tourist Matches (First-Class) Tourist Matches (Limited-Overs)	1 + other runs scored	1 + other runs scored
Friends Provident Trophy (50 overs) Pro 40 League (40 overs) Twenty20 Cup (20 overs) Second XI Trophy	2 + other runs scored + a free hit for a foot fault	1 + other runs scored

LIMITED-OVERS INTERNATIONALS CAREER RECORDS

These records, complete to 11 February 2007 (the conclusion of the Commonwealth Bank Trophy in Australia), include all players registered for county cricket in 2007 at the time of going to press, plus those who have appeared in LOI matches for ICC full member countries since 1 September 2005 or are in the originally selected XVs for those countries for the 2007 World Cup. They exclude all matches involving multinational teams, as well as any abandoned without a ball bowled, regardless of the toss having been made.

ENGLAND – BATTING AND FIELDING

	M	*I*	*NO*	*HS*	*Runs*	*Avge*	*100*	*50*	*Ct/St*
C.J.Adams	5	4	–	42	71	17.75	–	–	3
Kabir Ali	14	9	3	39*	93	15.50	–	–	1
J.M.Anderson	57	23	11	15	89	7.41	–	–	13
G.J.Batty	7	5	1	3	6	1.50	–	–	4
I.R.Bell	36	34	3	88	1172	37.80	–	9	6
I.D.Blackwell	34	29	2	82	403	14.92	–	1	8
R.S.Bopara	1	1	1	7*	7	–	–	–	–
T.T.Bresnan	4	4	1	20	51	17.00	–	–	1
S.C.J.Broad	5	3	3	8*	9	40.02	–	–	1
A.D.Brown	16	16	–	118	354	22.12	1	1	6
D.R.Brown	9	8	4	21	99	24.75	–	–	1
A.R.Caddick	54	38	18	36	249	12.45	–	–	9
G.Chapple	1	1	–	14	14	14.00	–	–	–
R.Clarke	20	13	–	39	144	11.07	–	–	11
P.D.Collingwood	112	101	22	120*	2690	34.05	4	13	63
A.N.Cook	2	2	–	41	80	40.00	–	–	–
D.G.Cork	32	21	3	31*	180	10.00	–	–	6
J.P.Crawley	13	12	1	73	235	21.36	–	2	1/1
R.D.B.Croft	50	36	12	32	345	14.37	–	–	11
J.W.M.Dalrymple	24	23	1	67	481	21.86	–	2	9
M.A.Ealham	64	45	4	45	716	17.46	–	–	9
A.Flintoff	112	100	14	123	2883	33.52	3	16	35
J.S.Foster	11	6	3	13	41	13.66	–	–	13/7
P.J.Franks	1	1	–	4	4	4.00	–	–	1
A.F.Giles	62	35	13	41	385	17.50	–	–	22
D.Gough	158	87	38	46*	609	12.42	–	–	24
S.J.Harmison	46	22	13	13*	67	7.44	–	–	8
G.A.Hick	120	118	15	126*	3846	37.33	5	27	64
M.J.Hoggard	26	6	2	7	17	4.25	–	–	5
R.C.Irani	31	30	5	53	360	14.40	–	1	6
R.L.Johnson	10	4	1	10	16	5.33	–	–	–
G.O.Jones	49	41	8	80	815	24.69	–	4	68/4
S.P.Jones	8	1	–	1	1	1.00	–	–	–
E.C.Joyce	12	12	–	107	319	26.58	1	1	3
R.W.T.Key	5	5	–	19	54	10.80	–	–	–
R.J.Kirtley	11	2	–	1	2	1.00	–	–	5
J.Lewis	12	7	2	9	33	6.60	–	–	–
A.G.R.Loudon	1	1	–	0	0	0.00	–	–	–
M.B.Loye	7	7	–	45	142	20.28	–	–	–
A.McGrath	14	12	2	52	166	16.60	–	1	4
D.L.Maddy	8	6	–	53	113	18.83	–	1	1
S.I.Mahmood	19	11	2	22*	83	9.22	–	–	1
P.A.Nixon	10	10	1	49	104	11.55	–	–	13/1
M.S.Panesar	9	3	2	6	6	6.00	–	–	2
K.P.Pietersen	40	34	8	116	1564	60.15	3	11	19

ENGLAND – BATTING AND FIELDING (continued)

	M	*I*	*NO*	*HS*	*Runs*	*Avge*	*100*	*50*	*Ct/St*
L.E.Plunkett	22	20	9	56	258	23.45	–	1	5
M.J.Prior	12	12	–	45	240	20.00	–	–	4/1
M.R.Ramprakash	18	18	4	51	376	26.85	–	1	8
C.M.W.Read	36	24	7	30*	300	17.64	–	–	41/2
I.D.K.Salisbury	4	2	1	5	7	7.00	–	–	1
O.A.Shah	18	18	2	62	294	18.37	–	2	6
R.J.Sidebottom	2	1	1	2*	2	–	–	–	–
C.E.W.Silverwood	7	4	–	12	17	4.25	–	–	–
J.N.Snape	10	7	3	38	118	29.50	–	–	5
V.S.Solanki	51	46	5	106	1097	26.75	2	5	16
A.J.Strauss	74	73	7	152	2156	32.66	2	14	26
G.P.Swann	1	–	–	–	–	–	–	–	–
C.T.Tremlett	6	3	–	8	16	5.33	–	–	–
M.E.Trescothick	123	122	6	137	4335	37.37	12	21	49
J.O.Troughton	6	5	1	20	36	9.00	–	–	1
A.J.Tudor	3	2	1	6	9	9.00	–	–	1
S.D.Udal	11	7	4	11*	35	11.66	–	–	1
M.P.Vaughan	77	74	10	90*	1773	27.70	–	15	24
A.G.Wharf	13	5	3	9	19	9.50	–	–	1
C.White	51	41	5	57*	568	15.77	–	1	12
M.H.Yardy	5	4	1	12*	30	10.00	–	–	1

ENGLAND – BOWLING

	O	*M*	*R*	*W*	*Avge*	*Best*	*4wI*	*R/Over*
Kabir Ali	112.1	4	682	20	34.10	4-45	1	6.08
J.M.Anderson	471.4	48	2280	86	26.51	4-25	6	4.83
G.J.Batty	60.2	1	294	4	73.50	2-40	–	4.87
I.R.Bell	14.4	0	88	6	14.66	3-9	–	6.00
I.D.Blackwell	205	8	877	24	36.54	3-26	–	4.27
R.S.Bopara	4	0	19	1	19.00	1-19	–	4.75
T.T.Bresnan	25	1	169	2	84.50	1-38	–	6.76
S.C.J.Broad	35.4	2	185	5	37.00	3-57	–	5.18
A.D.Brown	1	0	5	0	–	–	–	5.00
D.R.Brown	54	3	305	7	43.57	2-28	–	5.64
A.R.Caddick	489.3	66	1965	69	28.47	4-19	3	4.01
G.Chapple	4	0	14	0	–	–	–	3.50
R.Clarke	78.1	3	415	11	37.72	2-28	–	5.30
P.D.Collingwood	427.3	8	2134	58	36.79	6-31	3	4.99
D.G.Cork	295.2	17	1368	41	33.36	3-27	–	4.63
R.D.B.Croft	411	25	1743	45	38.73	3-51	–	4.24
J.W.M.Dalrymple	130	2	597	14	42.64	2-5	–	4.59
M.A.Ealham	537.5	32	2197	67	32.79	5-15	3	4.08
A.Flintoff	711.5	57	3070	121	25.37	4-14	5	4.31
P.J.Franks	9	0	48	0	–	–	–	5.33
A.F.Giles	476	17	2069	55	37.61	5-57	1	4.34
D.Gough	1403.3	120	6154	234	26.29	5-44	12	4.38
S.J.Harmison	407.1	25	2057	67	30.70	5-33	3	5.05
G.A.Hick	206	6	1026	30	34.20	5-33	1	4.98
M.J.Hoggard	217.4	13	1152	32	36.00	5-49	1	5.29
R.C.Irani	213.5	5	989	24	41.20	5-26	2	4.62
R.L.Johnson	67	7	239	11	21.72	3-22	–	3.56
S.P.Jones	58	9	275	7	39.28	2-43	–	4.74
R.J.Kirtley	91.3	4	481	9	53.44	2-33	–	5.25
J.Lewis	109.2	12	437	17	25.70	4-36	1	3.99
A.G.R.Loudon	6	0	36	0	–	–	–	6.00

ENGLAND – BOWLING (continued)

	O	M	R	W	Avge	Best	4wI	R/Over
A.McGrath	38	2	175	4	43.75	1-13	–	4.60
S.I.Mahmood	144.3	4	869	21	41.38	3-37	–	6.01
M.S.Panesar	74	4	341	9	37.88	2-35	–	4.60
K.P.Pietersen	14	0	91	1	91.00	1-4	–	6.50
L.E.Plunkett	172.1	6	1003	28	35.82	3-24	–	5.82
M.R.Ramprakash	22	0	108	4	27.00	3-28	–	4.90
I.D.K.Salisbury	31	1	177	5	35.40	3-41	–	5.70
R.J.Sidebottom	14	0	84	2	42.00	1-42	–	6.00
C.E.W.Silverwood	51	0	244	6	40.66	3-43	–	4.78
J.N.Snape	88.1	2	403	13	31.00	3-43	–	4.57
V.S.Solanki	18.3	0	105	1	105.00	1-17	–	5.66
A.J.Strauss	1	0	3	0	–	–	–	3.00
G.P.Swann	5	0	24	0	–	–	–	4.80
C.T.Tremlett	52.5	1	265	6	44.16	4-32	1	5.01
M.E.Trescothick	38.4	0	219	4	54.75	2-7	–	5.66
A.J.Tudor	21.1	1	136	4	34.00	2-30	–	6.42
S.D.Udal	102	4	400	9	44.44	2-37	–	3.92
M.P.Vaughan	110.4	2	562	12	46.83	4-22	1	5.07
A.G.Wharf	97.2	10	428	18	23.77	4-24	1	4.39
C.White	394	25	1725	65	26.53	5-21	2	4.37
M.H.Yardy	36	3	106	4	26.50	3-24	–	2.94

AUSTRALIA – BATTING AND FIELDING

	M	I	NO	HS	Runs	Avge	100	50	Ct/St
A.J.Bichel	67	36	13	64	471	20.47	–	1	19
N.W.Bracken	51	17	9	21*	142	17.75	–	–	11
S.R.Clark	23	8	5	16*	59	19.66	–	–	7
M.J.Clarke	98	86	20	105*	2867	43.43	2	21	36
M.J.Cosgrove	3	3	–	74	112	37.33	–	1	–
D.J.Cullen	5	1	1	2*	2	–	–	–	2
M.J.Di Venuto	9	9	–	89	241	26.77	–	2	1
B.R.Dorey	4	1	–	2	2	2.00	–	–	–
M.T.G.Elliott	1	1	–	1	1	1.00	–	–	–
A.C.Gilchrist	253	246	9	172	8381	35.36	13	48	373/45
J.N.Gillespie	97	39	16	44*	289	12.56	–	–	10
B.J.Haddin	18	16	1	70	374	24.93	–	1	25/4
I.J.Harvey	73	51	11	48*	715	17.87	–	–	17
M.L.Hayden	130	126	13	146	4619	40.87	6	29	54
B.W.Hilfenhaus	1	–	–	–	–	–	–	–	1
B.J.Hodge	10	10	1	99*	233	25.88	–	2	7
G.B.Hogg	92	54	22	71*	640	20.00	–	2	29
J.R.Hopes	9	3	–	43	84	28.00	–	–	3
M.E.K.Hussey	55	43	21	109*	1472	66.90	1	9	32
P.A.Jaques	4	4	–	94	121	30.25	–	1	1
M.G.Johnson	16	5	2	15	21	7.00	–	–	3
S.M.Katich	42	40	5	107*	1219	34.82	1	8	13
J.L.Langer	8	7	2	36	160	32.00	–	–	2/1
S.G.Law	54	51	5	110	1237	26.89	1	7	12
B.Lee	147	67	26	57	713	17.39	–	2	35
M.L.Lewis	7	1	1	4	4*	–	–	–	1
G.D.McGrath	234	66	37	11	110	3.79	–	–	33
D.R.Martyn	205	179	51	144*	5259	41.08	5	36	67
R.T.Ponting	265	259	31	164	9584	42.03	21	56	112
A.Symonds	158	125	23	156	3969	38.91	5	21	66
S.W.Tait	2	1	–	11	11	11.00	–	–	–

AUSTRALIA – BATTING AND FIELDING (continued)

	M	I	NO	HS	Runs	Avge	100	50	Ct/St
S.K.Warne	193	106	28	55	1016	13.02	–	1	80
S.R.Watson	51	37	12	79	706	28.24	–	4	11
C.L.White	10	7	2	45	89	17.80	–	–	3

AUSTRALIA – BOWLING

	O	M	R	W	Avge	Best	4wI	R/Over
A.J.Bichel	542.5	28	2463	78	31.57	7-20	3	4.53
N.W.Bracken	431.5	44	1880	89	21.12	5-67	3	4.35
S.R.Clark	194	9	1060	33	32.12	4-54	2	5.46
M.J.Clarke	212.2	2	1102	30	36.73	5-35	2	5.18
M.J.Cosgrove	5	0	13	1	13.00	1-1	–	2.60
D.J.Cullen	35.3	4	147	2	73.50	2-25	–	4.14
B.R.Dorey	27	2	146	2	73.00	1-12	–	5.40
J.N.Gillespie	857.2	79	3611	142	25.42	5-22	6	4.21
I.J.Harvey	546.3	29	2577	85	30.31	4-16	4	4.71
M.L.Hayden	1	0	18	0	–	–	–	18.00
B.W.Hilfenhaus	7	1	26	1	26.00	1-26	–	3.71
B.J.Hodge	3	0	16	0	–	–	–	5.33
G.B.Hogg	703.3	23	3159	112	28.21	5-32	2	4.49
J.R.Hopes	56	7	269	4	67.25	1-8	–	4.80
M.E.K.Hussey	32	2	167	2	83.50	1-22	–	5.21
M.G.Johnson	118	6	595	23	25.86	4-11	2	5.04
S.G.Law	134.3	3	635	12	52.91	2-22	–	4.72
B.Lee	1263.4	96	5940	260	22.84	5-22	16	4.70
M.L.Lewis	56.5	1	391	7	55.85	3-56	–	6.87
G.D.McGrath	2045.1	270	7882	351	22.45	7-15	16	3.85
D.R.Martyn	132.2	2	704	12	58.66	2-21	–	5.31
R.T.Ponting	25	0	104	3	34.66	1-12	–	4.16
A.Symonds	892	28	4437	119	37.28	5-18	3	4.97
S.W.Tait	20	1	94	3	31.33	2-68	–	4.70
S.K.Warne	1766.4	110	7514	291	25.82	5-33	13	4.25
S.R.Watson	335.5	11	1586	45	35.24	4-43	1	4.72
C.L.White	23	2	150	4	37.50	1-5	–	6.52

SOUTH AFRICA – BATTING AND FIELDING

	M	I	NO	HS	Runs	Avge	100	50	Ct/St
D.M.Benkenstein	23	20	3	69	305	17.94	–	1	3
N.Boje	113	69	18	129	1410	27.64	2	4	33
I.L.Bosman	8	8	–	88	202	25.25	–	1	3
J.Botha	11	6	3	46	98	32.66	–	–	6
M.V.Boucher	230	167	40	147*	3549	27.94	1	21	323/17
A.B.de Villiers	28	27	2	92*	784	31.36	–	5	11
H.H.Dippenaar	101	89	14	125*	3300	44.00	4	25	33
J.P.Duminy	8	8	2	60	144	24.00	–	1	4
H.H.Gibbs	197	193	14	175	6356	35.50	16	27	81
A.J.Hall	75	49	12	81	843	22.78	–	3	27
C.W.Henderson	4	–	–	–	–	–	–	–	–
J.H.Kallis	241	228	41	139	8420	45.02	14	58	94
J.M.Kemp	65	50	15	100*	1167	33.34	1	8	25
L.Klusener	171	137	50	103*	3576	41.10	2	19	35
G.J.P.Kruger	3	2	1	0*	0	0.00	–	–	1
C.K.Langeveldt	37	6	2	3	7	1.75	–	–	5
J.A.Morkel	8	6	1	23*	63	12.60	–	–	1
A.Nel	56	14	8	22	51	8.50	–	–	15

SOUTH AFRICA – BATTING AND FIELDING (continued)

	M	I	NO	HS	Runs	Avge	100	50	Ct/St
M.Ntini	142	34	18	42*	158	9.87	–	–	27
J.L.Ontong	20	11	1	32	98	9.80	–	–	10
A.N.Peterson	2	2	–	80	100	50.00	–	1	–
R.J.Peterson	33	13	2	36	135	12.27	–	–	7
S.M.Pollock	267	176	62	75	2866	25.14	–	11	99
N.Pothas	3	1	–	24	24	24.00	–	–	4/1
A.G.Prince	39	32	10	89*	833	37.86	–	2	23
A.G.Puttick	1	1	–	0	0	0.00	–	–	1
J.A.Rudolph	43	37	6	81	1157	37.32	–	7	11
G.C.Smith	102	100	6	134*	3683	39.18	6	22	49
D.W.Steyn	2	–	–	–	–	–	–	–	–
R.Telemachus	37	15	3	29	73	6.08	–	–	4
J.J.van der Wath	8	7	2	37*	85	17.00	–	–	2
M.van Jaarsveld	11	7	1	45	124	20.66	–	–	4
C.M.Willoughby	3	2	–	0	0	0.00	–	–	–
M.Zondeki	9	2	2	3*	4	–	–	–	3

SOUTH AFRICA – BOWLING

	O	M	R	W	Avge	Best	4wI	R/Over
D.M.Benkenstein	10.5	1	44	4	11.00	3-5	–	4.06
N.Boje	742.5	21	3352	95	35.28	5-21	3	4.51
J.Botha	73	1	361	7	51.57	2-49	–	4.94
J.P.Duminy	20	1	97	1	97.00	1-28	–	4.85
A.J.Hall	448.5	23	2034	78	26.07	4-23	3	4.53
C.W.Henderson	36.1	2	132	7	18.85	4-17	1	3.64
J.H.Kallis	1425.5	67	6848	219	31.26	5-30	4	4.80
J.M.Kemp	176.1	10	823	27	30.48	3-20	–	4.67
L.Klusener	1222.4	48	5751	192	29.95	6-49	7	4.70
G.J.P.Kruger	23	1	139	2	69.50	1-43	–	6.04
C.K.Langeveldt	284.1	17	1389	46	30.19	5-62	2	4.88
J.A.Morkel	44	1	212	7	30.28	2-23	–	4.81
A.Nel	454	43	2130	73	29.17	4-13	2	4.69
M.Ntini	1189	108	5211	229	22.75	6-22	10	4.38
J.L.Ontong	89.4	3	396	9	44.00	3-30	–	4.41
R.J.Peterson	196.4	4	931	16	58.18	2-26	–	4.73
S.M.Pollock	2324.4	270	8612	362	23.79	6-35	16	3.70
A.G.Prince	2	0	3	0	–	–	–	1.50
J.A.Rudolph	4	0	26	0	–	–	–	6.50
G.C.Smith	146	0	799	14	57.07	3-30	–	5.47
D.W.Steyn	8	0	90	1	90.00	1-58	–	11.25
R.Telemachus	319.4	23	1565	56	27.94	4-43	1	4.89
J.J.van der Wath	70.4	2	442	10	44.20	2-21	–	6.25
M.van Jaarsveld	5.1	1	18	2	9.00	1-0	–	3.48
C.M.Willoughby	28	2	148	2	74.00	2-39	–	5.28
M.Zondeki	67	4	350	8	43.75	2-46	–	5.22

WEST INDIES – BATTING AND FIELDING

† Excluding match abandoned without a ball bowled after toss

	M	I	NO	HS	Runs	Avge	100	50	Ct/St
C.S.Baugh	25	19	7	29	186	15.50	–	–	12/1
T.L.Best	11	7	3	24	44	11.00	–	–	3
I.D.R.Bradshaw	59	32	10	37	261	11.86	–	–	6
D.J.Bravo†	58	45	12	112*	791	23.96	1	2	24
D.C.Butler	5	4	3	13*	25	25.00	–	–	–

WEST INDIES – BATTING AND FIELDING (continued)

	M	*I*	*NO*	*HS*	*Runs*	*Avge*	*100*	*50*	*Ct/St*
S.Chanderpaul†	207	196	26	150	6459	37.99	5	44	59
S.Chattergoon	3	3	1	54*	63	31.50	–	1	1
C.D.Collymore	77	30	14	13*	82	5.12	–	–	12
F.H.Edwards	23	8	5	4*	18	6.00	–	–	2
R.R.Emrit	2	2	1	13	13	13.00	–	–	1
D.Ganga	35	34	1	71	843	25.54	–	9	11
C.H.Gayle†	155	153	9	153*	5641	39.17	15	28	74
O.D.Gibson	15	11	1	52	141	14.10	–	1	3
W.W.Hinds	114	107	9	127*	2835	28.92	5	14	28
B.C.Lara†	285	277	31	169	10079	40.97	19	61	112
R.N.Lewis	20	15	4	49	172	15.63	–	–	6
D.Mohammed	5	1	1	0*	0	–	–	–	1
R.S.Morton	34	31	3	110*	893	31.89	2	5	16
D.B.Powell	15	7	1	6	16	2.66	–	–	2
D.Ramdin	22	19	6	74*	357	27.46	–	1	24/2
M.N.Samuels	83	77	13	108*	1905	29.76	2	12	23
R.R.Sarwan†	114	107	23	115*	3724	44.33	3	24	33
L.M.P.Simmons	6	6	–	70	112	18.66	–	1	3
D.R.Smith†	58	48	2	68	717	15.58	–	2	20
D.S.Smith†	9	9	1	44	201	25.12	–	–	4
J.E.Taylor	28	9	5	9	28	7.00	–	–	9

WEST INDIES – BOWLING

	O	*M*	*R*	*W*	*Avge*	*Best*	*4wI*	*R/Over*
T.L.Best	84.2	3	427	13	32.84	4-35	1	5.06
I.D.R.Bradshaw	499.4	38	2132	76	28.05	3-15	–	4.26
D.J.Bravo	371.4	16	1970	62	31.77	4-39	1	5.30
D.C.Butler	41	3	188	3	62.66	1-25	–	4.58
S.Chanderpaul	119.2	0	617	14	44.07	3-18	–	5.17
S.Chattergoon	2	0	6	0	–	–	–	3.00
C.D.Collymore	615.4	41	2656	77	34.49	5-51	2	4.31
F.H.Edwards	179.3	16	839	26	32.26	6-22	1	4.67
R.R.Emrit	14	0	99	0	–	–	–	7.07
D.Ganga	0.1	0	4	0	–	–	–	24.00
C.H.Gayle	913.5	34	4220	134	31.49	5-46	4	4.61
O.D.Gibson	123.1	8	621	34	18.26	5-40	4	5.04
W.W.Hinds	157.3	3	837	28	29.89	3-24	–	5.31
B.C.Lara	8.1	0	61	4	15.25	2-5	–	7.46
R.N.Lewis	130.1	2	676	14	48.28	2-40	–	5.19
D.Mohammed	38.5	3	170	8	21.25	3-37	–	4.37
R.S.Morton	1	0	2	0	–	–	–	2.00
D.B.Powell	125	12	585	14	41.78	4-27	1	4.68
M.N.Samuels	448.1	9	2172	53	40.98	3-25	–	4.84
R.R.Sarwan	67.5	1	399	10	39.90	3-31	–	5.88
L.M.P.Simmons	1	0	9	0	–	–	–	9.00
D.R.Smith	311.2	17	1489	39	38.17	5-45	–	4.78
J.E.Taylor	235.2	12	1149	43	26.72	4-24	2	4.88

NEW ZEALAND – BATTING AND FIELDING

† Excluding matches abandoned without a ball bowled after toss

	M	I	NO	HS	Runs	Avge	100	50	Ct/St
A.R.Adams†	41	34	10	45	419	17.45	–	–	8
N.J.Astle††	221	217	14	145*	7090	34.92	16	41	83
S.E.Bond†	56	26	13	31*	198	15.23	–	–	10
C.L.Cairns	214	192	25	115	4881	29.22	4	25	66
S.P.Fleming††	264	255	19	134*	7569	32.07	7	45	127
J.E.C.Franklin†	54	38	11	45*	411	15.22	–	–	17
P.G.Fulton†	25	25	3	112	688	31.27	1	3	9
M.R.Gillespie†	11	7	4	11	33	11.00	–	–	1
J.M.How	6	5	–	66	141	28.20	–	2	2
B.B.McCullum†	100	81	15	56*	1411	21.37	–	4	120/10
C.D.McMillan††	182	172	14	105	4310	27.27	2	26	44
H.J.H.Marshall†	62	59	8	101*	1373	26.92	1	11	18
J.A.H.Marshall	8	8	–	50	85	10.62	–	1	–
C.S.Martin	9	6	1	3	6	1.20	–	–	3
M.J.Mason†	13	4	2	13*	22	11.00	–	–	2
K.D.Mills	65	37	18	44*	261	13.73	–	–	21
J.D.P.Oram	92	71	8	101*	1382	21.93	1	5	23
J.S.Patel	16	4	–	10	22	5.50	–	–	7
C.M.Spearman	51	50	–	86	936	18.72	–	5	15
S.B.Styris†	119	103	12	141	2642	29.03	3	15	46
R.L.Taylor†	15	14	1	128*	471	36.23	1	2	12
D.R.Tuffey†	75	40	20	20*	146	7.30	–	–	19
D.L.Vettori††	183	118	36	83	1204	14.68	–	3	46
L.Vincent	91	88	9	172	2164	27.39	2	10	36
P.J.Wiseman	15	7	5	16	45	22.50	–	–	2

NEW ZEALAND – BOWLING

	O	M	R	W	Avge	Best	4wI	R/Over
A.R.Adams	314.1	15	1643	53	31.00	5-22	3	5.22
N.J.Astle	808.2	28	3809	99	38.47	4-43	1	4.71
S.E.Bond	486.1	55	2141	106	20.19	6-19	9	4.40
C.L.Cairns	1355.2	80	6557	200	32.78	5-42	4	4.83
S.P.Fleming	4.5	0	28	1	28.00	1-8	–	5.79
J.E.C.Franklin	392	25	2018	53	38.07	5-42	1	5.14
M.R.Gillespie	94.2	11	483	13	37.15	3-39	–	5.12
C.D.McMillan	281.4	7	1532	44	34.81	3-20	–	5.43
C.S.Martin	73	4	397	11	36.09	3-62	–	5.43
M.S.Mason	121	10	633	18	35.16	4-24	1	5.23
K.D.Mills	537.5	50	2511	89	28.21	4-14	3	4.66
J.D.P.Oram	671.4	58	3090	100	30.90	5-26	4	4.60
J.S.Patel	136.4	2	694	23	30.17	3-11	–	5.07
C.M.Spearman	0.3	0	6	0	–	–	–	12.00
S.B.Styris	729.3	34	3441	107	32.15	6-25	4	4.71
R.L.Taylor	2	0	16	0	–	–	–	8.00
D.R.Tuffey	578.2	64	2693	90	29.92	4-24	2	4.65
D.L.Vettori	1425.1	56	5983	176	33.99	5-30	5	4.19
L.Vincent	0.2	0	3	0	–	–	–	9.00
P.J.Wiseman	75	0	368	12	30.66	4-45	1	4.91

INDIA – BATTING AND FIELDING

	M	I	NO	HS	Runs	Avge	100	50	Ct/St
A.B.Agarkar	178	107	26	95	1240	15.30	–	3	48
M.S.Dhoni	64	58	16	183*	1891	45.02	2	11	60/12
R.Dravid	304	282	35	153	9857	39.90	12	75	183/14
G.Gambhir	19	19	–	103	480	25.26	1	2	10
S.C.Ganguly	283	273	21	183	10342	41.03	22	63	96
Harbhajan Singh	145	75	21	46	687	12.72	–	–	41
W.Jaffer	2	2	–	10	10	5.00	–	–	–
M.Kaif	125	110	24	111*	2753	32.01	2	17	55
K.D.Karthik	11	7	–	63	145	20.71	–	1	10/1
M.Kartik	31	11	4	32*	89	12.71	–	–	10
Z.Khan	111	60	25	34*	457	13.05	–	–	26
A.Kumble	268	134	47	26	903	10.37	–	–	85
V.V.S.Laxman	86	83	7	131	2338	30.76	6	10	39
D.Mongia	55	49	7	159*	1196	28.47	1	4	21
A.Nehra	69	25	14	24	86	7.81	–	–	9
M.M.Patel	16	7	5	2*	6	3.00	–	–	1
I.K.Pathan	73	54	14	83	1006	25.15	–	5	12
R.R.Powar	18	11	4	54	117	16.71	–	1	1
S.K.Raina	36	28	5	81*	612	26.60	–	3	15
V.Sehwag	158	153	7	130	4602	31.52	7	24	66
J.Sharma	4	3	2	29*	35	35.00	–	–	3
R.P.Singh	20	8	5	9*	26	8.66	–	–	6
V.R.Singh	2	1	–	8	8	8.00	–	–	3
S.Sreesanth	26	9	4	3	7	1.40	–	–	2
S.R.Tendulkar	380	370	36	186*	14782	44.25	41	76	114
A.R.Uthappa	7	6	–	86	203	33.83	–	2	4
Y.Venugopal Rao	16	11	2	61*	218	24.22	–	1	6
J.P.Yadav	12	7	3	69	81	20.25	–	1	3
Yuvraj Singh	161	145	21	139	4296	34.64	7	25	54

INDIA – BOWLING

	O	M	R	W	Avge	Best	4wI	R/Over
A.B.Agarkar	1463.4	92	7402	270	27.41	6-42	11	5.05
R.Dravid	31	1	170	4	42.50	2-43	–	5.48
G.Gambhir	1	0	13	0	–	–	–	13.00
S.C.Ganguly	689.1	29	3484	93	37.46	5-16	3	5.05
Harbhajan Singh	1296.1	66	5349	168	31.83	5-31	4	4.12
M.Kartik	255	14	1312	27	48.59	3-36	–	5.14
Z.Khan	912.5	59	4493	154	29.17	4-19	6	4.92
A.Kumble	2386.5	109	10262	331	31.00	6-12	10	4.29
V.V.S.Laxman	7	0	40	0	–	–	–	5.71
D.Mongia	88.4	1	465	11	42.27	3-31	–	5.24
A.Nehra	577	38	2777	90	30.85	6-23	4	4.81
M.M.Patel	125.4	12	590	21	28.09	4-49	1	4.69
I.K.Pathan	592.3	41	2980	115	25.91	5-27	4	5.02
R.R.Powar	144.4	4	663	24	27.62	3-24	–	4.58
S.K.Raina	5.2	0	37	1	37.00	1-23	–	6.93
V.Sehwag	537.2	12	2809	70	40.12	3-25	–	5.22
J.Sharma	25	3	115	1	115.00	1-28	–	4.60
R.P.Singh	143	11	734	24	30.58	4-35	2	5.13
V.R.Singh	12	0	105	0	–	–	–	8.75
S.Sreesanth	211.3	11	1218	34	35.82	6-55	2	5.75
S.R.Tendulkar	1276.5	24	6439	147	43.80	5-32	6	5.04
J.P.Yadav	66	4	326	6	54.33	2-32	–	4.93
Yuvraj Singh	324.1	13	1590	42	37.85	4-6	1	4.90

PAKISTAN – BATTING AND FIELDING

	M	I	NO	HS	Runs	Avge	100	50	Ct/St
Abdul Razzaq	224	193	49	112	4388	30.47	2	22	30
Abdur Rehman	4	2	–	7	7	3.50	–	–	1
Arshad Khan	58	29	18	20	133	12.09	–	–	10
Azhar Mahmood	142	109	26	67	1519	18.30	–	3	37
Danish Kaneria	16	8	6	3*	6	3.00	–	–	2
Faisal Iqbal	18	16	2	100*	314	22.42	1	–	3
Iftikhar Anjum	25	14	13	19*	85	85.00	–	–	8
Imran Farhat	33	33	1	107	974	30.43	1	6	11
Imran Nazir	64	64	2	105*	1462	23.58	1	9	19
Inzamam-ul-Haq	371	344	52	137*	11627	39.81	10	83	109
Kamran Akmal	61	52	8	124	1098	24.95	3	1	53/9
Mohammad Akram	23	9	7	7*	14	7.00	–	–	8
Mohammad Asif	21	6	2	6	15	3.75	–	–	2
Mohammad Hafeez	43	43	1	92	819	19.50	–	4	17
Mohammad Sami	79	43	19	46	275	11.45	–	–	18
Mushtaq Ahmed	144	76	34	34*	399	9.50	–	–	30
Naved-ul-Hasan	60	39	14	29	340	13.60	–	–	12
Salman Butt	33	33	1	108*	962	30.06	3	3	9
Shahid Afridi	232	220	10	109	4945	23.54	4	27	84
Shoaib Akhtar	128	61	30	43	311	10.03	–	–	17
Shoaib Malik	133	117	15	143	3389	33.22	5	20	47
Umar Gul	25	4	1	17*	34	11.33	–	–	2
Yasir Arafat	7	5	1	27	48	12.00	–	–	1
Yasir Hamid	50	50	1	127*	1917	39.12	3	11	12
Younis Khan	147	142	18	144	3932	31.70	2	26	77
Yousuf Youhana, M.	228	216	32	141*	7801	42.39	12	52	48

PAKISTAN – BOWLING

	O	M	R	W	Avge	Best	4wI	R/Over
Abdul Razzaq	1602.5	91	7469	244	30.61	6-35	11	4.65
Abdur Rehman	32	4	119	6	19.83	2-20	–	3.71
Arshad Khan	470.3	27	1948	56	34.78	4-33	1	4.14
Azhar Mahmood	1032.4	57	4788	123	38.92	6-18	5	4.63
Danish Kaneria	129.2	9	589	12	49.08	3-31	–	4.55
Faisal Iqbal	3	0	33	0	–	–	–	11.00
Iftikhar Anjum	193.5	18	899	19	47.31	2-13	–	4.63
Imran Farhat	14.2	2	89	5	17.80	3-10	–	6.20
Imran Nazir	8.1	0	48	1	48.00	1-3	–	5.87
Inzamam-ul-Haq	9.4	1	64	3	21.33	1-0	–	6.61
Mohammad Akram	164.5	6	790	19	41.57	2-28	–	4.79
Mohammad Asif	165.4	23	678	21	32.28	3-28	–	4.09
Mohammad Hafeez	251.5	9	1116	33	33.81	3-17	–	4.43
Mohammad Sami	651.2	38	3237	111	29.16	5-10	4	4.96
Mushtaq Ahmed	1257.1	51	5361	161	33.29	5-36	4	4.26
Naved-ul-Hasan	461.4	22	2541	95	26.74	6-27	6	5.50
Salman Butt	6	0	42	0	–	–	–	7.00
Shahid Afridi	1526.4	46	7036	196	35.89	5-11	4	4.60
Shoaib Akhtar	1003.3	81	4638	202	22.96	6-16	9	4.62
Shoaib Malik	790.2	21	3520	103	34.17	4-19	1	4.45
Umar Gul	192.1	13	883	30	29.43	5-17	1	4.59
Yasir Arafat	39	0	233	4	58.25	1-28	–	5.97
Yasir Hamid	3	0	26	0	–	–	–	8.66
Younis Khan	15.1	0	101	1	101.00	1-24	–	6.65
Yousuf Youhana, M.	0.1	0	1	0	–	–	–	6.00

SRI LANKA – BATTING AND FIELDING

† Excluding match abandoned without a ball bowled after toss

	M	*I*	*NO*	*HS*	*Runs*	*Avge*	*100*	*50*	*Ct/St*
R.P.Arnold	167	144	37	103	3744	34.99	1	26	46
M.S.Atapattu†	265	257	32	132*	8468	37.63	11	59	70
C.M.Bandara	21	10	3	28*	88	12.57	–	–	4
U.D.U.Chandana	146	110	17	89	1626	17.48	–	5	77
L.H.D.Dilhara	8	8	–	29	77	9.62	–	–	3
T.M.Dilshan	107	89	19	117*	2022	28.88	1	8	53/1
C.R.D.Fernando†	102	38	24	13*	138	9.85	–	–	17
K.H.R.K.Fernando	7	5	3	23*	43	21.50	–	–	2
W.C.A.Ganegama	4	2	–	7	7	3.50	–	–	1
D.A.Gunawardana	61	61	1	132	1708	28.46	1	12	13
S.T.Jayasuriya†	375	365	17	189	11486	33.00	23	62	110
D.P.M.D.Jayawardena†	231	215	23	128	6096	31.75	8	33	113
C.K.Kapugedara†	17	14	1	50	203	15.61	–	1	4
M.D.N.Kulasekara	16	9	5	11	23	5.75	–	–	3
K.S.Lokuarachchi	18	15	3	69	199	16.58	–	1	4
M.F.Maharoof†	57	37	10	58*	522	19.33	–	1	13
S.L.Malinga†	26	12	7	15	44	8.80	–	–	3
J.Mubarak	20	19	–	61	315	16.57	–	2	6
M.Muralitharan†	279	132	49	27	488	5.87	–	–	110
P.D.R.L.Perera	18	6	2	4*	8	2.00	–	–	2
K.T.G.D.Prasad	3	1	–	8	8	8.00	–	–	–
T.T.Samaraweera	17	13	1	33	199	16.58	–	–	3
K.C.Sangakkara†	179	164	21	138*	5216	36.47	6	33	160/45
L.P.C.Silva	13	10	–	55	169	16.90	–	1	3
W.U.Tharanga†	41	39	–	120	1415	36.28	6	5	7
W.P.U.C.J.Vaas†	288	198	65	50*	1869	14.05	–	1	55
M.G.Vandort	1	1	–	48	48	48.00	–	–	–
D.N.T.Zoysa	95	47	21	47*	343	13.19	–	–	13

SRI LANKA – BOWLING

	O	*M*	*R*	*W*	*Avge*	*Best*	*4wI*	*R/Over*
R.P.Arnold	347.2	8	1683	37	45.48	3-47	–	4.84
M.S.Atapattu	8.3	0	41	0	–	–	–	4.82
C.M.Bandara	156.2	2	739	25	29.56	4-31	2	4.72
U.D.U.Chandana	1016.4	20	4790	151	31.72	5-61	5	4.71
L.H.D.Dilhara	47	3	221	6	36.83	2-30	–	4.70
T.M.Dilshan	311.4	7	1502	36	41.72	4-29	2	4.81
C.R.D.Fernando	720.3	33	3824	123	31.08	4-48	1	5.30
K.H.R.K.Fernando	39	4	159	6	26.50	3-12	–	4.07
W.C.A.Ganegama	11	0	88	2	44.00	2-27	–	8.00
S.T.Jayasuriya	2202	40	10483	285	36.78	6-29	10	4.76
D.P.M.D.Jayawardena	94.4	1	539	7	77.00	2-56	–	5.69
M.D.N.Kulasekara	114.5	8	507	9	56.33	2-19	–	4.41
K.S.Lokuarachchi	143.3	6	624	28	22.28	4-44	1	4.34
M.F.Maharoof	372.4	25	1750	70	25.00	6-14	2	4.69
S.L.Malinga	210.5	14	998	39	25.58	4-44	2	4.73
J.Mubarak	8	0	49	1	49.00	1-10	–	6.12
M.Muralitharan	2534.4	178	9710	421	23.06	7-30	19	3.83
P.D.R.L.Perera	138	9	753	19	39.63	3-23	–	5.45
K.T.G.D.Prasad	21	2	116	3	38.66	2-29	–	5.52
T.T.Samaraweera	112	2	509	10	50.90	3-34	–	4.54
W.P.U.C.J.Vaas	2363.3	247	9915	369	26.86	8-19	13	4.19
D.N.T.Zoysa	709.5	60	3213	108	29.75	5-26	3	4.52

ZIMBABWE – BATTING AND FIELDING

	M	I	NO	HS	Runs	Avge	100	50	Ct/St
A.M.Blignaut	51	40	8	63*	625	19.53	–	5	11
G.B.Brent	57	41	15	24	260	10.00	–	–	16
C.J.Chibhabha	22	22	–	67	609	27.68	–	4	8
E.Chigumbura	53	47	5	77*	1059	25.21	–	6	16
C.K.Coventry	11	10	–	74	199	19.90	–	1	5
K.M.Dabengwa	12	9	3	32	146	24.33	–	–	6
T.Duffin	22	22	–	88	534	24.27	–	3	6
S.M.Ervine	42	34	7	100	698	25.85	1	2	5
G.M.Ewing	7	7	–	46	97	13.85	–	–	3
A.Flower	213	208	16	145	6786	35.34	4	55	141/32
G.W.Flower	219	212	18	142*	6536	33.69	6	40	86
M.W.Goodwin	71	70	3	112*	1818	27.13	2	8	20
R.S.Higgins	11	8	2	7*	15	2.50	–	–	5
A.J.Ireland	25	13	5	8*	30	3.75	–	–	1
T.Kamungozi	4	3	2	0*	0	0.00	–	–	2
F.Kasteni	1	1	–	9	9	9.00	–	–	–
N.B.Mahwire	23	19	8	22*	117	10.63	–	–	6
H.Masakadza	39	39	2	75	712	19.24	–	5	14
S.Matsikenyeri	60	58	4	89	1046	19.37	–	4	18
T.M.K.Mawayo	2	2	–	14	24	12.00	–	–	–
K.Meth	5	3	–	53	73	24.33	–	1	–
C.B.Mpofu	18	11	6	4	17	3.40	–	–	2
T.V.Mufambisi	6	6	–	21	55	9.16	–	–	1
T.Mupariwa	19	17	6	33	149	13.54	–	–	5
M.L.Nkala	50	35	5	47	324	10.80	–	–	6
R.W.Price	26	12	5	20*	90	12.85	–	–	1
E.C.Rainsford	23	13	6	9*	37	5.28	–	–	5
H.P.Rinke	18	18	–	72	317	17.61	–	3	–
V.Sibanda	46	45	2	116	1009	23.46	1	7	18
H.H.Streak	187	157	55	79*	2901	28.44	–	13	45
G.M.Strydom	12	10	–	58	147	14.70	–	1	4
T.Taibu	83	70	15	96*	1400	25.45	–	7	73/8
B.R.M.Taylor	60	59	5	98	1514	28.03	–	10	35/11
P.Utseya	59	47	15	31	326	10.18	–	–	18
S.C.Williams	13	13	2	68	261	23.72	–	3	7

ZIMBABWE – BOWLING

	O	M	R	W	Avge	Best	4wI	R/Over
A.M.Blignaut	378.2	11	2021	49	41.22	4-43	2	5.34
G.B.Brent	451.1	26	2192	64	34.25	4-22	3	4.85
C.J.Chibhabha	43	1	289	4	72.25	2-39	–	6.72
E.Chigumbura	125.3	7	840	15	56.00	3-37	–	6.69
K.M.Dabengwa	52.3	0	268	7	38.28	3-19	–	5.10
S.M.Ervine	274.5	10	1561	41	38.07	3-29	–	5.67
G.M.Ewing	52	0	236	5	47.20	3-31	–	4.53
A.Flower	5	0	23	0	–	–	–	4.60
G.W.Flower	903.1	11	4187	104	40.25	4-32	2	4.63
M.W.Goodwin	41.2	1	210	4	52.50	1-12	–	5.08
R.S.Higgins	90.4	6	380	13	29.23	4-21	1	4.19
A.J.Ireland	214	13	1077	37	29.10	3-41	–	5.03
T.Kamungozi	30	–	163	5	32.60	2-55	–	5.43
N.B.Mahwire	147.3	12	775	21	36.90	3-29	–	5.25
H.Masakadza	57.1	2	308	10	30.80	3-39	–	5.38
S.Matsikenyeri	125	2	655	13	50.38	2-33	–	5.24
K.O.Meth	18	1	96	1	96.00	1-6	–	5.33

ZIMBABWE – BOWLING (continued)

	O	M	R	W	Avge	Best	4wI	R/Over
C.B.Mpofu	138.1	6	708	21	33.71	4-42	1	5.12
T.Mupariwa	170.3	14	865	33	27.21	4-61	1	5.07
M.L.Nkala	263.4	8	1570	22	71.36	3-12	–	5.95
R.W.Price	221.2	9	917	15	61.13	2-16	–	4.14
E.C.Rainsford	196	17	879	23	38.21	3-16	–	4.48
H.P.Rinke	46.1	2	273	8	34.12	2-11	–	5.90
V.Sibanda	15	0	87	2	43.50	1-12	–	5.80
H.H.Streak	1569	114	7065	237	29.81	5-32	8	4.50
G.M.Strydom	11	0	61	1	61.00	1-28	–	5.54
T.Taibu	14	1	61	2	30.50	2-42	–	4.35
B.R.M.Taylor	35	0	224	8	28.00	3-54	–	6.40
P.Utseya	505.1	29	2009	37	54.29	3-35	–	3.97
S.C.Williams	68.3	0	308	5	61.60	3-23	–	4.49

BANGLADESH – BATTING AND FIELDING

	M	I	NO	HS	Runs	Avge	100	50	Ct/St
Abdur Razzaq	36	22	13	21	142	15.77	–	–	9
Aftab Ahmed	53	53	6	92	1374	29.23	–	12	13
Alok Kapali	55	52	3	89*	964	19.67	–	5	21
Farhad Reza	12	10	2	50	231	28.87	–	1	5
Habibul Bashar	98	94	5	78	1963	22.05	–	13	21
Javed Omar	53	53	4	85*	1166	23.79	–	9	10
Khaled Mahmud	77	72	3	50	991	14.36	–	1	17
Khaled Masud	126	110	27	71*	1818	21.90	–	7	91/35
Manjural Rana	25	21	5	63	331	20.68	–	1	6
Mashrafe Mortaza	55	43	9	51*	556	16.35	–	1	18
Mehrab Hossain II	10	9	–	54	200	22.22	–	1	2
Mohammad Ashraful	86	81	6	100	1548	20.64	1	9	14
Mohammad Rafique	110	96	14	77	1124	13.70	–	2	22
Mohammad Sharif	9	9	5	13*	53	13.25	–	–	1
Mushfiqur Rahim	9	6	1	57	151	30.20	–	1	7/3
Mushfiqur Rahman	28	25	3	49	360	16.36	–	–	6
Nazmul Hossain	17	11	7	6*	30	7.50	–	–	4
Rajin Saleh	43	43	1	108*	1005	23.92	1	6	10
Saqibul Hasan	18	17	5	68	487	40.58	–	2	4
Shahadat Hossain	19	8	5	5*	15	5.00	–	–	1
Shahriar Nafiz	39	39	3	123*	1391	38.63	3	7	6
Syed Rasel	18	8	2	15	30	5.00	–	–	3
Tamim Iqbal	2	2	–	30	35	17.50	–	–	–
Tapash Baisya	54	41	13	35*	336	12.00	–	–	8
Tushar Imran	37	36	–	65	547	15.19	–	2	5

BANGLADESH – BOWLING

	O	M	R	W	Avge	Best	4wI	R/Over
Abdur Razzaq	320.3	25	1175	56	20.98	5-33	3	3.66
Aftab Ahmed	102	0	517	10	51.70	5-31	1	5.06
Alok Kapali	187.2	8	939	15	62.60	2-29	–	5.01
Farhad Reza	62	4	320	2	160.00	1-19	–	5.16
Habibul Bashar	29.1	0	142	1	142.00	1-31	–	4.86
Khaled Mahmud	564.1	30	2865	67	42.76	4-19	1	5.07
Manjural Rana	166	9	689	23	29.95	4-34	2	4.15
Mashrafe Mortaza	476.5	44	2172	79	27.49	6-26	3	4.55
Mehrab Hossain II	23.1	0	108	3	36.00	2-30	–	4.66
Mohammad Ashraful	56.4	1	344	10	34.40	3-26	–	6.07

BANGLADESH – BOWLING (continued)

	O	M	R	W	Avge	Best	4wI	R/Over
Mohammad Rafique	937	56	4117	106	38.83	5-47	3	4.39
Mohammad Sharif	83.1	5	424	10	42.40	3-40	–	5.09
Mushfiqur Rahman	222	18	983	19	51.73	2-21	–	4.42
Nazmul Hossain	127.3	9	731	18	40.61	4-40	1	5.73
Rajin Saleh	89.5	1	459	15	30.60	4-16	1	5.10
Saqibul Hossain	148.3	10	512	19	26.94	3-18	–	3.44
Shahadat Hossain	138.4	10	667	23	29.00	3-34	–	4.81
Syed Rasel	155.3	19	654	26	25.15	4-22	1	4.20
Tapash Baisya	421.5	17	2364	58	40.75	4-16	2	5.60
Tushar Imran	18	0	86	1	86.00	1-24	–	4.77

ASSOCIATES – BATTING AND FIELDING

	M	I	NO	HS	Runs	Avge	100	50	Ct/St
J.A.R.Blain (Scotland)	18	15	4	30*	155	14.09	–	–	5
D.R.Brown (Scotland)	13	13	1	50*	156	13.00	–	1	2
D.L.Hemp (Bermuda)	12	12	1	58	321	29.18	–	2	1
E.J.G.Morgan (Ireland)	6	6	–	115	360	60.00	1	2	1
N.J.O'Brien (Ireland)	7	7	–	53	130	18.57	–	1	5/2
N.S.Poonia (Scotland)	8	8	–	67	111	13.87	–	1	4
W.B.Rankin (Ireland)	1	–	–	–	–	–	–	–	1
R.N.ten Doeschate (Holland)	11	11	3	109*	441	55.12	1	2	4
A.R.White (Ireland)	8	4	–	40	78	19.50	–	–	3

ASSOCIATES – BOWLING

	O	M	R	W	Avge	Best	4wI	R/Over
J.A.R.Blain	131.1	2	735	23	31.95	4-37	1	5.60
D.R.Brown	89.5	3	488	14	34.85	3-37	–	5.43
D.L.Hemp	17	0	87	1	87.00	1-25	–	5.11
W.B.Rankin	4	0	25	0	–	–	–	6.25
A.R.White	36.1	1	196	4	49.00	2-31	–	5.41
R.N.ten Doeschate	84.3	2	442	20	22.10	4-31	2	5.23

COUNTY BENEFITS AWARDED FOR 2007

Derbyshire	G.Welch
Durham	P.D.Collingwood (Benefit) and A.Walker (Testimonial)
Essex	–
Glamorgan	–
Gloucestershire	J.Lewis
Hampshire	A.D.Mascarenhas
Kent	–
Lancashire	S.G.Law
Leicestershire	P.A.Nixon
Middlesex	D.C.Nash
Northamptonshire	D.J.G.Sales
Nottinghamshire	P.J.Franks
Somerset	–
Surrey	I.D.K.Salisbury
Sussex	R.R.Montgomerie
Warwickshire	S.J.Rouse
Worcestershire	V.S.Solanki
Yorkshire	–

TEST MATCH CAREER RECORDS

These records, complete to 1 May 2007, contain all players registered for county cricket in 2007 at the time of going to press, plus those who have played Test cricket since 22 September 2005 (Test No. 1767).

ENGLAND – BATTING AND FIELDING

	M	*I*	*NO*	*HS*	*Runs*	*Avge*	*100*	*50*	*Ct/St*
C.J.Adams	5	8	–	31	104	13.00	–	–	6
U.Afzaal	3	6	1	54	83	16.60	–	1	–
K.Ali	1	2	–	9	10	5.00	–	–	–
J.M.Anderson	16	23	15	21*	101	12.62	–	–	4
G.J.Batty	7	8	1	38	144	20.57	–	–	3
I.R.Bell	23	42	5	162*	1618	43.72	5	11	23
I.D.Blackwell	1	1	–	4	4	4.00	–	–	–
M.A.Butcher	71	131	7	173*	4288	34.58	8	23	61
A.R.Caddick	62	95	12	49*	861	10.37	–	–	21
R.Clarke	2	3	–	55	96	32.00	–	1	1
P.D.Collingwood	20	38	4	206	1460	42.94	3	4	27
A.N.Cook	14	26	2	127	1037	43.20	4	3	9
D.G.Cork	37	56	8	59	864	18.00	–	3	18
J.P.Crawley	37	61	9	156*	1800	34.61	4	9	29
R.D.B.Croft	21	34	8	37*	421	16.19	–	–	10
R.K.J.Dawson	7	13	3	19*	114	11.40	–	–	3
M.A.Ealham	8	13	3	53*	210	21.00	–	2	4
A.Flintoff	66	108	6	167	3331	32.65	5	24	44
J.S.Foster	7	12	3	48	226	25.11	–	–	17/1
J.E.R.Gallian	3	6	–	28	74	12.33	–	–	1
A.F.Giles	54	81	13	59	1421	20.89	–	4	33
D.Gough	58	86	18	65	855	12.57	–	2	13
S.J.Harmison	49	67	17	42	577	11.54	–	–	7
G.A.Hick	65	114	6	178	3383	31.32	6	18	90
M.J.Hoggard	62	86	27	38	444	7.52	–	–	23
R.C.Irani	3	5	–	41	86	17.20	–	–	2
R.L.Johnson	3	4	–	26	59	14.75	–	–	–
G.O.Jones	34	53	4	100	1172	23.91	1	6	128/5
S.P.Jones	18	18	5	44	205	15.76	–	–	4
R.W.T.Key	15	26	1	221	775	31.00	1	3	11
R.J.Kirtley	4	7	1	12	32	5.33	–	–	3
J.Lewis	1	2	–	20	27	13.50	–	–	–
A.McGrath	4	5	–	81	201	40.20	–	2	3
D.L.Maddy	3	4	–	24	46	11.50	–	–	4
S.I.Mahmood	8	11	1	34	81	8.10	–	–	–
J.Ormond	2	4	1	18	38	12.66	–	–	–
M.S.Panesar	13	19	9	26	86	8.60	–	–	2
M.M.Patel	2	2	–	27	45	22.50	–	–	2
K.P.Pietersen	23	44	2	158	2087	49.69	6	9	14
L.E.Plunkett	6	9	1	28	69	8.62	–	–	2
M.R.Ramprakash	52	92	6	154	2350	27.32	2	12	39
C.M.W.Read	15	23	4	55	360	18.94	–	1	48/6
M.J.Saggers	3	3	–	1	1	0.33	–	–	1
I.D.K.Salisbury	15	25	3	50	368	16.72	–	1	5
C.P.Schofield	2	3	–	57	67	22.33	–	1	–
O.A.Shah	1	2	–	88	126	63.00	–	1	1
R.J.Sidebottom	1	1	–	4	4	4.00	–	–	–
C.E.W.Silverwood	6	7	3	10	29	7.25	–	–	2
E.T.Smith	3	5	–	64	87	17.40	–	1	5
A.J.Strauss	36	68	2	147	2844	43.09	10	8	42
M.E.Trescothick	76	143	10	219	5825	43.79	14	29	95
A.J.Tudor	10	16	4	99*	229	19.08	–	1	3
S.D.Udal	4	7	1	33*	109	18.16	–	–	1

ENGLAND – BATTING AND FIELDING (continued)

	M	I	NO	HS	Runs	Avge	100	50	Ct/St
M.P.Vaughan	64	115	8	197	4595	42.94	15	14	37
C.White	30	50	7	121	1052	24.46	1	5	14

ENGLAND – BOWLING

	O	M	R	W	Avge	Best	5wI	10wM
C.J.Adams	20	5	59	1	59.00	1- 42	–	–
U.Afzaal	9	0	49	1	49.00	1- 49	–	–
K.Ali	36	5	136	5	27.20	3- 80	–	–
J.M.Anderson	463.3	98	1766	46	38.39	5- 73	2	–
G.J.Batty	232.2	34	733	11	66.63	3- 55	–	–
I.R.Bell	18	3	76	1	76.00	1- 33	–	–
I.D.Blackwell	19	2	71	0				
M.A.Butcher	150.1	27	541	15	36.06	4- 42	–	–
A.R.Caddick	2259.4	501	6999	234	29.91	7- 46	13	1
R.Clarke	29	11	60	4	15.00	2- 7	–	–
P.D.Collingwood	75	11	265	1	265.00	1- 33	–	–
D.G.Cork	1279.4	264	3906	131	29.81	7- 43	5	–
R.D.B.Croft	769.5	195	1825	49	37.24	5- 95	1	–
R.K.J.Dawson	186	20	677	11	61.54	4-134	–	–
M.A.Ealham	176.4	43	488	17	28.70	4- 21	–	–
A.Flintoff	2059.4	421	6201	190	32.63	5- 58	2	–
J.E.R.Gallian	14	1	62	0				
A.F.Giles	2030	397	5806	143	40.60	5- 57	5	–
D.Gough	1970.1	370	6503	229	28.39	6- 42	9	–
S.J.Harmison	1784	355	5670	185	30.64	7- 12	8	1
G.A.Hick	509.3	128	1306	23	56.78	4-126	–	–
M.J.Hoggard	2169	461	7093	235	30.18	7- 61	7	1
R.C.Irani	32	10	112	3	37.33	1- 22	–	–
R.L.Johnson	91.1	25	275	16	17.18	6- 33	2	–
S.P.Jones	470.1	78	1666	59	28.23	6- 53	3	–
R.J.Kirtley	179.5	50	561	19	29.52	6- 34	1	–
J.Lewis	41	9	122	3	40.66	3- 68	–	–
A.McGrath	17	1	56	4	14.00	3- 16	–	–
D.L.Maddy	14	1	40	0				
S.I.Mahmood	188.2	25	762	20	38.10	4- 22	–	–
J.Ormond	62	12	185	2	92.50	1- 70	–	–
M.S.Panesar	490.5	112	1416	42	33.71	5- 72	3	–
M.M.Patel	46	8	180	1	180.00	1-101	–	–
K.P.Pietersen	43	3	201	1	201.00	1- 11	–	–
L.E.Plunkett	167.2	27	601	16	37.56	3- 17	–	–
M.R.Ramprakash	149.1	16	477	4	119.25	1- 2	–	–
M.J.Saggers	82.1	20	247	7	35.28	2- 29	–	–
I.D.K.Salisbury	415.2	50	1539	20	76.95	4-163	–	–
C.P.Schofield	18	2	73	0				
R.J.Sidebottom	20	2	64	0				
C.E.W.Silverwood	138	27	444	11	40.36	5- 91	1	–
M.E.Trescothick	50	6	155	1	155.00	1- 34	–	–
A.J.Tudor	252	51	963	28	34.39	5- 44	1	–
S.D.Udal	99.2	13	344	8	43.00	4- 14	–	–
M.P.Vaughan	156	20	537	6	89.50	2- 71	–	–
C.White	659.5	119	2220	59	37.62	5- 32	3	–

TEST AUSTRALIA – BATTING AND FIELDING

	M	I	NO	HS	Runs	Avge	100	50	Ct/St
A.J.Bichel	19	22	1	71	355	16.90	–	1	16
N.W.Bracken	5	6	2	37	70	17.50	–	–	2
S.R.Clark	9	10	2	39	116	14.50	–	–	2
M.J.Clarke	26	39	5	151	1468	43.17	4	5	19
D.J.Cullen	1	–	–	–	–	–	–	–	–
M.T.G.Elliott	21	36	1	199	1172	33.48	3	4	14
A.C.Gilchrist	89	127	19	204*	5258	48.68	17	23	339/35
J.N.Gillespie	71	93	28	201*	1218	18.73	1	2	27
M.L.Hayden	88	157	13	380	7551	52.43	26	26	115
B.J.Hodge	5	9	2	203*	409	58.42	1	1	9
M.E.K.Hussey	16	26	6	182	1597	79.85	5	8	8
P.A.Jaques	2	3	–	66	96	32.00	–	1	1
M.S.Kasprowicz	38	54	12	25	445	10.59	–	–	16
S.M.Katich	22	36	3	125	1258	38.12	2	8	14
J.L.Langer	104	180	12	250	7674	45.67	23	30	72
S.G.Law	1	1	1	54*	54	–	–	1	1
B.Lee	58	63	13	64	1094	21.88	–	3	16
S.C.G.MacGill	39	43	9	43	347	10.20	–	–	16
G.D.McGrath	123	136	51	61	639	7.51	–	1	38
D.R.Martyn	67	109	14	165	4406	46.37	13	23	36
M.J.Nicholson	1	2	–	9	14	7.00	–	–	–
R.T.Ponting	109	181	25	257	9268	59.41	33	35	123
A.Symonds	13	19	–	156	518	27.26	1	2	13
S.K.Warne	144	197	17	99	3142	17.45	–	12	125
S.R.Watson	2	2	–	31	47	23.50	–	–	–

AUSTRALIA – BOWLING

	O	M	R	W	Avge	Best	5wI	10wM
A.J.Bichel	556	111	1870	58	32.24	5- 60	1	–
N.W.Bracken	185	53	505	12	42.08	4- 48	–	–
S.R.Clark	341.2	91	837	47	17.80	5- 55	1	–
M.J.Clarke	43.2	5	128	8	16.00	6- 9	1	–
D.J.Cullen	14	0	54	1	54.00	1- 25	–	–
M.T.G.Elliott	2	1	4	0				
J.N.Gillespie	2372.2	630	6770	259	26.13	7- 37	8	–
M.L.Hayden	9	0	40	0				
B.J.Hodge	2	0	8	0				
M.E.K.Hussey	5	0	23	0				
M.S.Kasprowicz	1190	246	3716	113	32.88	7- 36	4	–
S.M.Katich	109.5	10	406	12	33.83	6- 65	1	–
J.L.Langer	1	0	3	0				
S.G.Law	3	1	9	0				
B.Lee	2028.3	407	7204	229	31.45	5- 30	7	–
S.C.G.MacGill	1677.4	341	5305	189	28.06	8-108	11	2
G.D.McGrath	4856.4	1464	12144	560	21.68	8- 24	29	3
D.R.Martyn	58	15	168	2	84.00	1- 0	–	–
M.J.Nicholson	25	4	115	4	28.75	3- 56	–	–
R.T.Ponting	87.5	23	231	5	46.20	1- 0	–	–
A.Symonds	180	41	488	11	44.36	3- 50	–	–
S.K.Warne	6753	1753	17924	702	25.53	8- 71	37	10
S.R.Watson	25	5	85	2	42.50	1- 25	–	–

TEST — SOUTH AFRICA – BATTING AND FIELDING

	M	I	NO	HS	Runs	Avge	100	50	Ct/St
H.D.Ackerman	4	8	–	57	161	20.12	–	1	1
H.M.Amla	13	25	1	149	616	25.66	1	4	15
N.Boje	43	62	10	85	1312	25.23	–	4	18
J.Botha	1	1	1	20*	20	–	–	–	–
M.V.Boucher	101	143	18	125	3827	30.61	4	25	374/16
A.B.de Villiers	28	52	2	178	1757	35.14	3	10	41/1
H.H.Dippenaar	38	62	5	177*	1718	30.14	3	7	27
H.H.Gibbs	84	144	7	228	5943	43.37	14	24	85
A.J.Hall	21	33	4	163	760	26.20	1	3	16
P.L.Harris	4	7	1	11*	26	4.33	–	–	2
M.Hayward	16	17	8	14	66	7.33	–	–	4
C.W.Henderson	7	7	–	30	65	9.28	–	–	2
J.H.Kallis	106	180	28	189*	8347	54.91	24	44	101
J.M.Kemp	4	6	–	55	80	13.33	–	1	3
L.Klusener	49	69	11	174	1906	32.86	4	8	34
C.K.Langeveldt	6	4	2	10	16	8.00	–	–	2
M.Morkel	1	2	1	31*	58	58.00	–	–	–
A.Nel	27	31	7	23*	200	8.33	–	–	12
M.Ntini	75	86	24	32*	619	9.98	–	–	20
S.M.Pollock	107	156	39	111	3781	32.31	2	16	72
A.G.Prince	29	47	5	139*	1800	42.85	6	5	16
J.A.Rudolph	35	63	7	222*	2028	36.21	5	8	22
G.C.Smith	53	94	5	277	4273	48.01	11	18	62
D.W.Steyn	11	17	6	13	80	7.27	–	–	2
M.van Jaarsveld	9	15	2	73	397	30.53	–	3	11
C.M.Willoughby	2	–	–	–	–	–	–	–	–

SOUTH AFRICA – BOWLING

	O	M	R	W	Avge	Best	5wI	10wM
H.M.Amla	1	0	4	0				
N.Boje	1436.4	293	4265	100	42.65	5- 62	3	–
J.Botha	19.3	2	103	2	51.50	1- 26	–	–
M.V.Boucher	1.2	0	6	1	6.00	1- 6	–	–
A.B.de Villiers	33	6	99	2	49.50	2- 49	–	–
H.H.Dippenaar	2	1	1	0				
H.H.Gibbs	1	0	4	0				
A.J.Hall	500.1	95	1617	45	35.93	3- 1	–	–
P.L.Harris	117.1	20	314	11	28.54	4- 46	–	–
M.Hayward	470.1	91	1609	54	29.79	5- 56	1	–
C.W.Henderson	327	79	928	22	42.18	4-116	–	–
J.H.Kallis	2372.5	618	6718	212	31.68	6- 54	4	–
J.M.Kemp	79.5	20	222	9	24.66	3- 33	–	–
L.Klusener	1147.5	319	3033	80	37.91	8- 64	1	–
C.K.Langeveldt	166.3	27	593	16	37.06	5- 46	1	–
M.Morkel	24	1	111	3	37.00	3- 86	–	–
A.Nel	989.1	218	3023	97	31.16	6- 32	3	1
M.Ntini	2637.4	577	8465	308	27.48	7- 37	17	4
S.M.Pollock	4030.5	1217	9648	416	23.19	7- 87	16	1
A.G.Prince	13	1	31	1	31.00	1- 2	–	–
J.A.Rudolph	110.4	13	432	4	108.00	1- 1	–	–
G.C.Smith	210.5	27	750	8	93.75	2-145	–	–
D.W.Steyn	340	59	1325	42	31.54	5- 47	2	–
M.van Jaarsveld	7	0	28	0				
C.M.Willoughby	50	18	125	1	125.00	1- 47	–	–

TEST WEST INDIES – BATTING AND FIELDING

	M	*I*	*NO*	*HS*	*Runs*	*Avge*	*100*	*50*	*Ct/St*
I.D.R.Bradshaw	5	8	1	33	96	13.71	–	–	3
D.J.Bravo	19	35	1	113	1113	32.73	2	6	16
G.R.Breese	1	2	–	5	5	2.50	–	–	1
S.Chanderpaul	101	173	22	203*	6736	44.60	14	40	44
P.T.Collins	32	47	7	24	235	5.87	–	–	7
C.D.Collymore	26	45	25	16*	160	8.00	–	–	6
F.H.Edwards	25	41	11	20	131	4.36	–	–	4
D.Ganga	41	72	1	135	1938	27.29	3	9	25
C.H.Gayle	64	113	3	317	4259	38.71	7	26	66
O.D.Gibson	2	4	–	37	93	23.25	–	–	–
W.W.Hinds	45	80	1	213	2608	33.01	5	14	33
B.C.Lara	130	230	6	400*	11912	53.17	34	48	164
J.J.C.Lawson	13	21	6	14	52	3.46	–	–	3
R.N.Lewis	4	8	–	40	88	11.00	–	–	–
D.Mohammed	5	8	1	52	225	32.14	–	1	1
R.S.Morton	6	10	1	70*	235	26.11	–	2	7
D.B.Powell	19	29	–	16	167	5.75	–	–	1
D.Ramdin	15	27	5	71	577	26.22	–	4	38/1
M.N.Samuels	23	41	4	104	1044	28.21	1	7	9
R.R.Sarwan	65	118	8	261*	4268	38.80	9	26	46
D.R.Smith	10	14	1	105*	320	24.61	1	–	9
D.S.Smith	16	30	1	108	735	25.34	1	3	14
J.E.Taylor	10	16	3	23	109	8.38	–	–	–

WEST INDIES – BOWLING

	O	*M*	*R*	*W*	*Avge*	*Best*	*5wI*	*10wM*
I.D.R.Bradshaw	170.1	33	540	9	60.00	3- 73	–	–
D.J.Bravo	485.3	95	1540	39	39.48	6- 55	2	–
G.R.Breese	31.2	3	135	2	67.50	2-108	–	–
S.Chanderpaul	269.0	52	802	8	100.25	1- 2	–	–
P.T.Collins	1160.4	221	3671	106	34.63	6- 53	3	–
C.D.Collymore	919.1	226	2526	82	30.80	7- 57	4	1
F.H.Edwards	702.2	80	2791	63	44.30	5- 36	4	–
D.Ganga	31.0	2	106	1	106.00	1- 20	–	–
C.H.Gayle	804.2	170	2051	53	38.69	5- 34	2	–
O.D.Gibson	78.4	9	275	3	91.66	2- 81	–	–
W.W.Hinds	187.1	41	590	16	36.87	3- 79	–	–
B.C.Lara	10.0	1	28	0				
J.J.C.Lawson	394.0	55	1512	51	29.64	7- 78	2	–
R.N.Lewis	126.3	24	388	1	388.00	1- 67	–	–
D.Mohammed	177.3	20	668	13	51.38	3- 98	–	–
R.S.Morton	10.0	0	46	0				
D.B.Powell	605.3	118	2006	47	42.68	5- 25	1	–
M.N.Samuels	218.0	32	703	5	140.60	2- 49	–	–
R.R.Sarwan	310.0	33	1042	23	45.30	4- 37	–	–
D.R.Smith	108.3	20	344	7	49.14	3- 71	–	–
J.E.Taylor	297.4	56	1029	31	33.19	5- 50	2	–

WEST INDIES 'A' TEAM TO BRITAIN 2006

Full Names	*Birthdate*	*Birthplace*	*Team*	*Type*	*F-C Debut*
BANKS, Omari Ahmed Clemente	17.07.82	Anguilla	Leeward Is	RHB/OB	2000-01
BEST, Tino la Bertram	26.08.81	St Michael	Barbados	RHB/RFM	2001-02
BROWNE, Patrick Anderson	26.01.82	Bayfield	Barbados	RHB/WK	2001-02
CHATTERGOON, Sewnarine	03.04.81	Fyrish, Berbice	Guyana	LHB/LB	2000
HINDS, Ryan O'Neal	17.02.81	Holders Hill	Barbados	LHB/SLA	1998-99
JOSEPH, Sylvester Cleofoster	05.09.78	New Winthorpes, Antigua	Leeward Is	RHB/OB	2004
KELLY, Richard	19.02.84	Trinidad	Trinidad	LHB/RFM	2004-05
MOHAMMED, Dave	08.10.79	Princes Town	Trinidad	LHB/SLC	2000-01
MOHAMMED, Jason	23.09.86	Trinidad	Trinidad	RHB	2005-06
MORTON, Runako Shakur	22.07.78	Rawlins, Nevis	Leeward Is	RHB/OB	1996-97
POWELL, Daren Brentlyle	15.04.78	Malvenn	Jamaica	RHB/RFM	2000-01
RICHARDSON, Andrew Peter	06.09.81	Kingston	Jamaica	LHB/RFM	2002-03
SAMMY, Darren Julius Garvey	20.12.83	Micoud, St Lucia	Windward Is	RHB/RM	2002-03
SIMMONS, Lendl Mark Platter	25.01.85	Port-of-Spain	Trinidad	RHB/RMF	2001-02
SMITH, Dwayne Romel	12.01.83	Storey Gap	Barbados	RHB/RM	2001-02
SMITH, Devon Sheldon	21.10.81	Sauters, Grenada	Windward Is	LHB/OB	1998-99

TEST NEW ZEALAND – BATTING AND FIELDING

	M	*I*	*NO*	*HS*	*Runs*	*Avge*	*100*	*50*	*Ct/St*
A.R.Adams	1	2	–	11	18	9.00	–	–	1
N.J.Astle	81	137	10	222	4702	37.02	11	24	70
S.E.Bond	16	17	7	41*	138	13.80	–	–	6
C.D.Cumming	7	13	1	74	327	27.25	–	1	2
S.P.Fleming	104	177	10	274*	6620	39.64	9	41	159
J.E.C.Franklin	21	28	5	122*	505	21.95	1	1	9
P.G.Fulton	5	7	–	75	185	26.42	–	1	3
J.M.How	6	10	1	37	131	14.55	–	–	8
B.B.McCullum	25	39	3	143	1157	32.13	2	6	64/6
H.J.H.Marshall	13	19	2	160	652	38.35	2	2	1
C.S.Martin	33	44	21	7	52	2.26	–	–	9
K.D.Mills	7	12	3	31	120	13.33	–	–	2
J.D.P.Oram	22	39	8	133	1221	39.38	3	4	13
M.H.W.Papps	6	12	1	86	229	20.81	–	2	7
J.S.Patel	1	1	1	27*	27	–	–	–	1
M.S.Sinclair	27	46	5	214	1448	35.31	3	4	26
C.M.Spearman	19	37	2	112	922	26.34	1	3	21
S.B.Styris	27	44	4	170	1527	38.17	5	6	23
D.L.Vettori	72	103	15	137*	2242	25.47	2	13	36
P.J.Wiseman	25	34	8	36	366	14.07	–	–	11

NEW ZEALAND – BOWLING

	O	*M*	*R*	*W*	*Avge*	*Best*	*5wI*	*10wM*
A.R.Adams	31.4	5	105	6	17.50	3- 44	–	–
N.J.Astle	948	316	2143	51	42.01	3- 27	–	–
S.E.Bond	480.1	102	1636	74	22.10	6- 51	4	1
J.E.C.Franklin	596.1	110	2143	76	28.19	6-119	3	–
H.J.H.Marshall	1	0	4	0				
C.S.Martin	1031.2	220	3636	106	34.30	6- 54	7	1
K.D.Mills	173.3	50	534	17	31.41	4- 43	–	–
J.D.P.Oram	562.4	150	1451	42	34.54	4- 41	–	–
J.S.Patel	42	8	117	3	39.00	3-117	–	–
M.S.Sinclair	4	0	13	0				
S.B.Styris	316.4	75	973	20	48.65	3- 28	–	–
D.L.Vettori	2903.5	723	7740	228	33.94	7- 87	13	3
P.J.Wiseman	943.2	208	2903	61	47.59	5- 82	2	–

TEST

INDIA – BATTING AND FIELDING

	M	I	NO	HS	Runs	Avge	100	50	Ct/St
A.B.Agarkar	26	39	5	109*	571	16.79	1	–	6
P.Chawla	1	1	–	1	1	1.00	–	–	–
M.S.Dhoni	15	24	1	148	706	30.69	1	3	41/9
R.Dravid	106	180	22	270	9151	57.91	23	46	146
G.Gambhir	13	21	2	139	684	36.00	1	3	12
S.C.Ganguly	91	146	13	173	5435	40.86	12	27	62
Harbhajan Singh	57	79	18	66	986	16.16	–	2	30
W.Jaffer	17	32	–	212	1068	33.37	3	6	16
M.Kaif	13	22	3	148*	624	32.84	1	3	14
K.D.Karthik	11	15	1	93	346	24.71	–	2	34/4
M.Kartik	8	10	1	43	88	9.77	–	–	2
Z.Khan	45	60	14	75	578	12.56	–	1	11
A.Kumble	113	146	27	88	2049	17.21	–	4	50
V.V.S.Laxman	80	130	15	281	4878	42.41	10	27	86
M.M.Patel	7	9	3	13	32	5.33	–	–	4
I.K.Pathan	25	32	2	93	835	27.83	–	6	8
V.Sehwag	51	85	3	309	4072	49.65	12	11	43
R.P.Singh	2	3	2	6	6	6.00	–	–	–
V.R.Singh	4	5	1	29	46	11.50	–	–	1
S.Sreesanth	8	13	4	29*	126	14.00	–	–	1
S.R.Tendulkar	135	217	22	248*	10668	54.70	35	43	85
Yuvraj Singh	19	29	4	122	830	33.20	2	3	21

INDIA – BOWLING

	O	M	R	W	Avge	Best	5wI	10wM
A.B.Agarkar	809.3	168	2745	58	47.32	6-41	1	–
P.Chawla	14.1	3	53	1	53.00	1- 8	–	–
M.S.Dhoni	1	0	13	0				
R.Dravid	20	4	39	1	39.00	1-18	–	–
S.C.Ganguly	423.2	87	1441	26	55.42	3-28	–	–
Harbhajan Singh	2527	518	7108	238	29.86	8-84	19	4
W.Jaffer	11	3	18	2	9.00	2-18	–	–
M.Kaif	3	0	4	0				
M.Kartik	322	74	820	24	34.16	4-44	–	–
Z.Khan	1443.4	291	4793	134	35.76	5-29	3	–
A.Kumble	5949	1433	15675	547	28.65	10-74	33	8
V.V.S.Laxman	42	10	100	1	100.00	1-32	–	–
M.M.Patel	250	54	725	25	29.00	4-25	–	–
I.K.Pathan	846.2	185	2802	91	30.79	7-59	7	2
V.Sehwag	214.2	34	674	14	48.14	3-33	–	–
R.P.Singh	87	8	345	9	38.33	4-89	–	–
V.R.Singh	91.1	14	357	5	71.40	2-61	–	–
S.Sreesanth	284.5	70	961	37	25.97	5-40	1	–
S.R.Tendulkar	568.1	79	1926	38	50.68	3-10	–	–
Yuvraj Singh	24	1	90	1	90.00	1-25	–	–

PAKISTAN – BATTING AND FIELDING

	M	I	NO	HS	Runs	Avge	100	50	Ct/St
Abdul Razzaq	46	77	9	134	1946	28.61	3	7	15
Asim Kamal	12	20	1	99	717	37.73	–	8	10
Azhar Mahmood	21	34	4	136	900	30.00	3	1	14
Danish Kaneria	46	62	29	29	230	6.96	–	–	15
Faisal Iqbal	18	32	2	139	773	25.76	1	5	12
Hasan Raza	7	10	1	68	235	26.11	–	2	5
Iftikhar Anjum	1	1	1	9*	9	–	–	–	–
Imran Farhat	27	51	1	128	1655	33.10	2	11	30
Inzamam-ul-Haq	118	196	22	329	8812	50.64	25	46	81
Kamran Akmal	33	55	4	154	1521	29.82	4	5	108/18
Mohammad Akram	9	15	6	10*	24	2.66	–	–	4
Mohammad Asif	9	13	6	12*	40	5.71	–	–	2
Mohammad Hafeez	10	19	1	104	642	35.66	2	3	3
Mohammad Sami	30	46	11	49	382	10.91	–	–	7
Mushtaq Ahmed	52	72	16	59	656	11.71	–	2	23
Naved-ul-Hasan	9	15	3	42*	239	19.91	–	–	3
Salman Butt	14	26	–	122	777	29.88	2	4	7
Shabbir Ahmed	10	15	5	24*	88	8.80	–	–	3
Shahid Afridi	26	46	1	156	1683	37.40	5	8	10
Shahid Nazir	15	19	3	40	194	12.12	–	–	5
Shoaib Akhtar	43	63	12	47	541	10.60	–	–	11
Shoaib Malik	18	29	4	148*	941	37.64	1	5	8
Taufiq Umar	25	46	2	135	1729	39.29	4	9	33
Umar Gul	14	17	2	26	116	7.73	–	–	4
Yasir Hamid	20	39	3	170	1292	35.88	2	8	16
Younis Khan	53	95	6	267	4291	48.21	12	19	64
Yousuf Youhana, M.	75	126	9	223	6553	56.00	23	27	59

PAKISTAN – BOWLING

	O	M	R	W	Avge	Best	5wI	10wM
Abdul Razzaq	1168	220	3694	100	36.94	5- 35	1	–
Azhar Mahmood	502.3	109	1402	39	35.94	4- 50	–	–
Danish Kaneria	2172.2	419	6408	198	32.36	7- 77	12	2
Faisal Iqbal	1	0	7	0				
Hasan Raza	1	0	1	0				
Iftikhar Anjum	14	1	62	0				
Imran Farhat	49.1	3	218	3	72.66	2- 69	–	–
Inzamam-ul-Haq	1.3	0	8	0				
Mohammad Akram	246.1	36	859	17	50.52	5-138	1	–
Mohammad Asif	319	74	986	49	20.12	6- 44	4	1
Mohammad Hafeez	106	23	266	3	88.66	1- 11	–	–
Mohammad Sami	1042	171	3686	77	47.87	5- 36	2	–
Mushtaq Ahmed	2088.4	406	6100	185	32.97	7- 56	10	3
Naved-ul-Hasan	260.5	36	1044	18	58.00	3- 30	–	–
Salman Butt	4	0	18	0				
Shabbir Ahmed	429.2	97	1175	51	23.03	5- 48	2	–
Shahid Afridi	515.2	69	1640	47	34.89	5- 52	1	–
Shahid Nazir	372.2	71	1272	36	35.33	5- 53	1	–
Shoaib Akhtar	1259.2	220	4276	169	25.30	6- 11	12	2
Shoaib Malik	238.1	35	820	13	63.07	4- 42	–	–
Taufiq Umar	13	2	44	–				
Umar Gul	523.3	86	1868	61	30.62	5- 31	3	–
Yasir Hamid	1	–	5	–				
Younis Khan	44	7	169	2	84.50	1- 24	–	–
Yousuf Youhana, M.	1	–	3	–				

SRI LANKA – BATTING AND FIELDING

	M	I	NO	HS	Runs	Avge	100	50	Ct/St
M.S.Atapattu	88	152	15	249	5330	38.90	16	15	57
C.M.Bandara	8	11	3	43	124	15.50	–	–	4
T.M.Dilshan	39	63	7	168	2056	36.71	4	9	44
C.R.D.Fernando	24	31	10	16	124	5.90	–	–	8
D.A.Gunawardena	6	11	–	43	181	16.45	–	–	2
S.T.Jayasuriya	107	182	14	340	6791	40.42	14	30	78
H.A.P.W.Jayawardena	9	9	–	42	161	17.88	–	–	18/3
D.P.M.D.Jayawardena	85	140	10	374	6289	48.37	16	29	113
C.K.Kapugedara	6	11	1	63	221	22.10	–	2	3
M.D.N.Kulasekara	4	7	–	64	115	16.42	–	1	1
M.F.Maharoof	17	27	4	72	476	20.69	–	3	5
S.L.Malinga	21	28	11	26	132	7.76	–	–	7
J.Mubarak	8	14	1	48	236	18.15	–	–	10
M.Muralitharan	109	142	49	67	1115	11.98	–	1	57
T.T.Samaraweera	39	58	8	142	2089	41.78	5	13	30
K.C.Sangakkara	64	107	7	287	5064	50.64	12	22	146/20
L.P.C.Silva	2	4	1	152*	213	71.00	1	1	2
W.U.Tharanga	12	23	1	165	675	30.68	1	3	10
W.P.U.C.J.Vaas	96	140	26	74*	2554	22.40	–	11	28
M.G.Vandort	6	11	2	140	461	51.22	2	2	2

SRI LANKA – BOWLING

	O	M	R	W	Avge	Best	5wI	10wM
M.S.Atapattu	8	0	24	1	24.00	1- 9	–	–
C.M.Bandara	192	29	633	16	39.56	3-84	–	–
T.M.Dilshan	88	20	271	6	45.16	2- 4	–	–
C.R.D.Fernando	599.2	95	2201	69	31.89	5-42	3	–
S.T.Jayasuriya	1333.4	315	3281	96	34.17	5-34	2	–
D.P.M.D.Jayawardena	76.2	17	228	4	57.00	2-32	–	–
M.D.N.Kulasekara	101	20	302	4	75.50	2-45	–	–
M.F.Maharoof	357	78	1211	23	52.65	4-52	–	–
S.L.Malinga	586.1	80	2242	71	31.57	5-68	2	–
J.Mubarak	13	2	42	0				
M.Muralitharan	6063.4	1577	14492	669	21.66	9-51	57	19
T.T.Samaraweera	214.1	36	671	14	47.92	4-49	–	–
K.C.Sangakkara	1	0	4	0				
W.P.U.C.J.Vaas	3447.4	786	9216	313	29.44	7-71	11	2

SRI LANKA TEAM TO BRITAIN 2006

Full Names	*Birthdate*	*Birthplace*	*Team*	*Type*	*F-C Debut*
BANDARA, C. Malinga	31.12.79	Kalutara	Kalutara Town	RHB/LBG	1996-97
DILSHAN, Tillakaratne M.	14.10.76	Kalutara	Bloomfield	RHB/WK	1993-94
JAYASURIYA, Sanath T.	30.06.69	Matara	Bloomfield	LHB/SLA	1988-89
JAYAWARDENA, D.P. Mahela deS.	27.05.77	Colombo	Sinhalese	RHB/RM	1995-96
JAYAWARDENA, H.A. Prasanna W.	09.10.79	Colombo	Sebastianites	RHB/WK	1997-98
KAPUGEDARA, Chamara K.	24.02.87	Kandy	Colombo	RHB/RM	2005-06
KULASEKARA, M.D. Nuwan	22.07.82	Nittambuwa	Colts	RHB/RFM	2002-03
MAHAROOF, M. Farveez	07.09.84	Colombo	Bloomfield	RHB/RFM	2001-02
MALINGA, S. Lasith	28.09.83	Galle	Galle	RHB/RMF	2001-02
MUBARAK, Jehan	10.01.81	Washington, USA	Colombo	LHB/OB	1999-00
MURALITHARAN, Muthiah	17.04.72	Kandy	Tamil Union	RHB/OB	1989-90
SAMARAWEERA, Thilan T.	22.09.76	Colombo	Sinhalese	RHB/OB	1995-96
SANGAKKARA, Kumar C.	27.10.77	Colombo	Nondescripts	LHB/WK	1997-98
THARANGA, W. Upul	02.02.85	Balapitiya	Nondescripts	LHB/WK	2000-01
VAAS, W.P.U. Chaminda J.	27.01.74	Mattumagala	Colts	LHB/LFM	1990-91
VANDORT, Michael G.	19.01.80	Colombo	Colombo	LHB/RM	1998-99
ZOYSA, D. Nuwan T.	13.05.78	Colombo	Sinhalese	LHB/LFM	1996-97

TEST

ZIMBABWE – BATTING AND FIELDING

	M	I	NO	HS	Runs	Avge	100	50	Ct/St
S.M.Ervine	5	8	–	86	261	32.62	–	3	7
A.Flower	63	112	19	232*	4794	51.54	12	27	151/9
G.W.Flower	67	123	6	201*	3457	29.54	6	15	43
M.W.Goodwin	19	37	4	166*	1414	42.84	3	8	10
R.W.Price	18	30	7	36	224	9.73	–	–	3
H.H.Streak	65	107	18	127*	1990	22.35	1	11	17

ZIMBABWE – BOWLING

	O	M	R	W	Avge	Best	5wI	10wM
S.M.Ervine	95	18	388	9	43.11	4-146	–	–
A.Flower	0.3	0	4	0				
G.W.Flower	563	122	1537	25	61.48	4- 41	–	–
M.W.Goodwin	19.5	3	69	0				
R.W.Price	855.5	198	2475	69	35.86	6- 73	5	1
H.H.Streak	2259.5	595	6079	216	28.14	6- 73	7	–

BANGLADESH – BATTING AND FIELDING

	M	I	NO	HS	Runs	Avge	100	50	Ct/St
Abdur Razzak	1	2	–	15	15	7.50	–	–	–
Aftab Ahmed	10	20	1	82*	395	20.78	–	1	4
Alok Kapali	17	34	1	85	584	17.69	–	2	5
Enamul Haque II	10	18	11	9	28	4.00	–	–	2
Habibul Bashar	42	83	1	113	2838	34.60	3	24	19
Javed Omar	35	70	1	119	1525	22.10	1	6	7
Khaled Masud	41	79	9	103*	1361	19.44	1	3	75/8
Mashrafe Mortaza	20	37	4	48	283	8.57	–	–	5
Mohammad Ashraful	33	65	3	158*	1511	24.37	3	6	10
Mohammad Rafique	26	50	5	111	982	21.82	1	4	6
Mushfiqur Rahim	2	4	–	19	24	6.00	–	–	1
Nafis Iqbal	11	22	–	121	518	23.54	1	2	2
Rajin Saleh	17	33	1	89	930	29.06	–	6	11
Shahadat Hossain	7	14	5	13	55	6.11	–	–	3
Shahriar Nafis	6	12	–	138	402	33.50	1	2	6
Syed Rasel	4	8	2	19	30	5.00	–	–	–

BANGLADESH – BOWLING

	O	M	R	W	Avge	Best	5wI	10wM
Abdur Razzak	30	5	99	0				
Aftab Ahmed	35	4	176	3	58.66	1- 28	–	–
Alok Kapali	183.5	15	709	6	118.16	3- 3	–	–
Enamul Haque II	397.3	80	1198	32	37.43	7- 95	3	1
Habibul Bashar	39	1	195	0				
Javed Omar	1	0	12	0				
Mashrafe Mortaza	593.2	134	1871	50	37.42	4- 60	–	–
Mohammad Ashraful	139	8	623	9	69.22	2- 42	–	–
Mohammad Rafique	1205.3	272	3184	87	36.59	6- 77	7	–
Rajin Saleh	67	4	244	2	122.00	1- 9	–	–
Shahadat Hossain	178.3	21	793	16	49.56	5- 86	1	–
Syed Rasel	91.5	17	360	9	40.00	4-129	–	–

FIRST-CLASS CRICKET RECORDS

To the end of the 2006 season

TEAM RECORDS

HIGHEST INNINGS TOTALS

1107	Victoria v New South Wales	Melbourne	1926-27
1059	Victoria v Tasmania	Melbourne	1922-23
952-6d	Sri Lanka v India	Colombo	1997-98
951-7d	Sind v Baluchistan	Karachi	1973-74
944-6d	Hyderabad v Andhra	Secunderabad	1993-94
918	New South Wales v South Australia	Sydney	1900-01
912-8d	Holkar v Mysore	Indore	1945-46
910-6d	Railways v Dera Ismail Khan	Lahore	1964-65
903-7d	England v Australia	The Oval	1938
900-6d	Queensland v Victoria	Brisbane	2005-06
887	Yorkshire v Warwickshire	Birmingham	1896
863	Lancashire v Surrey	The Oval	1990
860-6d	Tamil Nadu v Goa	Panjim	1988-89

Excluding penalty runs in India, there have been 30 innings totals of 800 runs or more in first-class cricket. Tamil Nadu's total of 860-6d was boosted to 912 by 52 penalty runs.

HIGHEST SECOND INNINGS TOTAL

770	New South Wales v South Australia	Adelaide	1920-21

HIGHEST FOURTH INNINGS TOTAL

654-5	England v South Africa	Durban	1938-39

HIGHEST MATCH AGGREGATE

2376-37	Maharashtra v Bombay	Poona	1948-49

RECORD MARGIN OF VICTORY

Innings and 851 runs: Railways v Dera Ismail Khan	Lahore	1964-65

MOST RUNS IN A DAY

721	Australians v Essex	Southend	1948

MOST HUNDREDS IN AN INNINGS

6	Holkar v Mysore	Indore	1945-46

LOWEST INNINGS TOTALS

12	†Oxford University v MCC and Ground	Oxford	1877
12	Northamptonshire v Gloucestershire	Gloucester	1907
13	Auckland v Canterbury	Auckland	1877-78
13	Nottinghamshire v Yorkshire	Nottingham	1901
14	Surrey v Essex	Chelmsford	1983
15	MCC v Surrey	Lord's	1839
15	†Victoria v MCC	Melbourne	1903-04
15	†Northamptonshire v Yorkshire	Northampton	1908
15	Hampshire v Warwickshire	Birmingham	1922

† *Batted one man short*

There have been 27 instances of a team being dismissed for under 20.

LOWEST MATCH AGGREGATE BY ONE TEAM

34 (16 and 18)	Border v Natal	East London	1959-60

LOWEST COMPLETED MATCH AGGREGATE BY BOTH TEAMS

105	MCC v Australians	Lord's	1878

FEWEST RUNS IN AN UNINTERRUPTED DAY'S PLAY

95	Australia (80) v Pakistan (15-2)	Karachi	1956-57

TIED MATCHES

Before 1949 a match was considered to be tied if the scores were level after the fourth innings, even if the side batting last had wickets in hand when play ended. Law 22 was amended in 1948 and since then a match has been tied only when the scores are level after the fourth innings has been completed. There have been 56 tied first-class matches, five of which would not have qualified under the current law. The most recent are:

Warwickshire (446-7d & forfeit) v Essex (66-0d & 380)	Birmingham	2003
Worcestershire (262 & 247) v Zimbabweans (334 & 175)	Worcester	2003

BATTING RECORDS
HIGHEST INDIVIDUAL INNINGS

501*	B.C.Lara	Warwickshire v Durham	Birmingham	1994
499	Hanif Mohammed	Karachi v Bahawalpur	Karachi	1958-59
452*	D.G.Bradman	New South Wales v Queensland	Sydney	1929-30
443*	B.B.Nimbalkar	Maharashtra v Kathiawar	Poona	1948-49
437	W.H.Ponsford	Victoria v Queensland	Melbourne	1927-28
429	W.H.Ponsford	Victoria v Tasmania	Melbourne	1922-23
428	Aftab Baloch	Sind v Baluchistan	Karachi	1973-74
424	A.C.MacLaren	Lancashire v Somerset	Taunton	1895
405*	G.A.Hick	Worcestershire v Somerset	Taunton	1988
400*	B.C.Lara	West Indies v England	St John's	2003-04
394	Naved Latif	Sargodha v Gujranwala	Gujranwala	2000-01
385	B.Sutcliffe	Otago v Canterbury	Christchurch	1952-53
383	C.W.Gregory	New South Wales v Queensland	Brisbane	1906-07
380	M.L.Hayden	Australia v Zimbabwe	Perth	2003-04
377	S.V.Manjrekar	Bombay v Hyderabad	Bombay	1990-91
375	B.C.Lara	West Indies v England	St John's	1993-94
374	D.P.M.D.Jayawardena	Sri Lanka v South Africa	Colombo	2006
369	D.G.Bradman	South Australia v Tasmania	Adelaide	1935-36
366	N.H.Fairbrother	Lancashire v Surrey	The Oval	1990
366	M.V.Sridhar	Hyderabad v Andhra	Secunderabad	1993-94
365*	C.Hill	South Australia v NSW	Adelaide	1900-01
365*	G.St A.Sobers	West Indies v Pakistan	Kingston	1957-58
364	L.Hutton	England v Australia	The Oval	1938
359*	V.M.Merchant	Bombay v Maharashtra	Bombay	1943-44
359	R.B.Simpson	New South Wales v Queensland	Brisbane	1963-64
357*	R.Abel	Surrey v Somerset	The Oval	1899
357	D.G.Bradman	South Australia v Victoria	Melbourne	1935-36
356	B.A.Richards	South Australia v W Australia	Perth	1970-71
355*	G.R.Marsh	W Australia v S Australia	Perth	1989-90
355	B.Sutcliffe	Otago v Auckland	Dunedin	1949-50
353	V.V.S.Laxman	Hyderabad v Karnataka	Bangalore	1999-00
352	W.H.Ponsford	Victoria v New South Wales	Melbourne	1926-27
350	Rashid Israr	Habib Bank v National Bank	Lahore	1976-77

There have been 159 triple hundreds in first-class cricket, W.V.Raman (313) and Arjan Kripal Singh (302*) for Tamil Nadu v Goa at Panjim in 1988-89 providing the only instance of two batsmen scoring 300 in the same innings.

MOST HUNDREDS IN SUCCESSIVE INNINGS

6	C.B.Fry	Sussex and Rest of England	1901
6	D.G.Bradman	South Australia and D.G.Bradman's XI	1938-39
6	M.J.Procter	Rhodesia	1970-71

TWO DOUBLE HUNDREDS IN A MATCH

244	202*	A.E.Fagg	Kent v Essex	Colchester	1938

TRIPLE HUNDRED AND HUNDRED IN A MATCH

333	123	G.A.Gooch	England v India	Lord's	1990

DOUBLE HUNDRED AND HUNDRED IN A MATCH MOST TIMES

4	Zaheer Abbas	Gloucestershire	1976-81

TWO HUNDREDS IN A MATCH MOST TIMES

8	Zaheer Abbas	Gloucestershire and PIA	1976-82
8	R.T.Ponting	Tasmania, Australia and Australians	1992-2006
7	W.R.Hammond	Gloucestershire, England and MCC	1927-45

MOST HUNDREDS IN A SEASON

18	D.C.S.Compton	1947	16	J.B.Hobbs	1925

100 HUNDREDS IN A CAREER

	Total		*100th Hundred*	
	Hundreds	*Inns*	*Season*	*Inns*
J.B.Hobbs	197	1315	1923	821
E.H.Hendren	170	1300	1928-29	740
W.R.Hammond	167	1005	1935	679
C.P.Mead	153	1340	1927	892
G.Boycott	151	1014	1977	645
H.Sutcliffe	149	1088	1932	700
F.E.Woolley	145	1532	1929	1031
G.A.Hick	132	829	1998	574
L.Hutton	129	814	1951	619
G.A.Gooch	128	990	1992-93	820
W.G.Grace	126	1493	1895	1113
D.C.S.Compton	123	839	1952	552
T.W.Graveney	122	1223	1964	940
D.G.Bradman	117	338	1947-48	295
I.V.A.Richards	114	796	1988-89	658
Zaheer Abbas	108	768	1982-83	658
A.Sandham	107	1000	1935	871
M.C.Cowdrey	107	1130	1973	1035
T.W.Hayward	104	1138	1913	1076
G.M.Turner	103	792	1982	779
J.H.Edrich	103	979	1977	945
L.E.G.Ames	102	951	1950	915
G.E.Tyldesley	102	961	1934	919
D.L.Amiss	102	1139	1986	1081

MOST 400s: 2 – B.C.Lara, W.H.Ponsford
MOST 300s or more: 6 – D.G.Bradman; 4 – W.R.Hammond, W.H.Ponsford
MOST 200s or more: 37 – D.G.Bradman; 36 – W.R.Hammond; 22 – E.H.Hendren

MOST RUNS IN A MONTH

1294 (avge 92.42)	L.Hutton	Yorkshire	June 1949

MOST RUNS IN A SEASON

Runs			*I*	*NO*	*HS*	*Avge*	*100*	*Season*
3816	D.C.S.Compton	Middlesex	50	8	246	90.85	18	1947
3539	W.J.Edrich	Middlesex	52	8	267*	80.43	12	1947
3518	T.W.Hayward	Surrey	61	8	219	66.37	13	1906

The feat of scoring 3000 runs in a season has been achieved 28 times, the most recent instance being by W.E.Alley (3019) in 1961. The highest aggregate in a season since 1969 is 2755 by S.J.Cook in 1991.

1000 RUNS IN A SEASON MOST TIMES

28 W.G.Grace (Gloucestershire), F.E.Woolley (Kent)

HIGHEST BATTING AVERAGE IN A SEASON

(Qualification: 12 innings)

Avge			*I*	*NO*	*HS*	*Runs*	*100*	*Season*
115.66	D.G.Bradman	Australians	26	5	278	2429	13	1938
104.66	D.R.Martyn	Australians	14	5	176*	942	5	2001
103.54	M.R.Ramprakash	Surrey	24	2	301*	2278	8	2006
102.53	G.Boycott	Yorkshire	20	5	175*	1538	6	1979
102.00	W.A.Johnston	Australians	17	16	28*	102	–	1953
101.70	G.A.Gooch	Essex	30	3	333	2746	12	1990
100.12	G.Boycott	Yorkshire	30	5	233	2503	13	1971

FASTEST HUNDRED AGAINST AUTHENTIC BOWLING

35 min	P.G.H.Fender	Surrey v Northamptonshire	Northampton	1920

FASTEST DOUBLE HUNDRED

113 min	R.J.Shastri	Bombay v Baroda	Bombay	1984-85

FASTEST TRIPLE HUNDRED

181 min	D.C.S.Compton	MCC v NE Transvaal	Benoni	1948-49

MOST SIXES IN AN INNINGS

16	A.Symonds	Gloucestershire v Glamorgan	Abergavenny	1995

MOST SIXES IN A MATCH

20	A.Symonds	Gloucestershire v Glamorgan	Abergavenny	1995

MOST SIXES IN A SEASON

80	I.T.Botham	Somerset and England	1985

MOST FOURS IN AN INNINGS

72	B.C.Lara	Warwickshire v Durham	Birmingham	1994

MOST RUNS OFF ONE OVER

36	G.St A.Sobers	Nottinghamshire v Glamorgan	Swansea	1968
36	R.J.Shastri	Bombay v Baroda	Bombay	1984-85

Both batsmen hit for six all six balls of overs bowled by M.A.Nash and Tilak Raj respectively.

MOST RUNS IN A DAY

390*	B.C.Lara	Warwickshire v Durham	Birmingham	1994

There have been 19 instances of a batsman scoring 300 or more runs in a day.

LONGEST INNINGS

1015 min	R.Nayyar (271)	Himachal Pradesh v Jammu & Kashmir	Chamba	1999-00

HIGHEST PARTNERSHIPS FOR EACH WICKET

First Wicket

561	Waheed Mirza/Mansoor Akhtar	Karachi W v Quetta	Karachi	1976-77
555	P.Holmes/H.Sutcliffe	Yorkshire v Essex	Leyton	1932
554	J.T.Brown/J.Tunnicliffe	Yorkshire v Derbys	Chesterfield	1898

Second Wicket

576	S.T.Jayasuriya/R.S.Mahanama	Sri Lanka v India	Colombo (RPS)	1997-98
475	Zahir Alam/L.S.Rajput	Assam v Tripura	Gauhati	1991-92
465*	J.A.Jameson/R.B.Kanhai	Warwickshire v Glos	Birmingham	1974

Third Wicket

624	K.C.Sangakkara/D.P.M.D.Jayawardena	Sri Lanka v South Africa	Colombo	2006
467	A.H.Jones/M.D.Crowe	N Zealand v Sri Lanka	Wellington	1990-91
456	Khalid Irtiza/Aslam Ali	United Bank v Multan	Karachi	1975-76
451	Mudassar Nazar/Javed Miandad	Pakistan v India	Hyderabad	1982-83
445	P.E.Whitelaw/W.N.Carson	Auckland v Otago	Dunedin	1936-37
438*	G.A.Hick/T.M.Moody	Worcestershire v Hants	Southampton	1997

Fourth Wicket

577	V.S.Hazare/Gul Mahomed	Baroda v Holkar	Baroda	1946-47
574*	C.L.Walcott/F.M.M.Worrell	Barbados v Trinidad	Port-of-Spain	1945-46
502*	F.M.M.Worrell/J.D.C.Goddard	Barbados v Trinidad	Bridgetown	1943-44
470	A.I.Kallicharran/G.W.Humpage	Warwickshire v Lancs	Southport	1982

Fifth Wicket

464*	M.E.Waugh/S.R.Waugh	NSW v W Australia	Perth	1990-91
405	S.G.Barnes/D.G.Bradman	Australia v England	Sydney	1946-47
401	M.B.Loye/D.Ripley	Northants v Glamorgan	Northampton	1998

Sixth Wicket

487*	G.A.Headley/C.C.Passailaigue	Jamaica v Tennyson's	Kingston	1931-32
428	W.W.Armstrong/M.A.Noble	Australians v Sussex	Hove	1902
411	R.M.Poore/E.G.Wynyard	Hampshire v Somerset	Taunton	1899

Seventh Wicket

460	Bhupinder Singh jr/P.Dharmani	Punjab v Delhi	Delhi	1994-95
347	D.St E.Atkinson/C.C.Depeiza	W Indies v Australia	Bridgetown	1954-55
344	K.S.Ranjitsinhji/W.Newham	Sussex v Essex	Leyton	1902

Eighth Wicket

433	V.T.Trumper/A.Sims	Australians v C'bury	Christchurch	1913-14
313	Wasim Akram/Saqlain Mushtaq	Pakistan v Zimbabwe	Sheikhupura	1996-97
292	R.Peel/Lord Hawke	Yorkshire v Warwicks	Birmingham	1896

Ninth Wicket

283	J.Chapman/A.Warren	Derbys v Warwicks	Blackwell	1910
268	J.B.Commins/N.Boje	SA 'A' v Mashonaland	Harare	1994-95
251	J.W.H.T.Douglas/S.N.Hare	Essex v Derbyshire	Leyton	1921

Tenth Wicket

307	A.F.Kippax/J.E.H.Hooker	NSW v Victoria	Melbourne	1928-29
249	C.T.Sarwate/S.N.Banerjee	Indians v Surrey	The Oval	1946
239	Aqil Arshad/Ali Raza	Lahore Whites v Hyderabad	Lahore	2004-05
235	F.E.Woolley/A.Fielder	Kent v Worcs	Stourbridge	1909

35,000 RUNS IN A CAREER

	Career	*I*	*NO*	*HS*	*Runs*	*Avge*	*100*
J.B.Hobbs	1905-34	1315	106	316*	**61237**	50.65	197
F.E.Woolley	1906-38	1532	85	305*	**58969**	40.75	145
E.H.Hendren	1907-38	1300	166	301*	**57611**	50.80	170
C.P.Mead	1905-36	1340	185	280*	**55061**	47.67	153
W.G.Grace	1865-1908	1493	105	344	**54896**	39.55	126
W.R.Hammond	1920-51	1005	104	336*	**50551**	56.10	167
H.Sutcliffe	1919-45	1088	123	313	**50138**	51.95	149
G.Boycott	1962-86	1014	162	261*	**48426**	56.83	151
T.W.Graveney	1948-71/72	1223	159	258	**47793**	44.91	122
G.A.Gooch	1973-2000	990	75	333	**44846**	49.01	128
T.W.Hayward	1893-1914	1138	96	315*	**43551**	41.79	104
D.L.Amiss	1960-87	1139	126	262*	**43423**	42.86	102
M.C.Cowdrey	1950-76	1130	134	307	**42719**	42.89	107
A.Sandham	1911-37/38	1000	79	325	**41284**	44.82	107
L.Hutton	1934-60	814	91	364	**40140**	55.51	129
M.J.K.Smith	1951-75	1091	139	204	**39832**	41.84	69
W.Rhodes	1898-1930	1528	237	267*	**39802**	30.83	58
J.H.Edrich	1956-78	979	104	310*	**39790**	45.47	103
G.A.Hick	1983/84-2006	829	80	405*	**39460**	52.68	132
R.E.S.Wyatt	1923-57	1141	157	232	**39405**	40.04	85
D.C.S.Compton	1936-64	839	88	300	**38942**	51.85	123
G.E.Tyldesley	1909-36	961	106	256*	**38874**	45.46	102
J.T.Tyldesley	1895-1923	994	62	295*	**37897**	40.60	86
K.W.R.Fletcher	1962-88	1167	170	228*	**37665**	37.77	63
C.G.Greenidge	1970-92	889	75	273*	**37354**	45.88	92
J.W.Hearne	1909-36	1025	116	285*	**37252**	40.98	96
L.E.G.Ames	1926-51	951	95	295	**37248**	43.51	102
D.Kenyon	1946-67	1159	59	259	**37002**	33.63	74
W.J.Edrich	1934-58	964	92	267*	**36965**	42.39	86
J.M.Parks	1949-76	1227	172	205*	**36673**	34.76	51
M.W.Gatting	1975-98	861	123	258	**36549**	49.52	94
D.Denton	1894-1920	1163	70	221	**36479**	33.37	69
G.H.Hirst	1891-1929	1215	151	341	**36323**	34.13	60
I.V.A.Richards	1971/72-93	796	63	322	**36212**	49.40	114
A.Jones	1957-83	1168	72	204*	**36049**	32.89	56
W.G.Quaife	1894-1928	1203	185	255*	**36012**	35.37	72
R.E.Marshall	1945/46-72	1053	59	228*	**35725**	35.94	68
G.Gunn	1902-32	1061	82	220	**35208**	35.96	62

BOWLING RECORDS

ALL TEN WICKETS IN AN INNINGS

This feat has been achieved 78 times in first-class matches (excluding 12-a-side fixtures).

Three Times: A.P.Freeman (1929, 1930, 1931)

Twice: V.E.Walker (1859, 1865); H.Verity (1931, 1932); J.C.Laker (1956)

Instances since 1945:

W.E.Hollies	Warwickshire v Notts	Birmingham	1946
J.M.Sims	East v West	Kingston on Thames	1948
J.K.R.Graveney	Gloucestershire v Derbyshire	Chesterfield	1949
T.E.Bailey	Essex v Lancashire	Clacton	1949
R.Berry	Lancashire v Worcestershire	Blackpool	1953
S.P.Gupte	President's XI v Combined XI	Bombay	1954-55
J.C.Laker	Surrey v Australians	The Oval	1956

K.Smales	Nottinghamshire v Glos	Stroud	1956
G.A.R.Lock	Surrey v Kent	Blackheath	1956
J.C.Laker	England v Australia	Manchester	1956
P.M.Chatterjee	Bengal v Assam	Jorhat	1956-57
J.D.Bannister	Warwicks v Combined Services	Birmingham (M & B)	1959
A.J.G.Pearson	Cambridge U v Leicestershire	Loughborough	1961
N.I.Thomson	Sussex v Warwickshire	Worthing	1964
P.J.Allan	Queensland v Victoria	Melbourne	1965-66
I.J.Brayshaw	Western Australia v Victoria	Perth	1967-68
Shahid Mahmood	Karachi Whites v Khairpur	Karachi	1969-70
E.E.Hemmings	International XI v W Indians	Kingston	1982-83
P.Sunderam	Rajasthan v Vidarbha	Jodhpur	1985-86
S.T.Jefferies	Western Province v OFS	Cape Town	1987-88
Imran Adil	Bahawalpur v Faisalabad	Faisalabad	1989-90
G.P.Wickremasinghe	Sinhalese v Kalutara	Colombo	1991-92
R.L.Johnson	Middlesex v Derbyshire	Derby	1994
Naeem Akhtar	Rawalpindi B v Peshawar	Peshawar	1995-96
A.Kumble	India v Pakistan	Delhi	1998-99
D.S.Mohanty	East Zone v South Zone	Agartala	2000-01

MOST WICKETS IN A MATCH

19	J.C.Laker	England v Australia	Manchester	1956

MOST WICKETS IN A SEASON

Wkts		*Season*	*Matches*	*Overs*	*Mdns*	*Runs*	*Avge*
304	A.P.Freeman	1928	37	1976.1	423	5489	18.05
298	A.P.Freeman	1933	33	2039	651	4549	15.26

The feat of taking 250 wickets in a season has been achieved on 12 occasions, the last instance being by A.P.Freeman in 1933. 200 or more wickets in a season have been taken on 59 occasions, the last being by G.A.R.Lock (212 wickets, average 12.02) in 1957.

The highest aggregates of wickets taken in a season since the reduction of County Championship matches in 1969 are as follows:

Wkts		*Season*	*Matches*	*Overs*	*Mdns*	*Runs*	*Avge*
134	M.D.Marshall	1982	22	822	225	2108	15.73
131	L.R.Gibbs	1971	23	1024.1	295	2475	18.89
125	F.D.Stephenson	1988	22	819.1	196	2289	18.31
121	R.D.Jackman	1980	23	746.2	220	1864	15.40

Since 1969 there have been 50 instances of bowlers taking 100 wickets in a season.

MOST HAT-TRICKS IN A CAREER

7	D.V.P.Wright
6	T.W.J.Goddard, C.W.L.Parker
5	S.Haigh, V.W.C.Jupp, A.E.G.Rhodes, F.A.Tarrant

2000 WICKETS IN A CAREER

	Career	*Runs*	*Wkts*	*Avge*	*100w*
W.Rhodes	1898-1930	69993	**4187**	16.71	23
A.P.Freeman	1914-36	69577	**3776**	18.42	17
C.W.L.Parker	1903-35	63817	**3278**	19.46	16
J.T.Hearne	1888-1923	54352	**3061**	17.75	15
T.W.J.Goddard	1922-52	59116	**2979**	19.84	16
W.G.Grace	1865-1908	51545	**2876**	17.92	10
A.S.Kennedy	1907-36	61034	**2874**	21.23	15
D.Shackleton	1948-69	53303	**2857**	18.65	20
G.A.R.Lock	1946-70/71	54709	**2844**	19.23	14

	Career	Runs	Wkts	Avge	100w
F.J.Titmus	1949-82	63313	**2830**	22.37	16
M.W.Tate	1912-37	50571	**2784**	18.16	13+1
G.H.Hirst	1891-1929	51282	**2739**	18.72	15
C.Blythe	1899-1914	42136	**2506**	16.81	14
D.L.Underwood	1963-87	49993	**2465**	20.28	10
W.E.Astill	1906-39	57783	**2431**	23.76	9
J.C.White	1909-37	43759	**2356**	18.57	14
W.E.Hollies	1932-57	48656	**2323**	20.94	14
F.S.Trueman	1949-69	42154	**2304**	18.29	12
J.B.Statham	1950-68	36999	**2260**	16.37	13
R.T.D.Perks	1930-55	53771	**2233**	24.07	16
J.Briggs	1879-1900	35431	**2221**	15.95	12
D.J.Shepherd	1950-72	47302	**2218**	21.32	12
E.G.Dennett	1903-26	42571	**2147**	19.82	12
T.Richardson	1892-1905	38794	**2104**	18.43	10
T.E.Bailey	1945-67	48170	**2082**	23.13	9
R.Illingworth	1951-83	42023	**2072**	20.28	10
F.E.Woolley	1906-38	41066	**2068**	19.85	8
N.Gifford	1960-88	48731	**2068**	23.56	4
G.Geary	1912-38	41339	**2063**	20.03	11
D.V.P.Wright	1932-57	49307	**2056**	23.98	10
J.A.Newman	1906-30	51111	**2032**	25.15	9
A.Shaw	1864-97	24580	**2026+1**	12.12	9
S.Haigh	1895-1913	32091	**2012**	15.94	11

ALL-ROUND RECORDS
THE 'DOUBLE'

3000 runs and 100 wickets: J.H.Parks (1937)
2000 runs and 200 wickets: G.H.Hirst (1906)
2000 runs and 100 wickets: F.E.Woolley (4), J.W.Hearne (3), W.G.Grace (2), G.H.Hirst (2), W.Rhodes (2), T.E.Bailey, D.E.Davies, G.L.Jessop, V.W.C.Jupp, J.Langridge, F.A.Tarrant, C.L.Townsend, L.F.Townsend
1000 runs and 200 wickets: M.W.Tate (3), A.E.Trott (2), A.S.Kennedy

Most Doubles: 16 – W.Rhodes; 14 – G.H.Hirst; 10 – V.W.C.Jupp

Double in Debut Season: D.B.Close (1949) – aged 18, the youngest to achieve this feat.

The feat of scoring 1000 runs and taking 100 wickets in a season has been achieved on 305 occasions, R.J.Hadlee (1984) and F.D.Stephenson (1988) being the only players to complete the 'double' since the reduction of County Championship matches in 1969.

WICKET-KEEPING RECORDS
EIGHT DISMISSALS IN AN INNINGS

9	(8ct, 1st)	Tahir Rashid	Habib Bank v PACO	Gujranwala	1992-93
9	(7ct, 2st)	W.R.James	Matabeleland v Mashonaland CD	Bulawayo	1995-96
8	(8ct)	A.T.W.Grout	Queensland v W Australia	Brisbane	1959-60
8	(8ct)	D.E.East	Essex v Somerset	Taunton	1985
8	(8ct)	S.A.Marsh	Kent v Middlesex	Lord's	1991
8	(6ct, 2st)	T.J.Zoehrer	Australians v Surrey	The Oval	1993
8	(7ct, 1st)	D.S.Berry	Victoria v South Australia	Melbourne	1996-97
8	(7ct, 1st)	Y.S.S.Mendis	Bloomfield v Kurunegala Youth	Colombo	2000-01
8	(7ct, 1st)	S.Nath	Assam v Tripura (*on debut*)	Gauhati	2001-02
8	(8ct)	J.N.Batty	Surrey v Kent	The Oval	2004
8	(8ct)	Golam Mabud	Sylhet v Dhaka	Dhaka	2005-06

TWELVE DISMISSALS IN A MATCH

13	(11ct, 2st)	W.R.James	Matabeleland v Mashonaland CD	Bulawayo	1995-96
12	(8ct, 4st)	E.Pooley	Surrey v Sussex	The Oval	1868
12	(9ct, 3st)	D.Tallon	Queensland v NSW	Sydney	1938-39
12	(9ct, 3st)	H.B.Taber	NSW v South Australia	Adelaide	1968-69

MOST DISMISSALS IN A SEASON

128	(79ct, 49st)	L.E.G.Ames	1929

1000 DISMISSALS IN A CAREER

	Career	*Dismissals*	*Ct*	*St*
R.W.Taylor	1960-88	**1649**	1473	176
J.T.Murray	1952-75	**1527**	1270	257
H.Strudwick	1902-27	**1497**	1242	255
A.P.E.Knott	1964-85	**1344**	1211	133
R.C.Russell	1981-2004	**1320**	1192	128
F.H.Huish	1895-1914	**1310**	933	377
B.Taylor	1949-73	**1294**	1083	211
S.J.Rhodes	1981-2004	**1263**	1139	124
D.Hunter	1889-1909	**1253**	906	347
H.R.Butt	1890-1912	**1228**	953	275
J.H.Board	1891-1914/15	**1207**	852	355
H.Elliott	1920-47	**1206**	904	302
J.M.Parks	1949-76	**1181**	1088	93
R.Booth	1951-70	**1126**	948	178
L.E.G.Ames	1926-51	**1121**	703	418
D.L.Bairstow	1970-90	**1099**	961	138
G.Duckworth	1923-47	**1096**	753	343
H.W.Stephenson	1948-64	**1082**	748	334
J.G.Binks	1955-75	**1071**	895	176
T.G.Evans	1939-69	**1066**	816	250
A.Long	1960-80	**1046**	922	124
G.O.Dawkes	1937-61	**1043**	895	148
R.W.Tolchard	1965-83	**1037**	912	125
W.L.Cornford	1921-47	**1017**	675	342

FIELDING RECORDS

MOST CATCHES IN AN INNINGS

7	M.J.Stewart	Surrey v Northamptonshire	Northampton	1957
7	A.S.Brown	Gloucestershire v Nottinghamshire	Nottingham	1966

MOST CATCHES IN A MATCH

10	W.R.Hammond	Gloucestershire v Surrey	Cheltenham	1928

MOST CATCHES IN A SEASON

78	W.R.Hammond	1928	77	M.J.Stewart	1957

750 CATCHES IN A CAREER

1018	F.E.Woolley	1906-38	784	J.G.Langridge	1928-55
887	W.G.Grace	1865-1908	764	W.Rhodes	1898-1930
830	G.A.R.Lock	1946-70/71	758	C.A.Milton	1948-74
819	W.R.Hammond	1920-51	754	E.H.Hendren	1907-38
813	D.B.Close	1949-86			

UNIVERSITY MATCH RESULTS

Played: 161. Wins: Cambridge 56; Oxford 53. Drawn: 52. Abandoned: 1

In 2001, for the very first time, Cambridge hosted the University Match, cricket's oldest surviving first-class fixture, after the ECB's re-organisation of university cricket around six centres of excellence had removed it from Lord's. Dating from 1827 it has, wartime interruptions apart, been played annually since 1838. With the exception of five matches played in the area of Oxford (1829, 1843, 1846, 1848 and 1850), all the previous fixtures had been staged at Lord's. Since 2001 it has been played over four days rather than three.

In 2003, Oxford (with Brookes), Cambridge (with Anglia) and Durham were joined by Loughborough in playing three first-class matches against counties. The other two centres – Cardiff (with UWIC and Glamorgan), and Leeds (with Bradford and Leeds Metropolitan) – also play three counties apiece but without first-class status.

1827	Drawn	1876	Cambridge	1921	Cambridge	1968	Drawn
1829	Oxford	1877	Oxford	1922	Cambridge	1969	Drawn
1836	Oxford	1878	Cambridge	1923	Oxford	1970	Drawn
1838	Oxford	1879	Cambridge	1924	Cambridge	1971	Drawn
1839	Cambridge	1880	Cambridge	1925	Drawn	1972	Cambridge
1840	Cambridge	1881	Oxford	1926	Cambridge	1973	Drawn
1841	Cambridge	1882	Cambridge	1927	Cambridge	1974	Drawn
1842	Cambridge	1883	Cambridge	1928	Drawn	1975	Drawn
1843	Cambridge	1884	Oxford	1929	Drawn	1976	Oxford
1844	Drawn	1885	Cambridge	1930	Cambridge	1977	Drawn
1845	Cambridge	1886	Oxford	1931	Oxford	1978	Drawn
1846	Oxford	1887	Oxford	1932	Drawn	1979	Cambridge
1847	Cambridge	1888	Drawn	1933	Drawn	1980	Drawn
1848	Oxford	1889	Cambridge	1934	Drawn	1981	Drawn
1849	Cambridge	1890	Cambridge	1935	Cambridge	1982	Cambridge
1850	Oxford	1891	Cambridge	1936	Cambridge	1983	Drawn
1851	Cambridge	1892	Oxford	1937	Oxford	1984	Oxford
1852	Oxford	1893	Cambridge	1938	Drawn	1985	Drawn
1853	Oxford	1894	Oxford	1939	Oxford	1986	Cambridge
1854	Oxford	1895	Cambridge	1946	Oxford	1987	Drawn
1855	Oxford	1896	Oxford	1947	Drawn	1988	Abandoned
1856	Cambridge	1897	Cambridge	1948	Oxford	1989	Drawn
1857	Oxford	1898	Oxford	1949	Cambridge	1990	Drawn
1858	Oxford	1899	Drawn	1950	Drawn	1991	Drawn
1859	Cambridge	1900	Drawn	1951	Oxford	1992	Cambridge
1860	Cambridge	1901	Drawn	1952	Drawn	1993	Oxford
1861	Cambridge	1902	Cambridge	1953	Cambridge	1994	Drawn
1862	Cambridge	1903	Oxford	1954	Drawn	1995	Oxford
1863	Oxford	1904	Drawn	1955	Drawn	1996	Drawn
1864	Oxford	1905	Cambridge	1956	Drawn	1997	Drawn
1865	Oxford	1906	Cambridge	1957	Cambridge	1998	Cambridge
1866	Oxford	1907	Cambridge	1958	Cambridge	1999	Drawn
1867	Cambridge	1908	Oxford	1959	Oxford	2000	Drawn
1868	Cambridge	1909	Drawn	1960	Drawn	2001	Oxford
1869	Cambridge	1910	Oxford	1961	Drawn	2002	Drawn
1870	Cambridge	1911	Oxford	1962	Drawn	2003	Oxford
1871	Oxford	1912	Cambridge	1963	Drawn	2004	Oxford
1872	Cambridge	1913	Cambridge	1964	Drawn	2005	Oxford
1873	Oxford	1914	Oxford	1965	Drawn	2006	Oxford
1874	Oxford	1919	Oxford	1966	Oxford		
1875	Oxford	1920	Drawn	1967	Drawn		

CAMBRIDGE UNIVERSITY RECORDS

ALL FIRST-CLASS MATCHES

Highest Total	For 703-9d		v	Sussex	Hove	1890
	V 730-3		by	W Indians	Cambridge	1950
Lowest Total	For 30		v	Yorkshire	Cambridge	1928
	V 32		by	Oxford U	Lord's	1878
Highest Innings	For 254*	K.S.Duleepsinhji	v	Middlesex	Cambridge	1927
	V 304*	E.de C.Weekes	for	W Indians	Cambridge	1950
Highest Partnership						
(2nd wicket)	429*	J.G.Dewes/G.H.G.Doggart	v	Essex	Cambridge	1949
Best Innings Bowling	10-69	S.M.J.Woods	v	Thornton's XI	Cambridge	1890
Best Match Bowling	15-88	S.M.J.Woods	v	Thornton's XI	Cambridge	1890
Most Runs – Season		1581	D.S.Sheppard		(av 79.05)	1952
Most Runs – Career		4310	J.M.Brearley		(av 38.48)	1961-68
Most 100s – Season		7	D.S.Sheppard			1952
Most 100s – Career		14	D.S.Sheppard			1950-52
Most Wkts – Season		80	O.S.Wheatley		(av 17.63)	1958
Most Wkts – Career		208	G.Goonesena		(av 21.82)	1954-57

UNIVERSITY MATCH RECORDS

Highest Total	604		Oxford	2002
Lowest Total	39		Lord's	1858
Highest Innings	211	G.Goonesena	Lord's	1957
Best Innings Bowling	8-44	G.E.Jeffery	Lord's	1873
Best Match Bowling	13-73	A.G.Steel	Lord's	1878

Hat Tricks: F.C.Cobden (1870), A.G.Steel (1879), P.H.Morton (1880), J.F.Ireland (1911), R.G.H.Lowe (1926)

OXFORD UNIVERSITY RECORDS

ALL FIRST-CLASS MATCHES

Highest Total	For 651		v	Sussex	Hove	1895
	V 679-7d		by	Australians	Oxford	1938
Lowest Total	For 12		v	MCC	Oxford	1877
	V 24		by	MCC	Oxford	1846
Highest Innings	For 281	K.J.Key	v	Middlesex	Chiswick Park	1887
	V 338	W.W.Read	for	Surrey	The Oval	1888
Highest Partnership						
(3rd wicket)	408	S.Oberoi/D.R.Fox	v	Cambridge U	Cambridge	2005
Best Innings Bowling	10-38	S.E.Butler	v	Cambridge U	Lord's	1871
Best Match Bowling	15-65	B.J.T.Bosanquet	v	Sussex	Oxford	1900
Most Runs – Season		1307	Nawab of Pataudi sr		(av 93.35)	1931
Most Runs – Career		3319	N.S.Mitchell-Innes		(av 47.41)	1934-37
Most 100s – Season		6	Nawab of Pataudi sr			1931
Most 100s – Career		9	A.M.Crawley			1927-30
		9	Nawab of Pataudi sr			1928-31
		9	N.S.Mitchell-Innes			1934-37
		9	M.P.Donnelly			1946-47
Most Wkts – Season		70	I.A.R.Peebles		(av 18.15)	1930
Most Wkts – Career		182	R.H.B.Bettington		(av 19.38)	1920-23

UNIVERSITY MATCH RECORDS

Highest Total	610-5d		Cambridge	2005
Lowest Total	32		Lord's	1878
Highest Innings	247	S.Oberoi	Cambridge	2005
Best Innings Bowling	10-38	S.E.Butler	Lord's	1871
Best Match Bowling	15-95	S.E.Butler	Lord's	1871

Match Doubles: P.R.le Couteur (160 and 11-66 in 1910); G.J.Toogood (149 and 10-93 in 1985)

LIMITED-OVERS INTERNATIONALS RESULTS

1970-71 to 11 February 2007

These records exclude all matches involving multinational teams, as well as any abandoned without a ball bowled, regardless of the toss having been made.

	Opponents	*Matches*	*Won*											*Tied*	*NR*
			E	*A*	*SA*	*WI*	*NZ*	*I*	*P*	*SL*	*Z*	*B*	*Ass*		
England	Australia	**92**	37	51	–	–	–	–	–	–	–	–	–	2	2
	South Africa	**34**	11	–	21	–	–	–	–	–	–	–	–	1	1
	West Indies	**71**	30	–	–	37	–	–	–	–	–	–	–	–	4
	New Zealand	**58**	27	–	–	–	27	–	–	–	–	–	–	1	3
	India	**58**	26	–	–	–	–	30	–	–	–	–	–	–	2
	Pakistan	**63**	35	–	–	–	–	–	26	–	–	–	–	–	2
	Sri Lanka	**37**	19	–	–	–	–	–	–	18	–	–	–	–	–
	Zimbabwe	**30**	21	–	–	–	–	–	–	–	8	–	–	–	1
	Bangladesh	**7**	7	–	–	–	–	–	–	–	–	0	–	–	–
	Associates	**8**	8	–	–	–	–	–	–	–	–	–	0	–	–
Australia	South Africa	**65**	–	34	28	–	–	–	–	–	–	–	–	3	–
	West Indies	**113**	–	52	–	57	–	–	–	–	–	–	–	2	2
	New Zealand	**105**	–	75	–	–	27	–	–	–	–	–	–	–	3
	India	**83**	–	51	–	–	–	27	–	–	–	–	–	–	5
	Pakistan	**74**	–	43	–	–	–	–	27	–	–	–	–	1	3
	Sri Lanka	**62**	–	41	–	–	–	–	–	19	–	–	–	–	2
	Zimbabwe	**27**	–	25	–	–	–	–	–	–	1	–	–	–	1
	Bangladesh	**12**	–	11	–	–	–	–	–	–	–	1	–	–	–
	Associates	**9**	–	9	–	–	–	–	–	–	–	–	0	–	–
S Africa	West Indies	**39**	–	–	26	12	–	–	–	–	–	–	–	–	1
	N Zealand	**46**	–	–	27	–	15	–	–	–	–	–	–	–	4
	India	**54**	–	–	34	–	–	18	–	–	–	–	–	–	2
	Pakistan	**46**	–	–	31	–	–	–	14	–	–	–	–	–	1
	Sri Lanka	**44**	–	–	21	–	–	–	–	21	–	–	–	1	1
	Zimbabwe	**24**	–	–	21	–	–	–	–	–	2	–	–	–	1
	Bangladesh	**7**	–	–	7	–	–	–	–	–	–	0	–	–	–
	Associates	**11**	–	–	11	–	–	–	–	–	–	–	0	–	–
W Indies	New Zealand	**44**	–	–	–	23	17	–	–	–	–	–	–	–	4
	India	**90**	–	–	–	53	–	35	–	–	–	–	–	1	1
	Pakistan	**109**	–	–	–	63	–	–	44	–	–	–	–	2	–
	Sri Lanka	**42**	–	–	–	24	–	–	–	17	–	–	–	–	1
	Zimbabwe	**31**	–	–	–	23	–	–	–	–	7	–	–	–	1
	Bangladesh	**12**	–	–	–	10	–	–	–	–	–	0	–	–	2
	Associates	**8**	–	–	–	7	–	–	–	–	–	–	1	–	–
N Zealand	India	**75**	–	–	–	–	35	36	–	–	–	–	–	–	4
	Pakistan	**78**	–	–	–	–	29	–	47	–	–	–	–	1	1
	Sri Lanka	**65**	–	–	–	–	34	–	–	28	–	–	–	1	2
	Zimbabwe	**28**	–	–	–	–	19	–	–	–	7	–	–	1	1
	Bangladesh	**7**	–	–	–	–	7	–	–	–	–	0	–	–	–
	Associates	**6**	–	–	–	–	6	–	–	–	–	–	0	–	–
India	Pakistan	**108**	–	–	–	–	–	40	64	–	–	–	–	–	4
	Sri Lanka	**92**	–	–	–	–	–	47	–	36	–	–	–	–	9
	Zimbabwe	**49**	–	–	–	–	–	39	–	–	8	–	–	2	–
	Bangladesh	**14**	–	–	–	–	–	13	–	–	–	1	–	–	–
	Associates	**18**	–	–	–	–	–	16	–	–	–	–	2	–	–
Pakistan	Sri Lanka	**107**	–	–	–	–	–	–	65	38	–	–	–	1	3
	Zimbabwe	**34**	–	–	–	–	–	–	30	–	2	–	–	1	1
	Bangladesh	**18**	–	–	–	–	–	–	17	–	–	1	–	–	–
	Associates	**15**	–	–	–	–	–	–	15	–	–	–	0	–	–
Sri Lanka	Zimbabwe	**37**	–	–	–	–	–	–	–	30	6	–	–	–	1
	Bangladesh	**18**	–	–	–	–	–	–	–	17	–	1	–	–	–
	Associates	**10**	–	–	–	–	–	–	–	9	–	–	1	–	–
Zimbabwe	Bangladesh	**33**	–	–	–	–	–	–	–	–	18	15	–	–	–
	Associates	**25**	–	–	–	–	–	–	–	–	20	–	3	–	2
Bangladesh	Associates	**19**	–	–	–	–	–	–	–	–	–	12	7	–	–
Associates	Associates	**41**	–	–	–	–	–	–	–	–	–	–	40	–	1
		2512	221	392	227	309	216	301	349	233	79	31	54	21	79

MERIT TABLE OF ALL L-O INTERNATIONALS

1970-71 to 11 February 2007

	Matches	*Won*	*Lost*	*Tied*	*No Result*	*% Won (exc NR)*
South Africa	370	227	127	5	11	63.23
Australia	642	392	224	8	18	62.82
West Indies	559	309	229	5	16	56.90
Pakistan	652	349	282	6	15	54.78
England	458	221	218	4	15	49.88
India	641	301	310	3	27	49.02
Sri Lanka	514	233	259	3	19	47.07
New Zealand	512	216	270	4	22	44.08
Associate Members	211	54	153	–	4	26.08
Zimbabwe	318	79	226	4	9	25.56
Bangladesh	147	31	114	–	2	21.37

TEAM RECORDS
HIGHEST TOTALS

443-9	(50 overs)	Sri Lanka v Holland	Amstelveen	2006
438-9	(49.5 overs)	South Africa v Australia	Johannesburg	2005-06
434-4	(50 overs)	Australia v South Africa	Johannesburg	2005-06
418-5	(50 overs)	South Africa v Zimbabwe	Potchefstroom	2006-07
398-5	(50 overs)	Sri Lanka v Kenya	Kandy	1995-96
397-5	(44 overs)	New Zealand v Zimbabwe	Bulawayo	2005
392-6	(50 overs)	South Africa v Pakistan	Pretoria	2006-07
391-4	(50 overs)	England v Bangladesh	Nottingham	2005
376-2	(50 overs)	India v New Zealand	Hyderabad, India	1999-00
373-6	(50 overs)	India v Sri Lanka	Taunton	1999
371-9	(50 overs)	Pakistan v Sri Lanka	Nairobi	1996-97
368-5	(50 overs)	Australia v Sri Lanka	Sydney	2005-06
363-3	(50 overs)	South Africa v Zimbabwe	Bulawayo	2001-02
363-7	(55 overs)	England v Pakistan	Nottingham	1992
360-4	(50 overs)	West Indies v Sri Lanka	Karachi	1987-88
359-2	(50 overs)	Australia v India	Johannesburg	2002-03
359-5	(50 overs)	Australia v India	Sydney	2003-04
356-9	(50 overs)	India v Pakistan	Vishakhapatnam	2004-05
354-3	(50 overs)	South Africa v Kenya	Cape Town	2001-02
353-5	(50 overs)	India v New Zealand	Hyderabad, India	2003-04
353-6	(50 overs)	Pakistan v England	Karachi	2005-06
351-3	(50 overs)	India v Kenya	Paarl	2001-02
351-4	(50 overs)	Pakistan v South Africa	Durban	2006-07
350-6	(50 overs)	India v Sri Lanka	Nagpur	2005-06

The highest for Zimbabwe is 340-2 (v Namibia, Harare, 2002-03), and for Bangladesh 301-7 (v Kenya, Bogra, 2005-06).

HIGHEST TOTALS BATTING SECOND

WINNING:	438-9	(49.5 overs)	South Africa v Australia	Johannesburg	2005-06
LOSING:	344-8	(50.0 overs)	Pakistan v India	Karachi	2003-04

HIGHEST MATCH AGGREGATE

872-13	(99.5 overs)	South Africa v Australia	Johannesburg	2005-06

LARGEST RUNS MARGINS OF VICTORY

256 runs	Australia beat Namibia	Potschefstroom	2002-03
245 runs	Sri Lanka beat India	Sharjah	2000-01
233 runs	Pakistan v Bangladesh	Dhaka	1999-00
232 runs	Australia beat Sri Lanka	Adelaide	1984-85
224 runs	Australia beat Pakistan	Nairobi	2002
217 runs	Pakistan beat Sri Lanka	Sharjah	2001-02
210 runs	New Zealand beat USA	The Oval	2004
209 runs	South Africa beat West Indies	Cape Town	2003-04
208 runs	South Africa beat Kenya	Cape Town	2001-02

208 runs		Australia beat India	Sydney	2003-04
206 runs		New Zealand beat Australia	Adelaide	1985-86
206 runs		Sri Lanka beat Holland	Colombo (RPS).	2002-03
202 runs		England beat India	Lord's	1975
202 runs		South Africa beat Kenya	Nairobi	1996-97
202 runs		Zimbabwe beat Kenya	Dhaka	1998-99
200 runs		India beat Bangladesh	Dhaka	2002-03

LOWEST TOTALS (Excluding reduced innings)

35	(18.0 overs)	Zimbabwe v Sri Lanka	Harare	2003-04
36	(18.4 overs)	Canada v Sri Lanka	Paarl	2002-03
38	(15.4 overs)	Zimbabwe v Sri Lanka	Colombo (SSC)	2001-02
43	(19.5 overs)	Pakistan v West Indies	Cape Town	1992-93
45	(40.3 overs)	Canada v England	Manchester	1979
45	(14.0 overs)	Namibia v Australia	Potschefstroom	2002-03
54	(26.3 overs)	India v Sri Lanka	Sharjah	2000-01
54	(23.2 overs)	West Indies v South Africa	Cape Town	2003-04
55	(28.3 overs)	Sri Lanka v West Indies	Sharjah	1986-87
63	(25.5 overs)	India v Australia	Sydney	1980-81
64	(35.5 overs)	New Zealand v Pakistan	Sharjah	1985-86
65	(24.0 overs)	USA v Australia	Southampton	2004
65	(24.3 overs)	Zimbabwe v India	Harare	2005
68	(31.3 overs)	Scotland v West Indies	Leicester	1999
69	(28.0 overs)	South Africa v Australia	Sydney	1993-94
69	(22.5 overs)	Zimbabwe v Kenya	Harare	2005-06
70	(25.2 overs)	Australia v England	Birmingham	1977
70	(26.3 overs)	Australia v New Zealand	Adelaide	1985-86

The lowest for England is 86 (v A, Manchester, 2001), and for Bangladesh 76 (v SL, Colombo (SSC), 2002, and v I, Dhaka, 2002-03).

LOWEST MATCH AGGREGATES

73-11	(23.2 overs)	Canada (36) v Sri Lanka (37-1)	Paarl	2002-03
75-11	(27.2 overs)	Zimbabwe (35) v Sri Lanka (40-1)	Harare	2003-04
78-11	(20.0 overs)	Zimbabwe (38) v Sri Lanka (40-1)	Colombo (SSC)	2001-02

BATTING RECORDS

HIGHEST INDIVIDUAL INNINGS

194	Saeed Anwar	Pakistan v India	Madras	1996-97
189*	I.V.A.Richards	West Indies v England	Manchester	1984
189	S.T.Jayasuriya	Sri Lanka v India	Sharjah	2000-01
188*	G.Kirsten	South Africa v UAE	Rawalpindi	1995-96
186*	S.R.Tendulkar	India v New Zealand	Hyderabad	1999-00
183*	M.S.Dhoni	India v Sri Lanka	Jaipur	2005-06
183	S.C.Ganguly	India v Sri Lanka	Taunton	1999
181	I.V.A.Richards	West Indies v Sri Lanka	Karachi	1987-88
175*	Kapil Dev	India v Zimbabwe	Tunbridge Wells	1983
175	H.H.Gibbs	South Africa v Australia	Johannesburg	2005-06
173	M.E.Waugh	Australia v West Indies	Melbourne	2000-01
172*	C.B.Wishart	Zimbabwe v Namibia	Harare	2002-03
172	A.C.Gilchrist	Australia v Zimbabwe	Hobart	2003-04
172	L.Vincent	New Zealand v Zimbabwe	Bulawayo	2005
171*	G.M.Turner	New Zealand v East Africa	Birmingham	1975
169*	D.J.Callaghan	South Africa v New Zealand	Pretoria	1994-95
169	B.C.Lara	West Indies v Sri Lanka	Sharjah	1995-96
167*	R.A.Smith	England v Australia	Birmingham	1993
164	R.T.Ponting	Australia v South Africa	Johannesburg	2005-06
161	A.C.Hudson	South Africa v Holland	Rawalpindi	1995-96
159*	D.Mongia	India v Zimbabwe	Gauhati	2001-02
158	D.I.Gower	England v New Zealand	Brisbane	1982-83
157	S.T.Jayasuriya	Sri Lanka v Holland	Amstelveen	2006
156	B.C.Lara	West Indies v Pakistan	Adelaide	2004-05
156	A.Symonds	Australia v New Zealand	Wellington	2005-06
154	A.C.Gilchrist	Australia v Sri Lanka	Melbourne	1998-99

153*	I.V.A.Richards	West Indies v Australia	Melbourne	1979-80
153*	M.Azharuddin	India v Zimbabwe	Cuttack	1997-98
153*	S.C.Ganguly	India v New Zealand	Gwalior	1999-00
153*	C.H.Gayle	West Indies v Zimbabwe	Bulawayo	2003-04
153	B.C.Lara	West Indies v Pakistan	Sharjah	1993-94
153	R.Dravid	India v New Zealand	Hyderabad	1999-00
153	H.H.Gibbs	South Africa v Bangladesh	Potchefstroom	2002-03
152*	D.L.Haynes	West Indies v India	Georgetown	1988-89
152*	C.H.Gayle	West Indies v South Africa	Johannesburg	2003-04
152	C.H.Gayle	West Indies v Kenya	Nairobi	2001-02
152	S.R.Tendulkar	India v Namibia	Pietermaritzburg	2002-03
152	A.J.Strauss	England v Bangladesh	Nottingham	2005
152	S.T.Jayasuriya	Sri Lanka v England	Leeds	2006
151*	S.T.Jayasuriya	Sri Lanka v India	Bombay	1996-97
151	A.Symonds	Australia v Sri Lanka	Sydney	2005-06
150	S.Chanderpaul	West Indies v South Africa	East London	1998-99

The highest for Bangladesh is 123* by Shahriar Nafis (v Z, Jaipur, 2006-07).

HUNDRED ON DEBUT

D.L.Amiss	103	England v Australia	Manchester	1972
D.L.Haynes	148	West Indies v Australia	St John's	1977-78
A.Flower	115*	Zimbabwe v Sri Lanka	New Plymouth	1991-92
Salim Elahi	102*	Pakistan v Sri Lanka	Gujranwala	1995-96

Shahid Afridi scored 102 for P v SL, Nairobi, 1996-97, in his second match having not batted in his first.

Fastest 100	37 balls	Shahid Afridi (102)	P v SL	Nairobi	1996-97
Fastest 50	17 balls	S.T.Jayasuriya (76)	SL v P	Singapore	1995-96

CARRYING BAT THROUGH INNINGS (SIDE ALL OUT)

G.W.Flower	84*	Zimbabwe (205) v England	Sydney	1994-95
Saeed Anwar	103*	Pakistan (219) v Zimbabwe	Harare	1994-95
N.V.Knight	125*	England (246) v Pakistan	Nottingham	1996
R.D.Jacobs	49*	West Indies (110) v Australia	Manchester	1999
D.R.Martyn	116*	Australia (191) v New Zealand	Auckland	1999-00
H.H.Gibbs	59*	South Africa (101†) v Pakistan	Sharjah	1999-00
A.J.Stewart	100*	England (192) v West Indies	Nottingham	2000
Javed Omar	33*	Bangladesh (103) v Zimbabwe	Harare	2000-01

† One batsman retired hurt.

5000 RUNS IN A CAREER

		LOI	*I*	*NO*	*HS*	*Runs*	*Avge*	*100*	*50*
S.R.Tendulkar	I	380	370	36	186*	**14782**	44.25	41	76
Inzamam-ul-Haq	P	371	344	52	137*	**11627**	39.81	10	83
S.T.Jayasuriya	SL	375	365	17	189	**11486**	33.00	23	62
S.C.Ganguly	I	283	273	21	183	**10342**	41.03	22	63
B.C.Lara	WI	285	277	31	169	**10079**	40.97	19	61
R.Dravid	I	304	282	35	153	**9857**	39.90	12	75
R.T.Ponting	A	265	259	31	164	**9854**	42.03	21	56
M.Azharuddin	I	334	308	54	153*	**9378**	36.92	7	58
P.A.de Silva	SL	308	296	30	145	**9284**	34.90	11	64
Saeed Anwar	P	247	244	19	194	**8823**	39.21	20	43
D.L.Haynes	WI	238	237	28	152*	**8648**	41.37	17	57
M.E.Waugh	A	244	236	20	173	**8500**	39.35	18	50
M.S.Atapattu	SL	265	257	32	132*	**8468**	37.63	11	59
J.H.Kallis	SA	241	228	41	139	**8420**	45.02	14	58
A.C.Gilchrist	A	253	246	9	172	**8381**	35.36	13	48
M.Yousuf Youhana	P	228	216	32	141*	**7801**	42.39	12	52
S.P.Fleming	NZ	264	255	19	134*	**7569**	32.07	7	45
S.R.Waugh	A	325	288	58	120*	**7569**	32.90	3	45
A.Ranatunga	SL	269	255	47	131*	**7454**	35.83	4	49
Javed Miandad	P	233	218	41	119*	**7381**	41.70	8	50

		LOI	I	NO	HS	Runs	Avge	100	50
Salim Malik	P	283	256	38	102	**7171**	32.89	5	47
N.J.Astle	NZ	221	217	14	145*	**7090**	34.92	16	41
M.G.Bevan	A	232	196	67	108*	**6912**	53.58	6	46
G.Kirsten	SA	185	185	19	188*	**6798**	40.95	13	45
A.Flower	Z	213	208	16	145	**6786**	35.34	4	55
I.V.A.Richards	WI	187	167	24	189*	**6721**	47.00	11	45
Ijaz Ahmed	P	250	232	29	139*	**6564**	32.33	10	37
G.W.Flower	Z	219	212	18	142*	**6536**	33.69	6	40
A.R.Border	A	273	252	39	127*	**6524**	30.62	3	39
S.Chanderpaul	WI	207	196	26	150	**6459**	37.99	5	44
H.H.Gibbs	SA	197	193	14	175	**6356**	35.50	16	27
R.B.Richardson	WI	224	217	30	122	**6248**	33.41	5	44
D.P.M.D.Jayawardena	SL	232	215	23	128	**6096**	31.75	8	33
D.M.Jones	A	164	161	25	145	**6068**	44.61	7	46
D.C.Boon	A	181	177	16	122	**5964**	37.04	5	37
J.N.Rhodes	SA	245	220	51	121	**5935**	35.11	2	33
Ramiz Raja	P	198	197	15	119*	**5841**	32.09	9	31
C.L.Hooper	WI	227	206	43	113*	**5761**	35.34	7	29
C.H.Gayle	WI	155	153	9	153*	**5641**	39.17	15	28
W.J.Cronje	SA	188	175	31	112	**5565**	38.64	2	39
A.Jadeja	I	196	179	36	119	**5359**	37.47	6	30
D.R.Martyn	A	205	179	51	144*	**5259**	41.08	5	36
K.C.Sangakkara	SL	179	164	21	138*	**5216**	36.47	6	33
A.D.R.Campbell	Z	188	184	14	131*	**5185**	30.50	7	30
R.S.Mahanama	SL	213	198	23	119*	**5162**	29.49	4	35
C.G.Greenidge	WI	128	127	13	133*	**5134**	45.03	11	31

The most for England is 4677 in 162 innings by A.J.Stewart, and for Bangladesh 1963 (94) by Habibul Bashar.

15 HUNDREDS

		Inns	100	E	A	SA	WI	NZ	I	P	SL	Z	B	Ass
S.R.Tendulkar	I	370	**41**	1	7	3	4	4	–	5	7	5	–	5
S.T.Jayasuriya	SL	365	**23**	4	2	–	–	5	5	3	–	1	2	1
S.C.Ganguly	I	273	**22**	1	1	3	–	3	–	2	4	3	1	4
R.T.Ponting	A	259	**21**	3	–	2	1	4	4	1	4	1	1	–
Saeed Anwar	P	244	**20**	–	1	–	2	4	4	–	7	2	–	–
B.C.Lara	WI	277	**19**	1	3	3	–	2	–	5	2	1	1	1
M.E.Waugh	A	236	**18**	1	–	2	3	3	3	1	1	3	–	1
D.L.Haynes	WI	237	**17**	2	6	–	–	2	2	4	1	–	–	–
H.H.Gibbs	SA	193	**16**	2	2	–	4	1	2	1	1	1	1	1
N.J.Astle	NZ	217	**16**	2	1	1	1	–	5	2	–	3	–	1
C.H.Gayle	WI	153	**15**	2	–	3	–	–	4	1	–	2	1	2

The most for England is 12 by M.E.Trescothick in 122 innings, for Zimbabwe 7 by A.D.R.Campbell (184), and for Bangladesh 3 by Shahriar Nafis (39).

HIGHEST PARTNERSHIP FOR EACH WICKET

1st	286	W.U.Tharanga/S.T.Jayasuriya	Sri Lanka v England	Leeds	2006
2nd	331	S.R.Tendulkar/R.Dravid	India v New Zealand	Hyderabad (Ind)	1999-00
3rd	237*	R.Dravid/S.R.Tendulkar	India v Kenya	Bristol	1999
4th	275*	M.Azharuddin/A.Jadeja	India v Zimbabwe	Cuttack	1997-98
5th	223	M.Azharuddin/A.Jadeja	India v Sri Lanka	Colombo (RPS)	1997-98
6th	165	M.E.K.Hussey/B.J.Haddin	Australia v West Indies	Kuala Lumpur	2006-07
7th	130	A.Flower/H.H.Streak	Zimbabwe v England	Harare	2001-02
8th	138*	J.M.Kemp/A.J.Hall	South Africa v India	Cape Town	2006-07
9th	126*	Kapil Dev/S.M.H.Kirmani	India v Zimbabwe	Tunbridge Wells	1983
10th	106*	I.V.A.Richards/M.A.Holding	West Indies v England	Manchester	1984

BOWLING RECORDS
SIX WICKETS IN AN INNINGS

8-19	W.P.U.C.J Vaas	Sri Lanka v Zimbabwe	Colombo (SSC)	2001-02
7-15	G.D.McGrath	Australia v Namibia	Potschefstroom	2002-03
7-20	A.J.Bichel	Australia v England	Port Elizabeth	2002-03
7-30	M.Muralitharan	Sri Lanka v India	Sharjah	2000-01
7-36	Waqar Younis	Pakistan v England	Leeds	2001
7-37	Aqib Javed	Pakistan v India	Sharjah	1991-92
7-51	W.W.Davis	West Indies v Australia	Leeds	1983
6-12	A.Kumble	India v West Indies	Calcutta	1993-94
6-14	G.J.Gilmour	Australia v England	Leeds	1975
6-14	Imran Khan	Pakistan v India	Sharjah	1984-85
6-14	M.F.Maharoof	Sri Lanka v West Indies	Bombay	2006-07
6-15	C.E.H.Croft	West Indies v England	Kingstown	1980-81
6-16	Shoaib Akhtar	Pakistan v New Zealand	Karachi	2001-02
6-18	Azhar Mahmood	Pakistan v West Indies	Sharjah	1999-00
6-19	H.K.Olonga	Zimbabwe v England	Cape Town	1999-00
6-19	S.E.Bond	New Zealand v Zimbabwe	Harare	2005
6-20	B.C.Strang	Zimbabwe v Bangladesh	Nairobi	1997-98
6-22	F.H.Edwards	West Indies v Zimbabwe	Harare	2003-04
6-22	M.Ntini	South Africa v Australia	Cape Town	2005-06
6-23	A.A.Donald	South Africa v Kenya	Nairobi	1996-97
6-23	A.Nehra	India v England	Durban	2002-03
6-23	S.E.Bond	New Zealand v Australia	Port Elizabeth	2002-03
6-25	S.B.Styris	New Zealand v West Indies	Port-of-Spain	2002
6-25	W.P.U.C.J Vaas	Sri Lanka v Bangladesh	Pietermaritzburg	2002-03
6-26	Waqar Younis	Pakistan v Sri Lanka	Sharjah	1989-90
6-26	Mashrafe Mortaza	Bangladesh v Kenya	Nairobi	2006
6-27	Naved-ul-Hasan	Pakistan v India	Jamshedpur	2004-05
6-28	H.K.Olonga	Zimbabwe v Kenya	Bulawayo	2002-03
6-29	B.P.Patterson	West Indies v India	Nagpur	1987-88
6-29	S.T.Jayasuriya	Sri Lanka v England	Moratuwa	1992-93
6-30	Waqar Younis	Pakistan v New Zealand	Auckland	1993-94
6-31	P.D.Collingwood	England v Bangladesh	Nottingham	2005
6-35	S.M.Pollock	South Africa v West Indies	East London	1998-99
6-35	Abdul Razzaq	Pakistan v Bangladesh	Dhaka	2001-02
6-39	K.H.MacLeay	Australia v India	Nottingham	1983
6-41	I.V.A.Richards	West Indies v India	Delhi	1989-90
6-42	A.B.Agarkar	India v Australia	Melbourne	2003-04
6-44	Waqar Younis	Pakistan v New Zealand	Sharjah	1996-97
6-49	L.Klusener	South Africa v Sri Lanka	Lahore	1997-98
6-50	A.H.Gray	West Indies v Australia	Port-of-Spain	1990-91
6-55	S.Sreesanth	India v England	Indore	2005-06
6-59	Waqar Younis	Pakistan v Australia	Nottingham	2001
6-59	A.Nehra	India v Sri Lanka	Colombo (RPS)	2005

150 WICKETS IN A CAREER

		LOI	*Balls*	*R*	*W*	*Avge*	*Best*	*4w*	*R/Over*
Wasim Akram	P	356	18186	11812	**502**	23.52	5-15	23	3.89
M.Muralitharan	SL	279	15208	9710	**421**	23.06	7-30	19	3.83
Waqar Younis	P	262	12698	9919	**416**	23.84	7-36	27	4.68
W.P.U.C.J.Vaas	SL	288	14181	9915	**369**	26.86	8-19	13	4.19
S.M.Pollock	SA	267	13948	8612	**362**	23.79	6-35	16	3.70
G.D.McGrath	A	234	12271	7882	**351**	22.45	7-15	16	3.85
A.Kumble	I	268	14321	10262	**331**	31.00	6-12	10	4.29
J.Srinath	I	229	11935	8847	**315**	28.08	5-23	10	4.44
S.K.Warne	A	193	10600	7514	**291**	25.82	5-33	13	4.25
Saqlain Mushtaq	P	169	8770	6275	**288**	21.78	5-20	17	4.29
S.T.Jayasuriya	SL	375	13212	10483	**285**	36.78	6-29	10	4.76
A.A.Donald	SA	164	8561	5926	**272**	21.78	6-23	13	4.15
A.B.Agarkar	I	178	8782	7402	**270**	27.41	6-42	11	5.05
B.Lee	A	147	7582	5940	**260**	22.84	5-22	16	4.70
Kapil Dev	I	225	11202	6945	**253**	27.45	5-43	4	3.72
Abdul Razzaq	P	224	9617	7469	**244**	30.61	6-35	11	4.65

		LOI	Balls	R	W	Avge	Best	4w	R/Over
H.H.Streak	Z	187	9414	7065	**237**	29.81	5-32	8	4.50
D.Gough	E	158	8421	6154	**234**	26.29	5-44	12	4.38
M.Ntini	SA	142	7134	5211	**229**	22.75	6-22	10	4.38
C.A.Walsh	WI	205	10822	6915	**227**	30.46	5- 1	7	3.83
C.E.L.Ambrose	WI	176	9353	5430	**225**	24.13	5-17	10	3.48
J.H.Kallis	SA	241	8555	6848	**219**	31.26	5-30	4	4.80
C.J.McDermott	A	138	7460	5018	**203**	24.71	5-44	5	4.03
C.Z.Harris	NZ	248	10667	7613	**203**	37.50	5-42	3	4.28
Shoaib Akhtar	P	128	6021	4638	**202**	22.96	6-16	9	4.62
C.L.Cairns	NZ	214	8132	6557	**200**	32.78	5-42	4	4.83
B.K.V.Prasad	I	161	8129	6332	**196**	32.30	5-27	4	4.67
Shahid Afridi	P	232	9160	7036	**196**	35.89	5-11	4	4.60
S.R.Waugh	A	325	8883	6764	**195**	34.68	4-33	3	4.56
C.L.Hooper	WI	227	9573	6957	**193**	36.04	4-34	3	4.36
L.Klusener	SA	171	7336	5751	**192**	29.95	6-49	7	4.70
Aqib Javed	P	163	8012	5721	**182**	31.43	7-37	6	4.28
Imran Khan	P	175	7462	4845	**182**	26.62	6-14	4	3.90
D.L.Vettori	NZ	183	8551	5983	**176**	33.99	5-30	5	4.19
Harbhajan Singh	I	145	7777	5349	**168**	31.83	5-31	4	4.12
Mushtaq Ahmed	P	144	7543	5361	**161**	33.29	5-36	4	4.26
R.J.Hadlee	NZ	115	6182	3407	**158**	21.56	5-25	6	3.31
M.Prabhakar	I	130	6360	4534	**157**	28.87	5-33	6	4.27
M.D.Marshall	WI	136	7175	4233	**157**	26.96	4-18	6	3.54
Z.Khan	I	111	5477	4493	**154**	29.17	4-19	6	4.92
U.D.U.Chandana	SL	146	6100	4790	**151**	31.72	5-61	5	4.71

The most for Bangladesh is 106 by Mohammad Rafique (110 LOI).

HAT-TRICKS

Jalaluddin	Pakistan v Australia	Hyderabad	1982-83
B.A.Reid	Australia v New Zealand	Sydney	1985-86
C.Sharma	India v New Zealand	Nagpur	1987-88
Wasim Akram	Pakistan v West Indies	Sharjah	1989-90
Wasim Akram	Pakistan v Australia	Sharjah	1989-90
Kapil Dev	India v Sri Lanka	Calcutta	1990-91
Aqib Javed	Pakistan v India	Sharjah	1991-92
D.K.Morrison	New Zealand v India	Napier	1993-94
Waqar Younis	Pakistan v New Zealand	East London	1994-95
Saqlain Mushtaq	Pakistan v Zimbabwe	Peshawar	1996-97
E.A.Brandes	Zimbabwe v England	Harare	1996-97
A.M.Stuart	Australia v Pakistan	Melbourne	1996-97
Saqlain Mushtaq	Pakistan v Zimbabwe	The Oval	1999
W.P.U.C.J Vaas	Sri Lanka v Zimbabwe	Colombo (SSC)	2001-02
Mohammad Sami	Pakistan v West Indies	Sharjah	2001-02
W.P.U.C.J Vaas[1]	Sri Lanka v Bangladesh	Pietermaritzburg	2002-03
B.Lee	Australia v Kenya	Durban	2002-03
J.M.Anderson	England v Pakistan	The Oval	2003
S.J.Harmison	England v India	Nottingham	2004
C.K.Langeveldt	South Africa v West Indies	Bridgetown	2004-05
Shahadat Hossain	Bangladesh v Zimbabwe	Harare	2006
J.E.Taylor	West Indies v Australia	Bombay	2006-07
S.E.Bond	New Zealand v Australia	Hobart	2006-07

[1] The first three balls of the match. Took four wickets in opening over (W W W 4 wide W 0).

WICKET-KEEPING RECORDS
SIX DISMISSALS IN AN INNINGS

6	(6ct)	A.C.Gilchrist	Australia v South Africa	Cape Town	1999-00
6	(6ct)	A.J.Stewart	England v Zimbabwe	Manchester	2000
6	(5ct/1st)	R.D.Jacobs	West Indies v Sri Lanka	Colombo (RPS)	2001-02
6	(5ct/1st)	A.C.Gilchrist	Australia v England	Sydney	2002-03
6	(6ct)	A.C.Gilchrist	Australia v Namibia	Potchefstroom	2002-03
6	(6ct)	A.C.Gilchrist	Australia v Sri Lanka	Colombo (RPS)	2003-04
6	(6ct)	M.V.Boucher	South Africa v Pakistan	Cape Town	2006-07

100 DISMISSALS IN A CAREER

Total			LOI	*Ct*	*St*
418‡	A.C.Gilchrist	Australia	248	373	45
340	M.V.Boucher	South Africa	230	323	17
287‡	Moin Khan	Pakistan	211	214	73
233	I.A.Healy	Australia	168	194	39
220‡	Rashid Latif	Pakistan	164	182	38
207‡	R.S.Kaluwitharana	Sri Lanka	187	132	75
204‡	P.J.L.Dujon	West Indies	167	183	21
187	R.D.Jacobs	West Indies	146	159	28
186†‡	K.C.Sangakkara	Sri Lanka	136	142	44
165	D.J.Richardson	South Africa	122	148	17
165†‡	A.Flower	Zimbabwe	185	133	32
163†‡	A.J.Stewart	England	138	148	15
154‡	N.R.Mongia	India	139	110	44
136†‡	A.C.Parore	New Zealand	148	111	25
127†‡	B.B.McCullum	New Zealand	93	117	10
126	Khaled Masud	Bangladesh	125	91	35
124	R.W.Marsh	Australia	92	120	4
103	Salim Yousuf	Pakistan	86	81	22

† *Excluding catches taken in the field.* ‡ *Excluding matches when not wicket-keeper.*

FIELDING RECORDS
FIVE CATCHES IN AN INNINGS

5	J.N.Rhodes	South Africa v West Indies	Bombay	1993-94

100 CATCHES IN A CAREER

Total			*LOI*
156	M.Azharuddin	India	334
127	S.P.Fleming	New Zealand	264
127	A.R.Border	Australia	273
120	C.L.Hooper	West Indies	227
114	S.R.Tendulkar	India	380
113	D.P.M.D.Jayawardena	Sri Lanka	231
112	R.T.Ponting	Australia	265
112	B.C.Lara	West Indies	285
112	R.Dravid	India	304
111	S.R.Waugh	Australia	325
110	M.Muralitharan	Sri Lanka	279
110	S.T.Jayasuriya	Sri Lanka	375
109	R.S.Mahanama	Sri Lanka	213
109	Inzamam-ul-Haq	Pakistan	371
108	M.E.Waugh	Australia	244
105	J.N.Rhodes	South Africa	245
101	I.V.A.Richards	West Indies	187

The most for England is 64 by G.A.Hick (120 LOI) and 63 by P.D.Collingwood (112), for Zimbabwe 86 by GW Flower (219), and for Bangladesh 22 by Mohammad Rafique (110).

ALL-ROUND RECORDS
50 RUNS AND 5 WICKETS IN A MATCH

I.V.A.Richards	119	5-41	West Indies v New Zealand	Dunedin	1986-87
K.Srikkanth	70	5-27	India v New Zealand	Vishakhapatnam	1988-89
M.E.Waugh	57	5-24	Australia v West Indies	Melbourne	1992-93
L.Klusener	54	6-49	South Africa v Sri Lanka	Lahore	1997-98
Abdul Razzaq	70*	5-48	Pakistan v India	Hobart	1999-00
G.A.Hick	80	5-33	England v Zimbabwe	Harare	1999-00
Shahid Afridi	61	5-40	Pakistan v England	Lahore	2000-01
S.C.Ganguly	71*	5-34	India v Zimbabwe	Kanpur	2000-01
S.B.Styris	63*	6-25	New Zealand v West Indies	Port-of-Spain	2002
R.C.Irani	53	5-26	England v India	The Oval	2002
C.H.Gayle	60	5-46	West Indies v Australia	St George's	2002-03
P.D.Collingwood	112*	6-31	England v Bangladesh	Nottingham	2005

1000 RUNS AND 100 WICKETS

England	I.T.Botham (2113/145), A.Flintoff (2883/121).
Australia	S.P.O'Donnell (1242/108); A.Symonds (3969/119); S.K.Warne (1016/291); S.R.Waugh (7569/195)
South Africa	W.J.Cronje (5565/114); J.H.Kallis (8420/219); L.Klusener (3576/192); S.M.Pollock (2866/362)
West Indies	C.H.Gayle (5641/134); C.L.Hooper (5761/193); I.V.A.Richards (6721/118)
New Zealand	C.L.Cairns (4881/200); R.J.Hadlee (1751/158); C.Z.Harris (4379/203); J.D.P.Oram (1382/100); S.B.Styris (2642/107); D.L.Vettori (1204/176)
India	A.B.Agarkar (1240/270); Kapil Dev (3782/253); I.K.Pathan (1006/115); M.Prabhakar (1858/157); R.J.Shastri (3108/129); S.R.Tendulkar (14782/147)
Pakistan	Abdul Razzaq (4388/244); Azhar Mahmood (1519/123); Imran Khan (3709/182); Mudassar Nazar (2654/111); Shahid Afridi (4945/196); Shoaib Malik (3389/103); Wasim Akram (3717/502)
Sri Lanka	U.D.U.Chandana (1626/151); P.A.de Silva (9284/106); H.D.P.K.Dharmasena (1222/138); S.T.Jayasuriya (11486/285); W.P.U.C.J.Vaas (1869/369)
Zimbabwe	G.W.Flower (6536/104); H.H.Streak (2901/237)
Bangladesh	Mohammad Rafique (1124/106)

APPEARANCE RECORDS – 250 MATCHES

380	S.R.Tendulkar	India
375	S.T.Jayasuriya	Sri Lanka
371	Inzamam-ul-Haq	Pakistan
356	Wasim Akram	Pakistan
334	M.Azharuddin	India
325	S.R.Waugh	Australia
308	P.A.de Silva	Sri Lanka
304	R.Dravid	India
288	W.P.U.C.J.Vaas	Sri Lanka
285	B.C.Lara	West Indies
283	Salim Malik	Pakistan
283	S.C.Ganguly	India
279	M.Muralitharan	Sri Lanka
273	A.R.Border	Australia
269	A.Ranatunga	Sri Lanka
268	A.Kumble	India
267	S.M.Pollock	South Africa
265	M.S.Atapattu	Sri Lanka
265	R.T.Ponting	Australia
264	S.P.Fleming	New Zealand
262	Waqar Younis	Pakistan
253	A.C.Gilchrist	Australia
250	Ijaz Ahmed	Pakistan

The most for England is 170 by A.J.Stewart, for Zimbabwe 219 by G.W.Flower, and for Bangladesh 126 by Khaled Masud. The most consecutive appearances is 172 by A.Flower for Zimbabwe (Feb 1992-Apr 2001).

100 MATCHES AS CAPTAIN

LOI			*W*	*L*	*T*	*NR*	*% Won (exc NR)*
203	S.P.Fleming	New Zealand	88	103	1	11	45.83
193	A.Ranatunga	Sri Lanka	89	95	1	8	48.10
178	A.R.Border	Australia	107	67	1	3	61.14
174	M.Azharuddin	India	90	76	2	6	53.57
146	S.C.Ganguly	India	76	65	–	5	53.90
139	Imran Khan	Pakistan	75	59	1	4	55.55
138	W.J.Cronje	South Africa	99	35	1	3	73.33
134	R.T.Ponting	Australia	101	25	2	6	78.90
118	S.T.Jayasuriya	Sri Lanka	66	47	2	3	57.39
115	B.C.Lara	West Indies	55	54	–	6	50.45
109	Wasim Akram	Pakistan	66	41	2	–	60.55
108	I.V.A.Richards	West Indies	68	36	–	4	65.38
106	S.R.Waugh	Australia	67	35	3	1	63.80

The most for England is 56 by N.Hussain, for Zimbabwe 86 by A.D.R.Campbell, and for Bangladesh 56 by Habibul Bashar.

100 LOI UMPIRING APPEARANCES

171	D.R.Shepherd	England	09.06.1983	to	12.07.2005
158	R.E.Koertzen	South Africa	09.12.1992	to	09.02.2007
153	S.A.Bucknor	Jamaica	18.03.1989	to	09.02.2007
133	D.J.Harper	Australia	14.01.1994	to	09.02.2007
129	D.B.Hair	Australia	14.12.1991	to	07.02.2007
107	D.L.Orchard	South Africa	02.12.1994	to	07.12.2003
102	B.F.Bowden	New Zealand	23.03.1995	to	31.01.2007
103	S.J.A.Taufel	Australia	13.01.1999	to	11.02.2007
100	R.S.Dunne	New Zealand	06.02.1989	to	26.02.2002

WOMEN'S TEST CRICKET RECORDS

1934-35 to 1 May 2007

RESULTS SUMMARY

	Opponents	*Tests*	*Won by*									*Drawn*
			E	*A*	*NZ*	*SA*	*WI*	*I*	*P*	*SL*	*Ire*	
England	Australia	42	7	10	–	–	–	–	–	–	–	25
	New Zealand	23	6	–	0	–	–	–	–	–	–	17
	South Africa	6	2	–	–	0	–	–	–	–	–	4
	West Indies	3	2	–	–	–	0	–	–	–	–	1
	India	12	1	–	–	–	–	1	–	–	–	10
Australia	New Zealand	13	–	4	1	–	–	–	–	–	–	8
	West Indies	2	–	0	–	–	0	–	–	–	–	2
	India	9	–	4	–	–	–	0	–	–	–	5
New Zealand	South Africa	3	–	–	1	0	–	–	–	–	–	2
	India	6	–	–	0	–	–	0	–	–	–	6
South Africa	India	1	–	–	–	0	–	1	–	–	–	–
West Indies	India	6	–	–	–	–	1	1	–	–	–	4
	Pakistan	1	–	–	–	–	0	–	0	–	–	1
Pakistan	Sri Lanka	1	–	–	–	–	–	–	0	1	–	–
	Ireland	1	–	–	–	–	–	–	0	–	1	–
		129	18	18	2	0	1	3	0	1	1	85

	Tests	*Won*	*Lost*	*Drawn*	*Toss Won*
England	86	18	11	57	51
Australia	66	18	8	40	22
New Zealand	45	2	10	33	21
South Africa	10	–	4	6	6
West Indies	12	1	3	8	6†
India	34	3	6	25	16†
Pakistan	3	–	2	1	1
Sri Lanka	1	1	–	–	1
Ireland	1	1	–	–	–

† *Results of tosses in five of the six India v West Indies Tests in 1976-77 are not known*

TEAM RECORDS

HIGHEST INNINGS TOTALS

569-6d	Australia v England	Guildford	1998
525	Australia v India	Ahmedabad	1983-84
517-8	New Zealand v England	Scarborough	1996
503-5d	England v New Zealand	Christchurch	1934-35
497	England v South Africa	Shenley	2003
467	India v England	Taunton	2002
455	England v South Africa	Taunton	2003
440	West Indies v Pakistan	Karachi	2003-04
427-4d	Australia v England	Worcester	1998
426-7d	Pakistan v West Indies	Karachi	2003-04
426-9d	India v England	Blackpool	1986
414	England v New Zealand	Scarborough	1996
414	England v Australia	Guildford	1998
404-9d	India v South Africa	Paarl	2001-02
403-8d	New Zealand v India	Nelson	1994-95

The highest totals for countries not included above are:

316	South Africa v England	Shenley	2003
193-3d	Ireland v Pakistan	Dublin	2000

LOWEST INNINGS TOTALS

35	England v Australia	Melbourne	1957-58
38	Australia v England	Melbourne	1957-58
44	New Zealand v England	Christchurch	1934-35
47	Australia v England	Brisbane	1934-35
53	Pakistan v Ireland	Dublin	2000

The lowest innings totals for countries not included above are:

67	West Indies v England	Canterbury	1979
89	South Africa v New Zealand	Durban	1971-72
65	India v West Indies	Jammu	1976-77

BATTING RECORDS
1000 RUNS IN TESTS

			M	*I*	*NO*	*HS*	*Avge*	*100*	*50*
1935	J.A.Brittin	England	27	44	5	167	49.61	5	11
1594	R.Heyhoe-Flint	England	22	38	3	179	45.54	3	10
1301	D.A.Hockley	New Zealand	19	29	4	126*	52.04	4	7
1209	C.M.Edwards	England	16	29	1	117	43.17	3	6
1164	C.A.Hodges	England	18	31	2	158*	40.13	2	6
1110	S.Agarwal	India	13	23	1	190	50.45	4	4
1078	E.Bakewell	England	12	22	4	124	59.88	4	7
1007	M.E.Maclagan	England	14	25	1	119	41.95	2	6

HIGHEST INDIVIDUAL INNINGS ‡ *On debut*

242	Kiran Baluch	P v WI	Karachi	2003-04
214	M.Raj	I v E	Taunton	2002
209*	K.L.Rolton	A v E	Leeds	2001
204	K.E.Flavell	NZ v E	Scarborough	1996
204‡	M.A.J.Goszko	A v E	Shenley	2001
200	J.Broadbent	A v E	Guildford	1998
193	D.A.Annetts	A v E	Collingham	1987
190	S.Agarwal	I v E	Worcester	1986
189	E.A.Snowball	E v NZ	Christchurch	1934-35
179	R.Heyhoe-Flint	E v A	The Oval	1976
177	S.C.Taylor	E v SA	Shenley	2003
176*	K.L.Rolton	A v E	Worcester	1998
167	J.A.Brittin	E v A	Harrogate	1998
161*	E.C.Drumm	E v A	Christchurch	1994-95
160	B.A.Daniels	E v NZ	Scarborough	1996
158*	C.A.Hodges	E v NZ	Canterbury	1984
155*	P.F.McKelvey	NZ v E	Wellington	1968-69

FIVE HUNDREDS

				Opponents									
		M	*I*	*E*	*A*	*NZ*	*SA*	*WI*	*IND*	*P*	*SL*	*IRE*
5	J.A.Brittin (E)	27	44	–	3	1	–	–	1	–	–	–

HIGHEST PARTNERSHIP FOR EACH WICKET

1st	241	Kiran Baluch/Sajjida Shah	P v WI	Karachi	2003-04
2nd	235	E.A.Snowball/M.E.Hide	E v NZ	Christchurch	1934-35
3rd	309	L.A.Reeler/D.A.Annetts	A v E	Collingham	1987
4th	253	K.L.Rolton/L.C.Broadfoot	A v E	Leeds	2001
5th	138	J.Logtenberg/C.van der Westhuizen	SA v E	Shenley	2003
6th	132	B.A.Daniels/K.M.Leng	E v NZ	Scarborough	1996
7th	157	M.Raj/J.Goswami	I v E	Taunton	2002
8th	181	S.J.Griffiths/D.L.Wilson	A v NZ	Auckland	1989-90
9th	107	B.Botha/M.Payne	SA v NZ	Cape Town	1971-72
10th	119	S.Nitschke/C.R.Smith	A v E	Hove	2005

BOWLING RECORDS

50 WICKETS IN TESTS

Wkts			*M*	*Balls*	*Runs*	*Avge*	*Best*	*5wI*	*10wM*
77	M.B.Duggan	E	17	3734	1039	13.49	7- 6	5	–
68	E.R.Wilson	A	11	2885	803	11.80	7- 7	4	2
63	D.F.Edulji	I	20	5098†	1624	25.77	6- 64	1	–
60	M.E.Maclagan	E	14	3432	935	15.58	7- 10	3	–
60	C.L.Fitzpatrick	A	13	3603	1147	19.11	5-292	–	
57	R.H.Thompson	A	16	4304	1040	18.24	5- 33	1	–
56	S.Kulkarni	I	18	3320	1599	28.55	6- 99	5	–
55	J.Lord	NZ	15	3108	1049	19.07	6-119	4	1
50	E.Bakewell	E	12	2697	831	16.62	7- 61	3	1

† *Excludes balls bowled in Sixth Test v West Indies 1976-77*

TEN WICKETS IN A TEST

13-226	Shaiza Khan	P v WI	Karachi	2003-04
11- 16	E.R.Wilson	A v E	Melbourne	1957-58
11- 63	J.M.Greenwood	E v WI	Canterbury	1979
11-107	L.C.Pearson	E v A	Sydney	2002-03
10- 65	E.R.Wilson	A v NZ	Wellington	1947-48
10- 75	E.Bakewell	E v WI	Birmingham	1979
10- 78	J.Goswami	I v E	Taunton	2006
10-107	K.Price	A v I	Lucknow	1983-84
10-118	D.A.Gordon	A v E	Melbourne	1968-69
10-137	J.Lord	NZ v A	Melbourne	1978-79

SEVEN WICKETS IN AN INNINGS

8-53	N.David	I v E	Jamshedpur	1995-96
7- 6	M.B.Duggan	E v A	Melbourne	1957-58
7- 7	E.R.Wilson	A v E	Melbourne	1957-58
7-10	M.E.Maclagan	E v A	Brisbane	1934-35
7-18	A.Palmer	A v E	Brisbane	1934-35
7-24	L.Johnston	A v NZ	Melbourne	1971-72
7-34	G.E.McConway	E v I	Worcester	1986
7-41	J.A.Burley	NZ v E	The Oval	1966
7-51	L.C.Pearson	E v A	Sydney	2002-03
7-59	Shaiza Khan	P v WI	Karachi	2003-04
7-61	E.Bakewell	E v WI	Birmingham	1979

HAT-TRICKS

E.R.Wilson	Australia v England	Melbourne	1957-58
Shaiza Khan	Pakistan v West Indies	Karachi	2003-04

WICKET-KEEPING, FIELDING AND APPEARANCE RECORDS

25 DISMISSALS IN TESTS

Total			*Tests*	*Ct*	*St*
58	C.Matthews	Australia	20	46	12
43	J.Smit	England	21	39	4
36	S.A.Hodges	England	11	19	17
28	B.A.Brentnall	New Zealand	10	16	12

EIGHT DISMISSALS IN A TEST

9 (8ct, 1st)	C.Matthews	A v I	Adelaide	1990-91
8 (6ct, 2st)	L.Nye	E v NZ	New Plymouth	1991-92

SIX DISMISSALS IN AN INNINGS

8 (6ct, 2st)	L.Nye	E v NZ	New Plymouth	1991-92
6 (2ct, 4st)	B.A.Brentnall	NZ v SA	Johannesburg	1971-72

20 CATCHES IN THE FIELD IN TESTS

Total			*Tests*
25	C.A.Hodges	England	18
21	S.Shah	India	20
20	L.A.Fullston	Australia	12

25 TEST MATCH APPEARANCES

27	J.A.Brittin	England	1979-98

INTERNATIONAL TEST MATCH RESULTS

Matches completed by 1 May 2007

	Opponents	*Tests*	*Won by*										*Tied*	*Drawn*
			E	*A*	*SA*	*WI*	*NZ*	*I*	*P*	*SL*	*Z*	*B*		
England	Australia	316	97	131	–	–	–	–	–	–	–	–	–	88
	South Africa	130	54	–	26	–	–	–	–	–	–	–	–	50
	West Indies	134	38	–	–	52	–	–	–	–	–	–	–	44
	New Zealand	88	41	–	–	–	7	–	–	–	–	–	–	40
	India	94	34	–	–	–	–	17	–	–	–	–	–	43
	Pakistan	67	19	–	–	–	–	–	12	–	–	–	–	36
	Sri Lanka	18	8	–	–	–	–	–	–	5	–	–	–	5
	Zimbabwe	6	3	–	–	–	–	–	–	–	0	–	–	3
	Bangladesh	4	4	–	–	–	–	–	–	–	–	0	–	–
Australia	South Africa	77	–	44	15	–	–	–	–	–	–	–	–	18
	West Indies	102	–	48	–	32	–	–	–	–	–	–	1	21
	New Zealand	46	–	22	–	–	7	–	–	–	–	–	–	17
	India	68	–	32	–	–	–	15	–	–	–	–	1	20
	Pakistan	52	–	24	–	–	–	–	11	–	–	–	–	17
	Sri Lanka	18	–	11	–	–	–	–	–	1	–	–	–	6
	Zimbabwe	3	–	3	–	–	–	–	–	–	0	–	–	–
	Bangladesh	4	–	4	–	–	–	–	–	–	–	0	–	–
South Africa	West Indies	19	–	–	12	2	–	–	–	–	–	–	–	5
	New Zealand	33	–	–	18	–	4	–	–	–	–	–	–	11
	India	19	–	–	9	–	–	4	–	–	–	–	–	6
	Pakistan	14	–	–	7	–	–	–	3	–	–	–	–	4
	Sri Lanka	17	–	–	8	–	–	–	–	4	–	–	–	5
	Zimbabwe	7	–	–	6	–	–	–	–	–	0	–	–	1
	Bangladesh	4	–	–	4	–	–	–	–	–	–	0	–	–
West Indies	New Zealand	35	–	–	–	10	9	–	–	–	–	–	–	16
	India	82	–	–	–	30	–	11	–	–	–	–	–	41
	Pakistan	44	–	–	–	14	–	–	15	–	–	–	–	15
	Sri Lanka	10	–	–	–	2	–	–	–	5	–	–	–	3
	Zimbabwe	6	–	–	–	4	–	–	–	–	–	–	–	2
	Bangladesh	4	–	–	–	3	–	–	–	–	–	0	–	1
New Zealand	India	44	–	–	–	–	9	14	–	–	–	–	–	21
	Pakistan	45	–	–	–	–	6	–	21	–	–	–	–	18
	Sri Lanka	24	–	–	–	–	9	–	–	5	–	–	–	10
	Zimbabwe	13	–	–	–	–	7	–	–	–	0	–	–	6
	Bangladesh	4	–	–	–	–	4	–	–	–	–	0	–	–
India	Pakistan	56	–	–	–	–	–	8	12	–	–	–	–	36
	Sri Lanka	26	–	–	–	–	–	10	–	3	–	–	–	13
	Zimbabwe	11	–	–	–	–	–	7	–	–	2	–	–	2
	Bangladesh	3	–	–	–	–	–	3	–	–	–	0	–	–
Pakistan	Sri Lanka	32	–	–	–	–	–	–	15	7	–	–	–	10
	Zimbabwe	14	–	–	–	–	–	–	8	–	2	–	–	4
	Bangladesh	6	–	–	–	–	–	–	6	–	–	0	–	–
Sri Lanka	Zimbabwe	15	–	–	–	–	–	–	–	10	0	–	–	5
	Bangladesh	7	–	–	–	–	–	–	–	7	–	0	–	–
Zimbabwe	Bangladesh	8	–	–	–	–	–	–	–	–	4	1	–	3
		1829	298	319	105	149	62	89	103	47	8	1	2	646

	Tests	Won	Lost	Drawn	Tied	Toss Won
England	857	298	250	309	–	412
Australia	686	319	178	187	2	343
South Africa	320	105	115	100	–	153
West Indies	436	149	138	148	1	233
New Zealand	332	62	131	139	–	167
India	403	89	131	182	1	207
Pakistan	330	103	87	140	–	157
Sri Lanka	167	47	63	57	–	86
Zimbabwe	83	8	49	26	–	49
Bangladesh	44	1	39	4	–	22

INTERNATIONAL TEST CRICKET RECORDS

(To 1 May 2007)

TEAM RECORDS

HIGHEST INNINGS TOTALS

952-6d	Sri Lanka v India	Colombo (RPS)	1997-98
903-7d	England v Australia	The Oval	1938
849	England v West Indies	Kingston	1929-30
790-3d	West Indies v Pakistan	Kingston	1957-58
758-8d	Australia v West Indies	Kingston	1954-55
756-5d	Sri Lanka v South Africa	Colombo (SSC)	2006
751-5d	West Indies v England	St John's	2003-04
747	West Indies v South Africa	St John's	2004-05
735-6d	Australia v Zimbabwe	Perth	2003-04
729-6d	Australia v England	Lord's	1930
713-3d	Sri Lanka v Zimbabwe	Bulawayo	2003-04
708	Pakistan v England	The Oval	1987
705-7d	India v Australia	Sydney	2003-04
701	Australia v England	The Oval	1934
699-5	Pakistan v India	Lahore	1989-90
695	Australia v England	The Oval	1930
692-8d	West Indies v England	The Oval	1995
687-8d	West Indies v England	The Oval	1976
682-6d	South Africa v England	Lord's	2003
681-8d	West Indies v England	Port-of-Spain	1953-54
679-7d	Pakistan v India	Lahore	2005-06
676-7	India v Sri Lanka	Kanpur	1986-87
675-5d	India v Pakistan	Multan	2003-04
674-6	Pakistan v India	Faisalabad	1984-85
674	Australia v India	Adelaide	1947-48
671-4	New Zealand v Sri Lanka	Wellington	1990-91
668	Australia v West Indies	Bridgetown	1954-55
660-5d	West Indies v New Zealand	Wellington	1994-95
659-8d	Australia v England	Sydney	1946-47
658-8d	England v Australia	Nottingham	1938
658-9d	South Africa v West Indies	Durban	2003-04
657-7d	India v Australia	Calcutta	2000-01
657-8d	Pakistan v West Indies	Bridgetown	1957-58
656-8d	Australia v England	Manchester	1964
654-5	England v South Africa	Durban	1938-39
653-4d	England v India	Lord's	1990
653-4d	Australia v England	Leeds	1993

652-7d	England v India	Madras	1984-85
652-7d	Australia v South Africa	Johannesburg	2001-02
652-8d	West Indies v England	Lord's	1973
652	Pakistan v India	Faisalabad	1982-83
650-6d	Australia v West Indies	Bridgetown	1964-65

The highest for Zimbabwe is 563-9d (v WI, Harare, 2001), and for Bangladesh 488 (v Z, Chittagong, 2004-05).

LOWEST INNINGS TOTALS

†One batsman absent

26	New Zealand v England	Auckland	1954-55
30	South Africa v England	Port Elizabeth	1895-96
30	South Africa v England	Birmingham	1924
35	South Africa v England	Cape Town	1898-99
36	Australia v England	Birmingham	1902
36	South Africa v Australia	Melbourne	1931-32
42	Australia v England	Sydney	1887-88
42	New Zealand v Australia	Wellington	1945-46
42†	India v England	Lord's	1974
43	South Africa v England	Cape Town	1888-89
44	Australia v England	The Oval	1896
45	England v Australia	Sydney	1886-87
45	South Africa v Australia	Melbourne	1931-32
46	England v West Indies	Port-of-Spain	1993-94
47	South Africa v England	Cape Town	1888-89
47	New Zealand v England	Lord's	1958
47	West Indies v England	Kingston	2003-04

The lowest for Pakistan is 53† (v A, Sharjah, 2002-03), for Sri Lanka 71 (v P, Kandy, 1994-95), for Zimbabwe 54 (v SA, Cape Town, 2004-05), and for Bangladesh 86 (v SL, Colombo RPS, 2005-06).

BATTING RECORDS

4000 RUNS IN A TEST CAREER

Runs			*M*	*I*	*NO*	*HS*	*Avge*	*100*	50
11912	B.C.Lara	WI	130	230	6	400*	53.17	34	48
11174	A.R.Border	A	156	265	44	205	50.56	27	63
10927	S.R.Waugh	A	168	260	46	200	51.06	32	50
10668	S.R.Tendulkar	I	135	217	22	248*	54.70	35	43
10122	S.M.Gavaskar	I	125	214	16	236*	51.12	34	45
9268	R.T.Ponting	A	109	181	25	257	59.41	33	35
9151	R.Dravid	I	106	180	22	270	57.91	23	46
8900	G.A.Gooch	E	118	215	6	333	42.58	20	46
8832	Javed Miandad	P	124	189	21	280*	52.57	23	43
8812	Inzamam-ul-Haq	P	118	196	22	329	50.64	25	46
8540	I.V.A.Richards	WI	121	182	12	291	50.23	24	45
8463	A.J.Stewart	E	133	235	21	190	39.54	15	45
8347	J.H.Kallis	SA	106	180	28	189*	54.91	24	44
8231	D.I.Gower	E	117	204	18	215	44.25	18	39
8114	G.Boycott	E	108	193	23	246*	47.72	22	42
8032	G.St A.Sobers	WI	93	160	21	365*	57.78	26	30
8029	M.E.Waugh	A	128	209	17	153*	41.81	20	47
7728	M.A.Atherton	E	115	212	7	185*	37.70	16	46
7674	J.L.Langer	A	104	180	12	250	45.67	23	30

Runs			M	I	NO	HS	Avge	100	50
7624	M.C.Cowdrey	E	114	188	15	182	44.06	22	38
7558	C.G.Greenidge	WI	108	185	16	226	44.72	19	34
7551	M.L.Hayden	A	88	157	13	380	52.43	26	26
7525	M.A.Taylor	A	104	186	13	334*	43.49	19	40
7515	C.H.Lloyd	WI	110	175	14	242*	46.67	19	39
7487	D.L.Haynes	WI	116	202	25	184	42.29	18	39
7422	D.C.Boon	A	107	190	20	200	43.65	21	32
7289	G.Kirsten	SA	101	176	15	275	45.27	21	34
7249	W.R.Hammond	E	85	140	16	336*	58.45	22	24
7110	G.S.Chappell	A	87	151	19	247*	53.86	24	31
6996	D.G.Bradman	A	52	80	10	334	99.94	29	13
6971	L.Hutton	E	79	138	15	364	56.67	19	33
6868	D.B.Vengsarkar	I	116	185	22	166	42.13	17	35
6806	K.F.Barrington	E	82	131	15	256	58.67	20	35
6791	S.T.Jayasuriya	SL	107	182	14	340	40.42	14	30
6744	G.P.Thorpe	E	100	179	28	200*	44.66	16	39
6736	S.Chanderpaul	WI	101	173	22	203*	44.60	14	40
6620	S.P.Fleming	NZ	104	177	10	274*	39.64	9	41
6553	M.Yousuf Youhana	P	75	126	9	223	56.00	23	27
6361	P.A.de Silva	SL	93	159	11	267	42.97	20	22
6289	D.P.M.D.Jayawardena	SL	85	140	10	374	48.37	16	29
6227	R.B.Kanhai	WI	79	137	6	256	47.53	15	28
6215	M.Azharuddin	I	99	147	9	199	45.03	22	21
6149	R.N.Harvey	A	79	137	10	205	48.41	21	24
6080	G.R.Viswanath	I	91	155	10	222	41.93	14	35
5949	R.B.Richardson	WI	86	146	12	194	44.39	16	27
5943	H.H.Gibbs	SA	84	144	7	228	43.37	14	24
5825	M.E.Trescothick	E	76	143	10	219	43.79	14	29
5807	D.C.S.Compton	E	78	131	15	278	50.06	17	28
5768	Salim Malik	P	103	154	22	237	43.69	15	29
5764	N.Hussain	E	96	171	16	207	37.19	14	33
5762	C.L.Hooper	WI	102	173	15	233	36.46	13	27
5444	M.D.Crowe	NZ	77	131	11	299	45.36	17	18
5435	S.C.Ganguly	I	91	146	13	173	40.86	12	27
5410	J.B.Hobbs	E	61	102	7	211	56.94	15	28
5357	K.D.Walters	A	74	125	14	250	48.26	15	33
5345	I.M.Chappell	A	75	136	10	196	42.42	14	26
5334	J.G.Wright	NZ	82	148	7	185	37.82	12	23
5330	M.S.Atapattu	SL	88	152	15	249	38.90	16	15
5312	M.J.Slater	A	74	131	7	219	42.84	14	21
5258	A.C.Gilchrist	A	89	127	19	204*	48.68	17	23
5248	Kapil Dev	I	131	184	15	163	31.05	8	27
5234	W.M.Lawry	A	67	123	12	210	47.15	13	27
5200	I.T.Botham	E	102	161	6	208	33.54	14	22
5138	J.H.Edrich	E	77	127	9	310*	43.54	12	24
5105	A.Ranatunga	SL	93	155	12	135*	35.69	4	38
5064	K.C.Sangakkara	SL	64	107	7	287	50.64	12	22
5062	Zaheer Abbas	P	78	124	11	274	44.79	12	20
4882	T.W.Graveney	E	79	123	13	258	44.38	11	20
4878	V.V.S.Laxman	I	80	130	15	281	42.41	10	27
4869	R.B.Simpson	A	62	111	7	311	46.81	10	27
4794	A.Flower	Z	63	112	19	232*	51.54	12	27
4737	I.R.Redpath	A	66	120	11	171	43.45	8	31
4702	N.J.Astle	NZ	81	137	10	222	37.02	11	24
4656	A.J.Lamb	E	79	139	10	142	36.09	14	18
4595	M.P.Vaughan	E	64	115	8	197	42.94	15	14

Runs			M	I	NO	HS	Avge	100	50
4555	H.Sutcliffe	E	54	84	9	194	60.73	16	23
4554	D.J.Cullinan	SA	70	115	12	275*	44.21	14	20
4545	H.P.Tillekeratne	SL	83	131	25	204*	42.87	11	20
4537	P.B.H.May	E	66	106	9	285*	46.77	13	22
4502	E.R.Dexter	E	62	102	8	205	47.89	9	27
4455	E.de C.Weekes	WI	48	81	5	207	58.61	15	19
4415	K.J.Hughes	A	70	124	6	213	37.41	9	22
4409	M.W.Gatting	E	79	138	14	207	35.55	10	21
4406	D.R.Martyn	A	67	109	14	165	44.37	13	23
4399	A.I.Kallicharran	WI	66	109	10	187	44.43	12	21
4389	A.P.E.Knott	E	95	149	15	135	32.75	5	30
4378	M.Amarnath	I	69	113	10	138	42.50	11	24
4356	I.A.Healy	A	119	182	23	161*	27.39	4	22
4334	R.C.Fredericks	WI	59	109	7	169	42.49	8	26
4291	Younis Khan	P	53	95	6	267	48.21	12	19
4288	M.A.Butcher	E	71	131	7	173*	34.58	8	23
4273	G.C.Smith	SA	53	94	5	277	48.01	11	18
4268	R.R.Sarwan	WI	65	118	8	261*	38.80	9	26
4259	C.H.Gayle	WI	64	113	3	317	38.71	7	26
4236	R.A.Smith	E	62	112	15	175	43.67	9	28
4114	Mudassar Nazar	P	76	116	8	231	38.09	10	17
4072	V.Sehwag	I	51	85	3	309	49.65	12	11
4052	Saeed Anwar	P	55	91	2	188*	45.52	11	25

The most for Bangladesh is 2838 by Habibul Bashar (83 innings).

750 RUNS IN A SERIES

Runs			Series	M	I	NO	HS	Avge	100	50
974	D.G.Bradman	A v E	1930	5	7	–	334	139.14	4	–
905	W.R.Hammond	E v A	1928-29	5	9	1	251	113.12	4	–
839	M.A.Taylor	A v E	1989	6	11	1	219	83.90	2	5
834	R.N.Harvey	A v SA	1952-53	5	9	–	205	92.66	4	3
829	I.V.A.Richards	WI v E	1976	4	7	–	291	118.42	3	2
827	C.L.Walcott	WI v A	1954-55	5	10	–	155	82.70	5	2
824	G.St A.Sobers	WI v P	1957-58	5	8	2	365*	137.33	3	3
810	D.G.Bradman	A v E	1936-37	5	9	–	270	90.00	3	1
806	D.G.Bradman	A v SA	1931-32	5	5	1	299*	201.50	4	–
798	B.C.Lara	WI v E	1993-94	5	8	–	375	99.75	2	2
779	E.de C.Weekes	WI v I	1948-49	5	7	–	194	111.28	4	2
774	S.M.Gavaskar	I v WI	1970-71	4	8	3	220	154.80	4	3
765	B.C.Lara	WI v E	1995	6	10	1	179	85.00	3	3
761	Mudassar Nazar	P v I	1982-83	6	8	2	231	126.83	4	1
758	D.G.Bradman	A v E	1934	5	8	–	304	94.75	2	1
753	D.C.S.Compton	E v SA	1947	5	8	–	208	94.12	4	2
752	G.A.Gooch	E v I	1990	3	6	–	333	125.33	3	2

HIGHEST INDIVIDUAL INNINGS

400*	B.C.Lara	WI v E	St John's	2003-04
380	M.L.Hayden	A v Z	Perth	2003-04
375	B.C.Lara	WI v E	St John's	1993-94
374	D.P.M.D.Jayawardena	SL v SA	Colombo (SSC)	2006
365*	G.St A.Sobers	WI v P	Kingston	1957-58
364	L.Hutton	E v A	The Oval	1938
340	S.T.Jayasuriya	SL v I	Colombo (RPS)	1997-98
337	Hanif Mohammed	P v WI	Bridgetown	1957-58
336*	W.R.Hammond	E v NZ	Auckland	1932-33

334*	M.A.Taylor	A v P	Peshawar	1998-99
334	D.G.Bradman	A v E	Leeds	1930
333	G.A.Gooch	E v I	Lord's	1990
329	Inzamam-ul-Haq	P v NZ	Lahore	2001-02
325	A.Sandham	E v WI	Kingston	1929-30
317	C.H.Gayle	WI v SA	St John's	2004-05
311	R.B.Simpson	A v E	Manchester	1964
310*	J.H.Edrich	E v NZ	Leeds	1965
309	V.Sehwag	I v P	Multan	2003-04
307	R.M.Cowper	A v E	Melbourne	1965-66
304	D.G.Bradman	A v E	Leeds	1934
302	L.G.Rowe	WI v E	Bridgetown	1973-74
299*	D.G.Bradman	A v SA	Adelaide	1931-32
299	M.D.Crowe	NZ v SL	Wellington	1990-91
291	I.V.A.Richards	WI v E	The Oval	1976
287	R.E.Foster	E v A	Sydney	1903-04
287	K.C.Sangakkara	SL v SA	Colombo (SSC)	2006
285*	P.B.H.May	E v WI	Birmingham	1957
281	V.V.S.Laxman	I v A	Calcutta	2000-01
280*	Javed Miandad	P v I	Hyderabad	1982-83
278	D.C.S.Compton	E v P	Nottingham	1954
277	B.C.Lara	WI v A	Sydney	1992-93
277	G.C.Smith	SA v E	Birmingham	2003
275*	D.J.Cullinan	SA v NZ	Auckland	1998-99
275	G.Kirsten	SA v E	Durban	1999-00
274*	S.P.Fleming	NZ v SL	Colombo (SSC)	2002-03
274	R.G.Pollock	SA v A	Durban	1969-70
274	Zaheer Abbas	P v E	Birmingham	1971
271	Javed Miandad	P v NZ	Auckland	1988-89
270*	G.A.Headley	WI v E	Kingston	1934-35
270	D.G.Bradman	A v E	Melbourne	1936-37
270	R.Dravid	I v P	Rawalpindi	2003-04
270	K.C.Sangakkara	SL v Z	Bulawayo	2003-04
268	G.N.Yallop	A v P	Melbourne	1983-84
267*	B.A.Young	NZ v SL	Dunedin	1996-97
267	P.A.de Silva	SL v NZ	Wellington	1990-91
267	Younis Khan	P v I	Bangalore	2004-05
266	W.H.Ponsford	A v E	The Oval	1934
266	D.L.Houghton	Z v SL	Bulawayo	1994-95
262*	D.L.Amiss	E v WI	Kingston	1973-74
262	S.P.Fleming	NZ v SA	Cape Town	2005-06
261*	R.R.Sarwan	WI v B	Kingston	2004
261	F.M.M.Worrell	WI v E	Nottingham	1950
260	C.C.Hunte	WI v P	Kingston	1957-58
260	Javed Miandad	P v E	The Oval	1987
259	G.M.Turner	NZ v WI	Georgetown	1971-72
259	G.C.Smith	SA v E	Lord's	2003
258	T.W.Graveney	E v WI	Nottingham	1957
258	S.M.Nurse	WI v NZ	Christchurch	1968-69
257*	Wasim Akram	P v Z	Sheikhupura	1996-97
257	R.T.Ponting	A v I	Melbourne	2003-04
256	R.B.Kanhai	WI v I	Calcutta	1958-59
256	K.F.Barrington	E v A	Manchester	1964
255*	D.J.McGlew	SA v NZ	Wellington	1952-53
254	D.G.Bradman	A v E	Lord's	1930
254	V.Sehwag	I v P	Lahore	2005-06
253	S.T.Jayasuriya	SL v P	Faisalabad	2004-05

251	W.R.Hammond	E v A	Sydney	1928-29
250	K.D.Walters	A v NZ	Christchurch	1976-77
250	S.F.A.F.Bacchus	WI v I	Kanpur	1978-79
250	J.L.Langer	A v E	Melbourne	2002-03

The highest for Bangladesh is 158* by Mohammad Ashraful (v I, Chittagong, 2004-05).

20 HUNDREDS

					Opponents									
			200	*Inn*	*E*	*A*	*SA*	*WI*	*NZ*	*I*	*P*	*SL*	*Z*	*B*
35	S.R.Tendulkar	I	4	217	6	7	3	3	3	–	2	7	3	1
34	S.M.Gavaskar	I	4	214	4	8	–	13	2	–	5	2	–	–
34	B.C.Lara	WI	8	230	7	9	4	–	1	2	4	5	1	1
33	R.T.Ponting	A	4	181	7	–	7	6	2	4	4	1	1	1
32	S.R.Waugh	A	1	260	10	–	2	7	2	2	3	3	1	2
29	D.G.Bradman	A	12	80	19	–	4	2	–	4	–	–	–	–
27	A.R.Border	A	2	265	8	–	–	3	5	4	6	1	–	–
26	M.L.Hayden	A	2	157	5	–	6	5	1	3	1	3	2	–
26	G.St A.Sobers	WI	2	160	10	4	–	–	1	8	3	–	–	–
25	Inzamam-ul-Haq	P	2	196	5	1	–	4	3	3	–	5	2	2
24	G.S.Chappell	A	4	151	9	–	–	5	3	1	6	–	–	–
24	J.H.Kallis	SA	–	180	5	3	–	7	3	1	1	–	3	1
24	I.V.A.Richards	WI	3	182	8	5	–	–	1	8	2	–	–	–
23	M.Younis Youhana	P	4	126	6	1	–	7	1	4	–	–	2	2
23	R.Dravid	I	5	180	3	2	1	3	4	–	5	1	3	1
23	J.L.Langer	A	3	180	5	–	2	3	4	3	4	2	–	–
23	Javed Miandad	P	6	189	2	6	–	2	7	5	–	1	–	–
22	W.R.Hammond	E	7	140	–	9	6	1	4	2	–	–	–	–
22	M.Azharuddin	I	–	147	6	2	4	–	2	–	3	5	–	–
22	M.C.Cowdrey	E	–	188	–	5	3	6	2	3	3	–	–	–
22	G.Boycott	E	1	193	–	7	1	5	2	4	3	–	–	–
21	R.N.Harvey	A	2	137	6	–	8	3	–	4	–	–	–	–
21	G.Kirsten	SA	3	176	5	2	–	3	2	3	2	1	1	2
21	D.C.Boon	A	1	190	7	–	–	3	3	6	1	1	–	–
20	K.F.Barrington	E	1	131	–	5	2	3	3	3	4	–	–	–
20	P.A.de Silva	SL	2	159	2	1	–	–	2	5	8	–	1	1
20	M.E.Waugh	A	–	209	6	–	4	4	1	1	3	1	–	–
20	G.A.Gooch	E	2	215	–	4	–	5	4	5	1	1	–	–

The most for New Zealand is 17 by M.D.Crowe (131 innings), for Zimbabwe 12 by A.Flower (112), and for Bangladesh 3 by Habibul Bashar (83) and 3 by Mohammad Ashraful (65).

The most double hundreds by batsmen not included above is 6 by M.S.Atapattu (16 hundreds for Sri Lanka), 4 by L.Hutton (19 for England), 4 by C.G.Greenidge (19 for West Indies) and 4 by Zaheer Abbas (12 for Pakistan).

HIGHEST PARTNERSHIP FOR EACH WICKET

1st	413	V.Mankad/Pankaj Roy	I v NZ	Madras	1955-56
2nd	576	S.T.Jayasuriya/R.S.Mahanama	SL v I	Colombo (RPS)	1997-98
3rd	624	K.C.Sangakkara/D.P.M.D.Jayawardena	SL v SA	Colombo (SSC)	2006
4th	411	P.B.H.May/M.C.Cowdrey	E v WI	Birmingham	1957
5th	405	S.G.Barnes/D.G.Bradman	A v E	Sydney	1946-47
6th	346	J.H.W.Fingleton/D.G.Bradman	A v E	Melbourne	1936-37
7th	347	D.St E.Atkinson/C.C.Depeiza	WI v A	Bridgetown	1954-55
8th	313	Wasim Akram/Saqlain Mushtaq	P v Z	Sheikhupura	1996-97
9th	195	M.V.Boucher/P.L.Symcox	SA v P	Johannesburg	1997-98
10th	151	B.F.Hastings/R.O.Collinge	NZ v P	Auckland	1972-73
	151	Azhar Mahmood/Mushtaq Ahmed	P v SA	Rawalpindi	1997-98

BOWLING RECORDS

200 WICKETS IN TESTS

Wkts			*M*	*Balls*	*Runs*	*Avge*	*5 wI*	*10 wM*
702	S.K.Warne	A	144	40518	17924	25.53	37	10
669	M.Muralitharan	SL	109	36382	14492	21.66	57	19
560	G.D.McGrath	A	123	29140	12144	21.68	29	3
547	A.Kumble	I	113	35694	15675	28.65	33	8
519	C.A.Walsh	WI	132	30019	12688	24.45	22	3
434	Kapil Dev	I	131	27740	12867	29.64	23	2
431	R.J.Hadlee	NZ	86	21918	9612	22.30	36	9
416	S.M.Pollock	SA	107	24185	9648	23.19	16	1
414	Wasim Akram	P	104	22627	9779	23.62	25	5
405	C.E.L.Ambrose	WI	98	22104	8500	20.98	22	3
383	I.T.Botham	E	102	21815	10878	28.40	27	4
376	M.D.Marshall	WI	81	17584	7876	20.94	22	4
373	Waqar Younis	P	87	16224	8788	23.56	22	5
362	Imran Khan	P	88	19458	8258	22.81	23	6
355	D.K.Lillee	A	70	18467	8493	23.92	23	7
330	A.A.Donald	SA	72	15519	7344	22.25	20	3
325	R.G.D.Willis	E	90	17357	8190	25.20	16	–
313	W.P.U.C.J.Vaas	SL	96	20686	9216	29.44	11	2
309	L.R.Gibbs	WI	79	27115	8989	29.09	18	2
308	M.Ntini	SA	75	15826	8465	27.48	17	4
307	F.S.Trueman	E	67	15178	6625	21.57	17	3
297	D.L.Underwood	E	86	21862	7674	25.83	17	6
291	C.J.McDermott	A	71	16586	8332	28.63	14	2
266	B.S.Bedi	I	67	21364	7637	28.71	14	1
259	J.Garner	WI	58	13169	5433	20.97	7	–
259	J.N.Gillespie	A	71	14234	6770	26.13	8	–
252	J.B.Statham	E	70	16056	6261	24.84	9	1
249	M.A.Holding	WI	60	12680	5898	23.68	13	2
248	R.Benaud	A	63	19108	6704	27.03	16	1
246	G.D.McKenzie	A	60	17681	7328	29.78	16	3
242	B.S.Chandrasekhar	I	58	15963	7199	29.74	16	2
238	Harbhajan Singh	I	57	15162	7108	29.86	19	4
236	A.V.Bedser	E	51	15918	5876	24.89	15	5
236	Abdul Qadir	P	67	17126	7742	32.80	15	5
236	J.Srinath	I	67	15104	7196	30.49	10	1
235	M.J.Hoggard	E	62	13014	7093	30.18	7	1
235	G.St A.Sobers	WI	93	21599	7999	34.03	6	–
234	A.R.Caddick	E	62	13558	6999	29.91	13	1
229	B.Lee	A	58	12171	7204	31.45	7	–
229	D.Gough	E	58	11821	6503	28.39	9	–
228	R.R.Lindwall	A	61	13650	5251	23.03	12	–
228	D.L.Vettori	NZ	72	17423	7740	33.94	13	3
218	C.L.Cairns	NZ	62	11698	6410	29.40	13	1
216	C.V.Grimmett	A	37	14513	5231	24.21	21	7
216	H.H.Streak	Z	65	13559	6079	28.14	7	–
212	M.G.Hughes	A	53	12285	6017	28.38	7	1
212	J.H.Kallis	SA	106	14237	6718	31.68	4	–
208	Saqlain Mushtaq	P	49	14070	6206	29.83	13	3
202	A.M.E.Roberts	WI	47	11136	5174	25.61	11	2
202	J.A.Snow	E	49	12021	5387	26.66	8	1
200	J.R.Thomson	A	51	10535	5601	28.00	8	–

The most for Bangladesh 87 in 26 Tests by Mohammad Rafique.

35 WICKETS IN A SERIES

Wkts			Series	M	Balls	Runs	Avge	5 wI	10 wM
49	S.F.Barnes	E v SA	1913-14	4	1356	536	10.93	7	3
46	J.C.Laker	E v A	1956	5	1703	442	9.60	4	2
44	C.V.Grimmett	A v SA	1935-36	5	2077	642	14.59	5	3
42	T.M.Alderman	A v E	1981	6	1950	893	21.26	4	–
41	R.M.Hogg	A v E	1978-79	6	1740	527	12.85	5	2
41	T.M.Alderman	A v E	1989	6	1616	712	17.36	6	1
40	Imran Khan	P v I	1982-83	6	1339	558	13.95	4	2
40	S.K.Warne	A v V	2005	5	1517	797	19.92	3	2
39	A.V.Bedser	E v A	1953	5	1591	682	17.48	5	1
39	D.K.Lillee	A v E	1981	6	1870	870	22.30	2	1
38	M.W.Tate	E v A	1924-25	5	2528	881	23.18	5	1
37	W.J.Whitty	A v SA	1910-11	5	1395	632	17.08	2	–
37	H.J.Tayfield	SA v E	1956-57	5	2280	636	17.18	4	1
36	A.E.E.Vogler	SA v E	1909-10	5	1349	783	21.75	4	1
36	A.A.Mailey	A v E	1920-21	5	1465	946	26.27	4	2
36	G.D.McGrath	A v E	1997	6	1499	701	19.47	2	–
35	G.A.Lohmann	E v SA	1895-96	3	520	203	5.80	4	2
35	B.S.Chandrasekhar	I v E	1972-73	5	1747	662	18.91	4	–
35	M.D.Marshall	WI v E	1988	5	1219	443	12.65	3	1

The most for New Zealand is 33 by R.J.Hadlee (3 Tests v A, 1985-86), for Sri Lanka 30 by M.Muralitharan (3 Tests v Z, 2001-02), for Zimbabwe 22 by H.H.Streak (3 Tests v P, 1994-95), and for Bangladesh 18 by Enamul Haque II (2 Tests v Z, 2004-05).

15 WICKETS IN A TEST († *On debut*)

19- 90	J.C.Laker	E v A	Manchester	1956
17-159	S.F.Barnes	E v SA	Johannesburg	1913-14
16-136†	N.D.Hirwani	I v WI	Madras	1987-88
16-137†	R.A.L.Massie	A v E	Lord's	1972
16-220	M.Muralitharan	SL v E	The Oval	1998
15- 28	J.Briggs	E v SA	Cape Town	1888-89
15- 45	G.A.Lohmann	E v SA	Port Elizabeth	1895-96
15- 99	C.Blythe	E v SA	Leeds	1907
15-104	H.Verity	E v A	Lord's	1934
15-123	R.J.Hadlee	NZ v A	Brisbane	1985-86
15-124	W.Rhodes	E v A	Melbourne	1903-04
15-217	Harbhajan Singh	I v A	Madras	2000-01

The best analysis for South Africa is 13-132 by M.Ntini (v WI, Port-of-Spain, 2004-05), for West Indies 14-149 by M.A.Holding (v E, The Oval, 1976), for Pakistan 14-116 by Imran Khan (v SL, Lahore, 1981-82), for Zimbabwe 11-257 by A.G.Huckle (v NZ, Bulawayo, 1997-98), and for Bangladesh 12-200 by Enamul Haque II (v Z, Dhaka, 2004-05).

NINE WICKETS IN AN INNINGS

10-53	J.C.Laker	E v A	Manchester	1956
10-74	A.Kumble	I v P	Delhi	1998-99
9-28	G.A.Lohmann	E v SA	Johannesburg	1895-96
9-37	J.C.Laker	E v A	Manchester	1956
9-51	M.Muralitharan	SL v Z	Kandy	2001-02
9-52	R.J.Hadlee	NZ v A	Brisbane	1985-86
9-56	Abdul Qadir	P v E	Lahore	1987-88
9-57	D.E.Malcolm	E v SA	The Oval	1994
9-65	M.Muralitharan	SL v E	The Oval	1998
9-69	J.M.Patel	I v A	Kanpur	1959-60
9-83	Kapil Dev	I v WI	Ahmedabad	1983-84

9- 86	Sarfraz Nawaz	P v A	Melbourne	1978-79
9- 95	J.M.Noreiga	WI v I	Port-of-Spain	1970-71
9-102	S.P.Gupte	I v WI	Kanpur	1958-59
9-103	S.F.Barnes	E v SA	Johannesburg	1913-14
9-113	H.J.Tayfield	SA v E	Johannesburg	1956-57
9-121	A.A.Mailey	A v E	Melbourne	1920-21

The best analysis for Zimbabwe is 8-109 by P.A.Strang (v NZ, Bulawayo, 2000-01), and for Bangladesh 7-95 by Enamul Haque II (v Z, Dhaka, 2004-05).

HAT-TRICKS

F.R.Spofforth	Australia v England	Melbourne	1878-79
W.Bates	England v Australia	Melbourne	1882-83
J.Briggs	England v Australia	Sydney	1891-92
G.A.Lohmann	England v South Africa	Port Elizabeth	1895-96
J.T.Hearne	England v Australia	Leeds	1899
H.Trumble	Australia v England	Melbourne	1901-02
H.Trumble	Australia v England	Melbourne	1903-04
T.J.Matthews (2)[2]	Australia v South Africa	Manchester	1912
M.J.C.Allom[1]	England v New Zealand	Christchurch	1929-30
T.W.J.Goddard	England v South Africa	Johannesburg	1938-39
P.J.Loader	England v West Indies	Leeds	1957
L.F.Kline	Australia v South Africa	Cape Town	1957-58
W.W.Hall	West Indies v Pakistan	Lahore	1958-59
G.M.Griffin	South Africa v England	Lord's	1960
L.R.Gibbs	West Indies v Australia	Adelaide	1960-61
P.J.Petherick[1]	New Zealand v Pakistan	Lahore	1976-77
C.A.Walsh[3]	West Indies v Australia	Brisbane	1988-89
M.G.Hughes[3]	Australia v West Indies	Perth	1988-89
D.W.Fleming[1]	Australia v Pakistan	Rawalpindi	1994-95
S.K.Warne	Australia v England	Melbourne	1994-95
D.G.Cork	England v West Indies	Manchester	1995
D.Gough	England v Australia	Sydney	1998-99
Wasim Akram[4]	Pakistan v Sri Lanka	Lahore	1998-99
Wasim Akram[4]	Pakistan v Sri Lanka	Dhaka	1998-99
D.N.T.Zoysa[5]	Sri Lanka v Zimbabwe	Harare	1999-00
Abdul Razzaq	Pakistan v Sri Lanka	Galle	2000-01
G.D.McGrath	Australia v West Indies	Perth	2000-01
Harbhajan Singh	India v Australia	Calcutta	2000-01
Mohammad Sami	Pakistan v Sri Lanka	Lahore	2001-02
J.J.C.Lawson	West Indies v Australia	Bridgetown	2002-03
Alok Kapali	Bangladesh v Pakistan	Peshawar	2003
A.M.Blignaut	Zimbabwe v Bangladesh	Harare	2003-04
M.J.Hoggard	England v West Indies	Bridgetown	2003-04
J.E.C.Franklin	New Zealand v Bangladesh	Dhaka	2004-05
I.K.Pathan[6]	India v Pakistan	Karachi	2005-06

[1] *On debut.* [2] *Hat-trick in each innings.* [3] *Involving both innings.* [4] *In successive Tests.* [5] *His first 3 balls (second over of the match).* [6] *The fourth, fifth and sixth balls of the match.*

WICKET-KEEPING RECORDS

100 DISMISSALS IN TESTS†

Total			*Tests*	*Ct*	*St*
395	I.A.Healy	Australia	119	366	29
390	M.V.Boucher	South Africa	101	374	16
374	A.C.Gilchrist	Australia	89	339	35
355	R.W.Marsh	Australia	96	343	12

Total			*Tests*	*Ct*	*St*
270†	P.J.L.Dujon	West Indies	79	265	5
269	A.P.E.Knott	England	95	250	19
241†	A.J.Stewart	England	82	227	14
228	Wasim Bari	Pakistan	81	201	27
219	R.D.Jacobs	West Indies	65	207	12
219	T.G.Evans	England	91	173	46
201†	A.C.Parore	New Zealand	67	194	7
198	S.M.H.Kirmani	India	88	160	38
189	D.L.Murray	West Indies	62	181	8
187	A.T.W.Grout	Australia	51	163	24
176	I.D.S.Smith	New Zealand	63	168	8
174	R.W.Taylor	England	57	167	7
165	R.C.Russell	England	54	153	12
152	D.J.Richardson	South Africa	42	150	2
151†	A.Flower	Zimbabwe	55	142	9
147†	Moin Khan	Pakistan	66	127	20
145†	K.C.Sangakkara	Sri Lanka	47	125	20
141	J.H.B.Waite	South Africa	49	124	17
133	G.O.Jones	England	34	128	5
130	Rashid Latif	Pakistan	37	119	11
130	K.S.More	India	49	110	20
130	W.A.S.Oldfield	Australia	54	78	52
126	Kamran Akmal	Pakistan	33	108	18
119	R.S.Kaluwitharana	Sri Lanka	49	93	26
112†	J.M.Parks	England	43	101	11
107	N.R.Mongia	India	44	99	8
104	Salim Yousuf	Pakistan	32	91	13
101†	J.R.Murray	West Indies	31	98	3

The most for Bangladesh is 83 (75 ct, 8 st) by Khaled Masud in 41 Tests.

† Excluding catches taken in the field

25 DISMISSALS IN A SERIES

28	R.W.Marsh	Australia v England	1982-83
27 (inc 2st)	R.C.Russell	England v South Africa	1995-96
27 (inc 2st)	I.A.Healy	Australia v England (6 Tests)	1997
26 (inc 3st)	J.H.B.Waite	South Africa v New Zealand	1961-62
26	R.W.Marsh	Australia v West Indies (6 Tests)	1975-76
26 (inc 5st)	I.A.Healy	Australia v England (6 Tests)	1993
26 (inc 1st)	M.V.Boucher	South Africa v England	1998
26 (inc 2st)	A.C.Gilchrist	Australia v England	2001
26 (inc 2st)	A.C.Gilchrist	Australia v England	2006-07
25 (inc 2st)	I.A.Healy	Australia v England	1994-95
25 (inc 2st)	A.C.Gilchrist	Australia v England	2002-03

TEN DISMISSALS IN A TEST

11	R.C.Russell	England v South Africa	Johannesburg	1995-96
10	R.W.Taylor	England v India	Bombay	1979-80
10	A.C.Gilchrist	Australia v New Zealand	Hamilton	1999-00

SEVEN DISMISSALS IN AN INNINGS

7	Wasim Bari	Pakistan v New Zealand	Auckland	1978-79
7	R.W.Taylor	England v India	Bombay	1979-80
7	I.D.S.Smith	New Zealand v Sri Lanka	Hamilton	1990-91
7	R.D.Jacobs	West Indies v Australia	Melbourne	2000-01

FIVE STUMPINGS IN AN INNINGS

5	K.S.More	India v West Indies	Madras	1987-88

FIELDING RECORDS

100 CATCHES IN TESTS

Total			*Tests*	*Total*			*Tests*
181	M.E.Waugh	Australia	128	115	C.L.Hooper	West Indies	102
164	B.C.Lara	West Indies	130	113	D.P.M.D.Jayawardena	Sri Lanka	85
159	S.P.Fleming	New Zealand	104	112	S.R.Waugh	Australia	168
157	M.A.Taylor	Australia	104	110	R.B.Simpson	Australia	62
156	A.R.Border	Australia	156	110	W.R.Hammond	England	85
146	R.Dravid	India	106	109	G.St A.Sobers	West Indies	93
125	S.K.Warne	Australia	144	108	S.M.Gavaskar	India	125
123	R.T.Ponting	Australia	109	105	I.M.Chappell	Australia	75
122	G.S.Chappell	Australia	87	105	M.Azharuddin	India	99
122	I.V.A.Richards	West Indies	121	105	G.P.Thorpe	England	100
120	I.T.Botham	England	102	103	G.A.Gooch	England	118
120	M.C.Cowdrey	England	114	101	J.H.Kallis	South Africa	106
115	M.L.Hayden	Australia	88				

The most for Pakistan is 93 by Javed Miandad (124), for Zimbabwe 60 by A.D.R.Campbell (60) and for Bangladesh 19 by Habibul Bashar (42).

15 CATCHES IN A SERIES

15	J.M.Gregory	Australia v England	1920-21

SEVEN CATCHES IN A TEST

7	G.S.Chappell	Australia v England	Perth	1974-75
7	Yajurvindra Singh	India v England	Bangalore	1976-77
7	H.P.Tillekeratne	Sri Lanka v New Zealand	Colombo (SSC)	1992-93
7	S.P.Fleming	New Zealand v Zimbabwe	Harare	1997-98
7	M.L.Hayden	Australia v Sri Lanka	Galle	2003-04

FIVE CATCHES IN AN INNINGS

5	V.Y.Richardson	Australia v South Africa	Durban	1935-36
5	Yajurvindra Singh	India v England	Bangalore	1976-77
5	M.Azharuddin	India v Pakistan	Karachi	1989-90
5	K.Srikkanth	India v Australia	Perth	1991-92
5	S.P.Fleming	New Zealand v Zimbabwe	Harare	1997-98

APPEARANCE RECORDS

100 TEST MATCH APPEARANCES

			Opponents									
			E	*A*	*SA*	*WI*	*NZ*	*I*	*P*	*SL*	*Z*	*B*
168	S.R.Waugh	Australia	46	–	16	32	23	18	20	8	3	2
156	A.R.Border	Australia	47	–	6	31	23	20	22	7	–	–
144	S.K.Warne	Australia	36	–	24	19	20	14	15	13	1	2
135	S.R.Tendulkar	India	19	21	19	16	16	–	16	16	9	3
133	A.J.Stewart	England	–	33	23	24	16	9	13	9	6	–
132	C.A.Walsh	West Indies	36	38	10	–	10	15	18	3	2	–
131	Kapil Dev	India	27	20	4	25	10	–	29	14	2	–
130	B.C.Lara	West Indies	30	30	18	–	11	17	12	8	2	2
128	M.E.Waugh	Australia	29	–	18	28	14	14	15	9	1	–
125	S.M.Gavaskar	India	38	20	–	27	9	–	24	7	–	–

			Opponents									
			E	*A*	*SA*	*WI*	*NZ*	*I*	*P*	*SL*	*Z*	*B*
124	Javed Miandad	Pakistan	22	24	–	17	18	28	–	12	3	–
123	G.D.McGrath	Australia	30	–	17	23	14	11	17	8	1	2
121	I.V.A.Richards	West Indies	36	34	–	–	7	28	16	–	–	–
119	I.A.Healy	Australia	33	–	12	28	11	9	14	11	1	–
118	G.A.Gooch	England	–	42	3	26	15	19	10	3	–	–
118	Inzamam-ul-Haq	Pakistan	19	13	12	15	12	10	–	20	11	6
117	D.I.Gower	England	–	42	–	19	13	24	17	2	–	–
116	D.L.Haynes	West Indies	36	33	1	–	10	19	16	1	–	–
116	D.B.Vengsarkar	India	26	24	–	25	11	–	22	8	–	–
115	M.A.Atherton	England	–	33	18	27	11	7	11	4	4	–
114	M.C.Cowdrey	England	–	43	14	21	18	8	10	–	–	–
113	A.Kumble	India	16	14	19	17	11	–	12	15	7	2
110	C.H.Lloyd	West Indies	34	29	–	–	8	28	11	–	–	–
109	M.Muralitharan	Sri Lanka	13	10	15	10	12	15	14	–	14	6
109	R.T.Ponting	Australia	26	–	15	15	11	15	10	10	3	4
108	G.Boycott	England	–	38	7	29	15	13	6	–	–	–
108	C.G.Greenidge	West Indies	29	32	–	–	10	23	14	–	–	–
107	D.C.Boon	Australia	31	–	6	22	17	11	11	9	–	–
107	S.T.Jayasuriya	Sri Lanka	13	11	15	10	13	10	17	–	13	5
107	S.M.Pollock	South Africa	23	13	–	15	11	12	12	13	5	3
106	R.Dravid	India	12	18	15	17	9	–	12	11	9	3
106	J.H.Kallis	South Africa	20	17	–	18	12	8	11	12	6	2
104	S.P.Fleming	New Zealand	16	14	13	11	–	13	9	13	11	4
104	M.A.Taylor	Australia	33	–	11	20	11	9	12	8	–	–
104	J.L.Langer	Australia	21	–	11	18	14	14	13	8	3	2
104	Wasim Akram	Pakistan	18	13	4	17	9	12	–	19	10	2
103	Salim Malik	Pakistan	19	15	1	7	18	22	–	15	6	–
102	I.T.Botham	England	–	36	–	20	15	14	14	3	–	–
102	C.L.Hooper	West Indies	24	25	10	–	2	19	14	6	2	–
101	M.V.Boucher	South Africa	17	12	–	18	12	7	11	14	6	4
101	S.Chanderpaul	West Indies	21	12	14	–	11	18	13	2	6	4
101	G.Kirsten	South Africa	22	18	–	13	13	10	11	9	3	2
100	G.P.Thorpe	England	–	16	16	27	13	5	8	9	2	4

The most for Zimbabwe is 67 by G.W.Flower, and for Bangladesh 42 by Habibul Bashar.

100 CONSECUTIVE TEST APPEARANCES

153	A.R.Border	Australia	March 1979 to March 1994
107	M.E.Waugh	Australia	June 1993 to October 2002
106	S.M.Gavaskar	India	January 1975 to February 1987

50 TESTS AS CAPTAIN

			Won	*Lost*	*Drawn*	*Tied*
93	A.R.Border	Australia	32	22	38	1
80	S.P.Fleming	New Zealand	28	27	25	–
74	C.H.Lloyd	West Indies	36	12	26	–
57	S.R.Waugh	Australia	41	9	7	–
56	A.Ranatunga	Sri Lanka	12	19	25	–
54	M.A.Atherton	England	13	21	20	–
53	W.J.Cronje	South Africa	27	11	15	–
50	I.V.A.Richards	West Indies	27	8	15	–
50	M.A.Taylor	Australia	26	13	11	–

The most for India is 49 by S.C.Ganguly, for Pakistan 48 by Imran Khan, for Zimbabwe 21 by A.D.R.Campbell and H.H.Streak, and for Bangladesh 15 by Habibul Bashar.

TEST MATCH SCORES AND SERIES AVERAGES
BANGLADESH v SRI LANKA (1st Test)

At Divisional Stadium, Chittagong, on 28 February, 1, 2, 3 March 2006.
Toss: Bangladesh. Result: **SRI LANKA** won by eight wickets.
Debuts: None.

BANGLADESH

Javed Omar	c Samaraweera b Malinga	4		lbw b Fernando	31
Nafis Iqbal	b Bandara	34		c Sangakkara b Fernando	6
*Habibul Bashar	lbw b Bandara	29		lbw b Bandara	12
Shahriar Nafis	b Maharoof	27		c Fernando b Muralitharan	38
Mohammad Ashraful	c Tharanga b Muralitharan	136		c Tharanga b Muralitharan	1
†Khaled Masud	lbw b Muralitharan	6		c Dilshan b Muralitharan	15
Alok Kapali	c Tharanga b Muralitharan	16		lbw b Muralitharan	9
Mohammad Rafique	b Malinga	17		st Sangakkara b Muralitharan	40
Shahadat Hossain	c Tharanga b Malinga	13		c Malinga b Bandara	0
Syed Rasel	b Malinga	1	(11)	not out	2
Enamul Haque II	not out	3	(10)	lbw b Muralitharan	1
Extras	(B 11, LB 4, W 3, NB 15)	33		(B 13, LB 3, W 3, NB 7)	26
Total		**319**			**181**

SRI LANKA

M.G.Vandort	c Masud b Rasel	0	not out	64
W.U.Tharanga	c Ashraful b Rafique	42	c Shahriar b Rasel	19
†K.C.Sangakkara	c Ashraful b Haque	69	c and b Haque	46
*D.P.M.D.Jayawardena	c Shahadat b Rafique	30	not out	23
T.T.Samaraweera	c Javed b Shahadat	58		
T.M.Dilshan	lbw b Haque	22		
M.F.Maharoof	b Shahadat	72		
C.M.Bandara	not out	19		
C.R.D.Fernando	c Shahriar b Shahadat	6		
M.Muralitharan	c Shahriar b Shahadat	5		
S.L.Malinga	run out	0		
Extras	(LB 2, W 2, NB 11)	15	(B 4, LB 5, NB 2)	11
Total		**338**	(2 wickets)	**163**

SRI LANKA	O	M	R	W		O	M	R	W
Malinga	16.5	3	57	4		13	2	41	0
Maharoof	11	3	37	1		2	0	5	0
Fernando	17	4	50	0	(5)	4	1	10	2
Muralitharan	32	8	87	3		19.5	6	54	6
Bandara	13	0	61	2	(3)	20	2	55	2
Dilshan	2	0	12	0					
BANGLADESH									
Syed Rasel	18	1	75	1		8	4	18	1
Shahadat Hossain	22	3	83	4		8	1	39	0
Mohammad Rafique	29	6	76	2	(4)	8	0	28	0
Enamul Haque II	24.1	5	76	2	(3)	9	1	50	1
Alok Kapali	1	0	6	0		2	0	6	0
Mohammad Ashraful	3	0	20	0		2	0	13	0

FALL OF WICKETS

	B	SL	B	SL
Wkt	*1st*	*1st*	*2nd*	*2nd*
1st	4	0	47	25
2nd	76	86	56	115
3rd	81	149	68	–
4th	146	149	69	-
5th	210	178	122	-
6th	248	295	131	-
7th	293	316	135	-
8th	308	330	150	-
9th	314	338	168	-
10th	319	338	181	-

Umpires: Asad Rauf (*Pakistan*) (4) and S.A.Bucknor (*West Indies*) (109).
Referee: C.H.Lloyd (*West Indies*) (52). **Test No. 1783/6 (B41/SL157)**

BANGLADESH v SRI LANKA (2nd Test)

At Shaheed Chandu Stadium, Bogra, on 8, 9, 10, 11 March 2006.
Toss: Bangladesh. Result: **SRI LANKA** won by ten wickets.
Debuts: None.

BANGLADESH

Javed Omar	lbw b Muralitharan	35	c Sangakkara b Fernando	13
Nafis Iqbal	lbw b Muralitharan	26	c Sangakkara b Malinga	2
*Habibul Bashar	c Tharanga b Muralitharan	69	lbw b Malinga	73
Shahriar Nafis	c Sangakkara b Malinga	9	c Maharoof b Muralitharan	6
Mohammad Ashraful	b Bandara	24	c Jayawardena b Bandara	13
Mushfiqur Rahim	lbw b Muralitharan	2	c Sangakkara b Bandara	0
†Khaled Masud	c Sangakkara b Malinga	12	c Malinga b Muralitharan	6
Mohammad Rafique	c Muralitharan b Fernando	32	c Muralitharan b Malinga	64
Shahadat Hossain	c Muralitharan b Fernando	6	b Fernando	8
Enamul Haque II	not out	3	c Sangakkara b Fernando	3
Syed Rasel	c Bandara b Muralitharan	0	not out	1
Extras	(B 3, LB 5, NB 8)	16	(B 1, LB 4, W 2, NB 5)	12
Total		**234**		**201**

SRI LANKA

M.G.Vandort	lbw b Rasel	0	not out	40
W.U.Tharanga	c Masud b Shahadat	165	not out	71
C.M.Bandara	c Nafiz b Shahadat	2		
T.T.Samaraweera	c Masud b Shahadat	20		
†K.C.Sangakkara	lbw b Shahadat	0		
*D.P.M.D.Jayawardena	c Rahim b Ashraful	49		
T.M.Dilshan	b Rafique	33		
M.F.Maharoof	c Masud b Haque	7		
C.R.D.Fernando	lbw b Haque	5		
S.L.Malinga	c Nafiz b Shahadat	12		
M.Muralitharan	not out	8		
Extras	(B 5, LB 4, W 2, NB 4)	15	(LB 5, W 3, NB 1)	9
Total		**316**	(0 wickets)	**120**

SRI LANKA	O	M	R	W		O	M	R	W
Malinga	20	1	73	2		14.1	1	51	3
Maharoof	4	0	22	0					
Fernando	9	4	24	2	(2)	19	4	51	3
Muralitharan	30.5	8	79	3	(3)	13	1	62	2
Bandara	13	1	28	1	(4)	10	4	32	2
BANGLADESH									
Syed Rasel	20	8	50	1		5	0	21	0
Shahadat Hossain	21.3	2	86	5		8	2	43	0
Mohammad Rafique	32	9	84	1		9	2	32	0
Enamul Haque II	26	3	71	2		6	0	19	0
Mohammad Ashraful	4	1	16	1					

FALL OF WICKETS

Wkt	B *1st*	SL *1st*	B *2nd*	SL *2nd*
1st	52	4	15	–
2nd	85	13	29	–
3rd	106	43	46	–
4th	157	43	95	–
5th	172	167	95	–
6th	186	232	110	–
7th	208	251	162	–
8th	231	263	187	–
9th	233	305	198	–
10th	234	316	201	–

Umpires: Asad Rauf (*Pakistan*) (5) and K.Hariharan (*India*) (1).
Referee: C.H.Lloyd (*West Indies*) (53). **Test No. 1784/7 (B42/SL158)**

INDIA v ENGLAND (1st Test)

At Vidarbha C.A. Ground, Nagpur on 1, 2, 3, 4, 5 March 2006.
Toss: England. Result: **MATCH DRAWN**.
Debuts: India – S.Sreesanth; England – I.D.Blackwell, A.N.Cook, M.S.Panesar.

ENGLAND

A.J.Strauss	c Laxman b Sreesanth	28	c Dhoni b Pathan	46
A.N.Cook	b Pathan	60	not out	104
I.R.Bell	c Dravid b Harbhajan	9	c Dhoni b Pathan	1
K.P.Pietersen	b Sreesanth	15	c Dravid b Kumble	87
P.D.Collingwood	not out	134	not out	36
*A.Flintoff	lbw b Kumble	43		
†G.O.Jones	lbw b Pathan	14		
I.D.Blackwell	b Pathan	4		
M.J.Hoggard	c Dhoni b Sreesanth	11		
S.J.Harmison	st Dhoni b Harbhajan	39		
M.S.Panesar	lbw b Sreesanth	9		
Extras	(B 7, LB 7, W 1, NB 12)	27	(B 12, LB 7, W 2, NB 2)	23
Total		**393**	(3 wickets declared)	**297**

INDIA

W.Jaffer	c Flintoff b Hoggard	81	c Strauss b Flintoff	100
V.Sehwag	c Pietersen b Hoggard	2	b Hoggard	0
*R.Dravid	lbw b Hoggard	40	b Panesar	71
S.R.Tendulkar	lbw b Panesar	16	(6) not out	28
V.V.S.Laxman	lbw b Hoggard	0	(8) not out	0
M.Kaif	b Panesar	91		
†M.S.Dhoni	c Jones b Flintoff	5	(5) c Strauss b Harmison	16
I.K.Pathan	c Flintoff b Hoggard	2	(4) c Strauss b Flintoff	35
A.Kumble	c Cook b Harmison	58		
Harbhajan Singh	not out	0	(7) b Harmison	7
S.Sreesanth	lbw b Hoggard	1		
Extras	(B 17, LB 3, W 5, NB 2)	27	(LB 3)	3
Total		**323**	(6 wickets)	**260**

INDIA	O	M	R	W		O	M	R	W
Pathan	23	5	92	3		14	2	48	2
Sreesanth	28.5	6	95	4		10	2	36	0
Harbhajan Singh	34	5	93	2	(4)	30	6	79	0
Kumble	40	13	88	1	(3)	32	8	101	1
Tendulkar	2	0	11	0					
Sehwag					(5)	1	0	14	0
ENGLAND									
Hoggard	30.5	13	57	6		16	7	29	1
Harmison	27	5	75	1		17.2	4	48	2
Flintoff	29	10	68	1		17	2	79	2
Panesar	42	19	73	2		16	2	58	1
Blackwell	7	0	28	0		12	2	43	0
Bell	1	0	2	0					

FALL OF WICKETS

	E	I	E	I
Wkt	*1st*	*1st*	*2nd*	*2nd*
1st	56	11	95	1
2nd	81	140	97	168
3rd	110	149	221	198
4th	136	149	–	215
5th	203	176	–	252
6th	225	183	–	260
7th	244	190	–	–
8th	267	318	–	–
9th	327	322	–	–
10th	393	323	–	–

Umpires: Alim Dar (*Pakistan*) (28) and I.L.Howell (*South Africa*) (4).
Referee: R.S.Madugalle (*Sri Lanka*) (83). **Test No. 1785/92 (I394/E843)**

INDIA v ENGLAND (2nd Test)

At Mohali, Chandigarh, on 9, 10, 11, 12, 13 March 2006.
Toss: England. Result: **INDIA** won by nine wickets.
Debuts: India – P.Chawla, M.M.Patel.

ENGLAND

A.J.Strauss	c Dhoni b Pathan	18	c Dhoni b Kumble	13
A.N.Cook	lbw b Pathan	17	c Dhoni b Patel	2
I.R.Bell	b Kumble	38	c Dhoni b Kumble	57
K.P.Pietersen	c and b Patel	64	c Dravid b Harbhajan	4
P.D.Collingwood	b Kumble	25	c Dravid b Kumble	14
*A.Flintoff	c and b Patel	70	c Patel b Chawla	51
†G.O.Jones	b Kumble	52	b Patel	5
L.E.Plunkett	c Dhoni b Patel	0	lbw b Patel	1
M.J.Hoggard	not out	4	b Patel	4
S.J.Harmison	lbw b Kumble	0	st Dhoni b Kumble	13
M.S.Panesar	c Dravid b Kumble	0	not out	0
Extras	(LB 5, W 1, NB 6)	12	(LB 10, W 1, NB 6)	17
Total		**300**		**181**

INDIA

W.Jaffer	c Flintoff b Panesar	31	lbw b Hoggard	17
V.Sehwag	c Jones b Harmison	11	not out	76
*R.Dravid	b Flintoff	95	not out	42
S.R.Tendulkar	c Strauss b Flintoff	4		
Yuvraj Singh	c Bell b Hoggard	15		
†M.S.Dhoni	c Jones b Harmison	16		
I.K.Pathan	c Collingwood b Flintoff	52		
A.Kumble	b Plunkett	32		
Harbhajan Singh	c Jones b Flintoff	36		
P.Chawla	c Collingwood b Hoggard	1		
M.M.Patel	not out	11		
Extras	(LB 25, W 1, NB 8)	34	(B 4, LB 5)	9
Total		**338**	(1 wicket)	**144**

INDIA	O	M	R	W		O	M	R	W
Pathan	28	9	71	2		6	1	16	0
Patel	25	6	72	3		13	4	25	4
Harbhajan Singh	12	0	31	0		23	5	52	1
Chawla	9	1	45	0	(5)	5.1	2	8	1
Kumble	29.4	8	76	5	(4)	29	6	70	4
ENGLAND									
Hoggard	18	6	55	2	(2)	8	2	24	1
Harmison	28	9	60	2	(1)	4	1	10	0
Flintoff	22	3	96	4	(4)	5	0	11	0
Plunkett	9.2	1	37	1	(5)	2	0	22	0
Panesar	19	3	65	1	(3)	11	0	48	0
Collingwood						3	1	20	0

FALL OF WICKETS

	E	I	E	I
Wkt	*1st*	*1st*	*2nd*	*2nd*
1st	35	18	7	39
2nd	36	96	50	–
3rd	117	103	55	–
4th	157	134	88	–
5th	180	153	109	–
6th	283	229	116	–
7th	290	260	124	–
8th	300	313	139	–
9th	300	321	181	–
10th	300	338	181	–

Umpires: D.B.Hair (*Australia*) (70) and S.J.A.Taufel (*Australia*) (32).
Referee: R.S.Madugalle (*Sri Lanka*) (84). **Test No. 1786/93 (I395/E844)**

INDIA v ENGLAND (3rd Test)

At Wankhede Stadium, Bombay, on 18, 19, 20, 21, 22 March 2006.
Toss: India. Result: **ENGLAND** won by 212 runs.
Debuts: England – O.A.Shah.

ENGLAND

A.J.Strauss	c Dhoni b Harbhajan	128		c Dhoni b Patel	4
I.R.Bell	c Harbhajan b Sreesanth	18		c Dhoni b Sreesanth	8
O.A.Shah	c Dravid b Harbhajan	88		run out	38
K.P.Pietersen	c Dhoni b Sreesanth	39	(5)	c and b Kumble	7
P.D.Collingwood	c Dhoni b Sreesanth	31	(6)	c and b Harbhajan	32
*A.Flintoff	c Tendulkar b Kumble	50	(7)	st Dhoni b Kumble	50
†G.O.Jones	c Kumble b Sreesanth	1	(8)	c Pathan b Harbhajan	3
S.D.Udal	lbw b Patel	9	(4)	c Jaffer b Pathan	14
M.J.Hoggard	b Patel	0		lbw b Kumble	6
J.M.Anderson	c Yuvraj b Harbhajan	15		c Dravid b Kumble	6
M.S.Panesar	not out	3		not out	0
Extras	(B 5, LB 7, W 3, NB 3)	18		(B 1, LB 8, W 4, NB 10)	23
Total		**400**			**191**

INDIA

W.Jaffer	c Jones b Hoggard	11		lbw b Flintoff	10
V.Sehwag	c Shah b Hoggard	6	(7)	lbw b Anderson	0
*R.Dravid	c Jones b Anderson	52	(4)	c Jones b Flintoff	9
S.R.Tendulkar	c Jones b Anderson	1	(5)	c Bell b Udal	34
Yuvraj Singh	c Jones b Flintoff	37	(6)	c Collingwood b Flintoff	12
†M.S.Dhoni	run out	64	(8)	c Panesar b Udal	5
I.K.Pathan	c Hoggard b Udal	26	(2)	b Anderson	6
A.Kumble	lbw b Panesar	30	(3)	lbw b Hoggard	8
Harbhajan Singh	c Jones b Anderson	2		c Hoggard b Udal	6
S.Sreesanth	not out	29		not out	0
M.M.Patel	b Anderson	7		c Hoggard b Udal	1
Extras	(B 4, LB 7, NB 3)	14		(B 1, LB 4, W 1, NB 3)	9
Total		**279**			**100**

INDIA	O	M	R	W		O	M	R	W
Pathan	17	4	64	0		13	2	24	1
Sreesanth	22	5	70	4	(3)	13	3	30	1
Patel	29	4	81	2	(2)	13	2	39	1
Kumble	39	7	84	1		30.4	13	49	4
Harbhajan Singh	26.4	4	89	3		23	9	40	2
ENGLAND									
Hoggard	22	6	54	2		12	6	13	1
Flintoff	21	4	68	1	(4)	11	4	14	3
Anderson	19.1	8	40	4	(2)	12	2	39	2
Panesar	26	7	53	1	(3)	4	1	15	0
Udal	16	2	53	1		9.2	3	14	4

FALL OF WICKETS

	E	I	E	I
Wkt	*1st*	*1st*	*2nd*	*2nd*
1st	52	9	9	6
2nd	230	24	21	21
3rd	242	28	61	33
4th	326	94	73	75
5th	328	142	85	76
6th	333	186	151	77
7th	356	212	157	92
8th	356	217	183	99
9th	385	272	188	99
10th	400	279	191	100

Umpires: D.B.Hair (*Australia*) (71) and S.J.A.Taufel (*Australia*) (33).
Referee: R.S.Madugalle (*Sri Lanka*) (85).
Shah (50*) retired with cramp at 158 in the first innings and resumed at 326-4.

Test No. 1787/94 (I396/E845)

INDIA v ENGLAND 2005-06

INDIA – BATTING AND FIELDING

	M	I	NO	HS	Runs	Avge	100	50	Ct/St
R.Dravid	3	6	1	95	309	61.80	–	3	7
W.Jaffer	3	6	0	100	250	41.66	1	1	1
A.Kumble	3	4	0	58	128	32.00	–	1	2
S.Sreesanth	2	3	2	29*	30	30.00	–	–	–
I.K.Pathan	3	5	0	52	121	24.20	–	1	1
Yuvraj Singh	2	3	0	37	64	21.33	–	–	1
M.S.Dhoni	3	5	0	64	106	21.20	–	1	13/3
S.R.Tendulkar	3	5	1	34	83	20.75	–	–	1
V Sehwag	3	6	1	76*	95	19.00	–	1	–
Harbhajan Singh	3	5	1	36	51	12.75	–	–	2
M.M.Patel	2	3	1	11*	19	9.50	–	–	3

Played in one Test: P.Chawla 1; M.Kaif 91; V.V.S.Laxman 0, 0* (1 ct).

INDIA – BOWLING

	O	M	R	W	Avge	Best	5wI	10wM
M.M.Patel	80	16	217	10	21.70	4-25	–	–
S.Sreesanth	73.5	16	231	9	25.66	4-70	–	–
A.Kumble	200.2	56	468	16	29.25	5-76	1	–
I.K.Pathan	101	23	315	8	39.37	3-92	–	–
Harbhajan Singh	148.4	29	384	8	48.00	3-89	–	–

Also bowled: P.Chawla 14.1-3-53-1; V.Sehwag 1-0-14-0; S.R.Tendulkar 2-0-11-0.

ENGLAND – BATTING AND FIELDING

	M	I	NO	HS	Runs	Avge	100	50	Ct/St
P.D.Collingwood	3	6	2	134*	272	68.00	1	–	3
A.N.Cook	2	4	1	104*	183	61.00	1	1	1
A.Flintoff	3	5	–	70	264	52.80	–	4	3
A.J.Strauss	3	6	–	128	237	39.50	1	–	4
K.P.Pietersen	3	6	–	87	216	36.00	–	2	1
I.R.Bell	3	6	–	57	131	21.83	–	1	2
S.J.Harmison	2	3	–	39	52	17.33	–	–	–
G.O.Jones	3	5	–	52	75	15.00	–	1	10
M.J.Hoggard	3	5	1	11	25	6.25	–	–	3
M.S.Panesar	3	5	3	9	12	6.00	–	–	1

Played in one Test: J.M.Anderson 15, 6; I.D.Blackwell 4; L.E.Plunkett 0, 1; O.A.Shah 88, 38 (1 ct); S.D.Udal 9, 14.

ENGLAND – BOWLING

	O	M	R	W	Avge	Best	5wI	10wM
J.M.Anderson	31.1	10	79	6	13.16	4-40	–	–
S.D.Udal	25.2	5	67	5	13.40	4-14	–	–
M.J.Hoggard	106.5	40	232	13	17.84	6-57	1	–
A.Flintoff	105	23	336	11	30.54	4-96	–	–
S.J.Harmison	76.2	19	193	5	38.60	2-48	–	–
M.S.Panesar	118	32	312	5	62.40	2-73	–	–

Also bowled: I.R.Bell 1-0-2-0; I.D.Blackwell 19-2-71-0; P.D.Collingwood 3-1-20-0; L.E.Plunkett 11.2-1-59-1.

NEW ZEALAND v WEST INDIES (1st Test)

At Eden Park, Auckland, on 9, 10, 11, 12, 13 March 2006.
Toss: West Indies. Result: **NEW ZEALAND** won by 27 runs.
Debuts: P.G.Fulton, J.M.How – New Zealand. I.D.R.Bradshaw – West Indies.

NEW ZEALAND

H.R.H Marshall	c Edwards b Taylor	11		c Ganga b Bradshaw	1
J.M.How	run out	11		c Ramdin b Bradshaw	37
P.G.Fulton	c Ganga b Bradshaw	17		b Edwards	28
*S.P.Fleming	c Ramdin b Bradshaw	14		lbw b Bradshaw	33
N.J.Astle	c Ramdin b Smith	51	(7)	run out	13
S.B.Styris	not out	103	(5)	c Bradshaw b Edwards	5
†B.B.McCullum	b Smith	19	(8)	c Bravo b Gayle	74
D.L.Vettori	c Gayle b Smith	6	(9)	c sub (D.S.Smith) b Gayle	33
J.E.C.Franklin	c sub (R.S.Morton) b Gayle	14	(6)	b Gayle	20
S.E.Bond	b Gayle	3		not out	18
C.S.Martin	c Ramdin b Bradshaw	0		b Gayle	0
Extras	(B 4, LB 2, W 9, NB 11)	26		(LB 3, W 2, NB 5)	10
Total		**275**			**272**

WEST INDIES

C.H.Gayle	c McCullum b Styris	25		c Fleming b Astle	82
D.Ganga	c How b Martin	20		c How b Astle	95
I.D.R.Bradshaw	c How b Styris	0	(9)	c Fleming b Vettori	10
R.R.Sarwan	c Franklin b Bond	62	(3)	c Styris b Bond	4
B.C.Lara	c sub (C.Cachopa) b Bond	5	(4)	b Bond	0
*S.C.Chanderpaul	c McCullum b Franklin	13	(5)	c Fulton b Vettori	15
D.J.Bravo	c Bond b Martin	59	(6)	lbw b Bond	17
D.R.Smith	c McCullum b Martin	38	(7)	c Fleming b Bond	0
†D.Ramdin	c and b Vettori	9	(8)	c Franklin b Vettori	15
F.H.Edwards	c McCullum b Vettori	1	(11)	not out	2
J.E.Taylor	not out	4	(10)	b Bond	13
Extras	(LB 7, W 1, NB 13)	21		(B 1, LB 3, W 1, NB 5)	10
Total		**257**			**263**

WEST INDIES	O	M	R	W		O	M	R	W
Edwards	15	1	76	0		21	3	65	2
Bradshaw	23.1	3	73	3		34	10	83	3
Taylor	8	2	39	1		1	0	6	0
Smith	18	2	71	3	(5)	17	6	44	0
Gayle	5	0	10	2	(4)	30.1	5	71	4
NEW ZEALAND									
Bond	19	4	57	2		27.3	7	69	5
Franklin	21	4	83	1		14	1	46	0
Martin	17	1	80	3		16	5	39	0
Styris	7	1	23	2					
Vettori	7.2	3	7	2	(4)	35	11	92	3
Astle					(5)	10	4	13	2

FALL OF WICKETS

	NZ	WI	NZ	WI
Wkt	*1st*	*1st*	*2nd*	*2nd*
1st	23	47	11	148
2nd	31	48	66	157
3rd	54	49	73	182
4th	69	60	88	211
5th	140	90	118	216
6th	170	179	143	218
7th	199	237	146	221
8th	240	248	210	246
9th	261	252	272	251
10th	275	257	272	263

Umpires: D.J.Harper (*Australia*) (56) and R.E.Koertzen (*South Africa*) (71).
Referee: M.J.Procter (*South Africa*) (38).
Sarwan (4*) retired hurt at 157-1 in the second innings and resumed at 216-5.

Test No. 1788/33 (NZ325/WI427)

NEW ZEALAND v WEST INDIES (2nd Test)

At Basin Reserve, Wellington, on 17, 18, 19, 20 March 2006.
Toss: West Indies. Result: **NEW ZEALAND** won by ten wickets.
Debuts: None.

WEST INDIES				
C.H.Gayle	c McCullum b Franklin	30	lbw b Vettori	68
D.Ganga	c McCullum b Mills	15	c McCullum b Martin	23
R.S. Morton	lbw b Franklin	63	c Fleming b Franklin	7
B.C.Lara	c Fleming b Franklin	1	c Marshall b Astle	1
*S.C.Chanderpaul	c Fleming b Martin	8	c Fleming b Mills	36
D.J.Bravo	lbw b Franklin	9	c Astle b Martin	7
†D.Ramdin	b Franklin	2	b Vettori	7
R.N.Lewis	c Fleming b Martin	22	c Astle b Mills	40
I.R.Bradshaw	not out	20	c Styris b Franklin	2
D.B.Powell	c How b Mills	16	c How b Mills	7
F.H.Edwards	c Fleming b Mills	0	not out	0
Extras	(B 2, LB 1, NB 3)	6	(W 6, NB 11)	17
Total		**192**		**215**

NEW ZEALAND				
H.R.H Marshall	c Chanderpaul b Bradshaw	3	not out	23
J.M.How	b Edwards	0	not out	9
P.G.Fulton	c Ramdin b Powell	75		
*S.P.Fleming	c Bravo b Edwards	97		
N.J.Astle	c Ramdin b Powell	65		
S.B.Styris	c Morton b Powell	8		
†B.B.McCullum	c Ramdin b Powell	23		
D.L.Vettori	c Chanderpaul b Edwards	42		
J.E.C.Franklin	not out	28		
K.D.Mills	c Ramdin b Edwards	10		
C.S.Martin	b Edwards	0		
Extras	(LB 4, W 2, NB 15)	21	(NB 5)	5
Total		**372**	(0 wickets)	**37**

NEW ZEALAND	O	M	R	W		O	M	R	W
Martin	14	1	66	2		27	8	65	2
Franklin	20	7	53	5		21	8	64	2
Mills	19.4	7	53	3		9.5	2	29	3
Vettori	5	2	13	0	(5)	20	4	40	2
Astle	3	2	4	0	(4)	13	4	17	1
WEST INDIES									
Edwards	15.3	2	65	5					
Bradshaw	19	2	97	1	(2)	4	0	16	0
Powell	24	7	83	4	(1)	4.1	1	21	0
Gayle	18	4	46	0					
Lewis	29	8	70	0					
Morton	1	0	7	0					

FALL OF WICKETS	WI	NZ	WI	NZ
Wkt	*1st*	*1st*	*2nd*	*2nd*
1st	43	3	54	–
2nd	45	3	75	–
3rd	49	168	84	–
4th	80	207	113	–
5th	102	219	129	–
6th	108	246	156	–
7th	142	332	163	–
8th	165	335	189	–
9th	186	372	210	–
10th	192	372	215	–

Umpires: M.R.Benson (*England*) (7) and D.J.Harper (*Australia*) (57).
Referee: M.J.Procter (*South Africa*) (39). **Test No. 1789/34 (NZ326/WI428)**

NEW ZEALAND v WEST INDIES (3rd Test)

At McLean Park, Napier, on 25, 26, 27 (no play), 28 (no play), 29 March 2006.
Toss: New Zealand. Result: **MATCH DRAWN.**
Debuts: None.

WEST INDIES

C.H.Gayle	c Fulton b Martin	30
D.Ganga	b Bond	38
B.C.Lara	b Astle	83
R.S.Morton	not out	70
*S.C.Chanderpaul	run out	2
D.J.Bravo	not out	22
D.R.Smith		
†D.Ramdin		
I.R.Bradshaw		
D.B.Powell		
F.H.Edwards		
Extras	(LB 3, NB 8)	11
Total	(4 wickets)	**256**

NEW ZEALAND

H.R.H Marshall
J.M.How
P.G.Fulton
*S.P.Fleming
N.J.Astle
S.B.Styris
†B.B.McCullum
D.L.Vettori
J.E.C.Franklin
S.E.Bond
C.S.Martin

NEW ZEALAND	O	M	R	W
Bond	18	2	87	1
Franklin	15	1	66	0
Martin	10	2	39	1
Astle	14	5	23	1
Styris	13.1	5	27	0
Vettori	8	4	11	0

FALL OF WICKETS

	WI
Wkt	*1st*
1st	37
2nd	111
3rd	171
4th	189
5th	–
6th	–
7th	–
8th	–
9th	–
10th	–

Umpires: M.R.Benson (*England*) (8) and I.L.Howell (*South Africa*) (5).
Referee: M.J.Procter (*South Africa*) (40). **Test No. 1790/35 (NZ327/WI429)**

NEW ZEALAND v WEST INDIES 2005-06

NEW ZEALAND – BATTING AND FIELDING

	M	I	NO	HS	Runs	Avge	100	50	Ct/St
S.B.Styris	3	3	1	103*	116	58.00	1	–	2
S.P.Fleming	3	3	–	97	144	48.00	–	1	9
N.J.Astle	3	3	–	65	129	43.00	–	2	2
P.G.Fulton	3	3	–	75	120	40.00	–	1	2
B.B.McCullum	3	3	–	74	116	38.66	–	1	7
J.E.C.Franklin	3	3	1	28*	62	31.00	–	–	2
D.L.Vettori	3	3	–	42	81	27.00	–	–	1
S.E.Bond	2	2	1	18*	21	21.00	–	–	1
J.M.How	3	4	1	37	57	19.00	–	–	5
H.J.H.Marshall	3	4	1	23*	38	12.66	–	–	1
C.S.Martin	3	3	–	0	0	0.00	–	–	–

Played in one Test: K.D.Mills 10.

NEW ZEALAND – BOWLING

	O	M	R	W	Avge	Best	5wI	10wM
K.D.Mills	29.3	9	82	6	13.66	3-29	–	–
N.J.Astle	40	15	57	4	14.25	2-13	–	–
D.L.Vettori	75.2	24	163	7	23.28	3-92	–	–
S.B.Styris	20.1	6	50	2	25.00	2-23	–	–
S.E.Bond	64.3	13	213	8	26.62	5-69	1	–
C.S.Martin	84	17	289	8	36.12	3-80	–	–
J.E.C.Franklin	91	21	312	8	39.00	5-53	1	–

WEST INDIES – BATTING AND FIELDING

	M	I	NO	HS	Runs	Avge	100	50	Ct/St
R.S.Morton	2	3	1	70*	140	70.00	–	2	1
C.H.Gayle	3	5	–	82	235	47.00	–	2	1
D.Ganga	3	5	–	95	191	38.20	–	1	2
D.J.Bravo	3	5	1	59	114	28.50	–	1	2
D.R.Smith	2	2	–	38	38	19.00	–	–	–
B.C.Lara	3	5	–	83	90	18.00	–	1	–
S.Chanderpaul	3	5	–	36	74	14.80	–	–	2
D.B.Powell	2	2	–	16	23	11.50	–	–	–
I.D.R.Bradshaw	3	4	1	20*	32	10.66	–	–	1
D.Ramdin	3	4	–	15	33	8.25	–	–	8
F.H.Edwards	3	4	2	2*	3	1.50	–	–	1

Played in one Test: R.N.Lewis 22, 40; R.R.Sarwan 62, 4; J.E.Taylor 4*, 13.

WEST INDIES – BOWLING

	O	M	R	W	Avge	Best	5wI	10wM
C.H.Gayle	53.1	9	127	6	21.16	4-71	–	–
D.B.Powell	28.1	8	104	4	26.00	4-83	–	–
F.H.Edwards	51.3	6	206	7	29.42	5-65	1	–
D.R.Smith	35	8	115	3	38.33	3-71	–	–
I.D.R.Bradshaw	80.1	15	269	7	38.42	3-73	–	–
J.E.Taylor	9	2	45	1	45.00	1-39	–	–

Also bowled: R.N.Lewis 29-8-70-0; R.S.Morton 1-0-7-0.

SOUTH AFRICA v AUSTRALIA (1st Test)

At Newlands, Cape Town, on 16, 17, 18 March 2006.
Toss: South Africa. Result: **AUSTRALIA** won by seven wickets.
Debuts: Australia – S.R.Clark.

SOUTH AFRICA

*G.C. Smith	c Gilchrist b Clark	19	(2) lbw b Warne	16
A.B.de Villiers	b Kasprowicz	8	(1) c Gilchrist b Lee	7
H.H.Gibbs	b Clark	18	b Lee	0
J.H.Kallis	c Hayden b Clark	6	c Gilchrist b Clark	36
A.G.Prince	c Hayden b Lee	17	c Gilchrist b Clark	27
J.A.Rudolph	c Gilchrist b Kasprowicz	10	b Warne	41
†M.V.Boucher	c Gilchrist b Clark	16	c Langer b Kasprowicz	2
A.J.Hall	c Hayden b Lee	24	not out	34
N.Boje	lbw b Clark	31	c and b Clark	14
A.Nel	lbw b Lee	18	b Clark	4
M.Ntini	not out	17	c Kasprowicz b Warne	6
Extras	(LB 6, NB 15)	21	(W 3, NB 7)	10
Total		**205**		**197**

AUSTRALIA

J.L.Langer	lbw b Nel	16	b Ntini	34
M.L.Hayden	c Rudolph b Ntini	94	c Gibbs b Ntini	32
*R.T.Ponting	c Hall b Kallis	74	lbw b Ntini	1
D.R.Martyn	c Boucher b Kallis	22	not out	9
M.E.K.Hussey	c Boucher b Hall	6	not out	14
A.Symonds	c Nel b Boje	55		
†A.C.Gilchrist	c Smith b Kallis	12		
S.K.Warne	c De Villiers b Boje	7		
B.Lee	c Gibbs b Ntini	0		
M.S.Kasprowicz	not out	6		
S.R.Clark	c Gibbs b Nel	8		
Extras	(LB 7, W 1)	8	(LB 5)	5
Total		**308**	(3 wickets)	**95**

AUSTRALIA	O	M	R	W		O	M	R	W
Lee	14.5	2	37	3		17	5	47	2
Kasprowicz	13	0	44	2		12	0	39	1
Symonds	10	2	22	0					
Clark	17	3	55	5	(3)	16	7	34	4
Warne	9	0	41	0	(4)	18.5	1	77	3
SOUTH AFRICA									
Ntini	21	2	76	2	(2)	10	3	28	3
Nel	22.2	6	45	2	(1)	7	1	25	0
Hall	16	2	66	1		5	1	16	0
Boje	16	4	63	2		5.1	1	21	0
Kallis	12	0	51	3					

FALL OF WICKETS

	SA	A	SA	A
Wkt	*1st*	*1st*	*2nd*	*2nd*
1st	24	21	20	71
2nd	42	175	20	71
3rd	48	192	37	76
4th	61	214	75	–
5th	76	236	92	–
6th	104	272	108	–
7th	124	294	158	–
8th	148	294	179	–
9th	173	296	183	–
10th	205	308	197	–

Umpires: Alim Dar (*Pakistan*) (29) and B.R.Doctrove (*West Indies*) (6).
Referee: B.C.Broad (*England*) (18). **Test No. 1791/75 (SA307/A677)**

SOUTH AFRICA v AUSTRALIA (2nd Test)

At Kingsmead, Durban, 24, 25, 26, 27, 28 March 2006.
Toss: Australia. Result: **AUSTRALIA** won by 112 runs.
Debuts: None.

AUSTRALIA

J.L.Langer	c Boucher b Kallis	35	c Pollock b Boje	37
M.L.Hayden	c De Villiers b Ntini	0	c Boucher b Ntini	102
*R.T.Ponting	c Gibbs b Boje	103	c Boje b Pollock	116
D.R.Martyn	c Kallis b Ntini	57	not out	15
M.E.K.Hussey	lbw b Kallis	75		
B.Lee	c Boucher b Ntini	0		
A.Symonds	lbw b Nel	13		
†A.C.Gilchrist	c Boucher b Nel	2	(5) c Nel b Boje	24
S.K.Warne	c De Villiers b Pollock	36		
M.S.Kasprowicz	c De Villiers b Nel	7		
S.R.Clark	not out	13		
Extras	(B 9, LB 10, W 2, NB 7)	28	(LB 5, W 1, NB 7)	13
Total		**369**	(4 wickets declared)	**307**

SOUTH AFRICA

*G.C. Smith	c Langer b Lee	0	(2) c Langer b Warne	46
A.B.de Villiers	c Hayden b Clark	50	(1) st Gilchrist b Warne	40
H.H.Gibbs	b Kasprowicz	9	c Warne b Clark	17
J.H.Kallis	c and b Clark	114	lbw b Warne	7
A.G.Prince	c Symonds b Warne	33	c Hussey b Clark	7
J.A.Rudolph	c Hussey b Warne	13	c Langer b Warne	36
†M.V.Boucher	b Lee	19	not out	51
S.M. Pollock	c Gilchrist b Lee	1	b Lee	4
N.Boje	not out	6	c sub (M.J.Clarke) b Kasprowicz	48
A.Nel	c Hayden b Lee	5	c Hayden b Warne	14
M.Ntini	c Ponting b Lee	0	lbw b Warne	0
Extras	(LB 3, NB 14)	17	(B 5, LB 8, NB 14)	27
Total		**267**		**297**

SOUTH AFRICA	O	M	R	W		O	M	R	W
Pollock	32	11	73	1		19	4	55	1
Ntini	24	4	81	3		15	2	62	1
Nel	31	8	83	3	(4)	14	3	58	0
Kallis	21.1	8	52	2	(5)	8	0	40	0
Boje	19	1	61	1	(3)	26.4	4	87	2
AUSTRALIA									
Lee	19.4	5	69	5		22	6	65	1
Kasprowicz	14	0	60	1	(5)	12	2	51	1
Warne	25	2	80	2	(4)	35.5	9	86	6
Symonds	11	3	16	0	(3)	8	0	32	0
Hussey	1	0	2	0	(6)	1	0	4	0
Clark	18	4	37	2	(2)	21	6	46	2

FALL OF WICKETS

	A	SA	A	SA
Wkt	*1st*	*1st*	*2nd*	*2nd*
1st	0	0	49	91
2nd	97	10	250	98
3rd	198	144	278	122
4th	218	200	307	122
5th	219	226	–	146
6th	253	255	–	170
7th	259	256	–	181
8th	315	257	–	253
9th	327	267	–	292
10th	369	267	–	297

Umpires: S.A. Bucknor (*West Indies*) (110) and B.R.Doctrove (*West Indies*) (7).
Referee: B.C.Broad (*England*) (19). **Test No. 1792/76 (SA308/A678)**

SOUTH AFRICA v AUSTRALIA (3rd Test)

At The Wanderers, Johannesburg, on 31 March, 1, 2, 3, 4 April 2006.
Toss: South Africa. Result: **AUSTRALIA** won by two wickets.
Debuts: None.

SOUTH AFRICA

A.B.de Villiers	c Martyn b Clark	12		b Clark	4
H.H.Gibbs	b Kasprowicz	16		c Martyn b Warne	53
H.H.Dippenaar	c Gilchrist b Clark	32		c Hayden b Clark	20
*J.H.Kallis	b Lee	37		lbw b Clark	27
A.G.Prince	c Langer b Lee	93		c Symonds b Warne	9
J.A.Rudolph	c Hayden b Warne	25	(7)	c Gilchrist b Clark	0
†M.V.Boucher	lbw b Symonds	24	(8)	c Gilchrist b Lee	63
S.M.Pollock	c Ponting b Clark	8	(6)	c Gilchrist b Lee	44
N.Boje	c Langer b Kasprowicz	43		c Symonds b Warne	4
A.Nel	c Martyn b Lee	0		not out	18
M.Ntini	not out	0		b Lee	0
Extras	(LB 4, NB 9)	13		(B 6, LB 4, W 1, NB 5)	16
Total		**303**			**258**

AUSTRALIA

J.L.Langer	retired hurt	0			
M.L.Hayden	c Gibbs b Ntini	3	(1)	c De Villiers b Ntini	0
*R.T.Ponting	c De Villiers b Ntini	34		c Boucher b Kallis	20
D.R.Martyn	c Nel b Ntini	21		lbw b Pollock	101
M.E.K.Hussey	lbw b Boje	73	(2)	lbw b Boje	89
A.Symonds	lbw b Ntini	4	(5)	c Boucher b Kallis	29
†A.C.Gilchrist	c Rudolph b Nel	12	(6)	c Boucher b Ntini	0
S.K.Warne	c Pollock b Ntini	36	(7)	c Boucher b Ntini	3
B.Lee	c Boje b Ntini	64	(8)	not out	24
M.S.Kasprowicz	c Gibbs b Pollock	2		not out	7
S.R.Clark	not out	0	(9)	c Boucher b Ntini	10
Extras	(B 5, LB 14, W 2)	21		(B 1, LB 9, NB 1)	11
Total		**270**		(8 wickets)	**294**

AUSTRALIA	O	M	R	W		O	M	R	W
Lee	24	8	57	3		18.3	3	57	3
Clark	28	8	81	3		18	4	64	4
Kasprowicz	24.2	4	86	2		2	0	12	0
Warne	13	2	49	1	(6)	26	5	90	3
Symonds	8	2	26	1	(4)	5	0	18	0
Ponting					(5)	2	1	7	0
SOUTH AFRICA									
Ntini	18.5	2	100	6		26	4	78	4
Nel	15	2	42	1		2	1	4	0
Pollock	15	2	56	1		25.4	3	81	1
Kallis	10	2	43	0		18	6	44	2
Boje	4	1	10	1		19	5	65	1
De Villiers						1	0	12	0

FALL OF WICKETS

	SA	A	SA	A
Wkt	*1st*	*1st*	*2nd*	*2nd*
1st	26	12	9	0
2nd	38	68	55	33
3rd	97	73	100	198
4th	106	89	120	228
5th	161	106	130	229
6th	233	174	140	237
7th	251	242	186	258
8th	285	260	194	275
9th	303	270	258	–
10th	303	–	258	–

Umpires: S.A. Bucknor (*West Indies*) (111) and A.L Hill (*New Zealand*) (4).
Referee: B.C.Broad (*England*) (20).
Langer retired hurt at 0-0.

Test No. 1793/77 (SA309/A679)

SOUTH AFRICA v AUSTRALIA 2005-06

SOUTH AFRICA – BATTING AND FIELDING

	M	*I*	*NO*	*HS*	*Runs*	*Avge*	*100*	*50*	*Ct/St*
J.H.Kallis	3	6	–	114	227	37.83	1	–	1
M.V.Boucher	3	6	1	63	175	35.00	–	2	11
A.G.Prince	3	6	–	93	186	31.00	–	1	–
N.Boje	3	6	1	48	146	29.20	–	–	2
A.B.de Villiers	3	6	–	50	127	21.16	–	1	6
J.A.Rudolph	3	6	–	41	125	20.83	–	–	2
H.H.Gibbs	3	6	–	53	113	18.83	–	1	6
G.C.Smith	2	4	–	40	75	18.75	–	–	1
S.M.Pollock	2	4	–	44	57	14.25	–	–	2
A.Nel	3	6	1	18*	59	11.80	–	–	3
M.Ntini	3	6	2	17*	23	5.75	–	–	–

Played in one Test: H.H.Dippenaar 32, 20; A.J.Hall 24, 34* (1 ct).

SOUTH AFRICA – BOWLING

	O	*M*	*R*	*W*	*Avge*	*Best*	*5wI*	*10wM*
M.Ntini	114.5	17	425	19	22.36	6-100	1	1
J.H.Kallis	69.1	16	230	7	32.85	3- 51	–	–
A.Nel	91.2	21	257	6	42.83	3- 83	–	–
N.Boje	89.5	16	307	7	43.85	2- 63	–	–
S.M.Pollock	91.4	20	265	4	66.25	1- 55	–	–
A.J.Hall	21.0	3	82	1	82.00	1- 66	–	–

Also bowled: A.B.de Villiers 1-0-12-0.

AUSTRALIA – BATTING AND FIELDING

	M	*I*	*NO*	*HS*	*Runs*	*Avge*	*100*	*50*	*Ct/St*
M.E.K.Hussey	3	5	1	89	257	64.25	–	3	2
R.T.Ponting	3	6	–	116	348	58.00	2	1	2
D.R.Martyn	3	6	2	101	225	56.25	1	1	3
M.L.Hayden	3	6	–	102	231	38.50	1	1	8
J.L.Langer	3	5	1	37	122	30.50	–	–	6
B.Lee	3	4	1	64	88	29.33	–	1	–
A.Symonds	3	4	–	55	101	25.25	–	1	3
S.K.Warne	3	4	–	36	82	20.50	–	–	1
S.R.Clark	3	4	2	13*	31	15.50	–	–	2
M.S.Kasprowicz	3	4	2	7*	22	11.00	–	–	1
A.C.Gilchrist	3	5	–	24	50	10.00	–	–	11/1

AUSTRALIA – BOWLING

	O	*M*	*R*	*W*	*Avge*	*Best*	*5wI*	*10wM*
S.R.Clark	118.0	32	317	20	15.85	5-55	1	–
B.Lee	116.0	29	332	17	19.52	5-69	1	–
S.K.Warne	127.4	19	423	15	28.20	6-86	1	–
M.S.Kasprowicz	77.2	6	292	7	41.71	2-44	–	–
A.Symonds	42.0	7	114	1	114.00	1-26	–	–

Also bowled: M.E.K.Hussey 2-0-6-0, R.T.Ponting 2-1-7-0.

SRI LANKA v PAKISTAN (1st Test)

At Sinhalese Sports Club, Colombo, on 26 (*no play*), 27, 28, 29, 30 March 2006.
Toss: Pakistan. Result: **MATCH DRAWN.**
Debuts: None.

SRI LANKA

W.U.Tharanga	lbw b Asif	0	c Farhat b Kaneria	72
S.T.Jayasuriya	b Gul	6	c Akmal b Asif	13
†K.C.Sangakkara	b Asif	8	c Inzamam b Shoaib	185
*D.P.M.D.Jayawardena	c Akmal b Gul	1	c Razzak b Asif	82
T.T.Samaraweera	b Asif	4	c Farhat b Afridi	64
T.M.Dilshan	c Younis b Kaneria	69	not out	8
M.F.Maharoof	c Younis b Asif	46	not out	5
C.M.Bandara	b Kaneria	16		
C.R.D.Fernando	c Inzamam b Kaneria	16		
S.L.Malinga	c Inzamam b Afridi	8		
M.Muralitharan	not out	0		
Extras	(B 4, LB 6, W 1)	11	(B 10, LB 6, NB 3)	19
Total		**185**	(5 wickets declared)	**448**

PAKISTAN

Shoaib Malik	c Tharanga b Maharoof	13	not out	148
Imran Farhat	c Bandara b Malinga	69	c Jayawardena b Muralitharan	34
Younis Khan	c Sangakkara b Maharoof	0	b Muralitharan	8
Faisal Iqbal	c Maharoof b Malinga	2	lbw b Maharoof	60
*Inzamam-ul-Haq	c Sangakkara b Maharoof	31	c Dilshan b Muralitharan	48
Abdul Razzak	b Maharoof	8	not out	20
Shahid Afridi	b Muralitharan	14		
†Kamran Akmal	c Tharanga b Muralitharan	27		
Umar Gul	lbw b Muralitharan	2		
Mohammad Asif	b Malinga	0		
Danish Kaneria	not out	0		
Extras	(B 1, W 1, NB 8)	10	(B 6, LB 7, W 1, NB 5)	19
Total		**176**	(4 wickets)	**337**

PAKISTAN	O	M	R	W		O	M	R	W
Mohammad Asif	16	5	41	4		23	4	71	2
Umar Gul	12	2	41	2		20	1	73	0
Abdul Razzak	10	1	43	0	(6)	12	1	43	0
Danish Kaneria	17.5	3	44	3	(3)	36	5	138	1
Shahid Afridi	2	0	6	1		21	0	57	1
Shoaib Malik					(4)	15	2	48	1
Imran Farhat					(7)	1	0	2	0
SRI LANKA									
Malinga	12	3	30	3		13	3	44	0
Maharoof	15	2	52	4		23	8	70	1
Fernando	3	0	20	0	(4)	15	3	40	0
Bandara	7	1	32	0	(5)	14	4	35	0
Muralitharan	17.4	4	41	3	(3)	42	13	94	3
Jayasuriya					(6)	13	3	37	0
Dilshan						1	0	4	0

FALL OF WICKETS

	SL	P	SL	P
Wkt	*1st*	*1st*	*2nd*	*2nd*
1st	0	25	53	59
2nd	10	25	127	71
3rd	18	28	285	186
4th	26	122	429	267
5th	32	127	438	–
6th	143	138	–	–
7th	149	154	–	–
8th	162	160	–	–
9th	177	172	–	–
10th	185	176	–	–

Umpires: S.J.Davis (*Australia*) (8) and R.E.Koertzen (*South Africa*) (72).
Referee: A.G.Hurst (*Australia*) (7). **Test No. 1794/31 (SL159/P319)**

SRI LANKA v PAKISTAN (2nd Test)

At Asgiriya Stadium, Kandy on 3, 4, 5 April 2006.
Toss: Pakistan. Result: **PAKISTAN** won by eight wickets.
Debuts: Pakistan – Iftikhar Anjum

SRI LANKA

W.U.Tharanga	c Younis b Asif	10		b Asif	12
S.T.Jayasuriya	b Asif	14		absent hurt	–
†K.C.Sangakkara	c Iqbal b Kaneria	79	(2)	b Asif	16
*D.P.M.D.Jayawardena	c Farhat b Asif	4	(3)	b Razzak	15
T.T.Samaraweera	b Asif	65	(4)	b Asif	4
T.M.Dilshan	c Akmal b Kaneria	22	(5)	c Akmal b Asif	11
M.F.Maharoof	c Younis b Kaneria	7	(6)	lbw b Asif	1
C.M.Bandara	c Akmal b Asif	43	(7)	c Akmal b Razzak	4
M.D.N.Kulasekara	b Asif	13	(8)	c Gul b Razzak	6
S.L.Malinga	c Razzak b Kaneria	9	(9)	not out	0
M.Muralitharan	not out	1	(10)	c Gul b Razzak	0
Extras	(LB 4, W 1, NB 2, Pen 5)	12		(LB 3, W 1)	4
Total		**279**			**73**

PAKISTAN

Imran Farhat	c Jayasuriya b Kulasekara	23	c Jayawardena b Kulasekara	65
†Kamran Akmal	c Jayawardena b Muralitharan	33	c Sangakkara b Malinga	24
Younis Khan	c Samaraweera b Maharoof	35	not out	73
M.Yousuf Youhana	b Muralitharan	17	not out	14
*Inzamam-ul-Haq	run out	15		
Faisal Iqbal	lbw b Muralitharan	5		
Abdul Razzak	b Muralitharan	4		
Iftikhar Anjum	not out	9		
Umar Gul	c Sangakkara b Kulasekara	4		
Mohammad Asif	run out	0		
Danish Kaneria	c Sangakkara b Muralitharan	4		
Extras	(B 4, LB 9, W 1, NB 7)	21	(LB 3, NB 4)	7
Total		**170**	(2 wickets)	**183**

PAKISTAN	O	M	R	W		O	M	R	W
Mohammad Asif	23	7	44	6		12	6	27	5
Umar Gul	23	3	83	0	(3)	3	0	15	0
Iftikhar Anjum	11	1	54	0	(2)	3	0	8	0
Danish Kaneria	23.2	6	53	4					
Abdul Razzak	11	1	36	0	(4)	6.5	1	20	4
SRI LANKA									
Malinga	6	2	19	0	(3)	6.2	0	33	1
Maharoof	14	2	54	1	(1)	10	0	52	0
Kulasekara	16	3	45	2	(2)	12	3	34	1
Muralitharan	16.4	4	39	5		13	3	46	0
Bandara						2	0	15	0

FALL OF WICKETS

	SL	P	SL	P
Wkt	*1st*	*1st*	*2nd*	*2nd*
1st	18	57	22	38
2nd	27	71	40	152
3rd	61	121	46	–
4th	142	125	56	–
5th	178	140	57	–
6th	193	149	65	–
7th	238	162	72	–
8th	256	166	73	–
9th	271	166	73	–
10th	279	170	–	–

Umpires: S.J.Davis (*Australia*) (9) and D.J.Harper (*Australia*) (58).
Referee: A.G.Hurst (*Australia*) (8). **Test No. 1795/32 (SL160/P320)**

BANGLADESH v AUSTRALIA (1st Test)

At Narayanganj Osmani Stadium, Fatullah, on 9, 10, 11, 12, 13 April 2006.
Toss: Bangladesh. Result: **AUSTRALIA** won by three wickets.
Debuts: None.

BANGLADESH				
Javed Omar	lbw b Gillespie	27	c Gilchrist b Gillespie	18
Shahriar Nafis	b MacGill	138	b Lee	33
*Habibul Bashar	c Lee b MacGill	76	run out	7
Rajin Saleh	c sub (A.Symonds) b MacGill	67	c Hayden b Gillespie	33
Mohammad Ashraful	lbw b Gillespie	29	lbw b Clark	4
Aftab Ahmed	c Hayden b MacGill	29	lbw b MacGill	17
†Khaled Masud	st Gilchrist b MacGill	17	b Gillespie	0
Mohammad Rafique	b MacGill	6	lbw b Warne	14
Mashrafe Mortaza	lbw b MacGill	6	b Warne	0
Shahadat Hossain	not out	3	not out	1
Enamul Haque II	c Hayden b MacGill	0	lbw b Warne	0
Extras	(LB 16, W 2, NB 11)	29	(B10, LB 7, NB 4)	21
Total		**427**		**148**

AUSTRALIA				
M.L.Hayden	lbw b Mortaza	6	run out	72
M.E.K. Hussey	b Rafique	23	b Haque	37
*R.T.Ponting	lbw b Hossain	21	not out	118
D.R.Martyn	b Rafique	4	b Rafique	7
M.J.Clarke	b Haque	19	c Masud b Rafique	9
†A.C.Gilchrist	c Hossain b Rafique	144	b Rafique	12
S.K.Warne	c Masud b Haque	6	lbw b Rafique	5
B.Lee	lbw b Mortaza	15	c Masud b Mortaza	29
J.N.Gillespie	b Rafique	26	not out	4
S.R.Clark	lbw b Rafique	0		
S.C.G.MacGill	not out	0		
Extras	(LB 4, NB 1)	5	(B 4, LB 7, W 1, NB 2)	14
Total		**269**	(7 wickets)	**307**

AUSTRALIA	O	M	R	W		O	M	R	W
Lee	19	5	68	0		8	0	47	1
Clark	25	4	69	0	(4)	4	2	8	1
Gillespie	23	7	47	2	(2)	11	4	18	3
Warne	20	1	112	0	(5)	13	4	28	3
MacGill	33.3	2	108	8	(3)	13	4	30	1
Clarke	3	0	7	0		1	1	0	0
BANGLADESH									
Mashrafe Mortaza	22	3	56	2		22	7	51	1
Shahadat Hossain	14	2	48	1		20	5	67	0
Mohammad Rafique	32.2	9	62	5		38	6	98	4
Enamul Haque II	25	4	83	2		27	5	80	1
Mohammad Ashraful	1	0	11	0					
Rajin Saleh	1	0	5	0					

FALL OF WICKETS	B	A	B	A
Wkt	*1st*	*1st*	*2nd*	*2nd*
1st	51	6	48	64
2nd	238	43	58	173
3rd	265	50	66	183
4th	295	61	77	205
5th	351	79	124	225
6th	398	93	128	231
7th	416	156	147	277
8th	417	229	147	–
9th	424	268	147	–
10th	427	269	148	–

Umpires: Alim Dar (*Pakistan*) (30) and Nadeem Ghauri (*Pakistan*) (5).
Referee: J.J.Crowe (*New Zealand*) (10). **Test No. 1796/3 (B43/A680)**

BANGLADESH v AUSTRALIA (2nd Test)

At Chittagong Divisional Stadium on 16, 17, 18, 19, 20 April 2006.
Toss: Bangladesh. Result: **AUSTRALIA** won by an innings and 80 runs.
Debuts: Australia – D.J.Cullen; Bangladesh – Abdur Razzak.

BANGLADESH

Javed Omar	lbw b Gillespie	2	lbw b Lee	19
Shahriar Nafis	c Lee b Gillespie	0	c Gilchrist b Warne	79
*Habibul Bashar	c Jacques b Gillespie	9	c Hayden b Warne	49
Rajin Saleh	b MacGill	71	c Ponting b Warne	5
Mohammad Ashraful	c Hayden b Warne	6	b Warne	29
Aftab Ahmed	c Gilchrist b Warne	18	c Gilchrist b MacGill	18
†Khaled Masud	not out	34	lbw b MacGill	11
Mohammad Rafique	c Hayden b MacGill	19	c Warne b MacGill	65
Mashrafe Mortaza	c Gilchrist b Cullen	4	c Gillespie b Warne	1
Abdur Razzak	c Lee b MacGill	15	c Ponting b MacGill	0
Shahadat Hossain	c Gillespie b Warne	0	not out	3
Extras	(LB 10, W 3, NB 6)	19	(B7, LB 11, W 2, NB 5)	25
Total		**197**		**304**

AUSTRALIA

M.L.Hayden	c sub (Alok Kapali) b Rafique	29
P.A.Jaques	c Nafis b Rafique	66
J.N.Gillespie	not out	201
*R.T.Ponting	run out	52
M.E.K.Hussey	c Hossain b Aftab	182
M.J.Clarke	not out	23
S.K.Warne		
B.Lee		
†A.C.Gilchrist		
D.J.Cullen		
S.C.G.MacGill		
Extras	(B 10, LB 10, W 5, NB 3)	28
Total	(4 wickets declared)	**581**

AUSTRALIA	O	M	R	W	O	M	R	W
Lee	9	2	36	0	11	3	35	1
Gillespie	5	2	11	3	4	0	14	0
Warne	18.2	3	47	3	36	4	113	5
MacGill	22	4	68	3	22.2	3	95	4
Cullen	7	0	25	1	7	0	29	0
BANGLADESH								
Mashrafe Mortaza	26	3	114	0				
Shahadat Hossain	33	3	143	0				
Mohammad Rafique	48.3	11	145	2				
Abdur Razzak	30	5	99	0				
Rajin Saleh	8	0	32	0				
Aftab Ahmed	7	1	28	1				

FALL OF WICKETS

	B	A	B
Wkt	*1st*	*1st*	*2nd*
1st	0	67	25
2nd	11	120	127
3rd	17	210	137
4th	41	530	187
5th	102	–	201
6th	130	–	229
7th	152	–	230
8th	157	–	233
9th	193	–	235
10th	197	–	304

Umpires: Alim Dar (*Pakistan*) (31) and I.L.Howell (*South Africa*) (6).
Referee: J.J.Crowe (*New Zealand*) (11). **Test No. 1797/4 (B44/A681)**

SOUTH AFRICA v NEW ZEALAND (1st Test)

At Centurion Park, (Verwoerdburg), Pretoria, on 15, 16, 17, 18, 19 April 2006.
Toss: South Africa . Result: **SOUTH AFRICA** won by 128 runs.
Debuts: None.

SOUTH AFRICA					
*G.C.Smith	lbw b Franklin	45		lbw b Martin	7
H.H.Gibbs	b Mills	6		c Styris b Franklin	2
H.H.Dippenaar	c Fulton b Mills	52		c Fleming b Oram	16
J.H.Kallis	b Franklin	38		c Vettori b Styris	62
A.G.Prince	c Styris b Mills	9		c McCullum b Franklin	11
A.B.de Villiers	b Franklin	27		c Franklin b Oram	97
†M.V.Boucher	c Fleming b Martin	18		b Mills	21
S.M.Pollock	c Styris b Mills	24		lbw b Vettori	10
N.Boje	lbw b Franklin	23		c McCullum b Astle	31
D.W.Steyn	c Mills b Martin	13		not out	7
M.Ntini	not out	1		lbw b Vettori	16
Extras	(B 6, LB 4, W 3, NB 7)	20		(B 12, LB 2, NB 5)	19
Total		**276**			**299**

NEW ZEALAND					
H.J.H.Marshall	b Ntini	6		c Boucher b Ntini	25
P.G.Fulton	c Boucher b Pollock	14		c Boucher b Ntini	4
*S.P.Fleming	c and b Ntini	0	(4)	c Kallis b Steyn	6
S.B.Styris	c Gibbs b Ntini	17	(5)	c Boucher b Steyn	2
N.J.Astle	c Boucher b Steyn	4	(6)	c De Villiers b Ntini	2
J.D.P.Oram	c Pollock b Steyn	133	(7)	b Ntini	2
†B.B.McCullum	c Boje b Kallis	31	(8)	c Dippenaar b Steyn	33
D.L.Vettori	c Prince b Ntini	81	(9)	c Boucher b Steyn	38
J.E.C.Franklin	c Boucher b Ntini	8	(10)	not out	0
K.D.Mills	c Boje b Pollock	12	(3)	c Dippenaar b Ntini	0
C.S.Martin	not out	1		b Steyn	0
Extras	(LB 12, NB 8)	20		(LB 2, NB 6)	8
Total		**327**			**120**

NEW ZEALAND	O	M	R	W		O	M	R	W
Mills	18	7	43	4	(3)	21	5	57	1
Franklin	18	3	75	4	(1)	14	2	60	2
Martin	22.4	4	66	2	(2)	24	6	64	1
Oram	14	7	27	0		17	3	44	2
Vettori	18	2	44	0		15.1	0	42	2
Astle	5	2	11	0		5	1	15	1
Styris						2	0	3	1
SOUTH AFRICA									
Ntini	19	2	94	5		14	3	51	5
Steyn	18.4	1	95	2		17	4	47	5
Pollock	15	4	45	2		5	1	20	0
Kallis	9	1	41	1					
Boje	7	0	29	0					
Smith	3	1	11	0					

FALL OF WICKETS

	SA	NZ	SA	NZ
Wkt	*1st*	*1st*	*2nd*	*2nd*
1st	16	8	8	5
2nd	95	12	19	5
3rd	119	32	42	17
4th	130	38	73	23
5th	177	45	140	26
6th	197	89	194	28
7th	229	272	205	73
8th	233	280	270	119
9th	274	322	276	119
10th	276	327	299	120

Umpires: M.R.Benson (*England*) (9) and D.J.Harper (*Australia*) (59).
Referee: R.S.Madugalle (*Sri Lanka*) (86). **Test No. 1798/31 (SA310/NZ328)**

SOUTH AFRICA v NEW ZEALAND (2nd Test)

At Newlands, Cape Town, on 27, 28, 29, 30 April, 1 May 2006.
Toss: South Africa. Result: **MATCH DRAWN.**
Debuts: New Zealand – J.S.Patel.

NEW ZEALAND

M.H.W.Papps	b Nel	22		c Prince b Steyn	20
P.G.Fulton	c Boucher b Steyn	36		c Kallis b Ntini	11
*S.P.Fleming	b Prince	262			
S.B.Styris	c Dippenaar b Ntini	11	(3)	not out	54
N.J.Astle	lbw b Ntini	50	(4)	c Smith b Kallis	14
J.D.P.Oram	run out	13	(5)	not out	8
†B.B.McCullum	lbw b Ntini	5			
D.L.Vettori	c Nel b Ntini	11			
J.E.C.Franklin	not out	122			
J.S.Patel	not out	27			
C.S.Martin					
Extras	(B 3, LB 15, W 1, NB 15)	34		(B 1, LB 9, NB 4)	14
Total	(8 wickets declared)	**593**		(3 wickets)	**121**

SOUTH AFRICA

*G.C.Smith	c and b Patel	25
H.H.Dippenaar	b Patel	47
H.M.Amla	lbw b Vettori	149
J.H.Kallis	c Martin b Oram	71
A.G.Prince	not out	108
A.B.de Villiers	c Papps b Patel	13
†M.V.Boucher	c Fleming b Franklin	33
N.Boje	lbw b Franklin	0
A.Nel	lbw b Franklin	12
D.W.Steyn	st McCullum b Vettori	13
M.Ntini	run out	11
Extras	(B 15, LB 10, NB 5)	30
Total		**512**

SOUTH AFRICA	O	M	R	W		O	M	R	W
Ntini	43	5	162	4	(2)	8	2	25	1
Steyn	31	4	114	1	(1)	9	3	26	1
Nel	27	3	98	1		10	2	41	0
Kallis	15	4	45	0		5	3	5	1
Boje	29	4	89	0		5	1	14	0
Smith	17	2	61	0					
Amla	1	0	4	0					
Prince	2	0	2	1					
NEW ZEALAND									
Martin	20	7	62	0					
Franklin	33	5	95	3					
Vettori	63	10	147	2					
Patel	42	8	117	3					
Styris	10	2	33	0					
Oram	18	10	24	1					
Astle	2	0	9	0					

FALL OF WICKETS

	NZ	SA	NZ
Wkt	*1st*	*1st*	*2nd*
1st	50	36	34
2nd	62	108	41
3rd	82	252	81
4th	188	344	–
5th	237	361	–
6th	259	435	–
7th	279	435	–
8th	535	462	–
9th	–	495	–
10th	–	512	–

Umpires: M.R.Benson (*England*) (10) and E.A.R.de Silva (*Sri Lanka*) (31).
Referee: R.S.Madugalle (*Sri Lanka*) (87). **Test No. 1799/32 (SA311/NZ329)**

SOUTH AFRICA v NEW ZEALAND (3rd Test)

At The Wanderers, Johannesburg, on 5, 6, 7 May 2006.
Toss: South Africa. Result: **SOUTH AFRICA** won by four wickets.
Debuts: None.

NEW ZEALAND

M.H.W.Papps	b Ntini	0	c Hall b Kallis	15
J.M.How	c De Villiers b Steyn	0	lbw b Steyn	4
*S.P.Fleming	c Boucher b Ntini	46	c De Villiers b Kallis	37
S.B.Styris	c De Villiers b Ntini	0	c and b Steyn	42
N.J.Astle	c Kallis b Steyn	20	c Boucher b Steyn	45
J.D.P.Oram	lbw b Pollock	18	c Dippenaar b Steyn	27
†B.B.McCullum	c and b Ntini	0	c Boucher b Pollock	5
D.L.Vettori	lbw b Steyn	2	c De Villiers b Hall	60
J.E.C.Franklin	c Boucher b Hall	19	b Pollock	19
K.D.Mills	not out	0	not out	0
C.S.Martin	c Smith b Ntini	1	c Amla b Hall	0
Extras	(LB 9, W 1, NB 3)	13	(B 5, LB 17, W 3, NB 4)	29
Total		**119**		**283**

SOUTH AFRICA

*G.C.Smith	c McCullum b Franklin	63	c McCullum b Franklin	68
H.H.Dippenaar	b Martin	0	c McCullum b Martin	37
H.M.Amla	c Papps b Styris	56	b Mills	28
J.H.Kallis	b Martin	9	c How b Mills	13
A.G.Prince	c McCullum b Martin	4	not out	43
A.B.de Villiers	c Styris b Franklin	2	b Franklin	5
†M.V.Boucher	lbw b Franklin	0	b Franklin	6
S.M.Pollock	not out	32	not out	6
A.J.Hall	lbw b Martin	5		
D.W.Steyn	b Martin	2		
M.Ntini	c McCullum b Mills	8		
Extras	(NB 5)	5	(B 4, LB 5, W 2, NB 3)	14
Total		**186**	(6 wickets)	**220**

SOUTH AFRICA	O	M	R	W		O	M	R	W
Ntini	16	7	35	3	(2)	17	4	44	0
Steyn	12	3	43	3	(1)	22	3	91	4
Hall	9	2	21	1	(4)	12.5	1	50	2
Pollock	7	2	11	1	(5)	13	3	36	2
Kallis					(3)	14	1	40	2
NEW ZEALAND									
Martin	15	2	37	5		17	1	64	1
Franklin	13	2	87	3		13.3	0	67	3
Oram	4	0	20	0	(4)	2	0	8	0
Mills	8	0	30	1	(3)	11	3	49	2
Astle	2	0	11	0					
Styris	2	1	1	1	(5)	3	0	12	0
Vettori					(6)	1	0	11	0

FALL OF WICKETS

	NZ	SA	NZ	SA
Wkt	*1st*	*1st*	*2nd*	*2nd*
1st	0	1	9	69
2nd	0	99	40	130
3rd	2	131	82	156
4th	57	131	158	167
5th	78	139	177	180
6th	78	139	190	202
7th	82	139	239	–
8th	118	145	283	–
9th	118	161	283	–
10th	119	186	283	–

Umpires: E.A.R.de Silva (*Sri Lanka*) (32) and D.B.Hair (*Australia*) (72).
Referee: R.S.Madugalle (*Sri Lanka*) (88). **Test No. 1800/33 (SA312/NZ330)**

SOUTH AFRICA v NEW ZEALAND 2006-07

SOUTH AFRICA – BATTING AND FIELDING

	M	I	NO	HS	Runs	Avge	100	50	Ct/St
H.M.Amla	2	3	–	149	233	77.66	1	1	1
A.G.Prince	3	5	2	108*	175	58.33	1	–	2
G.C.Smith	3	5	–	68	208	41.60	–	2	2
J.H.Kallis	3	5	–	71	193	38.60	–	2	3
S.M.Pollock	2	4	2	32*	72	36.00	–	–	1
H.H.Dippenaar	3	5	–	52	152	30.40	–	1	4
A.B.de Villiers	3	5	–	97	144	28.80	–	1	5
N.Boje	2	3	–	31	54	18.00	–	–	2
M.V.Boucher	3	5	–	33	78	15.60	–	–	12
M.Ntini	3	4	1	16	36	12.00	–	–	2
D.W.Steyn	3	4	1	13	35	11.66	–	–	1

Played in one Test: A.J.Hall 5 (1 ct); H.H.Gibbs 6, 2 (1 ct); A.Nel 12 (1 ct).

SOUTH AFRICA – BOWLING

	O	M	R	W	Avge	Best	5wI	10wM
M.Ntini	117	23	411	20	20.55	5-35	3	1
S.M.Pollock	40	10	112	5	22.40	2-36	–	–
A.J.Hall	21.5	3	71	3	23.66	2-50	–	–
D.W.Steyn	109.4	18	416	16	26.00	5-47	1	–
J.H.Kallis	43	9	131	4	32.75	2-40	–	–

Also bowled: H.M.Amla 1-0-4-0; N.Boje 41-5-132-0; A.Nel 37-5-139-1; A.G.Prince 2-0-2-1; G.C.Smith 20-3-72-0.

NEW ZEALAND – BATTING AND FIELDING

	M	I	NO	HS	Runs	Avge	100	50	Ct/St
S.P.Fleming	3	5	–	262	351	70.20	1	–	3
J.E.C.Franklin	3	5	2	122*	168	56.00	1	–	1
J.D.P.Oram	3	6	1	133	201	40.20	1	–	–
D.L.Vettori	3	5	–	81	192	38.40	–	2	1
S.B.Styris	3	6	1	54*	126	25.20	–	1	4
N.J.Astle	3	6	–	50	135	22.50	–	1	–
P.G.Fulton	2	4	–	36	65	16.25	–	–	1
B.B.McCullum	3	5	–	33	74	14.80	–	–	7/1
M.H.W.Papps	2	4	–	22	57	14.25	–	–	2
K.D.Mills	2	4	2	12	12	6.00	–	–	1
C.S.Martin	3	4	1	1*	2	0.66	–	–	1

Played in one Test: J.M.How 0, 4 (1 ct); H.J.H.Marshall 6, 25; J.S.Patel 27* (1 ct).

NEW ZEALAND – BOWLING

	O	M	R	W	Avge	Best	5wI	10wM
K.D.Mills	58	15	179	8	22.37	4- 43	–	–
J.E.C.Franklin	91.3	12	384	15	25.60	4- 75	–	–
C.S.Martin	98.4	20	293	9	32.55	5- 37	1	–
J.S.Patel	42	8	117	3	39.00	3-117	–	–
J.D.P.Oram	55	20	123	3	41.00	2- 44	–	–
D.L.Vettori	97.1	12	244	4	61.00	2- 42	–	–

Also bowled: N.J.Astle 14-3-46-1; S.B.Styris 17-3-49-2.

ENGLAND v SRI LANKA (1st Test)

At Lord's, London, 11, 12, 13, 14, 15 May 2006.
Toss: England. Result: **MATCH DRAWN.**
Debuts: England – S.I.Mahmood; Sri Lanka – C.K.Kapugedara.

ENGLAND

M.E.Trescothick	c Jayawardena b Muralitharan	106
A.J.Strauss	c Jayawardena b Muralitharan	48
A.N.Cook	c Sangakkara b Maharoof	89
K.P.Pietersen	lbw b Vaas	158
M.J.Hoggard	b Vaas	7
P.D.Collingwood	b Muralitharan	57
*A.Flintoff	not out	33
†G.O.Jones	not out	11
L.E.Plunkett		
S.I.Mahmood		
M.S.Panesar		
Extras	(B 16, LB 7, W 4, NB 15)	42
Total	(6 wickets declared)	**551**

SRI LANKA

J.Mubarak	lbw b Hoggard	0		b Hoggard	6
W.U.Tharanga	lbw b Hoggard	10		c Jones b Panesar	52
†K.C.Sangakkara	c Trescothick b Mahmood	21		c Jones b Panesar	65
*D.P.M.D.Jayawardena	c Jones b Flintoff	61		c Jones b Flintoff	119
T.T.Samaraweera	lbw b Mahmood	0	(6)	c Jones b Mahmood	6
T.M.Dilshan	run out	0	(7)	c Trescothick b Plunkett	69
C.K.Kapugedara	lbw b Mahmood	0	(8)	c Jones b Flintoff	10
M.F.Maharoof	c and b Hoggard	22	(5)	c Pietersen b Mahmood	59
W.P.U.C.J.Vaas	c Trescothick b Hoggard	31		not out	50
M.D.N.Kulasekara	c Strauss b Flintoff	29		c Pietersen b Hoggard	64
M.Muralitharan	not out	0		not out	1
Extras	(LB 8, NB 10)	18		(B 9, LB 19, W 3, NB 5)	36
Total		**192**		(9 wickets)	**537**

SRI LANKA	O	M	R	W		O	M	R	W
Vaas	36	2	124	2					
Maharoof	28	4	125	1					
Kulasekara	25	3	89	0					
Muralitharan	48	10	158	3					
Dilshan	6	0	32	0					
ENGLAND									
Hoggard	14	4	27	4		46	11	110	2
Flintoff	17.3	2	55	2		51	11	131	2
Plunkett	11	0	52	0	(4)	31	10	85	1
Mahmood	13	2	50	3	(3)	35	5	118	2
Collingwood						9	2	16	0
Panesar						27	10	49	2

FALL OF WICKETS

	E	SL	SL
Wkt	*1st*	*1st*	*2nd*
1st	86	0	10
2nd	213	21	119
3rd	312	81	178
4th	329	81	291
5th	502	85	303
6th	502	85	371
7th	–	129	405
8th	–	131	421
9th	–	192	526
10th	–	192	–

Umpires: Alim Dar (*Pakistan*) (32) and R.E.Koertzen (*South Africa*) (73).
Referee: A.G.Hurst (*Australia*) (9). **Test No. 1801/16 (E846/SL161)**

ENGLAND v SRI LANKA (2nd Test)

At Edgbaston, Birmingham, on 25, 26, 27, 28 May 2006.
Toss: Sri Lanka. Result: **ENGLAND** won by six wickets.
Debuts: None.

SRI LANKA

M.G. Vandort	c Collingwood b Plunkett	9	c Jones b Plunkett	105
W.U.Tharanga	b Hoggard	0	c Jones b Hoggard	0
†K.C.Sangakkara	c Jones b Plunkett	25	c Collingwood b Panesar	18
*D.P.M.D.Jayawardena	c Jones b Plunkett	0	lbw b Hoggard	5
T.T.Samaraweera	c Collingwood b Hoggard	3	st Jones b Panesar	8
T.M.Dilshan	c Trescothick b Flintoff	27	lbw b Hoggard	59
M.F.Maharoof	c Jones b Mahmood	5	c and b Flintoff	13
W.P.U.C.J.Vaas	not out	30	c Collingwood b Plunkett	1
M.D.N.Kulasekara	c Trescothick b Mahmood	3	c Collingwood b Plunkett	0
S.L.Malinga	lbw b Panesar	26	c Strauss b Flintoff	2
M.Muralitharan	c Plunkett b Flintoff	1	not out	0
Extras	(LB 6, NB 6)	12	(LB 8, W 1, NB 11)	20
Total		**141**		**231**

ENGLAND

M.E.Trescothick	c Sangakkara b Muralitharan	27	lbw b Muralitharan	0
A.J.Strauss	run out	30	c Jayawardena b Muralitharan	16
A.N.Cook	lbw b Muralitharan	23	not out	34
K.P.Pietersen	lbw b Muralitharan	142	lbw b Muralitharan	13
M.J.Hoggard	b Vaas	3		
P.D.Collingwood	c Tharanga b Muralitharan	19	(5) c Sangakkara b Muralitharan	3
*A.Flintoff	b Malinga	9	(6) not out	4
†G.O.Jones	c Samaraweera b Muralitharan	4		
L.E.Plunkett	c Vandort b Muralitharan	0		
S.I.Mahmood	not out	0		
M.S.Panesar	lbw b Malinga	0		
Extras	(B 6, LB 13, NB 14, Pen 5)	38	(B 2, NB 9)	11
Total		**295**	(4 wickets)	**81**

ENGLAND	O	M	R	W		O	M	R	W
Hoggard	15	4	32	2		22	8	64	3
Flintoff	13.2	4	28	2		19	3	50	2
Plunkett	12	1	43	3		13.2	6	17	3
Mahmood	9	1	25	2	(5)	9	2	19	0
Panesar	2	0	7	1	(4)	28	6	73	2
Collingwood						2	2	0	0
SRI LANKA									
Vaas	16	6	30	1		7	2	12	0
Malinga	13.3	2	68	2		7	1	29	0
Maharoof	11	3	42	0					
Muralitharan	25	2	86	6	(3)	12.2	3	29	4
Kulasekara	13	2	45	0					
Dilshan					(4)	1	0	9	0

FALL OF WICKETS

	SL	E	SL	E
Wkt	*1st*	*1st*	*2nd*	*2nd*
1st	3	56	2	9
2nd	16	69	38	35
3rd	16	125	43	63
4th	25	169	56	73
5th	46	238	181	–
6th	65	290	219	–
7th	79	290	223	–
8th	82	233	223	–
9th	132	294	231	–
10th	141	295	231	–

Umpires: Alim Dar (*Pakistan*) (33) and D.B.Hair (*Australia*) (73).
Referee: A.G.Hurst (*Australia*) (10). **Test No. 1802/17 (E847/SL162)**

ENGLAND v SRI LANKA (3rd Test)

At Trent Bridge, Nottingham, on 2, 3, 4, 5 June 2006.
Toss: England. Result: **SRI LANKA** won by 134 runs.
Debuts: England – J.Lewis.

SRI LANKA

M.G.Vandort	b Lewis	1		b Hoggard	5
W.U.Tharanga	c Jones b Hoggard	34		c Cook b Panesar	46
†K.C.Sangakkara	c Jones b Flintoff	36		c Trescothick b Flintoff	66
*D.P.M.D.Jayawardena	c Jones b Flintoff	0		c Jones b Plunkett	45
T.M.Dilshan	c Jones b Lewis	8	(6)	c Jones b Hoggard	32
S.T.Jayasuriya	c Pietersen b Flintoff	4	(5)	lbw b Panesar	4
C.K.Kapugedara	c Strauss b Plunkett	14		c Cook b Plunkett	50
M.F.Maharoof	c Flintoff b Hoggard	13		b Panesar	6
W.P.U.C.J.Vaas	not out	38		not out	34
S.L.Malinga	c Pietersen b Lewis	21		b Panesar	22
M.Muralitharan	c Flintoff b Plunkett	33		c Strauss b Panesar	2
Extras	(B 4, LB 3, W 2, NB 20)	29		(B 1, LB 3, W 1, NB 5)	10
Total		**231**			**322**

ENGLAND

M.E.Trescothick	run out	24	b Muralitharan	31
A.J.Strauss	b Vaas	7	c Jayawardena b Muralitharan	55
A.N.Cook	b Malinga	24	lbw b Muralitharan	5
K.P.Pietersen	c Jayawardena b Muralitharan	41	c Dilshan b Muralitharan	6
P.D.Collingwood	lbw b Vaas	48	c Dilshan b Muralitharan	9
*A.Flintoff	c Jayawardena b Jayasuriya	1	c Dilshan b Muralitharan	0
†G.O.Jones	st Sangakkara b Muralitharan	19	b Muralitharan	6
L.E.Plunkett	b Jayasuriya	9	not out	22
M.J.Hoggard	c Jayawardena b Muralitharan	10	run out	4
J.Lewis	c Dilshan b Malinga	20	lbw b Muralitharan	7
M.S.Panesar	not out	0	lbw b Jayasuriya	26
Extras	(B 2, LB 13, W 3, NB 8)	26	(B 13, LB 1, W 1, NB 4)	19
Total		**229**		**190**

ENGLAND	O	M	R	W		O	M	R	W
Hoggard	17	3	65	2		22	4	71	2
Lewis	21	3	68	3		20	6	54	0
Plunkett	8.2	1	36	2	(5)	19	2	65	2
Flintoff	15	2	52	3	(3)	13	1	38	1
Panesar	5	3	3	0	(4)	37.1	13	78	5
Pietersen						2	0	12	0
SRI LANKA									
Vaas	26	5	71	2		9	1	28	0
Malinga	23.1	3	62	2		7	0	24	0
Muralitharan	31	10	62	3		30	10	70	8
Jayasuriya	11	4	19	2		22.5	3	54	1

FALL OF WICKETS

	SL	E	SL	E
Wkt	*1st*	*1st*	*2nd*	*2nd*
1st	2	25	6	84
2nd	84	39	100	104
3rd	85	73	143	111
4th	86	117	148	120
5th	97	118	191	120
6th	105	151	223	125
7th	129	184	238	132
8th	139	196	287	136
9th	169	229	320	153
10th	231	229	322	190

Umpires: D.B.Hair (*Australia*) (74) and R.E.Koertzen (*South Africa*) (74).
Referee: A.G.Hurst (*Australia*) (11). **Test No. 1803/18 (E848/SL163)**

ENGLAND v SRI LANKA 2006

ENGLAND – BATTING AND FIELDING

	M	I	NO	HS	Runs	Avge	100	50	Ct/St
K.P.Pietersen	3	5	–	158	360	72.00	2	–	4
A.N.Cook	3	5	1	89	175	43.75	–	1	2
M.E.Trescothick	3	5	–	106	188	37.60	1	–	6
A.J.Strauss	3	5	–	55	156	31.20	–	1	4
P.D.Collingwood	3	5	–	57	136	27.20	–	1	5
A.Flintoff	3	5	2	33*	47	15.66	–	–	4
L.E.Plunkett	3	3	1	22*	31	15.50	–	–	1
G.O.Jones	3	4	1	19	40	13.33	–	–	16/1
M.S.Panesar	3	3	1	26	26	13.00	–	–	–
M.J.Hoggard	3	4	–	10	24	6.00	–	–	1
S.I.Mahmood	2	1	1	0*	0	∞	–	–	–

Played in one Test: J.Lewis 20, 7.

ENGLAND – BOWLING

	O	M	R	W	Avge	Best	5wI	10wM
M.S.Panesar	99.1	32	210	10	21.00	5-78	1	–
M.J.Hoggard	136	34	369	15	24.60	4-27	–	–
L.E.Plunkett	94.4	20	298	11	27.09	3-17	–	–
A.Flintoff	128.5	23	354	12	29.50	3-52	–	–
S.I.Mahmood	66	10	212	7	30.28	3-50	–	–
J.Lewis	41	9	122	3	40.66	3-68	–	–

Also bowled: P.D.Collingwood 11-4-16-0; K.P.Pietersen 2-0-12-0.

SRI LANKA – BATTING AND FIELDING

	M	I	NO	HS	Runs	Avge	100	50	Ct/St
W.P.U.C.J.Vaas	3	6	4	50*	184	92.00	–	1	–
K.C.Sangakkara	3	6	–	66	231	38.50	–	2	3/1
D.P.M.D.Jayawardena	3	6	–	119	230	38.33	1	1	7
T.M.Dilshan	3	6	–	69	195	32.50	–	2	4
M.G.Vandort	2	4	–	105	120	30.00	1	–	1
M.D.N.Kulasekara	2	4	–	64	96	24.00	–	1	–
W.U.Tharanga	3	6	–	52	142	23.66	–	1	1
M.F.Maharoof	3	6	–	59	118	19.66	–	1	–
C.K.Kapugedara	2	4	–	50	74	18.50	–	1	–
S.L.Malinga	2	4	–	26	71	17.75	–	–	–
M.Muralitharan	3	6	3	33	37	12.33	–	–	–
T.T.Samaraweera	2	4	–	8	17	4.25	–	–	1

Played in one Test: S.T.Jayasuriya 4, 4; J.Mubarak 0, 6.

SRI LANKA – BOWLING

	O	M	R	W	Avge	Best	5wI	10wM
M.Muralitharan	146.2	35	405	24	16.87	8- 70	2	2
S.T.Jayasuriya	33.5	7	73	3	24.33	2- 19	–	–
S.L.Malinga	50.4	6	183	4	45.75	2- 62	–	–
W.P.U.C.J.Vaas	94	16	265	5	53.00	2- 71	–	–
M.F.Maharoof	39	7	167	1	167.00	1-125	–	–

Also bowled: T.M.Dilshan 7-0-41-0; M.D.N.Kulasekara 38-5-134-0.

WEST INDIES v INDIA (1st Test)

At Recreation Ground, St John's, Antigua, on 2, 3, 4, 5, 6 June 2006.
Toss: India. Result: **MATCH DRAWN.**
Debuts: India – V.R.Singh.

INDIA

W.Jaffer	c Ramdin b Edwards	1	b Bradshaw	212
V.Sehwag	c Lara b Collymore	36	c Gayle b Collymore	41
V.V.S.Laxman	c Ramdin b Bravo	29	c Bradshaw b Mohammed	31
*R.Dravid	c Lara b Collymore	49	c Bradshaw b Mohammed	62
Yuvraj Singh	b Mohammed	23	c Chanderpaul b Gayle	39
M.Kaif	c Ramdin b Bravo	13	not out	46
†M.S.Dhoni	c Lara b Collymore	19	c Ganga b Mohammed	69
A.Kumble	b Bravo	21		
S.Sreesanth	not out	29		
V.R.Singh	c Sarwan b Bravo	2		
M.M.Patel	b Edwards	0		
Extras	(LB 8, W 2, NB 9)	19	(LB 6, W 6, NB 9)	21
Total		**241**	(6 wickets declared)	**521**

WEST INDIES

C.H.Gayle	c Dravid b Kumble	72	lbw b Kumble	69
D.Ganga	lbw b Patel	9	c Yuvraj b Kumble	36
R.R.Sarwan	lbw b Kumble	58	c Kumble b Sreesanth	1
*B.C.Lara	c Yuvraj b Patel	18	lbw b Sreesanth	0
S.Chanderpaul	c Dhoni b Sehwag	24	c Dravid Kumble	62
D.J.Bravo	st Dhoni b Sehwag	68	c Dhoni b Sehwag	28
†D.Ramdin	c Dhoni b Patel	26	c Dravid b Sehwag	8
I.D.R.Bradshaw	c Yuvraj b Singh	33	c Dhoni b Patel	10
D.Mohammed	not out	19	b Kumble	52
F.H.Edwards	c Dhoni b Singh	4	not out	1
C.D.Collymore	lbw b Kumble	0	not out	1
Extras	(B 2, LB 14, W 2, NB 22)	40	(B 5, LB 8, NB 17)	30
Total		**371**	(9 wickets)	**298**

WEST INDIES	O	M	R	W		O	M	R	W
Edwards	18.5	3	53	2		5.4	2	16	0
Bradshaw	24	3	83	0	(3)	40	9	108	1
Collymore	17	7	27	3	(2)	23	8	50	1
Gayle	4	0	6	0	(6)	22	5	66	1
Bravo	22	9	40	4	(4)	26.2	4	98	0
Mohammed	7	1	24	1	(5)	29.5	3	162	3
Sarwan						4	0	15	0
INDIA									
Sreesanth	16	1	96	0	(2)	19	10	49	2
Patel	28	7	80	3	(1)	20	4	55	1
Singh	15	1	61	2	(4)	11	3	35	0
Kumble	27.3	6	86	3	(3)	34	8	107	4
Sehwag	12	2	32	2		11	2	39	2

FALL OF WICKETS

	I	WI	I	WI
Wkt	*1st*	*1st*	*2nd*	*2nd*
1st	10	18	72	67
2nd	51	137	147	68
3rd	72	159	350	72
4th	126	182	375	171
5th	155	255	419	202
6th	179	282	521	220
7th	180	331	–	226
8th	227	359	–	277
9th	231	370	–	297
10th	241	371	–	–

Umpires: Asad Rauf (*Pakistan*) (6) and S.J.A.Taufel (*Australia*) (34).
Referee: J.J.Crowe (*New Zealand*) (12). **Test No. 1804/79 (WI430/I397)**

WEST INDIES v INDIA (2nd Test)

At Beausejour Stadium, Gros Islet, St Lucia, on 10, 11, 12, 13, 14 June 2006.
Toss: India. Result: **MATCH DRAWN.**
Debuts: None.

INDIA

W.Jaffer	c Bravo b Collins	43
V.Sehwag	c and b Collins	180
V.V.S.Laxman	c Ramdin b Collins	0
*R.Dravid	c Lara b Sarwan	146
Yuvraj Singh	b Collins	2
M.Kaif	not out	148
†M.S.Dhoni	c Ganga b Bradshaw	9
I.K.Pathan	c Ganga b Gayle	19
A.Kumble	b Taylor	14
M.M.Patel		
V.R.Singh		
Extras	(B 4, LB 7, W 4, NB 12)	27
Total	(8 wickets declared)	**588**

WEST INDIES

C.H.Gayle	c Dhoni b Kumble	46		c Dhoni b Pathan	2
D.Ganga	lbw b Patel	16		b Kumble	26
R.R.Sarwan	lbw b Patel	0	(4)	b Dhoni b Patel	1
*B.C.Lara	lbw b Kumble	7	(3)	lbw b Sehwag	120
S.Chanderpaul	lbw b Pathan	30		c Pathan b Kumble	54
D.J.Bravo	c Dravid b Kumble	25		c Yuvraj b Kumble	47
†D.Ramdin	c Dhoni b Patel	30		not out	19
I.D.R.Bradshaw	c and b Sehwag	20		lbw b Patel	1
J.E.Taylor	c Kaif b Sehwag	23		not out	0
P.T.Collins	c Dravid b Sehwag	0			
C.D.Collymore	not out	2			
Extras	(B 5, LB 2, NB 9)	16		(LB 4, NB 15, Pen 5)	24
Total		**215**		(7 wickets)	**294**

WEST INDIES	O	M	R	W		O	M	R	W
Collins	28	5	116	4					
Taylor	24.2	4	88	1					
Bravo	10	0	66	0					
Collymore	21	1	92	0					
Bradshaw	26	6	80	1					
Sarwan	18	0	83	1					
Gayle	21	6	52	1					
INDIA									
Pathan	11	2	43	1		15	2	50	1
Patel	17	4	51	3		21	7	50	2
Kumble	30	12	57	3	(4)	42	10	98	3
Singh	10	3	23	0	(3)	11	0	39	0
Sehwag	16.1	5	33	3		30	9	48	1
Yuvraj Singh	1	0	1	0					

FALL OF WICKETS

	I	WI	WI
Wkt	*1st*	*1st*	*2nd*
1st	159	36	2
2nd	161	36	51
3rd	300	55	52
4th	306	106	181
5th	485	106	252
6th	517	167	276
7th	555	178	291
8th	588	209	–
9th	–	210	–
10th	–	215	–

Umpires: Asad Rauf (*Pakistan*) (7) and S.J.A.Taufel (*Australia*) (35).
Referee: J.J.Crowe (*New Zealand*) (13). **Test No. 1805/80 (WI431/I398)**

WEST INDIES v INDIA (3rd Test)

At Warner Park, Basseterre, St Kitts, on 22, 23, 24, 25, 26 June 2006.
Toss: West Indies. Result: **MATCH DRAWN.**
Debuts: None.

WEST INDIES

C.H.Gayle	b Patel	83	c Dhoni b Sreesanth	3
D.Ganga	b Patel	135	not out	66
R.R.Sarwan	lbw b Sreesanth	116	c Dravid b Sreesanth	23
*B.C.Lara	lbw b Patel	10	st Dhoni b Kumble	19
S.Chanderpaul	not out	97	c and b Kumble	11
D.J.Bravo	c Dhoni b Harbhajan	21	c Sreesanth b Kumble	9
M.N.Samuels	c Harbhajan b Sehwag	87	st Dhoni b Harbhajan	20
†D.Ramdin	c Jaffer b Harbhajan	3	not out	8
J.E.Taylor	c Yuvraj b Harbhajan	2		
P.T.Collins	c Dravid b Harbhajan	1		
C.D.Collymore	b Harbhajan	0		
Extras	(LB 14, W 1, NB 11)	26	(B 4, LB 7, W 1, NB 1)	13
Total		**581**	(6 wickets declared)	**172**

INDIA

W.Jaffer	c Lara b Bravo	60	c Gayle b Collins	54
V.Sehwag	c Lara b Collymore	31	lbw b Collymore	65
V.V.S.Laxman	c Ramdin b Collins	100	c Lara b Collins	63
*R.Dravid	lbw b Taylor	22	not out	68
Yuvraj Singh	c Ramdin b Taylor	0	(6) not out	8
M.Kaif	lbw b Taylor	0		
†M.S.Dhoni	lbw b Collymore	29	(5) c Gayle b Taylor	20
A.Kumble	c Collins b Collymore	43		
Harbhajan Singh	not out	38		
S.Sreesanth	c Lara b Collins	0		
M.M.Patel	c Ganga b Bravo	13		
Extras	(B 8, LB 5, NB 13)	26	(B 9, LB 8, W 1, NB 2)	20
Total		**362**	(4 wickets)	**298**

INDIA	O	M	R	W		O	M	R	W
Patel	32	4	134	3		7	0	43	0
Sreesanth	31	8	99	1		6	1	19	2
Kumble	47	8	140	0		12	0	60	3
Harbhajan Singh	44	6	147	5		7	0	39	1
Sehwag	16	3	47	1					
WEST INDIES									
Taylor	26	3	118	3	(2)	11	1	40	1
Collins	29.3	4	117	2	(1)	18	1	66	2
Collymore	25	4	63	3		15	3	40	1
Bravo	17.3	6	38	2	(5)	7	1	36	0
Gayle	2	0	3	0	(6)	14	2	31	0
Samuels	7	1	10	0	(4)	20	3	68	0

FALL OF WICKETS

	WI	I	WI	I
Wkt	*1st*	*1st*	*2nd*	*2nd*
1st	143	61	3	109
2nd	346	124	46	143
3rd	356	157	81	243
4th	371	159	102	273
5th	406	159	120	–
6th	562	220	152	–
7th	570	297	–	–
8th	576	311	–	–
9th	581	315	–	–
10th	581	362	–	–

Umpires: B.G.Jerling (*South Africa*) (1) and R.E.Koertzen (*South Africa*) (75).
Referee: J.J.Crowe (*New Zealand*) (14). **Test No. 1806/81 (WI432/I399)**

WEST INDIES v INDIA (4th Test)

At Sabina Park, Kingston, Jamaica, on 30 June, 1, 2, July 2006.
Toss: India. Result: **INDIA** won by 49 runs.
Debuts: None.

INDIA

W.Jaffer	b Taylor	1	c sub (R.S. Morton) b Taylor	1
V.Sehwag	c Sarwan b Collins	0	lbw b Taylor	4
V.V.S.Laxman	c sub (R.S.Morton) b Bravo	18	c Lara b Collymore	16
*R.Dravid	c Ramdin b Collymore	81	b Collymore	68
Yuvraj Singh	lbw b Taylor	19	c Lara b Collymore	13
M.Kaif	c Lara b Taylor	13	b Collins	6
†M.S.Dhoni	c Bravo b Collymore	3	b Taylor	19
A.Kumble	b Bravo	45	c Bravo b Collymore	10
Harbhajan Singh	not out	9	c Lara b Collymore	9
S.Sreesanth	b Taylor	0	c Lara b Taylor	16
M.M.Patel	c Ramdin b Taylor	0	not out	0
Extras	(B 2, LB 2, W 5, NB 2)	11	(B 4, LB 3, W 1, NB 1)	9
Total		**200**		**171**

WEST INDIES

C.H.Gayle	b Sreesanth	0		c Laxman b Sreesanth	0
D.Ganga	lbw b Harbhajan	40		b Sreesanth	16
*B.C.Lara	c Jaffer b Sreesanth	26		lbw b Patel	11
M.N.Samuels	st Dhoni b Kumble	2	(7)	lbw b Kumble	5
S.Chanderpaul	c Dhoni b Patel	10		lbw b Kumble	13
D.J.Bravo	c Yuvraj b Harbhajan	0		b Kumble	33
R.R.Sarwan	c Kaif b Harbhajan	7	(4)	c Dravid b Sreesanth	51
†D.Ramdin	c Yuvraj b Harbhajan	10		not out	62
J.E.Taylor	run out	6		lbw b Kumble	20
P.T.Collins	c Sehwag b Harbhajan	0		lbw b Kumble	3
C.D.Collymore	not out	0		c Dhoni b Kumble	0
Extras	(W 1, NB 1)	2		(LB 2, NB 3)	5
Total		**103**			**219**

WEST INDIES	O	M	R	W		O	M	R	W
Collins	19	7	34	1		22	8	61	1
Taylor	18.4	4	50	5		15	4	45	4
Bravo	24	3	68	2	(4)	4	1	10	0
Collymore	19	11	17	2	(3)	24.1	9	48	5
Chanderpaul	5	0	17	0					
Gayle	2	0	10	0					
INDIA									
Sreesanth	9	3	34	2		15	2	38	3
Patel	12	5	24	1		12	2	26	1
Kumble	8	3	32	1	(4)	22.4	3	78	6
Harbhajan Singh	4.3	0	13	5	(3)	16	3	65	0
Sehwag						4	0	10	0

FALL OF WICKETS

	I	WI	I	WI
Wkt	*1st*	*1st*	*2nd*	*2nd*
1st	1	0	1	0
2nd	3	42	6	27
3rd	34	53	49	29
4th	58	72	63	56
5th	78	80	76	126
6th	91	81	122	128
7th	184	88	141	144
8th	197	99	154	180
9th	200	103	171	219
10th	200	103	171	219

Umpires: B.G.Jerling (*South Africa*) (2) and R.E.Koertzen (*South Africa*) (76).
Referee: J.J.Crowe (*New Zealand*) (15). **Test No. 1807/82 (WI433/I400)**

WEST INDIES v INDIA 2006-07

WEST INDIES – BATTING AND FIELDING

	M	I	NO	HS	Runs	Avge	100	50	Ct/St
D.Ganga	4	8	1	135	344	49.14	1	1	4
S.Chanderpaul	4	8	1	97*	301	43.00	–	3	1
C.H.Gayle	4	8	–	83	275	34.37	–	3	3
D.Ramdin	4	8	3	62*	166	33.20	–	1	8
R.R.Sarwan	4	8	–	116	257	32.12	1	2	2
D.J.Bravo	4	8	–	68	231	28.87	–	1	3
M.N.Samuels	2	4	–	87	114	28.50	–	1	–
B.C.Lara	4	8	–	120	211	26.37	1	–	13
I.D.R.Bradshaw	2	4	–	33	64	16.00	–	–	2
J.E.Taylor	3	5	1	23	51	12.75	–	–	–
P.T.Collins	3	4	–	3	4	1.00	–	–	2
C.D.Collymore	4	6	3	2*	3	1.00	–	–	–

Played in one Test: F.H.Edwards 4, 1*; D.Mohammed 19*, 52.

WEST INDIES – BOWLING

	O	M	R	W	Avge	Best	5wI	10wM
C.D.Collymore	144.1	43	337	15	22.46	5- 48	1	–
J.E.Taylor	95	16	341	14	24.35	5- 50	1	–
F.H.Edwards	24.3	5	69	2	34.50	2- 53	–	–
P.T.Collins	116.3	25	394	10	39.40	4-116	–	–
D.J.Bravo	110.5	24	356	8	44.50	4- 40	–	–
D.Mohammed	36.5	4	186	4	46.50	3-162	–	–
C.H.Gayle	65	13	168	2	84.00	1- 52	–	–
I.D.R.Bradshaw	90	18	271	2	135.50	1- 80	–	–

Also bowled: S.Chanderpaul 5-0-17-0; M.N.Samuels 27-4-78-0; R.R.Sarwan 22-0-98-1.

INDIA – BATTING AND FIELDING

	M	I	NO	HS	Runs	Avge	100	50	Ct/St
R.Dravid	4	7	1	146	496	82.66	1	4	8
M.Kaif	4	6	2	148*	226	56.50	1	–	2
Harbhajan Singh	2	3	2	38*	56	56.00	–	–	1
W.Jaffer	4	7	–	212	372	53.14	1	2	2
V.Sehwag	4	7	–	180	357	51.00	1	1	2
V.V.S.Laxman	4	7	–	100	257	36.71	1	1	1
A.Kumble	4	5	–	45	133	26.60	–	–	2
M.S.Dhoni	4	7	–	69	168	24.00	–	1	13/4
Yuvraj Singh	4	7	1	39	104	17.33	–	–	7
S.Sreesanth	3	4	1	29*	45	15.00	–	–	1
M.M.Patel	4	4	1	13	13	4.33	–	–	–
V.R.V.Singh	2	1	–	2	2	2.00	–	–	–

Played in one Test: I.K.Pathan 19 (1 ct).

INDIA – BOWLING

	O	M	R	W	Avge	Best	5wI	10wM
V.Sehwag	89.1	21	209	9	23.22	3-33	–	–
Harbhajan Singh	71.3	9	264	11	24.00	5-13	2	–
A.Kumble	223.1	50	658	23	28.60	6-78	1	–
M.M.Patel	149	33	463	14	33.07	3-51	–	–
S.Sreesanth	96	25	335	10	33.50	3-38	–	–
I.K.Pathan	26	4	93	2	46.50	1-43	–	–
V.R.V.Singh	47	7	158	2	79.00	2-61	–	–

Also bowled: Yuvraj Singh 1-0-1-0.

ENGLAND v PAKISTAN (1st Test)

At Lord's, London, on 13, 14, 15, 16, 17 July 2006.
Toss: England. Result: **MATCH DRAWN.**
Debuts: None.

ENGLAND

M.E.Trescothick	c Akmal b Gul	16		b Gul	18
*A.J.Strauss	lbw b Razzaq	30		c Farhat b Kaneria	128
A.N.Cook	b Sami	105		c Yousuf b Gul	4
K.P.Pietersen	lbw b Razzaq	21		st Akmal b Afridi	41
P.D.Collingwood	st Akmal b Kaneria	186		c Butt b Kaneria	3
I.R.Bell	not out	100		run out	28
†G.O.Jones	lbw b Kaneria	18		c Akmal b Kaneria	16
L.E.Plunkett	c Farhat b Kaneria	0		c Akmal b Razzaq	28
M.J.Hoggard	lbw b Afridi	13		not out	12
S.J.Harmison	run out	2			
M.S.Panesar	not out	0			
Extras	(B 8, W 15, NB 14)	37		(B 5, LB 6, W 1, NB 6)	18
Total	(9 wickets declared)	**528**		(8 wickets declared)	**296**

PAKISTAN

Salman Butt	c Strauss b Harmison	10		lbw b Hoggard	0
Imran Farhat	b Plunkett	33		c Collingwood b Hoggard	18
Faisal Iqbal	c Collingwood b Harmison	0		c Cook b Panesar	48
Md Yousuf Youhana	c Jones b Harmison	202		lbw b Panesar	48
Mohammad Sami	c Jones b Hoggard	0			
*Inzamam-ul-Haq	b Plunkett	69	(5)	not out	56
Abdul Razzaq	c Jones b Harmison	22	(6)	not out	25
†Kamran Akmal	c Jones b Pietersen	58			
Shahid Afridi	c Bell b Hoggard	17			
Umar Gul	c Jones b Hoggard	0			
Danish Kaneria	not out	1			
Extras	(B 7, LB 14, W 7, NB 5)	33		(B 1, LB 8, W 6, NB 4)	19
Total		**445**		(4 wickets)	**214**

PAKISTAN	O	M	R	W		O	M	R	W
Mohammad Sami	28	4	116	1		6	1	23	0
Umar Gul	33	6	133	1		19	4	70	2
Abdul Razzaq	25	2	86	2	(4)	9.5	0	45	1
Danish Kaneria	52	6	119	3	(3)	30	4	77	3
Shahid Afridi	19.3	0	63	1		19	1	65	1
Imran Farhat	1	0	3	0		1	0	5	0
ENGLAND									
Hoggard	33	3	117	3		12	3	31	2
Harmison	29.3	6	94	4		15	3	43	0
Panesar	27	3	93	0	(4)	27	7	60	2
Plunkett	21	3	78	2	(3)	12	2	41	0
Collingwood	7	1	31	0	(6)	2	0	11	0
Pietersen	2	0	11	1	(5)	5	1	19	0

FALL OF WICKETS

	E	P	E	P
Wkt	*1st*	*1st*	*2nd*	*2nd*
1st	60	28	38	0
2nd	60	28	64	33
3rd	88	65	141	116
4th	321	68	146	141
5th	441	241	203	–
6th	469	300	250	–
7th	473	399	253	–
8th	515	435	296	–
9th	525	436	–	–
10th	–	445	–	–

Umpires: S.A.Bucknor (*West Indies*) (112) and S.J.A.Taufel (*Australia*) (36).
Referee: R.S.Madugalle (*Sri Lanka*) (89). **Test No. 1808/64 (E849/P321)**

ENGLAND v PAKISTAN (2nd Test)

At Old Trafford, Manchester on 27, 28, 29 July 2006.
Toss: Pakistan. Result: **ENGLAND** won by an innings and 120 runs.
Debuts: None.

PAKISTAN

†Kamran Akmal	c Trescothick b Harmison	4	c Jones b Harmison	4
Imran Farhat	c Pietersen b Harmison	0	c Bell b Panesar	34
Younis Khan	c Collingwood b Harmison	44	lbw b Panesar	62
M.Yousuf Youhana	c Jones b Panesar	38	st Jones b Panesar	15
*Inzamam-ul-Haq	c Pietersen b Harmison	0	c Cook b Panesar	13
Faisal Iqbal	c Jones b Panesar	3	c Trescothick b Panesar	29
Abdul Razzaq	b Harmison	9	c Jones b Harmison	13
Shahid Afridi	c Pietersen b Panesar	15	c Strauss b Harmison	17
Mohammad Sami	c Strauss b Harmison	1	c Jones b Harmison	0
Umar Gul	not out	1	c Jones b Harmison	13
Danish Kaneria	run out	0	not out	4
Extras	(LB 2, W 2)	4	(B 4, LB 4, W 6, NB 4)	18
Total		**119**		**222**

ENGLAND

M.E.Trescothick	c Akmal b Sami	5
*A.J.Strauss	c Akmal b Razzaq	42
A.N.Cook	lbw b Gul	127
K.P.Pietersen	c Farhat b Gul	38
P.D.Collingwood	c Sami b Gul	48
I.R.Bell	not out	106
†G.O.Jones	lbw b Sami	8
S.I.Mahmood	c and b Razzaq	12
M.J.Hoggard	lbw b Afridi	6
S.J.Harmison	c Akmal b Kaneria	26
M.S.Panesar	not out	3
Extras	(B 9, LB 10, W 7, NB 14)	40
Total	(9 wickets declared)	**461**

ENGLAND	O	M	R	W		O	M	R	W
Hoggard	9	1	30	0		14	2	52	0
Harmison	13	7	19	6		18.1	3	57	5
Mahmood	6	1	33	0		6	1	22	0
Collingwood	3	0	14	0					
Panesar	7.4	3	21	3	(4)	27	4	72	5
Pietersen					(5)	2	0	11	0
PAKISTAN									
Mohammad Sami	28	5	92	2					
Umar Gul	28	2	96	3					
Abdul Razzaq	19	4	72	2					
Danish Kaneria	37	8	106	1					
Shahid Afridi	21	0	76	1					

FALL OF WICKETS

	P	E	P
Wkt	*1st*	*1st*	*2nd*
1st	4	30	21
2nd	9	95	60
3rd	90	169	101
4th	90	288	117
5th	93	304	161
6th	93	321	174
7th	112	357	194
8th	113	384	194
9th	118	457	208
10th	119	–	222

Umpires: S.A.Bucknor (*West Indies*) (113) and S.J.A.Taufel (*Australia*) (37).
Referee: R.S.Madugalle (*Sri Lanka*) (90). **Test No. 1809/65 (E850/P322)**

ENGLAND v PAKISTAN (3rd Test)

At Headingley, Leeds, on 4, 5, 6, 7, 8 August 2006.
Toss: England. Result: **ENGLAND** won by 167 runs.
Debuts: None.

ENGLAND

M.E.Trescothick	c and b Sami	28	c Butt b Gul	58
*A.J.Strauss	c Younis b Nazir	36	c Akmal b Sami	116
A.N.Cook	c and b Gul	23	c Iqbal b Kaneria	21
K.P.Pietersen	c Nazir b Sami	135	b Kaneria	16
P.D.Collingwood	c Taufiq b Gul	31	b Nazir	25
I.R.Bell	b Kaneria	119	c Akmal b Sami	4
†C.M.W.Read	lbw b Gul	38	b Sami	55
M.J.Hoggard	b Gul	0	(9) c Younis b Nazir	8
S.I.Mahmood	b Gul	34	(8) c Akmal b Nazir	2
S.J.Harmison	c Sami b Kaneria	36	c sub (Imran Farhat) b Gul	4
M.S.Panesar	not out	5	not out	5
Extras	(B 13, LB 6, NB 11)	30	(B 8, LB 3, W 1, NB 19)	31
Total		**515**		**345**

PAKISTAN

Salman Butt	run out	20	c Trescothick b Hoggard	16
Taufiq Umar	c Read b Hoggard	7	c Cook b Panesar	11
Younis Khan	run out	173	b Panesar	41
M.Yousuf Youhana	c Read b Harmison	192	run out	8
*Inzamam-ul-Haq	hit wicket b Panesar	26	(7) st Read b Panesar	37
Faisal Iqbal	lbw b Collingwood	0	(5) c Read b Mahmood	11
†Kamran Akmal	c Trescothick b Mahmood	20	(6) c Read b Mahmood	0
Mohammad Sami	c Harmison b Panesar	19	run out	0
Shahid Nazir	not out	13	c Trescothick b Mahmood	17
Umar Gul	c Panesar b Mahmood	7	c Collingwood b Mahmood	0
Danish Kaneria	c Trescothick b Panesar	29	not out	0
Extras	(B 1, LB 20, W 5, NB 6)	32	(LB 6, W 5, NB 3)	14
Total		**538**		**155**

PAKISTAN	O	M	R	W		O	M	R	W
Mohammad Sami	26	1	135	2		21.3	4	100	3
Umar Gul	29	4	123	5		20	1	76	2
Shahid Nazir	28	7	101	1		14	4	32	3
Danish Kaneria	34	4	111	2		33	2	126	2
Taufiq Umar	2	0	8	0					
Salman Butt	4	0	18	0					
ENGLAND									
Hoggard	29	4	93	1		7	3	26	1
Harmison	30	1	142	1	(3)	15	3	62	0
Mahmood	24	4	108	2	(4)	8	2	22	4
Panesar	47.4	13	127	3	(2)	17.5	4	39	3
Pietersen	1	0	14	0					
Collingwood	10	1	33	1					

FALL OF WICKETS

	E	P	E	P
Wkt	*1st*	*1st*	*2nd*	*2nd*
1st	67	34	158	23
2nd	67	36	190	52
3rd	110	399	214	68
4th	192	447	237	80
5th	345	447	248	80
6th	347	451	299	112
7th	421	481	301	113
8th	445	489	323	148
9th	501	496	332	149
10th	515	538	345	155

Umpires: B.R.Doctrove (*West Indies*) (8) and D.B.Hair (*Australia*) (75).
Referee: R.S.Madugalle (*Sri Lanka*) (91). **Test No. 1810/66 (E851/P323)**

ENGLAND v PAKISTAN (4th Test)

At Kennington Oval, London, on 17, 18, 19, 20 August 2006.
Toss: Pakistan. Result: **ENGLAND** won by forfeiture.
Debuts: None.

ENGLAND

M.E.Trescothick	c Hafeez b Gul	6	c Akmal b Asif	4
*A.J.Strauss	c Akmal b Asif	38	lbw b Kaneria	54
A.N.Cook	lbw b Nazir	40	lbw b Gul	83
K.P.Pietersen	c Akmal b Asif	0	c Akmal b Nazir	96
P.D.Collingwood	lbw b Asif	5	not out	26
I.R.Bell	c Iqbal b Kaneria	9	not out	9
†C.M.W.Read	b Gul	33		
S.I.Mahmood	b Gul	15		
M.J.Hoggard	c Akmal b Asif	3		
S.J.Harmison	not out	8		
M.S.Panesar	b Gul	0		
Extras	(B 4, LB 5, NB 7)	16	(B 8, LB 3, NB 10, Pen 5)	26
Total		**173**	(4 wickets)	**298**

PAKISTAN

Mohammad Hafeez	c Strauss b Hoggard	95
Imran Farhat	c Trescothick b Hoggard	91
Younis Khan	c Read b Mahmood	9
M.Yousuf Youhana	c Read b Hoggard	128
*Inzamam-ul-Haq	c Strauss b Harmison	31
Faisal Iqbal	not out	58
†Kamran Akmal	c Collingwood b Harmison	15
Shahid Nazir	c Hoggard b Mahmood	17
Umar Gul	lbw b Panesar	13
Danish Kaneria	c Trescothick b Harmison	15
Mohammad Asif	c Cook b Harmison	0
Extras	(B 4, LB 9, W 11, NB 8)	32
Total		**504**

PAKISTAN	O	M	R	W		O	M	R	W
Mohammad Asif	19	6	56	4		17	1	79	1
Umar Gul	15.2	3	46	4		14	1	70	1
Shahid Nazir	11	1	44	1	(5)	8	1	26	1
Danish Kaneria	8	1	18	1		29	6	94	1
Mohammad Hafeez					(3)	4	1	13	0
ENGLAND									
Hoggard	34	2	124	3					
Harmison	30.5	6	125	4					
Mahmood	27	3	101	2					
Panesar	30	6	103	1					
Collingwood	6	0	29	0					
Pietersen	2	0	9	0					

FALL OF WICKETS

	E	P	E
Wkt	*1st*	*1st*	*2nd*
1st	36	70	8
2nd	54	148	115
3rd	54	325	218
4th	64	379	277
5th	91	381	–
6th	112	398	–
7th	158	444	–
8th	163	475	–
9th	173	504	–
10th	173	504	–

Umpires: B.R.Doctrove (*West Indies*) (9) and D.B.Hair (*Australia*) (76).
Referee: M.J.Procter (*South Africa*) (41). **Test No. 1811/67 (E852/P324)**

ENGLAND v PAKISTAN 2006

ENGLAND – BATTING AND FIELDING

	M	I	NO	HS	Runs	Avge	100	50	Ct/St
I.R.Bell	4	7	3	119	375	93.75	3	–	2
A.J.Strauss	4	7	–	128	444	63.42	2	1	5
A.N.Cook	4	7	–	127	403	57.57	2	1	4
P.D.Collingwood	4	7	1	186	324	54.00	1	–	5
K.P.Pietersen	4	7	–	135	347	49.57	1	1	3
C.M.W.Read	2	3	–	55	126	42.00	–	1	6/1
M.E.Trescothick	4	7	–	58	135	19.28	–	1	8
S.J.Harmison	4	5	1	36	76	19.00	–	–	1
S.I.Mahmood	3	4	–	34	63	15.75	–	–	–
G.O.Jones	2	3	–	18	42	14.00	–	–	11/1
M.S.Panesar	4	5	4	5*	13	13.00	–	–	1
M.J.Hoggard	4	6	1	13	42	8.40	–	–	1

Played in one Test: L.E.Plunkett 0, 28.

ENGLAND – BOWLING

	O	M	R	W	Avge	Best	5wI	10wM
S.J.Harmison	151.3	29	542	20	27.10	6- 19	2	1
M.S.Panesar	184.1	40	515	17	30.29	5- 72	1	–
S.I.Mahmood	71	11	286	8	35.75	4- 22	–	–
M.J.Hoggard	138	18	473	10	47.30	3-117	–	–
L.E.Plunkett	33	5	119	2	59.50	2- 78	–	–
K.P.Pietersen	12	1	64	1	64.00	1- 11	–	–
P.D.Collingwood	28	2	118	1	118.00	1- 33	–	–

PAKISTAN – BATTING AND FIELDING

	M	I	NO	HS	Runs	Avge	100	50	Ct/St
Mohd Yousuf Youhana	4	7	–	202	631	90.14	3	–	1
Younis Khan	3	5	–	173	329	65.80	1	1	2
Inzamam-ul-Haq	4	7	1	69	232	38.66	–	2	–
Imran Farhat	3	5	–	91	176	35.20	–	1	3
Faisal Iqbal	4	7	1	58*	149	24.83	–	1	2
Shahid Nazir	2	3	1	17	47	23.50	–	–	1
Abdul Razzaq	2	4	1	25*	69	23.00	–	–	1
Kamran Akmal	4	6	–	58	101	16.83	–	1	14/2
Shahid Afridi	2	3	–	17	49	16.33	–	–	–
Danish Kaneria	4	6	3	29	49	16.33	–	–	–
Salman Butt	2	4	–	20	46	11.50	–	–	2
Umar Gul	4	6	1	13	34	6.80	–	–	1
Mohammad Sami	3	5	–	19	20	4.00	–	–	3

Played in one Test: Mohammad Asif 0; Mohammad Hafeez 95 (1 ct); Taufiq Umar 7, 11 (1 ct).

PAKISTAN – BOWLING

	O	M	R	W	Avge	Best	5wI	10wM
Mohammad Asif	36	7	135	5	27.00	4- 56	–	–
Shahid Nazir	61	13	203	6	33.83	3- 32	–	–
Umar Gul	158.2	21	614	18	34.11	5-123	1	–
Abdul Razzaq	53.5	6	203	5	40.60	2- 72	–	–
Danish Kaneria	223	31	651	13	50.07	3- 77	–	–
Mohammad Sami	109.3	15	466	8	58.25	3-100	–	–
Shahid Afridi	59.3	1	204	3	68.00	1- 63	–	–

Also bowled: Imran Farhat 2-0-8-0; Mohammad Hafeez 4-1-13-0; Salman Butt 4-0-18-0; Taufiq Umar 2-0-8-0.

SRI LANKA v SOUTH AFRICA (1st Test)

At Sinhalese Sports Club, Colombo, on 27, 28, 29, 30, 31 July 2006.
Toss: South Africa. Result: **SRI LANKA** won by an innings and 153 runs.
Debuts: None.

SOUTH AFRICA

H.H.Gibbs	b Fernando	19	(7)	c and b Muralitharan	18
A.J.Hall	b Fernando	17		lbw b Muralitharan	64
J.A.Rudolph	c HAPD Jayawardena b Maharoof	29	(1)	c Kapugedara b Fernando	90
H.M.Amla	st HAPD Jayawardena b Muralitharan	19	(3)	lbw b Fernando	2
*A.G.Prince	c HAPD Jayawardena b Maharoof	1	(4)	c DPMD Jayawardena b Muralitharan	61
A.B.de Villiers	c Kapugedara b Muralitharan	65	(5)	lbw b Muralitharan	24
†M.V.Boucher	c Jayasuriya b Muralitharan	4	(6)	c and b Jayasuriya	85
N.Boje	lbw b Muralitharan	5		not out	33
A.Nel	lbw b Fernando	0		b Muralitharan	0
D.W.Steyn	b Fernando	0		b Muralitharan	4
M.Ntini	not out	0		b Malinga	16
Extras	(B 4, LB 6)	10		(B 11, LB 4, W 2, NB 20)	37
Total		**169**			**434**

SRI LANKA

W.U.Tharanga	c Boucher b Steyn	7
S.T.Jayasuriya	lbw b Steyn	4
K.C.Sangakkara	c Boucher b Hall	287
*D.P.M.D.Jayawardena	b Nel	374
T.M.Dilshan	lbw b Steyn	45
C.K.Kapugedara	not out	1
†H.A.P.W.Jayawardena		
M.F.Maharoof		
S.L.Malinga		
C.R.D.Fernando		
M.Muralitharan		
Extras	(B 17, LB 5, W 8, NB 8)	38
Total	(5 wickets declared)	**756**

SRI LANKA	O	M	R	W	O	M	R	W
Malinga	10	2	38	0	16.2	0	85	1
Maharoof	9	1	32	2	15	3	48	0
Fernando	13	2	48	4	24	6	69	2
Muralitharan	18.2	6	41	4	64	11	131	6
Dilshan					4	1	10	0
Jayasuriya					34	8	76	1

SOUTH AFRICA	O	M	R	W
Ntini	31	3	97	0
Steyn	26	1	129	3
Nel	25.1	2	114	1
Hall	25	2	99	1
Boje	65	5	221	0
Rudolph	7	0	45	0
Prince	2	0	7	0
De Villiers	4	0	22	0

FALL OF WICKETS

	SA	SL	SA
Wkt	*1st*	*1st*	*2nd*
1st	32	6	165
2nd	45	14	171
3rd	78	638	185
4th	80	751	234
5th	112	756	312
6th	128	–	350
7th	148	–	401
8th	151	–	404
9th	151	–	412
10th	169	–	434

Umpires: M.R.Benson (*England*) (11) and B.F.Bowden (*New Zealand*) (36).
Referee: J.Srinath (*India*) (1). **Test No. 1812/16 (SL165/SA3213)**

SRI LANKA v SOUTH AFRICA (2nd Test)

At P.Saravanamuttu Stadium, Colombo, on 4, 5, 6, 7, 8 August 2006.
Toss: South Africa. Result: **SRI LANKA** won by one wicket.
Debuts: None.

SOUTH AFRICA

H.H.Gibbs	lbw b Vaas	0		c Jayasuriya b Muralitharan	92
A.J.Hall	c Dilshan b Malinga	0		c HAPW Jayawardena b Maharoof	32
J.A.Rudolph	b Malinga	13		run out	15
H.M.Amla	lbw b Muralitharan	40		run out	8
*A.G.Prince	c HAPW Jayawardena b Muralitharan	86		c and b Muralitharan	17
A.B.de Villiers	c HAPW Jayawardena b Malinga	95		c Dilshan b Muralitharan	33
†M.V.Boucher	b Muralitharan	32		c Dilshan b Muralitharan	65
S.M.Pollock	not out	57		c Tharanga b Muralitharan	14
N.Boje	c Sangakkara b Maharoof	11		c HAPW Jayawardena b Muralitharan	15
D.W.Steyn	c Jayasuriya b Muralitharan	6		lbw b Muralitharan	0
M.Ntini	c Maharoof b Muralitharan	13		not out	5
Extras	(NB 8)	8		(B 9, LB 4, W 1, NB 1)	15
Total		**361**			**311**

SRI LANKA

W.U.Tharanga	c Boje b Ntini	2		c Gibbs b Ntini	0
S.T.Jayasuriya	c Gibbs b Ntini	47		c Amla b Boje	73
K.C.Sangakkara	c Amla b Ntini	14		c Amla b Pollock	39
*D.P.M.D.Jayawardena	b Boucher b Steyn	13		c Gibbs b Boje	123
T.M.Dilshan	b Ntini	4		c Gibbs b Boje	18
C.K.Kapugedara	b Boje	63		c De Villiers b Boje	13
†H.A.P.W.Jayawardena	b Steyn	42		lbw b Hall	30
M.F.Maharoof	b Steyn	56		not out	29
W.P.U.C.J.Vaas	c Boucher b Steyn	64		c De Villiers b Hall	4
S.L.Malinga	not out	8	(11)	not out	1
M.Muralitharan	c Hall b Steyn	0	(10)	b Hall	2
Extras	(LB 1, W 2, NB 5)	8		(B 4, LB 8, W 4, NB 4)	20
Total		**321**		(9 wickets)	**352**

SRI LANKA	O	M	R	W		O	M	R	W
Vaas	18	4	71	1		19	4	53	0
Malinga	18	4	81	3		12	1	55	0
Muralitharan	33.5	2	128	5	(4)	46.5	12	97	7
Maharoof	15	2	52	1	(3)	21	3	53	1
Jayasuriya	5	0	29	0		9	0	40	0
SOUTH AFRICA									
Ntini	21	3	84	4		7.2	2	13	1
Steyn	13.1	1	82	5		22.4	2	81	0
Pollock	16	4	52	0	(4)	19	2	60	1
Hall	15	7	31	0	(5)	25	3	75	3
Boje	20	6	71	1	(3)	39.3	11	111	4

FALL OF WICKETS	SA	SL	SA	SL
Wkt	*1st*	*1st*	*2nd*	*2nd*
1st	0	16	76	12
2nd	4	43	119	94
3rd	31	74	131	121
4th	70	85	161	164
5th	231	86	206	201
6th	256	191	207	279
7th	273	191	235	341
8th	307	308	280	348
9th	327	317	282	350
10th	361	321	311	–

Umpires: Alim Dar (*Pakistan*) (34) and B.F.Bowden (*New Zealand*) (37).
Referee: J.Srinath (*India*) (2). **Test No. 1813/17 (SL165/SA314)**

PAKISTAN v WEST INDIES (1st Test)

At Gaddafi Stadium, Lahore, on 11, 12, 13, 14 November 2006.
Toss: West Indies. Result: **PAKISTAN** won by nine wickets.
Debuts: None.

WEST INDIES

C.H.Gayle	lbw b Nazir	34		c Akmal b Gul	11
D.Ganga	c Younis b Gul	3		run out	5
R.R.Sarwan	c Younis b Nazir	3		lbw b Gul	23
*B.C.Lara	c Akmal b Gul	61		lbw b Hafeez	122
S.Chanderpaul	lbw b Nazir	5	(6)	c Yousuf b Nazir	81
D.J.Bravo	c Nazir b Kaneria	32	(7)	lbw b Gul	2
†D.Ramdin	c Hafeez b Kaneria	12	(8)	c Farhat b Kaneria	1
D.Mohammed	c Akmal b Gul	35	(9)	c Razzaq b Nazir	15
J.E.Taylor	lbw b Gul	8	(10)	c Akmal b Gul	8
F.H.Edwards	c Malik b Gul	2	(5)	c Younis b Nazir	10
C.D.Collymore	not out	1		not out	1
Extras	(LB 8, NB 2)	10		(LB 7, NB 5)	12
Total		**206**			**291**

PAKISTAN

Mohammad Hafeez	lbw b Taylor	57	lbw b Collymore	1
Imran Farhat	lbw b Taylor	9	not out	8
Younis Khan	c Sarwan b Edwards	11	not out	0
M.Yousuf Youhana	st Ramdin b Gayle	192		
*Inzamam-ul-Haq	b Mohammed	0		
Shoaib Malik	c Mohammed b Taylor	69		
Abdul Razzaq	c Ramdin b Taylor	5		
†Kamran Akmal	c Lara b Gayle	78		
Shahid Nazir	c Collymore b Mohammed	0		
Umar Gul	not out	16		
Danish Kaneria	c Ramdin b Mohammed	23		
Extras	(B 4, LB 7, W 6, NB 8)	25	(LB 4)	4
Total		**485**	(1 wicket)	**13**

PAKISTAN	O	M	R	W		O	M	R	W
Umar Gul	15.1	2	65	5		29	6	99	4
Shahid Nazir	14	4	42	3		20	8	63	3
Abdul Razzaq	7	2	22	0		7	2	19	0
Danish Kaneria	18	3	58	2		29	7	78	1
Shoaib Malik	2	0	11	0		5	1	14	0
Mohammad Hafeez						4	0	11	1
WEST INDIES									
Edwards	26	3	109	1	(2)	2.1	1	7	0
Taylor	33	7	115	4					
Collymore	25	6	63	0	(1)	3	2	2	1
Bravo	20	3	63	0					
Mohammed	31	4	98	3					
Gayle	10	3	24	2					
Sarwan	1	0	2	0					

FALL OF WICKETS

	WI	P	WI	P
Wkt	*1st*	*1st*	*2nd*	*2nd*
1st	41	16	16	2
2nd	41	45	20	–
3rd	46	133	56	–
4th	52	140	101	–
5th	96	279	238	–
6th	122	285	248	–
7th	174	433	251	–
8th	202	444	278	–
9th	203	446	288	–
10th	206	485	291	–

Umpires: E.A.R.de Silva (*Sri Lanka*) (33) and S.J.A.Taufel (*Australia*) (38).
Referee: R.S. Mahanama (Sri Lanka) (8). **Test No. 1814/42 (P325/WI434)**

PAKISTAN v WEST INDIES (2nd Test)

At Multan Cricket Stadium on 19, 20, 21, 22, 23 November 2006.
Toss: Pakistan. Result: **MATCH DRAWN**.
Debuts: None.

PAKISTAN

Mohammad Hafeez	c Ramdin b Taylor	36	b Taylor	18
Imran Farhat	c Lara b Bravo	74	run out	76
Younis Khan	c Morton b Taylor	56	c Ramdin b Mohammed	56
M.Yousuf Youhana	c Lara b Gayle	56	c Chanderpaul b Mohammed	191
*Inzamam-ul-Haq	c Ramdin b Taylor	31	lbw b Taylor	10
Shoaib Malik	c Bravo b Collymore	42	b Powell	4
Abdul Razzaq	not out	16	c Chanderpaul b Mohammed	80
†Kamran Akmal	c Bravo b Collymore	17	not out	2
Shahid Nazir	lbw b Taylor	7		
Umar Gul	c Bravo b Taylor	7		
Danish Kaneria	run out	0		
Extras	(B 9, LB 4, NB 2)	15	(B 8, LB 10, W 3, NB 3)	24
Total		**357**	(7 wickets)	**461**

WEST INDIES

C.H.Gayle	lbw b Kaneria	93
D.Ganga	lbw b Kaneria	82
*B.C.Lara	c Malik b Kaneria	216
R.S.Morton	lbw b Gul	5
S.Chanderpaul	c Razzaq b Nazir	14
D.J.Bravo	c Younis b Kaneria	89
†D.Ramdin	c Akmal b Nazir	11
D.Mohammed	st Akmal b Kaneria	36
D.B.Powell	lbw b Razzaq	9
J.E.Taylor	lbw b Razzaq	1
C.D.Collymore	not out	1
Extras	(B 9, LB 18, NB 7)	34
Total		**591**

WEST INDIES	O	M	R	W		O	M	R	W
Taylor	26	6	91	5		25	4	75	2
Collymore	31	9	67	2		28	9	66	0
Powell	14	4	50	0	(4)	20	6	47	1
Gayle	22	6	52	1	(3)	29	5	85	0
Bravo	19	6	41	1		13	3	40	0
Mohammed	11	1	39	0		27.4	4	101	3
Morton	1	0	4	0	(8)	3	0	20	0
Chanderpaul					(7)	2	0	9	0
PAKISTAN									
Umar Gul	38	13	96	1					
Shahid Nazir	29	2	103	2					
Danish Kaneria	46	7	181	5					
Abdul Razzaq	17.4	4	65	2					
Mohammad Hafeez	24	2	72	0					
Shoaib Malik	13	1	47	0					

FALL OF WICKETS

	P	WI	P
Wkt	*1st*	*1st*	*2nd*
1st	83	162	24
2nd	125	220	124
3rd	212	281	243
4th	250	302	284
5th	269	502	306
6th	315	523	458
7th	333	563	461
8th	346	583	–
9th	357	590	–
10th	357	591	–

Umpires: M.R.Benson (*England*) (12) and D.J.Harper (*Australia*) (60).
Referee: R.S. Mahanama (*Sri Lanka*) (9). **Test No. 1815/43 (P326/WI435)**

PAKISTAN v WEST INDIES (3rd Test)

At National Stadium, Karachi, on 27, 28, 29, 30 November, 1 December 2006.
Toss: Pakistan. Result: **PAKISTAN** won by 199 runs.
Debuts: None.

PAKISTAN

Mohammad Hafeez	b Collymore	18	c Ramdin b Taylor	104
Imran Farhat	c Ramdin b Bravo	47	c Ramdin b Powell	20
Younis Khan	run out	20	lbw b Gayle	38
M.Yousuf Youhana	lbw b Collymore	102	b Sarwan	124
*Inzamam-ul-Haq	c Chanderpaul b Ganga	18	not out	58
Shoaib Malik	lbw b Taylor	18	b Collymore	10
Abdul Razzaq	c Ramdin b Bravo	7	c Gayle b Sarwan	10
†Kamran Akmal	b Collymore	31		
Shahid Nazir	b Powell	0		
Umar Gul	b Powell	26		
Danish Kaneria	not out	7		
Extras	(B 1, LB 7, NB 2)	10	(B 13, LB 21, W 1)	35
Total		**304**	(6 wickets declared)	**399**

WEST INDIES

C.H.Gayle	c Razzaq b Gul	40	b Gul	2
D.Ganga	c Akmal b Razzaq	81	lbw b Nazir	2
*B.C.Lara	b Gul	0	c Malik b Gul	49
R.R.Sarwan	b Gul	0	retired hurt	35
S.Chanderpaul	c Farhat b Kaneria	36	lbw b Kaneria	69
R.S.Morton	c Farhat b Kaneria	21	c and b Kaneria	16
D.J.Bravo	c Akmal b Kaneria	8	c Younis b Nazir	26
†D.Ramdin	run out	50	not out	25
D.B.Powell	b Gul	1	c Younis b Kaneria	0
J.E.Taylor	c Akmal b Nazir	1	lbw b Razzaq	1
C.D.Collymore	not out	8	lbw b Razzaq	0
Extras	(B 5, LB 2, NB 7)	14	(B 5, LB 9, NB 5)	19
Total		**260**		**244**

WEST INDIES	O	M	R	W		O	M	R	W
Taylor	22	3	76	1		24	8	60	1
Collymore	21	6	57	3		22	10	52	1
Gayle	16	3	27	0	(5)	15	2	38	1
Powell	23.5	5	83	2	(3)	24	6	70	1
Bravo	14	6	33	2	(4)	19	1	68	0
Ganga	4	0	20	1					
Sarwan					(6)	17.5	0	70	2
Chanderpaul					(7)	2	0	7	0
PAKISTAN									
Umar Gul	24	5	79	4		19	2	89	2
Shahid Nazir	17	3	58	1		18	6	49	2
Danish Kaneria	35	12	62	3		26	6	69	3
Abdul Razzaq	16	5	44	1	(5)	12	5	23	2
Mohammad Hafeez	4	1	10	0					
Shoaib Malik					(4)	1	1	0	0

FALL OF WICKETS

	P	WI	P	WI
Wkt	*1st*	*1st*	*2nd*	*2nd*
1st	26	51	43	2
2nd	72	51	122	17
3rd	112	51	271	97
4th	178	114	365	126
5th	222	153	384	183
6th	239	190	399	227
7th	248	204	–	277
8th	265	213	–	236
9th	272	216	–	244
10th	304	260	–	–

Umpires: M.R.Benson (*England*) (13) and D.J.Harper (*Australia*) (61).
Referee: R.S. Mahanama (*Sri Lanka*) (10).
Sarwan retired hurt at 101-3 in the second innings. **Test No. 1816/44 (P327/WI436)**

PAKISTAN v WEST INDIES 2006-07

PAKISTAN – BATTING AND FIELDING

	M	I	NO	HS	Runs	Avge	100	50	Ct/St
Yousuf Youhana	3	5	–	192	665	133.00	4	1	1
Imran Farhat	3	6	1	76	234	46.80	–	2	3
Kamran Akmal	3	4	1	78	128	42.66	–	1	8/1
Mohammad Hafeez	3	6	–	104	234	39.00	1	1	1
Younis Khan	3	6	1	56	181	36.20	–	2	6
Abdul Razzaq	3	5	1	80	118	29.50	–	1	3
Inzamam-ul-Haq	3	5	1	58*	117	29.25	–	1	–
Shoaib Malik	3	5	–	69	143	28.60	–	1	3
Umar Gul	3	3	1	26	49	24.50	–	–	–
Danish Kaneria	3	3	1	23	30	15.00	–	–	1
Shahid Nazir	3	3	–	7	7	2.33	–	–	1

PAKISTAN – BOWLING

	O	M	R	W	Avge	Best	5wI	10wM
Umar Gul	125.1	28	428	16	26.75	5- 65	1	–
Shahid Nazir	98	23	315	11	28.63	3- 42	–	–
Danish Kaneria	154	35	448	14	32.00	5-181	1	–
Abdul Razzaq	59.4	18	173	5	34.60	2- 23	–	–

Also bowled: Mohammad Hafeez 32-3-93-1; Shoaib Malik 21-3-72-0.

WEST INDIES – BATTING AND FIELDING

	M	I	NO	HS	Runs	Avge	100	50	Ct/St
B.C.Lara	3	5	–	216	448	89.60	2	1	3
S.Chanderpaul	3	5	–	81	205	41.00	–	2	3
C.H.Gayle	3	5	–	93	180	36.00	–	1	1
D.Ganga	3	5	–	82	173	34.60	–	2	–
D.J.Bravo	3	5	–	89	157	31.40	–	1	3
D.Mohammed	2	3	–	36	86	28.66	–	–	1
D.Ramdin	3	5	1	50	99	24.75	–	1	9/1
R.R.Sarwan	2	4	1	35*	61	20.33	–	–	1
R.S.Morton	2	3	–	21	42	14.00	–	–	1
C.D.Collymore	3	5	4	8*	11	11.00	–	–	1
J.E.Taylor	3	5	–	8	19	3.80	–	–	–
D.B.Powell	2	3	–	9	10	3.33	–	–	–

Played in one Test: F.H.Edwards 2, 10.

WEST INDIES – BOWLING

	O	M	R	W	Avge	Best	5wI	10wM
J.E.Taylor	130	28	417	13	32.07	5-91	1	–
D.Mohammed	69.4	9	238	6	39.66	3-98	–	–
C.D.Collymore	130	42	307	7	43.85	3-57	–	–
C.H.Gayle	92	19	226	4	56.50	2-24	–	–
D.B.Powell	81.5	21	250	4	62.50	2-83	–	–
D.J.Bravo	85	19	245	3	81.66	2-33	–	–

Also bowled: S.Chanderpaul 4-0-16-0; F.H.Edwards 28.1-4-116-1; D.Ganga 4-0-20-1; R.S.Morton 4-0-24-0; R.R.Sarwan 18.5-0-72-2.

AUSTRALIA v ENGLAND (1st Test)

At Woolloongabba, Brisbane, on 23, 24, 25, 26, 27 November 2006.
Toss: Australia. Result: **AUSTRALIA** won by 277 runs.
Debuts: None.

AUSTRALIA

J.L.Langer	c Pietersen b Flintoff	82	not out	100
M.L.Hayden	c Collingwood b Flintoff	21	run out	37
*R.T.Ponting	lbw b Hoggard	196	not out	60
D.R.Martyn	c Collingwood b Giles	29		
M.E.K.Hussey	b Flintoff	86		
M.J.Clarke	c Strauss b Anderson	56		
†A.C.Gilchrist	lbw b Hoggard	0		
S.K.Warne	c Jones b Harmison	17		
B.Lee	not out	43		
S.R.Clark	b Flintoff	39		
G.D.McGrath	not out	8		
Extras	(B 2, LB 8, W 8, NB 7)	25	(LB 4, NB 1)	5
Total	(9 wickets declared)	**602**	(1 wicket declared)	**202**

ENGLAND

A.J.Strauss	c Hussey b McGrath	12	c sub (R.A.Broad) b Clark	11
A.N.Cook	c Warne b McGrath	11	c Hussey b Warne	43
I.R.Bell	c Ponting b Clark	50	lbw b Warne	0
P.D.Collingwood	c Gilchrist b Clark	5	st Gilchrist b Warne	96
K.P.Pietersen	lbw b McGrath	16	c Martyn b Lee	92
*A.Flintoff	c Gilchrist b Lee	0	c Langer b Warne	16
†G.O.Jones	lbw b McGrath	19	b McGrath	33
A.F.Giles	c Hayden b McGrath	24	c Warne b Clark	23
M.J.Hoggard	c Gilchrist b Clark	0	c Warne b Clark	8
S.J.Harmison	c Gilchrist b McGrath	0	c McGrath b Clark	13
J.M.Anderson	not out	2	not out	4
Extras	(B 2, LB 8, W 2, NB 6)	18	(B 8, LB 10, W 2, NB 11)	31
Total		**157**		**370**

ENGLAND	O	M	R	W		O	M	R	W
Harmison	30	4	123	1	(4)	12.1	1	54	0
Hoggard	31	5	98	2	(1)	11	2	43	0
Anderson	29	6	141	1	(2)	9	1	54	0
Flintoff	30	4	99	4	(3)	5	2	11	0
Giles	25	2	91	1		5	0	22	0
Bell	1	0	12	0					
Pietersen	9	1	28	0	(6)	3	0	14	0
AUSTRALIA									
Lee	15	3	51	1		22	1	98	1
McGrath	23.1	8	50	6		19	3	53	1
Clark	14	5	21	3		24.1	6	72	4
Warne	9	0	25	0		34	7	124	4
Hussey						1	0	5	0

FALL OF WICKETS

	A	E	A	E
Wkt	*1st*	*1st*	*2nd*	*2nd*
1st	79	28	68	29
2nd	141	28	–	36
3rd	198	42	–	91
4th	407	78	–	244
5th	467	79	–	271
6th	467	126	–	293
7th	500	149	–	326
8th	528	153	–	346
9th	578	154	–	361
10th	–	157	–	370

Umpires: B.F.Bowden (*New Zealand*) (38) and S.A.Bucknor (*West Indies*) (114).
Referee: J.J.Crowe (*New Zealand*) (16). **Test No. 1817/312 (A682/E853)**

AUSTRALIA v ENGLAND (2nd Test)

At Adelaide Oval on 1, 2, 3, 4, 5 December 2006.
Toss: England. Result: **AUSTRALIA** won by six wickets.
Debuts: None.

ENGLAND

A.J.Strauss	c Martyn b Clark	14	c Hussey b Warne	34
A.N.Cook	c Gilchrist b Clark	27	c Gilchrist b Clark	9
I.R.Bell	c and b Lee	60	run out	26
P.D.Collingwood	c Gilchrist b Clark	206	not out	22
K.P.Pietersen	run out	158	b Warne	2
*A.Flintoff	not out	38	c Gilchrist b Lee	2
†G.O.Jones	c Martyn b Warne	1	c Hayden b Lee	10
A.F.Giles	not out	27	c Hayden b Warne	0
M.J.Hoggard			b Warne	4
S.J.Harmison			lbw b McGrath	8
J.M.Anderson			lbw b McGrath	1
Extras	(LB 10, W 2, NB 8)	20	(B 3, LB 5, W 1, NB 2)	11
Total	(6 wickets declared)	**551**		**129**

AUSTRALIA

J.L.Langer	c Pietersen b Flintoff	4		c Bell b Hoggard	7
M.L.Hayden	c Jones b Hoggard	12		c Collingwood b Flintoff	18
*R.T.Ponting	c Jones b Hoggard	142		c Strauss b Giles	49
D.R.Martyn	c Bell b Hoggard	11	(5)	c Strauss b Flintoff	5
M.E.K.Hussey	b Hoggard	91	(4)	not out	61
M.J.Clarke	c Giles b Hoggard	124		not out	21
†A.C.Gilchrist	c Bell b Giles	64			
S.K.Warne	lbw b Hoggard	43			
B.Lee	not out	7			
S.R.Clark	b Hoggard	0			
G.D.McGrath	c Jones b Anderson	1			
Extras	(B 4, LB 2, W 1, NB 7)	14		(B 2, LB 2, W 1, NB 2)	7
Total		**513**		(4 wickets)	**168**

AUSTRALIA	O	M	R	W		O	M	R	W
Lee	34	1	139	1		18	3	35	2
McGrath	30	5	107	0		10	6	15	2
Clark	34	6	75	3	(4)	13	4	22	1
Warne	53	9	167	1	(3)	32	12	49	4
Clarke	17	2	53	0					
ENGLAND									
Hoggard	42	6	109	7		4	0	29	1
Flintoff	26	5	82	1		9	0	44	2
Harmison	25	5	96	0	(4)	4	0	15	0
Anderson	21.3	3	85	1	(5)	3.5	0	23	0
Giles	42	7	103	1	(3)	10	0	46	1
Pietersen	9	0	32	0		2	0	7	0

FALL OF WICKETS

	E	A	E	A
Wkt	*1st*	*1st*	*2nd*	*2nd*
1st	32	8	31	14
2nd	45	35	69	33
3rd	158	65	70	116
4th	468	257	73	121
5th	489	286	77	–
6th	491	384	94	–
7th	–	502	97	–
8th	–	505	105	–
9th	–	507	119	–
10th	–	513	129	–

Umpires: S.A.Bucknor (*West Indies*) (115) and R.E.Koertzen (*South Africa*) (77).
Referee: J.J.Crowe (*New Zealand*) (17). **Test No. 1818/313 (A683/E854)**

AUSTRALIA v ENGLAND (3rd Test)

At W.A.C.A. Ground, Perth, on 14, 15, 16, 17, 18 December 2006.
Toss: Australia. Result: **AUSTRALIA** won by 206 runs.
Debuts: None.

AUSTRALIA

J.L.Langer	b Panesar	37		b Hoggard	0
M.L.Hayden	c Jones b Hoggard	24		c Collingwood b Panesar	92
*R.T.Ponting	lbw b Harmison	2		c Jones b Harmison	75
M.E.K.Hussey	not out	74		c Jones b Panesar	103
M.J.Clarke	c and b Harmison	37		not out	135
A.Symonds	c Jones b Panesar	26		c Collingwood b Panesar	2
†A.C.Gilchrist	c Bell b Panesar	0		not out	102
S.K.Warne	c Jones b Panesar	25			
B.Lee	lbw b Panesar	10			
S.R.Clark	b Harmison	3			
G.D.McGrath	c Cook b Harmison	1			
Extras	(W 1, NB 4)	5		(LB 15, W 2, NB 1)	18
Total		**244**		(5 wickets declared)	**527**

ENGLAND

A.J.Strauss	c Gilchrist b Clark	42		lbw b Lee	0
A.N.Cook	c Langer b McGrath	15		c Gilchrist b McGrath	116
I.R.Bell	c Gilchrist b Lee	0		c Langer b Warne	87
P.D.Collingwood	c Hayden b McGrath	11		c Gilchrist b Clark	5
K.P.Pietersen	c Symonds b Lee	70		not out	60
*A.Flintoff	c Warne b Symonds	13	(7)	b Warne	51
†G.O.Jones	c Langer b Symonds	0	(8)	run out	0
S.I.Mahmood	c Gilchrist b Clark	10	(9)	lbw b Clark	4
M.J.Hoggard	c Hayden b Warne	4	(6)	b McGrath	0
S.J.Harmison	c Lee b Clark	23		lbw b Warne	0
M.S.Panesar	not out	16		b Warne	1
Extras	(W 1, NB 10)	11		(B 7, LB 8, W 6, NB 5)	26
Total		**215**			**350**

ENGLAND	O	M	R	W	O	M	R	W
Hoggard	12	2	40	1	20	4	85	1
Flintoff	9	2	36	0	19	2	76	0
Harmison	19	4	48	4	24	3	116	1
Panesar	24	4	92	5	34	3	145	3
Mahmood	7	2	28	0	10	0	59	0
Pietersen					5	1	31	0
AUSTRALIA								
Lee	18	1	69	2	22	3	75	1
McGrath	18	5	48	2	27	9	61	2
Clark	15.1	3	49	3	25	7	56	2
Warne	9	0	41	1	39.2	6	115	4
Symonds	4	1	8	2	9	1	28	0

FALL OF WICKETS

	A	E	A	E
Wkt	*1st*	*1st*	*2nd*	*2nd*
1st	47	36	0	0
2nd	54	37	144	170
3rd	69	55	206	185
4th	121	82	357	261
5th	172	107	365	261
6th	172	114	–	336
7th	214	128	–	336
8th	234	155	–	345
9th	242	175	–	346
10th	244	215	–	350

Umpires: Alim Dar (*Pakistan*) (35) and R.E.Koertzen (*South Africa*) (78).
Referee: J.J.Crowe (*New Zealand*) (18). **Test No. 1819/314 (A684/E855)**

AUSTRALIA v ENGLAND (4th Test)

At Melbourne Cricket Ground on 26, 27, 28 December 2006.
Toss: England. Result: **AUSTRALIA** won by an innings and 99 runs.
Debuts: None.

ENGLAND

A.J.Strauss	b Warne	50		c Gilchrist b Clark	31
A.N.Cook	c Gilchrist b Lee	11		b Clark	20
I.R.Bell	lbw b Clark	7		lbw b McGrath	2
P.D.Collingwood	c Ponting b Lee	28	(5)	c Langer b Lee	16
K.P.Pietersen	c Symonds b Warne	21	(4)	b Clark	1
*A.Flintoff	c Warne b Clark	13		lbw b Clark	25
†C.M.W.Read	c Ponting b Warne	3		not out	26
S.I.Mahmood	c Gilchrist b McGrath	0		lbw b Warne	0
S.J.Harmison	c Clarke b Warne	7		lbw b Warne	4
M.S.Panesar	c Symonds b Warne	4		c Clarke b Lee	14
M.J.Hoggard	not out	9		b Lee	5
Extras	(B 2, LB 1, NB 3)	6		(LB 12, W 1, NB 4)	17
Total		**159**			**161**

AUSTRALIA

J.L.Langer	c Read b Flintoff	27
M.L.Hayden	c Read b Mahmood	153
B.Lee	c Read b Flintoff	0
*R.T.Ponting	c Cook b Flintoff	7
M.E.K.Hussey	b Hoggard	6
M.J.Clarke	c Read b Harmison	5
A.Symonds	c Read b Harmison	156
†A.C.Gilchrist	c Collingwood b Mahmood	1
S.K.Warne	not out	40
S.R.Clark	c Read b Mahmood	8
G.D.McGrath	c Bell b Mahmood	0
Extras	(LB 6, W 1, NB 9)	16
Total		**419**

AUSTRALIA	O	M	R	W		O	M	R	W
Lee	13	4	36	2		18.5	6	47	4
McGrath	20	8	37	1		12	2	26	1
Clark	17	6	27	2		16	6	30	3
Symonds	7	2	17	0					
Warne	17.2	4	39	5	(4)	19	3	46	2
ENGLAND									
Hoggard	21	6	82	1					
Flintoff	22	1	77	3					
Harmison	28	6	69	2					
Mahmood	21.3	1	100	4					
Panesar	12	1	52	0					
Collingwood	3	0	20	0					
Pietersen	1	0	13	0					

FALL OF WICKETS

	E	A	E
Wkt	*1st*	*1st*	*2nd*
1st	23	44	41
2nd	44	44	48
3rd	101	62	49
4th	101	79	75
5th	122	84	90
6th	135	363	108
7th	136	365	109
8th	145	383	127
9th	146	417	146
10th	159	419	161

Umpires: Alim Dar (*Pakistan*) (36) and R.E.Koertzen (*South Africa*) (79).
Referee: R.S.Madugalle (*Sri Lanka*) (92). **Test No. 1820/315 (A685/E856)**

AUSTRALIA v ENGLAND (5th Test)

At Sydney Cricket Ground on 2, 3, 4, 5 January 2007.
Toss: England. Result: **AUSTRALIA** won by ten wickets.
Debuts: None.

ENGLAND

A.J.Strauss	c Gilchrist b Lee	29		lbw b Clark	24
A.N.Cook	c Gilchrist b Clark	20		c Gilchrist b Lee	4
I.R.Bell	b McGrath	71		c Gilchrist b Lee	28
K.P.Pietersen	c Hussey b McGrath	41		c Gilchrist b McGrath	29
P.D.Collingwood	c Gilchrist b McGrath	27		c Hayden b Clark	17
*A.Flintoff	c Gilchrist b Clark	89		st Gilchrist b Warne	7
†C.M.W.Read	c Gilchrist b Lee	2	(8)	c Ponting b Lee	4
S.I.Mahmood	c Hayden b Lee	0	(9)	b McGrath	4
S.J.Harmison	lbw b Clark	2	(10)	not out	16
M.S.Panesar	lbw b Warne	0	(7)	run out	0
J.M.Anderson	not out	0		c Hussey b McGrath	5
Extras	(LB 5, W 3, NB 2)	10		(B 2, LB 3, W 1, NB 3)	9
Total		**291**			**147**

AUSTRALIA

J.L.Langer	c Read b Anderson	26	not out	20
M.L.Hayden	c Collingwood b Harmison	33	not out	23
*R.T.Ponting	run out	45		
M.E.K.Hussey	c Read b Anderson	37		
M.J.Clarke	c Read b Harmison	11		
A.Symonds	b Panesar	48		
†A.C.Gilchrist	c Read b Anderson	62		
S.K.Warne	st Read b Panesar	71		
B.Lee	c Read b Flintoff	5		
S.R.Clark	c Pietersen b Mahmood	35		
G.D.McGrath	not out	0		
Extras	(LB 10, W 4, NB 6)	20	(LB 3)	3
Total		**393**	(0 wickets)	**46**

AUSTRALIA	O	M	R	W		O	M	R	W
McGrath	29	8	67	3	(2)	21	11	38	3
Lee	22	5	75	3	(1)	14	5	39	3
Clark	24	6	62	3		12	4	29	2
Warne	22.4	1	69	1		6	1	23	1
Symonds	6	2	13	0		5	2	13	0
ENGLAND									
Flintoff	17	2	56	1					
Anderson	26	8	98	3	(1)	4	0	12	0
Harmison	23	5	80	2	(2)	5	1	13	0
Mahmood	11	1	59	1	(3)	1.5	0	18	0
Panesar	19.3	0	90	2					

FALL OF WICKETS

	E	A	E	A
Wkt	*1st*	*1st*	*2nd*	*2nd*
1st	45	34	5	–
2nd	58	100	55	–
3rd	166	118	64	–
4th	167	155	98	–
5th	245	190	113	–
6th	258	260	114	–
7th	258	318	114	–
8th	282	325	122	–
9th	291	393	123	–
10th	291	393	147	–

Umpires: Alim Dar (*Pakistan*) (37) and B.F.Bowden (*New Zealand*) (39).
Referee: R.S.Madugalle (*Sri Lanka*) (93). **Test No. 1821/316 (A686/E857)**

AUSTRALIA v ENGLAND 2006-07

AUSTRALIA – BATTING AND FIELDING

	M	I	NO	HS	Runs	Avge	100	50	Ct/St
M.E.K.Hussey	5	7	2	103	458	91.60	1	4	5
R.T.Ponting	5	8	1	196	576	82.28	2	2	4
M.J.Clarke	5	7	2	135*	389	77.80	2	1	2
A.Symonds	3	4	–	156	232	58.00	1	–	3
M.L.Hayden	5	9	1	153	413	51.62	1	1	7
S.K.Warne	5	5	1	71	196	49.00	–	1	5
A.C.Gilchrist	5	6	1	102*	229	45.80	1	2	24/2
J.L.Langer	5	9	2	100*	303	43.28	1	1	5
B.Lee	5	5	2	43*	65	21.66	–	–	2
S.R.Clark	5	5	–	39	85	17.00	–	–	–
D.R.Martyn	2	3	–	29	45	15.00	–	–	3
G.D.McGrath	5	5	2	8*	10	3.33	–	–	1

AUSTRALIA – BOWLING

	O	M	R	W	Avge	Best	5wI	10wM
S.R.Clark	194.2	53	443	26	17.03	4-72	–	–
G.D.McGrath	209.1	65	502	21	23.90	6-50	1	–
S.K.Warne	241.2	43	698	23	30.34	5-39	1	–
B.Lee	196.5	32	664	20	33.20	4-47	–	–
A.Symonds	31	8	79	2	39.50	2- 8	–	–

Also bowled: M.J.Clarke 17-2-53-0; M.E.K.Hussey 1-0-5-0.

ENGLAND – BATTING AND FIELDING

	M	I	NO	HS	Runs	Avge	100	50	Ct/St
K.P.Pietersen	5	10	1	158	490	54.44	1	3	3
P.D.Collingwood	5	10	1	206	433	48.11	1	1	7
I.R.Bell	5	10	–	87	331	33.10	–	4	5
A.Flintoff	5	10	1	89	254	28.22	–	2	–
A.N.Cook	5	10	–	116	276	27.60	1	–	2
A.J.Strauss	5	10	–	50	247	24.70	–	1	3
A.F.Giles	2	4	1	27*	74	24.66	–	–	1
C.M.W.Read	2	4	1	26*	35	11.66	–	–	11/1
G.O.Jones	3	6	–	33	63	10.50	–	–	9
S.J.Harmison	5	9	1	23	73	9.12	–	–	1
M.S.Panesar	3	6	1	16*	35	7.00	–	–	–
J.M.Anderson	3	5	3	5	12	6.00	–	–	–
M.J.Hoggard	4	7	1	9*	30	5.00	–	–	–
S.I.Mahmood	3	6	–	10	18	3.00	–	–	–

ENGLAND – BOWLING

	O	M	R	W	Avge	Best	5wI	10wM
M.J.Hoggard	141	25	486	13	37.38	7-109	1	–
M.S.Panesar	89.3	8	379	10	37.90	5- 92	1	–
A.Flintoff	137	18	481	11	43.72	4- 99	–	–
S.I.Mahmood	51.2	4	264	5	52.80	4-100	–	–
S.J.Harmison	170.1	29	614	10	61.40	4- 48	–	–
J.M.Anderson	93.2	18	413	5	82.60	3- 98	–	–
A.F.Giles	82	9	262	3	87.33	1- 46	–	–

Also bowled: I.R.Bell 1-0-12-0; P.D.Collingwood 3-0-20-0; K.P.Pietersen 29-2-125-0.

NEW ZEALAND v SRI LANKA (1st Test)

At Lancaster Park, Christchurch, on 7, 8, 9 December 2006.
Toss: Sri Lanka. Result: **NEW ZEALAND** won by five wickets.
Debuts: Sri Lanka – L.P.C.Silva.

SRI LANKA

W.U.Tharanga	c How b Franklin	33	c Fleming b Bond	24
S.T.Jayasuriya	c Fleming b Bond	5	run out	10
K.C.Sangakkara	c Sinclair b Bond	4	not out	100
*D.P.M.D.Jayawardena	c Franklin b Bond	8	c Fleming b Franklin	0
C.K.Kapugedara	lbw b Franklin	37	c Oram b Bond	1
L.P.C.Silva	b Franklin	0	c Vettori b Bond	0
†H.A.P.W.Jayawardena	c How b Martin	7	run out	11
W.P.U.C.J.Vaas	c McCullum b Oram	4	c McCullum b Oram	0
M.F.Maharoof	c Fleming b Oram	15	c McCullum b Bond	7
S.L.Malinga	not out	7	c McCullum b Franklin	0
M.Muralitharan	c Astle b Martin	14	run out	8
Extras	(LB 13, W 1, NB 6)	20	(LB 5, NB 4)	9
Total		**154**		**170**

NEW ZEALAND

C.D.Cumming	b Muralitharan	43	c HAPW Jayawardena b Vaas	43
J.M.How	lbw b Malinga	0	lbw b Muralitharan	11
M.S.Sinclair	c HAPW Jayawardena b Vaas	36	c Sangakkara b Muralitharan	4
*S.P.Fleming	c Kapugedara b Maharoof	48	lbw b Vaas	0
N.J.Astle	lbw b Muralitharan	2	lbw b Muralitharan	24
J.D.P.Oram	c Silva b Vaas	1	not out	12
†B.B.McCullum	b Vaas	0	not out	14
D.L.Vettori	c DPMD Jayawardena b Malinga	63		
J.E.C.Franklin	lbw b Muralitharan	0		
S.E.Bond	lbw b Muralitharan	1		
C.S.Martin	not out	0		
Extras	(LB 5, NB 7)	12	(B 1, LB 1, W 5, NB 4)	11
Total		**206**	(5 wickets)	**119**

NEW ZEALAND	O	M	R	W		O	M	R	W
Bond	13	2	43	3		19.1	5	63	4
Martin	16.4	2	37	2		11	2	38	0
Franklin	12	0	30	3		13	1	34	2
Oram	10	5	30	2		7	1	19	1
Astle	1	0	1	0	(6)	1	0	1	0
Vettori					(5)	2	0	10	0
SRI LANKA									
Vaas	18	4	49	3		12	3	33	2
Malinga	19.4	2	43	2		4	1	35	0
Maharoof	14	3	44	1	(4)	3	0	15	0
Muralitharan	34	7	65	4	(3)	14	5	34	3

FALL OF WICKETS

	SL	NZ	SL	NZ
Wkt	*1st*	*1st*	*2nd*	*2nd*
1st	11	3	18	58
2nd	17	73	44	66
3rd	37	106	45	66
4th	87	108	46	68
5th	87	113	46	103
6th	106	113	74	–
7th	110	188	80	–
8th	121	190	99	–
9th	132	206	143	–
10th	154	206	170	–

Umpires: B.G.Jerling (*South Africa*) (3) and S.J.A.Taufel (*Australia*) (39).
Referee: J.Srinath (*India*) (3). **Test No. 1822/23 (NZ331/SL166)**

NEW ZEALAND v SRI LANKA (2nd Test)

At Basin Reserve, Wellington, on 15, 16, 17, 18 December 2006.
Toss: Sri Lanka. Result: **SRI LANKA** won by 217 runs.
Debuts: None.

SRI LANKA

W.U.Tharanga	c McCullum b Martin	7	lbw b Martin	20
S.T.Jayasuriya	c Fleming b Martin	0	c Fleming b Vettori	31
†K.C.Sangakkara	not out	156	c Franklin b Bond	8
*D.P.M.D.Jayawardena	b Martin	0	c Sinclair b Vettori	31
C.K.Kapugedara	c Sinclair b Oram	5	b Vettori	27
L.P.C.Silva	c Fleming b Franklin	61	not out	152
H.A.P.W.Jayawardena	lbw b Vettori	25	c sub (S.M.Mills) b Martin	37
W.P.U.C.J.Vaas	c McCullum b Bond	0	c McCullum b Vettori	47
M.F.Maharoof	c McCullum b Vettori	4	lbw b Vettori	1
S.L.Malinga	c Sinclair b Vettori	0	lbw b Vettori	0
M.Muralitharan	c and b Bond	0	st McCullum b Vettori	0
Extras	(B 1, LB 1, NB 8)	10	(LB 7, NB 4)	11
Total		**268**		**365**

NEW ZEALAND

C.D.Cumming	b Maharoof	13	c Sangakkara b Muralitharan	20
J.M.How	lbw b Malinga	26	lbw b Malinga	33
M.S.Sinclair	b Malinga	6	c DPMD Jayawardena b Muralitharan	37
*S.P.Fleming	c HAPW Jayawardena b Malinga	0	c Sangakkara b Malinga	27
N.J.Astle	b Malinga	17	lbw b Muralitharan	9
†B.B.McCullum	b Muralitharan	43	b Muralitharan	17
D.L.Vettori	b Malinga	0	(8) lbw b Muralitharan	51
J.D.P.Oram	lbw b Muralitharan	1	(7) lbw b Vaas	4
J.E.C.Franklin	lbw b Muralitharan	1	c Silva b Muralitharan	44
S.E.Bond	lbw b Muralitharan	8	c Sangakkara b Maharoof	6
C.S.Martin	not out	0	not out	4
Extras	(B 7, LB 6, NB 2)	15	(B 9, LB 7, W 11, NB 7)	34
Total		**130**		**286**

NEW ZEALAND	O	M	R	W		O	M	R	W
Bond	16	1	85	2		19	3	67	1
Martin	13	2	50	3		23	1	98	2
Franklin	12	2	46	1	(4)	25	8	63	0
Oram	3	0	10	1					
Vettori	14	1	53	3	(3)	42.3	6	130	7
Astle	7	2	22	0					
SRI LANKA									
Vaas	4	0	8	0		18	2	64	1
Malinga	18	4	68	5		16	1	62	2
Maharoof	5	2	10	1		11	1	47	1
Muralitharan	12.1	3	31	4		34.1	9	87	6
Jayasuriya						6	3	10	0

FALL OF WICKETS

	SL	NZ	SL	NZ
Wkt	*1st*	*1st*	*2nd*	*2nd*
1st	0	30	44	56
2nd	27	40	62	60
3rd	41	40	62	115
4th	81	66	100	139
5th	202	75	168	156
6th	239	85	262	161
7th	240	90	350	163
8th	251	98	356	259
9th	259	116	365	278
10th	268	130	365	286

Umpires: B.G.Jerling (*South Africa*) (4) and S.J.A.Taufel (*Australia*) (40).
Referee: J.Srinath (*India*) (4). **Test No. 1823/24 (NZ332/SL167)**

SOUTH AFRICA v INDIA (1st Test)

At The Wanderers, Johannesburg, on 15, 16, 17, 18, December 2006.
Toss: India. Result: **INDIA** won by 123 runs.
Debuts: None.

INDIA

W.Jaffer	lbw b Ntini	9	c Smith b Nel	4
V.Sehwag	c Boucher b Pollock	4	c Gibbs b Nel	33
*R.Dravid	c Smith b Kallis	32	c Boucher b Pollock	1
S.R.Tendulkar	c De Villiers b Kallis	44	b Pollock	14
V.V.S.Laxman	c Boucher b Ntini	28	c Smith b Ntini	73
S.C.Ganguly	not out	51	c Boucher b Ntini	25
†M.S.Dhoni	c Pollock b Ntini	5	c Boucher Pollock	18
A.Kumble	c Kallis b Nel	6	c Prince b Nel	1
Z.Khan	lbw b Pollock	9	c Boucher b Ntini	37
S.Sreesanth	c Amla b Pollock	0	not out	6
V.R.Singh	c and b Pollock	29	run out	11
Extras	(LB 15, W 11, NB 6)	32	(B 2, LB 10, W 1)	13
Total		**249**		**236**

SOUTH AFRICA

*G.C.Smith	lbw b Sreesanth	5	(2) c Sehwag b Sreesanth	10
H.H.Gibbs	c Sehwag b Khan	0	(1) c Tendulkar b Khan	0
H.M.Amla	c Laxman b Sreesanth	0	c Dhoni b Sreesanth	17
J.H.Kallis	c Laxman b Sreesanth	12	c Ganguly b Sreesanth	27
A.G.Prince	c Dhoni b Kumble	24	b Kumble	97
A.B.de Villiers	c Sehwag b Khan	6	run out	17
†M.V.Boucher	b Sreesanth	5	lbw b Khan	23
S.M.Pollock	lbw b Sreesanth	5	b Kumble	40
A.Nel	c Khan b Singh	21	lbw b Kumble	6
M.Ntini	b Kumble	0	(11) c Sehwag b Khan	8
D.W.Steyn	not out	0	(10) not out	6
Extras	(B 2, W 3, NB 1)	6	(LB 8, NB 19)	27
Total		**84**		**278**

SOUTH AFRICA	O	M	R	W		O	M	R	W
Steyn	10.1	3	26	0					
Ntini	18	1	57	3	(1)	15.4	2	77	3
Pollock	17.5	7	39	4		16	4	33	3
Nel	18.5	5	45	1	(2)	19	4	58	3
Kallis	15	0	67	2	(4)	11	2	30	0
Smith						3	0	26	0
INDIA									
Khan	10	3	32	2		22.5	5	79	3
Sreesanth	10	3	40	5		25	8	59	3
Singh	3.1	0	8	1		18	4	67	0
Kumble	2	1	2	2	(5)	20	4	54	3
Ganguly					(4)	1	0	11	0

FALL OF WICKETS

	I	SA	I	SA
Wkt	*1st*	*1st*	*2nd*	*2nd*
1st	14	5	20	0
2nd	14	5	37	22
3rd	83	5	41	34
4th	110	21	61	48
5th	156	33	119	120
6th	167	38	147	164
7th	188	45	148	231
8th	205	84	218	245
9th	205	84	219	264
10th	249	84	236	278

Umpires: M.R.Benson (*England*) (14) and D.J.Harper (*Australia*) (62).
Referee: R.S.Mahanama (*Sri Lanka*) (11). **Test No. 1824/17 (SA315/I401)**

SOUTH AFRICA v INDIA (2nd Test)

At Kingsmead, Durban, on 26, 27, 28, 29, 30 December 2006.
Toss: South Africa. Result: **SOUTH AFRICA** won by 174 runs.
Debuts: South Africa – M.Morkel.

SOUTH AFRICA

*G.C.Smith	c Tendulkar b Khan	5	b Sreesanth	58
A.B.de Villiers	c Tendulkar b Sreesanth	9	c Laxman b Singh	47
H.M.Amla	lbw b Khan	1	lbw b Sreesanth	0
H.H.Gibbs	c Dhoni b Sreesanth	63	c sub (K.D.Karthik) b Kumble	9
A.G.Prince	c Laxman b Sreesanth	121	c Ganguly b Sreesanth	0
†M.V.Boucher	b Sreesanth	53	lbw b Khan	8
S.M.Pollock	c Sehwag b Singh	11	not out	63
A.J.Hall	lbw b Kumble	0	lbw b Sreesanth	21
A.Nel	b Kumble	0		
M.Morkel	not out	31	(9) c Singh b Sehwag	27
M.Ntini	lbw b Kumble	16		
Extras	(LB 3, W 1, NB 14)	18	(B 5, LB 8, W 7, NB 12)	32
Total		**328**	(8 wickets declared)	**265**

INDIA

W.Jaffer	c De Villiers b Ntini	26	c Nel b Ntini	28
V.Sehwag	c De Villiers b Nel	0	c Smith b Ntini	8
*R.Dravid	lbw b Nel	11	c Boucher b Ntini	5
S.R.Tendulkar	c Boucher b Ntini	63	lbw b Ntini	0
V.V.S.Laxman	not out	50	b Nel	15
S.C.Ganguly	c Gibbs b Ntini	0	c Gibbs b Ntini	26
†M.S.Dhoni	c De Villiers b Morkel	34	c Boucher b Nel	47
A.Kumble	c Boucher b Morkel	0	c Amla b Hall	11
Z.Khan	c Amla b Morkel	2	c Hall b Nel	21
S.Sreesanth	c Boucher b Hall	28	c Boucher b Hall	10
V.R.Singh	c Boucher b Pollock	4	not out	0
Extras	(B 1, LB 7, W 2, NB 12)	22	(B 2, LB 1, W 1, NB 4)	8
Total		**240**		**179**

INDIA	O	M	R	W		O	M	R	W
Khan	23	7	83	2		20	5	65	1
Sreesanth	24	4	109	4		19	3	79	4
Singh	13	1	60	1		10	2	64	1
Kumble	28.3	1	62	3		16	4	37	1
Ganguly	3	1	11	0					
Sehwag						2.4	1	7	1
SOUTH AFRICA									
Nel	23	5	60	2		16	4	57	3
Ntini	15	4	41	3		19	6	48	5
Morkel	18	1	86	3	(4)	6	0	25	0
Pollock	14.5	10	17	1	(3)	9	5	20	0
Hall	7	0	28	1		5.1	1	26	2

FALL OF WICKETS

	SA	I	SA	I
Wkt	*1st*	*1st*	*2nd*	*2nd*
1st	8	5	99	14
2nd	13	35	108	34
3rd	28	61	121	38
4th	122	125	121	45
5th	222	125	140	83
6th	256	179	143	85
7th	257	179	213	101
8th	257	183	265	160
9th	296	235	–	179
10th	328	240	–	179

Umpires: Asad Rauf (*Pakistan*) (8), M.R.Benson (*England*) (15) and I.L.Howell (*South Africa*) (7).
Referee: R.S.Mahanama (*Sri Lanka*) (12). **Test No. 1825/18 (SA316/I402)**

SOUTH AFRICA v INDIA (3rd Test)

At Newlands, Cape Town, on 2, 3, 4, 5, 6 January 2007.
Toss: India. Result: **SOUTH AFRICA** won by five wickets.
Debuts: South Africa – P.L.Harris.

INDIA

W.Jaffer	c Kallis b Steyn	116		c De Villiers b Ntini	2
†K.D.Karthik	c Amla b Harris	63	(7)	not out	38
*R.Dravid	c Boucher b Pollock	29		c and b Harris	47
S.R.Tendulkar	c Kallis b Harris	64	(5)	lbw b Pollock	14
V.V.S.Laxman	b Steyn	13	(6)	run out	1
S.C.Ganguly	c Amla b Pollock	66	(4)	c Gibbs b Kallis	46
V.Sehwag	c Ntini b Harris	40	(2)	c Boucher b Steyn	4
A.Kumble	lbw b Pollock	0		c Gibbs b Steyn	6
Z.Khan	st Boucher b Harris	1		run out	1
S.Sreesanth	c Gibbs b Pollock	3		c Kallis b Steyn	4
M.M.Patel	not out	0		c Pollock b Steyn	0
Extras	(B 5, LB 4, W 2, NB 8)	19		(LB 5, NB 1)	6
Total		**414**			**169**

SOUTH AFRICA

*G.C.Smith	c Sehwag b Kumble	94	(2)	c Karthik b Khan	55
A.B.de Villiers	c Karthik b Sreesanth	1	(1)	c Karthik b Khan	22
H.M.Amla	c Karthik b Sreesanth	63		lbw b Kumble	10
J.H.Kallis	c Patel b Tendulkar	54	(5)	c Dravid b Khan	32
A.G.Prince	b Kumble	26	(6)	not out	38
H.H.Gibbs	c Jaffer b Sehwag	7	(7)	not out	0
†M.V.Boucher	c Karthik b Patel	50			
S.M.Pollock	c Ganguly b Khan	31	(4)	c Laxman b Khan	37
P.L.Harris	not out	11			
D.W.Steyn	b Kumble	1			
M.Ntini	lbw b Kumble	0			
Extras	(B 7, LB 13, W 1, NB 14)	35		(B 11, LB 1, NB 5)	17
Total		**373**		(5 wickets)	**211**

SOUTH AFRICA	O	M	R	W		O	M	R	W
Steyn	27	12	58	2	(2)	7	0	30	4
Ntini	26	4	107	0	(1)	8	1	29	1
Pollock	29.1	9	75	4		15	5	24	1
Kallis	12	4	36	0	(5)	12	0	31	1
Harris	37	3	129	4	(4)	22	6	50	1
INDIA									
Khan	20	3	74	1		21	2	62	4
Sreesanth	24	9	58	2		13	2	50	0
Kumble	42.3	6	117	4		25	4	74	1
Patel	20	5	43	1		1	0	2	0
Sehwag	12	0	31	1		1	0	8	0
Tendulkar	10	2	30	1		3.1	2	3	0

FALL OF WICKETS	I	SA	I	SA
Wkt	*1st*	*1st*	*2nd*	*2nd*
1st	153	14	6	36
2nd	202	173	6	55
3rd	240	177	90	127
4th	269	260	114	132
5th	337	260	115	209
6th	395	281	121	–
7th	395	350	147	–
8th	398	372	165	–
9th	407	373	169	–
10th	414	373	169	–

Umpires: Asad Rauf (*Pakistan*) (9) and D.J.Harper (*Australia*) (63).
Referee: R.S.Mahanama (*Sri Lanka*) (13). **Test No. 1826/19 (SA317/I403)**

SOUTH AFRICA v INDIA 2006-07

SOUTH AFRICA – BATTING AND FIELDING

	M	I	NO	HS	Runs	Avge	100	50	Ct/St
A.G.Prince	3	6	1	121	306	61.20	1	1	1
G.C.Smith	3	6	–	94	227	37.83	–	3	4
S.M.Pollock	3	6	1	63*	187	37.40	–	1	3
J.H.Kallis	2	4	–	54	125	31.25	–	1	4
M.V.Boucher	3	5	–	53	139	27.80	–	2	15/1
A.B.de Villiers	3	6	–	47	102	17.00	–	–	5
H.H.Gibbs	3	6	1	63	79	15.80	–	1	6
H.M.Amla	3	6	–	63	91	15.16	–	1	5
A.Nel	2	3	–	21	27	9.00	–	–	1
D.W.Steyn	2	3	2	6*	7	7.00	–	–	–
M.Ntini	3	4	–	16	24	6.00	–	–	1

Played in one Test: A.J.Hall 0, 21 (1 ct); P.L.Harris 11* (1 ct); M.Morkel 31*, 27.

SOUTH AFRICA – BOWLING

	O	M	R	W	Avge	Best	5wI	10wM
S.M.Pollock	101.5	40	208	13	16.00	4- 39	–	–
A.J.Hall	12.1	1	54	3	18.00	2- 26	–	–
D.W.Steyn	44.1	15	114	6	19.00	4- 30	–	–
M.Ntini	101.4	18	359	15	23.93	5- 48	1	–
A.Nel	76.5	18	220	9	24.44	3- 57	–	–
P.L.Harris	59	9	179	5	35.80	4-129	–	–
M.Morkel	24	1	111	3	37.00	3- 86	–	–
J.H.Kallis	50	6	164	3	54.66	2- 67	–	–

Also bowled: G.C.Smith 3-0-26-0.

INDIA – BATTING AND FIELDING

	M	I	NO	HS	Runs	Avge	100	50	Ct/St
S.C.Ganguly	3	6	1	66	214	42.80	–	2	3
V.V.S.Laxman	3	6	1	73	180	36.00	–	2	5
S.R.Tendulkar	3	6	–	64	199	33.16	–	2	3
W.Jaffer	3	6	–	116	185	30.83	1	–	1
M.S.Dhoni	2	4	–	47	104	26.00	–	–	3
R.Dravid	3	6	–	47	125	20.83	–	–	1
V.Sehwag	3	6	–	40	89	14.83	–	–	6
V.R.V.Singh	2	4	1	29	44	14.66	–	–	1
Z.Khan	3	6	–	37	71	11.83	–	–	1
S.Sreesanth	3	6	1	28	51	10.20	–	–	–
A.Kumble	3	6	–	11	24	4.00	–	–	–

Played in one Test: K.D.Karthik 63, 38* (5 ct); M.M.Patel 0*, 0 (1 ct).

INDIA – BOWLING

	O	M	R	W	Avge	Best	5wI	10wM
S.Sreesanth	115	29	395	18	21.94	5- 40	1	–
A.Kumble	134	20	346	14	24.71	4-117	–	–
Z.Khan	116.5	25	395	13	30.38	4- 62	–	–
V.R.V.Singh	44.1	7	199	3	66.33	1- 8	–	–

Also bowled: S.C.Ganguly 4-1-22-0; M.M.Patel 21-5-45-1; V.Sehwag 15.4-1-46-2; S.R.Tendulkar 13.1-4-33-1.

SOUTH AFRICA v PAKISTAN (1st Test)

At Centurion Park, (Verwoerdburg), Pretoria, on 11, 12, 13, 14, 15 January 2007.
Toss: Pakistan. Result: **SOUTH AFRICA** won by seven wickets.
Debuts: None.

PAKISTAN

Mohammad Hafeez	c Boucher b Ntini	19		c Smith b Kallis	15
Imran Farhat	c Amla b Ntini	26		c De Villiers b Harris	68
Yasir Hamid	c Ntini b Nel	65		c Boucher b Kallis	9
Younis Khan	c Nel b Pollock	68		lbw b Pollock	38
*Inzamam-ul-Haq	c Amla b Ntini	42		c De Villiers b Pollock	35
Faisal Iqbal	c Boucher b Kallis	1		c Gibbs b Harris	9
†Kamran Akmal	c Pollock b Nel	29		c Gibbs b Harris	15
Shahid Nazir	c Gibbs b Ntini	15	(9)	b Ntini	40
Naved-ul-Hasan	c and b Nel	30	(8)	c Prince b Pollock	33
Danish Kaneria	c Kallis b Ntini	0		c Gibbs b Harris	23
Mohammad Asif	not out	1		not out	8
Extras	(B 6, LB 6, W 2, NB 3)	17		(LB 5, NB 4)	9
Total		**313**			**302**

SOUTH AFRICA

A.B.de Villiers	c Younis b Asif	4	(2)	c Younis b Asif	12
*G.C.Smith	c Akmal b Asif	0	(1)	lbw b Hafeez	32
H.M.Amla	c Akmal b Asif	71		not out	64
J.H.Kallis	c Younis b Asif	18	(5)	not out	60
A.G.Prince	st Akmal b Kaneria	138			
H.H.Gibbs	lbw b Naved	94			
†M.V.Boucher	c and b Kaneria	2			
S.M.Pollock	not out	39			
P.L.Harris	b Kaneria	3	(4)	c Faisal b Asif	7
A.Nel	b Naved	5			
M.Ntini	c Younis b Asif	5			
Extras	(LB 13, NB 25)	38		(B 8, LB 4, NB 12)	24
Total		**417**		(3 wickets)	**199**

SOUTH AFRICA	O	M	R	W		O	M	R	W
Ntini	24	3	83	5	(2)	16	2	78	1
Nel	26.5	3	100	3	(1)	22	6	69	0
Pollock	18	5	38	1		22	7	60	3
Kallis	15	3	55	1		16	0	44	2
Harris	13	2	25	0		20.2	6	46	4
PAKISTAN									
Mohammad Asif	27.5	4	89	5		14	2	56	2
Naved-ul-Hasan	17	2	92	2		7	3	21	0
Shahid Nazir	20	1	96	0		3	1	13	0
Danish Kaneria	41	8	97	3		24.5	5	61	0
Mohammad Hafeez	11	1	24	0		12	2	36	1
Imran Farhat	1	0	6	0					

FALL OF WICKETS

	P	SA	P	SA
Wkt	*1st*	*1st*	*2nd*	*2nd*
1st	48	3	41	20
2nd	50	8	58	67
3rd	183	53	115	80
4th	193	143	154	–
5th	204	356	175	–
6th	256	358	187	–
7th	276	383	199	–
8th	300	386	255	–
9th	311	391	283	–
10th	313	417	302	–

Umpires: S.A.Bucknor (*West Indies*) (116) and B.R.Doctrove (*West Indies*) (10).
Referee: B.C.Broad (*England*) (21). **Test No. 1827/12 (SA318/P328)**

SOUTH AFRICA v PAKISTAN (2nd Test)

At St George's Park, Port Elizabeth, on 19, 20, 21, 22 January 2007.
Toss: South Africa. Result: **PAKISTAN** won by five wickets.
Debuts: None.

SOUTH AFRICA

A.B.de Villiers	c Akmal b Akhtar	2	(2)	b Asif	15
*G.C.Smith	c Younis b Kaneria	28	(1)	c Inzamam b Asif	10
H.M.Amla	c Akmal b Akhtar	5		b Sami	16
J.H.Kallis	c Akmal b Akhtar	24		lbw b Asif	91
A.G.Prince	c Farhat b Sami	2		lbw b Kaneria	22
H.H.Gibbs	lbw b Kaneria	2		c Younis b Asif	40
†M.V.Boucher	c Younis b Kaneria	35		c Younis b Asif	46
S.M.Pollock	c Sami b Akhtar	4		c and b Kaneria	36
A.Nel	c Kaneria b Asif	10		not out	23
M.Ntini	not out	0	(11)	c Hamid b Kaneria	18
P.L.Harris	c Hamid b Asif	4	(10)	c sub (Faisal Iqbal) b Kaneria	0
Extras	(LB 3, NB 5)	8		(B 3, LB 5, NB 6)	14
Total		**124**			**331**

PAKISTAN

Mohammad Hafeez	c Amla b Ntini	13		lbw b Pollock	32
Imran Farhat	c De Villiers b Ntini	0		c Kallis b Ntini	7
Younis Khan	c Gibbs b Ntini	45	(4)	not out	67
Yasir Hamid	c De Villiers b Ntini	2	(3)	run out	6
M.Yousuf Youhana	lbw b Pollock	32		c Gibbs b Pollock	18
†Kamran Akmal	c Prince b Nel	33	(7)	not out	57
Mohammad Sami	c Boucher b Ntini	10			
*Inzamam-ul-Haq	not out	92	(6)	lbw b Ntini	1
Shoaib Akhtar	c Boucher b Kallis	4			
Danish Kaneria	c Gibbs b Pollock	1			
Mohammad Asif	b Ntini	7			
Extras	(B 4, LB 11, W 5, NB 1, Pen 5)	26		(LB 1, W 1, NB 1)	3
Total		**265**		(5 wickets)	**191**

PAKISTAN	O	M	R	W		O	M	R	W
Shoaib Akhtar	11	2	36	4					
Mohammad Asif	9	2	34	2	(1)	38	16	76	5
Danish Kaneria	14	3	36	3		51.2	14	105	4
Mohammad Sami	6	1	15	1	(2)	29	5	90	1
Imran Farhat					(4)	7	0	20	0
Mohammad Hafeez					(5)	8	0	32	0
SOUTH AFRICA									
Nel	23	2	68	1		14	2	63	0
Ntini	21	6	59	6		19	6	50	2
Kallis	13	0	56	1	(4)	6	0	17	0
Pollock	14	2	42	2	(3)	13	4	47	2
Harris	5	1	20	0		5.3	0	13	0

FALL OF WICKETS

	SA	P	SA	P
Wkt	*1st*	*1st*	*2nd*	*2nd*
1st	9	0	18	29
2nd	27	17	30	35
3rd	40	19	61	48
4th	49	79	117	87
5th	58	135	195	92
6th	83	135	205	–
7th	89	166	285	–
8th	120	184	289	–
9th	120	191	290	–
10th	124	265	331	–

Umpires: B.R.Doctrove (*West Indies*) (11) and P.D.Parker (*Australia*) (7).
Referee: B.C.Broad (*England*) (22). **Test No. 1828/13 (SA319/P329)**

SOUTH AFRICA v PAKISTAN (3rd Test)

At Newlands, Cape Town, on 26, 27, 28 January 2007.
Toss: South Africa. Result: **SOUTH AFRICA** won by five wickets.
Debuts: None.

PAKISTAN

Mohammad Hafeez	c De Villiers b Ntini	10	c Prince b Steyn	10
Imran Farhat	c Smith b Kallis	20	lbw b Steyn	13
Yasir Hamid	c Kallis b Ntini	7	c Prince b Hall	35
Younis Khan	c De Villiers b Kallis	8	c Boucher b Ntini	0
M.Yousuf Youhana	c Prince b Ntini	83	b Hall	18
*Inzamam-ul-Haq	c Boucher b Hall	6	c Boucher b Steyn	22
†Kamran Akmal	c De Villiers b Steyn	0	st Boucher b Harris	6
Mohammad Sami	c Boucher b Kallis	4	c Amla b Kallis	31
Shahid Nazir	c Harris b Ntini	3	c Boucher b Kallis	27
Danish Kaneria	c Boucher b Kallis	0	not out	1
Mohammad Asif	not out	0	c Prince b Harris	6
Extras	(LB 2, W 6, NB 8)	16	(B 6, LB 2, W 5, NB 4)	17
Total		**157**		**186**

SOUTH AFRICA

H.H.Dippenaar	lbw b Asif	0	(2) c Akmal b Kaneria	3
*G.C.Smith	c Inzamam b Nazir	64	(1) lbw b Asif	33
H.M.Amla	c Akmal b Asif	2	(4) c Akmal b Asif	3
J.H.Kallis	c Akmal b Sami	28	(5) b Nazir	51
A.G.Prince	c Hamid b Kaneria	19	(6) not out	59
A.B.de Villiers	b Kaneria	11	(7) not out	4
P.L.Harris	c Younis b Asif	1	(3) lbw b Kaneria	0
†M.V.Boucher	not out	40		
A.J.Hall	c Akmal b Kaneria	4		
D.W.Steyn	run out	3		
M.Ntini	lbw b Sami	0		
Extras	(B 4, LB 4, W 1, NB 2)	11	(B 4, LB 4)	8
Total		**183**	(5 wickets)	**161**

SOUTH AFRICA	O	M	R	W		O	M	R	W
Steyn	11	3	40	1	(2)	13	3	47	3
Ntini	13.1	2	44	4	(1)	10	2	41	1
Kallis	11	1	42	4		7	0	36	2
Hall	8	2	29	1		7	1	23	2
Harris						14.2	2	31	2
PAKISTAN									
Mohammad Asif	16	2	53	3		21	8	43	2
Mohammad Sami	9	1	41	2	(5)	1	0	9	0
Shahid Nazir	8	0	37	1	(2)	9	1	42	1
Danish Kaneria	20	6	44	3	(3)	28	9	52	2
Mohammad Hafeez					(4)	5	1	7	0

FALL OF WICKETS

	P	SA	P	SA
Wkt	*1st*	*1st*	*2nd*	*2nd*
1st	13	0	17	30
2nd	27	12	28	36
3rd	47	92	44	36
4th	54	107	83	39
5th	81	128	92	156
6th	90	133	111	–
7th	150	133	121	–
8th	155	140	176	–
9th	157	183	179	–
10th	157	183	186	–

Umpires: S.A.Bucknor (*West Indies*) (117) and P.D.Parker (*Australia*) (8).
Referee: B.C.Broad (*England*) (23). **Test No. 1829/14 (SA320/P330)**

SOUTH AFRICA v PAKISTAN 2006-07

SOUTH AFRICA – BATTING AND FIELDING

	M	*I*	*NO*	*HS*	*Runs*	*Avge*	*100*	*50*	*Ct/St*
A.G.Prince	3	5	1	138	240	60.00	1	1	6
J.H.Kallis	3	6	1	91	272	54.40	–	3	3
H.H.Gibbs	2	3	–	94	136	45.33	–	1	7
M.V.Boucher	3	4	1	46	123	41.00	–	–	11/1
S.M.Pollock	2	3	1	39*	79	39.50	–	–	1
H.M.Amla	3	6	1	71	161	32.20	–	2	4
G.C.Smith	3	6	–	64	167	27.83	–	1	2
A.Nel	2	3	1	23*	38	19.00	–	–	2
A.B.de Villiers	3	6	1	15	48	9.60	–	–	7
M.Ntini	3	4	1	18	23	7.66	–	–	1
P.L.Harris	3	6	–	7	15	2.50	–	–	1

Played in one Test: H.H.Dippenaar 0, 3; A.J.Hall 4; D.W.Steyn 3.

SOUTH AFRICA – BOWLING

	O	*M*	*R*	*W*	*Avge*	*Best*	*5wI*	*10wM*
A.J.Hall	15	3	52	3	17.33	2- 23	–	–
M.Ntini	103.1	21	355	19	18.68	6- 59	2	–
D.W.Steyn	24	6	87	4	21.75	3- 47	–	–
P.L.Harris	58.1	11	135	6	22.50	4- 46	–	–
S.M.Pollock	67	18	187	8	23.37	3- 60	–	–
J.H.Kallis	68	4	250	10	25.00	4- 42	–	–
A.Nel	85.5	13	300	4	75.00	3-100	–	–

PAKISTAN – BATTING AND FIELDING

	M	*I*	*NO*	*HS*	*Runs*	*Avge*	*100*	*50*	*Ct/St*
Younis Khan	3	6	1	68	226	45.20	–	2	9
Inzamam-ul-Haq	3	6	1	92*	198	39.60	–	1	2
Yousuf Youhana	2	4	–	83	151	37.75	–	1	–
Kamran Akmal	3	6	1	57*	140	28.00	–	1	10/1
Imran Farhat	3	6	–	68	134	22.33	–	1	1
Shahid Nazir	2	4	–	40	85	21.25	–	–	–
Yasir Hamid	3	6	–	65	124	20.66	–	1	3
Mohammad Hussain	2	3	–	32	52	17.33	–	–	–
Mohammad Hafeez	2	3	–	19	47	15.66	–	–	–
Mohammad Sami	2	3	–	31	45	15.00	–	–	1
Mohammad Asif	3	5	3	8*	22	11.00	–	–	–
Danish Kaneria	3	5	1	23	25	6.25	–	–	3

Played in one Test: Faisal Iqbal 1, 9 (1 ct); Naved-ul-Hasan 30, 33; Shoaib Akhtar 4.

PAKISTAN – BOWLING

	O	*M*	*R*	*W*	*Avge*	*Best*	*5wI*	*10wM*
Shoaib Akhtar	11	2	36	4	9.00	4- 36	–	–
Mohammad Asif	125.5	34	351	19	18.47	5- 76	2	–
Danish Kaneria	179.1	45	395	15	26.33	4-105	–	–
Mohammad Sami	45	7	155	4	38.75	2- 41	–	–
Naved-ul-Hasan	24	5	113	2	56.50	2- 92	–	–
Shahid Nazir	40	3	188	2	94.00	1- 37	–	–

Also bowled: Imran Farhat 8-0-26-0; Mohammad Hafeez 23-3-60-1; Mohammad Hussain 13-1-39-0.

LEADING TEST AGGREGATES 2006

1000 RUNS

	M	I	NO	HS	Runs	Avge	100	50
M.Yousuf Youhana (P)	11	19	1	202	1788	99.33	9	3
K.P.Pietersen (E)	14	26	1	158	1343	53.72	4	6
R.T.Ponting (A)	10	18	3	196	1333	88.86	7	4
K.C.Sangakkara (SL)	11	20	2	287	1242	69.00	4	4
Younis Khan (P)	11	20	2	119	1179	65.50	3	6
P.D.Collingwood (E)	14	26	4	206	1121	50.95	3	2
R.Dravid (I)	11	20	4	146	1079	67.43	3	7
A.J.Strauss (E)	14	26	–	128	1031	39.65	3	3
A.N.Cook (E)	13	24	2	127	1013	46.04	4	3

RECORD CALENDAR YEAR RUNS AGGREGATE

	M	I	NO	HS	Runs	Avge	100	50
M.Yousuf Youhana (P)(2006)	11	19	1	202	1788	99.33	9	3

1000 RUNS IN DEBUT CALENDAR YEAR

	M	I	NO	HS	Runs	Avge	100	50
M.A.Taylor (A) (1989)	11	20	1	219	1219	64.15	4	5
A.N.Cook (E) (2006)	13	24	2	127	1013	46.04	4	3

50 WICKETS

	M	O	R	W	Avge	Best	5wI	10wM
M.Muralitharan (SL)	11	588.4	1521	90	16.90	8-70	9	5
A.Kumble (I)	11	588.3	1811	53	34.16	6-78	2	–
M.J.Hoggard (E)	14	521.5	1560	51	30.58	7-109	2	–
M.Ntini (SA)	9	324.5	1164	50	23.28	6-100	4	2

RECORD CALENDAR YEAR WICKETS AGGREGATE

	M	O	R	W	Avge	Best	5wI	10wM
M.Muralitharan (SL)(2006)	11	588.4	1521	90	16.90	8-70	9	5
S.K.Warne (A)(2005)	14	691.4	2043	90	22.70	6-46	6	2

40 WICKET-KEEPING DISMISSALS

	M	Dis	Ct	St
G.O.Jones (E)	11	48	46	2
M.S.Dhoni (I)	11	43	35	8
Kamran Akmal (P)	12	42	37	5

RECORD CALENDAR YEAR DISMISSALS AGGREGATE

	M	Dis	Ct	St
I.A.Healy (A)(1993)	16	67	58	9
M.V.Boucher (SA)(1998)	13	67	65	2

RECORD CALENDAR YEAR CATCHES AGGREGATE (non wicket-keepers)

	M	Ct
S.P.Fleming (NZ)(1997)	10	28

---

50 TEST UMPIRING APPEARANCES

117	S.A.Bucknor	(Jamaica)	28.04.1989 to 28.01.2007
92	D.R.Shepherd	(England)	01.08.1985 to 07.06.2005
79	R.E.Koertzen	(South Africa)	26.12.1992 to 28.12.2006
76	D.B.Hair	(Australia)	25.01.1992 to 20.08.2006
73	S.Venkataraghavan	(India)	29.01.1993 to 20.01.2004
66	H.D.Bird	(England)	05.07.1973 to 24.06.1996
63	D.J.Harper	(Australia)	28.11.1998 to 06.01.2007

TEST MATCH CHAMPIONSHIP SCHEDULE

Months indicate the start of a series. Number of Tests in brackets.
All series involving Zimbabwe are subject to confirmation.

2007	**May**	**England host West Indies (4)**
		Bangladesh host India (2)
	Jun	Sri Lanka host Bangladesh (2)
	Jul	**England host India (3)**
	Aug	Zimbabwe host South Africa (2)
	Sep	Pakistan host South Africa (2)
	Nov	**Sri Lanka host England (3)**
		Australia host Sri Lanka (2)
		India host Pakistan (3)
		South Africa host New Zealand (2)
		Zimbabwe host West Indies (2)
	Dec	Australia host India (4)
		South Africa host West Indies (4)
2008	**Feb**	**New Zealand host England (3)**
		Pakistan host Australia (3)
		Bangladesh host South Africa (2)
	Mar	India host South Africa (3)
		West Indies host Sri Lanka (3)
	Apr	West Indies host Australia (4)
	May	**England host New Zealand (3)**
		Zimbabwe host India (2)
	Jul	**England host South Africa (4)**
		Australia host Bangladesh (2)
		Sri Lanka host India (3)
	Oct	India host Australia (4)
	Nov	**India host England (3)**
		Australia host New Zealand (2)
		South Africa host Bangladesh (2)
		Sri Lanka host Zimbabwe (2)
	Dec	Australia host South Africa (3)
		Pakistan host India (3)
		New Zealand host West Indies (3)
		Bangladesh host Sri Lanka (2)
2009	**Feb**	**West Indies host England (4)**
		South Africa host Australia (3)
		New Zealand host India (3)
		Zimbabwe host Sri Lanka (2)
	Apr	Bangladesh host West Indies (2)
	May	**England host Zimbabwe (2)**
	Jun	**England host Australia (5)**
	Jul	Sri Lanka host Pakistan (3)
		Zimbabwe host New Zealand (2)
	Aug	Sri Lanka host New Zealand (3)
		Zimbabwe host Bangladesh (2)
	Oct	Bangladesh host Zimbabwe (3)
	Nov	**South Africa host England (4)**
		Australia host Pakistan (3)
		India host Sri Lanka (3)
	Dec	Australia host West Indies (3)
		Bangladesh host India (2)
		Pakistan host New Zealand (3)
2010	**Jan**	New Zealand host Bangladesh (2)
	Feb	**Pakistan host England (4)**
		New Zealand host Australia (3)
		India host South Africa (3)
	Mar	West Indies host Zimbabwe (2)
	May	**England host Bangladesh (2)**
		West Indies host South Africa (4)
		Zimbabwe host India (2)
	Jul	**England host West Indies (4)**
	Sep	Pakistan host Bangladesh (2)
		South Africa host Zimbabwe (2)
	Oct	Bangladesh host New Zealand (2)
		Pakistan host South Africa (3)
	Nov	**Australia host England (5)**
		India host New Zealand (3)
		Sri Lanka host West Indies (3)
	Dec	South Africa host India (3)
		New Zealand host Pakistan (3)
		Bangladesh host Zimbabwe (2)
2011	**Apr**	Bangladesh host Australia (2)
		West Indies host India (4)
	May	**England host Sri Lanka (3)**
		West Indies host Pakistan (2)
	Jun	Australia host Zimbabwe (2)
	Jul	**England host India (4)**
		Zimbabwe host Bangladesh (2)
	Aug	Sri Lanka host Australia (3)
	Sep	South Africa host Australia (3)
		Zimbabwe host Pakistan (2)
	Oct	Pakistan host Sri Lanka (3)
		Bangladesh host West Indies (2)
	Nov	Australia host New Zealand (2)
		India host West Indies (3)
	Dec	Australia host India (4)
		New Zealand host Zimbabwe (2)
		Bangladesh host Pakistan (2)
		South Africa host Sri Lanka (3)
2012	**Jan**	**Bangladesh host England (2)**
	Feb	**Zimbabwe host England (2)**
		New Zealand host South Africa (3)
	Mar	West Indies host Australia (4)
		India host Pakistan (3)
	Apr	West Indies host New Zealand (3)

CHAMPIONSHIP TABLE

(As at 1 May 2007)

		Rating
1	Australia (1)	135
2	England (2)	114
3	Pakistan (4)	108
4	India (3)	107
5	Sri Lanka (7)	102
6	South Africa (6)	102
7	New Zealand (5)	93
8	West Indies (8)	72
9	Zimbabwe (9)	28
10	Bangladesh (10)	2

March 2006 positions in brackets

MAJOR ICC EVENTS

Sep 2008	Champions Trophy
Jun 2009	T20 World Championship
Feb/Mar 2011	World Cup

SECOND XI CHAMPIONSHIP FIXTURES 2007

(Three Days)

Date	Venue	Match
APRIL		
Tue 17	Leeds	Yorks v Durham
Wed 18	Derby	Derbys v Lancs
	Uxbridge	Middx v MCC YC
Tue 24	Southampton	Hants v Essex
	Reigate Priory	Surrey v Yorks
	Hove	Sussex v Durham
	Ombersley	Worcs v MCC YC
MAY		
Tue 1	*tba*	Glam v Lancs
	Cheam	Surrey v Warwks
Wed 2	Belper Meadows	Derbys v Notts
	Hinckley	Leics v Northants
Tue 8	Manchester	Lancs v Durham
	Radlett	MCC YC v Glam
	Birmingham	Warwks v Yorks
Wed 9	Denby	Derbys v Scotland
	Hinckley	Leics v Surrey
	Uxbridge (VL)	Middx v Hants
	Kidderminster	Worcs v Somerset
Tue 15	Southampton	Hants v Sussex
	Knowle & Dorridge	Warwks v Leics
	Ombersley	Worcs v Derbys
Wed 16	Gowerton	Glam v Glos
	Taunton	Somerset v Surrey
Tue 22	Radlett	MCC YC v Northants
	Caythorpe	Notts v Scotland
	Taunton Vale	Somerset v Glos
	Moseley	Warwks v Hants
Wed 23	Sutton	Surrey v Lancs
Tue 29	Southend	Essex v Northants
	Todmorden	Yorks v Leics
Wed 30	Canterbury	Kent v Sussex
	Alderley Edge	Lancs v Scotland
	Taunton	Somerset v Middx
	Stratford-upon-Avon	Warwks v Durham
	Kidderminster	Worcs v Surrey
JUNE		
Tue 5	Tynemouth	Durham v MCC YC
	Bishop's Stortford	Essex v Middx
	Leicester	Leics v Derbys
	Stamford Bridge	Yorks v Scotland
Wed 6	Taunton Vale	Somerset v Worcs
	The Oval	Surrey v Hants
Mon 11	Derby	Derbys v Surrey
	Stowe S	Northants v Middx
	Notts Sports Club	Notts v Durham
Wed 13	Southport	Lancs v Glos
	North Perrott	Somerset v MCC YC
	Hove	Sussex v Yorks
Tue 19	Dunstall	Derbys v Warwks
	Stirlands	Sussex v Essex
Wed 20	Bournemouth SC	Hants v Glam
Mon 25	Longhirst	Durham v Worcs
JULY		
Tue 17	Coggleshall	Essex v Surrey
Wed 18	Sheffield (Abbeydale Pk)	Yorks v Derbys
Tue 24	Chelmsford	Essex v Hants
	Bristol	Glos v Somerset
	Blackpool	Lancs v Derbys
	Radlett	Middx v Kent
	Barnt Green	Worcs v Northants
Wed 25	Swallwell	Durham v Scotland
	Whitgift S	Surrey v Sussex
Tue 31	Bristol	Glos v Middx
	Beckenham	Kent v MCC YC
	Milton Keynes	Northants v Warwks
	Stirlands	Sussex v Hants
AUGUST		
Wed 1	Durham (Racecourse)	Durham v Surrey
	Ombersley	Worcs v Leics
Tue 7	Hatherley & Reddings	Glos v Surrey
	Kidderminster	Worcs v Warwks
Wed 8	Manchester	Lancs v Yorks
	Uxbridge (VL)	MCC YC v Middx
	Notts Sports Club	Notts v Derbys
	Stowe S	Northants v Leics
	Taunton Vale	Somerset v Hants
Mon 13	*tba*	Derbys v Durham
	Southampton	Hants v Kent
Tue 14	Crosby	Lancs v Northants
	Notts Sports Club	Notts v Worcs
	Horsham	Sussex v Glos
	York	Yorks v Warwks
Wed 15	Panteg	Glam v Somerset
	Radlett	MCC YC v Surrey
	Southgate	Middx v Essex
Mon 20	Chester-le-Street	Durham v Yorks
Tue 21	Hinckley	Leics v MCC YC
	Wimbledon	Surrey v Kent
	Walmley	Warwks v Lancs
Wed 22	Northampton	Northants v Notts
	Taunton	Somerset v Essex
Tue 28	Chesterfield	Derbys v Northants
	Usk	Glam v Sussex
	Cheltenham C	Glos v MCC YC
	Basingstoke	Hants v Warwks
	Beckenham	Kent v Essex
Wed 29	Chester-le-Street	Durham v Lancs
	Hinckley	Leics v Notts
	Guildford	Surrey v Middx
SEPTEMBER		
Tue 4	Radlett	MCC YC v Durham
Wed 5	Southampton	Hants v Glos
	Beckenham	Kent v Sussex
	Uxbridge	Middx v Glam
	Kenilworth Wardens	Warwks v Notts
	Leeds	Yorks v Lancs
Tue 11	Halstead	Essex v MCC YC
	Liverpool	Lancs v Notts
	Hinckley	Leics v Durham
	Hove	Sussex v Somerset
	Stamford Bridge	Yorks v Worcs

SECOND XI TROPHY FIXTURES 2007

Date	Venue	Match
JUNE		
Tue 12	Neath	Glam v Worcs
Thu 14	Worcester	Worcs v Glam
Fri 15	Sutton	Surrey v Hants
Mon 25	Belper Meadows	Derbys v Leics
	Billericay	Essex v Northants
Tue 26	Banstead	Surrey v MCC YC
	Bradford & Bingley	Yorks v Leics
Wed 27	Bishop's Stortford	Essex v Minor Co
Thu 28	Tonbridge S	Kent v Surrey
	Ealing	Middx v Minor Co
	Hinckley	Leics v Derbys
	Barnt Green	Worcs v Somerset
Fri 29	Todmorden	Lancs v Yorks
	Uxbridge (VL)	MCC YC v Hants
JULY		
Mon 2	Newport	Glam v Somerset
	Southampton	Hants v Sussex
	Stowe S	Northants v Notts
	Leeds (Weetwood)	Yorks v Durham
Tue 3	Glossop	Derbys v Lancs
	Hinckley	Leics v Durham
	Milton Keynes	Minor Co v Notts
	Purley	Surrey v Kent
	Horsham	Sussex v MCC YC
	Dorridge	Warwks v Worcs
Wed 4	Seaton Carew	Durham v Yorks
	Southampton	Hants v MCC YC
	Unsworth	Lancs v Derbys
	Radlett	Middx v Essex
	Milton Keynes	Minor Co v Northants
Thu 5	Port Talbot	Glam v Warwks
	Ealing	Middx v Northants
	Taunton	Somerset v Glos
	Horsham	Sussex v Surrey
Fri 6	Tondu	Glam v Glos
	Southampton	Hants v Surrey
	Middleton	Lancs v Durham
	Radlett	MCC YC v Kent
Mon 9	Derby	Derbys v Yorks
	Stockton	Durham v Lancs
	Bristol (WICC)	Glos v Worcs
	Canterbury	Kent v MCC YC
	Milton Keynes	Northants v Essex
	Taunton	Somerset v Warwks
	Horsham	Sussex v Hants
Tue 10	Bristol	Glos v Somerset
	Canterbury	Kent v Hants
	Hinckley	Leics v Yorks
	Richmond	Middx v Notts
Wed 11	Alvaston & Boulton	Derbys v Durham
	Wickford	Essex v Notts
	Haydock	Lancs v Leics
	Milton Keynes	Northants v Middx
	Normandy	Surrey v Sussex
	Himley	Worcs v Warwks
Thu 12	Basingstoke	Hants v Kent
	Milton Keynes	Minor Co v Essex
	Leeds	Yorks v Lancs
Fri 13	South Shields	Durham v Derbys
	Bristol	Glos v Glam
	Beckenham	Kent v Sussex
	Uxbridge (VL)	MCC YC v Surrey
	Milton Keynes	Minor Co v Middx
	Worksop C	Notts v Essex
	Harborne	Warwks v Somerset
Mon 16	Seaton Carew	Durham v Leics
	Bristol	Glos v Warwks
	Uxbridge (VL)	MCC YC v Sussex
	Notts Unity	Notts v Middx
	North Perrott	Somerset v Glam
Tue 17	Worcester RGS	Worcs v Glos
	Sheffield United	Yorks v Derbys
Wed 18	Notts Sports Club	Notts v Northants
	Stirlands	Sussex v Kent
	Leamington	Warwks v Glam
Thu 19	Hinckley	Leics v Lancs
	Northampton	Northants v Minor Co
	Taunton Vale	Somerset v Worcs
	Birmingham	Warwks v Glos
Fri 20	Coggleshall	Essex v Middx
	Notts Sports Club	Notts v Minor Co
AUGUST		
Mon 6	*tba*	Semi-Finals
SEPTEMBER		
Mon 3	*tba*	FINAL

MINOR COUNTIES FIXTURES 2007

MCCA CHAMPIONSHIP

Date	Match	Venue
MAY		
27-29	Wiltshire v Wales	Trowbridge
JUNE		
10-12	Beds v Staffs	Luton
	Herts v Lincs	Radlett
	Cheshire v Devon	Chester (Boughton H)
	Cornwall v Dorset	Truro
	Cmbland v Suffolk	Sedbergh S
	Nthmbland v Cambs	Benwell Hill
	Oxon v Herefords	Challow & Childrey
	Shropshire v Berkshire	Bridgnorth
24-26	Beds v Herts	Dunstable
	Berkshire v Cheshire	Finchampstead
	Bucks v Nthmbland	Gerrards Cross
	Cambs v Norfolk	March
	Devon v Wiltshire	Bovey Tracey
	Dorset v Herefords	Bournemouth (DP)
	Lincs v Cmbland	Sleaford
	Shropshire v Cornwall	Shifnal
	Suffolk v Staffs	Ipswich (Ransomes)
	Wales v Oxon	Swansea
JULY		
8-10	Beds v Bucks	Bedford Modern S
	Berkshire v Wales	Falkland

	Dorset v Cheshire	Bournemouth (DP)
	Herefords v Devon	Colwall
	Oxon v Shropshire	Banbury
	Suffolk v Nthmbland	Bury St Edmunds
	Staffs v Lincs	Longton
	Wiltshire v Cornwall	Corsham
9-11	Cmbland v Norfolk	Netherfield
15-17	Cambs v Herts	Fenner's
22-24	Bucks v Cmbland	Slough
	Cheshire v Wiltshire	Alderley Edge
	Cornwall v Oxon	Camborne
	Herefords v Berkshire	Eastnor
	Herts v Staffs	Bishop's Stortford
	Lincs v Beds	Cleethorpes
	Norfolk v Nthmbland	Norwich (MP)
	Shropshire v Dorset	Bomere Heath
	Suffolk v Cambs	Mildenhall
	Wales v Devon	Swansea
29-31	Norfolk v Bucks	Norwich (MP)
AUGUST		
5-7	Berkshire v Dorset	Reading
	Bucks v Suffolk	Burnham
	Cambs v Beds	March
	Devon v Cornwall	Budleigh Salterton
	Norfolk v Lincs	Norwich (MP)
	Nthmbland v Herts	Jesmond
	Oxon v Cheshire	Banbury
	Staffs v Cmbland	Knypersley
	Wales v Herefords	Pontarddulais
	Wiltshire v Shropshire	South Wiltshire
19-21	Cheshire v Shropshire	Nantwich
	Cornwall v Berkshire	St Austell
	Cmbland v Cambs	Keswick
	Devon v Oxon	Exmouth
	Dorset v Wales	Bournemouth (DP)
	Herefords v Wiltshire	Brockhampton
	Herts v Bucks	Long Marston
	Lincs v Suffolk	Grantham
	Nthmbland v Beds	Jesmond
	Staffs v Norfolk	Walsall
SEPTEMBER		
9-12	CHAMPIONSHIP FINAL (*E Div Winners*)	

MCCA KNOCK-OUT TROPHY

Group 1	Group 2	Group 3	Group 4
Cheshire	Bedfordshire	Berkshire	Buckinghamshire
Cumberland	Lincolnshire	Cornwall	Cambridgeshire
Herefordshire	Norfolk	Devon	Hertfordshire
Northumberland	Northumberland	Dorset	Oxfordshire
Shropshire	Staffordshire	Wales	Wiltshire

April 29
Herefords v Shropshire (1) Kington
Nthmbland v Cmbland (1) S Northumberland
Norfolk v Lincs (2) Norwich (MP)
Berkshire v Wales (3) Thatcham
Dorset v Devon (3) Bournemouth (DP)
Bucks v Herts (4) Slough
Cambs v Oxon (4) March
May 6
Cheshire v Nthmbland (1) Grappenhall
Beds v Norfolk (2) Ampthill
Suffolk v Staffs (2) Ipswich S
Cornwall v Dorset (3) St Just
Devon v Berkshire (3) Exmouth
Oxon v Bucks (4) Aston Rowant
Wiltshire v Cambs (4) Devizes
May 7
Staffordshire v Beds (2) Leek
May 13
Herefords v Cheshire (1) Colwall
Shropshire v Cmbland (1) Shrewsbury
Lincs v Beds (2) Bracebridge Heath
Norfolk v Suffolk (2) Norwich (MP)
Berkshire v Cornwall (3) Falkland
Wales v Devon (3) Mumbles
Bucks v Wiltshire (4) Ascott Park
Herts v Oxon (4) Long Marston
May 20
Cheshire v Shropshire (1) Christleton
Nthmbland v Herefords (1) Benwell Hill
Staffs v Norfolk (2) Leek
Suffolk v Lincs (2) Woodbridge S
Cornwall v Wales (3) Falmouth
Cambs v Bucks (4) Wisbech
Wiltshire v Herts (4) Trowbridge
May 21
Cmbland v Herefords (1) Workington
May 28
Dorset v Berkshire (3) Bournemouth (DP)
June 3
Cmbland v Cheshire (1) Barrow
Shropshire v Nthmbland (1) Oswestry
Beds v Suffolk (2) Flitwick
Lincs v Staffs (2) Lincoln (Lindum)
Devon v Cornwall (3) Instow
Wales v Dorset (3) Abergavenny
Herts v Cambs (4) North Mymms
Oxon v Wiltshire (4) Radley College
July 1 *(Reserve JULY 2)* **SEMI-FINALS**
Winner (4) v Winner (2) *(tba)*
Winner (1) v Winner (3) *(tba)*
August 27 *(Reserve SEPT 16)* **FINAL LORD'S**

REPRESENTATIVE MATCHES

August 16 – MCCA v MCC at Trowbridge
August 17 – MCCA v Cricket Victoria Emerging Players XI at Trowbridge

PRINCIPAL FIXTURES 2007

CC1	Liverpool Vic County Championship (1st Div)	P40	NatWest Pro40 League
CC2	Liverpool Vic County Championship (2nd Div)	T20	Twenty20 Cup
FCF	First-Class Friendly	TM	npower Test Match
FPT	Friends Provident Trophy	UCCE	Univ Centre of Cricketing Excellence
LOI	NatWest Limited-Overs International	F	Floodlit

Fri 13 – Mon 16 April

FCF	Lord's	MCC v Sussex

Sat 14 – Mon 16 April

	Southampton	Hampshire v Cardiff UCCE
FCF	Taunton	Somerset v Loughboro' UCCE
	The Oval	Surrey v Leeds/Brad UCCE
FCF	Cambridge	Cambridge UCCE v Northants
FCF	Durham	Durham UCCE v Notts
FCF	Oxford	Oxford UCCE v Middlesex

Wed 18 – Sat 21 April

CC2	Chelmsford	Essex v Derbyshire
CC2	Nottingham	Notts v Leics
CC2	Taunton	Somerset v Middlesex
CC1	The Oval	Surrey v Yorkshire
CC1	Hove	Sussex v Kent
CC1	Birmingham	Warwks v Lancashire
CC1	Worcester	Worcs v Durham

Wed 18 – Fri 20 April

FCF	Oxford	Oxford UCCE v Glamorgan

Sun 22 April

FPT	Southampton	Hampshire v Middlesex
FPT	Manchester	Lancashire v Worcs
FPT	Leicester	Leics v Durham
FPT	Nottingham	Notts v Yorkshire
FPT	Taunton	Somerset v Glamorgan
FPT	The Oval	Surrey v Kent
FPT	Birmingham	Warwks v Northants
FPT	Dublin	Ireland v Glos

Wed 25 – Sat 28 April

CC2	Chelmsford	Essex v Glamorgan
CC2	Bristol	Glos v Notts
CC2	Leicester	Leicester v Somerset
CC2	Lord's	Middlesex v Northants
CC1	The Oval	Surrey v Hampshire
CC1	Birmingham	Warwks v Sussex
CC1	Leeds	Yorkshire v Durham

Wed 25 – Fri 27 April

FCF	Durham	Durham UCCE v Lancashire
	Canterbury	Kent v Cardiff UCCE
FCF	Worcester	Worcs v Loughboro' UCCE
FCF	Cambridge	Cambridge UCCE v Derbyshire

Sun 29 April

FPT	Chester-le-St	Durham v Derbyshire
FPT	Chelmsford	Essex v Hampshire
FPT	Manchester	Lancashire v Warwks
FPT	Lord's	Middlesex v Glamorgan
FPT	Northampton	Northants v Notts
FPT	Taunton	Somerset v Sussex
FPT	The Oval	Surrey v Glos
FPT	Worcester	Worcs v Leics
FPT	Belfast	Ireland v Kent
FPT	Edinburgh	Scot v Yorkshire

Wed 2 – Sat 5 May

CC1	Southampton	Hampshire v Yorkshire
CC1	Canterbury	Kent v Sussex
CC1	Manchester	Lancashire v Surrey
CC1	Worcester	Worcs v Warwks
CC2	Nottingham	Notts v Glamorgan
CC2	Bristol	Glos v Leics
CC2	Northampton	Northants v Essex
CC2	Taunton	Somerset v Derbyshire

Wed 2 – Fri 4 May

FCF	Durham	Durham UCCE v Durham

Sun 6 May

FPT	Chelmsford	Essex v Kent
FPT	Manchester	Lancashire v Northants
FPT	Leicester	Leics v Scotland
FPT	Lord's	Middlesex v Glos
FPT	Taunton	Somerset v Ireland
FPT	Worcester	Worcs v Notts

Mon 7 May

FPT	Derby	Derbyshire v Warwks
FPT	Chester-le-St	Durham v Lancashire
FPT	Bristol	Glos v Sussex
FPT	Southampton	Hampshire v Ireland
FPT	Canterbury	Kent v Middlesex
FPT	Northampton	Northants v Scotland
FPT	Leeds	Yorkshire v Leics

Tue 8 – Fri 11 May

CC2	Northampton	Northants v Somerset

Tue 8 – Thu 10 May

	Hove	Sussex v Cardiff UCCE

Wed 9 – Sat 12 May

CC2	Derby	Derbyshire v Leics
CC1	Chester-le-St	Durham v Kent
CC1	Southampton	Hampshire v Lancashire
CC2	Nottingham	Notts v Middlesex
CC1	The Oval	Surrey v Warwks
CC1	Leeds	Yorkshire v Worcs

Wed 9 – Fri 11 May

	Bristol	Glos v Leeds/Brad UCCE
FCF	Cambridge	Cambridge UCCE v Essex

Fri 11 May

FPT	[F]Hove	Sussex v Glamorgan

Sat 12 – Mon 14 May

FCF	Taunton	Somerset v West Indians

Sun 13 May

FPT	Derby	Derbyshire v Northants
FPT	Bristol	Glos v Hampshire
FPT	Nottingham	Notts v Warwks
FPT	The Oval	Surrey v Middlesex
FPT	Leeds	Yorkshire v Worcs
FPT	Dublin	Ireland v Essex

Tue 15 – Fri 18 May

CC1	Manchester	Lancashire v Worcs

Wed 16 – Sat 19 May

CC2	Derby	Derbyshire v Middlesex
CC2	Bristol	Glos v Glamorgan
CC2	Leicester	Leics v Essex
CC1	Hove	Sussex v Surrey
CC1	Birmingham	Warwks v Durham

Wed 16 – Fri 18 May

FCF	Leeds	Yorkshire v Loughboro' UCCE

Thu 17 – Mon 21 May

TM1	**Lord's**	**ENGLAND v WEST INDIES**

Fri 18 May

FPT	[F]Southampton	Hampshire v Somerset

Sun 20 May

FPT	Chelmsford	Essex v Middlesex
FPT	Bristol	Glos v Somerset
FPT	Southampton	Hampshire v Sussex
FPT	Canterbury	Kent v Glamorgan
FPT	Manchester	Lancashire v Yorkshire
FPT	Northampton	Northants v Durham
FPT	Birmingham	Warwks v Leics
FPT	Worcs	Worcs v Derbyshire
FPT	Edinburgh	Scotland v Notts

Tue 22 May

FPT	[F]Hove	Sussex v Surrey

Wed 23 – Sat 26 May

CC1	Chester-le-St	Durham v Yorkshire
CC2	Swansea	Glamorgan v Middlesex
CC1	Canterbury	Kent v Hampshire
CC2	Northampton	Northants v Derbyshire
CC2	Nottingham	Notts v Essex
CC2	Taunton	Somerset v Glos

Wed 23 – Fri 25 May

FCF	Oxford	OUCCE v Leics

Thu 24 – Sun 27 May

CC1	Worcester	Worcs v Sussex

Fri 25 – Tue 29 May

TM2	**Leeds**	**ENGLAND v WEST INDIES**

Sun 27 May

FPT	Swansea	Glamorgan v Essex
FPT	Manchester	Lancashire v Scotland
FPT	Northampton	Northants v Leics
FPT	Taunton	Somerset v Kent
FPT	The Oval	Surrey v Ireland

Mon 28 May

FPT	Chester-le-St	Durham v Scotland
FPT	Bristol	Glos v Essex
FPT	Cresselly	Glamorgan v Surrey
FPT	Leicester	Leics v Lancashire
FPT	Hove	Sussex v Ireland
FPT	Nottingham	Notts v Derbyshire
FPT	Birmingham	Warwks v Yorkshire

Wed 30 May – Sat 2 June

CC2	Swansea	Glamorgan v Essex
CC2	Oakham S	Leics v Notts
CC2	Lord's	Middlesex v Somerset
CC1	Whitgift S	Surrey v Kent
CC1	Hove	Sussex v Lancashire
CC1	Birmingham	Warwks v Hampshire

Thu 31 May

FPT	[F]Derby	Derbyshire v Yorkshire

Fri 1 – Mon 4 June

CC2	Gloucester	Glos v Northants

Fri 1 June

FPT	Chester-le-St	Durham v Worcs

Fri 1 – Sun 3 June

FCF	Durham	MCC v West Indians

Sun 3 June

FPT	Swansea	Glamorgan v Hampshire
FPT	Oakham S	Leics v Notts
FPT	Lord's	Middlesex v Somerset
FPT	Whitgift S	Surrey v Essex
FPT	Hove	Sussex v Kent
FPT	Worcester	Worcs v Warwks
FPT	Leeds	Yorkshire v Durham
FPT	Edinburgh	Scotland v Derbyshire

Tue 5 – Fri 8 June

CC2	Derby	Derbyshire v Glos
CC2	Swansea	Glamorgan v Notts

Wed 6 – Sat 9 June

CC1	Chester-le-St	Durham v Lancashire
CC2	Chelmsford	Essex v Northants
CC1	Tunbridge W	Kent v Yorkshire
CC2	Taunton	Somerset v Leics
CC1	Arundel	Sussex v Hampshire
CC1	Worcester	Worcs v Surrey

Wed 6 – Fri 8 June

–	Leeds (Weetwood)	Leeds/Bradford UCCE v Warwks

Thu 7 – Mon 11 June

TM3	**Manchester**	**ENGLAND v WEST INDIES**

Sun 10 June

FPT	Derby	Derbyshire v Lancashire
FPT	Chester-le-St	Durham v Notts
FPT	Colwyn Bay	Glamorgan v Glos
FPT	Tunbridge W	Kent v Hampshire
FPT	Northampton	Northants v Worcs

FPT	Bath	Somerset v Surrey
FPT	Arundel	Sussex v Essex
FPT	Dublin	Ireland v Middlesex
FPT	Edinburgh	Scotland v Warwks
Wed 13 June		
FPT	Chelmsford	Essex v Somerset
FPT	Southampton	Hampshire v Surrey
FPT	Tunbridge W	Kent v Glos
FPT	Leicester	Leics v Derbyshire
FPT	Lord's	Middlesex v Sussex
FPT	Nottingham	Notts v Lancashire
FPT	Birmingham	Warwks v Durham
FPT	Worcester	Worcs v Scotland
FPT	Leeds	Yorkshire v Northants
FPT	Belfast	Ireland v Glamorgan
Fri 15 – Tue 19 June		
TM4	**Chester-le-St**	**ENGLAND v WEST INDIES**
Fri 15 – Mon 18 June		
CC2	Bristol	Glos v Somerset
CC1	Southampton	Hampshire v Durham
CC1	Manchester	Lancashire v Kent
CC2	Lord's	Middlesex v Essex
CC2	Northampton	Northants v Leics
CC2	Nottingham	Notts v Derbyshire
CC1	Birmingham	Warwks v Worcs
CC1	Leeds	Yorkshire v Sussex
Wed 20 June (*No Reserve Days*)		
FPT		Semi-Finals
Thu 21 June		
	Worcester	England A v West Indians
Fri 22 June		
T20	[F]Derby	Derbyshire v Notts
T20	[F]Chelmsford	Essex v Sussex
T20	[F]Cardiff	Glamorgan v Glos
T20	[F]Southampton	Hampshire v Kent
T20	Manchester	Lancashire v Durham
T20	Leicester	Leics v Yorkshire
T20	Northampton	Northants v Worcs
T20	The Oval	Surrey v Middlesex
T20	Birmingham	Warwks v Somerset
Sat 23 June		
T20	Canterbury	Kent v Essex
T20	Nottingham	Notts v Lancashire
Sun 24 June		
[T20]	Derby	Derbyshire v West Indians
T20	Taunton	Somerset v Northants
T20	The Oval	Surrey v Hampshire
T20	Hove	Sussex v Middlesex
T20	Birmingham	Warwks v Glamorgan
Mon 25 June		
T20	[F]Derby	Derbyshire v Durham
T20	Bristol	Glos v Worcs
T20	Southgate	Middlesex v Hampshire
T20	Nottingham	Notts v Leics
T20	Leeds	Yorkshire v Lancashire
Tues 26 June		
T20	[F]Cardiff	Glamorgan v Somerset
T20	Canterbury	Kent v Sussex
T20	Birmingham	Warwks v Northants
[T20]	Arundel	PCA Masters v West Indians
Wed 27 June		
T20	Chester-le-St	Durham v Leics
T20	[F]Southampton	Hampshire v Sussex
T20	Manchester	Lancashire v Yorkshire
T20	Uxbridge	Middlesex v Kent
T20	Nottingham	Notts v Derbyshire
T20	Taunton	Somerset v Glos
T20	Worcester	Worcs v Warwks
Thu 28 June		
[T20]	The Oval	England v West Indies
T20	[F]Chelmsford	Essex v Surrey
T20	[F]Cardiff	Glamorgan v Northants
Fri 29 June		
[T20]	The Oval	England v West Indies
T20	[F]Derby	Derbyshire v Leics
T20	Chester-le-St	Durham v Lancashire
T20	[F]Chelmsford	Essex v Kent
T20	Bristol	Glos v Warwks
T20	[F]Southampton	Hampshire v Middlesex
T20	Nottingham	Notts v Yorkshire
T20	Taunton	Somerset v Glamorgan
T20	[F]Hove	Sussex v Surrey
T20	Worcester	Worcs v Northants
Sat 30 June – Tue 3 July		
FCF	Cambridge	Cambridge U v Oxford U
Sat 30 June		
T20	Leicester	Leics v Notts
T20	Leeds	Yorkshire v Durham
Sun 1 July		
LOI	Lord's	England v West Indies
T20	Southampton	Hampshire v Essex
T20	Manchester	Lancashire v Derbyshire
T20	Worcester	Worcs v Glos
Mon 2 July		
T20	[F]Cardiff	Glamorgan v Warwks
T20	Beckenham	Kent v Surrey
T20	Leicester	Leics v Derbyshire
T20	Milton Keynes	Northants v Glos
Tue 3 July		
T20	Chester-le-St	Durham v Yorkshire
T20	Lord's	Middlesex v Surrey
T20	Taunton	Somerset v Worcs
T20	[F]Hove	Sussex v Essex
Wed 4 July		
LOI	Birmingham	England v West Indies
T20	Bristol	Glos v Somerset
T20	Beckenham	Kent v Middlesex
T20	Leicester	Leics v Durham

T20	Northampton	Northants v Warwks
T20	Leeds	Yorkshire v Notts
Thu 5 July		
T20	[F]Derby	Derbyshire v Lancashire
T20	[F]Chelmsford	Essex v Hampshire
T20	The Oval	Surrey v Sussex
T20	Worcester	Worcs v Glamorgan
Fri 6 July		
T20	Chester-le-St	Durham v Notts
T20	Bristol	Glos v Glamorgan
T20	Manchester	Lancashire v Leics
T20	Lord's	Middlesex v Essex
T20	Northampton	Northants v Somerset
T20	The Oval	Surrey v Kent
T20	Hove	Sussex v Hampshire
T20	Birmingham	Warwks v Worcs
T20	Leeds	Yorkshire v Derbyshire
Sat 7 – Tue 10 July		
FCF	Hove	Sussex v Indians
Sat 7 July		
LOI	Nottingham	England v West Indies
	Lord's	Cambridge U v Oxford U
Sun 8 – Wed 11 July		
CC2	Chelmsford	Essex v Notts
CC1	Southampton	Hampshire v Warwks
CC1	Manchester	Lancashire v Yorkshire
CC2	Leicester	Leics v Glamorgan
CC2	Southgate	Middlesex v Derbyshire
CC2	Northampton	Northants v Glos
CC1	The Oval	Surrey v Durham
CC1	Worcester	Worcs v Kent
Tue 10 – Thu 12 July		
FCF	Arundel	MCC v Sri Lanka A
Fri 13 – Sun 15 July		
FCF	Chelmsford	England A v Indians
Fri 13 – Mon 16 July		
CC2	Nottingham	Notts v Glos
CC2	Taunton	Somerset v Northants
CC1	Hove	Sussex v Durham
CC1	Birmingham	Warwks v Yorkshire
Fri 13 July		
P40	[F]Worcester	Worcs v Hampshire
Sat 14 July		
	Worcester	Worcs v Sri Lanka A
P40	Leicester	Leics v Kent
Sun 15 July		
P40	Manchester	Lancashire v Essex
Mon 16 July		
	Canterbury	Kent v Sri Lanka A
P40	[F]Derby	Derbyshire v Glamorgan
Tue 17 and Wed 18 July		
T20		Quarter-Finals

Thu 19 – Mon 23 July		
TM1	**Lord's**	**ENGLAND v INDIA**
Thu 19 – Sat 21 July		
FCF	Hove	Sussex v Sri Lanka A
Fri 20 – Mon 23 July		
CC2	Derby	Derbyshire v Glamorgan
CC1	Chester-le-St	Durham v Hampshire
CC1	Canterbury	Kent v Warwks
CC2	Leicester	Leics v Middlesex
CC2	Taunton	Somerset v Essex
CC1	Worcester	Worcs v Lancashire
CC1	Leeds	Yorkshire v Surrey
Sun 22 July		
P40	Cheltenham	Glos v Northants
Tue 24 July		
P40	Cheltenham	Glos v Lancashire
P40	[F]Birmingham	Warwks v Notts
Weds 25 – Fri 27 July		
FCF	Birmingham	Warwks v Sri Lanka A
Wed 25 – Sat 28 July		
CC2	Chesterfield	Derbyshire v Somerset
CC2	Abergavenny	Glamorgan v Leics
CC2	Cheltenham	Glos v Essex
CC1	Southampton	Hampshire v Sussex
CC1	Guildford	Surrey v Worcs
CC1	Scarborough	Yorkshire v Kent
Wed 25 July		
P40	[F]Northampton	Northants v Lancashire
Thu 26 – Sun 29 July		
CC2	Northampton	Northants v Notts
Thu 26 July		
P40	[F]Chester-le-St	Durham v Middlesex
Fri 27 – Tue 31 July		
TM2	**Nottingham**	**ENGLAND v INDIA**
Sun 29 July		
P40	Chesterfield	Derbyshire v Kent
P40	Ebbw Vale	Glamorgan v Middlesex
P40	Cheltenham	Glos v Warwks
P40	Southampton	Hampshire v Essex
P40	Guildford	Surrey v Durham
P40	Worcester	Worcs v Sussex
P40	Scarborough	Yorkshire v Somerset
	Liverpool (*tbc*)	Lancashire v Sri Lanka A
Mon 30 July		
P40	Lord's	Middlesex v Leics
Tue 31 July – Fri 3 August		
CC1	Chester-le-St	Durham v Warwks
CC2	Cheltenham	Glos v Derbyshire
CC1	Liverpool	Lancashire v Sussex
CC2	Lord's	Middlesex v Glamorgan
Tue 31 July		
	Leeds	Yorkshire v Sri Lanka A

Wed 1 August		
P40	[F]Southampton	Hampshire v Notts
Thu 2 August		
P40	[F]Chelmsford	Essex v Worcs
Fri 3 – Sun 5 August		
FCF	Leicester	Sri Lanka A v Indians
Sat 4 August		
T20	Birmingham	Semi-Finals & Final
Sun 5 August		
P40	Lord's	Middlesex v Surrey
P40	Nottingham	Notts v Worcs
P40	Taunton	Somerset v Derbyshire
Mon 6 August		
P40	[F]Hove	Sussex v Glos
Tue 7 August		
P40	[F]Derby	Derbyshire v Leics
Wed 8 – Fri 10 August		
FCF	Chester-le-St	Durham v Sri Lanka A
Wed 8 – Sat 11 August		
CC2	Southend	Essex v Glos
CC2	Colwyn Bay	Glamorgan v Northants
CC1	Southampton	Hampshire v Worcs
CC1	Canterbury	Kent v Surrey
CC2	Nottingham	Notts v Somerset
CC1	Hove	Sussex v Warwks
Wed 8 Aug		
P40	[F]Leeds	Yorkshire v Middlesex
Thu 9 – Mon 13 August		
TM3	**The Oval**	**ENGLAND v INDIA**
Thu 9 – Sun 12 August		
CC2	Leicester	Leics v Derbyshire
CC1	Leeds	Yorkshire v Lancashire
Sun 12 August		
P40	Southend	Essex v Warwks
P40	Colwyn Bay	Glamorgan v Somerset
P40	Canterbury	Kent v Durham
P40	Nottingham	Notts v Northants
P40	Hove	Sussex v Hampshire
Tue 14 – Fri 17 August		
CC1	Chester-le-St	Durham v Surrey
CC2	Cardiff	Glamorgan v Somerset
CC2	Northampton	Northants v Middlesex
CC1	Birmingham	Warwks v Kent
CC1	Worcester	Worcs v Yorkshire
Tue 14 August		
P40	[F]Manchester	Lancashire v Sussex
Wed 15 August		
P40	[F]Nottingham	Notts v Essex
Thu 16 August		
tbc	Glasgow	Scotland v India
Sat 18 August		
FPT	Lord's	Final (*Reserve 19 Aug*)
	Northampton	England A v Indians
Sun 19 August		
P40	Leicester	Leics v Yorkshire
P40	Northampton	Northants v Hampshire
P40	Taunton	Somerset v Durham
P40	The Oval	Surrey v Derbyshire
P40	Birmingham	Warwks v Sussex
Mon 20 August		
P40	[F]Cardiff	Glamorgan v Yorkshire
Tues 21 August		
LOI	[F]Southampton	England v India
Tue 21 – Fri 24 August		
CC1	Canterbury	Kent v Worcs
CC1	Manchester	Lancashire v Hampshire
CC1	The Oval	Surrey v Sussex
Wed 22 – Sat 25 August		
CC2	Colchester	Essex v Leics
CC2	Cardiff	Glamorgan v Derbyshire
CC2	Lord's	Middlesex v Glos
CC2	Nottingham	Notts v Northants
CC1	Scarborough	Yorkshire v Warwks
Fri 24 August		
LOI	[F]Bristol	England v India
Sat 25 August		
P40	Worcester	Worcs v Lancashire
Sun 26 August		
P40	Chester-le-St	Durham v Leics
P40	Colchester	Essex v Sussex
P40	Lord's	Middlesex v Kent
P40	Nottingham	Notts v Glos
P40	Scarborough	Yorkshire v Surrey
Mon 27 August		
LOI	Birmingham	England v India
P40	Chester-le-St	Durham v Yorkshire
P40	Canterbury	Kent v Somerset
P40	The Oval	Surrey v Glamorgan
Tue 28 – Fri 31 August		
CC1	Canterbury	Kent v Lancashire
Tue 28 August		
P40	[F]Taunton	Somerset v Leics
Wed 29 August – Sat 1 September		
CC1	Chester-le-St	Durham v Worcs
CC2	Lord's	Middlesex v Notts
Wed 29 August		
P40	[F]Southampton	Hampshire v Warwks
Thu 30 August		
LOI	[F]Manchester	England v India
Thu 30 August – Sun 2 September		
CC2	Derby	Derbyshire v Essex
CC1	Southampton	Hampshire v Surrey
CC 2	Leicester	Leics v Glos
CC2	Taunton	Somerset v Glamorgan
Fri 31 August		
P40	[F]Hove	Sussex v Northants

Sat 1 September
P40 Birmingham Warwks v Lancashire

Sun 2 September
LOI Leeds England v India
P40 Manchester Lancashire v Notts
P40 Northampton Northants v Warwks

Mon 3 September
P40 [F]Chelmsford Essex v Glos

Tue 4 September
P40 [F]Derby Derbyshire v Durham
P40 [F]Canterbury Kent v Surrey

Wed 5 September
LOI The Oval England v India

Wed 5 – Sat 8 September
CC2 Chelmsford Essex v Somerset
CC2 Bristol Glos v Middlesex
CC2 Leicester Leics v Northants
CC1 Hove Sussex v Yorkshire
CC1 Worcester Worcs v Hampshire

Thu 6 – Sun 9 September
CC2 Derby Derbyshire v Notts
CC1 Blackpool Lancashire v Durham
CC1 Birmingham Warwks v Surrey

Fri 7 September
P40 [F]Cardiff Glamorgan v Kent

Sat 8 September
LOI Lord's England v India

Sun 9 September
P40 Southampton Hampshire v Glos
P40 Canterbury Kent v Yorkshire
P40 Leicester Leics v Glamorgan
P40 Worcester Worcs v Northants

Mon 10 September
P40 [F]Southgate Middlesex v Derbyshire

Tue 11 – Fri 14 September
CC1 Chester-le-St Durham v Sussex
CC1 Southampton Hampshire v Kent
CC1 Manchester Lancashire v Warwks
CC2 Southgate Middlesex v Leics
CC2 Northampton Northants v Glamorgan

Tue 11 September
P40 [F]The Oval Surrey v Somerset

Thu 13 September
P40 [F]Bristol Glos v Worcs

Sat 15 September
P40 Chester-le-St Durham v Glamorgan
P40 Leicester Leics v Surrey
P40 Taunton Somerset v Middlesex
P40 Leeds Yorkshire v Derbyshire

Sun 16 September
P40 Manchester Lancashire v Hampshire
P40 Northampton Northants v Essex
P40 Hove Sussex v Notts
P40 Birmingham Warwks v Worcs

Wed 19 – Sat 22 September
CC2 Derby Derbyshire v Northants
CC2 Chelmsford Essex v Middlesex
CC2 Cardiff Glamorgan v Glos
CC1 Canterbury Kent v Durham
CC2 Taunton Somerset v Notts
CC1 The Oval Surrey v Lancashire
CC1 Hove Sussex v Worcs
CC1 Leeds Yorkshire v Hampshire

Sun 23 September
P40 Play-Off

UNDER-19 CRICKET

TEST MATCH SERIES
England v Pakistan

TM1 Worcester Sat 4 – Tue 7 August
TM2 Derby Fri 10 – Mon 13 August

LIMITED-OVERS INTERNATIONALS
England v Pakistan
LOI Shenley Thu 16 August
LOI Shenley Fri 17 August
LOI Northampton Mon 20 August
LOI Leicester Wed 22 August
LOI Leicester Thu 23 August

WOMEN'S CRICKET

LIMITED-OVERS INTERNATIONALS

England v New Zealand
T20 Bath Sun 12 August
T20 Bath Mon 13 August
T20 Taunton Thu 16 August
LOI Taunton Fri 17 August
LOI Stratford Sun 19 August
LOI Derby Thu 23 August
LOI Blackpool Sun 26 August
LOI Blackpool Mon 27 August
LOI Shenley Thu 30 August

First published in 2007
by HEADLINE PUBLISHING GROUP

Cover photographs:
(*Front and Spine*) Ian Bell © Getty Images/Mike Hewitt;
(*Back*) Sachin Tendulkar © Getty Images/AFP/Manan Vatsyayana

1

ISBN 978 0 7553 1476 8

Headline's policy is to use papers that are natural, renewable and recyclable products and made from wood grown in sustainable forests. The logging and manufacturing processes are expected to conform to the environmental regulations of the country of origin.

Typeset in Times by
Letterpart Limited, Reigate, Surrey

Printed and bound in Great Britain by
Clays Ltd, St Ives plc

HEADLINE PUBLISHING GROUP
A division of Hachette Livre UK Ltd
338 Euston Road
London NW1 3BH
www.headline.co.uk
www.hodderheadline.com